SOTHIS PRESS

Sothis Press aims to completely reimagine the public domain book with an emphasis on universal access to captivatingly designed print editions. We believe that technology will enable every single book ever published to be perpetually accessible in beautiful print form. Sothis is beauty in ubiquity.

www.sothis.press
1 Waterhouse Square, London, ECIN 2ST

Lawrence Livermore National Laboratory and Sandia National Laboratories

United States Department of Energy

SOTHIS PRESS

ISBN 978-1-83548-914-7

This edition is published by Sothis Press © 2023. The company is registered in England and Wales. The Company Number is 14900389.

28

Final Environmental Impact Statement

Lawrence Livermore National Laboratory and Sandia National Laboratories — Livermore Sites

Livermore, California

U.S. Department of Energy

July 1982

This repo ... le copy.

Available ... U. S. Department of Commerce, Springfield, Virginia 2...

A99
A01

Codes are used for pricing all publications. The code is determined by the number of pages in the publication. Information pertaining to the pricing codes can be found in the current issues of the following publications, which are generally available in most libraries: *Energy Research Abstracts, (ERA); Government Reports Announcements* and Index (*GRA* and I); *Scientific and Technical Abstract Reports (STAR);* and publication, NTIS-PR-360 available from (NTIS) at the above address.

Final Environmental Impact Statement

Lawrence Livermore National Laboratory and Sandia National Laboratories — Livermore Sites

Livermore, California

U.S. Department of Energy
Washington, D.C. 20545

July 1982

This report has been reproduced directly from the best available copy.

Available from the National Technical Information Service, U. S. Department of Commerce, Springfield, Virginia 22161.

Price:	Printed Copy	A99
	Microfiche	A01

Codes are used for pricing all publications. The code is determined by the number of pages in the publication. Information pertaining to the pricing codes can be found in the current issues of the following publications, which are generally available in most libraries: *Energy Research Abstracts, (ERA); Government Reports Announcements* and Index (*GRA* and I); *Scientific and Technical Abstract Reports (STAR);* and publication, NTIS-PR-360 available from (NTIS) at the above address.

UU-Z, I

Final Environmental Impact Statement

Lawrence Livermore National aboratory and Sandia National b s — Livermore Sites

Livermore, California

U.S. Department of Energy
Washington, D.C. 20545

July 1982

COVER SHEET

FINAL ENVIRONMENTAL IMPACT STATEMENT
DOE/EIS-0028

(a) Lead Agency: The Department of Energy.

(b) Proposed Action: Lawrence Livermore National Laboratory and Sandia National Laboratories, Livermore, at Livermore, California.

(c) For Further Information Contact: (1) Mr. Gordon C. Facer, Deputy Director, Division of Safety, Environment, and Emergency Actions, Office of Military Application, Office of the Assistant Secretary for Defense Programs, Mail Station DP-226, Germantown Building, Washington, D.C. 20585, (301) 353-3011, (2) Dr. Robert J. Stern, Acting Director, Office of Environmental Compliance, Office of the Assistant Secretary, Environmental Protection, Safety, and Emergency Preparedness.

<u>For Copies of the EIS Contact</u>: Mr. Gordon C. Facer at the address noted above.

(d) Designation: Final EIS.

(e) Abstract: The statement assesses the potential impacts associated with current operation of the Lawrence Livermore National Laboratory and Sandia National Laboratories, Livermore, adjacent sites. This includes the impacts from postulated accidents associated with the activities. Various effluents including radioactive ones are released to the environment. However, a continuing, comprehensive monitoring program is carried out to assist in the control of hazardous effluents. Alternatives considered to current operation of the laboratories include: (1) shutdown and decommissioning, (2) total or partial relocation, (3) scaling down those operations having greatest impact, and (4) wider use of alternate technologies having reduced impact.

Foreword

This environmental impact statement has been prepared to further the purposes of the National Environmental Policy Act of 1969, as amended. It is intended that this document be used to assist future agency planning and decision making associated with activities at the Livermore site, Livermore, California.

On July 16, 1976, ERDA published a notice in the Federal Register that a draft environmental statement was under preparation on its Livermore operations. Comments and suggestions were solicited concerning material to be included in this statement. One comment letter was received in response to that notice.

In September 1978 the Department of Energy, formerly the Energy Research and Development Administration (ERDA), issued the draft environmental impact statement (DEIS), which assessed the impact of continued operation at the Livermore site. This DEIS was distributed for public review and comment to federal and state agencies, local governments, and other individuals and groups known to have an interest in the site. A 90-day comment period was established which closed on December 22, 1978.

A total of 26 comment letters were received from government agencies, organizations, and individuals. A staff statement was prepared in March 1979 in response to these comments. Copies of this staff statement were sent to those who prepared written comments and others who requested them.

During the comment period numerous requests were made for a public hearing to afford an opportunity for further comment on the DEIS. In response to these requests a public hearing was held at the Granada High School in Livermore on April 12, 1979. Specific issues raised at this hearing were recorded in the Hearing Transcript and Record. Copies of these documents, including the presiding board's statement and the written responses, have been distributed to all hearing participants and are available in DOE Public Document rooms.

The present EIS contains the changes made in the DEIS as a result of the comment letters received, the concerns voiced at the public hearing, and those issues identified by the Hearing Board which it considered to be critical to future decision-making at the Livermore site. The delay between the draft and final statement is due to the extensive geological/seismological studies performed at and around the Livermore site. Although the studies are still not complete, adequate information is now available to show that the design-basis earthquake will probably be less severe than that presently used. All the critical facilities have been evaluated for their resistance to the present design-basis earthquake.

Terms used in the EIS are defined in Appendix 1A, and the principal preparers are listed in Appendix 1B.

CONTENTS

LIST OF FIGURES

LIST OF TABLES

SUMMARY

1.1. BACKGROUND

The Lawrence Livermore National Laboratory (LLNL) and Sandia National Laboratories-Livermore (SNLL) are located on adjacent sites about 65 km east of San Francisco in the Livermore Valley in southern Alameda County, approximately 5 km east of the City of Livermore. The sites occupy a combined area of 3.29 km^2. Open agricultural areas surround the Livermore site. Site 300, located about 19 km southeast of Livermore, is operated by LLNL as a nonnuclear high-explosives site. Hydrodynamic tests are conducted here in support of nuclear weapons development.

Prior to World War II, the Livermore site was farmland and was used for grain production and cattle grazing. In 1942, the Navy established the Livermore Naval Air Station on the property. This property was transferred to the Atomic Energy Commission [now the Department of Energy (DOE)] in 1951 as a site for the Material Test Accelerator. The present LLNL was established in 1952 and SNLL was established in 1956.

A brief description is presented of LLNL and SNLL facilities which have programmatic operations with a potential for environmental impacts. Plans for future land use in accordance with the Livermore Site Development Plan are described. A description of new facilities planned is presented.

Nuclear weapons research and development has always been the primary mission of the Livermore operations. However, today's programs include magnetic fusion research, biomedical studies, and laser fusion and laser isotope separation research. Most recently, programs to develop nonnuclear energy technologies have been established at Livermore.

Activities undertaken at Livermore include the nuclear weapons development program; energy programs in geothermal development, coal gasification, combustion research, and solar energy; and magnetic and laser fusion energy research. Other Livermore operations include: 1) a large, high-speed computer facility which, in addition to application in weapons development, magnetic fusion, laser and energy research calculations, has been used for a variety of nonenergy projects such as developing predictive computer models of atmospheric pollution in the San Francisco Bay Area; 2) on-site facilities for the Graduate Center for Applied Science, a unit of the College of Engineering, University of California at Davis; and 3) an atmospheric release advisory capability for forecasting cloud trajectories, concentrations, and population doses resulting from a nuclear accident within the United States.

Population distributions are given for the public within 1.6 km, 16 km, and 80 km. These distributions are given to illustrate the number of people who might be affected by accidental release of either radioactive or otherwise hazardous material. The nearest urban residential area is 0.8 km from the west perimeter of the DOE property. Total present population within 80 km of the Livermore operations is approximately 5 million.

The DOE Livermore National Laboratories are located in a tectonically active region. Within the Livermore Valley and adjacent areas there is evidence of recent seismic activity along the Calaveras, Las Positas, and Greenville Faults as well as Quaternary movements of several other faults. Recent geologic studies have located a strand of the Las Positas Fault within SNLL. Three other faults have been postulated to cross the LLNL site. However, recent trenching showed no evidence of these three faults.

Major active faults in the vicinity of LLNL and SNLL are the San Andreas Fault, with a maximum credible earthquake (MCE) of 8.5 as measured on the Richter scale, which passes within 58 km; the Hayward Fault, with an MCE of 7.0 and at a distance of 32 km; and the Calaveras Fault, with an MCE of 7.3 and a closest distance of 17 km. The Greenville and Las Positas Faults have been investigated and found to be active. The Las Positas Fault has been mapped as passing through SNLL about 1 km south of LLNL. A strand of the Greenville Fault has been mapped about 1 km northeast of LLNL.

Permanent buildings were designed in accordance with the seismic design requirements of the Uniform Building Code (UBC) in force at the time of construction. However, the seismic resistance of critical facilities at LLNL were evaluated using a more conservative design-basis earthquake having a horizontal ground acceleration of 0.8 g. Because of the location of the Las Positas Fault, SNLL engaged the engineering and consulting firm of URS/John A. Blume & Associates, Engineers, to perform a geological investigation of the SNLL site and a structural investigation of the Tritium Research Laboratory (TRL). Remedial measures for seismic upgrade for the TRL recommended in the Blume report were performed.

Some additional geological studies have been deemed necessary as part of the review and improvement of the design-basis earthquake for LLNL facilities. These investigations include geologic mapping along the Greenville and Las Positas Fault zones and in other selected areas, in addition to subsurface exploration within LLNL. This work is being integrated with ongoing seismological, hydrological, and geophysical investigations as part of an LLNL Site Seismic Safety Program.

The climate of the Livermore Valley is characterized by mild, rainy winters and warm, dry summers. Severe weather is rare. Tornados do not pose a local threat as severe as extreme winds. Extreme wind has been defined as 49 m/s, based upon a mean recurrence interval of 10,000 years. For Site 300, the criterion is increased to 54 m/s because of possible channeling through the site. All critical facilities at Livermore and Site 300 will withstand the extreme wind.

An archaeological reconnaissance of the Livermore site, conducted by Archaeological Consulting and Research Services of Mill Valley, California, indicated no evidence of archaeological resources. An intensive archaeological survey was conducted at Site 300 which located several sites of aboriginal and historical activity.

The radiological background of the Livermore site is predominately determined by the activity levels of naturally occurring uranium, thorium, and potassium in local soils. Accordingly, on-site measurements of radiation exposure rates do not differ significantly from those made immediately off-site or within the Livermore Valley. Several minor incidents involving releases of radioactivity have occurred at LLNL during the past 25 years that have resulted in local surface contamination. These areas have been paved to eliminate possible spread of contamination. The total area so treated was about 300 m^2 and involved less than 0.1 μCi of plutonium. Environmental monitoring surveys detected low-level plutonium and americium contamination in an on-site area east of the LLNL waste treatment area. The source of this contamination is proabably due to local radioactivity releases connected with the solar evaporators used in volume reduction of intermediate-level liquid waste. These evaporators are no longer used for volume reduction of radioactive waste. Although levels above normal background radioactivity have occasionally been detected at perimeter air filter samples during solar evaporator operations, these filters now show typical global fallout levels of airborne plutonium. This would indicate that the contaminated soil is not being resuspended to an extent which influences site perimeter concentrations.

1.2. ENVIRONMENTAL IMPACT

Most of the property occupied by the Livermore laboratories has been diverted from its original agricultural land use for 40 years. Neither the present operations nor those planned for the immediate future impact on prime or unique farmland. None of the land immediately surrounding the Livermore laboratories is prime or unique farmland.

Requirements for consumption of natural resources and energy include water, natural gas, and electrical power. In 1979, water usage was 9.5×10^5 m^3; natural gas usage was 1.5×10^7 m^3; and electrical power consumption was 870 TJ.

Acquisition of additional property around LLNL is under consideration. Recently SNLL acquired approximately 0.1 km^2 of agricultural land joining the eastern boundary to provide for future expansion. All construction activities take place on land controlled by LLNL and SNLL. Consequently, with the exception of increased traffic on East Avenue (the main entrance to either site), the environmental impact of these activities on the community (such as noise and dust) is negligible.

Waste management at Livermore includes the categories of radioactive waste, sanitary waste, chemical (nonradioactive) waste, excess property, salvage and reclamation, and land fill operations.

Section 3.5 describes radioactive waste management procedures at LLNL. Some radioactive wastes generated by SNLL are also processed at LLNL. Liquid radioactive wastes are treated at LLNL's Building 514 facility to reduce activity levels to as low as practicable below standards set in DOE Order 5480.1A. Following this treatment, the material is released to the sanitary sewer system. Concentrations of radioactivity in the sewage effluent, which is discharged to the City of Livermore's sewer system, is continuously monitored. In 1980 a total of 5 Ci of tritium were released to the sewer. During this same period 2.8×10^{-4} Ci of ^{239}Pu were released. Liquid waste not amenable to further treatment is transferred to a vacuum evaporator for volume reduction. Solar evaporation used for these reductions prior to 1974 has been discontinued, because of the possible release of activity during the transfer of dry radioactive residues. Dry solid waste is transferred to Department of Transportation (DOT)-approved shipping containers and released to a contractor who ships it to a DOE-approved burial or storage facility. During 1979, approximately 376 m^3 of radioactive waste was shipped from LLNL. While no radioactive waste is permanently stored or buried at the Livermore sites, land burials of solid wastes containing depleted uranium are made at Site 300 using 10 CFR 20.304 as guidance.

Sanitary waste from DOE's Livermore laboratories is treated at the Livermore Water Reclamation Plant. This is a 220-liter/s tertiary sewage treatment plant serving the residential, commercial, and industrial users in Livermore. The sanitary effluent from DOE operations contributes about 7% of the total sewage treated. There have been several accidental releases of toxic and radioactive materials to the sanitary sewer from the Livermore laboratories. (These releases and their impact are listed in Appendix 3A.) For each such incident, corrective measures were instituted to prevent a recurrence. Some of these were chemical releases from the plating shops, or were pH excursions due to discharges from a variety of sources at LLNL or SNLL. A neutralization/ion-exchange facility to process the plating shop wastes is now in service. The Livermore Site sewage effluent is continuously monitored for pH as well as radioactivity.

The largest radiological impact from Livermore operations is from LLNL's 14-MeV neutron generator in Building 212. In 1980 the maximum annual fence line dose from this source was 166 mrem. A survey of potential exposures, including those to motorists and bicyclists on East Avenue and users of the Sandia parking lot, indicates that no one is exposed to more than 10 mrem per year from these operations. Radioactive airborne effluents include ^{41}Ar, from the LLNL reactor, Building 281; $^{13}N_2$-$^{15}O_2$ from LLNL's linear accelerator, Building 194; and $^{3}H_2$ principally from LLNL's Building 331. During 1980 the estimated maximum annual fence line doses from ^{41}Ar, ^{13}N-^{15}O, and ^{3}H were 1.3, 2.1, and

0.4 mrem, respectively. In 1980 the LLNL reactor was shutdown and the fuel elements were removed. Airborne particulate radioactivity is removed from effluent air using high-efficiency particulate air (HEPA) filters. In 1980 3 μCi of ^{239}Pu was released from the LLNL plutonium facility due to improper mounting of a HEPA filter.

A study of the sociological impact of DOE operations on the community of Livermore shows that the greatest impact occurred during the late 1950s and early 1960s. During this time, the DOE operations accounted for a larger percentage of the City's population than at present. As a result, LLNL and SNLL employees living in Livermore created strong demands for housing, and accounted for significant increases in school enrollments and local businesses. Since 1967, the majority of the City's growth has been due to the trend of living in suburbia and working in surrounding urban areas. At present, LLNL and SNLL employees and their families account for approximately 30% of the City's population.

Section 3.9 includes an analysis of maximum credible accidents that could occur at Livermore. These are postulated to occur under worst-case conditions. These maximum credible accidents include a tritium release, a nuclear criticality accident, a ^{244}Cm spill, a building fire, and a release of chlorine. All critical facilities have been evaluated for their ability to withstand natural accidents--such as earthquakes, flooding, and high winds. The consequences of such natural accidents are not greater than the ones described.

The postulated tritium accident involves 1.2 MCi of tritium released from either Tritium Facility, all of which is in the form of HTO (tritiated water). The maximum site boundary dose of 5.3 rem occurs from this postulated release from SNLL building 968 at the SNLL northeast perimeter. This is within the 10 CFR 100 guideline of 25 rem for a maximum whole body accidental dose.

The maximum credible nuclear criticality accident is postulated to involve plutonium in LLNL Building 332 and would result in a fission yield of 10^{18} fissions. The maximum fission product dose at the LLNL's west site boundary would be 0.08 rem whole body (submersion) and 0.58 rem thyroid (inhalation). These doses are well below the guideline of 25 rem whole body and 300 rem to the thyroid as a result of an accident.

The maximum credible spill is postulated to involve 15 g of ^{244}Cm dispersed through a workroom in LLNL's Building 251. The total integrated dose to the pulmonary region of a person standing in the center line of the cloud during its passage at the west site boundary would be 5.6 rem. This dose is within the guidelines of 10 CFR 100.

A large building fire having severe environmental consequences, such as destroying the containment features in facilities containing radioactivity, is not likely because of automatic fire protection (sprinklers) and/or fire-resistant building construction. Fires are most likely to occur in the wooden buildings used as offices. The major off-site consideration of such a fire would be a smoke cloud and the possibility of sparks and burning brands.

Most of the toxic chemicals at Livermore are used in such small quantities that their accidental release would have no credible off-site environmental impact. The largest container of toxic material in use at LLNL is the standard 68-kg chlorine cylinder used to chlorinate the LLNL swimming pool. Release of a full cylinder of this material to the atmosphere would not produce acute health effects off-site. Accidental releases of toxic chemicals to the sanitary sewer have occurred from "bright dip" tanks (a chromic acid solution containing copper), which are located in shop areas throughout the Laboratory. Similar toxic chemical releases have also originated from LLNL's Plating Shop. Some of these releases temporarily reduced the treatment capability at the Livermore Water Reclamation Plant. The frequency of these releases has now been minimized by engineering and administrative controls. The sewage effluent is now continuously monitored for pH, and provisions are available for the temporary diversion of sewage at the treatment plant in the event of an accidental release.

Radioactive materials that are transported by DOE contractors are handled in two ways. If transportation is intra-site, radioactive materials are double-contained (two contamination barriers). Department of Transportation regulations are followed if radioactive materials are moved off-site, such as a transfer of materials from the Livermore Site to Site 300. In either case the containers are capable of withstanding the maximum credible transportation accident.

Appendix 3B describes the LLNL Disaster Control Plan, which contains procedures to mitigate the consequences of accidents.

1.3. UNAVOIDABLE ADVERSE ENVIRONMENTAL IMPACTS

Environmental impacts which are considered unavoidable consequences of ongoing operations include 1) continued commitment of land to government use, 2) utilization of natural resources and energy, 3) Laboratory traffic on East Avenue, and 4) operational release of radioactive and nonradioactive effluents.

1.4. ALTERNATIVES

Alternatives considered to DOE Livermore operations have been 1) "no action," which for ongoing operations is plant shutdown and decommissioning, 2) total or partial plant relocation, 3) scaling down those operations having the greatest impact, and 4) wider use of alternate technologies having reduced impact.

1.5. RELATIONSHIP BETWEEN SHORT-TERM USES AND LONG-TERM PRODUCTIVITY

Historically, the lands now occupied by the Livermore Laboratories was used for agriculture. At Site 300 the commitment of land is principally as undeveloped buffer zone. Thus, the present use allows for easy conversion back to agricultural use. The Livermore Valley sites (LLNL and SNLL) are extensively built up, precluding return to agriculture. However, much of the surrounding land is zoned for industry, indicating that local governments feel the most appropriate long-term use of these lands is not agricultural but industrial.

1.6. RELATIONSHIPS OF THE LIVERMORE OPERATIONS TO LAND USE PLANS, POLICIES, AND CONTROLS

The Livermore operations are in agreement with the City of Livermore's General Plan for land use. These operations are also not in conflict with any known land use plans, policies, or controls of the State of California or Alameda County.

1.7. IRREVERSIBLE AND IRRETRIEVABLE COMMITMENT OF RESOURCES

Irreversible and irretrievable commitments of resources include those resources consumed during DOE operations and those that cannot be expected to revert to a natural state if DOE-owned structures were removed. Although not anticipated in the foreseeable future, these facilities could be decommissioned and much of the equipment recovered for use elsewhere. Small areas of the LLNL site exhibit radiation levels slightly above background. These areas would require decontamination as part of decommissioning.

1.8. ENVIRONMENTAL TRADE-OFF ANALYSIS

A qualitative environmental trade-off analysis is performed in Section 9, which balances the costs and benefits of each of the alternatives considered in Section 5.

Based on the discussion of the general alternatives available and the information presented in the other sections of this assessment, it is concluded that DOE operations at Livermore should continue in the present manner in research and development. Such action provides the capability 1) to use any new technologies that are developed through the present programs, and 2) to continually review and upgrade DOE programs to minimize any possible adverse environmental impacts.

2. BACKGROUND

Chapter 2 of the DEIS has been updated and revised in response to review and comment by federal, state, and municipal agencies and by private citizens. Major changes are as follows:

- Section 2.1.8 on Environmental Monitoring has been expanded to give greater emphasis on water and soil sampling and analysis. The 1980 annual environmental monitoring report for the Livermore site has been included as Appendix 2A to provide the reader with outlines of the procedures used and typical data obtained.
- Section 2.3.1, Population Distribution and Land Use, has been updated using data supplied by the Association of Bay Area Governments and Alameda County.
- By far the most significant change has been in Section 2.3.3, Geology and Seismicity. This section has been completely rewritten. The results of the Livermore site seismic study, which is being carried out to better define the seismic safety of critical facilities at Livermore, will be published as a separate report which is scheduled to be completed in 1982.

2.1. DETAILED DESCRIPTION

2.1.1. Location

The Lawrence Livermore National Laboratory (LLNL) and the Sandia National Laboratories-Livermore (SNLL) are located about 65 km east of San Francisco at the southeast end of the Livermore Valley in southern Alameda County. The City of Livermore is located about 5 km to the west. LLNL occupies essentially all (2.54 km^2) of Section 12, T3S, R2E of the USGS Altamont Quadrangle, California, while Sandia occupies 0.75 km^2 of the north half of Section 13 of the same quadrangle. The LLNL property also has an open storm drain right-of-way extending northward from the northwest corner of the site to the Western Pacific tracks, a distance of 317 m, covering an area of 5700 m^2 of land. Figure 2-1 shows the location of these laboratories with respect to the City of Livermore. Lands to the north, west and south are zoned industrial, although present usage is mostly agricultural. Land immediately to the east is zoned agricultural and is currently used as pasture.

Site 300, located about 19 km southeast of Livermore in the sparsely populated hills of the Diablo Range, is operated by LLNL as a high-explosives test facility. This site, covering an area of about 27 km^2, is roughly rectangular in shape with its southern boundary being adjacent to Corral Hollow

Figure 2-1. DOE Livermore site (looking west toward Livermore, 1981).

Road. About one-sixth of the Site lies in Alameda County. The remainder is in San Joaquin County. Figure 2-2 shows the location of Site 300 with reference to Livermore.

2.1.2. Prior Land Use

Prior to World War II the land now occupied by the two laboratories was used for light agriculture and cattle grazing. In March of 1942 the Navy purchased the property as a site for establishing a training base, subsequently known as the Livermore Naval Air Station. (See Fig. 2-3.) Part of the area now occupied by SNLL contained a Navy landfill disposal site.

Prior land use at Site 300 was limited to sheep and cattle grazing, due to the rugged terrain. Most of the area at Site 300 is characterized by steep, smooth hills and deep ravines, with elevations ranging from 150 m at the southwest corner along the Corral Hollow valley floor to over 500 m in the northwest sector.

SNLL began operations on a 0.3-km^2 site. One parcel was part of the Naval Air Station property and the other parcel was purchased dry farmland. In 1970, two additional parcels (0.35 km^2) of agricultural land were purchased for SNLL development. An additional purchase of approximately 0.1 km^2 was made during 1979.

2.1.3. History

2.1.3.1. Establishment of LLNL. The first Russian nuclear test in 1949 led to the establishment of LLNL. Plans were then being made at the Los Alamos National Laboratory to construct a fusion bomb. These plans and the Russians' first detonation of a fission device emphasized the need for a continuing supply of fissionable material. Large uranium deposits had not yet been found in the United States and this country was reluctant to depend on foreign sources. In January of 1950, construction of the fusion bomb was ordered. Shortly thereafter, Dr. E. O. Lawrence was authorized to construct an accelerator to demonstrate the feasibility of using high-energy neutrons to produce nuclear materials such as tritium and plutonium. This was the mission of the Materials Test Accelerator (MTA).

The search for a suitable location for this accelerator was soon narrowed to the Livermore Valley. Since, no such plans existed for the use of the naval air station, the Department of Defense volunteered to transfer the site to the Atomic Energy Commission (AEC). Although this transfer was dated January 5, 1951, the California Research and Development Corporation (a subsidiary of Standard Oil of California) moved onto the Livermore site in June of 1950 and began construction of the MTA,

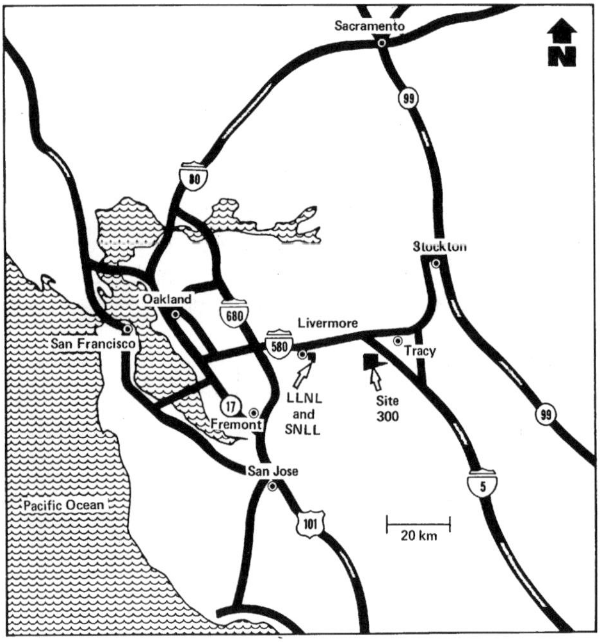

Figure 2-2. Location of LLNL, SNLL, and Site 300 with respect to Livermore and surrounding communities.

Figure 2-3. Livermore Naval Air Station (1944).

under a contract with the AEC. However, due to changes in technology this accelerator was never operated for its intended purpose.

In 1951, the University of California Radiation Laboratory (UCRL) at Berkeley began using some of the facilities in support of the Los Alamos National Laboratory (Los Alamos). In February of 1952, Livermore was selected as a second nuclear weapons laboratory. The Site was activated in July 1952 by an eight-man staff from Berkeley.

Soon after LLNL was established, it was recognized that an additional site would be required for high explosives tests in connection with the nuclear weapons programs at Livermore. Such a site should be in a remote area, but as near LLNL as possible. Accordingly, in July 1953 LLNL submitted a proposal for Site 300 (originally identified as the Corral Hollow Site) to be located about 19 km southeast of Livermore. The original site covered an area of approximately 8 km^2. Experiments with high explosives were conducted there beginning in 1955. It was enlarged in 1957 to its present area of 27 km^2.

Engineering research and development associated with nuclear ordnance originated at Los Alamos. Ordnance engineering was separated from nuclear design activities at Los Alamos when Sandia National Laboratories was established at Albuquerque in 1949. Since then Sandia has been operated through a contract between the Western Electric Company and the U. S. Department of Energy (DOE), formerly the Energy Research and Development Administration (ERDA), and before that the AEC.

In 1956 Sandia established a branch at Livermore, Sandia National Laboratories-Livermore (SNLL), to provide a closer working relationship with LLNL.

2.1.3.2. Objectives. LLNL's primary mission is the design of nuclear weapons. However, other programs have been added when the technical expertise and facilities at Livermore seemed appropriate for their undertaking. These additional programs include controlled thermonuclear research, biomedical studies, and laser fusion and laser isotope separation research. In addition, the Laboratory now has a program to investigate nonnuclear energy technologies and another involving environmental studies. Present funding for these latter two programs comes from DOE and other sources.

SNLL's principal objective is research, development, and design of nuclear weapons systems, excluding the nuclear components. Major activities include tritium research; arming, fusing, and firing systems; and aerodynamic and structural elements used in U.S. nuclear bombs and warheads. Components in these systems include power supplies, timing mechanisms, radars, switches, and other classified elements which make up the intricate actuating and control mechanisms. Energy-related activities are conducted in combustion and solar research. Sandia's responsibilities are carried out jointly between its Livermore and Albuquerque locations.

2.1.4. Significant Accomplishments

In the field of nuclear explosives development, extensive LLNL contributions began with a fundamental breakthrough in the late 1950s that permitted the development of strategic warheads small enough to fit into missiles. Since that time, LLNL and SNLL have been responsible for the development of the warheads for the present strategic missiles, notably Polaris, Poseidon, and Minuteman. Similarly, their contributions to the understanding of nuclear weapons enabled development of the Spartan warhead (tested at Amchitka), and made marked improvements in the survivability of offensive missile systems. SNLL has become increasingly involved in the design and development of command, control, and security systems for nuclear weapons.

In magnetic confinement fusion research, LLNL developed a new technique for stabilizing a mirror plasma. This enabled demonstration of a principle crucial to the mirror program, namely, that plasma confinement time increases with plasma temperature. Coupled with other recent LLNL high-density experiments, this research lends credence to the belief that the scientific feasibility of the mirror approach to fusion could be demonstrated in the early 1980s. LLNL's laser fusion program passed a major milestone by obtaining experimental evidence that thermonuclear neutrons are produced in laser-driven implosions. Advances in solid-state laser materials and other improvements promise a four-to-eightfold increase in laser power per dollar invested, compared with what has been available before. In 1975 the laser program increased its target irradiation facilities by putting in operation the half-terawatt JANUS laser and the one-terawatt CYCLOPS laser.

LLNL has made extensive innovations in new computer languages, software concepts, and detailed programs tying together varied computer equipment into a total system. A nuclear physics effort has produced extensive new information and refinements relating to nuclear energy states and processes relevant to energy generation. The theory, which provides the basis for hope that laser fusion may be achieved at practical laser-energy levels, provides major motivation to the expanding experimental program. Entirely new techniques in machining, especially to previously unattained tolerances and accuracies, have been developed.

2.1.5. Operations and Facility Descriptions

2.1.5.1. LLNL. LLNL is organized along programmatic lines to achieve balanced progress on the concurrent projects. Functionally, the staff is divided into scientific, support, and administrative categories. Responsibility for each of the major programs is assigned to an associate director.

Depending on the nature of the program, each division will obtain technical assistance from support departments such as engineering, computations, and chemistry.

Each of the programs has been provided buildings to house assigned personnel as well as to provide laboratory and shop facilities. However, in many cases support departments will work on programmatic assignments in their own facilities since their activities may be common to several programs or the necessary equipment (such as the large computers in the Computations Department and the specialized machines in the Mechanical Shops) cannot be profitably duplicated.

Figure 2-4 shows the current layout of the LLNL site. In 1968, a long-range development plan was adopted by the Laboratory and the AEC. The plan is currently being implemented on the site and provides for an orderly development and effective use of the remaining "open" area.

2.1.5.2. Site 300. Site 300 is divided into a general-service area located in the southeastern corner of the Site adjacent to Corral Hollow Road and six programmatic operation areas distributed throughout the Site (see Fig. 2-5).

General-Service Area--This area contains nine major buildings which house all administrative and support functions, such as Site Administration, Police/Security, Fire Department, Medical, Crafts and Plant Engineering, Stores, Mechanical and Electrical Engineering, Cafeteria, and Service Station.

Programmatic Facilities--The six basic programmatic operations include:

- High explosives (HE) formulation and manufacture. This work is performed in three facilities comprising six major buildings and five utility/support buildings and magazines.
- HE processing. Eight major buildings and 29 utility/support buildings and magazines are used in these operations.
- Dynamic testing. Seven HE firing sites (bunkers), three explosive storage magazines, and 17 support/storage buildings are used for this function.
- Environmental testing. Ten buildings house equipment for static and dynamic tests. These tests may involve plutonium and mock explosives, but plutonium and live explosives are not permitted within a test assembly or concurrently within a facility.
- Experiments not involving HE. From time to time experiments are performed at the Site which do not require the use of HE. They are located at Site 300 because they may require more space or more isolation or have other special requirements such that cannot be met at LLNL.
- Occasionally, Site 300 is used to perform experiments or provide space for outside groups.

Figure 2-5 is a map of Site 300.

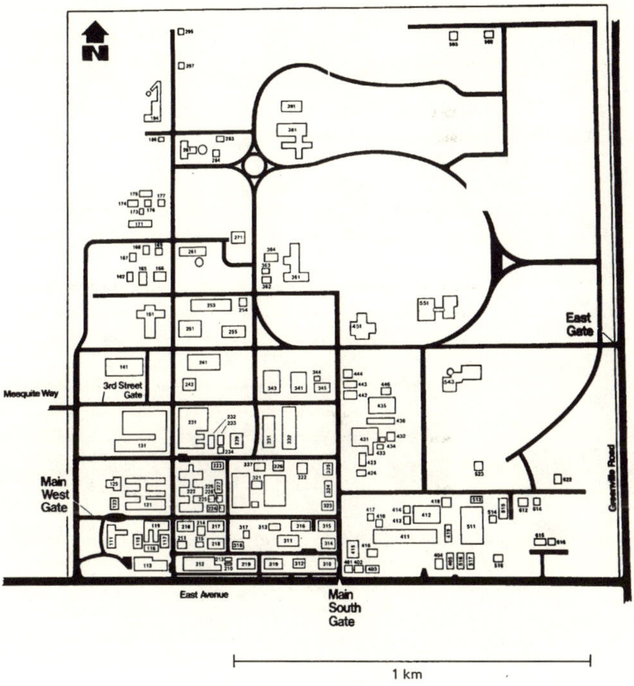

Figure 2-4. Layout of LLNL site.

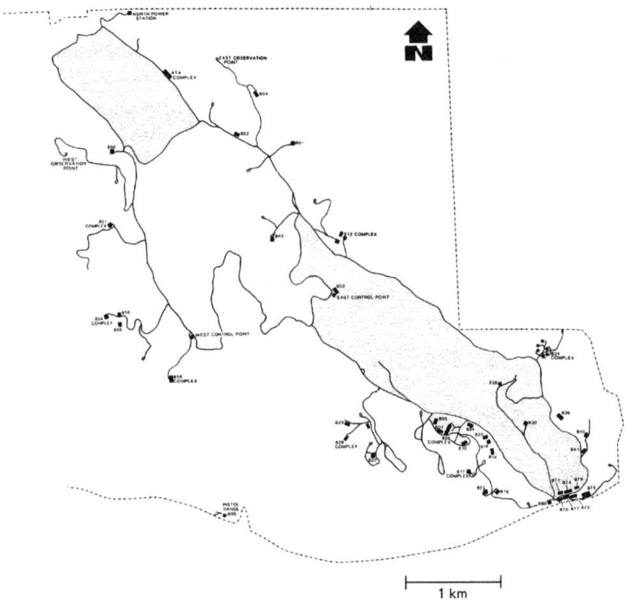

Figure 2-5. Layout of Site 300.

2.1.5.3. SNLL. The SNLL site is essentially divided into two different work areas as shown in Fig. 2-6. The Office and Laboratory Area is used to provide office, shop, laboratory, and support space. This area is the most heavily populated at SNLL.

The Office and Laboratory Area includes a vault for the storage of classified and unclassified radioactive materials. The laboratories in this area are: laboratories for electronics, telemetry, nucleonics, optical electronics, powder metallurgy, hydrogen effects, microelectronics, glass, and joining.

The Maintenance Shops and Storage Area are used for plant maintenance offices and shops, support facilities, raw stock storage, and a hold area for storing equipment. A small hold area used for the temporary storage of solid radioactive wastes is also located in this area. The carpentry and sheet metal shops were recently moved into this area from the Office and Laboratory Area.

2.1.6. Facilities Having Environmental Impact Significance

Operations within most facilities at LLNL and SNLL have no significant environmental impact. During normal operations several facilities release effluents having small but measurable levels of radioactive or nonradioactive contaminants. Other facilities handle radioactive materials in sufficient quantity that special containment features and operating procedures are required to assure that the radioactivity is not released to the environment.

Listed below are brief descriptions of these facilities. Where applicable, actions taken or planned for reducing the effects of effluents are noted. A detailed analysis of maximum credible accidents is given in Section 3.9. Normal impacts are described in Section 3.5.1.

2.1.6.1. LLNL Building 194--Electron Positron Accelerator. The Electron-Positron Linear Accelerator (LINAC) located in the northwest quarter of LLNL is a significant tool in the continuing neutron physics research effort and in the Laboratory's work involving photo nuclear cross-section and activation measurements. The 100-MeV LINAC produces the world's highest positron intensity and the world's highest variable-energy monochromatic gamma-ray flux.

Shielding and personnel barriers control on-site exposure from the accelerator's beam. Gaseous radioactive effluents ($^{15}O_2$ and $^{13}N_2$) are released through a 30-m stack.

2.1.6.2. LLNL Building 212--Accelerator Building. A number of medium-energy accelerators are housed in Building 212 at LLNL, which borders East Avenue. One of these units has off-site environmental implications--the Insulating Core Transformer Accelerator (ICT). The ICT is an air-insulated

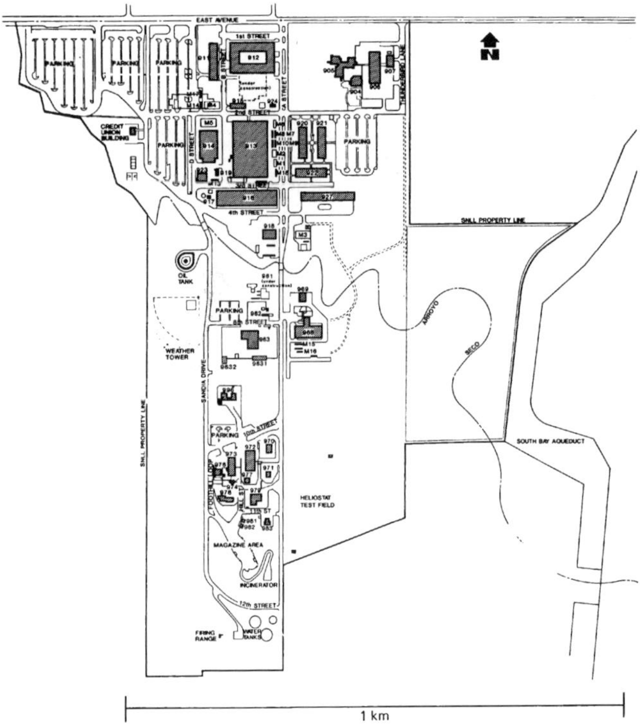

Figure 2-6. Layout of SNLL site.

variable-energy machine designed to accelerate protons and deuterons up to 500 keV. The machine is used mainly to generate 14-MeV neutrons by means of the $^{3}H(d,n)\,^{3}He$ reaction.

Beam currents in excess of 9-mA average current are obtainable. Pulsed modes of operation in the microsecond and nanosecond ranges are also available for neutron time-of-flight measurements. The ICT is housed in a concrete enclosure with 460-mm-thick concrete walls and roof. The entrance is a 460-mm-thick interlocked power-operated door.

The ICT has been used in radiation-damage studies in support of the Magnetic Fusion Energy (MFE) program. Flux rates at which the 14-MeV generator was operated for these studies have been responsible for above-background neutron and gamma exposure rates at the LLNL south boundary fence. Most of these high-flux operations are now conducted at Building 292, the Rotating Target Neutron Source (RTNS), located in the northwest quadrant of LLNL. Because of this, fenceline radiation dose at Building 212 was reduced from a maximum of 1020 mrem in 1975 to 166 in 1980.

2.1.6.3. LLNL Building 231--LLNL Central Vault. Building 231, in the southwest quadrant of LLNL, is the Laboratory's Central Vault. Activities in the building include receiving, shipping, and storage of plutonium, uranium and certain isotopes, and degreasing and oxidation of uranium. The vault is air-conditioned. Ventilation is a once-through system which maintains a negative pressure differential between the vault and the outside environment. All supply air ducts have fire dampers. The exhaust air is filtered through two high-efficiency particulate air (HEPA) filters in series. The facility is equipped with smoke detectors, a sprinkler system, and radiation and criticality alarms. Administrative controls and the safety design features within the vault make a nuclear criticality accident or radioactivity spill affecting the off-site environment extremely improbable.

2.1.6.4. LLNL Building 251--Nuclear Chemistry Operations. This facility in the southwest quadrant of LLNL primarily handles, processes, and stores multicurie quantities of the actinides. Operations within the building are conducted in specialized enclosures governed by strict administrative procedures.

Activities in Building 251 vary according to programmatic requirements but, in general, fall into two major categories. The first relates to the diagnostic activities associated with the underground testing of nuclear devices. The second category involves basic research devoted to a better understanding of the nuclear behavior of the heavy elements. Such activities as preparation of accelerator targets, providing ultrapure isotopic standards, and understanding the early characteristics of fission are examples of the research function of this facility. Although normal operations within Building 251 have no off-site environmental impacts, the scenario for a maximum credible radioactive spill discussed in Section 3.9 involves this facility. Modifications have recently been completed to upgrade ventilation and exhaust systems and incorporate structural modifications to improve seismic resistance. These changes reduce the possible impact on off-site environment from operations in Building 251 far below the spill described in Section 3.9.

2.1.6.5. LLNL Building 281--Pool-Type Reactor. Building 281 in the northwest quadrant of LLNL housed the Livermore Pool-Type Reactor (LPTR). Due to lack of projected need, the reactor was shutdown in 1980 and the fuel elements removed. The principal environmental impact from the reactor was the site boundary radiation dose from ^{41}Ar, which was produced in normal operation by activation of argon in the ambient air within the reactor containment building. The 1980 ^{41}Ar release corresponded to an estimated site perimeter radiation dose of 1.3 mrem. DOE Order 5480.1A allows a maximum annual dose off-site of 500 mrem. With the reactor shutdown, there is no ^{41}Ar produced or released.

2.1.6.6. LLNL Building 331--Tritium Research Facility. Building 331, the Tritium Research Facility located in the southwest quadrant of LLNL, is a facility designed for experimental work with radioactive gases and their compounds. The primary radioactive gas is tritium. Normal operations involve the use of multigram quantities of tritium in a variety of forms. Building ventilation is designed to maintain air flow toward zones of higher hazard. The building was constructed in two increments; each increment is monitored by a separate set of room air monitors, stack-effluent monitors, ventilation-loss detectors, and associated alarm panels. Each increment has its own 30-m stack. Tritium released through these stacks under normal operating conditions during 1980 accounted for an estimated annual site boundary radiation dose of less than 1 mrem--less than 0.2% of the DOE 5480.1A standard. Due to a change in programmatic funding, a major portion of the Building 331 facility has been decommissioned. Those operations remaining were consolidated in the north end (Increment II) of the building. Decommissioned laboratory space in Increment I will be used by other LLNL programs. Also being planned is a major upgrade of the building ventilation system that will provide for collection and retention of the small quantities of tritium currently released during routine operations. A second system is being designed to retain nonroutine releases of tritium that may occur in the event of failure of part of the handling system. These innovations will further reduce potential releases of tritium from this facility.

2.1.6.7. LLNL Building 332--Plutonium Facility. Building 332, the Plutonium Facility, is located in the southwest quadrant of LLNL just east of Building 331. The building is a two-story concrete structure, with laboratory work areas, a change room, and a storage vault on the first floor and a fan loft on the second. Operations within the building vary according to nuclear weapons programmatic requirements, but in general include testing of plutonium-bearing engineering assemblies, development of plutonium fabrication techniques, and basic and applied plutonium metallurgy. Building 332 activities include investigations involving americium and curium. The americium and curium are in the form of metals and oxides. The quantity of these isotopes is limited by the dose to personnel in the building under normal conditions and not environmental concerns. Safety procedures for the handling of these materials are similar to those developed for plutonium though more stringent. A one-story increment with basement has been added on the east side of Building 332. In this increment all exhaust air is filtered through multiple HEPA filters. The older portion of the building, has been upgraded by installing additional HEPA filters and temperature-activated water sprinklers in all room exhaust ducts. These modifications will reduce further any possible impact on the environment from operations in this facility.

2.1.6.8. LLNL Building 419--Decontamination. Building 419, which is located in the southeast quadrant of LLNL, contains facilities for removing radioactive or otherwise hazardous contaminants from assorted equipment. Soak tanks, steam guns, mechanical abrasives, ultrasonics and a vapor degreaser use mechanical, chemical, and heat energy to effect decontamination. Liquid wastes generated in these operations are transferred to Building 514 (Liquid Waste Treatment). Equipment that cannot be decontaminated is transferred to Building 612 (Solid Waste) for disposal. Process air from Building 419 is filtered through HEPA filters before release to the atmosphere.

2.1.6.9. LLNL Building 514--Liquid Waste Treatment Plant. Building 514 in the southeast quadrant of LLNL receives retention tank waste that may contain either radioactive or hazardous chemicals at concentrations which cannot be released directly to the sanitary sewer. This large-volume, low-level radioactive liquid waste is treated by a coagulation-fluocculation method that uses a diatomaceous-earth rotary-drum filter to remove the radioactivity and heavy metals from the liquid. The used diatomaceous earth is packaged as solid radioactive waste. A wiped-film evaporator is being installed to handle the somewhat higher-level radioactive liquid waste that is collected in carboys. The radioactive residue from the evaporator is packaged as solid radioactive waste.

Release of untreated liquid waste to the sewer through equipment failure or human error is potentially present in this plant. However, administrative controls and safety features have minimized this potential for environmental impact. Section 3.5 provides more detailed information on Building 514 operations.

2.1.6.10. LLNL Building 612--Waste Disposal. Radioactive solid waste and nonradioactive chemical waste are packaged and held for shipment at Building 612 on the LLNL site northeast of Building 514. Bagged radioactive waste contained in steel drums is delivered to Building 612 from a number of facilities at LLNL and SNLL. Using a hydraulically operated compactor the transuranium-contaminated waste is reduced in volume by a 3:1 ratio, while all other wastes are reduced 4:1. Compacting is done, with local ventilation, exhausted through a HEPA filter. The stack exhaust and the work area atmosphere are monitored continuously. The packaged radioactive waste is presently being transported to the Nevada Test Site for burial. The nonradioactive chemicals are pumped into drums that are trucked by a commercial waste handler to an approved Class I landfill disposal site. This waste-handling facility has had no measurable environmental impact on the off-site environment.

2.1.6.11 Site 300 Operations. At Site 300 there has been no evidence of off-site contamination due to particulate debris from operations at the high explosive bunkers. In 1972 a special study was made to determine to what extent the natural $^{235}U/^{238}U$ ratio in soil was perturbed by the use of depleted uranium in experiments at Site 300.[2-1] Based on isotopic uranium analyses of soils collected throughout the Site it was found that perturbation of the normal $^{235}U/^{238}U$ ratio was essentially restricted to areas adjacent to the firing bunkers. Indeed, samples collected more than about 500 m from these bunkers showed no measurable impact from depleted uranium usage. Depending on meteorological conditions, off-site impacts from annoying noises or overpressures can occur. To minimize these impacts meteorological measurements are made twice daily to set a limit on the weight of high explosives that can be detonated without impact on populated areas. To monitor the correctness of these limits, four microbarograph sensors are maintained in or near Tracy (see Fig. 2-2). The probability of overpressure is greatest in this area because of the direction of the prevailing winds.

2.1.6.12. SNLL Vaults. Security vaults are provided at SNLL for the receipt and storage of radioactive or special nuclear material. One has been established in the warehouse (Building 927) and a small one within the Tritium Research Laboratory (Building 968).

Contents of the 927 Vault vary because of changing needs of the work. They include depleted uranium-containing mock-ups of weapons (weapon-like configurations without the explosives or fissile materials needed to produce nuclear yield), and small, sealed radioactive sources not presently being used. On rare occasions, weapon mock-ups containing fissile materials are stored for short periods of time (up to 1 week) in the Building 927 Vault. These units never contain high explosives and are therefore incapable of producing nuclear yield. Tritium is not stored in the 927 Vault. Presently, the small quantities of tritium at SNLL are kept in the labs where they are used or in the Building 968 Vault.

2.1.6.13. SNLL Tritium Research Laboratory. Building 968, the SNLL Tritium Research Laboratory, is a 25-m x 55-m single-story concrete laboratory building designed for tritium research experiments involving more than 0.1 gram of tritium. The maximum quantity of tritium allowed in an experiment is 120 g (1.2 MCi). These experiments are performed in sealed glove boxes. Automatic decontamination systems remove tritium from glove boxes and vacuum pumps.

Tritium detectors and alarm systems monitor room air, glove boxes, and the stack effluent. These data are collected, displayed, and stored in a computer in the control room. This computer provides for a "stand alone" overview and control of the safety systems. A once-through high-flow ventilation system moves air from clean areas to areas of increasing contamination potential and discharges the building exhaust through a 30-m stack. Tritium released through this stack during 1980 accounted for an estimated annual site boundary radiation dose of less than 1 mrem--less than 0.2% of the DOE 5480.1A standard. Building 968 is scheduled for seismic upgrading which will consist of installing roof ties and external buttresses for lateral bracing. A hardened vault for tritium storage will also be added.

2.1.7. Current and Future Planning and Land Use

2.1.7.1. Livermore Site Development Plan. The Livermore Site Development Plan is a guide for the orderly development of LLNL as it experiences growth or replacement of its temporary and outdated facilities with new, permanent ones. The current allocation of land for programmatic use at the LLNL site is shown in Fig. 2-7.

The World War II buildings that remain on the site have outlived their expected life (30 years). These facilities are expensive to maintain, are generally not properly located to provide the housing where it is needed, and do not always adequately fulfill programmatic requirements. Plans include replacing these buildings with new facilities.

In addition to the World War II buildings, there are many trailers on site. These trailers can generally be located to provide the space where it is needed, but they are expensive to maintain. Where possible, they will be replaced with permanent facilities.

Future building sites are provided for in the Site Development Plan to allow for potential expansion. A new northwest entrance to LLNL is under consideration, augmenting the west entrance at Mesquite, to provide better access from Interstate 580 and the northern and eastern parts of Livermore. It is estimated that this entrance would require the purchase of a strip of farmland 335 m long by 37 m wide.

2.1.7.2. New Facilities: Proposed Major Facilities. The following paragraphs describe proposed major new facilities at LLNL, Site 300, and SNLL. With the exception of those effects typical of

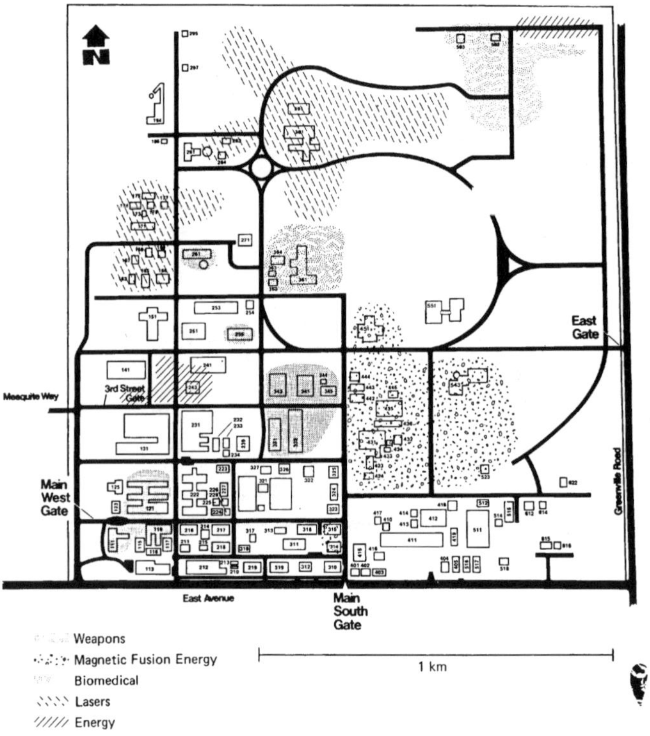

Figure 2-7. Programmatic use of LLNL site.

construction, it is anticipated that none of these will have significant environmental impact. Each proposed project will be examined, analyzed, and evaluated in relation to the policies, objectives, and requirements of CEQ (40CFR, 1500-1508) and DOE Guidelines for Compliance with NEPA (FR 45, No. 62, pp. 20695-20710, March 28, 1980).

2.1.7.2.1 LLNL--Bioenvironmental Office and Laboratory Building (BOLB). The proposed Bioenvironmental Building will be located on the east side of the main laboratory/office building (B-361). The project consists of a separate 3960-m^2 two-story laboratory/office building, and a single-story 418-m^2 library/office addition to the existing building. These facilities will provide for the consolidation of programs and relieve overcrowding.

2.1.7.2.2. LLNL--Laser Fusion Facility Addition. Building 391, which currently houses the laser fusion test facility SHIVA, will be expanded to accept the SHIVA upgrade called NOVA. The addition will be approximately 10,700 m^2 gross floor area and the facility will be used to further investigate inertial confinement fusion techniques.

2.1.7.2.3. LLNL--Fusion Target Development Facility (FTDF). Building 298, which will be programmatically associated with Building 391, will house the Fusion Target Development facility. The facility will consist of a single-story building with approximately 5400 m^2 gross area located northwest of Building 391. This facility will be used as a central location for fusion target fabrication, characterization, and assembly.

2.1.7.2.4. LLNL--Laser Fusion Office Building. This two-story structure, Building 481, will have a gross floor area of 5100 m^2 and will house 200 scientific and other personnel associated with laser fusion research. Many of these workers are presently housed in temporary buildings directly south of Building 381. Building 481 will be east of Building 381 and an upper-level enclosed corridor connecting the two is planned.

2.1.7.2.5. LLNL--Laser Isotope Separation Facility. This facility, Building 482, will provide a multistory structure totaling approximately 8400 m^2 of gross area to be located east of Building 381 (Laser Fusion Office Building). Work in this facility will permit the investigation of new uranium-enrichment processes.

2.1.7.2.6. LLNL--Materials R & D Facility (MRDF). The Materials Research and Development Facility (MRDF), Building 235, is proposed in order to expand and consolidate R & D efforts in the weapons related areas of metallurgy, plastics, and inorganic materials. The project includes a new facility to be located east of existing Building 231 and north of Building 239. The MRDF has a gross area of 6800 m^2 and will provide laboratory and office space for 179 people.

2.1.7.2.7. LLNL--Management Support Center, Core II (MSC-II). The MSC-II will be a T-shaped structure of 10,220 m^2 and will house Data Processing, Business Services, Procurement, Accounting, Forms and Records, and Mail Services for the Laboratory. The facility will have three floors, and will be located north of Building 551 (Core I).

2.1.7.2.8. LLNL--Mirror Fusion Test Facility-B (MFTF-B). This project provides for: (1) design, fabrication, and installation of added major components to comprise a large tandem mirror test apparatus; (2) modifications of existing buildings to house and support a magnetic mirror fusion test device; (3) construction of a light laboratory building of approximately 1430 m^2 and (4) construction of an office wing of approximately 3200 m^2. These proposed changes are an extension of the original MFTF concept scheduled for FY 1978-1981.

2.1.7.2.9. LLNL--High-Explosives Application Facility (HEAF) B-351. The proposed HEAF, Building 351, will make it possible to integrate, centralize, and extend many high explosives (HE) activities currently conducted at LLNL. The new facility will contain approximately 8800 m^2, of which 5600 m^2 will be underground. HEAF facilities located underground include spaces for HE storage, precision shot assembly and instrumentation, contact and remote control of HE operations in support of test firings, enclosed firing chambers, and a high-velocity gas gun. The remainder of the facility will be above grade and will contain office, drafting, library, data reduction, and conference space for the HE program staff. The HEAF will be located north of Building 341.

2.1.7.2.10. LLNL--Earth Sciences Facility (ESF). The proposed Earth Sciences Facility will be a two-story structure with a floor area of about 7400 m^2. It will provide office space and light laboratory space for 275 people, including conference and auditorium areas, library, computer centers, work areas, and other support areas. The building will be sited west of Building 151.

2.1.7.2.11. LLNL--National Atmospheric Release Advisory Center (NARAC). This project will consist of approximately 2300 m^2 of office space for 50 additional personnel, and space for computers and associated support equipment. NARAC is a real-time regional scale system for predicting the transport, diffusion, and deposition of radionuclides released to the atmosphere. The proposed facility will be north of Building 151.

2.1.7.2.12. LLNL--Nuclear Test Technology Complex (NTTC). The NTTC will be a multistory structure with laboratories and related offices located on the first floor and basement levels. The majority of the office facilities will be located on the second floor. The proposed new facility will have approximately 16,000 m^2 of floor space, and will be located west of Building 111. The project provides part of the facilities which are required to meet the objectives of future test programs .

2.1.7.2.13. LLNL--Weapons Technology Complex, Phase 1. This project will provide a seven-story addition to the east side of existing Building 111. It will contain approximately 4200 m^2 and will house 150 scientists and engineers. The building addition will support the future test program.

2.1.7.2.14. LLNL--Non-Destructive Evaluation Facility Addition (NDEF). This project provides for a three-story laboratory/office addition to Building 239 with basement levels which tie into the existing floor levels. The addition will have approximately 4800 m^2 of floor area. The basement and first-floor levels will provide space for radiographic applications and advanced studies in ultrasonics, laser holography, and radiation gaging. The second- and third-floor levels will be devoted to computer operations and offices.

2.1.7.2.15. LLNL--Large Optics Diamond Turning Machine Facility (LODTMF). The LODTMF will be a single-story structure with a total floor area of 1500 m^2. The majority of the floor space (1020 m^2) will be used for the Large Optics Diamond Turning Machine (LODTM), a new 75,000-pound lathe which will be able to machine laser optics weighing up to one metric ton with an average accuracy of one-millionth of an inch. The remainder of the building will be used for offices, restrooms, supply room, computers, and conference areas.

2.1.7.2.16. Site 300--Flash Radiography Facility (FXR). The Flash Radiography Facility at Site 300 will meet present and future needs to gather more definitive information on the implosion behavior of modern nuclear weapons in order to optimize their design. The proposed FXR will be a two-story reinforced concrete building housing a 15-MeV linear induction accelerator and related electrical equipment. Sufficient flux will be provided by the accelerator to penetrate any of the presently contemplated weapon designs which require high-density materials. The proposed facility will be coupled to Building 801A, but structurally separate to facilitate construction and to minimize operational conflicts.

2.1.7.2.17. Site 300--Weaponization Facilities Project (WFP). The proposed WFP will provide increased capability to test, record, and evaluate new weapon configurations and support items, and will correct equipment and facility limitations which have been noted over the past several years. The proposed actions include the construction of five new support buildings near existing facilities and modifications to Building 823B. The new buildings are:

- Building 823A, Office and Control Building.
- Building 832E, Test Specimen Inspection Building.
- Building 834M, Thermal Test Building.
- Building 836D, Electrodynamic Exciter Building.
- Building 854J, Dynamic Shock Test Building.

2.1.7.2.18. Site 300--Advanced Test Accelerator (ATA) Project. The ATA Project will consist of a Control and Support Building, a Beam Tube Building having three sections (accelerator, beam transport, experimental tank), and an adjacent building housing the power supplies and associated cables, diagnostic equipment, etc. A cooling tower will be constructed in the vicinity of the Control and Support Building. Electrical power will be supplied from the North Power Station. Cooling water will be supplied to the ATA from on-site wells.

The ATA is a linear charged-particle (electron) accelerator and will be used to investigate particle beam theory and operating parameters.

2.1.7.2.19. Site 300--High-Explosives Machining Facility (HEMF). This facility will be located in the explosives processing area and will provide approximately 1500 m^2 of space. It will have eight explosives machining and inspection cells with four adjacent control rooms, a double magazine, and a storage, handling, and support building.

2.1.7.2.20. SNLL--Computer Facilities Addition. This project is to provide 1200 m^2 of additional computer facilities space contiguous to the existing 1338-m^2 underground computer facility. The increasingly sophisticated weapon development responsibilities as well as newer activities (e.g., safeguards, solar energy, combustion research) will place increasing demands on Sandia computing capabilities. The SNLL plans provide for an orderly growth in computer capabilities to match this demand.

2.1.7.3. Long-Range Site Development Plan. In 1968, a long-range development plan was prepared for LLNL. This plan addressed the overall development pattern, on-site zoning, the reorganization of existing areas, and the function of future areas. In the years since its adoption the plan has continued to provide basic guidelines. Many of the details of the plan have been altered to reflect the changing needs of the Laboratory, but the basic criteria have remained unchanged.

Table 2-1. LLNL environmental monitoring sampling and analysis schedule.

Sample	Location	Analysis	Collection frequency	Number collected	Analysis frequency
Air	LLNL perimeter	Gross alpha	Weekly	6	Weekly
		Gross beta	•		•
		Gamma scan		6	Monthly composite
		^{238}Pu, ^{239}Pu			•
		^{137}Cs			
		^{235}U, ^{238}U			
		Be			
		HTO	Monthly	-	
	Liv. Valley	Gross alpha	Weekly	10	Weekly
		Gross beta	-	10	-
		^{238}Pu, ^{239}Pu		-	
	Site 300	Gross alpha		10	
		Gross beta		10	
		Gamma scan		10	
		^{238}Pu, ^{239}Pu		10	
		^{137}Cs		10	
		^{235}U, ^{238}U		10	
		Be		10	
Soil	Liv. Valley	Gamma scan	Annually	20	Annually
		^{238}Pu, ^{239}Pu	-	20	-
	Site 300	Gamma scan	•	11	
		^{238}Pu, ^{239}Pu		11	
Sewage	LLNL effluent	Gross alpha	Daily		Daily
		Gross beta	Daily		Daily
		HTO	-		-
		^{137}Cs	•	1	Monthly composite
		^{239}Pu			-
		Cu, Cr			
		F			

Table 2-1. (Continued)

		BOD, COD, N, Hg, Se, CN, B	Quarterly	1	Quarterly
	Site 300	BOD, COD, N Hg, Se, CN, B, etc.			
	Liv. Water Reclamation Plant effluent	Gross alpha	Daily		
		Gross beta	"		
		HTO	Daily		
		^{137}Cs	"		
		^{239}Pu			
Water	Liv. Valley	Gross alpha	Quarterly	8	Quarterly
		Gross beta			
		HTO	"	8	
	Site 300	Gross alpha			
		Gross beta			
		HTO			
	Wells	Gross alpha			
		Gross beta			
		HTO			
	Wells	Gross alpha	Monthly	2	Monthly
		Gross beta	"		"
		HTO			
Vege-tation	Livermore Valley	HTO		10	
	Site 300	HTO			
Milk	Livermore Valley	Gamma scan			
		HTO		-	
TLDs	LLNL perim.		Quarterly	12	Quarterly
	Livermore Valley			41	

The long-range Site Development Plan introduced the curving, loop road pattern. Within the pattern established by these roads, the LLNL site was zoned according to population and function. The core of the Site, enclosed by the inner loop road, was zoned for general Laboratory-support functions such as the Business Office, Technical Information, Plant Engineering, and the unclassified Computer Center. Between the inner and outer loop roads were sites for the various programmatic offices and laboratories.

Prior to 1968 existing buildings were often surrounded by a sea of asphalt. Reorganization usually involved establishing a service yard that was common to all facilities in the block. Portions of each block were zoned for limited automobile parking and for pedestrian access. Landscaped green belts that ran through several of the blocks contained pedestrian/ bicycle pathways. Formal landscaping was limited to main entrances to buildings.

The Laser Program area is the first new programmatic area developed in accordance with the function unit concept of the long-range plan. The Laser Fusion Research Facility (Building 381) and the High-Energy Laser Laboratory (Building 391) were the first two installations. Building 381 in particular was designed for additional buildings toward the east.

Long-range plans at SNLL include a laboratory building adjacent to the combustion research facility on the east side of Building 912. The construction site selected for this facility follows the general plan of locating offices and laboratories in a grouping near the front of the property, while the test facilities are located at a greater distance from the street.

2.1.8. ENVIRONMENTAL MONITORING

2.1.8.1. General. Contamination control efforts at LLNL and SNLL place maximum emphasis on controlling effluents at the source. Because of the proximity of the two laboratories, the environmental monitoring program maintained by LLNL serves to determine the effectiveness of control measures at both sites. The LLNL monitoring program uses analytical techniques capable of detecting the activity of numerous radionuclides in the environment at natural background levels. At present, the radionuclides of concern include the transuranic elements, products of neutron activation, fission products, and tritium. Table 2-1 shows a sampling schedule indicating the frequency and number of the various samples collected.

The results of this monitoring program are reported to DOE on an annual basis.[2-1] The 1980 Annual Report is included as Appendix 2A. The program includes the analysis of various types of environmental samples that have been collected within the Livermore Valley and Site 300.

The following is a summary of the current program to indicate its breadth and scope. Changes are expected as knowledge in specific areas increases and as the specific operations are changed.

2.1.8.2. Air Sampling. Particulate air sampling is conducted with 16 continuously operating air sampling stations strategically located within 16 km of the Livermore site. Filters are changed weekly and are subjected to gross alpha, gross beta, and gamma spectral analyses. Some of these filters also undergo radiochemical analyses for ^{238}Pu, ^{239}Pu, ^{137}Cs, ^{235}U, and ^{238}U.

Tritiated water (HTO) in air measurements are made at LLNL perimeter locations and east and west of the TRL. Water vapor is collected in silica gel samplers. The water collected is recovered by freeze-drying and the HTO is measured by liquid scintillation counting.

2.1.8.3. Water Sampling. The water sampling program is designed to monitor the effectiveness of pollution control measures at the Livermore site. Surface sources such as ponds, creeks, arroyos, and reservoirs are sampled at quarterly intervals. Site 300 water samples are collected from on-site wells, springs, and ponds. Rainfall samples are composited at monthly intervals during the rainy season, usually from November through April. Municipally operated wells plus purchased water from Alameda County Flood Control and Water Conservation District Zone 7 are sources of domestic water for the cities of Livermore, Pleasanton, and Dublin within the Livermore-Amador Valley. Water sold to California Water Service, which serves the City of Livermore, comes from the South Bay Aqueduct. Purchased water for Pleasanton and Dublin may be supplied either from Zone 7 well fields in the area or from the aqueduct. Water samples are routinely collected from the Patterson Reservoir, which is fed by the South Bay Aqueduct. As part of LLNL's groundwater quality monitoring program, a number of on-site wells have been drilled. Analysis of water from these wells will document any potential impact the Livermore operation might have on local groundwater quality. Annual samples are also collected from Zone 7 wells throughout the Valley. Radioactive measurements made on these samples demonstrate that the Livermore site has no measurable impact on drinking water in the Livermore Valley. The maximum radioactivity found in any of these samples was 6.8% of the concentration guides found in DOE Order 5480.1A. Appendix 2A, the environmental monitoring report for 1980, contains the most recent results of these measurements.

Surface drainage from the Livermore Valley flows westward in several arroyos that feed Alameda Creek, which discharges into the San Francisco Bay. Aquifers in the Niles Cone area of Alameda County are recharged by water from Alameda Creek. These aquifers serve as a domestic water source for the City of Fremont. (See Fig 2-2).

The Livermore site's sanitary waste is treated at the City of Livermore's Water Reclamation Plant (LWRP), a 200-liter/s tertiary sewage treatment plant that serves residential, commercial, and industrial water users in Livermore. The salt content of the LWPR effluent presented a problem for both local groundwater quality and that of the Niles Cone aquifers. Accordingly, as part of the Livermore-Amador Valley Wastewater Management program, a pipeline was constructed to transport wastewater out of the valley with discharge into the San Francisco Bay. The Livermore sewage plant was connected to this pipeline on February 8, 1980. Prior to the pipeline the LWRP effluent was used for irrigation of municipal property; any excess was discharged to the nearby Arroyo Las Positas. Because this effluent contains low levels of tritium arising from normal Livermore Site operational releases to the sanitary sewer system, tritium measurements have been made on well-water samples collected near the LWRP. The average concentration was less than .07% of the DOE 5480.1A concentration guide. All concentrations were well below the guide.

Results of the most recent measurements are contained in Appendix 2A. Although the LWRP effluent is still used for summer irrigation of municipal property, it is no longer discharged to the arroyo, thus eliminating the principal means of tritium movement to nearby ground water.

2.1.8.4. Sewer Effluent Sampling. Sewer effluents from SNLL and LLNL are combined and the combined flows are continuously monitored for pH and radioactivity before leaving the Livermore site at the northwest corner of LLNL. Daily samples are collected of the combined effluent and the treated effluent from the Livermore Water Reclamation Plant. These samples are analyzed for gross alpha and beta radioactivity and ^{3}H, ^{238}Pu, ^{239}Pu, ^{137}Cs, and other selected isotopic analyses are done on a monthly composite of these samples. In 1977, SNLL also installed an effluent monitoring system that has the capability to continuously record its pH. During 1979, LLNL installed an on-line monitoring system for detecting metals in the sewer effluent using x-ray fluorescence.[2-2]

2.1.8.5. Soil Sampling. The environmental monitoring program includes an annual soil sampling schedule to measure the concentration of various radionuclides that have been deposited within the Livermore Valley or Site 300, either as a result of global fallout from past atmospheric tests or possibly from Livermore site operations. Analyses include those for plutonium, uranium, and fission products. Collected annually since 1972, these analyses are part of a surveillance program to document any changes in environmental levels of radioactivity that may have occurred, and to evaluate any increase that may have resulted from site operations. Appendix 2A contains a description of the procedures and the data obtained in 1980 as well as an independent check by the California Department of Health.

When the program was begun, one of the objectives was to establish a data base for the concentration of those radionuclides near the Livermore Site and Site 300. Data for manmade radionuclides were expressed in deposition units (concentration per unit area), so that the data could be compared with that of Hardy and Krey.[2-3] Soil samples were collected to a depth of 25 cm, because it is implied when using deposition units that the sample has been collected to sufficient depth to account for essentially all the activity. Since 1972, when the objective has been to document changes in concentrations, more shallow sampling has been employed. Sampling to a depth of 1 cm was first attempted, but it was found to be difficult to reproduce a 1-cm-deep sample under the wide variety of soil conditions encountered in the field. Accordingly, in recent years all samples have been collected to a depth of 5 cm to reduce the error in sampling depth.

The sampling procedure now used at the Livermore site is typical of procedures used at many nuclear facilities. The procedure is the procedure outlined by the Nuclear Regulatory Commission's Regulatory Guide 4.5.

Although resuspended respirable particles of plutonium in the air are the most significant environmental impact, the procedures for determining the airborne respirable particle concentration from resuspension of respirable particles in the soil is difficult and uncertain.

There has been considerable interest in determining plutonium in the respirable dust fraction of soil according to the method developed by Johnson.[2-4]

Johnson's method, which consists of sweeping the soil surface, has been criticized because the technique is not reproducible with respect to the depth of the sampling, and because the physical and chemical treatment following collection materially alters the particle size distribution from that found in the soil.[2-5]

Airborne plutonium is measured at nine locations in the Livermore valley (see Appendix 2A). The soil sampling is an indicator of changes in deposited plutonium. The method in use measures those changes more reproducibly than is possible by the respirable dust method.

2.1.8.6. Vegetation and Milk Sampling. Vegetation samples are collected from various locations in the Livermore Valley on a monthly basis, and are subjected to tritium analyses. Goat milk samples are collected monthly from some nearby farms, and are condensed and analyzed for tritium and gamma emitters.

2.1.8.7. Background Radiation Measurements. Thermoluminescent dosimeters (TLDs) are employed at 54 stations for measuring the radiation background in the near vicinity of the Livermore site. These dosimeters are read every three months.

2.2. PURPOSE AND NEED

2.2.1. National Defense

Nuclear weapons development has always been the largest program at both LLNL and SNLL. This development started with fundamental advances in nuclear weapon design in the 1950s, and range from the early warheads to those currently being developed. These advances made the multiple independent reentry vehicle (MIRV) possible, which in turn provided the U.S. with a strong position in achieving international arms limitation agreements. The ultimate purpose of a vigorous nuclear weapons development program is the determent of nuclear war and political use of military force short of warfare in ways that are inimical to U.S. interests.

2.2.2. Other Activities

Other activities undertaken at the Livermore site include:

- Energy research and development
- Biomedical research
- Computer science
- Graduate Center of Applied Science
- Atmospheric Release Advisory Capability (ARAC)
- Visitor's Center

2.2.2.1. Energy--Long-Term Purpose and Need. Since it was established in 1952, LLNL has maintained active programs aimed at improving the nation's civilian energy position. Controlled thermonuclear research (CTR), now called magnetic fusion energy, started when LLNL was founded. In the early 1960s, LLNL started to explore the laser approach to controlled thermonuclear reactions. This experience, combined with the emerging national energy problem, led LLNL in 1970 to expand its work to include other nonnuclear energy studies.

2.2.2.1.1. Magnetic Fusion Energy. The Lawrence Livermbre National Laboratory is one of the pioneering centers of Magnetic Fusion Energy (MFE) research, which is a program exploring the generation of electricity through nuclear fusion in superhot hydrogen gases that are confined magnetically.

The Livermore program is now focused on one of the major magnetic confinement methods, the "magnetic mirror." This approach has been under development at LLNL since the early 1950s. One major mirror experiment (the 2XII-B) is the most advanced in a series of machines that, for nearly 20 years, have provided important information on the behavior of hot hydrogen gas or plasma. Several recent experimental and theoretical breakthroughs have occurred that now put the mirror program in a position to take a major step forward. The principal issues of energy scaling, startup in a steady magnetic field, and control of microstability have all been addressed with favorable results. These new results give the greatest encouragement to date that the ultimate goal of a pure-fusion DT mirror reactor can be achieved, and they provide the basis for preparing for a DT burning experimental mirror reactor to be operational in the 1980s.

To further the national MFE effort, and since the Laboratory had extensive experience in the use of large timesharing computational systems, Livermore was selected as the site of a national center for MFE computations. The center provides all U.S. MFE laboratories timesharing access to major computers.

2.2.2.1.2. Laser Technologies. The LLNL laser fusion program recently passed a major milestone in obtaining direct experimental evidence that thermonuclear neutrons were produced in laser-driven implosions. During 1975 there was a stepup in target irradiation facilities--both the half-terawatt JANUS laser and the one-terawatt CYCLOPS became operational. In addition, a 30-TW facility, Shiva, became operational in 1977 and Nova, a 200-300-TW device, is under construction.

In laser isotope separation, LLNL demonstrated the first macroscopic laser enrichment of uranium. More important for the future, LLNL researchers have demonstrated several other uranium-enrichment techniques utilizing economic ionization sources such as infrared lasers and electric fields. These enrichment techniques also apply to the isotopes of many other elements as well. It is expected that continued developments in these separation techniques will result in more efficient processes and processes applicable to a wider range of elements.

2.2.2.2. Energy--Near-Term Purpose and Need

2.2.2.2.1. Underground Coal Gasification. When coal is heated in the presence of oxygen and steam, it gives off a mixture of combustible gases that are much cleaner-burning and much easier to transport than coal. LLNL has been engaged in a series of field experiments at its Hoe Creek, Wyoming, test site to evaluate methods of gasifying thick seams of coal in situ (underground). After purification, these gases could be introduced into existing pipelines and used as a substitute for natural gas.

2.2.2.2.2. Underground Oil Shale Retorting. By heating oil shale underground to about 400°C, organic material bound in the rock structure decomposes, forming shale oil, a petroleum-like liquid. The most valuable deposits of oil shale in the United States lie in Colorado's Piceance Basin. This one basin contains shale oil equivalent to about three times the proved oil reserves of the entire Middle East. LLNL is exploring ways of retorting the shale underground.

2.2.2.2.3. Solar Energy. American industry burns the equivalent of 30 million barrels of oil annually just to heat water for chemical and manufacturing processes. Considerable oil can be saved by using solar energy to heat water. LLNL has designed two inexpensive solar water heaters for industrial use.

The first type of solar heater to produce hot water is the shallow solar pond. Essentially, this is a large, flat, water-filled plastic bag with a black bottom and a clear top. The bag, 4 m wide and 60 m long, is filled to a depth of 5 to 10 cm of water each morning. During the day, the water absorbs heat and reaches temperatures as high as 60°C (140°F) and is drained into an insulating tank at night.

LLNL is also developing and testing a simple concentrating solar collector. It is an inflated cylinder of thin-film plastic with a clear upper half and an aluminized lower half, which serves as a reflector. This collector surrounds a horizontal pipe that is coated and insulated. Solar energy is concentrated into the pipe by the reflector. Water passing through the pipe is heated to 170°C and is used either as hot water or flashed into steam.

2.2.2.2.4. Metal-Air Power Cells for Automobiles. In the United States, about 25% of our national energy budget goes for transportation, with virtually all this energy coming from petroleum. Battery power for automobiles is being studied again because these batteries could be recharged by power plants operating on domestic coal or uranium rather than petroleum. The difficulty with conventional batteries is that they do not offer performance comparable to that of an internal combustion engine.

A metal-air power cell converts chemical energy to electrical energy by oxidizing a replaceable negative metal electrode. Tests have shown that experimental aluminum-air cells offer high energy and power densities and suggest that they might provide the range, speed, and acceleration of conventional internal combustion engines now used in compact cars.

LLNL is doing basic electrochemistry research developing an aluminum-air power cell and evaluating the potential of other metal-air cells in automotive propulsion systems.

2.2.2.3. Biomedical and Environmental Research. The biomedical phase of this program, which began in 1963, deals with the biophysics, genetics, and molecular biology of cellular toxicology. Chromosome aberrations, genetic mutation, reproductive biology, and cellular kinetics are the main emphases, with a heavy commitment to instrumentation development in biophysical cell studies.

Benefits from biomedical and environmental research have resulted from a comprehensive study of the implications to man of radioactivity and other energy-related effluents in the biosphere.

Laboratory and field investigations are being conducted in marine biology, terrestrial ecology, and atmospheric sciences.

Specific benefits derived from biomedical and environmental research at Livermore include the following:

- The discovery that the high-speed, laser-based flow systems could be applied effectively to chromosome analysis and sorting has created a powerful new analytical tool.
- A complementary image-analysis system for chromosome measurement, the locally developed CYDAC, reached the point of initial clinical applications--a prenatal diagnosis for a possible birth defect, and quantitative confirmation of a microscopic chromosome defect in leukemia.
- A research project established the extreme sensitivity of mouse germ cells to radiation damage caused by low levels of tritium; the effort is now being extended to similar studies of the effects of energy-related environmental chemicals.
- A substantial study was initiated using mammalian cell systems to develop new methods of identifying environmental chemicals which are mutagenic or carcinogenic.
- A new project was begun to use fluorescent chemical tags for cellular enzymes which might serve as indicators of the transformation of cells from the normal to the malignant state. The application of such indicators would be in cancer diagnosis and the detection of environmental carcinogens.
- Analysis of crops, litter, soil and groundwater to determine cycling mechanisms for radionuclides in the environment and to formulate models for predicting the dose to people returning to Enewetak Atoll in the Marshall Islands. These studies represent DOE's program to determine rehabilitation plans and long-term use for the Atoll.
- Significant progress was made in the ability to understand and model such complex systems as man's potential influence on the climate, the effects of chemicals on stratospheric ozone, rainout, and fallout, and the transport of toxic materials through the atmosphere. In particular, this last project prompted a decision to establish the ARAC (see Section 2.2.2.6) computer network, based at Livermore and connected to other DOE laboratories, for real-time prediction of the movement of such materials in the event of a release.
- A sophisticated, user-oriented air quality model was made available to the Bay Area Air Quality Management District for that agency's use in making land-use decisions based on environmental impact.

2.2.2.4. Computer Science. LLNL operates one of the largest high-speed computer facilities in the world. This facility is in continuous use, with nearly 500 terminals available for essentially simultaneous computations by Laboratory employees under an LLNL timesharing system.

In addition to classified computations, these computers have been used in such programs as generating computer models of atmospheric pollution in the San Francisco Bay Area, studies of national transportation systems, and metropolitan traffic movements.

2.2.2.5. Graduate Center for Applied Science. This graduate center, established at Livermore in 1963, is a unit of the College of Engineering of the University of California at Davis. A total of 346 graduate degrees (including both Masters and PhDs) have been awarded under the Department of Applied Science (DAS). Approximately 25 LLNL staff members currently serve as DAS faculty members or lecturers.

The school was initially located in classrooms on East Avenue near the southeast corner of the LLNL site. However, a new 1000-m^2 building is now in service in the northeast quadrant of LLNL adjacent to Greenville Road. Funding for the construction of this permanent facility was shared by the University of California and the Hertz Foundation.

2.2.2.6. Atmospheric Release Advisory Capability (ARAC). The Atmospheric Release Advisory Capability (ARAC) service directed by LLNL has three main functions: (1) to provide support to designated DOE facilities during an accidental release of radionuclides; (2) to support the DOE Emergency Response Team in the event of potential or actual releases of radionuclides; and (3) to provide the Federal Aviation Administration (FAA) with dose assessments whenever aircraft could possibly intercept nuclear debris clouds from foreign atmospheric nuclear tests.

The ARAC central facility receives meteorological data from the Air Force Global Weather Central (AFGWC). In an accident situation the meteorological data collected nearest the accident site are used to predict cloud trajectories, concentrations, and population doses. At present, ARAC has two-way communications with AFGWC, the LLNL computer center, four DOE installations, the DOE Emergency Response Team and the FAA.

Following the Three Mile Island accident in March of 1979, ARAC assisted by generating predictions of radioactive isotope distribution. This assistance was of paramount importance in the effective deployment of ground and aerial monitoring teams, and in estimating the time dependent source term by comparing close-in measurements with these predictions.

2.2.2.7. Visitors Center. A 232-m^2 Visitors Center and badge service to unclassified LLNL areas was opened at the east (Greenville Road) entrance on July 31, 1976. Facilities include a theater and an exhibit hall. Approximately 15,000 people visit the Center each year.

2.3. CHARACTERISTICS OF EXISTING ENVIRONMENT

2.3.1. Population Distribution and Land Use

This discussion of population distribution in relation to the DOE Livermore laboratories is intended to clarify the existing patterns of population density and changes in these patterns which are likely to occur in the Livermore Valley. The population density is described to a distance of 80 km. However, the description of the land use here is limited to the more immediate surroundings of the Laboratories where either the existing land use might be impacted by DOE operations or where changes in land use might affect these operations. The immediate area probably does not extend beyond 16 km and becomes increasingly important as the boundaries of LLNL and SNLL are approached.

2.3.1.1. On-Site Population of LLNL and SNLL. At the present time the on-site population of LLNL, consisting of employees, contractors, outside agency personnel, and visitors, is between 7000 and 8000 persons. SNLL has approximately 1000 persons on site. The total number of persons on site varies according to the time of day and the number away from their normal work areas (on sick leave, vacation, travel, etc.).

2.3.1.2. Population Within 16 Kilometers of Facilities. The DOE Livermore laboratories are abutted on all sides by agricultural land with low residential density. The nearest urban residential area is 0.8 km from the west perimeters. There are a few homes at the Laboratory's boundaries. The city limits of Livermore, however, presently extend to the west side of these Laboratories, and future development may bring urban densities closer. The Livermore General Plan, 1976-2000, envisions continued industrial development to the north and east, and a residential population of approximately 9500 in the 2.6-km^2 area immediately to the west of LLNL. The foothill areas to the east and south of the Laboratories will remain agricultural.

Figure 2-8 shows the immediate environs of the DOE Livermore laboratories and residences within 1.6 km of the approximate center of the properties. A similar 3.2-km radius would include only agricultural land except for the portions of Livermore urban and Alameda County unincorporated residential development to the west, and an area of light industrial development to the northwest along North Vasco Road. The region north of the Southern Pacific Railroad is part of the City of Livermore and is presently zoned for future commercial/industrial development. Estimated populations by sectors of direction and distance to a distance of 16 km from the DOE Livermore laboratories are given in Fig. 2-9. This figure is based on the 1970 census. The present population is about 15% higher.

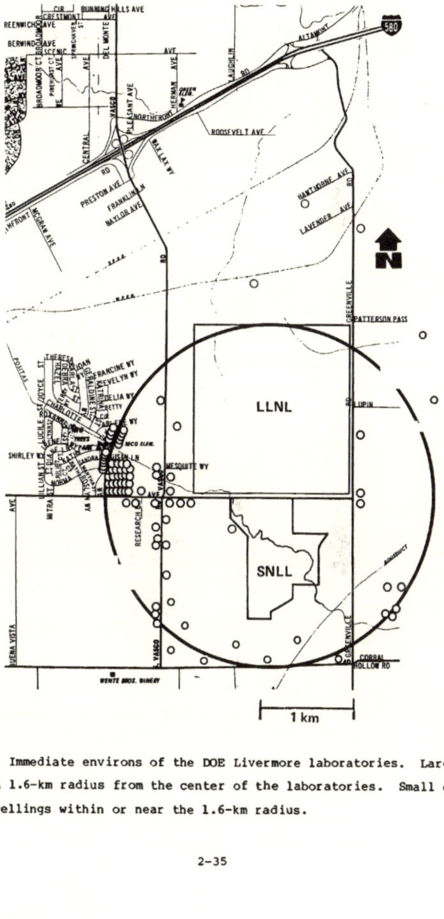

Figure 2-8. Immediate environs of the DOE Livermore laboratories. Large circle represents a 1.6-km radius from the center of the laboratories. Small circles represent dwellings within or near the 1.6-km radius.

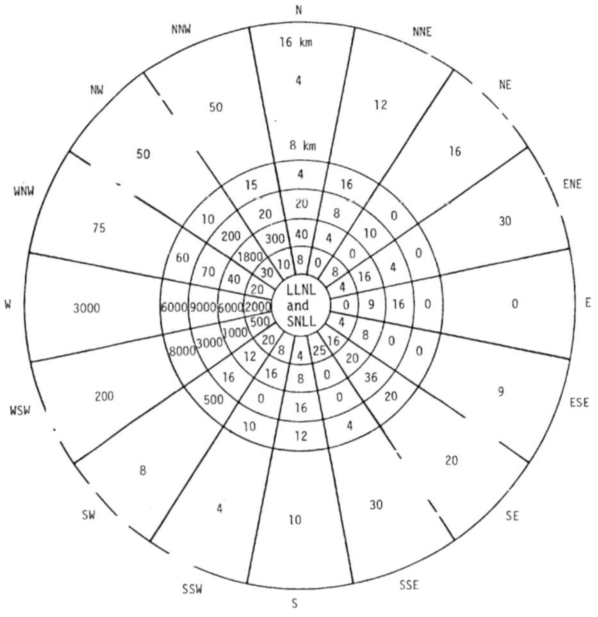

1.6-km arcs are shown to 8 km.

Figure 2-9. Estimated population distribution within 16 km of LLNL and SNLL (1970 census data).

2.3.1.3. Extended Regional Population. The regions to the west of LLNL and SNLL are the most heavily populated, with the City of Livermore (50,000)* extending from 3 to 10 km west and partly to the north. Pleasanton (36,000),* Dublin (15,000),* and San Ramon (21,000)* are the only other urban concentrations in the Livermore-Amador Valley, but just over the low ridges to the west are the densely populated San Francisco-Oakland and San Jose urbanized areas. Other urban concentrations at similar extended distances are Concord-Walnut Creek and Pittsburg-Antioch to the north, and the cities of Tracy, Stockton, and Manteca in the predominantly agricultural Central Valley to the east.

The hills ringing the Livermore Valley from the north toward Mt. Diablo through the east toward Altamont Pass and the south toward Mt. Hamilton are very sparsely populated.

Figure 2-10 shows estimated populations by 22.5-degree sectors with 16-km radius increments to a distance of 80 km from the Livermore site. This distribution was derived by plotting data from the Association of Bay Area Government's "Projection 79" (April 1979) in which 1975 data were projected to 1980. In making this projection, estimates of city census divisions in their respective geographical locations were utilized. Figure 2-11 shows a summary of these data. The total population within 80 km of the site is approximately 5 million.

2.3.1.4. Population Projections. Population growth in the Bay Area, along with the rest of the state, has been at a greater rate than for the nation as a whole, at least since 1900. Before the 1940s, the major growth was in the close-in, or bayshore, parts of San Francisco, Alameda, Contra Costa, Marin, and San Mateo counties. Since that time, the increase in number of places to work in new centers and an improved highway and rapid transit systems have led to the spread of medium- or low-density residential developments (tract homes) to virtually all remaining areas where development and sales are economically feasible. Efforts by local and regional agencies to limit this growth through control of its rate or through planning for alternate land uses such as "open space" or continued agricultural use have not so far modified this trend in any large sense. A recent Alameda County zoning ordinance limits the construction of new homes in the unincorporated areas of the eastern part of the county to sites of 0.4 km^2 or more. There are a number of pre-existing smaller homesteads along Mines and Tesla Roads; here a 0.02 km^2 limitation applies. This should tend to reduce change in the population of these areas, as long as they do not become part of an incorporated city.

While the DOE Livermore Laboratories brought some growth to the Livermore area when they began operations, an accelerated growth occurred during the 1960s when the area increasingly became a home for commuters to the large cities to the west. The most rapid growth in the Livermore-Amador Valley

* These population figures are from the Livermore, Dublin, Pleasanton, and San Ramon Chambers of Commerce, 1979.

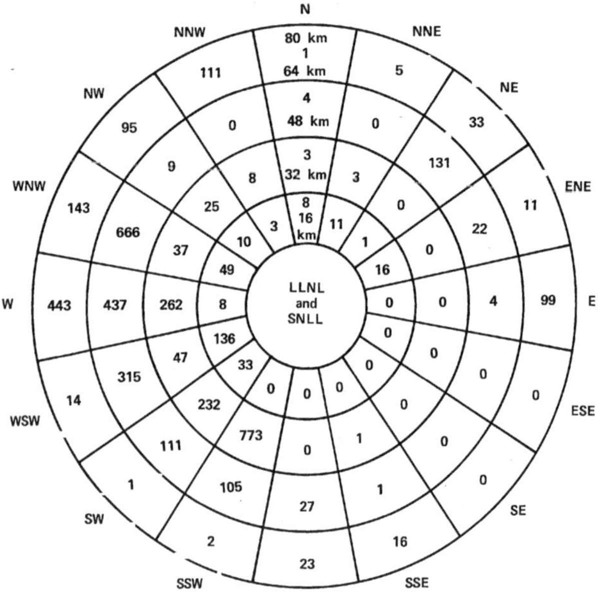

Figure 2-10. Estimated population distribution (in thousands) within 80 km of LLNL and SNLL (1975 population data projected to 1980).

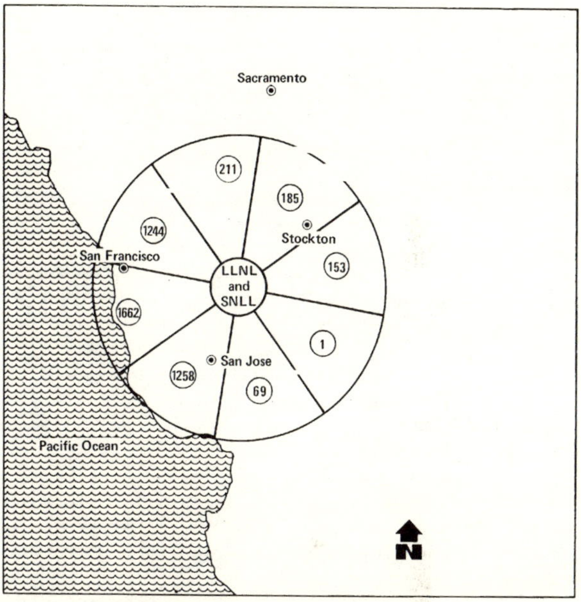

Figure 2-11. Estimated population distribution by sectors (in thousands) within 80 km of LLNL and SNLL.

has been in residential dwellings, mostly of single-family type, but with some concentrations of two-story apartment houses. At present, light industrial development is occurring in the Pleasanton and Dublin areas to the west. Such development has proceeded at a slower pace in the Livermore area. The voters of the Valley passed an initiative measure requiring future building permits to be issued only when assurance could be given that the new construction would not overburden the capacities of water, sewage, or school services.

Table 2-2 gives the 1970 U.S. Census populations of counties lying all or partly within 80 km of the Laboratory, with projections for every decade to the year 2000.

2.3.1.5. Land Use. The rural areas of the Livermore-Amador Valley are occupied by vineyards, orchards, irrigated pasture, many small farms, and larger tracts devoted to grains and hay. The hilly terrain surrounding the valley is used for cattle and sheep pasture. Dairying is not intensive in the Livermore-Amador Valley, but is prominent in the San Joaquin Valley to the east. During 1979, 1,900,000 chickens (broilers and fryers) were commercially grown in the Livermore Valley.

There is a large complex of gravel quarries just east of Pleasanton. Numerous mines in the surrounding hills are no longer active, but there are several producing oil wells located about 0.8 km east of LLNL on Patterson Pass Road.

The California Aqueduct and its facilities are important in the area. A branch, the South Bay Aqueduct, carries water destined for the San Jose area around the east and south margins of the valley, passing very close to the southeast corner of LLNL and adjacent to the east boundary. The Del Valle and San Antonio Reservoirs to the south and southwest serve this aqueduct as reserve storage and watershed contributors.

2.3.1.6. Transportation Routes. The major artery through the Livermore-Amador Valley is Interstate 580, which feeds traffic from the Bay Area to the Central Valley. With its connection to Interstate 5, it forms the major route between the Bay Area and Los Angeles. The average daily vehicle flow is 48,500.* The interchanges at Vasco Road and Greenville Road about 1.6 km north of LLNL serve as the major routes from most points, other than Livermore, to the Laboratories. Interstate 680 connects the San Jose Area with Interstate 80 at Cordelia, passing through Pleasanton and Dublin at the west end of the valley.

---

*California Division of Highways' estimate for I-580 at First Street Interchange. This is the total traffic count for one year divided by 365. There are, of course, seasonal and daily variations, especially due to the importance of this route for recreational travel.

Table 2-2. Projected populations of counties lying all or partly within 80 km of LLNL.

County	Area (km^2)	% Urban	Population (thousands), 1970 census	% Change, 1960-1970	1980[a]	1990[a]	2000[a]
Alameda	1898	99.0	1074	6.5	1116	1182	1263
Contra Costa	1901	93.6	558	17.0	642	751	845
Marin	1347	92.4	208	12.4	229	266	294
Merced	5133	50.0	106	19.7	126[b]	154	177
Napa	1963	58.0	80	27.5	99	110	118
Sacramento	2544	95.1	638	18.2	745[b]	877	976
San Francisco	117	100.0	714	-7.4	657	640	648
San Joaquin	3649	76.9	292	13.0	317[b]	363	415
San Mateo	1176	98.2	557	6.4	584	615	658
Santa Clara	3372	97.5	1074	25.0	1249	1390	1513
Santa Cruz	1137	75.2	124	42.8	176[b]	248	310
Solano	2141	93.0	174	14.3	223	322	379
Sonoma	4090	58.7	205	46.4	270	342	426
Stanislaus	1295	70.1	195	20.5	250[b]	309	364
Totals	31,765	82.5	5999	14.2	6683	7569	8386

[a] These projections are based on data in "Projections 79," published by Association of Bay Area Governments, April 1979.

[b] From State of California Department of Finance, "Population Estimates of California Cities and Counties," January 1979.

The Livermore area is served by main lines of the Southern Pacific and Western Pacific Railroads. As shown in Fig. 2-8, these lines pass just north of LLNL, but neither LLNL nor SNLL has spur tracks. Both lines carry freight only, with some 15 trains a day passing through the Valley.

The Livermore Municipal Airport, 10 km west of the Laboratories, is the nearest public airport. It has a 1200-m paved runway with clear approach zones and runway lights. The Laboratory operates flight service with a Fairchild F-27 turbo-prop transport aircraft to the Nevada Test Site and other locations from here. Nearby airports with scheduled airline service are Oakland, San José, San Francisco, and Stockton.

2.3.2. Natural Surface Features

Two arroyos (Arroyo Seco and Arroyo Las Positas) traverse these properties. Arroyo Seco flows to the west across the Sandia site south of the office and laboratory area, northwest along the western edge of the property, and then crosses the southwest corner of LLNL. Prior to the construction of the LLNL Building 113 Computer Complex in 1966, this arroyo crossed East Avenue and turned westward to a point now occupied by the multi-story portion of the building. To permit the present construction, the arroyo channel was diverted to the south. It now runs along East Avenue to a point west of the construction where it meets the original channel.

Arroyo Las Positas originates in the Livermore hills east of LLNL. It is normally dry most of the year. Originally, this arroyo crossed the northwest section of the LLNL site, entering from a point on Greenville Road between Patterson Pass Road and Lupin Way (formerly Doutherty Lane). In 1965, as part of an erosion control program, the arroyo was routed to the corner of the project and then west along the north perimeter to an outlet at the northwest corner. This outlet, which constitutes the principal pathway for LLNL's surface drainage, runs north to the Western Pacific tracks, then westward where it joins Arroyo Seco.

The LLNL Master Site Plan (discussed in 2.1.7.3) calls for the construction of a small lake in the center of the site. The principal flow of the Arroyo Las Positas (originating east of the site and presently channeled north to the northeast corner of the site as described above) will be then rerouted to feed this lake during the rainy season.

2.3.3. Geology and Seismicity

Following the April 1979 hearings on the draft EIS, the sections of the EIS dealing with geology and seismicity were considerably expanded in recognition of the public interest in the seismic setting of the Livermore sites. A site seismic safety program (Appendix 2B) was initiated in January 1979 to identify and characterize geologic hazards at LLNL. The final report of that program and a public information meeting are scheduled for October 1982.

2.3.3.1. Summary. Locations in the Livermore Valley are subject to ground motions from large seismic events on the San Andreas, Hayward, and Calaveras Faults, which are the major known active faults in the San Francisco Bay area.

The San Andreas Fault is capable of very strong earthquakes of which the best known example was the San Francisco earthquake of 1906, of magnitude 8.3. Activities on the Hayward (passing through Hayward in a NW-SE direction) Fault have probably produced seismic magnitudes of up to 7.5.

Along the east side of the Livermore Valley closer to the Livermore sites is the active Greenville fault. The largest recorded (or remembered) earthquake in the eastern Livermore Valley area occurred during a sequence of earthquakes on the Greenville fault in January and February 1980. This earthquake had a magnitude of 5.5 to 5.9. Several smaller faults have been observed in the Livermore Valley. The closest of these is the Las Positas fault, which passes through the Sandia Livermore site from southwest to northeast. This fault shows evidence of some late Pleistocene and possibly Holocene activity. Several other faults have been identified but they are believed to be inactive.

Seismic hazards have been estimated during past investigations of regional and local seismicity. John A. Blume and Associates, a professional engineering firm, concluded that the maximum hazard would be from a magnitude 5.7 earthquake on a nearby strand of the Tesla fault at a location about 2.5 miles from the site. Other engineers concluded that a somewhat larger magnitude 6.5 earthquake on the Tesla fault would constitute the maximum hazard. Seismic hazards associated with the Greenville and Las Positas faults are currently being investigated.

Future earthquakes would cause damage mainly through the ground acceleration forces they create, with the most serious damage resulting from accelerations at frequencies to which structures are resonant. High-frequency instrumental peak accelerations perhaps as high as 1.25g would have minor effect. The maximum horizontal sustained accelerations would cause the greatest damage. The estimates of these maximum accelerations range from 0.5g to 0.8g.

The critical facilities at LLNL and SNLL have been examined and strengthened (or are being strengthened) so that accelerations as large as 0.8g would not destroy the confinement integrity even though the operational capabilities might be damaged.

2.3.3.2. Regional Setting. LLNL and SNLL are located in the southeastern portion of the Livermore Valley. The Livermore Valley is an east-west trending topographic and structural depression cutting across the structural grain of the Central California Diablo Range.

The Diablo Range consists predominantly of highly deformed metamorphic and igneous rocks of the Jurassic-Cretaceous Franciscan assemblage. The range is generally bounded on the west by the active San Andreas Fault system and on the east by the ancient Coast Range Thrust Fault system as shown in Fig. 2-12.[2-6, 2-7] The San Andreas Fault is a right-lateral strike-slip fault system along which slip is occurring between the oceanic Pacific Plate of the earth's crust and the continental North American Crustal Plate. The Coast Range Thrust Fault system marks the location of an extinct subduction zone along which rocks of the Franciscan Assemblage and marine sedimentary rocks of Cretaceous through late Tertiary age are now juxtaposed.[2-7] These marine sedimentary rocks are exposed in the Altamont Hills east of LLNL and SNLL where they consist dominantly of sandstone, shale, and claystone with minor amounts of conglomerate, tuff, and coal-bearing strata.[2-8]

Western Central California is a tectonically active region as demonstrated by historic seismicity[2-9] and active deformation.[2-10] Major active faults in the region include the San Andreas Fault and two of its major branches, the Hayward Fault zone and the Calaveras Fault zone. The locations of these faults with respect to LLNL and SNLL are shown in Figure 2-12. Data concerning the extent of these faults, maximum credible earthquakes, and anticipated resulting bedrock accelerations for the LLNL and SNLL sites have been compiled and are presented in Table 2-3.

2.3.3.3. Geology in Vicinity of LLNL and SNLL

2.3.3.3.1. Rocks. Livermore Valley itself is underlain by up to 4000 ft of predominantly continental alluvial deposits of late Tertiary and Quaternary age.[2-12] These sediments consist of interstratified, lenticular and locally cemented, clay, silt, sand and gravel. Some tuff beds occur near the base of the section. Hydrocarbon exploratory well P-1, located about 1000 ft west of SNLL as shown in Fig. 2-13, penetrated approximately 2420 ft of these materials before reaching "basement" rocks of the Franciscan assemblage.[2-13]

The California Department of Water Resources (CDWR) recognized some areal variations in the composition of the alluvial deposits beneath Livermore Valley during their studies of the ground water resources of the Valley area.[2-12, 2-14] Beneath the eastern portion of the Valley, near LLNL and SNLL, well logs show that the alluvium is highly heterogeneous, the result of deposition from many small streams. In the southern portion of the Valley, adjacent to present-day major stream channels, the alluvial deposits consist dominantly of sand and gravel. This portion of the Valley is a major ground water recharge area.[2-15] In the western portion of the Valley, these gravel beds alternate with thick deposits of lacustrine clay, while the alluvial deposits along the northern margin of the

Table 2-3. Seismic hazard data for major regional faults.

Fault	Length[a] (km)	Maximum[a] earthquake (M)	Closest approach distance (km)	Bedrock[b] acceleration (g)
San Andreas	1200	8.5	58	0.4
Hayward	72	7.0	32	0.35
Calaveras	115	7.3	17	0.5

[a] From Ref. 2-9.
[b] From Ref. 2-11.

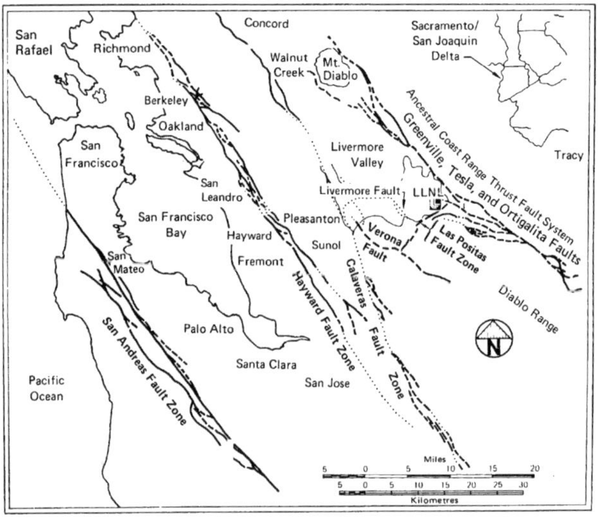

Figure 2-12. Major fault zones of the San Francisco Bay area. The great San Andreas zone, lying to the west of the Bay, is one of the chief tectonic features of the earth. It is capable of very strong earthquakes--for example, the San Francisco earthquake of 1906, of magnitude 8.3. The Hayward and Calaveras zones, lying between the Livermore Valley and the Bay, are parts of the San Andreas system, branching off from the main fault some distance south of the Bay. These faults, too, are active and have produced strong earthquakes, probably up to magnitude 7.5. The Greenville, Tesla and Ortigalita Faults, located to the east of LLNL, may be the remnants of the Coast Range Thrust Fault. The Livermore Valley earthquake sequence that began on January 24, 1980 gives evidence that these faults are periodically active. The Verona, Livermore, and Las Positas Faults are additional elements in Livermore Valley geology, although their tectonic significance is uncertain.

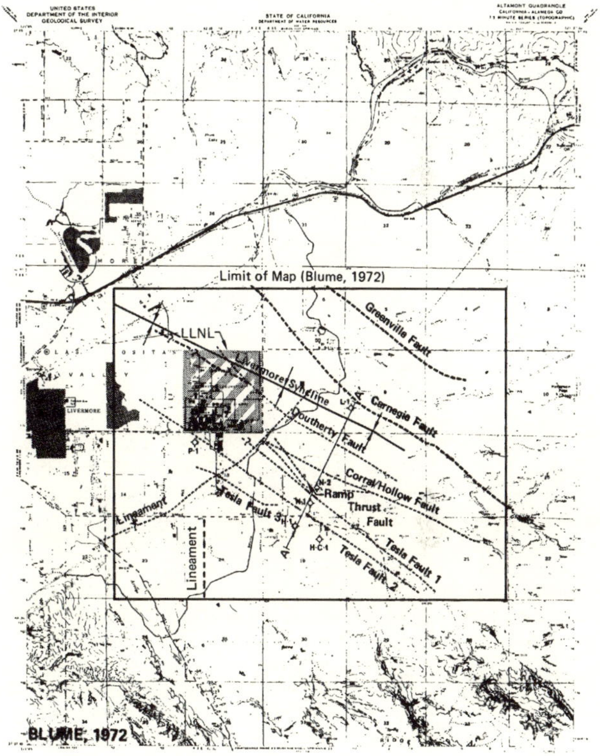

Figure 2-13. Folding and faulting as mapped by Blume (1972).[2-13]

Valley are predominantly fine-grained and represent deposition from small streams draining from the hills north and east of the Valley.[2-12, 2-14]

Huey[2-8] subdivided these Late Tertiary and Quaternary sediments into an older unit, the Livermore Formation, and younger Quaternary terrace deposits and undifferentiated alluvium. Herd[2-16] remapped the eastern two-thirds of the Livermore Valley and proposed additional subdivisions. He mapped the older, frequently deformed, alluvial deposits as the Livermore Formation and recognized four subdivisions of the Late Quaternary alluvium based on soil series, soil profile development, and correlations of terrace surfaces. Herd regarded recent floodplain alluvium and stream gravels as Holocene materials based on their deposition by the modern stream regimen.

LLNL and the northerly portions of SNLL have been constructed on a gently northwest-sloping land surface. The surface is underlain by alluvial deposits mapped by Herd as Holocene and late Quaternary in age. Logs of exploratory holes drilled for building foundation studies and drillers' logs from cathodic protection and water wells on the LLNL site reveal a heterogeneous assemblage of alluvial deposits consistent with the regional findings of the CDWR.[2-12, 2-14]

The southern portion of the SNLL site is hilly; mapping by Herd interprets this area as underlain by older alluvial terrace deposits and deformed beds of the Livermore Formation.[2-16] These two areas of contrasting physiography and stratigraphy are separated by a prominent break in slope that extends northeast-southwest across SNLL and adjacent areas.

2.3.3.3.2. Faults. The active Calaveras Fault bounds the western margin of the Livermore Valley[2-13] and the Greenville Fault zone, whose activity was clearly established by the earthquake on January 24, 1980, bounds the eastern margin of the Valley.[2-17] In addition to these principal geologic structures, various investigators have located or postulated 14 additional named and numerous unnamed minor faults beneath Livermore Valley and adjacent areas.[2-8, 2-12, 2-13, 2-16] Fault locations have generally been based on surface mapping, interpretations of air photos and well logs, and recognition of presumed ground water barriers. Some geophysical studies have been performed but field work has generally not included exploratory trenches or boreholes except in the western Livermore Valley, where the Calaveras Fault has been extensively studied as a result of the mandate of the State of California's Alquist-Priolo Act.[2-18] A study by URS/Blume and Associates[2-19] included the excavation of ten trenches within SNLL across locations of the Las Positas Fault as mapped by Herd[2-16] and the second strand of the Tesla Fault as mapped by Blume and Associates.[2-13]

Because of ambiguities in available indirect data and poor exposures in important areas, differing interpretations of the Valley fault pattern have been offered by past investigators. Two examples of these differences are shown in the fault maps of Blume and Associates and Herd, presented as Figs. 2-13 and 2-14, respectively.

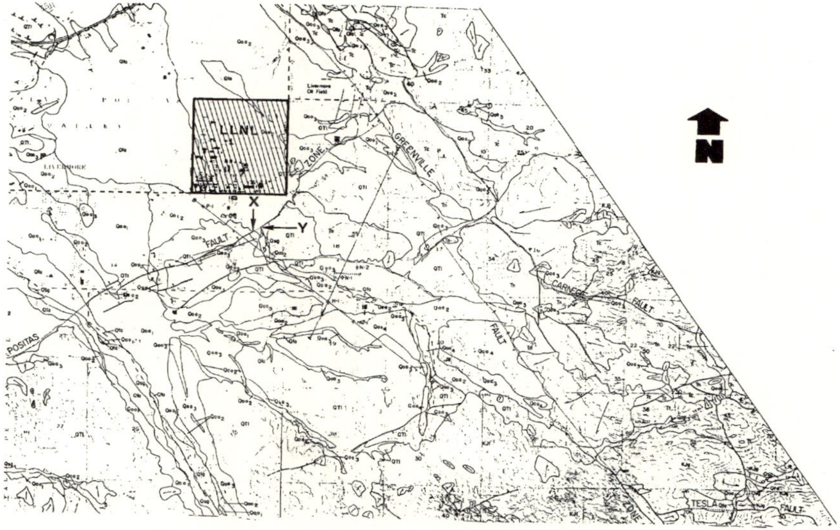

Figure 2-14. Geology and faulting as mapped by Herd (1977).[2-16] An essential difference from Huey and Blume is the replacing of the northwest-southeast tending strands of the Tesla system by southwest-northeast tending strands of the Las Positas zone in the region south of the LLNL site. Locations X and Y are exposures of the Las Positas Fault zone discussed in the text.

In order to resolve these ambiguities and obtain a more precise understanding of the geology of the Valley, LLNL geoscience personnel have reviewed all available geologic literature pertinent to Valley geology and tectonics, performed regional field reconnaissance studies, and conducted an extensive program of exploratory trenching and detailed mapping of key exposures within and near LLNL and SNLL.[2-20] As a result of these reviews and detailed studies, the following summary of geologic hazards has been developed for the area surrounding LLNL and SNLL.

2.3.3.3.3. Evidence for Active Faults. As previously stated, historic seismicity and geologic evidence for displacement of Holocene materials demonstrate the activity of the Calaveras and Greenville Fault zones. Discontinuous surface faulting occurred during the January 24, 1980, earthquake on the Greenville Fault zone and additional surface effects were noted following a strong aftershock on January 26, 1980. As documented by Bonilla and others,[2-21] the zone of surface rupture extended from the vicinity of the intersection of Greenville Road and I-580 2.6 km north of LLNL northwest for approximately 6.4 km to a point west of North Vasco Road near the Alameda-Contra Costa County line. Movements along the main Greenville Fault and several of its branches were observed within the zone. The sense of relative movement varied from place to place and the maximum offset observed was about 70 mm. Tokarz and Shaw[2-22] have estimated the ground acceleration at LLNL during the January 24, 1980 earthquake as 0.2-0.3g.

Geologic evidence developed during LLNL field investigations indicates late Quaternary and possibly Holocene displacement along a portion of the Las Positas Fault zone mapped by Herd.[2-16, 2-20] Oblique slickensides on a shear exposed in a stream bank outcrop on the southwest side of the Arroyo Seco within SNLL property indicate strike-slip movement (location X in Fig. 2-14). A ^{14}C age date of 17,400 $\pm$ 250 years was obtained for a wood sample preserved in displaced, locally altered, alluvial deposits exposed in exploratory trench E-3 excavated across another strand of the Las Positas Fault zone (location Y in Fig. 2-14). The horizon from which the wood sample was obtained was located near the bottom of trench E-3 but evidence for displacement of overlying, younger beds including an unaltered, fresh-appearing, gravel horizon was observed in the trench.

The Las Positas Fault zone appears to cross SNLL along the break in slope that separates the hilly southern portion of the site from the nearly flat, gently sloping area to the north. URS/Blume and Associates[2-19] excavated nine exploratory trenches along this slope break and reported evidence for faulting in some of the trenches but not in others.

The features mapped by Herd as establishing the extent of the Las Positas Fault zone are most evident in an area that extends roughly 2 km northeast and southwest from SNLL. However, Herd mapped the fault as extending about 3 km northeast and about 12 km southwest of SNLL along the southern margin of the Livermore Valley.

Displacements of late Pleistocene and Holocene materials have occurred along strands of the Verona Fault zone in southwestern Livermore Valley although the nature of movements along this fault is unclear.[2-23]

There is evidence for local displacement of Quaternary materials along the Carnegie, Livermore, Williams and Valle Faults[2-12, 2-24] and possibly the Patterson Pass Fault.[2-20]

Direct geologic evidence is lacking for activity along other faults projected beneath the Livermore Valley by previous investigators and some of these faults may not exist at all. However, indirect evidence such as interpretations of well logs, possible ground water barriers, and geophysical data suggest that several may be present in older materials.

Exploratory trenching studies by LLNL geoscientists do not support the existence of the Doutherty and Corral Hollow faults in later Quaternary materials, which are present across the locations mapped by previous investigators.[2-12, 2-14, 2-20] These trenching studies have also found no evidence for the existence of Strand 2 of the Tesla Fault as projected toward LLNL and SNLL by some previous investigators. The exploratory trench across the mapped trace of Strand 2 of the Tesla Fault was excavated in late Quaternary terrace and alluvial deposits and exposed unfaulted beds of the much older Livermore Formation along most of its length.

2.3.3.3.4. Other Geologic Hazards. Review of existing geologic and geotechnical data for the LLNL and SNLL sites indicates that the possibility for secondary seismic effects such as soil liquefaction or similar phenomena is remote. The presence of dense, poorly sorted materials beneath LLNL and SNLL and the position of the water table at depths generally in excess of 16 m support this judgment. No instances of ground failures that could be attributed to liquefaction or related phenomena were observed in Livermore Valley following the great San Francisco earthquake in 1906[2-25] and none were noted following the January 24, 1980, event. The nearly flat land surface that underlies LLNL and most of SNLL precludes the possibility of large-scale landsliding within the two Laboratories. Such minor erosion and slumping as may occur along stream or ditch banks or in the hilly southern portion of SNLL as a result of severe storms would be local in extent and readily mitigated before any possible structural hazards could develop.

As discussed in the program and work schedule for the LLNL Site Seismic Safety assessment presented in Appendix 2B, some additional geological studies have been deemed necessary or desirable as part of the review and improvement of the Design Basis Earthquake for LLNL facilities. These investigations include field mapping along the Greenville and Las Positas Fault zones and in other selected areas. Additional subsurface exploration will also be conducted within LLNL. This work will be integrated with ongoing seismological, hydrological, and geophysical investigations.

2.3.3.4. Seismicity. The largest earthquake in the immediate area occurred in 1861 and has been assigned a Richter magnitude of 6.0 to 7.5. Contemporary accounts indicate that the event was felt most severely in the town of Livermore, but these reports also indicate that the earthquake was located on the Calaveras fault system, probably in the San Ramon Valley. The largest instrumentally recorded earthquakes in the Livermore Valley occurred during the Greenville earthquake sequence of January-February 1980. The two largest of these earthquakes were accorded local magnitudes of about 5.5 to 5.9 by the USGS and the U. C. Berkeley seismographic stations. Epicenters for this sequence ranged between 2 and 20 km deep and were near faults in the Greenville system. Prior to these events, low-level seismicity had been routinely recorded in the valley since 1969 by the USGS Northern California seismic net, but the events could not be unambiguously assigned to any of the postulated fault systems in the Valley. In the absence of positive evidence to the contrary, LLNL considered all mapped faults to be potentially active in the determination of the Design Basis Earthquake.[2-11, 2-26] A local seismic net has been installed to complement the existing USGS net and provide better information regarding seismic locations and fault mechanisms.

2.3.3.4.1. Design-Basis Earthquake. Earthquakes have two ways of causing damage to structures: surface offset and ground shaking. Large shallow earthquakes may cause ground rupture which, if it occurs beneath a building, can damage it. The hazard due to surface rupture has been discussed in the preceding section on geology.

The ground shaking results from seismic waves emanating from the slipping fault. This ground shaking causes structures to vibrate. Depending on the intensity of shaking and the stiffness, strength, and resonant frequencies of the structure, damage could occur. The intensity and the general characteristics of the shaking at the site where the structure is located depend principally on the local soil conditions, the distance to the earthquake, and the earthquake magnitude.

Therefore, in order to assess the seismic hazard for a structure, one must:

(1) Determine the location of important active faults and/or regions of diffuse seismicity.

(2) Postulate the maximum size (magnitude) of earthquake possible for each fault.

(3) Estimate the potential ground shaking at the building site for each earthquake.

The methodology for estimating ground shaking due to earthquakes located on more distant faults, those greater than about 10 km from a site, is well established. For these faults, one begins by estimating the maximum possible magnitude of an earthquake on that fault, or the greatest amount of energy that fault can release in an earthquake. This is commonly estimated according to relationships between the observed magnitudes of earthquakes and the observed rupture lengths of the faults. In these studies the rupture length is the length of the portion of the fault that has slipped during a given earthquake. Although for any given length the observed magnitude varies, the trend is obvious: the greater the rupture length, the greater the magnitude.

To use such a relationship to predict the maximum future earthquake of which a given fault is capable, one has to judge the fraction of the total length of a fault zone that can slip in any single earthquake. In observations on earthquakes in California, this fraction has commonly been 1/5 to 1/2. The larger the fraction of total length one uses as the rupture length, the larger would be the estimated magnitude. For distant faults potential surface offset is not a safety concern. Only faults that are less than 0.5 km from the building site are considered to have any potential for causing surface rupture at the building.

Having located a distant fault and estimated the magnitude of the maximum earthquake that could occur along the fault, the next step is to estimate the severity of ground motion that this earthquake could produce at the site in question. For use in structural analyses, the ground shaking is generally expressed in terms of a maximum or peak horizontal acceleration measured in terms of "g." The acceleration equal to the acceleration produced by the earth's gravitational field, approximately equal to 9.8 m/s^2 at sea level, is one "g." For example, a horizontal force equal to 1.0 times the weight of the structure acting horizontally would produce a horizontal acceleration of 1.0g. Associated with this peak acceleration is a "response spectrum."[2-27] The former reflects only the high-frequency level of shaking while the latter reflects the entire frequency content of the motion. Peak vertical ground shaking is often approximated as 2/3 the maximum horizontal.[2-28]

To estimate ground motion from earthquake sources less than 10 km from a building site, the first two steps are the same as for the more distant faults. However, the ground motion is more complex and the recorded data are so sparse and widely scattered that the relationships between earthquake magnitude and acceleration at short distances are more uncertain.

The general response spectrum can be estimated by a variety of methods. Basically, the methods involve generating many response spectra plots using a selected data base of recorded strong motion earthquake records, all normalized to a peak acceleration for the site. The response spectra are then enveloped and the resulting spectrum becomes the final ground-shaking criterion for evaluating the building's structural integrity.

A general discussion of the problem of making estimates of the ground shaking when the fault is very near the site is given in Bernreuter and Tokarz.[2-26] Estimates are made by considering all of the recorded strong ground motion and applying judgment. In particular, considerable judgment must be applied to estimate response of the local soils compared to sites where very intense ground motion have been observed, and to assess the potential for focusing of seismic waves. The fact that the

Livermore site is a deep-soil site would probably reduce the very intense high-frequency peak ground motion in comparison with a bedrock site such as Pacoima dam.

2.3.3.4.2. Interpretations of the Seismic Hazard. The Design-Basis Earthquake (DBE) for the Livermore Site considers two possibilities: (1) a larger, more probable future earthquake associated with the more distant fault zones to the west of the site--the San Andreas, Hayward, and Calaveras--and (2) a smaller, less probable future earthquake associated with the local faults in the general vicinity of the site. For the more distant fault zones, one needs to consider only the effects of strong ground motion on the structural integrity or safety of buildings. For the local fault systems, both strong ground motion and the possibility of surface offset are considered. As discussed in the preceding section, on-site geology, drilling, and trenching has produced no evidence to substantiate the possibility of a surface offset beneath any Livermore Site facilities; therefore, the evaluation of the seismic hazard to LLNL from local faults need only consider the effects of strong ground motion. Appendix 2B contains the work schedule and outlines additional studies that are in progress and will improve the Design-Basis Earthquake determination for the LLNL site.

Strong Ground Motion. On four different occasions between 1971 and 1974, the geological and seismological evidence has been examined with a view to defining a DBE for the Livermore site. These examinations are documented in Blume,[2-27] Bernreuter and Tokarz,[2-26] Blume,[2-13] and Wight.[2-11] The salient points of these four analyses are summarized below.

Blume[2-27]: As part of the planning for Increment 3 of the LLNL plutonium facility, Blume established a DBE to be used to establish preliminary seismic design criteria. The investigation addressed the potential seismic hazard from both the faults within Livermore Valley and the more distant major faults to the west. Based on a geological and seismological literature survey and limited local field explorations, Blume concluded that the faults near the Laboratory were inactive and the controlling DBE should be based on a postulated earthquake associated with the more distant faults to the west-- San Andreas, Hayward, and Calaveras. Blume postulated DBEs with magnitudes of 8.3, 7.5, and 7.0 on these faults respectively. He used several of the standard methods to calculate a maximum acceleration for the Livermore site. Blume also indicated that a "reasonably conservative prediction of the maximum ground motion that would be produced at the site by any of these earthquakes is 0.4g." Blume also specified an associated response spectrum.

Bernreuter and Tokarz[2-26]: This study reflected the results of the authors' detailed review of the 1971 Blume report plus their own independent assessment of the seismic hazard for Livermore site. The fundamental difference between these two studies was their assessment of the activity of the local fault system. To be conservative, these LLNL staff members assumed that the local fault system (in particular the Tesla fault) was active, whereas Blume had considered the local fault system as inactive.

Bernreuter and Tokarz derived maximum accelerations for the Livermore site from both the distant major fault zones to the west and for the fault system local to the LLNL site. Their values are summarized below.

On the basis of past seismic activity and statistical correlations (similar to those used by Blume in 1971), they assigned maximum Richter magnitudes of 8.3 to the San Andreas fault (equivalent to the San Francisco earthquake of 1906) and 7.5 to the Hayward and Calaveras. To estimate the maximum ground accelerations at LLNL due to earthquakes on these distant faults, they used three different methods and recommended the largest acceleration value developed from each fault: 0.4g from the San Andreas and Hayward faults and 0.5g from the Calaveras.

The physical picture of faulting at the site used by Bernreuter and Tokarz [2-26] was that drawn by Blume on the basis of the 1971 field investigation for the proposed plutonium laboratory. An essential feature of this picture was the projection of both the Tesla and Corral Hollow faults as transecting the LLNL site. Although Blume had found no evidence of faulting onto the LLNL site, the projections resulted from connecting features, previously reported by others, which are suggestive of faulting southeast and northwest of the site. For the purpose of predicting maximum possible ground motions due to potential earthquakes on those faults, Bernreuter and Tokarz felt that the LLNL site must be considered as being at the earthquake epicenter and not at some mitigating distance from it.

For the less well-characterized local fault system, the historic seismic records are brief and sparse. Careful review indicated that these faults were capable of producing earthquakes with Richter magnitudes in the range of 5 to 7. Within this range, Bernreuter and Tokarz observed, "close-in the actual magnitude . . . of the earthquake is not so important from the engineering aspect since the maximum ground acceleration and response spectra will be much the same. The duration will be different. The larger the earthquake magnitude, the longer its duration. Certainly it seems highly unlikely that the fault system near the Laboratories site would have a magnitude 7 earthquake; however, since the site is at the epicenter, if the magnitude is in the range of 5 to 7 it makes little difference except on duration. An upper limit of magnitude 6.5 is estimated as the largest earthquake that will occur on the fault system under the Laboratories site."

To estimate the maximum ground acceleration that might occur at the LLNL site at the epicenter of an earthquake on one of the local faults, Bernreuter and Tokarz used a statistical treatment of data for peak acceleration vs epicentral distance recorded for about 20 earthquakes. Their analysis indicated that a ground motion similar to that recorded at the Pacoima Dam during the 1971 San Fernando earthquake could reasonably be considered representative of ground motion in epicentral regions. Their statistics indicated that "the peak g level of 1.25g from the Pacoima Dam is not unreasonable for a maximum peak g level from an earthquake." However, more important from the structural viewpoint "are the number of oscillations at 0.8g. For earthquakes located on the local faults it is estimated that the peak g level will be 0.8-1.25g. Certainly one could expect that 0.8-g level would create considerable energy, while the higher spikes would not greatly influence the spectra." Their recommended spectrum for the response of structures on the LLNL site to shaking due to an earthquake on a local fault was one derived from the Pacoima Dam record, with the peak over 1g reduced to 0.8g. To illustrate this, Fig. 2-15 shows the trace of acceleration versus time that was recorded at Pacoima Dam during the San Fernando earthquake of February 9, 1971. In the acceleration record, note that there is an extreme peak that stands out far beyond the level of sustained acceleration. Such high load applied very briefly and only once is not the kind of load that tests the structural quality of a building, since the building does not have time to respond to it. Earthquake damage in a structure is a cumulative effect, developing over a period of several seconds; it does not occur instantaneously. Therefore, as far as structural response and damage are concerned, the "effective acceleration" which can cause damage is not the single spike but rather the highest level attained repeatedly during the whole period of strong shaking. This effective peak acceleration is the ground shaking level that has been considered in the LLNL DBE.

Although Bernreuter and Tokarz concluded that the intensity of ground shaking at the LLNL site would be greatest for earthquakes on the local faults, and therefore recommended a DBE with a maximum ground acceleration of 0.8g, they stressed that earthquakes on the San Andreas, Hayward, and Calaveras faults were also important "because first, the duration of maximum shaking is much longer than that of earthquakes on the local faults and second, they are more likely to occur."

<u>Blume</u>[2-13]: The recommendations developed in this investigation established the seismic design criteria to which Increment 3 of the plutonium facility was designed--specifically, a maximum horizontal ground acceleration of 0.5g and the response spectrum shown in Fig. 2-16.

Faulting in the vicinity of the Laboratory site was investigated. Figure 2-13 reflects the critical findings of this investigation. Blume concluded that the earlier described Tesla fault system was composed of three strands--called Tesla fault No. 1, Tesla fault No. 2, and Tesla fault No. 3--and represented the largest fault system near LLNL. Based on his judgments of its surface expressions in the hills to the southeast, Blume concluded that this local fault system was probably also the most recently active, even though the evidence from wells N-1 and N-2 (Fig. 2-13) suggested that, nearer the LLNL site, the Tesla fault No. 1 had long been inactive. Hence, their DBE for LLNL was defined as the largest earthquake the Tesla fault could produce.

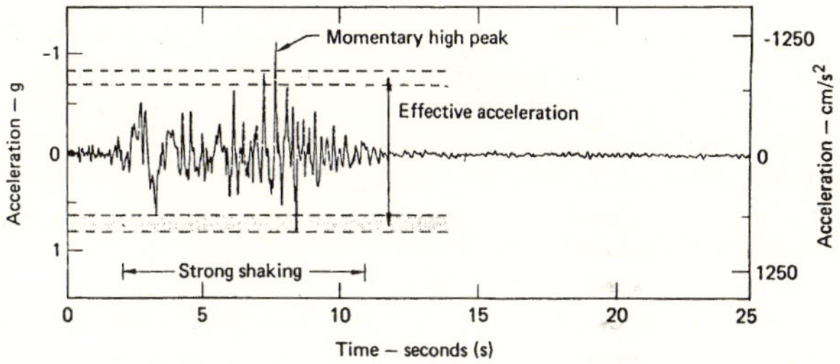

Figure 2-15. Acceleration vs time as recorded at Pacoima Dam during the San Fernando earthquake of February 9, 1971. Damage to buildings is caused by strong shaking over a period of several seconds, not by one or two very brief high accelerations.

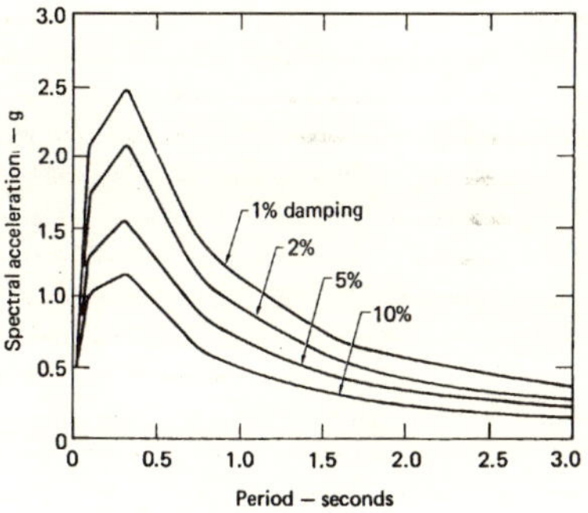

Figure 2-16. Design-basis response spectrum recommended by Blume & Associates after their major investigation of faulting at the LLNL site.

Blume & Associates based their estimate of earthquake magnitude on estimates of the total length and rupture length of the Tesla fault No. 2. They chose as the southeasterly end of this independently acting segment the point where it intersects the Greenville fault about 11 miles southwest from the LLNL site. To estimate the total length of this branch, not knowing its northwesterly extent, they conservatively assumed that it continued out under the Livermore Valley another 5 miles NW of the site, for a total length of 16 miles.

To estimate the rupture length, Blume applied a theoretical factor of 1/3 (judgments of this factor vary, as mentioned above), tempered by an empirical observation that, since a 4-mile stretch of Arroyo Seco appeared to be a surface lineament of Tesla fault No. 2, 4 miles was representative of a typical rupture length on the fault. To be more conservative, they chose 6 miles (about 10 km) as the rupture length on the Tesla fault for the purpose of estimating the magnitude of the earthquake.

From an empirical relationship between surface rupture length and magnitude, Blume selected 5.7 as the magnitude of the earthquake that the largest, nearest fault could produce. From the observed dip of the Tesla fault and an estimated focal depth of 5 miles, they calculated that the nearest epicenter of an earthquake on Tesla fault No. 2 would be 2-1/2 miles from the center of the site. Finally, from a compilation of acceleration data observed near the epicenters of earthquakes, Blume & Associates arrived at 0.5g as a conservative estimate of the maximum ground acceleration to which a structure like Building 332 on the LLNL site could be subjected by an earthquake.

In summary, as the result of this investigation, Blume indicated an agreement with Bernreuter and Tokarz that the Tesla fault is the largest active fault near the Laboratory. However, he assigned an earthquake magnitude of 5.7 as the largest possible earthquake for the Tesla. Further, based on published data by Boore and Page[2-29] relating to acceleration levels near faults that have moved during moderate-sized earthquakes, Blume estimated a peak ground acceleration of 0.5g. These estimates of earthquake magnitude and DBE acceleration are lower than the Bernreuter and Tokarz estimates of magnitude 6.5 and maximum acceleration value of 0.8 g and differ from Blume's prior estimate of 0.4g for the DBE. The DBE for the plutonium facility was therefore modified to 0.5g.[2-27] Finally, Blume still found no evidence for potential surface faulting at the site of the plutonium facility.

Wight[2-11]: The purpose of this report, published by LLNL two years after Blume's investigation,[2-13] was to define the seismic hazard at LLNL in a manner consistent with the Atomic Energy Commission's requirements for the format and content of safety analysis reports for nuclear power plants. The AEC had requested that such reports be prepared as well for other structures whose integrity was essential to the health and safety of the public.

For the San Andreas, Hayward, and Calaveras faults, Wight estimated magnitudes by means of statistical correlations of magnitude with fracture length, taking the fracture length to be half the total length of the fault. This led to magnitudes of 8.3, 7.5, and 7.5, respectively. To estimate ground accelerations at the LLNL site, he followed the method of first estimating bedrock accelerations on the basis of acceleration-distance-magnitude relationships and then calculating a surface acceleration by means of a mathematical model of the soil layers. By this procedure Wight arrived at values of 0.5g for the maximum acceleration in the bedrock and 0.32g for the maximum acceleration on the surface at the LLNL site due to earthquakes on the distant major faults to the west.

In examining the local fault system, Wight[2-11] used the mapping of Blume[2-13] as shown in Fig. 2-13. As Blume & Associates had, Wight chose the Tesla fault as the one potentially capable of producing the maximum seismic effects at the LLNL site. However, Wight judged the total active length of the Tesla fault to be 34 km, or about 21 miles, as compared with Blume's 16 miles. In estimating earthquake magnitude, Wight applied the same relationship of magnitude to fracture length as he had used for the more distant faults, taking the fracture length to be half the total length, rather than one third as Blume had. As a result of these differences, Wight's fracture length for the Tesla fault was 17 km, or about 10-1/2 miles, whereas Blume's had been only 6 miles. This led to an estimated maximum earthquake magnitude on the Tesla fault of 6.5, which agreed with the estimate of Bernreuter and Tokarz but was greater than Blume's 5.7.

Wight's approach to estimating maximum surface accelerations due to this local earthquake was also similar to Bernreuter and Tokarz's, in that the magnitude of the earthquake is considered to be less important than the proximity of the site to the epicenter. Wight noted that close in "the dependence of peak acceleration on magnitude is weak," that "the correlation of peak acceleration with site geology is low," and that recent "data, calculations, and observations clearly indicate that accelerations approaching 1.0g are possible in near-epicentral regions for earthquakes of all magnitudes." Emphasizing the evidence of the Pacoima dam record, Wight estimated, as Bernreuter and Tokarz had done, that the peak acceleration at the LLNL site due to an earthquake on the local fault system could be 0.8g.

Impact of the Las Positas Fault. Both Blume[2-13] and Wight[2-11] considered the Tesla fault, as mapped in Fig. 2-13, to be the local fault on which to place the design basis earthquake. However, if Herd's mapping of the Las Positas and Tesla systems, as shown in Fig. 2-14, is correct, the Las Positas zone truncates Tesla fault No. 1, and eliminates Tesla fault No. 2 altogether, since, except for the presence of the arroyo, postulated evidence for strand 2 of the Tesla fault zone can be accounted for by the presence of Las Positas fault. Also, the Las Positas itself would become the largest, nearest fault, and so by that criterion would be the one on which to base the DBE for the LLNL site. If this is the case, the DBE ground motion levels generated by the Las Positas fault should not exceed those previously established. The rupture length (and hence the potential earthquake magnitude) of the Las Positas fault is constrained by the 20-km distance between the Calaveras system on the west and the Greenville fault on the east, and the Las Positas is no closer to the LLNL site than the postulated Tesla fault No. 2. Therefore, these DBE ground motion levels would be about the same. Additional studies (Appendix 2B) are underway to improve the DBE determination for the LLNL site.

2.3.3.4.3. Critical Facility Earthquake Response. All critical facilities at LLNL have been evaluated for seismic integrity using the Blume response spectrum anchored at 0.5g peak ground acceleration (PGA). Additionally, these critical facilities have been reviewed for a 0.8g PGA by an extrapolation of the analysis results of the 0.5g PGA review. The objective of these reviews is to insure confinement of radioactive and toxic materials contained within these structures. With this objective in mind, the assessment of these facilities was done using allowable stresses and element capacity levels higher than those specified in the Uniform Building Code (UBC). Stress levels and material capacities used were based on test data, ultimate strength concrete values and steel yield values. The objective was to make a realistic assessment of the actual building capacities could be made. As a result of this approach, yielding and damage of building elements is permitted as long as this does not lead to structural collapse or a loss of safety related functions. It is anticipated that repair will be required following a 0.5g or 0.8g PGA event before the facility is returned to routine operation. Safety reviews of all critical facilities has been completed. The results of seismic analysis for these reviews at LLNL are summarized below:

Building 231 Vault. Analysis indicates no modifications required for this structure to insure confinement at the 0.5g and 0.8g PGA levels.

Building 251. Analysis of this structure indicated insufficient capacity in roof-to-wall connections, roof chord stresses, shear wall stresses and out-of-plane bending of shear walls.

As a result of these findings, design modifications have been implemented to "harden" a portion of the building so that radioactive and toxic materials may be stored and handled safely. Furthermore, changes were made in Building 251 operations to limit the amount of radioactivity that might be released in a major earthquake before construction of the "hardened" portion of the facility was completed.

Building 281. The analysis of this facility indicated some yielding of reinforcing steel in the reactor shield could be expected, but no structural collapse was predicted. Also, the heat-exchange support and bridge-crane support were found to be deficient. Modifications to both of these structures have since been made, additionally, this pool-type reactor was decommissioned in 1980.

Building 331. Evaluation of this facility at the 0.5g and 0.8g PGA levels indicated deficiencies in the stack supports and roof-to-wall and wall-to-foundation connections. Additionally, shear transfer through the wall pilasters was questionable. Modifications to the stacks (addition of support guys) were made and design modifications have been proposed to upgrade the roof-to-wall, wall-to-floor connections and pilaster shear transfer capacity.

Building 332. The evaluation of this structure to the 0.5g and 0.8g PGA earthquake levels indicated deficiencies in the Increment I loft structure and the mechanical equipment room. Modifications were made to upgrade the loft to the 0.5g PGA level; however, a re-evaluation of this portion of the facility still indicates some local yielding with anchor bolt and connection failures occurring as well as problems with the connection capacities of the precast tilt-up exterior wall panels. Additional modifications are still required in this area, although no collapse of the loft structure is anticipated.

Modifications to the mechanical equipment room have recently been completed, significantly increasing its seismic capacity.

As a result of safety concerns regarding this building following the January 1980 Greenville earthquake sequence, the DOE has insituted an independent review of Building 332. Results of this review will soon be available.

Work is currently underway to provide an extensive seismic instrumentation system for this facility. This will enable us to better determine the response of the building and potential force levels experienced in the event of future earthquakes.

Recent modifications to portions of the ventilation system and optical pipes, and airlocks have been designed and constructed to withstand the DBE.

2.3.4. Surface Water Hydrology

The three water systems considered as having a potential hydrological effect on the Livermore site are:

- Storm water.
- South Bay Aqueduct.
- Del Valle Reservoir.

Figures 2-1, 2-2, and 2-6 show the location of the Site and local natural drainage channels. Some of the arroyos and creeks in the Livermore Valley area have only minimal flow from October to

April, the area's typical rainy season. Storm water is channeled through storm sewers and open ditches designed to accommodate a maximum flow expected in a ten-year interval. Storm water is directed north to the nearby Arroyo Las Positas via an open storm-drain right-of-way from the northwest corner of the site to the Western Pacific tracks, a distance of 317 m. A much smaller percentage of the stormwater flows southwest to the Arroyo Seco. However, SNLL storm drainage water is all channeled to the Arroyo Seco.

The South Bay Aqueduct transfers water from Byron, California, to Santa Clara County through a system of pipelines and aqueducts. The aqueduct is an open channel as it traverses the eastern edge of Livermore Valley about 1.6 km southeast of the LLNL site and adjacent to the SNLL east boundary. Demand for this water includes local domestic and agricultural users plus surrounding counties.

Del Valle Reservoir is located about 11 km southwest of the site. This 9.5×10^7-m^3 reservoir provides water conservation, flood control, and supply to surrounding counties. The Livermore site is outside the floodplain of the Del Valle dam.

A detailed discussion of local surface hydrology is included in Appendix 2C.

2.3.5. Groundwater Hydrology

The Livermore Valley is a major groundwater source area.[2-14, 2-15] Sandy-gravelly aquifer horizons alternate with fine-grained, relatively impermeable beds and groundwater occurs both under confined and unconfined conditions. Both the Quaternary alluvial sequence and the Livermore Formation are sources of water supplies sufficient for urban, industrial, and agricultural use.

Quality of Livermore Valley groundwater varies, but is generally suitable for most uses. Groundwater in the central and southern portions of the Livermore Valley is replenished by percolation from Arroyo Valle and Arroyo Mocho and is of good quality. Groundwater in the northern and eastern Livermore Valley contains substantially higher mineral concentrations than that found in other portions of the Valley. For example, areas of high boron and fluoride concentrations occur in ground waters in the northeastern Livermore Valley, north of LLNL and SNLL.[2-14]

The CDWR[2-14] subdivided the Livermore Valley groundwater basin into 12 sub-basins based on variations in groundwater occurrence, movement, and quality. The sub-basins appeared to be separated by partial ground water barriers, most of which were believed to be faults. Difficulties in assessing characteristics of the groundwater basin were described together with the uncertainties that exist.[2-14]

The eastern Livermore Valley is underlain by water-bearing strata, mostly of alluvial origin. Faults and stratigraphic variations affect the movement of ground water and divide the Livermore

Valley ground water basin into sub-basins. Ground water recharge occurs in uplands east and southeast of the LLNL-SNLL site. The flow of this groundwater is inferred to be to the northwest, in two fault-defined sub-basins; one of these sub-basins is beneath LLNL. Some of this groundwater ultimately is discharged by seepage at the surface some 3.5 km northwest of the site. The remaining groundwater moves an undetermined distance west of the discharge site. It is not known if this groundwater is ultimately contained in the eastern Livermore Valley or if it flows west into other groundwater sub-basins of the Livermore Valley. Additional details regarding the occurrence and movement of groundwater near the DOE Livermore laboratories are included in Appendix 2D and plans for an additional hydrogeologic study are outlined in Appendix 2B.

2.3.6. Site 300 Hydrology

The drainage divide for the coastal ranges in this area is the Diablo Range. Since Site 300 lies on the eastern flank of this range, all of the runoff from the Site flows to the San Joaquin Valley. Most of the Site runoff flows into Corral Hollow Creek. Corral Hollow Creek is an intermittent stream carrying water only in the rainy season, and it flows toward the San Joaquin River.

2.3.7. Meteorology

2.3.7.1. General Climate. The Livermore Valley is flat and roughly bowl-shaped, about 21 km long and 7 to 11 km wide, and surrounded by hills that are 300 to 600 m high. The general area has a "Mediterranean scrub woodland" climate[2-13] that is characterized by mild, rainy winters (about 380 mm of rain) from October to April and warm, dry summers. Sunshine is abundant throughout the year since the winter rains are of a showery nature. Snow is very rare. Winter storms are a result of migratory low-pressure systems that become detached from the semi-permanent Aleutian Low and move over or north of the area. Following the passage of the migratory low, skies typically clear as the Eastern Pacific High builds inland. Occasionally, under these conditions, strong northerly surface winds with gusts up to 30 m/s are observed for a day or two. The summer is consistently warm and dry. A sea breeze typically develops during the afternoon when modified ocean air moves through the passes to the west; although the effect upon maximum temperatures is slight, the breeze persists into the early evening and brings cool night-time temperatures. The strength of this sea breeze rarely exceeds 13 m/s in Livermore. The spring and autumn seasons are typically transitional periods when no exceptional meteorological phenomena occur.

2.3.7.2. Severe Weather. The Livermore Valley rarely experiences severe weather. The greatest recorded daily rainfall is about 90 mm. Thunderstorms occur less than 5 days per year and are not intense; hail occurs even less frequently. Strong winds with gusts to about 30 m/s occur a few times each fall and winter, usually following the passage of a low pressure system.

In a study conducted by Smith and Mirabella[2-30] the tornado recurrence interval was estimated to be about 1 per 292,000 yrs or 3×10^{-6} per year. A more recent study by McDonald, Minor, and Mehta[2-31] indicates that extreme winds pose a more significant threat of structural damage in the central California area than do tornados. Since extreme wind probability distributions are based on data from widely scattered weather stations, and because Livermore and Site 300 are less than 32 km apart, the same data were used to develop extreme wind criteria for the two locations. For the Livermore site, McDonald, Minor, and Mehta[2-31] defined the extreme wind as 49 m/s based on a mean recurrence interval of 10,000 years. For Site 300, the windspeed criterion is increased by 10 percent to 54 m/s because of the possibility of channeling of the wind through the Site.

2.3.7.3. Air Pollution Potential. Because of its location, surrounded by hills, the Livermore Valley has more days of high photochemical smog levels (oxidant) than most of the other air pollution sampling stations in the San Francisco Bay Area. Such smog is generated from automobile emissions; it is estimated that about one-third of the ambient Livermore smog is imported into the Valley from upwind metropolitan areas.

2.3.7.4. Local Meteorology

2.3.7.4.1. Station Summary. Tables 2-4 and 2-5 are taken from the National Weather Service compilation for Livermore and are based on data observed from 1931 to 1960. As a check on these normals, temperature and precipitation data observed at the County Fire Department about 5.6 km to the west-southwest of the DOE site were tabulated and are shown for 1969-1971 in Table 2-6. The data source was the Climatological Data for California, published monthly by the National Oceanic and Atmospheric Administration (NOAA). It is apparent that these two tables are similar enough that no significant climatic change is obvious. The Lawrence Livermore National Laboratory is similar to the NOAA sub-station in topography, soil type, etc., so that the values in Tables 2-4 and 2-5 may be considered representative of the site.

2.3.7.4.2. Wind Direction and Speed. Winds have not been measured at NOAA's climatological sub-station in Livermore. Wind observations were taken at LLNL for several years by instruments

Table 2-4. Climatological temperature summary for Livermore (1931-1960 normals).[a]

	No. years	Jan	Feb	Mar	Apr	May	June	July	Aug	Sept	Oct	Nov	Dec	Annual
Highest, °C	30	24	25	27	34	39	43	44	44	46	39	32	26	46
Mean daily maximum, °C	30	13.6	15.6	17.9	21.4	24.7	28.2	32.0	31.3	30.6	25.6	19.5	14.6	22.9
Mean daily, °C	30	7.8	9.4	11.3	13.8	16.6	19.4	22.0	21.6	20.8	17.0	11.9	8.6	15.0
Mean daily minimum, °C	30	2.1	3.3	4.7	6.3	8.6	10.7	12.1	11.6	11.0	8.4	4.3	2.7	7.2
Lowest, °C	30	-7	-5	-4	-1	0	4	5	5	12	-2	-4	-7	-7
Degree days	30	326	249	217	137	74	18	0	0	7	50	193	302	1572
Number days above 32°C	19	0	0	0	+[b]	3	8	17	14	12	4	+	0	58
Number days below 0°C	19	15	9	4	+	+	0	0	0	0	+	4	23	55

[a] Elevation 166 m (545 ft), latitude 37°39'N, longitude 181°47'W. Wind: Calm 24%, W 19%, SW 16%, NW 7%, NE 12%.
[b] + = More than 0 but less than 1.

Table 2-5. Climatological precipitation summary (mm) for Livermore (1931-1960 normals).[a]

	No. years	Jan	Feb	Mar	Apr	May	June	July	Aug	Sept	Oct	Nov	Dec	Annual
Greatest monthly	30	207	172	129	95	70	15	6.1	4.1	48	47	151	258	258
Mean monthly	30	77	68	49	29	12	2.5	0.3	0.5	3.0	15	37	73	31
Greatest daily	30	88	37	51	46	18	10	4.1	3.8	39	21	78	83	88
No. days 0.3-2.5 mm	30	11	10	9	5	3	+[b]	+	+	1	3	6	10	58
No. days 2.5 mm or more	7	7	6	4	4	2	+	0	0	+	1	2	5	31
No. days 12.7 mm or more	10	2	2	1	1	+	0	0	0	+	+	1	3	10
Snowfall	30	2.5	T[c]	T	0	0	0	0	0	0	0	T	T	2.5

[a] Elevation 166 m (545 ft), latitude 37°39'N, longitude 181°47'W. Wind: Calm 24%, W 19%, SW 16%, NW 7%, NE 12%.
[b] + = more than 0 but less than 1.
[c] T = trace.

Table 2-6. 1969-1971 Summary of temperature and precipitation observations at County Fire Department, Livermore, California.

	Jan	Feb	Mar	Apr	May	Jun	Jul	Aug	Sept	Oct	Nov	Dec	Annual
Temperature (°C)													
Mean maximum	14.2	16.0	19.3	20.4	25.8	27.4	33.4	33.7	32.4	24.8	19.7	14.2	23.4
Mean minimum	3.0	3.1	3.4	4.0	8.4	10.8	11.9	11.4	10.7	6.5	4.3	2.3	6.7
Average	8.6	9.6	11.4	12.3	17.2	19.1	22.7	22.6	21.6	15.7	12.0	8.3	15.0
Absolute maximum	21	24	28	32	38	37	42	42	43	37	29	21	43
Absolute minimum	-6	-3	-6	-2	2	4	7	7	3	-2	-4	-4	-6
Precipitation (mm)	108.7	53.1	31.5	25.4	5.8	2.8	0.0	0.0	1.0	13.2	52.3	92.2	388.6

mounted atop a telephone pole. No maintenance records nor calibration reports of these instruments are available. Furthermore, trees gradually grew up around the pole during the past ten years. Consequently, these measurements are not deemed to be reliable for obtaining a representative wind summary. In 1971, an instrumented 40-m telescoping tower was installed in an open area in the northwest section of the Laboratory.

The predominant wind direction throughout the year and especially during the dry season is from the southwest through west. During the wet season, post-frontal anti-cyclonic flow occurs often enough to cause north-northeast and northeast winds of comparable frequency to the southwest through west directions. The most common windspeeds during all seasons are 5 to 7 m/s from the southwest through west. This relatively high speed is caused by channeling of the winds through passes in hills to the west. The wet season winds from the north-northeast and northeast are most common in the 2 to 3 m/s range, but winds of 11 to 16 m/s occur with nearly half that frequency. In general, the strongest winds blow during the wet season from the north-northeast and northeast. Figure 2-17 shows the typical annual average wind pattern for LLNL and SNLL.

2.3.7.4.3. Atmospheric Stability. The wind records mentioned above were used to estimate Pasquill-Gifford stability categories using the method described by Slade.[2-32] In the dry season D and E stabilities are of nearly equal prominence (about 70% combined frequency); during the wet season E stability is observed nearly 40% of the time. A summary of the dry and wet season tables is given in Table 2-7.

2.3.7.4.4. Humidity and Fog. Long-term records of humidity and fog are not available in the Livermore Valley.

Data summarized by the Weather Bureau[2-33] indicate that heavy fog (visibility less than 0.4 km) occurs on some 27 days per year. The monthly frequency is rather uniform at 2 or 3 days per month, except for 4 days in January and 1 day in March. Radiation fogs are more prevalent in late fall and early winter. High fog (coastal fog that is lifted in passing over the western hills) is prevalent on many spring and summer mornings but rarely reaches the ground in the vicinity of the LLNL site.

2.3.7.5. On-Site Meteorological Measurements Program. The Livermore site maintains a meteorological program for rapidly assessing critical meteorological parameters that may be used to estimate potential doses to individuals in the off-site environment in the event of an accidental release of hazardous materials into the atmosphere. (The meteorological measurements program provides input to the ARAC system described in paragraph 2.2.2.6). The program includes meteorological instrumentation

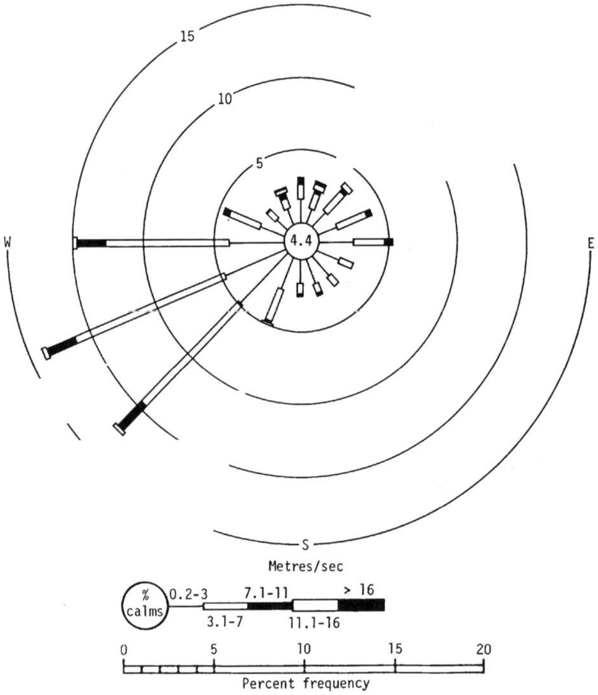

Figure 2-17. Annual wind rose for LLNL and SNLL. Length of line shows percent frequency (4.4% calm).

Table 2-7. Summary of wind frequency tables by stability categories.[a]

	Category[b]					
	A	B	C	D	E	F
Dry season						
Most frequent direction	WSW, W	WSW, W	WSW, W	SW, WSW	SW, WSW	SW
Frequency (%)	~34	~48	~55	~62	~57	29
Speed (m/s)	3	3	4	5	5	5
Least frequent direction	ESE,SE,SSE	SE, SSE	ESE,SE	SE,NW	SE	SSE
Frequency (%)	5	~3	~2	~2	<1	0
Speed (m/s)	2	1-2	2	3-4	4	3
Highest avg speed (m/s)	3	4	5	8	10	8
Direction	WNW,NW	WNW	N	NNW	NNW	NNW
Frequency	7-9	7	4	2	3	10
Lowest avg speed (m/s)	2	2	2	2	2	0
Direction	S	SSE	SE	S	E	SSE
Frequency	7	2	1	1	1	0
Wet season						
Most frequent direction	N	E	WSW,W	WSW,W	WSW,W	E
Frequency (%)	9	11	~25	~28	~32	15
Speed (m/s)	2	3	4	5	5-6	6
Least frequent direction	ESE	SSW	N	NNW	NNW	NW
Frequency (%)	3	4	2	2	1	<1
Speed (m/s)	2	3	4	3	4	2
Highest avg speed (m/s)	3	~3	4	5	7	12
Direction	NW	WSW,W,WNW	WSW	WSW	NNE	NNE
Frequency (%)	5	~28	12	14	4	9
Lowest avg speed (m/s)	2	2	3	3	3	2
Direction	ESE	SE,SSE	SSW,NNW	SSE	ESE,SE	NNW
Frequency (%)	3	~9	3-4	2	8	1

[a] Values rounded to nearest whole number.

[b] A = Extremely unstable conditions. B = Moderately unstable conditions. C = Slightly unstable conditions. D = Neutral conditions (applicable to heavy overcast, day or night). E = Slightly stable conditions. F = Moderately stable conditions.

near the LLNL's north perimeter and near the southwest corner of the SNLL property, where the measurements accurately represent the overall meteorology and are not influenced by building structures. The instruments are attached to 40-m telescoping towers; measurements of wind direction and speed and temperature are recorded at both 10 and 40 m. At LLNL temperatures are also measured at 2 m and the temperature differential between 2 m and 40 m is recorded.

The sensors consist of a lightweight Climet bivane for measuring horizontal and vertical wind direction fluctuations within accuracies of $\pm 3^{o}$ and $\pm 1^{o}$ respectively, and a cup anemometer for measuring the wind speed to an accuracy of 67 mm/s above the 220 mm/s threshold speed. In addition, a thermistor temperature sensor is placed in a wind-aspirated shield to prevent exposure of the sensor to direct solar radiation and to prevent air from stagnating about the thermistor. Ambient temperatures may be measured to within $0.2^{o}C$ with this type of sensor. The associated electronics for processing the data from LLNL, Site 300 (2.3.7.6), and SNLL are located in a building near the LLNL tower. Both standard chart records and digital (magnetic tape) data are currently used for recording. The sensors are replaced with serviced and recalibrated units every six months to ensure reliable operation.

2.3.7.6. Meteorology at Site 300. LLNL has operated a climatological observation station at Site 300 for many years. At the present time, this station measures and records surface temperature, pressure, humidity, and precipitation. Wind speed and direction and temperature data for Site 300 are collected from a meteorological tower located at this station. The tower is instrumented at a height of 20 m with sensors described in 2.3.7.5.

The mean annual precipitation is about 290 mm, although wide variation occurs from year to year. Most of the precipitation falls between the months of October and April in the form of rain, although a light dusting of snow can occur on the coldest days. Localized thunderstorms with the threat of lightning are infrequent. Maximum temperatures in the winter months, November to February, average around $13^{o}C$. During these months, the minimum temperatures are never much below the freezing level. Relative humidity is about 85 to 90% at night, decreasing to 60 or 70% during the afternoon. Winds are predominantly from the west and average about 5 to 7 m/s in the winter months.

The dry season extends from May through September. Daytime temperatures in the high 30's and low 40's are common in the middle of the summer. The relative humidity ranges from about 30 to 50% in the driest part of the year in the fall. Persistent westerly winds are characteristic of this area from spring to fall. Marine air flows through the canyons into the San Joaquin Valley and results in moderately strong winds in the afternoon and evening.

2.3.8. Biotic Species at SNLL and LLNL

The biological features of the area occupied by SNLL and LLNL have been examined at length. The plants, mammals, birds, amphibians, reptiles, arachnids, and crustaceans identified on the site are listed in Appendix 2E.

2.3.9. Biotic Species at Site 300

The Site 300 area is primarily a grassland community. The topography of the Site consists of moderate to steep hillside slopes covered with various annual grasses. Many biotic species favor this community. Insects such as spiders, beetles, grasshoppers, and crickets abound in the area. Mammals in the community are represented by many species of rodents such as mice, gophers, and squirrels which feed on the plants of the grassland and on the insects. Rabbits feed exclusively on the plant vegetation and deer browse throughout the area. Several varieties of lizards inhabit the area, feeding primarily on insects. Several types of snakes are also common, feeding on small mammals, birds and their eggs, lizards, and other snakes. Other predatory species such as the badger, fox, and coyote search for prey in this community. A listing of plants and animals observed at Site 300 is shown in Appendix 2E.

The grassland habitat shows a limited resident bird population due to the lack of shelter from predators. However, the area is important to many species of birds which, though roosting and nesting elsewhere, are dependent on the abundant supply of seeds and insects. The grassland also provides a suitable hunting ground for birds of the Raptores Order which include rodents and small birds in their diet. In 1975 approximately 100 acres of land on the east side of Site 300 was released as surplus property and deeded to the California Department of Fish and Game for use as a wildlife preserve.

Site 300 is thought to be the only natural location for a rare species of wildflower, *Amsinckia grandiflora*. The plant, which grows to a height of about 25 cm, was first discovered in the 1880s and was thought to be extinct until a patch was discovered at the Corral Hollow site in 1938. The area is presently roped off. The plant appears to meet the criteria to place it on the endangered species list according to the Endangered Species Act of 1973. As required by the Act, the U.S. Fish and Wildlife Service is considering establishing an area at Site 300 as Critical Habitat for this plant. A survey was conducted by an independent consultant (EG&G) to investigate the occurrence and status of endangered plants and animals (such as the San Joaquin Kit Fox) at Site 300. This study showed no new populations of *Amsinckia grandiflora* and no evidence that LLNL activities were impacting adversely on the known population of the species. There was also no evidence that the San Joaquin Kit Fox is present at Site 300. A report of this investigation is contained in Appendix 2E.

2.3.10. Archaeological and Historical Sites

An archaeological reconnaissance of the Livermore site was conducted by the Archaeological Consulting and Research Services of Mill Valley, California. It indicated no evidence of archaeological resources on either the LLNL or the SNLL properties. Inspection of the archaeological records on file with the Archaeological Research Facility of the University of California at Berkeley, and the records on file with the Laboratory of Archaeological Research at San Francisco State University, revealed no previously recorded archaeological sites in the area occupied by the Laboratories.

While no surface visible evidence of archaeological sites has ever been noted at LLNL or SNLL, and none was found during excavation, the possibility of buried or otherwise obscured remains is always present. If any future land modification should show any such evidence, Federal law (the Antiquities Act of 1906, as amended) requires that it be reported to the Secretary of the Interior so that appropriate steps can be taken to preserve the values so encountered.

A Class III cultural resources inventory was performed at Site 300 (Appendix 2F). Twenty-four cultural resource properties and twenty-five site types were located and recorded. Of the prbperties three are prehistoric, 20 historic, and one is both prehistoric and historic. Historic petroglyphs and structures are the most frequent site types.

The majority of the sites are of low significance. Four of the sites are potential resources for the National Register of Historic Places. The California Office of Historic Preservation is currently evaluating these sites.

2.3.11. Radiological Background Characteristics

The radiological background at the Livermore site is predominately determined by the activity levels of naturally occurring uranium, thorium, and potassium in the soil. Table 2-8 shows the natural radionuclide content of soils collected in a relatively undisturbed section of open land in the northeast portion of the LLNL site. Sample locations are shown in Fig. 2-18. Terrestrial gamma radiation exposure rates derived from the analyses vary from 5 to 7 μR/h, with a median of 5.8 μR/h. An exposure rate range of 3 to 7 μR/h was observed in a survey in the off-site vicinity.[2-35] At present, the exposure rate from ^{137}Cs, the principal global fallout radionuclide from past weapons tests, is about 0.1 μR/h, or about 1-2% of that of the median from natural terrestrial sources. The inferred local radiation exposure rate from cosmic rays is estimated to be 3.8 μR/h, based on an average site elevation of 182 m and using the data of Lowder and

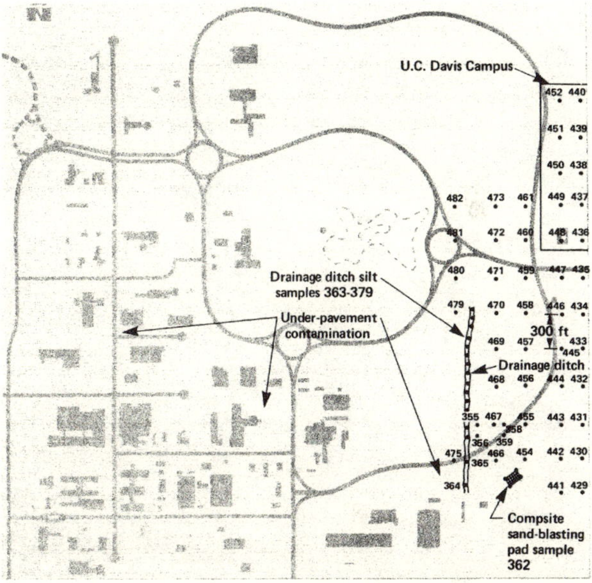

Figure 2-18. Locations of on-site soil sampling.

Table 2-8. Naturally occurring radionuclides in LLNL soils.[a]

Location	Activity (pCi/g)		
	^{238}Uranium	^{232}Thorium	^{40}Potassium
436	0.52	0.69	12.7
437	0.57	0.71	13.6
438	0.55	0.67	11.9
439	0.65	0.68	14.3
440	0.41	0.71	13.6
448	0.85	0.77	15.2
449	0.60	1.07	12.5
450	0.79	0.99	13.3
451	0.73	1.00	12.6
452	0.65	0.80	11.8
Average	0.63	0.81	13.2
Maximum	0.85	1.07	15.2
Minimum	0.41	0.67	11.8

[a] Exposure rates in μR/h at 1 m above the ground can be calculated from these activities using the conversion factor derived by Beck[2-34]:

^{238}U + daughters	1.82 (μR/h)/(pCi/g)
^{232}Th + daughters	2.82 (μR/h)/(pCi/g)
^{40}K	0.179 (μR/h)/(pCi/g)

Beck,[2-36] who relate cosmic radiation with elevation. The median total exposure rate (terrestrial plus cosmic) thus is 9.7 μR/h, comparable to a median value of 9.4 μR/h observed in a survey of environmental radiation backgrounds in the United States.[2-37]

With few exceptions, contributions of DOE operations to radiological soil contamination are below the limit of detection of field survey instrumentation. However, at LLNL a number of minor incidents involving radioactivity have occurred during the past 25 years that have resulted in local on-site surface contamination. Contaminated material in these areas, either pavement or exposed soil, was usually dug up, packaged in steel drums, and disposed of as contaminated waste. Since the areas were either known or suspected to contain traces of residual contamination, the locations were paved to eliminate the possible spread of contamination. The total area so treated was about 300 m^2 and involved less than 0.1 μCi of plutonium. These areas are also identified in Fig. 2-18.

Plutonium and americium contamination has been found in a few soil samples collected on-site east of the LLNL waste disposal area. The locations are shown in Fig. 2-18 and the activity levels for the respective samples are shown in Tables 2-8 and 2-9. The source of contamination is probably due to local radiation incidents connected with the solar evaporators used in volume reduction of intermediate-level liquid waste. These evaporators are no longer used for radioactive waste.

2.3.12. Aerial Radiation Survey

During the summer of 1975 an aerial radiation survey was conducted over the LLNL and SNLL sites and at Site 300. This survey was performed for DOE by EG&G, Inc.,[2-38] utilizing the EG&G Aerial Radiological Measuring System (ARMS). The survey employed an array of 40 NaI(Tl) scintillation detectors, 127 mm in diameter by 51 mm thick, mounted externally on a helicopter platform. Surveys were conducted at an elevation of 45 m at air speeds of approximately 30 m/s. Flight lines were flown visually with the aid of aerial photographs taken just prior to the radiation survey. The results of the survey were presented in the form of radiation isopleths plotted over photographs of the respective areas. Eleven areas within the LLNL and SNLL Complex were found to have radiation levels above background. The source of elevated radioactivity in each of these locations is shown in Table 2-10. None of these represent a radiation hazard to workers in the area. At Site 300 elevated activity levels were detected in the vicinity of three of the high-explosive firing tables. These levels are due to depleted uranium (a byproduct of ^{235}U enrichment) used in experiments at the Site. Data obtained from the fly-over confirm the results of annual soil sampling, namely, that shot debris is restricted to within 500 m of the bunkers. The levels ranged from the normal background of 0.1 μR/hr to 0.5 μR/hr.

Table 2-9. Plutonium content of soils collected at locations shown in Fig. 2-18.

Sample No.[a]		Activity (μCi/g)
429		$9.18 \times 10^{-8} \pm 27\%$[b]
430		$8.65 \times 10^{-8} \pm 24\%$
431		$1.13 \times 10^{-7} \pm 23\%$
432		$2.05 \times 10^{-7} \pm 13\%$
433		$2.86 \times 10^{-8} \pm 12\%$
434		$6.12 \times 10^{-8} \pm 12\%$
435		$3.00 \times 10^{-8} \pm 17\%$
436		$1.15 \times 10^{-8} \pm 19\%$
437		$5.36 \times 10^{-9} \pm 26\%$
438		$1.22 \times 10^{-8} \pm 18\%$
439		$5.32 \times 10^{-9} \pm 24\%$
440		$1.29 \times 10^{-8} \pm 13\%$
441		$1.09 \times 10^{-7} \pm 14\%$
442		$1.17 \times 10^{-7} \pm 13\%$
443		$3.26 \times 10^{-8} \pm 23\%$
444		$1.12 \times 10^{-7} \pm 16\%$
445		$1.56 \times 10^{-8} \pm 15\%$
446		$1.93 \times 10^{-8} \pm 7\%$
447		$1.67 \times 10^{-8} \pm 16\%$
448		$1.04 \times 10^{-8} \pm 21\%$
449		$2.16 \times 10^{-8} \pm 16\%$
450		$3.28 \times 10^{-9} \pm 40\%$
451		$1.26 \times 10^{-8} \pm 20\%$
452		$9.19 \times 10^{-9} \pm 24\%$
453	No sample at this location	
454		$3.73 \times 10^{-8} \pm 12\%$
455		$4.41 \times 10^{-8} \pm 16\%$
456		$1.74 \times 10^{-7} \pm 12\%$
457		$1.30 \times 10^{-7} \pm 12\%$
458		$1.96 \times 10^{-8} \pm 13\%$[b]
459		$1.18 \times 10^{-8} \pm 13\%$
460		$1.91 \times 10^{-8} \pm 32\%$
461		$1.05 \times 10^{-8} \pm 32\%$
462		$1.22 \times 10^{-9} \pm 42\%$
463		$5.59 \times 10^{-9} \pm 33\%$
464		$6.13 \times 10^{-9} \pm 24\%$
465	No sample at this location	
466		$4.03 \times 10^{-8} \pm 11\%$
467		$3.92 \times 10^{-7} \pm 10\%$
468		$1.17 \times 10^{-6} \pm 6.4\%$
469		$1.38 \times 10^{-8} \pm 16\%$

Table 2-9. (Continued)

Sample No.[a]		Activity (μCi/g)
470		$5.09 \times 10^{-8} \pm 11\%$
471		$2.26 \times 10^{-8} \pm 16\%$
472		$6.35 \times 10^{-9} \pm 25\%$
473		$1.51 \times 10^{-8} \pm 18\%$
474	No sample at this location	
475		$9.59 \times 10^{-7} \pm 7.2\%$
476	No sample at this location	
477	No sample at this location	
478	No sample at this location	
479		$3.76 \times 10^{-8} \pm 11\%$
480		$5.68 \times 10^{-8} \pm 11\%$
481		$1.23 \times 10^{-8} \pm 20\%$
482	No sample at this location	

[a] All samples are 50 mm in depth.
[b] All error limits are at the 2σ level.

Table 2-10. Identification of sources of radiation detected by the ARMS flyover at LLNL-SNLL.

Location	Source
Building 612, LLNL (Dry Waste Processing)	Three concrete blocks unshielded at top containing various radioactive reactor wastes.
Taxi Strip, LLNL (Waste storage)	Two waste carboys originating with the LPTR reactor and Building 251 (Diagnostic Chemistry).
Building 321, LLNL (Materials Fabrication Shop)	A pallet of drums containing depleted uranium chips was found to be the primary source of radiation in the storage yard.
Building 212, LLNL (Accelerators)	Radiation levels due to induced radioactivity in parts in the source storage room.
Building 251, LLNL (Diagnostic Chemistry)	Activity due to a ^{85}Kr source in building.
Building 194, LLNL (Electron-Positron Accelerator)	Elevated levels due to $^{15}O_2$ and $^{13}N_2$ in stack exhaust gases.
Building 233, LLNL (Classified storage area)	
Building 281, LLNL (LPTR reactor)	Elevated levels due to concrete blocks containing activated parts from the reactor--principally ^{60}Co from stainless steel. Also identified ^{41}Ar in downwind stack exhaust.
Building 9143, SNLL (Radiography)	Elevated radiation due to a variety of shielded sources including a 75-Ci ^{60}Co source. Also contains 1400 kg of depleted uranium.
Building 9122, SNLL	Depleted uranium.
Building 921, SNLL (Vault)	Depleted uranium, ^{235}U, and various shielded sources.

While it is clear that LLNL operations have produced a detectable increase in uranium near the firing bunkers, the areas affected are well within Site boundaries and the uranium levels observed constitute no health hazard.

References

2-1. W. J. Silver, C. L. Lindeken, A. Conover, and J. H. White, Environmental Monitoring at the Lawrence Livermore Laboratory--1978 Annual Report, Lawrence Livermore National Laboratory, Livermore, CA, UCRL-50027-78 (1979).

2-2. J. L. Cate, Jr., M. Auyong, and D. W. Rueppel, A Prototype On-Line X-Ray Fluorescence Analyzer for Detecting Metals in Sewage, Lawrence Livermore National Laboratory, Livermore, CA, UCRL-81954 (1979).

2-3. E. P. Hardy and P. W. Krey, "Determining the Accumulated Deposit of Radionuclides by Soil Sampling and Analysis," Proceedings of the Plutonium Symposium held at Los Alamos Scientific Laboratory August 4-5, 1971, Los Alamos National Laboratory, Los Alamos, NM, LA-4756 (1971).

2-4. C. J. Johnson, R. R. Tidball, and R. C. Severson, Science 193, 488 (1976).

2-5. J. A. Hayden, "Size Fractionation Methods--Measuring Plutonium in Respirable Dust," Science 202, 753 (1978).

2-6. B. M. Page, "Geology of the Coast Ranges of California," in Geology of Northern California, E. H. Bailey, Ed., California Division of Mines and Geology, Bulletin 190 (1966).

2-7. E. H. Bailey, M. C. Blake, Jr., and D. L. Jones, "Character and Significance of the Ophiolitic Crust that Forms the Basis of the Great Valley Sequence in Western California," in Abstracts with Programs (Cordilleran Section), Vol. 2, No. 2 (Geological Society of America, 1970), pp. 68-69.

2-8. A. S. Huey, Geology of the Tesla Quadrangle, California, California Division of Mines, Bulletin 140 (1948).

2-9. R. L. Wesson, E. J. Helley, K. R. Lajoie, and C. M. Wentworth, "Faults and Future Earthquakes," in Studies for Seismic Zonation of the San Francisco Bay Region, R. D. Borcherdt, Ed., U. S. Geological Survey Prof. Paper 941-A (1975), pp. 5-30.

2-10. J. N. Alt, "Analysis of Repeated Geodetic Leveling Data for the Livermore Valley Area, Alameda County, California," in Abstracts with Programs (Cordilleran Section), Geological Society of America 75th Annual Meeting, San Jose, CA (1979), pp. 65-66.

2-11. L. H. Wight, A Geological and Seismological Investigation of the Lawrence Livermore Laboratory Site, Lawrence Livermore National Laboratory, Livermore, CA, UCRL-51592 (1974).

2-12. California Department of Water Resources, Livermore and Sunol Valleys, Evaluation of Ground Water Resources, CDWR Bulletin 118-2, Appendix A: Geology (State of California, The Resources Agency, Sacramento, CA, 1966).

2-13. John A. Blume and Associates, Inc., Investigation of Faulting at the Lawrence Livermore Laboratory, report to Lawrence Livermore National Laboratory by John A. Blume and Associates, Inc., San Francisco, CA (1972).

2-14. California Department of Water Resources, Evaluation of Ground Water Resources, Livermore and Sunol Valleys, CDWR Bulletin 118-2, Geology (State of California, The Resources Agency, Sacramento, CA, 1974).

2-15. Alameda County Planning Department, Draft Environmental Impact Report, Livermore-Amador Valley Quarry Reclamation Plan (Alameda County Planning Department, Hayward, CA, 1979).

2-16. D. G. Herd, Geologic Map of the Las Positas, Greenville and Verona Faults, Eastern Alameda County, CA, U. S. Geological Survey Open-File Report 77-689 (1977).

2-17. R. S. Cockerham, F. W. Lester, and W. L. Ellsworth, A Preliminary Report on the Livermore Valley Earthquake Sequence, January 24-February 26, 1980, U. S. Geological Survey Open-File Report 80-714 (1980).

2-18. J. E. Slosson, State of California Special Studies Zones, Dublin Quadrangle, California Division of Mines and Geology, unnumbered map, scale 1:24,000 (1974).

2-19. URS/John A. Blume and Associates, Inc., Seismic and Geologic Investigations of the Sandia Livermore Laboratory Site and Structural Investigations of the Tritium Research Facility, report to Sandia Laboratories-Livermore by URS/John A. Blume and Associates, Inc., San Francisco, CA (1978).

2-20. D. W. Carpenter, K. R. Puchlik, A. L. Ramirez, J. L. Wagoner, K. D. Knouss, and P. W. Kasameyer, Status Report on the Geology of the Lawrence Livermore National Laboratory Site and Adjacent Areas, Lawrence Livermore National Laboratory, Livermore, CA, UCRL-53065 (1980).

2-21. M. G. Bonilla, J. J. Lienkaemper, and J. C. Tinsley, Surface Faulting near Livermore, California, Associated with the January 1980 Earthquakes, U. S. Geological Survey Open-File Report 80-523 (1980).

2-22. F. J. Tokarz and G. Shaw, Seismic Safety of the LLL Plutonium Facility (Bldg. 332), Lawrence Livermore National Laboratory, Livermore, CA, UCRL-52786 (1980).

2-23. S. Rice, E. Stephens, and C. Real, Geologic Evaluation of the General Electric Test Reactor Site, Vallecitos, Alameda County, California, California Division of Mines and Geology, Special Publication 56 (1979).

2-24. California Department of Water Resources, Reevaluation of Seismic Hazards for Clifton Court Forebay, Bethany Dams and Reservoir, Patterson Reservoir, Del Valle Dam and Lake Del Valle (State of California, The Resources Agency, Sacramento, CA, 1979).

2-25. T. L. Youd and S. N. Hoose, Historic Ground Failures in Northern California Triggered by Earthquakes, U. S. Geological Survey Prof. Paper 993 (1978).

2-26. D. L. Bernreuter and F. J. Tokarz, Design Basis Earthquakes for the Lawrence Livermore National Laboratory, Lawrence Livermore National Laboratory, Livermore, CA, UCRL-51193 (1972).

2-27. John A. Blume and Associates, Inc., Plutonium Laboratory, Lawrence Livermore Laboratory--Geologic, Seismologic and Foundation Investigation, report to Maker and Martens, Architects, by John A. Blume and Associates, Inc., San Francisco, CA (1971).

2-28. N. M. Newmark, J. A. Blume, and K. K. Kaput, "Seismic Design Spectra for Nuclear Power Plants," J. Power Division, Proc. ASCE 99 (PO2), pp. 287-303 (1973).

2-29. D. M. Boore and R. A. Page, Accelerations Near Faults That Have Moved Through Moderate-Sized Earthquakes, U. S. Geological Survey Open-File Report (1972).

2-30. T. B. Smith and V. A. Mirabella, Characteristics of California Tornadoes, Lawrence Livermore National Laboratory, Livermore, CA, UCRL-13533 (1972).

2-31. J. R. McDonald, J. E. Minor, and K. C. Mehta, Development of a Design Basis Tornado and Structural Design Criteria for Lawrence Livermore Laboratory's Site 300, California, Lawrence Livermore National Laboratory, Livermore, CA, UCRL-13667 (1975).

2-32. D. H. Slade, Ed., Meteorology and Atomic Energy (U.S. Atomic Energy Commission/Division of Technical Information, 1968). Also available as TID-24190 from Clearing House for Federal Scientific and Technical Information, National Bureau of Standards, U. S. Dept. of Commerce, Springfield, VA 22151.

2-33. U. S. Weather Bureau, Expected Meteorological Conditions for the Livermore Research Laboratory of the AEC (U. S. Weather Bureau Scientific Service Division, Washington, D. C., 1952).

2-34. H. L. Beck, J. DeCamp, and C. Gogolak, In-Situ Ge(Li) and NaI(TL) Gamma-Ray Spectrometry, U. S. Atomic Energy Commission, HASL-258 (1972).

2-35. C. L. Lindeken, P. H. Gudiksen, J. W. Meadows, K. O. Hamby, and L. R. Anspaugh, Environmental Levels of Radioactivity in Livermore Valley Soils, Lawrence Livermore National Laboratory, Livermore, CA, UCRL-74424 (1973).

2-36. W. M. Lowder and H. L. Beck, "Cosmic-Ray Ionization in the Lower Atmosphere," J. Geo. Phys. Res. 71, 4611 (1966).

2-37. C. L. Lindeken, K. R. Peterson, D. E. Jones, and R. E. McMillen, Geographical Variations in Environmental Radiation Background in the United States, Lawrence Livermore National Laboratory, Livermore, CA, UCRL-73822 (1972).

2-38. An Aerial Radiological Survey of the Lawrence Livermore Laboratory, EG&G, EGG-1182-1693 (1975).

3. ENVIRONMENTAL IMPACT

3.1. INTRODUCTION

Chapter 3 of the DEIS has been updated and revised in response to review and comment by federal, state, and municipal agencies and by private citizens. Major changes are:

- Section 3.5.3, Chemical Waste Management, has been expanded to include more information regarding the disposal of environmentally hazardous chemical wastes.
- Section 3.7, Health and Safety Aspects of Livermore Operations, now contains information on the radiological impact of Livermore site operations on employees, on local water supplies, and on agricultural crops. A 5-year data base has been included to provide the reader with a means for evaluating past radioactive effluent releases.
- Section 3.9, Accident Analysis, contains added information on the number and mode of radioactive shipments in and out of the Livermore site. The methodology employed in estimating radiation dose is also outlined.

3.2. PAST, CURRENT, AND FUTURE LAND USE

The major environmental impact to the Livermore property occurred during World War II when this general farming and cattle-grazing property was converted to a Naval air station (see 2.1.2). Construction of landing strips and the addition of streets and buildings completely altered the property so that it was no longer suitable for farming or cattle grazing.

The past, current, and future land use for the Livermore site is described in sections 2.1.6 and 2.1.7. The use of the land is about the same as for the air base in that buildings, concrete, and asphalt will continue to prevent its use for general farming and cattle grazing.

The major present environmental impact of the DOE Livermore laboratories is from the approximate total of 8000 employees and their utilization of natural resources, energy and effects on the nearby community. This is discussed in section 4.

At Site 300, prior land use was sheep and cattle grazing since the land was generally too hilly for cultivation. Because of the size of the Site and the distance between high explosive test areas, DOE's impact due to construction and land use is small. Operations at Site 300 in terms of future land use depend on requirements of the weapons program.

In 1973 approximately 100 acres on the east side of Site 300 was declared excess property. This property was subsequently transferred to the California Department of Fish and Game for use as an ecological reserve. Prior to release a radiological survey was made in compliance with AEC requirements for disposal of land. A terrestrial radiation survey was made at a nominal height of one meter above the soil surfaces using a portable survey instrument. Soil samples were also collected and analyzed for uranium. The terrestrial radiation exposure rates, which varied from 4.0 to 6.5 μR/h, were typical of natural background radiation from soils in this area. Likewise the concentration of one to three parts per million of uranium were within the range observed in northern California.

3.3. RESOURCES AND ENERGY

3.3.1. Water Use

The primary supply of potable water for the Livermore site--both LLNL and SNLL--is obtained from the City of San Francisco's Hetch-Hetchy water system. The water is used for domestic and plant purposes, and for fire protection. It is pumped out of the Hetch-Hetchy Coast Range tunnel at the Mocho Shaft into two standpipe tanks, from which it is delivered under gravity flow via a 25-cm, 10-km-long pipeline to three water storage tanks located on a hill at the south end of the Sandia Livermore site. Delivery capacity is approximately 4.92 m^3 per minute. Water storage capacity in the three tanks is 4.6×10^3 m^3.

Water is delivered from the storage tanks by gravity and distributed throughout the LLNL and Sandia sites via an underground piping grid system with mains on most streets within the developed areas of the two sites. Distribution mains are 20-35 cm in diameter, and there are sectionalizing valves at most intersections. Hydrants are located throughout the system at a maximum spacing of 152 m.

In addition to the Hetch-Hetchy water supply, an emergency supply is available from Zone 7 of the Alameda County Flood Control and Water Conservation District for standby and emergency services. Water from the Zone 7 system can be delivered into the site water distribution system by a pumping plant which is connected to the Zone 7 main at the north boundary of the Livermore Site.

Water consumption has always shown a wide seasonal variation. The magnitude of these changes are indicated in Fig. 3-1. Greatest water use occurs in July or August (irrigation) and the lowest use in December, January, and February. The variation ranges from about 50,000 m^3 in a winter month to a peak of near 125,000 m^3 per month during the summer.

The total annual use of water increased with the growth at the Livermore site until 1969, at which time the combined population of LLNL and SNLL was 7053. In 1970, the total water use was higher

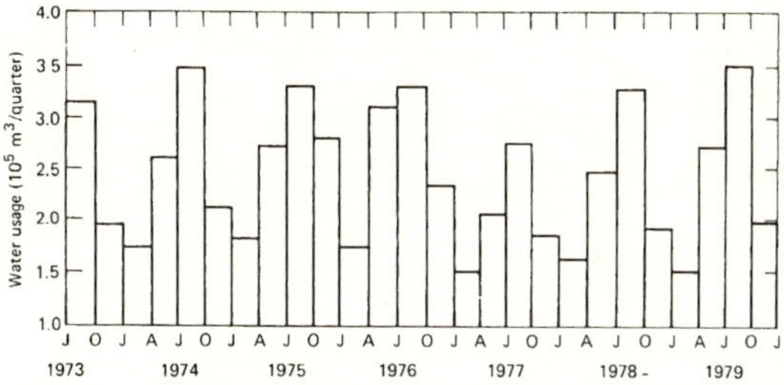

Figure 3-1. Seasonal water consumption by LLNL, Site 300, and SNLL.

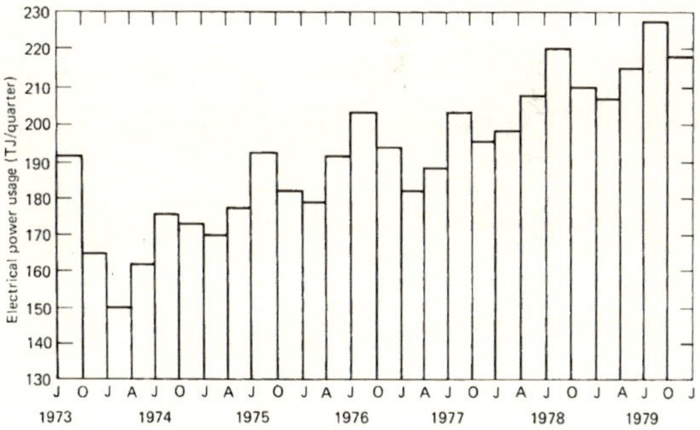

Figure 3-2. Seasonal use of electrical power by LLNL, Site 300, and SNLL.

(1.1×10^6 m^3, 0.3% of the average Hetch Hetchy Aqueduct annual flow) even though the population was less. In recent years, water use has stabilized at about 1.0×10^6 m^3.

3.3.2. Electrical Energy Use

Power at 115 kV is delivered to LLNL by Pacific Gas and Electric Company through two overhead transmission lines. Power at 13.8 kV is delivered to SNLL from LLNL through two underground distribution lines. The electrical power consumption of the Livermore site grew each year between 1964 and 1972. The use of electrical power more than tripled over that 8-year span even though the sustained population growth was less than 10%. The surge of increased power consumption is partly attributed to bringing on-line new buildings and adding increments to existing buildings. At the same time, significant power increases occurred due to the Magnestic Fusion Power and Laser programs. Following the energy conservation programs inititated by DOE in the last half of 1973, electrical power use decreased in 1974 (see Fig. 3-2). Conservation efforts have continued to act as a damper on power consumption; however, the addition of new building areas and the electrical energy requirements of new and existing programs increased the electrical power in 1978.

3.3.3. Fuel Use

3.3.3.1. Natural Gas. Natural gas, supplied by the Pacific Gas and Electric Company, is used to heat most of the buildings at LLNL and SNLL as well as supplying fuel for shop equipment and special research operations.

Natural gas use at LLNL and SNLL has generally followed a pattern of growth year by year as the number of buildings and square feet of occupancy have increased. In 1974, a decrease in natural gas usage was accomplished as a direct result of energy conservation measures and mild winter weather (see Fig. 3-3). Installation of automatic controls on building heating, ventilation, and air conditioning systems and continued energy conservation measures nearly offset the additional heating load of new building areas occupied in 1979.

At LLNL about 7% of the natural gas usage (for the computer facilities and adjacent buildings) is provided by Pacific Gas and Electric on a noninterruptable basis. The balance of LLNL and all of SNLL are subject to natural gas curtailment during periods of high demand. Approximately 15% (16 of 109) of the gas fired boilers at LLNL and SNLL have been equipped for burning either propane or No. 2 fuel oil during periods of interrupted gas service. To provide heating during periods of interrupted service for natural gas, some of the boilers at both LLNL and SNLL have been equipped for burning either propane or No. 2 fuel oil.

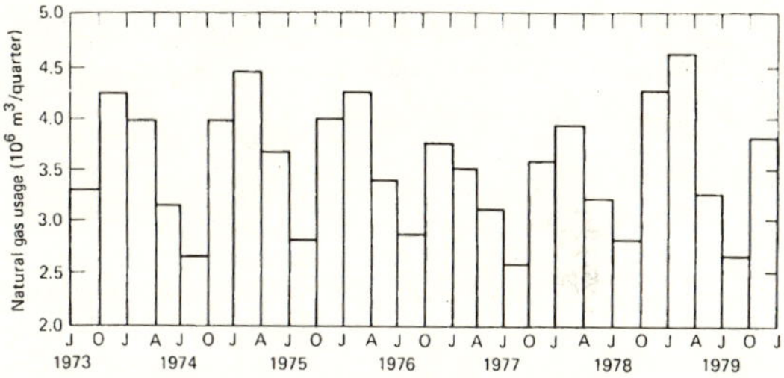

Figure 3-3. Seasonal use of natural gas by LLNL and SNLL.

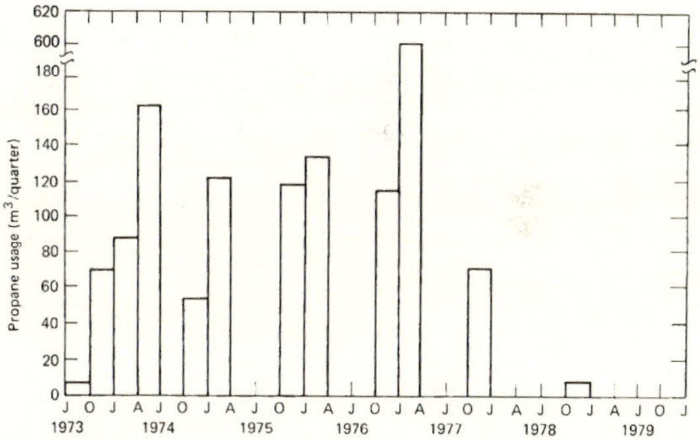

Figure 3-4. Seasonal use of propane by LLNL. High propane consumption in the first quarter of 1977 was due to Pacific Gas & Electric's curtailment of natural gas during unusually coal weather.

3.3.3.2. Propane Gas. At LLNL a propane-air plant delivers propane-air mixed gas into the site gas distribution system during natural gas curtailment periods. The existing plant capacity of 1.6 m^3/s of mixed gas is adequate for supplying those buildings where dual fuel capability is impractical. The total propane storage capacity of 220 m^3 at Building 622 and 680 m^3 at Camp Parks will take care of the LLNL site for about 25 days on a curtailment basis. (See Fig. 3-4 for propane use by LLNL.) The LLNL propane-air supply does not extend to SNLL.

3.3.3.3. Oil. Approximately 600 m^3 of heating oil can be stored by LLNL (including 223 m^3 at Site 300) and about 640 m^3 by SNLL. At present, most of the storage capacity is in above-ground tankage. The largest tank, with a capacity of about 570 m^3, is located at SNLL. An earth berm surrounds this tank to contain unexpected oil spills. Use is being made of mobile tankers for fuel oil storage at several buildings at LLNL. Future plans call for installation of underground tanks at these locations and for new construction. Figures 3-5 and 3-6 show the amounts of fuel oil used for building heat and for equipment usage respectively.

3.3.3.4. Gasoline. Figure 3-7 shows the use of gasoline at DOE's Livermore site for the period 1973 through 1979. The use of increased gasoline can relate to the increased number of employees; more employees will use more taxi service, outside travel, and more trucks for equipment movement. Although the amount of gasoline used has increased, the energy conservation program has proved effective in minimizing this increase. The motor pool has planned the use of small nonhighway type electric and gasoline vehicles, reserving the larger sedans for off-site trips whenever possible. In addition, the large on-site use of bicycles conserves gasoline.

3.3.3.5. Jet Fuel. Jet fuel is used by the turbo-prop plane leased by LLNL for flights to the Nevada Test Site (NTS). The plane makes two flights a day; however, if there is a special project at NTS, additional flights might be made. The fuel usage is shown in Fig. 3-8. The fluctuations occur as a function of activity at NTS, the weather, and the downtime of the aircraft.

3.4. CONSTRUCTION ACTIVITIES

3.4.1. Environmental Impact

The environmental impact of construction is considered from the standpoint of land use, community effects, and commitment of resources. Several major construction projects have been completed at the

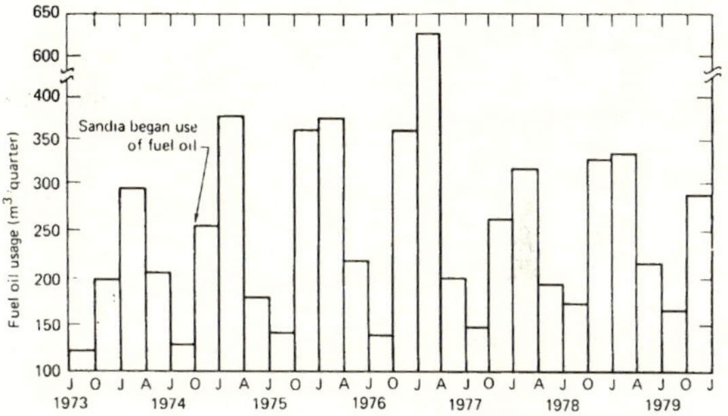

Figure 3-5. Seasonal use of fuel oil by LLNL, Site 300, and SNLL. High oil consumption in the first quarter of 1977 was due to Pacific Gas & Electric's curtailment of natural gas during unusually cold weather.

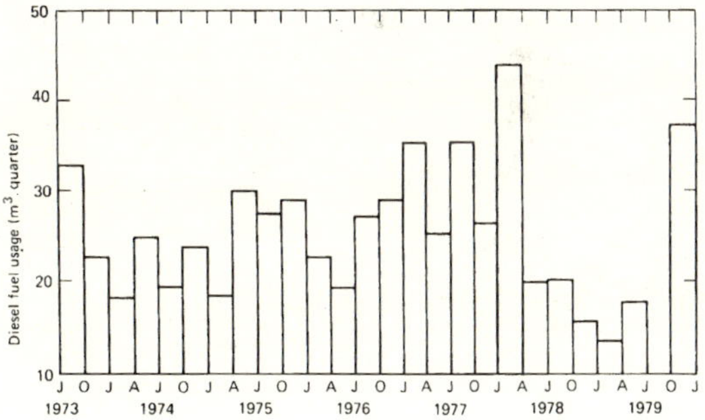

Figure 3-6. Seasonal use of diesel fuel by LLNL and Site 300 for owned equipment.

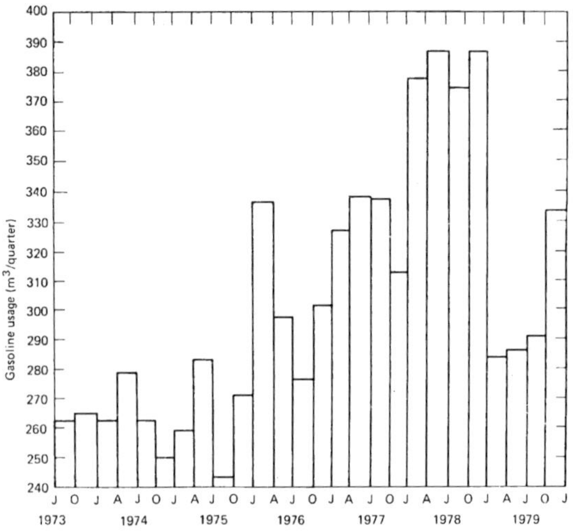

Figure 3-7. Seasonal use of gasoline by LLNL, Site 300, and SNLL.

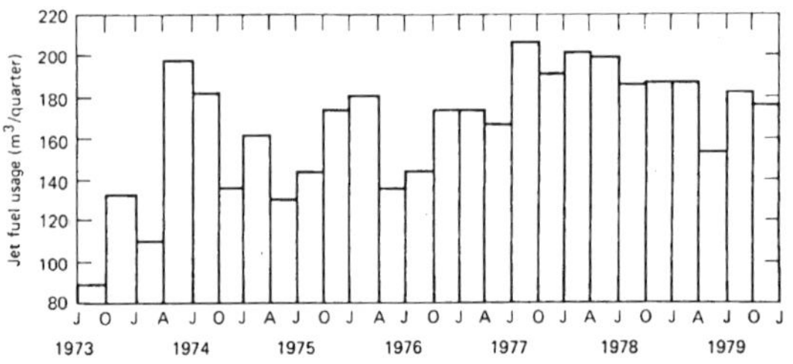

Figure 3-8. Seasonal use of jet fuel by LLNL.

Livermore site in recent years. Accordingly, it is possible to evaluate these activities in the light of present-day concern on the part of the public.

3.4.2. Land Use

At LLNL the construction now underway, or planned for the future, uses the present site, which has been committed to government use for over 30 years. Sandia's purchase of land in 1970 and 1979 may be repeated in the future as operational requirements dictate. In new construction at either LLNL or SNLL, siting is carefully considered to assure that such construction does not result in destruction of trees or native plants. Consideration is given to erosion control and site drainage. All construction includes funds for landscaping.

As a result of grading for the air field by the Navy in World War II, the LLNL site is reasonably level. Consequently, there are no natural hills that must be cut down in preparation for construction. Certain buildings require substantial excavation to provide for either underground earth shielding or basement facilities. Soil that is not required for backfill is moved to one of several soil stockpile areas on site.

A survey (section 2.3.10) showed no evidence of archaeological resources on the Livermore site that might be destroyed by construction.

3.4.3. Community Effects

The construction activities at the DOE Livermore laboratories take place in secured areas not used by the public. Excavated soil is used on site so the community is not exposed to the noise and dust caused by trucking this soil to off-site disposal areas. At LLNL, the trees along the western perimeter act as a sight barrier. Also, the agricultural lands on the west and north act as space barriers. Since construction is all on site, all residents in the vicinity have full access to their properties.

Construction at the Livermore site causes heavier traffic on city streets, particularly East Avenue. On any given day of the work week, there may be up to 200 construction contractor personnel on the site. Since there are about 2500 DOE operating contractor employee cars in the parking lots on any work day, construction employees account for less than a 10% maximum increase in traffic. Major construction jobs are awarded through open bid; however, most of the subcontractors are from the Bay Area with approximately 20% coming directly from the Livermore Valley area.

Materials used in construction represent irretrievable commitment of resources (see Section 8). Competition for materials used in new construction has little local impact on residential construction. Lumber, which is the prime material in residential construction, is not used to a great extent in DOE construction. Construction projects are competing for concrete and steel, but no construction at Livermore enjoys any priority in material procurement.

3.5. WASTE MANAGEMENT

Waste management at the DOE Livermore laboratories includes the following categories:

- Radioactive waste.
- Sanitary waste.
- Chemical waste.
- Excess properties, salvage, and reclamation.
- Nonhazardous waste landfill.

3.5.1. Radioactive Waste Management

Unlike a production facility, the varied research programs at LLNL and SNLL produce a continually changing amount and type of radioactive waste. Compaction and packaging of SNLL radioactive wastes are performed in Building 969. Radioactive wastes are shipped to NTS for disposal and chemical wastes are collected by a commercial waste disposal firm. The subparagraphs that follow describe LLNL procedures, but apply equally to SNLL with respect to material collection.

Collection of Radioactive Solid Waste. Operations in a glove box produce contaminated articles such as laboratory glassware, transfer containers, small equipment, absorbent paper, rubber gloves, etc. These items are placed in an uncontaminated secondary container within the box. All such containers are removed from the box by bagging the container in plastic (bagging out). The plastic-bagged items are placed in covered, metal containers (garbage cans), which are lined with a plastic bag and a paper inner bag.

Radioactive solid waste generated in areas other than glove boxes is placed directly in the metal waste containers:

- When a contaminated waste collector is full, the plastic bag is sealed and placed in a covered metal drum.

- The filled drums are transferred to the solid waste disposal facility (Building 612) where the contaminated waste is compacted in drums using a hydraulic press.
- Drums containing quantities of transuranium nuclides in which the specific activity of the drum contents exceed 10 nCi/g are accumulated for transfer to NTS for long-term retrievable (above-ground) storage. Drums containing waste in the nonretrievable category (<10 nCi/g) are transferred periodically to a land burial site at NTS.

Radioactive, Liquid Waste in a Building with a Retention-Tank System. Paths for these liquid wastes are as follows:

- Laboratory sinks, lavatories, janitors' sinks, and floor sumps drain to retention tanks outside the building. This system helps prevent the inadvertent release of radioactivity to the sanitary sewer.
- When a tank is full, drainage from the building is switched to another tank and a sample is withdrawn from the filled tank and analyzed for radioactivity.
- If the activity is below standards set by DOE Order 5480.1A and is considered to be as low as practicable, the liquid waste is released to the sanitary sewer.
- If the activity exceeds these criteria, the liquid waste is transferred to a portable tank and moved to the waste treatment area. The liquid waste is either added to a holding tank to await normal decontamination treatment, or it is segregated and decontaminated individually by a method appropriate for the radionuclides present.

Radioactive Liquid Waste in Carboys. Paths for these liquid wastes are as follows:

- Dilutions, rinses, excess solution, etc. are collected in a glass or plastic carboy protected by a metal secondary container, located in the work area.
- When a carboy is nearly full, it is loosely capped and moved outside the building to a designated collection area. The carboys are periodically collected and moved to the waste treatment area where they are evaluated for treatment procedure, and scheduled for the treatment indicated.

Radioactive wastes originate in over 20 buildings in which many different operations are performed. However, five of these facilities are responsible for producing the bulk of all radioactive waste.

Radioactive wastes are products of:

- Chemical laboratory research and analytical processes.
- Accelerator operations.
- Mechanical operations.

Radioactive Airborne Effluents. At the Livermore site, and typically at all DOE contractor facilities, HEPA (high-efficiency particulate air) filters are used in exhaust air systems to assure that hazardous particulate matter is not released to the environment. All facilities handling plutonium, uranium, and beryllium are equipped with these filters. In buildings such as Nuclear Chemistry Operations (Section 2.1.6.4) and the Plutonium Facility (Section 2.1.6.7), exhaust air from the glove boxes is double-filtered. Following this filtration the air enters a manifold system and is filtered a third time before being exhausted to the outside atmosphere.

Before being installed, every HEPA filter is tested for efficiency using a monodispersed 0.3-μm aerosol of dioctylphthalate (DOP). To be acceptable, the efficiency for removing 0.3-μm particles must be 99.97%. As this size is the most difficult size to remove, particles larger or smaller than 0.3 μm will be removed with efficiencies greater than 99.97%. After installation, the HEPA filters are tested in-place to assure that filter damage has not occurred during installation and that the filters are properly gasketed. Spent filters are disposed of as solid radioactive waste.

3.5.1.1. Summary of Radioactive-Waste-Producing Operations. Chemical laboratory research and analytical processes primarily involve analyses or studies of radionuclides, which produce contaminated liquid and solid waste. A few operations involve separation of high-level material for diagnostics and for transplutonic-element studies. Chemical engineering research and development operations contribute low-level liquid and solid waste.

3.5.1.2. Major Sources of Radioactive Wastes. The four major producers of radioactive waste at LLNL are

- 100-MeV Linear Accelerator--Building 194.
- Heavy Element Chemistry--Building 251.
- Metallurgy Chemistry--Building 332.
- Light Isotope Chemistry--Building 331.

The types of waste material and the method of generation at each of these facilities are described in sections 3.5.1.3 through 3.5.1.7.

3.5.1.3. 100-MeV Linear Accelerator (LINAC)--Building 194.

3.5.1.3.1. Solid Waste. Solid waste is generated primarily by the activation of various components and equipment around the 100-MeV LINAC. When removed from the facility, these items are normally packaged and sent to Building 612 for disposal.

3.5.1.3.2. Liquid Waste. There is very little liquid waste generated at the 100-MeV LINAC. There are two cooling-water loops used to cool various components and targets at the accelerator; however, these are essentially closed-loop systems and the generated activation products are retained within the systems.

3.5.1.3.3. Airborne Effluents. The primary gaseous effluents at the 100-MeV LINAC are $^{15}O_2$ and $^{13}N_2$, which are produced by (γ, η) reactions on these elements in the air. The remainder of the airborne effluent is generated primarily by the activation of dust particles in the air. The effluent air stream passes through high-efficiency filters before it is discharged to the stack. The $^{15}O_2$ and $^{13}N_2$ pass through the filters; however, only a trace amount of the activated dust appears on the downstream side of the filters.

The effluent stream is continuously monitored for particulate radioactivity. A flow-through ionization chamber is used to measure the $^{15}O_2$ and $^{13}N_2$ activity. In 1980 the releases from this facility resulted in a dose of 2.1 mrem/yr at the site boundary.

3.5.1.4. Nuclear Chemistry Operations--Building 251.

3.5.1.4.1. Solid Waste. Transuranic-contaminated solid waste material is normally generated during hot-cell or glove-box operations. In either case, the material is transferred out of the enclosure into a primary container free of contamination on the outer surface. Following an estimate of the identity and quantity of radionuclides present, the material is placed in a secondary container usually consisting of a heavy paper sack, plus a heavy plastic bag. This bag, when full, is sealed in a metal 210-liter drum and sent to the solid-waste handling area (Building 612) for final disposal. Larger items, such as pumps, manipulators, or enclosures, also are packaged and sent to Building 612 for disposal.

3.5.1.4.2. Liquid Waste. Highly contaminated liquid waste is processed within the building. Processing consists of transferring the liquid from its point of origin to a central waste block through double-walled polyethylene lines. The liquid is then solidified by addition of a cement-vermiculite mixture. When filled, the waste block is capped off and turned over to Waste Management (Building 612) for final disposal. Moderately contaminated liquids are placed in polyethylene waste jugs and sent to Building 514 for treatment and disposal. All water discharged from Building 251 is held in retention tanks until it is analyzed for radioactivity. This is achieved by a central collection system that directs all water, except sanitary sewage, to two 4-m^3 retention tanks. Water flow to the tanks is continuously monitored for gross contamination by a scintillation detection system. The detector is set to alarm at twice background. All water in the tanks is held until laboratory analyses show that contamination levels are within acceptable discharge limits. If the water exceeds discharge limits, it is transferred via tank truck to Building 514 for treatment prior to disposal.

3.5.1.4.3. Airborne Effluents. Airborne particulate waste generated by work performed in the various glove boxes and hot cells consists of alpha-contaminated particulates. Air from the glove boxes passes through double HEPA filters at the glove box and then is exhausted through manifolds to stacks on the roof top, where the air is again filtered through HEPA filters. Continuous particulate sampling is done on all Building 251 exhausts. Gaseous waste from the several hot cells is treated similarly except that continuous monitoring is provided at the discharge point to provide gross release detection capability. Detection is provided by in-line proportional detectors for alpha contaminants and NaI detectors for gamma emitters. Room air is continuously sampled for particulate contamination and is discharged through exhaust ducts to the roof where it is filtered through filters rated at 95% by NBS stain test (60-65% by 0.3-M DOP smoke). These filters are being replaced with double HEPA filtration as part of the planned upgrading of this facility (see 2.1.6.4).

3.5.1.5. Plutonium Facility--Building 332.

3.5.1.5.1. Solid Waste. Plutonium-contaminated solid waste is generated and handled by methods similar to those described for Building 251. All waste barrels are assayed for plutonium content (by means of a rotating-drum scanner) before leaving the building. The scanner consists of a 76 x 76-mm NaI(Tl) detector connected to a multi-channel analyzer and recorder. Details of the system are described in Hazards Control Progress Reports.[3-1,3-2]

3.5.1.5.2. Liquid Waste. All recoverable highly and moderately contaminated liquid waste is sent to Building 514 for treatment and disposal. Water from within the facility is retained in two 4-m^3 tanks until analysis indicates that contamination levels are within sanitary sewage discharge limits. Water is then released to the sanitary sewer. If contamination levels exceed the limits, the water is transferred to Waste Disposal for treatment prior to disposal.

3.5.1.5.3. Airborne Effluents. Alpha-contaminated particulate waste is generated by operations in the glove boxes used for continuing processes and experimental work. The glove box exhaust is passed through double HEPA filters. The exhaust air is again passed through a HEPA filter before being discharged to the atmosphere. All exhaust air is continuously monitored for particulate radioactivity. Room air exhaust is filtered through double HEPA filters and temperature-activated water spray nozzles are installed in room exhaust ducts. These features reduce further any possible impact on the environment (see 2.1.6.7).

3.5.1.6. Tritium Technology--Building 331. Tritium waste is generated within Building 331 by the various experimental operations performed there and takes the form of tritiated hydrogen gas (HT), tritiated water (HTO), or solids or liquids contaminated with HT or HTO.

3.5.1.6.1. Solid Waste. Solid waste is generally doubly contained, placed in metal drums, and sent to the Solid Waste Disposal facility (Building 612) for disposal.

3.5.1.6.2. Liquid Waste. There is no liquid waste retention tank system in Building 331. The majority of low-level liquid waste (less than 5 Ci/y) is released to the sanitary sewer. The majority of intermediate-level (1 to 10 Ci/liter) liquid waste is vacuum pump oil (approximately 400 liters/y). This oil is placed in 4-liter metal cans and packed in a sorbent inside 210-liter drums (limited to 200 Ci/drum), which are disposed of as solid waste. Some other liquids are placed in small plastic bottles, which are then placed in 4-liter metal cans, and the void volume filled with a sorbent. The metal cans are then disposed of as solid waste. Contamination levels of the liquid waste in the metal cans normally vary from 100 mCi/liter to 10 Ci/liter. The remaining radioactive liquid waste (less than 5000 Ci/y) is collected in 20-liter bottles and sent to the waste treatment facility.

3.5.1.6.3. Airborne Effluents. Stack effluents from the facility are continuously monitored for possible tritium release by drawing aliquots of the total flow through ion chambers. Both analog and digital integrator ion chamber output are provided. In addition, the relative concentration of HTO and HT in the effluent are measured using a molecular sieve method. In 1980, 2218 Ci of tritium (65% as HTO) were released.

3.5.1.7. Waste Management Facilities. The waste management facilities consist of:

- Retention-tank systems located in buildings where significant quantities of liquid waste could become contaminated. All effluent from sinks and floor drains is retained in 4- to 40-m^3 tanks until the radioactivity status is determined. If the radioactivity is not as low as practicable, the liquid is transferred to a portable tank and sent to the liquid decontamination facility at Building 514. Each retention system has at least two tanks so that operations can proceed while the radioactivity of the filled tank is being determined.

- Carboy or small tank accumulations of intermediate-level (1 to 10^6 μCi/liter) liquid waste at any location and of low-level (<1 μCi/liter) liquid waste at buildings without retention tank systems. These wastes are sent to the Solid Waste Disposal Facility and stored there prior to treatment.
- A collection and decontamination plant at Building 514 for treatment of low-level radioactive liquid waste.
- A facility in the waste treatment area that is presently used for the accumulation of intermediate-level liquid waste.
- A collection, packaging, and disposal facility at Building 612 where solid contaminated waste is prepared for shipment to a commercial underground storage site.
- A decontamination facility in which contaminated articles are cleaned of radioactivity.

3.5.1.8. Liquid Waste Treatment Plant Description. The Liquid Waste Treatment Plant receives building retention tank waste that was shown by analysis to exceed permissible dump limits. The liquid waste is transported in 4-m^3 portable plastic-lined steel tanks. This liquid waste is transferred to a 110-m^3 holding tank to await decontamination treatment. Four 5.7-m^3 plastic-lined steel tanks are used for decontamination, primarily by the coagulation-flocculation method.

The slurry from several treatments is accumulated in one tank and vacuum-filtered through diatomaceous earth on a rotary drum filter. The filter cake is collected in plastic-lined drums and sent to the Solid Waste Disposal Facility. A drum typically shows a gamma radiation of 1 mR/h at the surface and may contain 100 μCi of alpha emitters and 150 μCi of beta emitters, with an overall specific activity of about 2 nCi/g. The vacuum filtering produces dry-appearing flakes that contain about 45% water. No separation is expected since diatomaceous earth can absorb three times its weight of water without appearing wet. Centrifuging samples of filtered sludge produces a 10% volume separation of liquid. Tests to determine if the vibration from transportation to the underground storage site releases free liquid have not shown any free liquid.

Liquid waste with known specific contaminants can be treated by a method more suitable for that material than the regular coagulation-flocculation treatment. Equipment exists for special filtration, carbon absorption, ion exchange, centrifugal extraction, reverse osmosis, and distillation.

3.5.1.9. Solid Waste Disposal. The solid waste packaging, holding, and shipment activities are housed in Building 612 and its fenced and paved yard area. The contaminated waste accumulated in drums at the generating buildings is delivered to Building 612. The bagged waste is compacted using a hydraulic press and then sealed, marked, and recorded. Transuranium (TRU) contaminated waste is packaged in hot-dipped galvanized DOT Specification 17-H drums. These drums are intended to comply with the 20-year retrieval policy of the DOE. Other waste is packaged in drums with yellow exteriors. The yellow drums are moved to the yard area and the galvanized drums are stored in Building 612 to await shipment to a DOE-approved storage site at NTS. Drum shipments are made about twice a year.

The compressor plate of the hydraulically operated compactor is constructed with an integral hood-type controlled ventilation system exhausted through a HEPA filter. The stack exhaust and the work area atmosphere are monitored continuously during compacting operations.

Objects that could damage a drum during compaction or do not fit in a drum are accumulated in steel containers 1.8 m in diameter and 2.1 m high. When one is filled, a gasketed steel lid is bolted in place and the container is moved to the yard area to await shipment. Objects too large for these containers are packaged in specially constructed containers which are sealed by welding the cover plate.

3.5.1.10. Waste Storage. There is no waste storage facility at the Livermore site. Radioactive waste is transferred to an off-site, DOE-approved storage facility.

3.5.1.11. Effluent Control Systems. The primary control system for preventing the release of excessive amounts of radioactivity to the environment in waste liquids is the network of retention tank systems. These tanks are located at the buildings where the waste liquids are generated. The systems are designed so that all fluids entering the building sinks or floor drains are collected in a tank that is isolated from the domestic sewer lines. An alarm system announces when a tank is full and fluid flow is switched manually or automatically to another tank. A laboratory analysis of a sample from the filled tank governs the disposition of the contents.

All domestic sewer effluent leaves the site at the northwest boundary where a sampling station provides continuous monitoring.[3-3] Samples are also collected at this location for detailed laboratory analysis. A 51-x-51-mm NaI detector monitors continually for medium- and high-energy gamma emitters and a 3-x-127-mm diam NaI crystal monitors continuously for low-energy gamma emitters.[3-3] The minimum detectable concentration of ^{239}Pu is 30 nCi/liter. If contaminants in the effluent exceed preset limits, an alarm sounds at the Fire Station which is manned continuously. The contamination status is evaluated by a health physicist. A three-hour period elapses between the alarm and the arrival of the effluent at the Livermore Water Reclamation Plant (LWRP), so there is time for evaluation of the alternatives. Upon notification, the LWRP personnel will divert the effluent into one of their holding ponds. No diversion for radioactive release has been required.

The diverted sewage would be disposed of in accordance with the concentration found in the holding pond. The most likely occurrence is a release that would exceed the standards for drinking water by a small factor.

The LWRP is prepared to dispose of such sewage by a controlled release from the pond into the sewage treatment stream to assure an adequate dilution factor.

In the unlikely event of a large release that results in significant contamination in the holding pond, the corrective action would be dictated by the level of contamination and the radionuclide involved.

3.5.1.12. Site Administrative Limits on Effluents. The policy of the Laboratories is to maintain concentration of their liquid and airborne radioactive effluents to as low as reasonably achievable below the standards set by DOE Order 5480.1A. The current policy regarding liquid effluent tank releases is to discharge no more than a total of 5 µCi of alpha activity, 50 µCi of beta activity, and 20 mCi of tritium activity per day to the sanitary sewer. Factors considered in making this decision are as follows:

- The total quantity of radioactivity involved.
- Whether or not there has been an attempt to remove the radioactivity from the waste solution.
- The ability to remove the radioactivity from the waste solution.
- The current available storage and treatment capacity at the Liquid Treatment Facility.

Releases of radioactivity to the sanitary sewer system are usually more than 1000 times less than permissible levels, and it is expected that this will hold true as new facilities are constructed. These guidelines and considerations are applied in an effort to minimize discharges of radioactivity to the Livermore Water Reclamation Plant.

3.5.1.13. Radioactive Waste Releases. Airborne and liquid radioactive effluents released at the Livermore site in 1980 are shown in Table 3-1. Both normal and accidental releases are included (see Appendix 2A). However, liquid releases should be reduced as new treatment equipment is installed. During 1979, 376 m^3 of packaged radioactive solid waste was shipped from Livermore. Of this total, 33 m^3 was TRU waste. Three shipments of TRU waste were made to NTS during 1979. At Site 300, radioactive waste is restricted to depleted-uranium-contaminated high-explosive debris, which is buried on-site as described in Section 3.5.6.

Table 3-1. Airborne and liquid radioactive effluents released in 1980 at the Livermore site.

Effluent	Discharge (Ci)
Airborne:	
$^{3}H_2$	2305
^{41}Ar	165
^{13}N - ^{15}O	1656
Unidentified β-α	5.1×10^{-5}
Liquid:	
HTO	
^{239}Pu	2.8×10^{-4}

3.5.2. Sanitary Waste Management

3.5.2.1. General. Sanitary sewage from SNLL flows into the LLNL sewer system and the effluent of both laboratories is treated at the LWRP. The sewage is continuously monitored for pH and radioactivity as it leaves the LLNL site to detect any potentially hazardous release soon enough to permit the sewage to be diverted into holding ponds at the treatment plant. Any diverted sewage is held until analyses show what, if any, special treatment is needed before the sewage can be treated in the municipal plant. In addition to the continuous sampling, composite sewage samples are collected daily and analyzed for radioactive materials and toxic metals.

The term "sanitary sewage" includes all liquid wastes except: radioactive wastes, toxic chemical wastes, and process wastes from the plating shop and printed-circuit-etching facility. Radioactive and toxic wastes are collected either in suitable small containers or in larger waste retention tanks, and disposed of by the Toxic Waste Control Group. Plating shop and printed-circuit-facility process wastes are now treated in a neutralization/ion-exchange facility. This purification system produces "reclaimed" water suitable for reuse in plating shop processes.

Administrative controls are used to minimize the release of radioactive and toxic wastes to the sanitary sewage system. These controls include:

- Notice labels attached to sinks connected to the sanitary sewer advising personnel to contact Hazards Control for disposal of hazardous wastes.
- Instructions for proper disposal of wastes discussed in building Operational Safety Procedures and in the LLNL Health and Safety Manual.
- Periodic review of waste disposal techniques by Hazards Control technicians assigned to the area.
- Investigation of releases into the sewer system that are detected by the continuous monitoring system, employee reports, or other means. Formal incident reports are prepared for potentially serious releases and steps are taken to prevent recurrence.
- Use of the LLNL Safety-Wise publication (a leaflet which is distributed throughout the Laboratory) and Industrial Hygiene briefings to LLNL employees regarding proper disposal of wastes, details of past releases, and the importance of keeping potentially hazardous materials out of the sanitary sewer.

Rainwater and irrigation runoff water are not connected to the sanitary sewers. Runoff is collected in open ditches that flow to the northwest corner of the LLNL site. After leaving LLNL, the water flows through other ditches until it reaches the Arroyo Las Positas. Effluent blow-down water from LLNL cooling towers was formerly discharged into the storm water ditches. However, starting in

1975, these discharges were connected to the sanitary sewer system and are treated at LWRP. The following is a brief description of the sewer system, the municipal treatment plant, analytical tests performed, and significant releases that have occurred in the past.

3.5.2.2. Sewer System. The sanitary sewer system network has three primary elements (see Figs. 3-9 and 3-10). The portion of the southern half of the LLNL site that was built by the Navy, including SNLL, has sewer lines that flow by gravity westward along East Avenue to the southwest corner of the LLNL site. The rest of the southern half of LLNL has gravity flow lines running northwestward to the west end of 5th Street. Sewage from the northern half of LLNL flows by gravity to the northwest corner of LLNL. The combined sewage from the southwest, 5th Street, and northwest flows by gravity through a new line to the City of Livermore's 525-mm industrial park sewer line about 2 km to the northwest.

3.5.2.3. Livermore Water Reclamation Plant (LWRP). The LWRP is a 200-liter/s tertiary sewage plant serving the residential, commercial, and industrial users in Livermore. Sanitary sewage from the DOE site contributes 7%, about 15 liters/s, of the total sewage treated at the plant. Sewage entering the plant flows into the "primary settling tanks" where most solids drop out and grease floats to the surface. Next, the sewage is pumped over two "trickling filter" units where aerobic bacteria growing on filter rock oxidize dissolved organic matter in the sewage. The sewage then enters an "activated sludge" aeration tank where microbes suspended in the sewage further oxidize organics to purify the waste. After aeration, the sewage flows to the "final sedimentation tank" where the suspended microbes settle out. The treated sewage is filtered through charcoal filters, and chlorinated and dechlorinated before being released from the plant. Treated water is used as required for irrigation on the golf course, airport, and nearby agricultural land. Treated water is also supplied to the California Department of Transportation for irrigation of landscaping on I-580. The balance is discharged into a pipeline and transported to San Francisco Bay (see 2.1.8.3).

Solids from the settling tanks are pumped to anaerobic digesters where bacteria break down the organics to yield "stabilized sludge," plus methane and CO_2. This sludge is dried in open beds, and buried in a local landfill. The methane is used for in-plant heating as required, or burned as waste.

The plant also has two emergency holding basins with a total capacity of 1.5×10^5 m^3 or about six days of average flow for retention of sewage in case of plant malfunctions, a potentially harmful release into the sewer system, or other problems. Additionally, the basins are used to equalize the treatment load, storing sewage during peak production periods for release into the system during periods of low flow. Since the ponds are located at the treatment plant, any releases into the

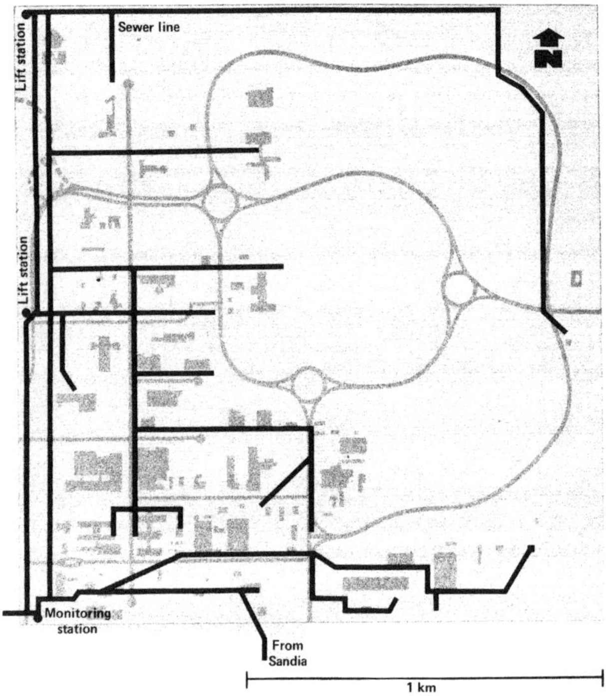

Figure 3-9. LLNL site sanitary sewer system.

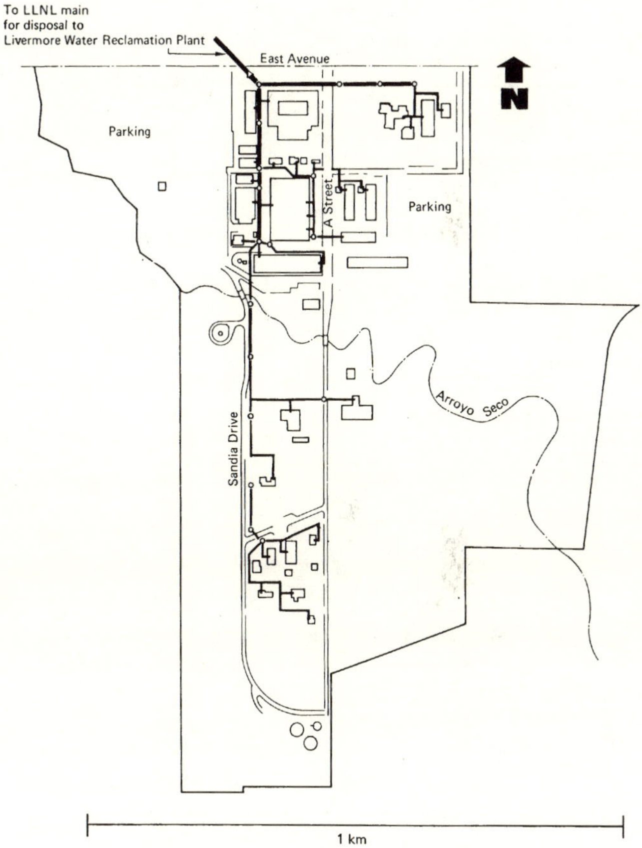

Figure 3-10. SNLL site sanitary sewer system.

sewer are diluted by the total city flow by the time they are diverted. Based on the experience in dealing with past incidents requiring diversions, the LWRP has had little difficulty dealing with the treatment of most releases from the Laboratories. Radioactivity, other than tritium, is usually retained in the sludge. For the DOE site to duplicate the retention and treatment capability now provided by the LWRP does not appear to be cost effective, considering the low frequency with which need for diversion occurs.

3.5.2.4. Sewage Monitoring. For rapid identification of potentially harmful releases into the sewer, a continuous stream of 40 liters/min is pumped to a small building at LLNL housing detection instrumentation. Inside this building, the sewage is piped through a 26-liter lead-shielded tank that contains a recording pH meter, a low-energy NaI (Tl) detector, and a higher energy NaI (Tl) detector.[3-3] Output of these radiation detectors provides a capability for detection of radionuclides commonly used at the Laboratory. The sewage stream also flows through an x-ray fluorescence monitor capable of detecting transition metals such as copper and chromium.[3-4]

Audio alarms from the pH meter, the two radiation detectors and the x-ray fluorescence monitor are received in the LLNL firehouse, which is continuously manned. The flow time between LLNL and the LWRP permits ample time to investigate the source of alarm and to evaluate the problem. Based on past experience, the LWRP plant can be notified in time to divert sewage into holding ponds for subsequent treatment if required.

3.5.2.4.1. Collection of Sample. A small sewage sample is picked up every 4-5 min by a revolving scoop (a Trebler sampler) and collected for later analysis. These composite samples are collected daily and analyzed as indicated in Table 2-1.

3.5.2.4.2. Discharge Limits. Limitations on discharges of industrial wastes are contained in Livermore Ordinance No. 586. This ordinance prohibits discharge of any material that interferes with operation or maintenance of the sewer system or treatment plant, or that causes the City to discharge treated effluent that violates established standards. It also contains the specific discharge limitations listed below:

- Any liquid or vapor having a temperature higher than 66°C.
- Any waste containing more than 200 ppm of fat, oil, or grease that is petroleum-ether soluble.
- Any gasoline, benzene, naphtha, fuel oil, or other flammable or explosive liquid, solid, or gas.
- Any garbage, except if properly ground with a mechanical garbage grinder.

- Any ashes, cinders, sand, or other solid viscous substance capable of causing obstruction to the flow in sewers or other interferences with the operation of the sewage works.
- Any waste or water with a pH lower than 6.8 or higher than 8.0.
- Any water or waste containing an increase of total dissolved solids greater than 325 ppm or chloride greater than 75 ppm during a single-cycle use of the water supply.
- Any water or waste having a Biochemical Oxygen Demand (BOD) greater than 300 ppm.
- Any water or waste containing more than 300 ppm of suspended solids.
- Any radioactive wastes except where:
  - The waste is discharged in strict conformity with current DOE recommendations for safe disposal of radioactive wastes.
  - The discharging of radioactive waste will not cause injury to personnel or damage to the sewage works.
- Any waters intended to be used to dilute waste discharge to avoid violation of the above limits.

Discharges from LLNL and SNLL meet the requirements of Ordinance 586 except for intermittent variation of pH above or below the 6.8 to 8.0 permitted range. Serious variations cause the pH monitor at LLNL to alarm so that the LWRP operators can be notified to take corrective action to divert the potentially harmful sewage. In the six years since the existing monitoring/alarm system has been operating, no damage to the treatment plant or receiving waters has occurred due to releases from the DOE Livermore laboratories.

3.5.2.5. Sewer Release Incidents. There have been several incidents of toxic or radioactive material releases into the sanitary sewer. These incidents are listed in Appendix 3A. For each incident, corrective measures were recommended to prevent a recurrence. Because most of the releases were from the plating shop, the special process waste treatment system described earlier (see 3.5.2.1) was installed. This unit significantly reduced the incidence rate of low- or high-pH discharges. However, the rapid warning provided by the continuous monitoring station provides the time needed to evaluate other possible sources of pH excursion and to recommend diversion if necessary.

3.5.3. Chemical Waste Management

Research quantities of liquid, solid, and gaseous nonradioactive chemicals are used at the Livermore site. Because of the diversity in the variety of chemicals handled it has not been practical to establish treatment facilities for these materials. At present, areas generating larger quantities of chemical waste include LLNL Buildings 131, 322, and 325 (printed-circuit facility, plating shop and ion exchange, respectively) and SNLL's Building 913 (plating shop, and printed circuit facilities). Between 10,000 and 20,000 gal of acid rinsewater waste containing copper, chromium, and nickel is generated at the Livermore site each month. About 5000 gal of alkaline brine is generated per month from regenerating ion-exchange columns used for producing low-conductivity water. In 1978 about 30,000 gal of mixed acids, bases, and solvent waste were generated. Of the latter about 30% was nitric acid, about 25% chromic acid, and the balance was miscellaneous chemicals, including the research quantities noted above. These chemical wastes are packaged in state and federally approved containers and transported by licensed contractors to Class I chemical waste disposal sites.

3.5.4. Excess Properties, Salvage, and Reclamation Operation

3.5.4.1. General. Material not needed for use by LLNL personnel may be disposed of in a number of ways. (This is summarized in Fig. 3-11.) If the item is being removed from a radioactive materials area, it must first be monitored by Hazards Control and tagged with the type of radiation, level, and date. If it is determined that the item is contaminated, it is sent to the decontamination group to be decontaminated. If the radiation level cannot be brought down to meet applicable standards, the item is disposed of as radioactive waste.

Items not from a radiation area and items that have been determined by Hazards Control not to be contaminated, or have been decontaminated, can be sent to one of two places. Capital equipment must be sent to the Redeployment Center, and all other items may be sent to the Reclamation and Salvage Section.

The Redeployment Center evaluates its condition and the Laboratory's need for a particular item. If it is determined to be of potential value to LLNL or other government agencies, it is sent to the Excess Property Section. Materials that cannot be repaired or have no potential value to anyone are sent to Reclamation and Salvage.

3.5.4.2. Excess Property at LLNL and SNLL. Excess materials are listed and this list is circulated on the LLNL site for 30 days. If no need is found, the materials are reported on a list to DOE and circulated another 30 days. Items still not used are reported to the General Services Office in San Francisco. This list is circulated to other federal agencies for 60 days. If the materials are not needed by other federal agencies, they are then reclassified as federal surplus and made available for 15 days for donation to state education agencies or other organizations specified by federal surplus

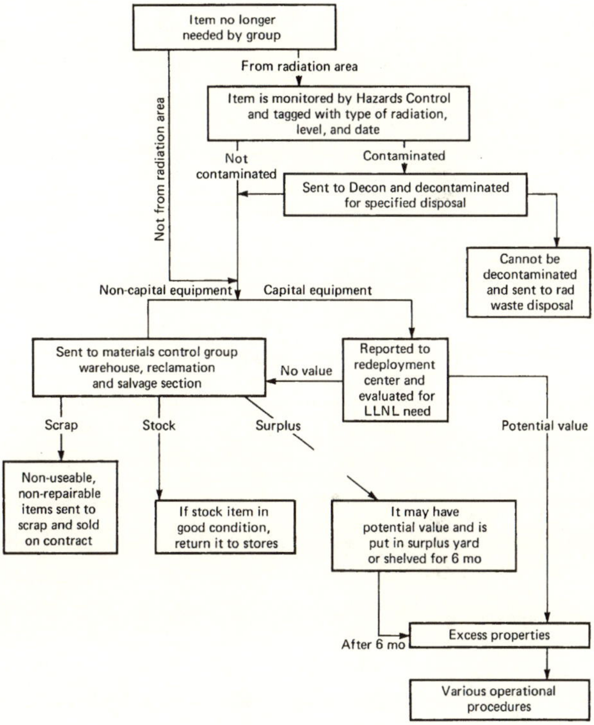

Figure 3-11. Disposal of excess material.

guidelines. The materials remaining throughout this series are taken to the Concord site of the Alameda Defense Properties Disposal Office where they can be sold or stored. At SNLL, a similar procedure is employed, but items to be excessed are listed through the Sandia Property Control Division at Albuquerque.

3.5.4.3. Reclamation and Salvage. Non-capital materials are evaluated by Reclamation and Salvage for condition and need. If the item is a stock item (currently stocked by LLNL Supply Department) and is in good condition, it is returned to stock for reissue. An item may be sent for repair before returning to stock. Materials that are not in stock condition but still may have some future value to LLNL are held in the surplus yard or surplus shelves in the Materials Control warehouse. After 6 months, the surplus items are turned over to the Excess Property Section and processed as described above.

Materials that are non-repairable and non-usable are first disassembled for salvageable parts, then sent to scrap.

Scrap materials are sold by bid. Metals are segregated by type of metal (ferrous, copper, etc.) and sold by bulk weight on 3-month contracts. The exception is mercury, which is collected and redistilled (by outside contract) for LLNL reuse. Solvents and oils are stored in 210-liter drums and sold on a yearly contract. Tires are collected and sold on contract as accumulated. Paper and unclassified IBM cards are sold on a yearly contract. Scrap lumber is made available to LLNL personnel on Saturday mornings.

3.5.4.4. Space Used for Excess Properties, Salvage, and Reclamation. The reclamation and salvage operation uses approximately 93 m^2 of inside storage space and 1900 m^2 of outside storage area. The excess properties operation uses approximately 110 m^2 of inside storage area and 460 m^2 of outside storage area.

3.5.4.5. Decontamination. Building 419 is LLNL's decontamination center for the removal of radioactive and toxic contaminants from equipment. Soak tanks, steam guns, mechanical abrasives, ultrasonics, and a vapor degreaser use mechanical, chemical, and heat energy to remove undesirable contaminants. All wastes generated in the cleaning operation are transferred to Waste Management. Discharged air is passed through double HEPA filters and monitored. As required, SNLL equipment can also be decontaminated at this facility.

3.5.5. Nonhazardous Waste Landfill

LLNL generates approximately 44 m^3 of waste per work day which is transported to the Alameda County sanitary landfill site. This debris consists primarily of 8 m^3 of shredded computer printout paper, 24 m^3 of waste paper and garbage, and 12 m^3 of wood and other construction rubble. All such waste is covered immediately with several feet of clean earth. Compaction is performed by large dirt-moving equipment. Burning is not permitted. No radioactive or toxic materials are sent to the landfill.

SNLL generates approximately 6 m^3 of waste per day, consisting of about 2.5 m^3 of computer printout paper, waste paper, and garbage, 2.5 m^3 of cardboard, and the balance wood and rubble. SNLL waste is also transported to the Alameda County sanitary landfill site.

3.5.6. Waste Management at Site 300

3.5.6.1. Solid Radioactive or Chemical Wastes. Solid wastes resulting from detonation of test assemblies constitute the principal source of radioactive or chemical wastes at Site 300. Most of these assemblies contain depleted uranium and beryllium, although a few have contained natural uranium or thorium. A limited number of experiments involving tritium have also been conducted at the Site.

Solid waste consisting of contaminated rubble is collected from the gravel-covered firing table after each shot. It is estimated that most of the uranium in the test assembly is associated either with this debris, or remains in the gravel. That uranium debris is limited to areas adjacent to the firing bunkers was confirmed by the EG&G aerial radiological survey in 1975 (described in section 2.3.12) and soil analyses (described in Appendix 2A).

Firing table gravel and the associated debris are buried in designated disposal areas within Site 300. These burials are made in accordance with the Code of Federal Regulations, Title 10, Part 20, Paragraph 20.304, which permits land burials of radioactivity equivalent to 300 kg of depleted uranium per year. Each firing bunker maintains records of the uranium and beryllium in the test assemblies expended on its firing table. Based on these records the firing table gravel is removed to the disposal pit when an estimated total of 300 kg of uranium is contained in this gravel and in the contaminated rubble previously trucked to the pit. The pits are in the form of a trench. Gravel and rubble containing the estimated 300 kg of uranium are covered with 1.2 m of soil and a soil barrier 1.8 m wide is established between trenches. Disposal areas are surveyed and located on the Site map as indicated by the circles in Fig. 3-12.

Depleted uranium is a byproduct in the process by which enriched uranium (enriched in ^{235}U) is produced from natural uranium. In a preliminary step of this process, uranium decay products

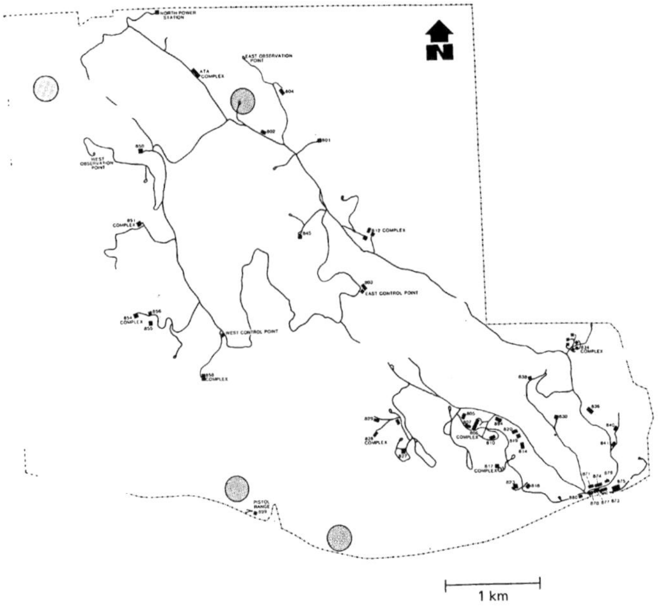

Figure 3-12. Site 300 disposal areas.

including radium are chemically separated from the uranium. Because the radiological hazard from uranium is predominantly due to radium and its decay products there is essentially no radiation hazard associated with the land burial of depleted uranium at Site 300. Starting with radium-free uranium, it takes over a million years for the ^{226}Ra activity to grow back into equilibrium with the parent ^{238}U, as shown by the following tabulation.

Time after separation (years)	% Equilibrium
$\times 10^4$	0.072
$\times 10^5$	7.9
$\times 10^6$	90.6
$\times 10^6$	100.0

High-explosive wastes generated in formulation and processing are collected from the firing tables and periodically burned in a remote burn area on the Site.

At one time solid waste from Livermore, consisting largely of bulky items from radiation workplaces at LLNL and from large animal experiments conducted at LLNL and LBL, were buried at Site 300. Approximately 100,000 ft^3 of waste was buried at the Site 300 Pistol Range Pit between 1964 and 1973. Animal wastes and carcasses contaminated with short-lived radionuclides accounted for 23,000 ft^3 of the total volume. The animal burial practice was stopped in 1973 when large animal experiments were discontinued. The remaining 77,000 ft^3 of waste buried consisted of compressed drums, capacitors, glove boxes, beryllium-contaminated filters and equipment, gas bottles, assorted waste chemicals, and other scrap metal primarily from the Taxi Strip and Salvage storage areas. Burial of this type of waste was discontinued in 1970 as a result of an LLNL policy change.

3.5.6.2. Liquid Chemical Wastes. Liquid wastes from high-explosive processing are passed through clarifiers (settling tanks). Clarified liquid is then pumped to holding ponds where it is evaporated. Solids are treated as solid high-explosive waste.

3.5.6.3. Sanitary Wastes. In all areas except the General Service Area (GSA), sanitary wastes are handled by individual septic tanks or chemical toilets. All septic tanks are equipped with leach fields.

A sanitary sewer system is provided in the GSA area with the sewage piped to an asphalt lined, oxidation pond at the southeast corner of the Site. This pond has a surface area of about 4000 m^2. It was designed to accommodate a population of approximately 200. At present, the personnel assigned to the GSA area number about 100. The depth of the liquid is maintained between 1 and 1.5 m. During the summer months, water must be added to the pond to maintain the minimum level. A smaller overflow pond was constructed to provide additional capacity during the winter when evaporation is minimal.

Samples of the oxidation pond are analyzed on a quarterly basis as part of the environmental monitoring program for Site 300.

3.6. SITE 300 OPERATIONS

LLNL's nonnuclear explosive tests are conducted at Site 300. The handling of radioactive and toxic material and the detonation of high-explosive assemblies containing these materials are the principal sources of possible environmental impact.

There are no tests at Site 300 involving high-explosive assemblies that contain fissile material. However, as noted in section 2.1.5.2, static (e.g. temperature cycling) and dynamic (e.g., vibration and impulse) tests are performed at Site 300 that do involve plutonium. Two sealed barriers are required for static tests and three such barriers are required for dynamic tests, and the ventilating exhaust air from these test facilities is passed through HEPA filters. No breach of any barriers are expected in any of these tests involving fissile material. All such tests are verification design tests and are not tests to failure. The shipment or transfer of explosives and radioactive material other than depleted or natural uranium and thorium in the same container or to the same facility at Site 300 is prohibited.

An environmental monitoring program is maintained to ensure that the LLNL controls are indeed restricting effluent releases to levels well below appropriate standards. Because of the remoteness of this site, these experiments can be performed with minimal off-site impact from annoying noises or damaging overpressures (667 pascals or 0.1 psi for a tightly-fitted window glass.) Based on meteorological measurements made twice daily, a limit is set on the weight of high explosives that can be detonated without impact in populated areas. The Laboratory uses an offsite, overpressure limit of 40 pascals (0.006 psi) for areas 4.8 km (3.0 mi) beyond the detonation point. To monitor the correctness of these limits, four microbarograph sensors are maintained in or near Tracy. The probability of overpressure is greatest in this area due to the direction of the prevailing winds. In 1976, there was one incident involving a noticeable overpressure which was caused by an unexpected change in the direction of the upper winds. There were no complaints of damage.

An ecology study was made at Site 300 in 1974 to determine if LLNL operations have had a measurable impact on plants and animals native to the area. The ecosystem is dominated by perennial grasslands. Small rodents abound which are preyed upon by snakes, raptors, and a variety of carnivorous mammals. The study involved collection of plants and animals in the vicinity of the high-explosive firing bunkers. Similar sample groups were also collected during this period about 10 km west of the Site. This direction (normally upwind) and distance gave reasonable assurance that the latter samples would represent background conditions unaffected by LLNL operations.

Analysis of the data showed that while tritium, beryllium, and uranium were present in some plants and animals, in general the levels measured in the biota on Site 300 were not significantly different from those found in the control samples collected about 10 km west of Site 300.

As noted in 2.3.9, in 1975 approximately 100 acres on the east side at Site 300 was transferred to the California Department of Fish and Game for use as a wildlife preserve. A radiological survey of this property was made in 1973 prior to the release and in compliance with AEC requirements for disposal of land. A terrestrial survey was made using a sensitive gamma detector (sodium iodide) with readings made at a nominal height of one meter above the soil surface. Soil samples were also collected for uranium analyses. The terrestrial radiation exposure rates, which vary from 4.0 to 6.5 μR/h, are typical for natural background for soils in this area. Likewise, the variation of one to three parts per million in the total uranium is within the range observed in northern California.

Other impacts such as noise pollution from DOE high-explosive testing are negligible due to the distance of the firing bunkers from the eastern site perimeter. The closest bunker, Bunker 812, which is located in a deep ravine, is nearly three quarters of a mile from the perimeter. Concentrations of airborne beryllium at sampling points between this bunker and the east site boundary are less than 1% of that specified as the permissible standard.

It was concluded from these measurements that Site 300 operations had no measurable impact on the area up to 1973. Since that time, annual surveys near the site perimeters have not indicated off-site impact. No construction is presently planned along the east perimeter.

3.7. HEALTH AND SAFETY IMPACTS OF LIVERMORE OPERATIONS

3.7.1. Radiological Impact

The radiological impact of the DOE Livermore laboratories is being assessed, on a continuing basis, by LLNL's Hazards Control Department. An annual environmental monitoring report documents the levels of radioactive materials observed in air, water, soil and vegetation samples collected in the vicinity of the Livermore Site. Radiation dose rate measurements using thermoluminescent dosimeters are also made both at the site perimeter and in the off-site vicinity. Appendix 2A contains results of the Livermore environmental monitoring program for 1980. Table 3-2 shows annual airborne and liquid effluents released during the 5-year period 1976 through 1980. These data serve as a data base

Table 3-2. Airborne and liquid radioactive effluents released at Livermore during the 5-year period 1976-1980.

	Annual releases (Ci)					
	1976	1977	1978	1979	1980	5-year av
Airborne radioactive effluents:						
^{41}Ar	470	378	766	383	165	432
$^{3}H_2$	3990	5200	5361	4505	2305	4272
^{13}N - ^{15}O	1035	987	1444	829	1656	1190
Liquid radioactive effluents:						
HTO	10	13	8	[illegible]	[illegible]	[illegible]
^{239}Pu	1.5×10^{-4}	3.6×10^{-4}	8.6×10^{-4}	9.8×10^{-4}	2.8×10^{-4}	5.3×10^{-4}

Table 3-3. Airborne ^{239}Pu and HTO concentrations at the LLNL site boundary: a 5-year data base.

	^{239}Pu (10^{-17} µCi/ml)						HTO (10^{-11} µCi/ml)					
Location[a]	1976	1977	1978	1979	1980	Av[b]	1976	1977	1978	1979	1980	Av[b]
[illegible]	1.0	2.2	2.8	1.1	0.6	1.5	6.0	4.2	3.5	3.8	2.7	4.0
[illegible]	0.7	2.4	2.7	0.9	0.5	1.4	7.7	5.4	5.6	4.6	5.6	5.6
12	0.9	2.4	3.0	1.7	0.5	1.7	14.2	11.9	10.1	6.1	9.6	9.6
13	0.7	1.8	2.3	1.1	0.4	1.3	4.1	2.7	2.7	3.8	3.2	3.2
14	2.8	4.2	5.3	2.3	1.4	3.2	10.1	7.2	5.3	4.8	6.4	6.4
15	1.3	1.8	2.4	1.0	0.5	1.4	6.7	4.4	3.8	3.4	3.4	4.3
Av	1.2	2.5	3.1	1.4	0.6	1.8	8.1	6.0	5.7	4.4	5.9	5.6

[a] See Appendix 2A for sampling locations.
[b] This column shows the 5-year average by location as well as (last entry) the 5-year average of all locations.

Table 3-4. Annual radiation doses at the LLNL south site boundary (mrem).

	1976	1977	1978	1979	1980
Dose	893	877	230	176	148

to better evaluate the radiological impact of current Livermore operations. The increase in ^{41}Ar in 1978 compared with 1977 is due to additional running time of the pool-type reactor (Building 281) connected with LLNL work in the National Uranium Resource Evaluation (NURE) program. The decrease in ^{41}Ar in 1979 reflects the termination of LLNL participation in NURE. Likewise, increase in the ^{13}N - ^{15}O levels in 1978 and 1980 resulted from physics experiments requiring extended accelerator running times at Building 194. In 1979 the accelerator was shut down for about 3 months, explaining the decrease in ^{13}N - ^{15}O. Table 3-3 shows a 5-year tabulation of airborne plutonium and tritium concentrations measured at the LLNL site boundary. The concentrations of plutonium are within the range attributable to global fallout and less than 0.1% of the guideline standard (DOE Order 5480.1A). The highest annual average tritium-in-air concentration is also less than 0.1% of the DOE guideline.

The largest potential for radiological impact due to DOE operations at Livermore has been from LLNL's 14-MeV neutron generator in Building 212. In past years, this facility has been used in high-flux radiation damage studies in support of the magnetic fusion energy program. These experiments resulted in elevated gamma and neutron dose rates at the south perimeter of LLNL (East Avenue).

Many of these high-flux experiments are now performed at the rotating target neutron source (RTNS) in Building 292 located in the northwest quadrant of LLNL. Table 3-4 shows the decrease in radiation dose rates at the south site boundary since 1977.

Since the maximum allowable dose to any member of the public is 500 mrem per year, the potential for radiation exposure from operations at Building 212 was evaluated. When the generator is operating, the dose rate is about 0.1 mrem/h in the SNLL parking lot opposite Building 212. Assuming that an individual spent 45 minutes a day in this parking lot, and the high-flux runs were made 125 days a year (both conservative estimates), the estimated parking lot annual dose would be 9.4 mrem. Other potential exposures might have involved motorists and bicyclists on East Avenue and personnel in the credit union building on the Sandia parking lot. However, radiation measurements show that none of these exposures could have resulted in an annual dose exceeding the parking lot example.

The ICT is located at the east end of Building 212. A radiation monitoring station has been maintained for several years at the fence line on East Avenue opposite this accelerator. Another accelerator, the Cyclograff, located in the center of the building, may also contribute to elevated site boundary radiation. A.C. Transit now has a bus stop on East Avenue adjacent to Building 212. This bus stop is closer to the Cyclograff than it is to the ICT. Radiation measurements made at the bus stop using hand-held instruments varied depending on the experiments performed at the Cyclograff. To better document possible exposures, a duplicate of the radiation monitoring station at the ICT has been established at the bus stop.

Concern has been expressed over the potential for Laboratory radioactive effluents contaminating the drinking water supply for the City of Livermore. Livermore obtains about 1/3 of its annual domestic water supply from groundwater wells and purchases the balance from the Alameda County Flood Control District Zone 7. Zone 7 diverts water from the South Bay Aqueduct to fill the Patterson Reservoir. Water from the Patterson Reservoir is sampled at quarterly intervals and analyzed for gross alpha, gross beta, and tritium activities. Typical results of these analyses are shown in Appendix 2A as Location 15 in Tables 14, 16, and 18. Samples from Livermore city water are identified in the same tables as Location 19. Both locations show radioactivity levels in the range of natural background and well below standards set by EPA, indicating that the Livermore Laboratories have no discernable effect on local drinking water supplies.

Concern has also been expressed over the potential of accidental releases of plutonium contaminating the South Bay Aqueduct. Even under the worst-case conditions, which include the loss of the Building 332 HEPA filters, the plutonium concentration in the water of the aqueduct would be 0.3% of the permissible levels in drinking water, or 9.74×10^{-8} µCi/ml.

LLNL samples wells belonging to the Alameda County Flood Control District Zone 7 in order to monitor ground water (wells) in the Livermore Valley. This program is designed to determine the extent tritium in the treated effluent from the LWRP migrates into ground water. Tritium activities in all samples collected were below the DOE guide for water in uncontrolled areas (DOE Order 5480.1A).

As a means of evaluating the possible impact of Laboratory effluents on locally grown foodstuff, the tritium content of Livermore Valley wines has been compared with other wines from California and with European wines. The tritium levels of local wines have been found to be within the range of both the European wines and surface waters throughout the world, and somewhat higher than in those California wines produced from grapes grown outside the Valley. (See Appendix 2A.)

Honey produced from vegetation grown in the Livermore Valley has also been analyzed for tritium. The tritium content of locally produced honey was found to be similar to honey produced elsewhere. (See Appendix 2A.)

3.7.2. Impacts of Laboratory Operations on Employees

At Livermore, experts representing all safety disciplines provide safety guidance to both employees and management in planning, establishing, and maintaining a low-risk work environment. Safety teams monitor all Livermore operations to detect and evaluate hazards. Emergency response personnel are trained to control accidents or other emergencies. Research is conducted in such areas as fire safety, radiation detection and protection, chemical hazards, and respiratory protection.

During the history of the Livermore site, there have been nine fatal job-related injuries. All of these resulted from transportation accidents (auto, helicopter, airplane). Falls or falling objects striking personnel are the most frequent cause of lost-time accidents. Less than one percent of the lost-time injuries are caused by toxic materials or radiation.

The beryllium-monitoring program is typical of the Livermore site's attention to possible exposure to hazardous chemicals. Continuously operating air samplers provide filter samples from which the atmospheric working environment of all areas handling beryllium is evaluated. Swipe samples are also periodically collected from these areas.

Livermore programs involve the use of a wide variety of radioactive and radiation-producing equipment. Radiation dosimeters are issued to all employees and to visitors who may enter specified buildings. These dosimeters record both natural background and any occupational radiation to which the employee was exposed. Subtractions are made for average exposures received from natural sources. Table 3-5 shows the radiation dose distribution for LLNL employees covering the period from 1975 through 1979.

The maximum permissible whole-body dose for radiation workers is 5000 mrem/year (DOE Order 5480.1A). In the Livermore area, the natural background radiation dose from cosmic rays, terrestrial radiation, and radiation from radionuclide in the body is about 80 mrem/year. The table shows that few LLNL employees receive occupational radiation doses in excess of that received from natural sources.

3.7.2.1. <u>The LLNL Melanoma Study</u>. In late 1976 medical doctors specializing in the treatment of malignant melanoma reported to the Resource for Cancer Epidemiology (RCE) of the California Department of Health Services that an unusual number of their patients were employees of LLNL. Concurrently but independently the LLNL Medical Department began gathering information to determine whether or not employees of LLNL were experiencing an unusual risk of melanoma.

It was soon apparent that the RCE was better equipped to conduct a meaningful study and by July of 1977 initial planning for the investigation and negotiations for the necessary employee data file were completed.

The RCE study was completed in 1980. An LLNL committee was formed in 1980 to study detailed aspects of the problem. The California Legislative Audit Committee and a DOE committee have reviewed the RCE study. The DOE committee summarizes the problem and makes conclusions and recommendations as follows: "The number of cases of malignant melanoma of the skin in employees of the Lawrence Livermore National Laboratory reported during the period 1972-1977 exceeds the reported incidence rate in the surrounding two county general population by a factor of between three and four. The incidence rate in the immediately surrounding communities was not elevated during this time period.

Table 3-5. Occupational radiation dose distribution for LLNL employees (%).

Whole-body dose (mrem)	Year				
	1975	1976	1977	1978	1979
Not detectable over background	86	86	86	88	90.2
100	11	11	12	10	8.5
100-499	2.4	2.5	1.5	1.7	1.0
500-2000	0.5	0.5	0.5	0.3	0.3
2000-5000	<0.1	0.0	0.0	0.0	<0.1

"Preliminary efforts to explain the excess have not succeeded so far in implicating any specific cause. The possibility cannot be excluded that the excess may ultimately prove to reflect the influence of socioeconomic factors and lifestyle, rather than exposure to a cancer-causing agent in the workplace. It should be noted that the incidence of malignant melanoma has been rising rapidly in fair-skinned people throughout the world.

"The occupational safety, industrial hygiene, and medical programs in the Laboratory appear to be well conceived and well conducted. Unless a causative factor is identified in the Laboratory environment, no protective health measures above and beyond the existing industrial hygiene, safety, and medical surveillance programs appear to be warranted at this time.

"The Laboratory should be encouraged in its efforts to investigate the important problems associated with the observed incidence of malignant melanoma. It should be requested to submit a formal plan, which should include provision for more complete record systems for identifying employees who may be exposed to potentially carcinogenic chemical and physical agents. Also the Laboratory's plan should be coordinated with the research activities of the Resource for Cancer Epidemiology Section of the California State Department of Health Services and contain a target timetable for issuing periodic progress reports.

"The Department of Energy should support the further epidemiological investigations of the Resource for Cancer Epidemiology. A proposal should be solicited from the Resource which avoids duplication with the efforts of the Laboratory but which addresses collaborative arrangements.

"The above recommendations for research proposals are contingent on appropriate peer review. In addition, ongoing studies of the incidence of malignant melanoma in Laboratory employees should receive continuing review by outside experts."

Presently the DOE is funding a case control study being conducted by the RCE. This study assumes that the causative factor is an occupational exposure and uses extensive interviews and questionnaires to determine any significant historical differences between melanoma victims and matched controls.

LLNL is also funding four studies by the LLNL Biomedical and Environmental Research Division:

1. A death-certificate survey of all LLNL employees from 1963 to present to compare LLNL and California mortality rates.
2. A melanoma-incidence study of former LLNL employees using the mail questionnaire and the California Cancer Registry.
3. An expanded study of LLNL records to examine possible associations between melanoma and such factors as job classification, length of employment, radiation exposure, project assignment, work locations, and physical characteristics of the employee.

4. A collaboration with the Kaiser Foundation Research Institute to compare melanoma incidence and melanoma-associated factors in LLNL employees and non-LLNL employees who use the same prepaid medical plan.

The RCE study and the first three LLNL studies are scheduled for completion by January 1983. The fourth LLNL study is scheduled for completion by January 1984. The results of all these studies will be published in the open literature.

3.8. SOCIOLOGICAL AND ECONOMIC IMPACT

3.8.1. Employment and Population

The Lawrence Livermore National Laboratory of the University of California began operations in 1952 with a staff of approximately 320 people and has grown to over 8000 employees. Sandia Laboratories-Livermore began operations in 1956 with a staff of 15 and has grown to approximately 1000 employees. The City of Livermore has also grown considerably from a small town of 4000 in 1950 to approximately 50,000 in 1979. Much of the early growth of the city can be shown to be the direct result of the growth of the DOE Livermore laboratories. The late 1950s and early 1960s show the greatest effect of these laboratories on the City of Livermore population, while from 1967 the majority of the city's growth is due to the trend of living in suburbia and working in the urban areas (such as Oakland, Berkeley, Hayward, and San Francisco).

The growth of the DOE Livermore laboratories and the City of Livermore can be seen in Fig. 3-13. The city has had a constant growth while the Laboratories' population began fluctuating in 1967. These variations reflect budgetary and programming changes, which in particular were responsible for the decreases in 1970, 1971, and 1973. The effect of the DOE Livermore laboratories can be seen by the proportion of employees to Livermore residents. Figure 3-13 shows that in recent years the Laboratories' population has remained quite steady. The Livermore population continued to increase, indicating that the trend to suburban living and commuting to urban areas was the major contribution input to this increase.

Only minimum sociological and economic impacts are expected from the new construction planned for the laboratories. These impacts are expected to be similar to those from other recent construction programs, and no major effects are anticipated. Each new construction project is evaluated for these impacts and appropriate documentation prepared.

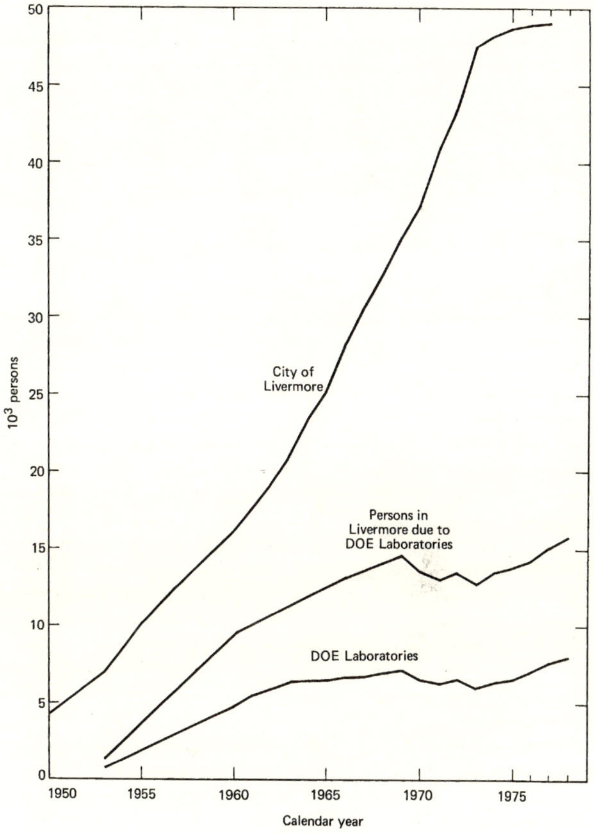

Figure 3-13. Populations of the city of Livermore and the DOE Livermore laboratories.

3.8.2. Equal Opportunity and Training Programs

It is the policy of the DOE laboratories to provide applicants and employees the right to equal employment opportunities and not to engage in discriminatory practices against any person employed or seeking employment because of race, color, religion, marital status, sex, or age. It is the intention of the respective Laboratories' management to measure performance of this policy against specific objectives and to move affirmatively towards full and equal participation of all employees in the opportunity available. The programs of Equal Opportunity Employment are offered to assist in the recruiting, training, and educating of minority and female employees.

3.8.3. Community Participation

The LLNL Fire Department participates in the Twin Valley (Livermore and Amador Valleys) Mutual Aid Agreement, under which LLNL equipment and personnel are dispatched as required within the area. A similar but less formal agreement exists for mutual assistance throughout Alameda County.

3.8.4. Technological Impact

The DOE Livermore laboratories, through research and development programs, have made and are continuing to make technological advances in areas of impact to society. The most significant impacts have been from the weapons development programs. This is described in detail in section 2.1.3. The other significant programs are energy resources development and environmental modeling. In the energy development program, laser fusion and controlled thermonuclear reactions (fusion power) are being studied in order to develop a workable fusion power plant for the production of electricity. Other areas of energy research are in situ coal gasification, recovery of natural gas following massive hydraulic fracturing, the in situ processing of oil shale, use of shallow ponds as solar heat collectors, combustion research, central solar receiver project, and magnetic fusion studies.

3.8.5. Traffic and Transportation

The transportation modes used by employees of the Laboratories varies but consists primarily of automobiles. Recognizing that continued increase in auto use contributes to the local potential for air pollution, car pooling and busing have been encouraged for several years. Following the 1979 fuel shortage and the accompanying rise in the price of gasoline there has been increased employee interest in alternatives to the single-occupancy automobile. Introducing the owner-operated van pool concept at Livermore has been highly successful, particularly for those riders who live at a considerable distance from the site.

Based on August 1979 data, employees regularly using transportation other than single-occupancy auto are distributed as follows:

car pooling	1667
van pooling	607
bus fleet	294
transit riders	180
bicycles	625
total	3373

There were 8050 employees at Livermore at the time, so those using alternatives to the single-occupancy auto account for approximately 42% of the overall staff.

The Road Department of the Alameda County Public Works Agency estimates current full-volume (two-way) average vehicles per day traffic on East Avenue, Vasco Road, and Greenville Road as follows:

East Avenue	
East of Vasco Road*	10,500 vehicles per day
West of Vasco Road	12,500 vehicles per day
South Vasco Road	
North of East Avenue	6,500
South of East Avenue	1,800
Greenville Road	
North of East Avenue	1,500
South of East Avenue	800

Based on a 1976 survey by the California Department of Transportation, the DOE Livermore laboratories contribute about 80% of the total vehicular count on East Avenue east of Vasco Road. Laboratory traffic on Vasco Road is included either in the East Avenue count or the Mesquite Way counts. A typical 24-hour both-way total count on Mesquite is 1650 vehicles. Peak period counts (7:00-8:30 am and 4:00-5:30 pm) indicate that less than 300 vehicles arrive from or depart toward the East Avenue/Greenville Road intersection.

---

*Location of the traffic counter on East Avenue/Vasco Road intersection.

3.8.6. Economic Impact

The economic impact of the Laboratories on the City of Livermore is very strong, although the influence of the Laboratories is decreasing due to the increase in population and the number of other industries in Livermore. The economic profile of Livermore shows an average increase of 6.6% per year in the money received from business licenses. In 1971 the base for determining the business license fee was changed and the figures for 1971-75 fiscal years have been adjusted to the average increase (see Fig. 3-14). The actual dollar volume of taxable transactions has an average annual increase of 12.2%.

The impact of the Laboratories may be seen in Table 3-6. This table shows the annual payroll of the DOE Livermore laboratories from 1960 through 1979. The dollar value of this payroll spent in Livermore has been estimated, assuming 1) a direct relation between payroll and the percentage of Laboratory employees living in Livermore, and 2) that 30% of the employees' income is available to be spent on retail taxable sales. With these assumptions, Table 3-6 shows in the early and mid-sixties the Laboratories accounted for approximately 30 to 35% of the total taxable sales, but as the city has continued to grow and the Laboratories stabilized this percentage has dropped to about 22%.

The economic impact of the Laboratories is still very important to the Public School System in Livermore since the city is granted impact aid for students whose parents work on federal installations. The Livermore School District includes students from 39 federal installations with the largest percentage (approximately 65%) being related to the Laboratories. The percentage of the enrolled students related to the Laboratories in the school district has decreased since 1966. The proportion of impact aid relative to the total expenditures has also decreased as shown in Fig. 3-15.

3.9. ACCIDENT ANALYSIS

The following paragraphs discuss the environmental impact of accidents at the Livermore laboratories. Section 3.9.1 deals with the accidents that have occurred. Section 3.9.2 treats some larger generic accidents that might occur (although the probability is extremely remote) and estimates their maximum off-site consequence. Section 3.9.3 summarizes efforts to mitigate the consequences of any accident.

3.9.1. Accident Experience

Each accident that occurs at LLNL or SNLL is documented and investigated to determine its cause. Based upon these investigations, corrective action is taken to minimize their recurrence. Some of

Table 3-6. Impact of DOE Livermore laboratories' payrolls on Livermore.

Year	(A) Total payroll x10^3	(B) Total employees	(C) Employees residing in Livermore	(D)[a] Payroll to (C) x10^3	(E) Taxable transactions x10^3	(F)[b]
1960	34,672	4,767	2,643	19,223	14,415	40.0
1961	40,744	5,507	(2,001)[c]	(15,227)	15,107	(30.2)
1962	44,074	5,884	(2,102)	(15,856)	17,653	(26.9)
1963	48,996	6,332	(2,144)	(17,270)	22,225	(23.9)
1964	55,861	6,404	(2,621)	(22,290)	24,914	(26.8)
1965	59,260	6,431	(2,759)	(25,619)	28,834	(26.6)
1966	63,570	6,731	3,674	35,899	30,590	35.2
1967	68,125	6,724	(3,006)	(31,040)	34,034	(27.4)
1968	73,414	6,895	3,939	41,940	41,852	30.0
1969	79,947	7,053	4,052	45,930	46,196	29.5
1970	87,015	6,513	3,756	50,181	46,245	32.6
1971	86,335	6,272	3,593	49,458	52,673	28.2
1972	88,674	6,550	3,742	50,659	58,199	26.1
1973	96,570	6,097	3,530	55,916	64,594	26.0
1974	98,504	6,329	3,767	58,629	71,524	24.6
1975	112,604	6,516	3,814	65,982	80,825	24.5
1976	131,000	6,896	3,951	80,848	93,415	26.0
1977	148,336	7,511	4,214	86,213	114,626	22.6
1978	169,400	7,940	4,360	92,995	129,060	21.6
1979	199,911	8,178	4,268	104,331	141,265	22.1

[a] D = (A/B) x C. This assumes a direct proportion of payroll to proportion of employees residing in Livermore.

[b] F = (D x 30%)/E. This shows the percentage of taxable transactions resulting from Livermore residents who are employees of the DOE Livermore laboratories. It is assumed that 30% of the payroll to these employees is available for spending in Livermore, including all categories of retail stores and consumer services.

[c] Numbers in parentheses are based on LLNL data only.

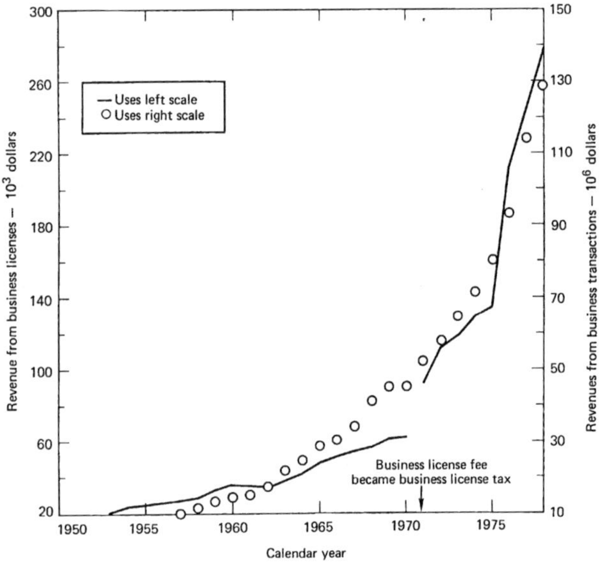

Figure 3-14. Economic profile of the city of Livermore.

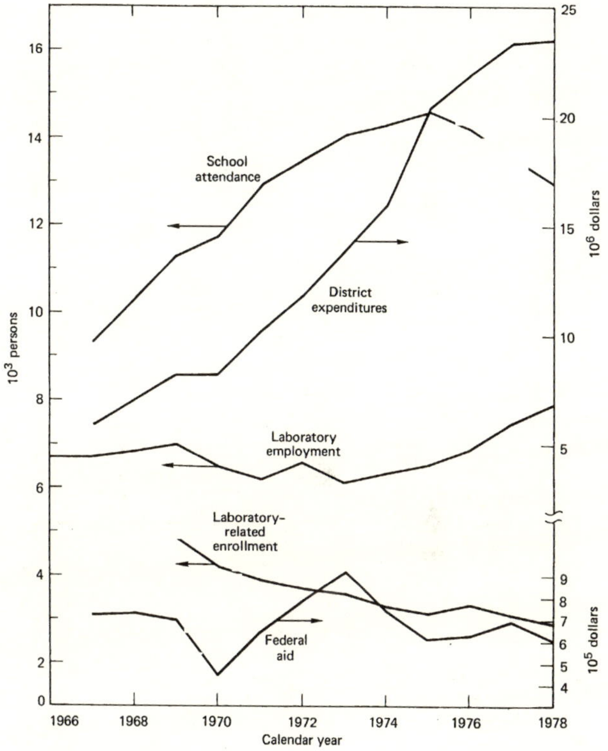

Figure 3-15. Impact of the DOE Livermore laboratories on the Livermore school system. (Arrows indicate the appropriate scale for each line.)

these accidents resulted in the release of radioactive or toxic materials to the environment. None of the accidents involved exposure to the public in excess of the appropriate radiation or concentration guides (DOE Order 5480.1A). A listing of these accidents is given in Appendix 3A.

3.9.2. Analysis of Postulated Accidents

All critical facilities have been evaluated for their capacity to withstand natural phenomena (earthquake, wind) and maintain confinement for their inventory of radioactive materials. As a result of these analyses and subsequent facility modifications, natural phenomena accidents should not have greater environmental effects than the human error accidents discussed here. Although highly unlikely, it is possible that human error will result in the release of some fraction of that inventory. The postulated accidents described below involve the maximum amounts handled in one operation and are assumed to occur in conditions that maximize offsite effect in order to estimate an upper bound of the consequences of accidents at the Livermore site.

3.9.2.1. HTO Release. This paragraph analyzes a hypothetical 1.2-MCi HTO release following rupture of a vessel and oxidation of the T_2 gas from Building 331 at LLNL or Building 968 at SNLL. Historically, 1.2 MCi represents the largest quantity of tritium ever handled at one time and is the maximum authorized for a single operation. The release and its consequences are considered unlikely for the following reasons:

- Currently, there are no operations planned involving this amount of tritium in one container or a single glove box.
- The release of this much tritium would require the simultaneous failure of the primary vessel, a glove box, and the decontamination system (see Sections 2.1.6.6 and 2.1.6.13).
- Previous experience with large tritium releases has shown that most of the material remains as tritium gas, which is 400 times less hazardous than tritiated water vapor (see DOE Order 5480.1A).
- An east wind maximizes the population dose and nearest-neighbor dose, but is not the most prevalent wind direction.

However, this analysis does place an upper limit on the consequences of a tritium release at either LLNL or SNLL.

Table 3-7 gives the ratio of concentration to release rate (χ/Q) for various distances west of Building 331 or Building 968. The χ/Q's were derived from wind speed, direction, and variability measurements using Gaussian diffusion equations.[3-5] These measurements were made at 30-min

Table 3-7. Values of χ/Q^a at various distances west of the tritium research facilities.

Meteorology data base	Condition	Distance downwind (km)						
		SB[b]	1	2	5	10	20	50
Annual	Median	1.2×10^{-5}	1.1×10^{-5}	7.5×10^{-6}	2.9×10^{-6}	1.2×10^{-6}	5.5×10^{-7}	1.7×10^{-7}
	95th percentile[c]	2.6×10^{-5}	2.5×10^{-5}	1.8×10^{-5}	1.0×10^{-5}	4.6×10^{-6}	2.2×10^{-6}	8.0×10^{-7}
Dry season	Median	2.0×10^{-5}	1.9×10^{-5}	1.2×10^{-5}	4.6×10^{-6}	1.9×10^{-6}	8.5×10^{-7}	2.8×10^{-7}
	95th percentile	8.5×10^{-5}	4.6×10^{-5}	3.6×10^{-5}	2.4×10^{-5}	1.2×10^{-5}	6.0×10^{-6}	2.1×10^{-6}
Wet season	Median	1.1×10^{-5}	1.0×10^{-5}	6.5×10^{-6}	2.6×10^{-6}	1.1×10^{-6}	4.8×10^{-7}	1.5×10^{-7}
	95th percentile	1.8×10^{-5}	1.7×10^{-5}	1.2×10^{-5}	5.0×10^{-6}	2.5×10^{-6}	1.1×10^{-6}	4.0×10^{-7}

[a] Units are s/m^3.
[b] Site boundary.
[c] Means the probability is 0.95 that the actual χ/Q will be less than that stated.

intervals for one year at a 40-m meteorological tower at the Livermore site. Table 3-8 gives downwind concentrations assuming that the 1.2 MCi are released uniformly over a 10-min interval. Table 3-8 also gives the estimated doses to persons standing directly under the centerline of the cloud during its entire passage. The conversion constant from concentration to dose, 3.7×10^{-14} $(rem/m^3)/(pCi/s)$ was derived by assuming:

- A biological half-life of 8.5 days.[3-6]
- An average energy per decay of 5.7 keV.[3-7]
- The critical receptor is body water (43 kg).[3-7]
- The breathing rate is 20 liters/min.[3-8]
- Absorption of HTO through bare skin is at 1/2 the inhalation rate.
- Clothing cuts the absorption to 3/10 the inhalation rate.
- All the HTO inhaled is absorbed by the lungs.[3-8]
- The quality factor for tritium betas is one.[3-9]

A maximum site boundary dose of 5.3 rem occurs at the SNLL northeast perimeter. For comparison, the Code of Federal Regulations, Title 10, Chapter 100 uses an accidental whole body exposure dose of 25 rem at the site boundary as a power-reactor siting criterion.

The maximum dose to an off-site resident is 3.8 rem. The EPA has drafted criteria for planning protective actions following radiological accidents that could present a hazard to the public.[3-10] In these criteria, EPA recommends that protective action be considered if the actions could reduce whole body doses 1 to 5 rem. The higher guide (5 rem) is a mandatory level at which effective actions should be taken to protect the general public unless the action would have greater risk than the anticipated dose.

The Laboratories are considering protective actions for nearby residents. However, the consequence of this postulated accident is not serious, even without protective action since the dose estimates for the tritium release are conservative. They assume that the individual, or population in each sector, stood outside under the cloud centerline and that all of the tritium is in the form of HTO. Table 3-9 gives the population dose in the downwind sector. Even the maximum doses are only about 1/4 of the population dose from natural radiation background.

3.9.2.2. Magnitude of Postulated Criticality Accident. It is postulated that the criticality accident occurs at LLNL's Building 332 (the Plutonium Facility) and involves a fission yield of 10^{18} fissions. Building 332 was chosen because most of the Livermore site's work with fissile materials is done there.

Table 3-8. Estimated concentrations and doses downwind (east wind) from a 1.2 MCi/10 min HTO release from the tritium research facilities.

Meteorology data base	Condition	Distance downwind (km)						
		SB[a]	1	2	5	10	20	50
Concentration (Ci/m^3)								
Annual	Median	2.4×10^{-2}	2.2×10^{-2}	1.5×10^{-2}	5.8×10^{-3}	2.4×10^{-3}	1.1×10^{-3}	3.4×10^{-4}
	95th percentile[b]	5.2×10^{-2}	5.0×10^{-2}	3.6×10^{-2}	2.0×10^{-2}	9.6×10^{-3}	4.4×10^{-3}	1.6×10^{-3}
Dry season	Median	4.0×10^{-2}	3.8×10^{-2}	2.4×10^{-2}	9.2×10^{-3}	3.8×10^{-3}	1.7×10^{-3}	5.6×10^{-4}
	95th percentile	3.6×10^{-2}	9.2×10^{-2}	7.2×10^{-2}	4.8×10^{-2}	2.4×10^{-2}	1.2×10^{-2}	4.2×10^{-3}
Wet seas o	Median	2.2×10^{-2}	2.0×10^{-2}	1.3×10^{-2}	5.2×10^{-3}	2.2×10^{-3}	9.6×10^{-4}	3.0×10^{-4}
	95th percentile	4.6×10^{-3}	3.4×10^{-2}	2.4×10^{-2}	1.0×10^{-2}	5.0×10^{-3}	2.2×10^{-3}	8.0×10^{-4}
Doses (rem)								
Annual	Median	5.3×10^{-1}	4.9×10^{-1}	3.2×10^{-1}	1.3×10^{-1}	5.3×10^{-2}	2.3×10^{-2}	7.5×10^{-3}
	95th percentile	1.2	1.1	8.0×10^{-1}	4.4×10^{-1}	2.1×10^{-1}	9.8×10^{-2}	3.5×10^{-2}
Dry season	Median	8.9×10^{-1}	8.4×10^{-1}	5.3×10^{-1}	2.0×10^{-1}	8.4×10^{-2}	3.8×10^{-2}	1.2×10^{-2}
	95th percentile	3.8	2.0	1.6	1.1	5.3×10^{-1}	2.6×10^{-1}	9.3×10^{-2}
Wet seas o	Median	4.9×10^{-1}	4.4×10^{-1}	2.9×10^{-1}	1.1×10^{-1}	4.9×10^{-2}	2.1×10^{-2}	1.8×10^{-2}
	95th percentile	7.8×10^{-1}	7.5×10^{-1}	5.3×10^{-1}	2.3×10^{-1}	1.1×10^{-1}	4.9×10^{-2}	1.8×10^{-2}

[a] Site boundary.
[b] Means the probability is 0.95 that the actual dose will be less than that stated.

Table 3-9. Population dose to 1.2×10^6 persons downwind of the tritium research facilities following a 1.2-MCi HTO release in an east wind.

Meteorological data base	Condition	Population dose (man-rem)
Annual	Median	11,000
	95th percentile[a]	46,000
Dry season	Median	33,000
	95th percentile	126,000
Wet season	Median	10,000
	95th percentile	31,000

[a] Means the probability is 0.95 that the estimated dose will be less than that stated.

Aspinall,[3-11] Woodcock,[3-12] and Stratton[3-13] have analyzed theoretical and actual yield data for criticality accidents. Actual accidents involving solid plutonium, as handled in 332, have yields lower than the 10^{18}-fission accident analyzed here. Woodcock[3-12] estimates the maximum potential magnitude of a criticality accident involving solid plutonium as 10^{18} fissions. To place an upper bound on the effects of a criticality accident, we have used Woodcock's[3-12] theoretical estimate.

At t + 1 min, the total quantity of fission products remaining after a 10^{18}-fissions accident is approximately 2.5 x 10^5 Ci. At t + 10 min, the total activity will have decayed to 1.5 x 10^4 Ci. By far the largest portion of the fission products will be in the nonvolatile form. The volatile isotopes which are the most significant when considering possible release to the environment are given in Table 3-10.

3.9.2.2.1. Effects of Fission-Product Release to the Environment. As indicated in 3.9.2.2, about 1.5 x 10^4 Ci of fission-product activity would be present at t + 10 min after the postulated 10^{18}-fission criticality accident. The Nuclear Regulatory Commission has suggested[3-14] that for plutonium criticality accidents involving solutions of plutonium, the following release fractions be used: 100% for noble gases, 25% for halogens, and 1% for all remaining fission products. Solid plutonium criticalities will release a smaller percentage of fission products so that the assumed release fractions are conservative. Air exhausted from facilities most likely to suffer a criticality accident passes through HEPA filters to ensure minimum release of particulates to the environment.

By assuming that a release occurs uniformly over a 10 min period and by using the median and 95%-probability χ/Q values given in Table 3-11 one can calculate the concentrations and possible doses to persons downwind. Possible dose pathways that should be considered include submersion, inhalation, and forage-cow-milk. Important nuclides and appropriate dose conversion constants are given in Table 3-12. The dose conversion constants were obtained from various sources, but primarily from Ng.[3-15]

The doses are calculated for an east wind and thus demonstrate the maximum environmental effect. The most probable wind direction is west to southwest. The hills near the site, north, east, and south, will reduce ground-level concentrations on their far sides. Population densities are highest in the sectors west of LLNL (see Figs. 2-9 and 2-10).

To determine the concentration of these isotopes at various distances downwind along the line of release and the resulting integrated dose, three sets of tables are provided to cover annual (Tables 3-13 and 3-14), wet season (Tables 3-15 and 3-16), and dry season (Tables 3-17 and 3-18) conditions. The radioiodine and cesium (from xenon decay) tend to attach themselves to particulates

Table 3-10. Volatile isotopes from 10^{18}-fissions accident.

^{131}I (8.05 d)	0.75
^{132}I (2.4 h)	3.3
^{133}I (20.5 h)	18
^{134}I (52.5 m)	450
^{135}I (6.68 h)	48
^{135m}Xe (15 m)	395
^{138}Xe (17 m)	1050
^{87}Kr (1.3 h)	112
^{83m}Kr (1.86 h)	13.5
^{88}Kr (2.8 h)	69.5
^{84m}Kr (4.4 h)	18.5
^{135}Xe (9.2 h)	36.4
^{133m}Xe (2.3 d)	0.2
^{133}Xe (5.27 d)	2.7
^{131m}Xe (12.0 d)	0.06
^{85}Kr (10.4 y)	0.002

Table 3-11. Values of χ/Q^a at various distances west of Building 332.

Meteorology data base	Condition	Distance downwind (km)						
		SB[b]	1	2	5	10	20	50
Annual	Median	7.0×10^{-5}	3.1×10^{-5}	9.4×10^{-6}	2.1×10^{-6}	6.6×10^{-7}	2.2×10^{-7}	4.2×10^{-8}
	95th percentile[c]	2.7×10^{-4}	1.0×10^{-4}	2.6×10^{-5}	4.9×10^{-6}	1.3×10^{-6}	3.8×10^{-7}	5.3×10^{-8}
Dry season	Median	7.6×10^{-5}	3.1×10^{-5}	9.0×10^{-6}	1.9×10^{-6}	5.4×10^{-7}	1.5×10^{-7}	2.3×10^{-8}
	95th percentile	4.5×10^{-4}	1.7×10^{-4}	4.2×10^{-5}	7.0×10^{-6}	1.8×10^{-6}	4.6×10^{-7}	7.2×10^{-8}
Wet season	Median	6.9×10^{-5}	3.1×10^{-5}	9.4×10^{-6}	2.1×10^{-6}	6.9×10^{-7}	2.1×10^{-7}	4.7×10^{-8}
	95th percentile	2.6×10^{-4}	1.0×10^{-4}	2.7×10^{-5}	5.0×10^{-6}	1.4×10^{-6}	4.5×10^{-7}	9.1×10^{-8}

[a] Units are s/m^3.
[b] Site boundary (0.69 km from Building 332).
[c] Means the probability is 0.95 that the actual χ/Q will be less than that stated.

Table 3-12. Nuclides of importance released during a maximum credible accident.

Nuclide	Half-life (h)	Source strength[a] (pCi/s)	Dose conversion constant $\frac{rem/m^2}{pCi/s}$	Dose conversion constant $\frac{rem/m^2}{pCi}$	Pathway	Organ affected
^{87}Kr	1.27	1.8×10^{11}	2.6×10^{-13}		Submersion	Whole body
^{88}Kr	2.8	1.2×10^{11}	5.0×10^{-13}		Submersion	Whole body
^{131}I	194.	3.2×10^{8}	3.4×10^{-10}		Inhalation	Thyroid
				2.7×10^{-5}	Forage-cow-milk	Thyroid
^{133}I	21.	7.5×10^{9}	9.2×10^{-11}		Inhalation	Thyroid
				6.0×10^{-7}	Forage-cow-milk	Thyroid
^{134}I[b]	0.87	1.8×10^{11}	5.8×10^{-12}		Inhalation	Thyroid
^{135}I[b]	6.7	2.0×10^{10}	2.8×10^{-11}		Inhalation	Thyroid
^{135}Xe	9.2	6.0×10^{10}	7.5×10^{-14}		Submersion	Whole body
^{135m}Xe	0.26	6.5×10^{11}	1.3×10^{-13}		Submersion	Whole body
^{138}Xe	0.28	1.7×10^{12}	7.2×10^{-14}		Submersion	Whole body
^{138}Cs	0.53	c	7.2×10^{-14}		Submersion	Whole body

[a] Assume 10-min release.
[b] Half-life too short to be of importance in forage-cow-milk pathway.
[c] ^{138}Cs forms from decay of ^{138}Xe and is not released at time of accident.

Table 3-13. Concentration (pCi/m^3) of nuclides of importance at various distances west of Building 332, based on the annual east wind meteorological summary.

Nuclide	Condition	Distance downwind (km)						
		SB[a]	1	2	5	10	20	50
^{87}Kr	Median	1.2×10^7	5.0×10^6	1.5×10^6	2.5×10^5	5.8×10^4	9.4×10^3	2.2×10^2
	95th percentile[b]	4.1×10^7	1.6×10^7	4.0×10^6	6.3×10^5	1.1×10^5	1.6×10^4	9.9×10^2
^{88}Kr	Median	8.2×10^6	3.6×10^6	1.1×10^6	2.3×10^5	5.8×10^4	1.3×10^4	1.0×10^3
	95th percentile	3.0×10^7	1.2×10^7	2.9×10^6	5.0×10^5	1.1×10^5	2.2×10^4	1.6×10^3
^{131}I	Median	2.2×10^4	9.9×10^3	3.0×10^3	6.7×10^2	2.1×10^2	70	13
	95th percentile	8.6×10^4	3.2×10^4	8.3×10^3	1.6×10^3	4.2×10^2	1.2×10^2	17
^{133}I	Median	5.3×10^5	2.3×10^5	7.0×10^4	1.5×10^4	4.8×10^3	1.5×10^3	2.5×10^2
	95th percentile	2.0×10^6	7.5×10^5	2.0×10^5	3.6×10^4	9.8×10^3	2.3×10^3	3.3×10^2
^{134}I	Median	1.2×10^7	5.0×10^6	1.4×10^6	2.2×10^5	4.0×10^4	4.9×10^3	45
	95th percentile	4.0×10^7	1.5×10^7	3.6×10^6	5.4×10^5	7.9×10^4	8.8×10^3	2.9×10^2
^{135}I	Median	1.4×10^6	6.2×10^5	1.8×10^5	3.8×10^4	1.2×10^4	3.4×10^3	4.4×10^2
	95th percentile	5.4×10^6	2.0×10^6	5.0×10^5	9.2×10^4	2.4×10^4	5.0×10^3	5.8×10^2
^{135}X	Median	4.1×10^6	1.9×10^6	5.5×10^5	1.2×10^5	3.6×10^4	1.1×10^4	1.6×10^3
	95th percentile	1.6×10^7	6.0×10^6	1.6×10^6	2.8×10^5	7.2×10^4	1.6×10^4	2.1×10^3
^{135m}Xe	Median	3.6×10^7	1.4×10^7	3.0×10^6	2.3×10^5	1.1×10^4	1.8×10^2	2.0×10^{-2}
	95th percentile	1.0×10^8	3.8×10^7	7.8×10^6	5.7×10^5	3.0×10^4	1.5×10^3	4.2
^{138}Xe	Median	9.4×10^7	3.7×10^7	8.3×10^6	6.8×10^5	3.7×10^4	7.3×10^2	4.8×10^{-2}
	95th percentile	2.7×10^8	1.0×10^8	2.2×10^7	1.7×10^6	9.9×10^4	5.4×10^3	15
^{138}Cs	Median	8.7×10^7	3.6×10^7	9.2×10^6	1.2×10^6	1.5×10^5	1.0×10^4	14
	95th percentile	2.8×10^8	1.0×10^8	2.4×10^7	2.9×10^6	3.4×10^5	2.2×10^4	3.5×10^2

[a] Site boundary (0.69 km).
[b] Means the probability is 0.95 that the concentration will be less than that stated.

Table 3-14. Estimated downwind doses (rem) from nuclides of importance, based on the annual east wind meteorological summary.

Nuclide	Pathway	Condition	Distance downwind (km)						
			SB[a]	1	2	5	10	20	50
^{87}Kr	Submersion	Median	1.9×10^{-3}	8.1×10^{-4}	2.3×10^{-4}	3.9×10^{-4}	9.0×10^{-6}	1.5×10^{-6}	3.4×10^{-8}
		95th percentile[b]	6.5×10^{-3}	2.5×10^{-1}	6.2×10^{-4}	9.8×10^{-5}	1.7×10^{-5}	2.4×10^{-6}	1.5×10^{-7}
^{88}Kr	Submersion	Median	2.4×10^{-3}	1.1×10^{-3}	3.2×10^{-4}	6.8×10^{-5}	1.7×10^{-5}	4.0×10^{-6}	3.0×10^{-7}
		95th percentile	9.0×10^{-3}	3.5×10^{-3}	8.6×10^{-4}	1.5×10^{-4}	3.3×10^{-5}	6.5×10^{-6}	4.7×10^{-7}
^{131}I	Inhalation	Median	4.6×10^{-3}	2.0×10^{-3}	6.1×10^{-4}	1.4×10^{-4}	4.3×10^{-5}	1.4×10^{-5}	2.7×10^{-6}
		95th percentile	1.8×10^{-2}	6.5×10^{-3}	1.7×10^{-3}	3.2×10^{-4}	8.5×10^{-5}	2.5×10^{-5}	3.5×10^{-6}
	Forage-cow-milk	Median	3.6	1.6	4.9×10^{-1}	1.1×10^{-1}	3.4×10^{-2}	1.1×10^{-2}	2.2×10^{-3}
		95th percentile	14	5.2	1.3	2.5×10^{-1}	6.7×10^{-2}	2.0×10^{-2}	2.7×10^{-3}
^{133}I	Inhalation	Median	2.9×10^{-2}	1.3×10^{-2}	3.9×10^{-3}	8.3×10^{-4}	2.6×10^{-4}	8.3×10^{-5}	1.4×10^{-5}
		95th percentile	1.1×10^{-1}	4.1×10^{-2}	1.1×10^{-2}	2.0×10^{-3}	5.4×10^{-4}	1.2×10^{-4}	1.8×10^{-5}
	Forage-cow-milk	Median	1.9	8.4×10^{-1}	2.5×10^{-1}	5.4×10^{-2}	1.7×10^{-2}	5.4×10^{-3}	9.5×10^{-4}
		95th percentile	7.0	2.7	7.0×10^{-1}	1.3×10^{-1}	3.5×10^{-2}	8.1×10^{-3}	1.2×10^{-3}
^{134}I	Inhalation	Median	4.1×10^{-2}	1.8×10^{-2}	4.8×10^{-3}	7.5×10^{-4}	1.4×10^{-4}	1.7×10^{-5}	1.6×10^{-7}
		95th percentile	1.4×10^{-1}	5.2×10^{-2}	1.3×10^{-2}	1.9×10^{-3}	2.8×10^{-4}	3.1×10^{-5}	1.0×10^{-6}
^{135}I	Inhalation	Median	2.3×10^{-2}	1.0×10^{-2}	3.1×10^{-3}	6.4×10^{-4}	1.9×10^{-4}	5.7×10^{-5}	7.4×10^{-6}
		95th percentile	9.1×10^{-2}	3.4×10^{-2}	8.4×10^{-3}	1.5×10^{-3}	4.0×10^{-4}	8.4×10^{-5}	9.7×10^{-6}
^{135}Xe	Submersion	Median	1.9×10^{-4}	8.4×10^{-5}	2.5×10^{-5}	5.4×10^{-6}	1.6×10^{-6}	4.9×10^{-7}	4.0×10^{-8}
		95th percentile	7.0×10^{-4}	2.7×10^{-4}	7.0×10^{-5}	1.3×10^{-5}	3.2×10^{-6}	7.3×10^{-7}	9.5×10^{-8}
^{135m}Xe	Submersion	Median	2.8×10^{-3}	1.1×10^{-3}	2.3×10^{-4}	1.8×10^{-5}	8.6×10^{-7}	1.4×10^{-7}	1.6×10^{-12}
		95th percentile	8.1×10^{-3}	2.9×10^{-3}	6.1×10^{-4}	4.4×10^{-5}	2.3×10^{-6}	1.2×10^{-7}	3.2×10^{-10}
^{138}Xe	Submersion	Median	4.0×10^{-3}	1.6×10^{-3}	3.6×10^{-4}	2.9×10^{-5}	1.6×10^{-6}	3.2×10^{-8}	2.1×10^{-12}
		95th percentile	1.2×10^{-2}	4.4×10^{-3}	9.5×10^{-4}	7.2×10^{-5}	4.3×10^{-6}	2.4×10^{-7}	6.5×10^{-10}
^{138}Cs	Submersion	Median	3.7×10^{-3}	1.6×10^{-3}	4.0×10^{-4}	5.3×10^{-5}	6.7×10^{-6}	4.5×10^{-7}	6.0×10^{-10}
		95th percentile	1.2×10^{-2}	4.5×10^{-3}	1.0×10^{-3}	1.3×10^{-4}	1.5×10^{-5}	9.7×10^{-7}	1.5×10^{-8}

[a] Site boundary (0.69 km).
[b] Means the probability is 0.95 that the dose will be less than that stated.

Table 3-15. Downwind concentrations (pCi/m^3) of nuclides of importance, based on the wet-season east wind meteorological summary.

Nuclide	Condition	Distance downwind (km)						
		SB[a]	1	2	5	10	20	50
^{87}Kr	Median	1.2×10^7	5.2×10^6	1.5×10^6	2.7×10^5	6.5×10^4	1.2×10^2	3.6×10^2
	95th percentile[b]	4.1×10^7	1.6×10^7	4.0×10^6	6.5×10^5	1.6×10^5	3.1×10^4	16
^{88}Kr	Median	8.0×10^6	3.6×10^6	1.1×10^6	2.2×10^5	6.1×10^4	1.6×10^4	1.3×10^3
	95th percentile	3.0×10^7	1.2×10^7	2.9×10^6	5.2×10^5	1.3×10^5	3.5×10^4	3.7×10^3
^{131}I	Median	2.2×10^4	9.9×10^3	3.0×10^3	6.7×10^2	2.2×10^2	67	15
	95th percentile	8.3×10^4	3.2×10^4	8.7×10^3	1.6×10^3	4.5×10^2	1.4×10^2	29
^{133}I	Median	5.1×10^5	2.3×10^5	7.0×10^4	1.6×10^4	5.0×10^3	1.7×10^3	2.9×10^2
	95th percentile	2.0×10^6	7.5×10^5	2.0×10^5	3.8×10^4	1.1×10^4	3.2×10^3	5.9×10^2
^{134}I	Median	1.2×10^7	5.0×10^6	1.4×10^6	2.3×10^5	4.7×10^4	6.5×10^3	83
	95th percentile	4.0×10^7	1.5×10^7	3.6×10^6	5.8×10^5	1.3×10^5	2.0×10^4	5.4×10^2
^{135}I	Median	1.4×10^6	6.2×10^5	1.8×10^5	4.0×10^4	1.2×10^4	3.6×10^3	5.2×10^2
	95th percentile	2.4×10^6	1.2×10^6	3.6×10^5	7.2×10^4	2.0×10^4	5.6×10^3	8.4×10^2
^{135}Xe	Median	4.1×10^6	1.9×10^6	5.3×10^5	1.2×10^5	3.8×10^4	1.2×10^4	1.9×10^3
	95th percentile	1.6×10^7	6.0×10^6	1.6×10^6	2.9×10^5	7.8×10^4	2.3×10^4	4.0×10^3
^{135m}Xe	Median	3.6×10^7	1.5×10^7	3.3×10^6	2.9×10^5	1.8×10^4	3.6×10^2	2.6×10^{-2}
	95th percentile	1.0×10^8	3.8×10^7	8.5×10^6	9.1×10^5	8.5×10^4	3.3×10^3	5.7
^{138}Xe	Median	9.5×10^7	3.9×10^7	1.1×10^7	8.3×10^5	5.8×10^4	1.4×10^3	1.0×10^{-1}
	95th percentile	2.9×10^8	6.0×10^8	2.2×10^7	2.6×10^6	2.6×10^5	1.2×10^4	20
^{138}Cs	Median	7.4×10^7	3.8×10^7	9.7×10^6	1.4×10^6	2.0×10^5	1.5×10^4	35
	95 percentile	2.8×10^8	1.1×10^8	2.5×10^7	3.5×10^6	6.2×10^5	6.6×10^4	5.2×10^2

[a] Site boundary (0.69 km).
[b] Means the probability is 0.95 that the concentration will be less than that stated.

Table 3-16. Estimated downwind doses (rem) from nuclides of importance, based on the wet-season east wind meteorological summary.

			Distance downwind (km)						
Nuclide	Pathway	Condition	SB[a]	1	2	5	10	20	50
^{87}Kr	Submersion	Median	1.9×10^{-3}	8.1×10^{-4}	2.3×10^{-4}	4.2×10^{-5}	1.0×10^{-5}	1.8×10^{-6}	5.6×10^{-8}
		95th percentile[b]	6.5×10^{-3}	2.5×10^{-3}	6.2×10^{-4}	1.0×10^{-4}	2.4×10^{-5}	4.8×10^{-6}	2.4×10^{-7}
^{88}Kr	Submersion	Median	2.4×10^{-3}	1.1×10^{-3}	3.2×10^{-4}	6.5×10^{-5}	1.8×10^{-5}	4.7×10^{-6}	4.0×10^{-7}
		95th percentile	9.0×10^{-3}	3.5×10^{-3}	8.6×10^{-4}	1.5×10^{-4}	4.0×10^{-5}	1.0×10^{-5}	1.1×10^{-6}
^{131}I	Inhalation	Median	4.5×10^{-3}	2.0×10^{-3}	6.1×10^{-4}	1.4×10^{-4}	4.5×10^{-5}	1.4×10^{-5}	3.1×10^{-6}
		95th percentile	1.7×10^{-2}	6.5×10^{-3}	1.8×10^{-3}	3.3×10^{-4}	9.1×10^{-5}	2.9×10^{-5}	5.9×10^{-6}
	Forage-cow-milk	Median	3.6	1.6	4.9×10^{-1}	1.1×10^{-1}	3.6×10^{-2}	1.1×10^{-2}	2.4×10^{-3}
		95th percentile	13	5.2	1.4	2.6×10^{-1}	7.3×10^{-2}	2.3×10^{-2}	4.7×10^{-3}
^{133}I	Inhalation	Median	2.8×10^{-2}	1.3×10^{-2}	3.9×10^{-3}	8.7×10^{-4}	2.7×10^{-4}	9.1×10^{-5}	1.6×10^{-5}
		95th percentile	1.1×10^{-1}	4.1×10^{-2}	1.1×10^{-2}	2.0×10^{-3}	5.8×10^{-4}	1.7×10^{-4}	3.3×10^{-5}
	Forage-cow-milk	Median	1.8	8.4×10^{-1}	2.5×10^{-1}	5.7×10^{-2}	1.8×10^{-2}	5.9×10^{-3}	1.1×10^{-3}
		95th percentile	7.0	2.7	7.3×10^{-1}	1.3×10^{-1}	3.8×10^{-2}	1.1×10^{-2}	2.1×10^{-3}
^{134}I	Inhalation	Median	4.0×10^{-2}	1.8×10^{-2}	4.9×10^{-3}	8.1×10^{-4}	1.6×10^{-4}	2.3×10^{-5}	2.9×10^{-7}
		95th percentile	1.4×10^{-1}	5.3×10^{-2}	1.3×10^{-2}	2.0×10^{-3}	4.4×10^{-4}	6.9×10^{-5}	1.9×10^{-6}
^{135}I	Inhalation	Median	2.3×10^{-2}	1.0×10^{-2}	3.1×10^{-3}	6.7×10^{-4}	2.0×10^{-4}	6.0×10^{-5}	8.7×10^{-6}
		95th percentile	4.0×10^{-2}	2.0×10^{-2}	6.0×10^{-3}	1.2×10^{-3}	3.4×10^{-4}	9.4×10^{-5}	1.4×10^{-5}
^{135}Xe	Submersion	Median	1.8×10^{-4}	8.4×10^{-5}	2.5×10^{-5}	5.4×10^{-6}	1.7×10^{-6}	5.4×10^{-7}	8.4×10^{-8}
		95th percentile	7.0×10^{-4}	2.7×10^{-4}	7.0×10^{-5}	1.3×10^{-5}	3.5×10^{-6}	1.1×10^{-6}	1.8×10^{-7}
^{135m}Xe	Submersion	Median	2.8×10^{-3}	1.2×10^{-3}	2.5×10^{-4}	2.2×10^{-5}	1.4×10^{-6}	2.8×10^{-8}	2.0×10^{-12}
		95th percentile	8.1×10^{-3}	8.0×10^{-3}	6.6×10^{-4}	7.1×10^{-5}	6.6×10^{-6}	2.5×10^{-7}	4.4×10^{-10}
^{138}Xe	Submersion	Median	4.1×10^{-3}	1.7×10^{-3}	4.6×10^{-4}	3.6×10^{-5}	2.5×10^{-6}	6.2×10^{-8}	4.6×10^{-12}
		95th percentile	1.2×10^{-2}	4.4×10^{-3}	9.5×10^{-4}	1.1×10^{-4}	1.1×10^{-5}	5.0×10^{-7}	818×10^{-10}
^{138}Cs	Submersion	Median	3.7×10^{-3}	1.6×10^{-3}	4.2×10^{-4}	5.9×10^{-5}	6.5×10^{-6}	6.7×10^{-7}	1.5×10^{-9}
		95th percentile	1.2×10^{-2}	4.6×10^{-3}	1.1×10^{-3}	1.5×10^{-4}	2.7×10^{-5}	2.8×10^{-6}	2.2×10^{-8}

[a] Site boundary (0.69 km).
[b] Means the probability is 0.95 that the dose will be less than that stated.

Table 3-17. Downwind concentrations (pCi/m^3) of nuclides of importance based on the dry-season east wind meteorological summary.

Nuclide	Condition	Distance downwind (km)						
		SB[a]	1	2	5	10	20	50
^{87}Kr	Median	1.3×10^7	5.0×10^6	1.3×10^6	1.8×10^5	2.9×10^4	2.7×10^3	17
	95th percentile[b]	6.8×10^7	2.5×10^7	5.9×10^6	8.1×10^5	1.4×10^5	1.7×10^4	3.6×10^2
^{88}Kr	Median	8.8×10^6	3.6×10^6	9.7×10^5	1.7×10^5	3.7×10^4	6.5×10^3	2.0×10^2
	95th percentile	4.9×10^7	1.9×10^7	4.4×10^6	6.8×10^5	1.4×10^5	2.8×10^4	1.4×10^3
^{131}I	Median	2.4×10^4	9.9×10^3	2.9×10^3	6.1×10^2	1.7×10^2	48	7.4
	95th percentile	1.4×10^5	5.4×10^4	1.3×10^4	2.2×10^3	5.8×10^2	1.5×10^2	23
^{133}I	Median	5.7×10^5	2.3×10^5	6.7×10^4	1.4×10^4	3.8×10^3	9.8×10^2	1.3×10^2
	95th percentile	3.3×10^6	1.3×10^6	3.1×10^5	5.1×10^4	1.3×10^4	3.2×10^3	4.4×10^2
^{134}I	Median	1.2×10^7	4.7×10^6	1.2×10^6	1.4×10^5	1.6×10^4	9.7×10^2	1.3
	95th percentile	6.5×10^7	2.3×10^7	5.4×10^6	6.7×10^5	9.7×10^4	8.6×10^3	86
^{135}I	Median	1.5×10^6	6.2×10^5	1.7×10^5	3.4×10^4	8.6×10^3	2.0×10^3	1.5×10^2
	95th percentile	8.6×10^6	3.4×10^6	8.0×10^5	1.3×10^5	3.0×10^5	6.8×10^3	6.8×10^2
^{135}Xe	Median	4.5×10^6	1.9×10^6	5.3×10^5	1.0×10^5	2.8×10^4	6.6×10^3	6.0×10^2
	95th percentile	2.6×10^7	1.0×10^7	8.4×10^5	3.9×10^5	9.6×10^4	2.2×10^4	2.5×10^3
^{135m}Xe	Median	3.3×10^7	1.1×10^7	1.9×10^6	7.2×10^4	9.1×10^2	3.1	2.1×10^{-5}
	95th percentile	1.6×10^8	5.6×10^7	1.0×10^7	6.2×10^5	2.1×10^4	4.0×10^2	4.4
^{138}Xe	Median	9.0×10^7	3.1×10^7	5.3×10^6	2.2×10^5	3.6×10^3	16	9.0×10^{-5}
	95th percentile	4.3×10^8	1.5×10^8	2.9×10^7	1.9×10^6	7.3×10^4	1.6×10^3	2.0×10^{-1}
^{138}Cs	Median	8.8×10^7	3.4×10^7	7.3×10^6	6.3×10^5	4.1×10^4	9.5×10^2	7.8×10^{-2}
	95th percentile	4.5×10^8	1.7×10^8	3.5×10^7	3.6×10^6	3.5×10^5	1.8×10^4	35

[a] Site boundary (0.69 km).
[b] Means the probability is 0.95 that the concentration will be less than that stated.

Table 3-18. Estimated downwind doses (rem) from nuclides of importance, based on the dry-season east wind meteorological summary.

Nuclide	Pathway	Condition	Distance downwind (km)						
			SB[a]	1	2	5	10	20	50
^{87}Kr	Submersion	Median	2.0×10^{-3}	7.9×10^{-4}	2.0×10^{-4}	2.8×10^{-5}	4.5×10^{-6}	4.2×10^{-7}	2.6×10^{-9}
		95th percentile[b]	1.1×10^{-2}	3.9×10^{-3}	9.3×10^{-4}	1.3×10^{-4}	2.2×10^{-5}	2.7×10^{-6}	5.6×10^{-8}
^{88}Kr	Submersion	Median	2.6×10^{-3}	1.1×10^{-3}	2.9×10^{-4}	5.0×10^{-5}	1.1×10^{-5}	1.9×10^{-6}	6.1×10^{-8}
		95th percentile	1.5×10^{-2}	5.8×10^{-3}	1.3×10^{-3}	2.1×10^{-4}	4.3×10^{-5}	8.3×10^{-6}	4.3×10^{-7}
^{131}I	Inhalation	Median	5.0×10^{-3}	2.0×10^{-3}	5.9×10^{-4}	1.2×10^{-4}	3.5×10^{-5}	9.8×10^{-6}	1.5×10^{-6}
		95th percentile	2.9×10^{-2}	1.1×10^{-2}	2.7×10^{-3}	4.6×10^{-4}	1.2×10^{-4}	3.0×10^{-5}	4.7×10^{-6}
	Forage-cow-milk	Median	3.9	1.6	4.7×10^{-1}	9.8×10^{-2}	2.8×10^{-2}	7.8×10^{-3}	1.2×10^{-3}
		95th percentile	23	8.8	2.2	3.6×10^{-1}	9.3×10^{-2}	2.4×10^{-2}	3.7×10^{-3}
^{133}I	Inhalation	Median	3.1×10^{-2}	1.3×10^{-2}	3.7×10^{-3}	7.5×10^{-4}	2.1×10^{-4}	5.4×10^{-5}	7.0×10^{-6}
		95th percentile	1.8×10^{-1}	7.0×10^{-2}	1.7×10^{-2}	2.8×10^{-3}	7.0×10^{-4}	1.7×10^{-4}	2.4×10^{-5}
	Forage-cow-milk	Median	2.1	8.4×10^{-1}	2.4×10^{-1}	4.9×10^{-2}	1.4×10^{-2}	3.5×10^{-3}	4.6×10^{-4}
		95th percentile	12	4.6	1.1	1.8×10^{-1}	4.6×10^{-2}	1.1×10^{-2}	1.6×10^{-3}
^{134}I	Inhalation	Median	4.3×10^{-2}	1.6×10^{-2}	4.0×10^{-3}	4.9×10^{-4}	5.7×10^{-5}	3.4×10^{-6}	4.6×10^{-9}
		95th percentile	2.3×10^{-1}	8.1×10^{-2}	1.9×10^{-2}	2.3×10^{-3}	3.4×10^{-4}	3.0×10^{-5}	3.0×10^{-7}
^{135}I	Inhalation	Median	2.5×10^{-1}	1.0×10^{-2}	2.9×10^{-3}	5.7×10^{-4}	1.4×10^{-4}	3.4×10^{-5}	2.6×10^{-6}
		95th percentile	1.4×10^{-2}	5.7×10^{-2}	1.3×10^{-2}	2.2×10^{-3}	5.0×10^{-4}	1.1×10^{-4}	1.1×10^{-5}
^{135}Xe	Submersion	Median	2.0×10^{-3}	8.4×10^{-5}	2.4×10^{-5}	4.6×10^{-6}	1.2×10^{-6}	3.0×10^{-7}	2.7×10^{-8}
		95th percentile	1.2×10^{-3}	4.6×10^{-4}	3.8×10^{-5}	1.8×10^{-5}	4.3×10^{-6}	1.0×10^{-6}	1.1×10^{-7}
^{135m}Xe	Submersion	Median	2.6×10^{-3}	8.6×10^{-4}	1.5×10^{-4}	5.6×10^{-6}	7.1×10^{-8}	2.4×10^{-10}	1.7×10^{-15}
		95th percentile	1.2×10^{-2}	4.4×10^{-3}	8.1×10^{-4}	4.9×10^{-5}	1.6×10^{-6}	3.1×10^{-8}	3.4×10^{-12}
^{138}Xe	Submersion	Median	3.9×10^{-3}	1.3×10^{-3}	2.3×10^{-4}	9.5×10^{-6}	1.5×10^{-7}	7.1×10^{-10}	3.9×10^{-15}
		95th percentile	1.8×10^{-2}	6.6×10^{-3}	1.2×10^{-3}	8.1×10^{-5}	3.2×10^{-6}	6.9×10^{-8}	8.8×10^{-12}
^{138}Cs	Submersion	Median	3.8×10^{-3}	1.5×10^{-3}	3.1×10^{-4}	2.7×10^{-5}	1.8×10^{-6}	4.1×10^{-8}	3.4×10^{-12}
		95th percentile	1.9×10^{-2}	7.3×10^{-3}	1.5×10^{-3}	1.6×10^{-4}	1.5×10^{-5}	7.9×10^{-7}	1.5×10^{-9}

[a] Site boundary (0.69 km).

[b] Means the probability is 0.95 that the dose will be less than that stated.

and deposit on the ground. The concentrations given have not accounted for reduction due to upwind deposition and are therefore conservative values. Doses from dry deposition of these nuclides are considered to be negligible due to the short half-lives of the nuclides and to the smaller dose conversion constants for surface deposition compared to inhalation and submersion.

It should be noted that the Livermore Valley is not a milk-producing area, and very few milk cows exist within a few kilometers of the site. At any rate, protective measures (replacing milk) could be taken in the event of an accident. Pasture meat doses were not considered because of short half-lives.

Table 3-19 gives doses at the LLNL west site boundary. The importance of eliminating the forage-cow-milk pathway dose by milk replacement is obvious. (At present, no milk cows are pastured near the west perimeter.) The maximum doses of 0.08 rem whole body (submersion) and 0.58 rem thyroid (inhalation) are well below power-reactor siting criteria of 25 rem for a maximum whole body dose and 300 rem for a thyroid dose in an accident (Code of Federal Regulations, Title 10, Chapter 100). Also, these maximum doses are below those recommended by the Environmental Protection Agency for considering protective action of populations at risk.[3-9]

Table 3-20 gives the population dose over the 1,209,000 people in the sector west of the site (see Fig. 2-10). The numbers are conservative since the calculation assumed that every person stood on the centerline of the cloud during its passage. The forage-cow-milk pathway is not considered to add to population exposure west of the site since the milk supply is almost entirely produced elsewhere. Even the maximum estimates are less than 1% of the man-rem dose of approximately 124,000 from natural background.

3.9.2.2.2. Effect of Rainfall on Doses. The radioiodines and ^{138}Cs atoms attach themselves to particulates in the atmosphere and are subject to washout during rainfall. The effect of such washout has been evaluated for the wet season (November-April). The following assumptions have been made:

- A rain rate of 3 mm/h.
- A deposition velocity of 1 cm/s.
- Stability category "D" during rainfall.

Rainfall will decrease the air concentrations (submersion and inhalation doses) of particulate-bound nuclides; there will then be a corresponding increase in the surface deposition.

The following conclusions were reached:

- The rainfall-induced external gamma doses, integrated to infinite time, are less than the inhalation doses at all distances to 50 km for all radioiodines. This result is primarily due to the lower dose conversion constants for external gamma.

Table 3-19. Doses (rem) at the west site boundary, estimated for three meteorological summaries of east winds.

Pathway	Annual		Wet season		Dry season	
	Median	95th percentile[a]	Median	95th percentile	Median	95th percentile
Submersion	0.015	0.048	0.015	0.048	0.015	0.076
Inhalation	0.098	0.36	0.099	0.31	0.10	0.58
Forage-cow-milk	5.5	21.0	5.4	20.0	6.0	35.0

[a] Means the probability is 0.95 that the actual meteorology will provide better diffusion and higher winds than those used here.

Table 3-20. Population doses (man-rem) in the sector west of the Laboratory, for three meteorological summaries of east winds. Population base is 1,209,000 people.

Pathway	Annual		Wet season		Dry season	
	Median	95th percentile[a]	Median	95th percentile	Median	95th percentile
Submersion	4		4	19		11
Inhalation	53	110	58	130	37	150

[a] Means the probability is 0.95 that the actual meteorology will provide better diffusion so that the doses will be less than shown.

- The forage-cow-milk pathway doses for ^{131}I and ^{133}I are increased by precipitation-scavenging by factors which increase with distance downwind. The maximum enhancement factor is about 1 at the site boundary and about 6 at 50 km.
- ^{138}Xe decays to ^{138}Cs; the latter becomes attached to particulates and is available for scavenging. For the 95th-percentile meteorology, the dose enhancement of ^{138}Cs from rainfall is less than a factor of 2 as far out as 50 km.
- Submersion doses are enhanced by attachment of ^{138}Cs particles to fog droplets; the enhancement factor for the 5% probability level is about 1 near the site boundary, increasing to about 2 at 50 km downwind. Radioiodine inhalation doses increased by a factor of 2. Although the droplets, which typically have diameters of 8 to 20 μm,[3-16] are too large to be readily inhaled, They are absorbed in the GI tract after being swallowed.[3-17]

3.9.2.3. Maximum Credible Spill. The maximum credible spill at Livermore is postulated to involve the accidental release of transuranic elements, since large quantities of these materials are handled in Buildings 251 and 332 at LLNL.

For purposes of analyzing this spill, it is assumed that 15 g of ^{244}Cm, as curium oxide, are dispersed throughout a work room in Building 251 (possibly the result of a fire and/or explosion). Fifteen grams, or 1250 Ci, is the largest amount of alpha activity ever expected to be in a single room. Even then, it is within a single glove box for a very short time, until it can be divided into smaller amounts and distributed to other locations within the facility. Again, it is extremely unlikely that this much activity could be involved in a spill. The worst past spills in Building 251 have involved curie amounts approximately 1000 times smaller than this. Present building procedures limit operations to 30 Ci of material at one time, except for rare instances where greater quantities are necessary. Although more transuranic material is usually present in Building 332, resulting in a greater potential hazard, the containment features of this building are superior to those of Building 251. As noted in Section 2.1.6.4, Building 251 is being upgraded.

The amount of ^{244}Cm spilled on the floor of the room that becomes airborne and a respiratory hazard will depend primarily on particle size. The material used in Building 251 is a powdered oxide of curium. No direct measurements concerning what fraction of this material would become airborne have been made; however, the oxide is nominally 400-mesh and it has been estimated that not more than 10% of the particles have a median diameter less than 2 μm. For purposes of this analysis it is assumed that 1.5 grams of the oxide is in the particle-size range of 0.5 μm to 2 μm and therefore respirable. With respect to the fraction that becomes airborne Mishima and Schwendiman[3-18] conclude that for plutonium oxide 0.05% is a satisfactory, safe value for estimating the fraction of material that becomes airborne and consequently a respiratory hazard. We believe that this percentage of airborne material represents a conservative estimate for a Building 251 spill also. Correcting for airborne and respirable fractions, we get a total quantity of respirable airborne ^{244}Cm of 0.0008 g, which is 61 mCi.

The present building filters are of a type that retain 95% (that is, they pass 5%) of the particulates when tested by the National Bureau of Standards stain test. This is equivalent to a retention of 60-65% by the dioctalphthalate (DOP) test. This means that the filters currently installed in Building 251 will pass at the most, 40% of the airborne curium oxide in the spill room to the outside atmosphere.

Thus, for a 10-min release period:

$$\frac{(6.1 \times 10^{-2} \text{ Ci})\ (0.4)(10^{6}\ \mu\text{Ci/Ci})}{(10 \text{ min})60 \text{ s/min}} = 41\ \mu\text{Ci/s}$$

released to the outside atmosphere. At the west site boundary, we apply the diffusion value that is exceeded only 5% of the time, $\chi/Q = 1.3 \times 10^{-3}$ s/m^3. The concentration of curium at the LLNL site boundary is then 5.2×10^{-2} μCi/m^3 during the 10-min release. We next calculate the amount of insoluble curium permanently lodged in the pulmonary region of a person breathing this fence-line cloud and determine the resulting radiation dose. Values found in the International Commission on Radiological Protection's (ICRP) Publication 19, <u>The Metabolism of Compounds of Plutonium and Other Actinides</u> (May 1972), are used for the calculation

Breathing rate = 2×10^4 cm^3/min,

Fraction retained long-term = 0.15,

Mass of pulmonary region = 600 g,

Effective energy per disintegration = 60 MeV,

Half residence time in pulmonary region = 500 days.

The total integrated dose to the pulmonary region from breathing the fence-line cloud during its passage is 5.6 rem. However, the maximum pulmonary dose to the nearest resident is 2.9 rem. For specific organ doses, the range of 1 to 5 rem (whole body) suggested by the EPA for considering protective action can be increased to 3 to 15 rem by applying the guidance of DOE 0524. Since this guidance specifies that allowable doses to specific organs are three times higher than those for the whole body, evacuation is not considered necessary. Off-site dose consequences would be considerably reduced by the current requirement which limits the activity removed from storage to 30 Ci.

Performing a similar analysis for Building 332 involving 4 kg of plutonium would result in a total integrated dose of 4 mrem to the lung. Therefore, the worse credible spill would involve ^{244}Cm in Building 251.

3.9.2.4. Explosions. Review of the potential for an explosion at the DOE Livermore site shows that the most serious one would result from heat-induced rupture and explosion of the 114-m^3 propane tanks at the LLNL Propane Storage Facility near Building 622. These explosions would result in structural damage both on and off site. However, because the tanks are equipped with temperature-activated water deluge systems, such explosions are not considered a credible accident. Other explosions would cause on-site building damage but would not result in significant off-site effects. Radioactive releases as a consequence of an explosion are considered to be no greater than those of radioactive accidents already postulated.

3.9.2.5. Fires. A large building fire having severe environmental consequences, such as destroying the containment features in facilities containing radioactivity, is not likely because of automatic fire protection (sprinklers) and/or fire-resistant building construction. Even if fires did involve areas containing radioactivity, radioactivity releases would not be expected to exceed those already postulated.

Fires are most likely to occur in wooden buildings used as offices, which were built by the Navy. The major off-site consideration of such a fire would be a smoke cloud and the possibility of sparks and burning brands.

The probability of a fire occurring and the consequences of a fire should it occur are mitigated by a full-time Fire Department based at LLNL in Building 324.

3.9.2.6. Release of Chlorine. Most of the toxic materials used at Livermore are used in such small quantities that their accidental release would prove hazardous only to people close to the release, e.g., in the same work room or building.

The largest container of toxic material in use at Livermore is a standard cylinder containing 68 kg of chlorine used to chlorinate the LLNL swimming pool. Figure 3-16 shows the downwind concentrations that would probably not be exceeded (with 95% probability) if a full chlorine cylinder ruptured and all the gas leaked out during a 20-min interval (20 minutes is an estimate of the time to empty a cylinder through a moderate crack).

Note that 1 ppm is the recommended maximum concentration for continuous occupational exposure[3-19] and 300 ppm is the approximate concentration at which severe acute health effects will occur.[3-20] Thus, people will probably smell the chlorine up to 2 km away, but only people in the building with the cylinder will be injured.

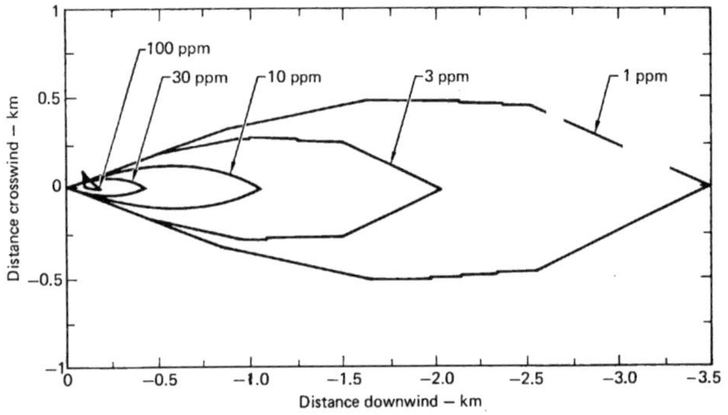

Figure 3-16. Chlorine-concentration isopleth resulting from a 60-g/s release; 95% of the time, concentrations will be less than shown.

3.9.2.7. Transportation of Radioactive Materials. Most of the radioactive shipments entering and leaving LLNL or SNLL are handled by common or contract carriers. Shipping and packaging procedures are set for these carriers by the Department of Transportation (DOT) and will not be considered here.

Radioactive materials that are transported by DOE contractors are handled in two ways. If transportation is intrasite, radioactive materials are double-contained (two contamination barriers). DOT regulations are followed if radioactive materials are moved off-site, including transfer of materials from the Livermore site to Site 300. Table 3-21, covering inbound and outbound shipments of nuclear and other radionuclide shipments at LLNL, shows that the majority of shipments are made by air. An analysis of outbound shipments of radionuclides indicates that materials most frequently shipped are multi-curie ^{192}Ir sources. These shipments are made either to source-production facilities (^{192}Ir has a 74-day half-life) or to the Nevada Test Site where the sources are used in radiography. With the exception of ^{60}Co sources, which are also in the multi-curie range, the remaining shipments cover a wide range of radionuclides, usually at μCi levels.

In section 3.3.3.5 it was noted that DOE operates a flight service between the Livermore Airport and test sites in Nevada. In the past, occasional air shipments of plutonium have been made between Livermore and Nevada, and between DOE's Rocky Flats plant in Colorado and Livermore. Justification for these shipments was based on programmatic need.

Public Law 94-187, effective December 31, 1975, prohibited air transportation of plutonium by DOE or its contractors (except for purposes of national security, public health and safety, or emergency maintenance operations) until such time as ". . . a safe container (package) has been developed and tested which will not rupture under crash- and blast-testing equivalent to the crash and explosion of a high-flying aircraft."

A container developed for the Nuclear Regulatory Commission and DOE has now been approved for use in shipping plutonium by air. Following evaluation by the Aeronautics and Space Engineering Board of the National Research Council, the Council issued a certificate of Compliance No. 0361, dated September 5, 1978. This certificate has an expiration date of September 30, 1983. At present, the Livermore site has no plans for routinely shipping plutonium by air.

There has been only one special air shipment of plutonium from Livermore to date. Several small plutonium sources totaling less than 40 μCi were shipped by air to England for calibration of medical equipment. Approval for this shipment was obtained from DOE Headquarters.

Air flights involving plutonium are now further restricted in accordance with a revision of 10 CFR Part 871, which limits air shipments of plutonium for national security purposes. More specific circumstances are established which would qualify an air shipment to be made for national security reasons and specify that such shipments must be approved by designated managers of DOE Operation Offices. Revised Parts 871.1, 871.3, and 871.4 would read as follows:

Table 3-21. Number of shipments of nuclear materials and other radionuclides to and from LLNL, by mode of transportation.[a]

	Commercial air	DOE contract air	LLNL plane	Commercial truck	DOE truck	Total
Nuclear materials[b]						
Inbound	415	298	46	121	126	1006
Outbound	232	62	89	85	346	814
Total	647	360	135	206	472	1820
Other radionuclides						
Inbound	450		106	129	45	732
Outbound	201	2	51	61	179	494
Total	651	[illegible]	157	190	224	1226

[a] Covers a period from January 1976 through August 1979.
[b] Nuclear materials include normal uranium, depleted uranium, ^{233}U, ^{235}U, ^{238}Pu, ^{239}Pu, ^{242}Pu, ^{241}Am, ^{243}Am, ^{246}Cm, ^{252}Bk, ^{6}Li, ^{2}H, ^{3}H, ^{232}Th and ^{237}Np.

(A) The following DOE air shipments of plutonium are considered as being made for the purposes of national security within the meaning of Section 502(2) of Public Law 94-187:

(1) Shipments made in support of the development, production testing, sampling, maintenance, repair modification or retirement of atomic weapons or devices;

(2) Shipments made pursuant to international agreements for cooperation for mutual defense purposes;

(3) Shipments necessary to respond to an emergency situation involving a possible threat to the national security.

(B) The managers of DOE's Albuquerque, San Francisco, Oak Ridge, Savannah River, and Nevada Operations Offices may authorize air shipments within Subsection (A)(1), on a case by case basis, provided that matter falls within their respective scope of responsibility and that they determine that such shipment is required by air either because:

(1) The delay resulting from using ground transportation methods would have serious adverse impact upon a national security requirement

(2) Safeguards or safety considerations dictate the use of air transportation;

(3) The nature of the item to be shipped necessitates the use of air transportation in order to avoid possible damage which may be expected from other available transportation environments; or

(4) The nature of the items being shipped necessitates rapid shipment by air in order to preserve the chemical, physical, or isotopic properties of the item."

3.9.2.7.1. Transportation Accidents. Packages used to transport materials in support of LLNL operations are designed to prevent the loss or dispersal of their contents under both hypothetical accident and normal transport conditions. These packages include shipments of enriched, depleted, and natural uranium, plutonium, americium, tritium, and other radionuclides. Although most of the shipments shown in Table 3-21 involve μCi quantities of radioactivity, some involve larger quantities. Table 3-22 summarizes these larger-quantity shipments. The data are from 1977 but quantities are not markedly different at present. In order to estimate conservatively the risks of transportation accidents, all transuranics (TRU) were assumed to be ^{239}Pu. Since almost all large-quantity uranium shipments are ^{238}U, all isotopes of uranium are combined and expressed as ^{238}U.

Under certain abnormal conditions, releases of radionuclides to the environment could occur. The NRC provides guidance on various accident severity categories, their probability of occurrence, and the means to assess these accidents through the RADTRAN computer code developed by Sandia Corporation.[3-21] The resulting radiation doses will be overestimated because it is assumed that all

Table 3-22. Average large-quantity shipments of radioactive materials to and from LLNL, 1977.

Material	Outbound			Inbound		
	Curies per shipment	Miles per shipment	Number of shipments	Curies per shipment	Miles per shipment	Number of shipments
U	0.47	1760	129	0.023	810	264
TRU	120	1350	75	92	1530	89
^{3}H	1400	1660	11	850	2500	[illegible]
^{192}Ir	57	1050	14	84	2010	20

the shipments were transported by truck, through suburban areas. In reality, over half the shipments were sent by air transport, which has a lower accident probability. The shipments sent by truck are driven through rural areas, which have lower population density, and therefore less population at risk. Maximum doses for each of the four types of large-quantity shipment are listed in Tables 3-23 and 3-24, by three of eight accident severity categories. Accident severity categories run from the most probable accident which is least likely to release radioactive material (Category III) to a very severe, highly improbable accident (Category VIII) which would release material from most types of containers. The table is limited to three categories to prevent overlap of somewhat redundant information but yet provides the range of possible maximum doses from various accidents. Category III was chosen because Categories I and II are assumed to release no material. Category VI was chosen as an intermediate category and Category VIII was chosen to give maximum possible doses. (Categories I-IV include 99.6% of all possible accidents in an overall accident rate of 1.06×10^{-6} accidents per km under normal circumstances.[3-22]) Maximum individual doses in category VIII are probably overestimated by RADTRAN because it assumes (for meteorological dispersion) a line source extending to 10 m above the surface. However, a true Category VIII accident[3-22] includes a sustained fire (in addition to a high crush force) which would cause the effluent plume to rise considerably, thus ensuring significant dilution before the maximum dose to an individual is given.

Included in Tables 3-23 and 3-24 is an annual radiological risk value. This takes into account the total expected population dose from each accident and multiplies that value by the probability of that accident occurring to give an annual expected man-rem value from accidental releases caused by transportation accidents.

As illustrated by the data, maximum doses from the accidents in Category III for incoming and outgoing shipments lead to small maximum individual and population doses. Much larger doses are encountered in Category VI and VIII accidents. When multiplied by the risk probabilities, however, Category VIII risks are less than Category VI risks.

The annual radiological risk (man-rem) in Tables 3-23 and 3-24 is much less than the population doses (man-rem) that might occur due to a maximum credible accident (Table 3-9), or the annual population dose to the sector west of the Livermore site (Table 3-20). The highest annual radiological risk of 0.027 man-rem is a small proportion of the approximately 124,000 man-rem due to natural radiation.

3.9.3. Emergency Preparedness

The consequences of almost all emergencies are altered by emergency response action. Health and Safety Technicians, safety professionals, a full-time Fire Department, a Medical Department, and/or a

Table 3-23. Radiological consequences from potential accidents involving transportation of radioactive materials--inbound.

Accident category	U	TRU	^{3}H	^{192}Ir
Category III				
Max. individual dose (rem)	2.1×10^{-4}	2.8	0.001	0.004
Critical organ	Lung	Bone	Whole body	Whole body
Population dose (man-rem)	0.02	1.3	0.001	0.007
Annual radiological risk (man-rem)	1.6×10^{-5}	0.028	1.5×10^{-6}	3.1×10^{-6}
Category VI				
Max. individual dose (rem)	0.021	279	0.1	3.5
Critical organ	Lung	Bone	Whole body	Whole body
Population dose (man-rem)	0.16	430	0.14	0.7
Annual radiological risk (man-rem)	1.3×10^{-5}	0.022	1.2×10^{-6}	1×10^{-5}
Category VIII				
Max. individual dose (rem)	0.021	229	0.1	3.5
Critical organ	Lung	Bone	Whole body	Whole body
Population dose (man-rem)	0.16	430	0.14	0.68
Annual radiological risk (man-rem)	4.3×10^{-8}	1×10^{-4}	4.1×10^{-9}	3.5×10^{-8}

Table 3-24. Radiological consequences from potential accidents involving transportation of radioactive materials--outbound.

Accident category	U	TRU	^{3}H	^{192}Ir
Category III				
Max. individual dose (rem)	0.004	3.6	0.002	0.002
Critical organ	Lung	Bone	Whole body	Whole body
Population dose (man-rem)	0.033	5.6	0.002	0.005
Annual radiological risk (man-rem)	4×10^{-4}	0.027	2×10^{-6}	3.2×10^{-6}
Category VI				
Max. individual dose (rem)	0.4	360	0.017	2.4
Critical organ	Lung	Bone	Whole Body	Whole body
Population dose (man-rem)	3.2	56	0.23	0.46
Annual radiological risk (man-rem)	3×10^{-4}	0.002	1.6×10^{-6}	2.5×10^{-6}
Category VIII				
Max. individual dose (rem)	0.4	360	0.017	2.4
Critical organ	Lung	Bone	Whole body	Whole body
Population dose (man-rem)	3.2	56	0.23	0.46
Annual radiological risk (man-rem)	9.3×10^{-7}	7.3×10^{-6}	5.3×10^{-9}	8.7×10^{-9}

Disaster Control Organization are prepared to respond at any time to mitigate the consequences of any accident at the Laboratories. The LLNL Disaster Control Plan, Appendix 3B, summarizes the response to any accident, shows how the Disaster Control Organization is composed and how it is mobilized, and outlines some of the emergency equipment used to cope with and alter the course of an accident. SNLL has a similar emergency plan with sections covering organization and control, warning signals, national emergencies, local emergencies, nuclear weapons or materials incidents/accidents, shutdown and restoration of operations, evacuation, shelter, and defense.

Limiting the emergency preparedness discussion to on-site procedures does not imply that DOE plans are not coordinated with those of local or state agencies for incidents having the potential for off-site consequences. None of the credible accidents described in section 3.9.2 is considered to require off-site action other than notification and monitoring. DOE assesses potential incidents at the Livermore site that might affect the public and coodinates its planning with appropriate agencies having the authority for the protection of public health and safety. Under the DOE Radiological Assistance Plan, DOE makes available its resources, such as personnel, equipment, facilities, data acquisition network, etc., to such state and local authorities. DOE is in agreement with the State Health Department, Radiologic Health Section, relative to the notification and response procedures concerning radiological incidents occurring in California. Accordingly, in the event of a radiological incident that may affect the off-site public, DOE will notify the State Radiologic Health Section via the State Office of Emergency Services' 24-hour telephone station in Sacramento. DOE will coordinate the deployment of its resources at the incident scene in support to the local agency in charge. DOE's radiological assistance does not in any way abridge state or local authority, but works in cooperation with state/local officials in radiological emergency operations.

LLNL has mutual aid agreements with the cities of Livermore and Pleasanton, and with Alameda County. A mutual aid agreement also exists between the Livermore Site and Valley Memorial Hospital. Laboratory emergency forces are prepared to notify local and county officials if an emergency requires off-site actions. The LLNL emergency dispatch center has a number of communication modes connecting it with local emergency centers. These include the Radio Mutual Aid Frequency with Livermore and Pleasanton fire departments and Alameda County emergency control center and the microwave telephone which connects LLNL with all other emergency dispatch centers in the area.

3.10. SAFEGUARDS AND SECURITY

The objectives of the Department of Energy's integrated Safeguards and Security plan are to:

1. Prevent successful malevolent acts involving nuclear materials or facilities, so as to protect the public against risk of death, injury, and property damage that could arise from such acts;

2. Protect classified information from unauthorized disclosures; and

3. Protect government property from theft or malevolence.

In order to carry out these objectives, DOE has developed a capability to characterize and assess current threats with the purpose of obtaining an in-depth understanding of the attributes of potential adversaries, and to apply that understanding to identifying the spectrum of adversaries to be addressed. Various forms of potential actions against nuclear facilities are then evaluated for attractiveness to these potential adversaries. The knowledge gained is directed to (1) developing conceptual approaches which optimize the mix of safeguards and security features into cost-effective safeguards systems, and (2) adapting techniques for modeling and evaluating the effectiveness of these potential systems at selected facilities. The data derived is then used to focus development, test, and evaluation of safeguards equipment and modular systems to meet identified safeguards and security requirements. The developed technology is evaluated in the laboratory and in prototypic operating environments to ensure proper performance prior to installation in an operating facility. As further assurance of adequate protection, the DOE also maintains a strong independent assessment capability to inspect and evaluate safeguards and security systems to assure that they are meeting current requirements and to determine if existing requirements are adequate under current threat conditions.

The objectives of the safeguards and security system at the Livermore site are (1) to assure that government-owned source and nuclear materials are not diverted to unauthorized uses, and (2) to protect DOE facilities against malevolent acts consistent with environmental, health, and safety standards. These objectives are accomplished within an integrated safeguards and security system which includes the elements of physical security, material control, and material accountability.

In their systems role, physical protection procedures and measures provide for immediate detection of special nuclear material misappropriation along with a redundant capability for such immediate detection in the material control procedures. Accountability systems provide primarily for a final evidence that the other two systems have achieved their purpose and, in the event they have not, the accountability systems provide data to facilitate tracking events and isolating the location where the other systems failed.

Physical protection follows the guidelines in DOE Interim Management Directive (IMD) 6102, Physical Protection of Classified Matter and Information. This IMD provides guidance for areas such as access control, detection of intrusion, protective personnel, and protection of classified matter in use, in storage, and in transit.

The access controls at Livermore include personnel identification and physical barriers. The physical barriers consist of cyclone fencing topped with barbed wire. Security guards are at each entrance and at the accesses to restricted areas. Personnel identification is by photo-identification badge which each employee must present to a guard for verification on entering or exiting from any area. Authorized escorts are required when a visitor requests access to a security area. The security personnel also reserve the right to examine packages and briefcases upon entrance or exit to ensure that prohibited materials are not brought into controlled areas nor classified matter removed. Patrols are made on off-working hours to provide security at all times.

Intrusion-detection equipment is used to increase efficiency, reduce guard-force costs, and to complement the other physical barriers. Protective-personnel requirements listed in detail in the DOE IMD 6102 are size and ability to use firearms, tear gas, communications systems, and other protective equipment. Classified material is maintained in security areas while in use; in security containers while in storage; or under protective services while in transit. Unauthorized entry to any area of LLNL or SNLL is forbidden, and warning signs are posted to alert the public of the consequences thereof.

Material control and accounting include process design, material control accounting, measurement of physical inventories, auditing, and statistical programs designed to provide an accurate knowledge of the quantities, location, and disposition of material. Material control begins with the receiving, on-site transportation, and shipment of special nuclear material. It includes operations of vaults for the storage of material and the physical inventories of such vaults. Special nuclear material must also be under observation when in use, in open storage, or in its container, by at least two cleared and authorized persons who may be doing other work but who can give an alarm in time to prevent unauthorized removal. Annual inventories are conducted in those areas outside the vaults where materials are being processed. Accountability systems are composed of those systems which involve bookkeeping data on the location of special nuclear material inventories, and those procedures used to verify, through measurements, the physical inventory of special nuclear material as compared with bookkeeping records.

References

3-1. Hazards Control Progress Report No. 35, Lawrence Livermore National Laboratory, Livermore, CA, UCRL-50007-69-3 (1969).

3-2. Hazards Control Progress Report No. 36, Lawrence Livermore National Laboratory, Livermore, CA, UCRL-50007-70-1 (1970).

3-3. J. L. Cate and T. O. Hoeger, "A Radioisotope Monitoring System for Sewage Effluent," American Ind. Hyg. Journal, October 1972, p. 693.

3-4. J. L. Cate Jr., M. Auyong, and D. W. Rueppel, A Prototype On-Line X-Ray Fluorescence Analyzer for Detecting Metals in Sewage, Lawrence Livermore National Laboratory, Livermore, CA, UCRL-81954 (1979).

3-5. O. H. Slade, Ed., Meterology and Atomic Energy (U. S. Atomic Energy Commission, 1968), p. 97.

3-6. K. F. Wylie, W. A. Bigler, and G. R. Grove, "Biological Half-life of Tritium in Man," Health Physics 9, 911 (1963).

3-7. K. Z. Morgan and J. E. Turner, Principles of Radiation Protection (John Wiley & Sons, New York, 1967), pp. 335-336.

3-8. Report of Committee II on Permissible Dose for Internal Radiation, International Commission on Radiological Protection, Publication 2 (Pergamon Press, Oxford, 1967).

3-9. Basic Radiation Protection Criteria (National Council on Radiation Protection and Measurements, P.O. Box 30175, Washington, DC, 20014, 1971), p. 83.

3-10. U. S. Environmental Protection Agency, Manual of Protective Action Guides and Protective Actions for Nuclear Incidents, U. S. Environmental Protection Agency, Office of Radiation Programs, Washington DC 20460, EPA 520/1-75-001 (1975).

3-11. K. J. Aspinall and J. T. Daniels, Review of UKAEA Criticality Detection and Alarm Systems, AHSB (S), R92 (1965).

3-12. E. R. Woodcock, Potential Magnitude of Criticality Accidents, AHSB, RPR14 (1966).

3-13. W. R. Stratton, A Review of Criticality Accidents, LA-3611 (1967).

3-14. U. S. Nuclear Regulatory Commission, Assumptions Used for Evaluating the Potential Consequences of Accidental Nuclear Criticality in a Plutonium Processing and Full Fabrication Plant, NRC Regulatory Guide 3.35 (May 1977).

3-15. Y. C. Ng et al., Prediction of the Maximum Dosage to Man from the Fallout of Nuclear Devices, IV: Handbook for Estimating the Internal Dose from Radionuclides Released to the Biosphere, Lawrence Livermore National Laboratory, Livermore, CA, UCRL-50163 (1968).

3-16. E. J. Mack, W. J. Eadie, C. W. Rogers, W. C. Kochmond, and R. J. Pilie, A Field Investigation and Numerical Simulation of Coastal Fog, Calspan Corporation, CJ-5055-M-1; NTIS No. N73-18648.

3-17. Limits for Intakes of Radionuclides by Workers, International Commission on Radiological Protection, Publication 30, Part I (Pergamon Press, 1979).

3-18. J. Mishima and L. C. Schwendiman, The Amount and Characteristics of Plutonium Made Airborne Under Thermal Stress, Battelle Northwest Laboratories, Richland, WA, BNWL-SA-3379 (1970).

3-19. Threshold Limit Values for Chemical Substances and Physical Agents in the Workroom Environment (American Conference of Governmental Industrial Hygienists, Cincinnati, Ohio, 1977), p. 12.

3-20. F. A. Patty, Industrial Hygiene and Toxicology, Vol. II (Interscience Publishers, New York, 1963), p. 847.

3-21. J. M. Taylor and S. L. Daniel, RADTRAN: A Revised Computer Code to Analyze Transportation of

3-22. Radioactive Material, Sandia National Laboratories, Albuquerque, NM (to be published).

U. S. Nuclear Regulatory Commission, Final Environmental Statement on Transportation of Radioactive Material by Air and Other Modes, NUREG-0170, Vol. 1 & 2 (1977).

4. UNAVOIDABLE ADVERSE ENVIRONMENTAL IMPACTS

Environmental impacts described in Section 3 which are unavoidable consequences of on-going operations at DOE Livermore laboratories are:

- Land use.
- Utilization of natural resources and energy.
- Laboratory-generated traffic on East Avenue.
- Impact of operational releases of radioactive and nonradioactive effluents.
- Radiation doses to the public.

4.1. LAND USE

Land use discussed in Section 3.2 involves the commitment of approximately 30 km^2 (including Site 300) to government use. Such a commitment curtails for an indefinite period diversity and range of potential uses of the property. As noted, the present use of the land at Livermore was not the initial commitment to government use; when the Atomic Energy Commission took over the property it was an "abandoned airfield" held by the Department of Defense. Since LLNL began operations in 1952, site improvements in buildings and landscaping have converted much of the area to a campus environment. SNLL has made similar improvements since 1956. Accordingly, if diversion from its pre-World War II use as an agricultural area is to be considered adverse, DOE's Livermore site improvements are balancing mitigating factors which should be considered beneficial. New construction is anticipated to have only minimal environmental effects. These will be similar to other recent programs which have had no major environmental effect (see section 2.1.7.2).

4.2. NATURAL RESOURCES AND ENERGY

4.2.1. Water

During 1979, LLNL and SNLL used 9.6×10^5 m^3 of domestic water, essentially unchanged from the 9.5×10^5 m^3 used in 1978, and only slightly higher than the 8.5×10^5 m^3 used in 1977 during the California drought. As described in section 2, this supply comes from the Hetch Hetchy line serving San Francisco. The above quantity is about 0.25% of that used by San Francisco during the same period.

4.2.2. Electrical Power

During 1979, LLNL and SNLL consumed 870 TJ of electricity, up from the 830 TJ used in 1978. Increased usage of electric power is due to additional staff and the requirements of the resulting programmatic effort.

4.2.3. Natural Gas

During 1979, LLNL and SNLL consumed 1.5 x 10^7 m^3 of natural gas. The consumption was unchanged from the quantity used in 1978.

4.3. LABORATORY-GENERATED TRAFFIC ON EAST AVENUE

Although vehicular traffic may enter LLNL from either Vasco Road on the west or Greenville Road on the east, the greatest traffic is on East Avenue. Most of this traffic is due to LLNL and SNLL personnel; on an average work day there are more than 2500 automobiles in the parking lots. Truck traffic also uses East Avenue, since most of these obtain access permits to LLNL at the South Main Gate Pass Office and must enter through this gate.

During morning and evening peak periods such traffic is an adverse impact to residents living on East Avenue. Cost of maintaining the roadbed is increased due to DOE laboratories' traffic.

4.4. OPERATIONAL RELEASES OF RADIOACTIVE AND NONRADIOACTIVE EFFLUENTS

Accidental releases of both radioactive and nonradioactive effluents were discussed in section 3.9. Accidents due to human error (including inadequate engineering controls) can be minimized. This section addresses those releases that, although technologically reduced to the lowest practicable level, occur as a consequence of normal programmatic activities.

4.4.1. Radioactive Releases

Radioactive airborne and liquid releases from the Livermore site in 1980 are listed in Table 3-1.

4.4.2. Nonradioactive Releases

There are no significant airborne releases of hazardous nonradioactive materials. As noted,[2-1] LLNL perimeter air filters are analyzed for beryllium content to detect possible releases of this material from beryllium machining operations. The data indicated levels approximately three orders of magnitude below those set as applicable standards (40 CFR, Part 61). At Site 300, release of radioactive and toxic materials to the environment is an unavoidable consequence of high-explosive tests involving these materials. However, as noted in section 2, air samplers are continuously operated at ten locations within the boundaries of the site. Analyses of these samples show concentrations well below DOE guide levels. Indeed, the beryllium levels observed can be accounted for by resuspension of surface soil containing naturally occurring beryllium. Accordingly, the off-site environmental impact from radioactive or toxic materials resulting from Site 300 operations is negligible.

Similarly, due to the remoteness of the Site, there is little off-site impact from annoying noises or damaging overpressures. Based on meteorological measurements made twice daily, a limit is set on the weight of high explosives that can be detonated without impact on populated areas. In spite of these precautions there are occasional incidents involving a noticeable overpressure, which are caused by an unexpected shift in the direction of the upper winds. Such incidents are rare, but must be considered unavoidable environmental impacts. At Livermore research levels of chemicals are periodically released via laboratory fume hoods. Experience has shown that these releases constitute no off-site environmental concern. There have been occasional pH excursions in both LLNL and SNLL sewer effluents, some of which have required diversion at the Livermore Water Reclamation Plant. These incidents are listed in Appendix 3A.

4.5. RADIATION DOSE TO THE PUBLIC

This matter has been addressed in section 3.7. The largest potential for radiological dose on man from DOE's Livermore operations is from LLNL's 14-MeV neutron generator in Building 212. Radioactive airborne effluents include ^{41}Ar from the LLNL reactor, Building 281; ^{13}N – ^{15}O from LLNL's linear accelerator, Building 194; and ^{3}H, principally from LLNL's Building 331.

The basic subject of this environmental statement is the question of whether the present and proposed operations at the two DOE laboratories in Livermore, California, can be carried on without causing unacceptable environmental impacts.

Based upon the evaluation of environmental impacts presented in this statement, it appears that these laboratory operations can continue with adequate assurance of environmental safety. Nevertheless, DOE has examined the following alternative courses of action:

- Plant shutdown and site decommissioning.
- Total or partial plant relocation.
- Scaling down those operations having the greatest potential for adverse environmental impact.
- Use of alternate technologies having reduced environmental impact.

5.2. PLANT SHUTDOWN AND SITE DECOMMISSIONING

Plant shutdown and site decommissioning would eliminate the environmental impacts arising from both normal operations and those resulting from potential accidents. Such action would jeopardize the attainment of present national goals in national defense. Even if this step were taken, decommissioning of the Livermore site would involve decontamination of several large facilities, and continual radiological safety surveillance in the vicinity of such areas as the Site 300 burial areas. Thus, plant shutdown may not permit unrestricted use of these facilities.

Such a shutdown would also cause a loss of much of the capital investment in facilities and equipment and a significant socioeconomic loss to nearby communities.

5.3. TOTAL OR PARTIAL PLANT RELOCATION

Some parts of the work carried out at LLNL parallel research carried out elsewhere. Similarly, some parts of the work done at SNLL relate to work done at Sandia National Laboratories-Albuquerque and elsewhere. While these efforts are not duplicative, the existence of other weapons laboratories is a basis for considering the feasibility and practicality of the alternatives of plant relocation.

The sociological and economic impact on the Livermore area resulting from total relocation of LLNL and SNLL would be difficult to balance against possible environmental benefits. As noted in section 3.8.1, the population of Livermore has increased from about 4000 to nearly 50,000 since LLNL began operation in 1952. Today the Livermore Valley is part of the Bay Area suburbia, and many people live here and work elsewhere. However, about 50% of the LLNL and SNLL staff of approximately 8,200 live in the Livermore area. Assuming an average family size of four, then about 20% of the Livermore area's population is directly dependent on DOE employment. Regardless of the relocation site (assuming it to be beyond reasonable commute distance), many people would elect to stay in Livermore and seek employment elsewhere. Employment for the specialized talents of many staff members would be difficult to find. Consequently, many of those who did not move with the Laboratory would be forced to leave Livermore. Such action would adversely affect local business and property values.

The time required for orderly site relocation would result in major programmatic interruption. In nuclear weapons development programs, these delays would affect Defense Department planning, scheduling, budget commitments, and our nuclear defense position would deteriorate. Similar delays would be experienced by energy and biomedical programs. Finding alternate utilization for the physical plant facilities would pose a problem. With the exception of the office-type structures, most of the DOE buildings have special design features unique to a given program requirement. For the most part, these buildings would require major modification for nonnuclear application. The air pollution potential of the Livermore Valley precludes the use of the property by heavy industry. Accordingly, available options for its land use are limited to agriculture and light industry.

5.3.1. Partial Relocation

Operations such as the 14-MeV neutron accelerator (in Building 212), Nuclear Chemistry Operations (Building 251), Tritium Research Facility (Building 331), and the Plutonium Facility (Building 332) at LLNL and Sandia's Tritium Research Facility all have potential for adverse impact. These operations could be relocated at the Nevada Test Site (NTS). Such a location might seem attractive because NTS is an area geographically remote from population centers and is owned and operated by DOE. Furthermore, many areas within NTS have been exposed to the impact of previous nuclear testing. As a result, the additional radiation impact of the operations listed above would be minimal.

However, such action is not a logical or desirable alternative. Discounting the cost of relocating and staffing the above facilities, the geographical separation from Livermore would reduce them to satellite operations. As such, work performance on those projects would lose the benefit of the close proximity to highly unique support activities and other scientific projects that on-site facilities enjoy, and which is essential for smooth programmatic progress.

5.3.2. Relocation Within the Livermore Site

Relocating an operation to reduce its environmental impact is seldom cost-effective compared with instituting properly designed engineering and management controls. However, there are exceptions, and LLNL's 14-MeV neutron accelerator in Building 212 is a case in point. This building, which was used as a drill hall by the Navy in World War II, is within 30 m of the southern perimeter fence adjacent to East Avenue. Because of its proximity to a public thoroughfare (East Avenue), the operation of the neutron accelerator at higher flux rates is prohibited by the high cost of adequate shielding. Most of these experiments are now performed in a new facility (Building 292) in the northwest quadrant of LLNL.

5.4. OPERATIONAL MODIFICATION

Modifying those operations having the greatest potential for adverse environmental impact is a practical alternative. At the two Livermore laboratory facilities, emphasis is placed on direct measures to reduce possible environmental impact rather than on simple workload reduction. An effective effluent-reduction program based on good engineering and proper management is reducing the environmental impacts without sacrificing plant productivity.

At Livermore, the effort in any given research area is regulated by programmatic need. Some of these programs have a significant potential for adverse environmental impact. Those in this category receive special attention to assure that environmental effects are reduced to the minimum. As an example, large quantities of beryllium were processed at Livermore during the late 1950s and early 1960s in support of a specific program. These operations, performed in gloved enclosures, were thoroughly monitored to assure that airborne beryllium was not released. As a result of those precautions, after the program was complete, beryllium contamination was limited to the enclosures and process lines. Recent soil samples taken at LLNL site perimeters show beryllium levels typical of those naturally occurring in Livermore Valley soils.

In other instances, the scale of operations has been reduced, which resulted in lessening the environmental impact. In the fall of 1973 methods were being considered for reducing the levels of ^{41}Ar released by LLNL's pool-type reactor. However, when the operating schedules were reduced from two shifts per day to one shift, the fence-line doses were also reduced. In 1974 use of a neutron-absorbing gadolinium paint in the east thermal column combined with the shorter operating schedule further reduced the ^{41}Ar released to the environment. Through this succession of measures the problem of ^{41}Ar production was reduced to the lowest practicable level and far less than the permissable standard. Due to a lack of projected need this reactor was shut down in 1980.

5.5. USE OF ALTERNATE TECHNOLOGIES

Since DOE's operations at Livermore are of a research nature and are subject to change with programmatic requirements, there is usually little opportunity to choose between technologies. Often it is because a technology has been developed that an operation can be undertaken at all. Each new operation is reviewed for possible adverse environmental impacts, and procedures are incorporated to minimize any such possible effects.

LLNL and SNLL have been quick to shift to alternate equipment or methods when technological or environmental advantages appeared. In fact, these two laboratories have been innovative in devising better techniques and in finding improved technologies.

6. RELATIONSHIPS BETWEEN SHORT-TERM USES AND LONG-TERM PRODUCTIVITY

Prior to World War II the present DOE property at Livermore was used for cattle grazing and occasional planting of grain used principally for cattle feed. Similarly, prior to its acquisition in 1955, the Site 300 area was used for grazing. For the most part the steep terrain at the latter site prevented its being tilled.

Since World War II the Livermore site has been committed to non-agricultural use, first as the Naval Air Station, and later as the site of the Lawrence Livermore Laboratory and the Sandia Laboratory.

These Livermore properties could be used for home construction; however, without the DOE Laboratories there would be less need for additional housing. It is also possible to return these properties to agricultural uses, but it would not appear cost-effective to destroy the Laboratory buildings, utilities, and streets to convert the area to such use. Indeed, the Alameda County Planning Commission has zoned some of the land surrounding the Livermore site for industrial use, indicating that the county has determined the land's highest value can be realized by industrial development, not agriculture.

Due to the nature of the high-explosive work at Site 300, there is considerable distance separating the facilities. Consequently, only a small fraction of the total land area is occupied by buildings and returning the land to use for grazing would be relatively easy.

The Livermore Area General Plan is based on an increase in population to 173,536 by 1990. This, coupled with reports from other agencies, indicates that the expected long-term function of the Livermore Valley is to provide suburban housing, some agriculture, and light industry for the forseeable future. Thus the long-term productivity of the land will be maximized if DOE property continues as a research institution or if the buildings and facilities are used for some form of industry.

7. RELATIONSHIPS OF THE LIVERMORE OPERATIONS TO LAND USE PLANS, POLICIES, AND CONTROLS

Land usage at these sites does not appear to be in conflict with any known state, county, or city land use plans, policies, or controls.

The Livermore General Plan has been recently revised. Citizen's committees have participated in formulating goals for the new General Plan, which include

- A Livermore area growth rate near the national average of 1.8%.
- Preserving the rural and native character of the Livermore area.
- Planning a feeling of openness in urban areas.

The growth rate of the laboratories and the implementation of their long-range plans are in balance with provisions of this Livermore General Plan.

The proposed new entrance to LLNL from Vasco Road (section 2.1.7.3) has been reviewed by Alameda County and the City of Livermore and is consistent with their plans. Since some of the land surrounding the Livermore laboratories has been judged to be prime or unique farmland, the impact of the new entrance was reviewed using the Council of Environmental Quality guidance.[7-1]

The land needed for the new access road, which is privately owned, is not now being farmed and there are no plans to use it as such. The Alameda County Planning Commission has determined that the land's highest value can be realized by industry and has zoned the area for industrial development. Accordingly, plans for the road construction are proceeding.

There are no known potential conflicts with plans of any other agency in continuing operation of Site 300.

The Association of Bay Area Governments Regional Plan 1970-1990 proposed public ownership of a permanent open-space area for recreational and scenic value to the public; areas west and south of Site 300 may be designated for this purpose. The Alameda County General Plan proposes major park and recreation uses along Tesla Road west of the Site. The San Joaquin General Plan for open space uses designates Corral Hollow Road as a recreational route. There does not appear to be any conflict with the Site if any or all of these plans mature.

In summary, although the DOE laboratories, located on federal property, are surrounded by land that is undergoing change with respect to local use planning, the LLNL and SNLL sites do not conflict with and are integrated into local land use master plans.

Reference

7-1. Executive Office of the President, Council on Environmental Quality, Analysis of Impacts on Prime and Unique Farmland in Environmental Impact Statements, Memorandum for Heads of Agencies, August 30, 1976.

8. IRREVERSIBLE AND IRRETRIEVABLE COMMITMENT OF RESOURCES

Irreversible and irretrievable commitments of resources include those consumed by LLNL and SNLL operations and those that cannot be reasonably expected to revert to a natural state if the DOE structures were removed.

Total investment in plant and equipment at the DOE Livermore laboratories is currently estimated at about $1.5 billion. This represents the current replacement cost of each facility constructed and equipped during the period from 1952 through September 30, 1979 (1956 to September 30, 1979 for Sandia). Although not anticipated in the foreseeable future, these facilities could be demolished and much of the equipment recovered for use, and the land returned to its pre-World War II use.

As discussed in section 2.3.11, small areas within LLNL exhibit radiation levels slightly above background; these would require decontamination in event the site were decommissioned. Decontamination costs could not be predicted accurately until such time as specific decommissioning requirements become known.

Resources consumed or used by DOE's Livermore operations are discussed in section 3.3. In summary, use during 1979 was as follows:

- Manpower 6906 man-years
- Water 9.6×10^5 m^3
- Natural gas 1.5×10^7 m^3
- Fuel oil 988 m^3
- Electricity 870 TJ
- Gasoline 1528 m^3
- Diesel 118 m^3
- Jet fuel 761 m^3

9. ENVIRONMENTAL TRADE-OFF ANALYSIS

9.1. INTRODUCTION

The economic and environmental costs associated with the continuing and future operation of the DOE laboratories at Livermore must be weighed against the national security and the technical, environmental, and socioeconomic cultural benefits to be derived from this proposed action. The projected costs for LLNL and SNLL operations are considered to be commensurate with the magnitude of the effort involved. As previously demonstrated in this EIS, the environmental impacts resulting from these operations are limited. As discussed in sections 3 and 4, these costs include the following items:

- The temporary use is required of approximately 30 km^2 of land originally used for grazing and now occupied by the Laboratory facilities and testing area.
- There will be the continued impact of over 8000 employees and their families on the neighboring community.
- A slight continued potential for accidents is inherent with research and development operations.
- Contamination with radioactive materials will be minimized as much as is possible, but the potential will continue for possible small radiation dosage.
- There will be continued resource utilization including manpower, water, electrical power, and fossil fuels, as summarized in section 8.

Conversely, the benefits of continued operation of the Laboratories as discussed in section 2 include:

- Increased national security from nuclear weapons development.
- Energy-systems development programs are directed toward systems to produce power. These include studies of fusion systems of both the magnetic and inertial (laser) containment types and fossil fuel, geothermal, and solar development programs.
- Other technological development programs of value to the nation are those of laser isotope separation, electronic systems, and improved chemical explosives.
- Biomedical, radiobiological, and radioecological studies and innovations in computer languages indicate future benefits.

These benefits clearly substantiate the need for continued operation in the light of national defense and energy requirements.

A qualitative comparison of the costs and benefits of the alternatives discussed in section 5 can be made as follows. The analysis balances the costs and benefits of the present operations as described in sections 2, 3, 4, 6, 7, and 8 (which is the alternative of taking no action) against the different alternative actions described in section 5.

9.2. ALTERNATIVES

- Plant Shutdown and Site Decommissioning. This alternative would result in the termination of operations in weapons development and energy research at Livermore and the elimination of any potential environmental damage. The cost of this alternative would involve facility decontamination and disposal of radioactive materials. Benefits from this action would be elimination of both radioactive and nonradioactive effluents to the Livermore Valley environment. Penalties of this alternative would be a downshift in the national defense and energy research efforts, and the termination of the missions of DOE's Livermore Laboratories. Such an alternative would also result in an economic impact due to the loss of about 8000 jobs in the area.
- Total or Partial Relocation. The cost of relocation would be extremely high since new construction of facilities would be necessary and personnel changes would involve much time and effort. The cost of maintaining the programs at another site would be at least comparable to those at the present site. Since the environmental impact from the Livermore operations is minimal, relocation is not a cost-effective alternative.
- Operational Modification. This alternative would involve modifying those operations with the greatest potential for adverse environmental impacts. Benefits would be the reduction of some environmental impact; however, the penalty would be programmatic interruption during such modifications and the cost of such modifications.
- Use of Alternate Technologies. This alternative would result in continuing the present operations of the DOE laboratories in research and development with the capability to use the technologies developed through these operations. Benefits of this alternative are an optimization of the programmatic effort at Livermore, and the protection of the population and the environment by emphasizing those technologies which minimize the adverse environmental impacts.

9.3. CONCLUSION

Based on the discussion of the general alternatives available and the information presented in the other sections of this assessment, it is concluded that DOE operations at Livermore should continue in the present manner in research and development. Such action provides the capability to use any new technologies that are developed through the present programs, and continually review and upgrade the programs to minimize any possible adverse environmental impacts.

10. COMMENTS

The Department of Energy (DOE) issued a Draft Environmental Impact Statement (DEIS) on the Livermore Site in September 1978. That DEIS (DOE/EIS-0028-D) assessed the environmental impact associated with current and continuing operation of both the Lawrence Livermore National Laboratory (LLNL) and the Sandia National Laboratories-Livermore (SNLL). Public review and comment on the DEIS were invited with the closing date for receiving comments being December 22, 1978. A total of 26 comment letters were received from government agencies, organizations and individuals. To provide further opportunity for public comment, a public hearing on the DEIS was held in Livermore on April 12, 1979.

Major substantive issues raised through letters received and at the public hearing concerned: (1) earthquake safety of continued operations of the laboratories on the Livermore site, (2) employee health effects associated with Livermore operations, (3) the maximum credible accident, (4) cost-benefit analysis of Livermore operations, (5) emergency response plans, and (6) the transportation of radioactive materials in and out of the Livermore site.

This section contains the comment letters and the response to each.

DEPARTMENT OF HEALTH, EDUCATION, AND WELFARE
PUBLIC HEALTH SERVICE
FOOD AND DRUG ADMINISTRATION
ROCKVILLE, MARYLAND 20857

:78

Mr. W. H. Pennington
Director
Division of Program Review
and Coordination
Office of NEPA Affairs
Department of Energy
Washington, D.C. 20545

Dear Mr. Pennington:

The Department of Health, Education, and Welfare has reviewed the health aspects of the Draft Environmental Impact Statement, DOE/EIS-0028D, Livermore Site, Livermore, California and has the following comments to offer.

Chapter 2, Section 2.1.8 Environmental Monitoring

The environmental monitoring program as outlined should provide sufficient data for determining the effectiveness of control measures at LLL and SLL. The sampling frequency and analyses for the radionuclides of concern should provide early warning of any unplanned releases to the environment.

Chapter 3, Section 3.5.1 Radioactive Waste Management

Radioactive waste from the varied research programs at LLL and SLL is described for the major sources. Sufficient detail has not been provided to fully assess each source. However, it appears from the presentation that the system for handling the liquid and solid waste and the airborne effluent is adequate for protecting the health and safety of the workers and the public. The data on airborne and liquid radioactive effluents released in 1976 as shown in Table 3-1 are within acceptable limits and would support such a conclusion.

Chapter 3, Section 3.7 Radiological Impact

Sufficient data are not presented to permit a detailed evaluation of the radiological impact from operations at the DOE Livermore laboratories. However, the limited data presented indicates that the annual dose to the nearest downwind resident from all DOE gaseous effluents is estimated to be less than 2 mrem. This dose is well within acceptable radiation protection guidelines. It is also stated in this section that the radiological impact is assessed on a continuing basis by LLL's Hazards Control Department, and the results are presented in an annual report. It is noted that the only reference to the findings is that in 1976 all levels of radioactivity observed were well below the appropriate concentration guides. Additional data would be helpful in assessing the environmental impact.

Chapter 3, Section 3.9 Accident Analysis

The discussions and presentation of data on consequences of postulated accidents has adequately assessed the issues that impact on public health and safety. However, it is noted from Table 3-16 that the dose from the forage-cow-milk pathway is higher than desirable. Milk replacement is a protective action that can be taken after an unplanned release; however it should not be depended upon to reduce the population dose to the exclusion of adding additional controls to reduce the source.

Continued normal operations at the Livermore site can be expected to result in an minimal environmental impact and to provide for protection of the public health and safety.

Sincerely yours,

Bernard Shleien for

Charles L. Weaver
Consultant
Bureau of Radiological Health

Department of Energy
Washington, D.C. 20545

DEC 4 1978

G. Facer, DP
A. Schoen, EV
J. Swinebroad, EV
R. Stern, EV
S. Miller, OGC
D. Smith, AD
R. Miller, AL
C. Lindeken, LLL (2)
J. Jeutten, SAN

Library, Room 1223, 20 Mass Avenue
G. Dennis, AL
G. Pitchford, CH (2)
R. Blackledge, ID
J. Felton, OR
T. Bauman, RL
D. Cook, SAN
D. Peek, SR
D. Jackson, NV

COMMENTS ON DRAFT ENVIRONMENTAL IMPACT STATEMENT, DOE/EIS-0028-D, LIVERMORE SITE, LIVERMORE, CALIFORNIA, SEPTEMBER 1978

Attached for your information or placement in your respective public document room for public inspection is a copy of comment letter No. 1 received on the subject draft statement from Mr. Charles L. Weaver, Consultant, Bureau of Radiological Health, Department of Health, Education, and Welfare, dated November 8, 1978.

W. H. Pennington
Division of NEPA Affairs
Office of Environmental Compliance
and Overview/EV

Attachment

Response to Letter 1

DOE RESPONSE TO LETTER FROM THE DEPARTMENT OF HEALTH, EDUCATION AND WELFARE

In response to your comments on sections 2.1.8 and 3.7, we have included the 1980 LLNL Environmental Monitoring Report.

Regarding your comments on section 3.5.1, the cumulative radioactive waste impacts for the entire site are found in Table 3-1 and in section 2.1.6.10. Since the total impact is small, we have not provided impacts for each source.

As to your comment on section 3.9, the Livermore Valley has no pastured dairy herds so the population exposure following a criticality accident from the forage-cow-milk pathway is limited to a few individuals who maintain family milk cows (and only if those cows are not on purchased feed). We take all reasonable precautions to reduce the risk of all accidents, especially nuclear criticalities. Dose reduction through milk replacement is only one of those precautions.

UNITED STATES DEPARTMENT OF AGRICULTURE

SOIL CONSERVATION SERVICE

2828 Chiles Road, Davis, CA 95616

November 8, 1978

W. H. Pennington, Director
Division of Program Review
and Coordination
Office of NEPA Affairs
Department of Energy
Washington, D. C. 20545

Dear Mr. Pennington:

We acknowledge receipt of the draft environmental impact statement for Livermore Site, Livermore in Alameda County, California, that was addressed to Mr. Barry R. Flamm and then referred to the Soil Conservation Service for review and comment.

We have reviewed the above draft and have the following comments.

Provisions for erosion control and water management during construction were not adequately addressed nor were the effects of water discharge from project lands.

We suggest you consider the following erosion control measures.

1. During construction, surface runoff should be collected on site and disposed to the point of discharge in order that it will not effect the normal flow in any stream or water course. Where drainage swales are used to divert surface water away from buildings, etc., they should be sodded or planted to prevent excessive erosion.

2. On site 300, debris basins should be constructed to trap and store sediment from eroding areas in order to protect stream channels below the installation from damage by excessive sedimentation and chemical pollution.

We appreciate the opportunity to review and comment on this proposed project.

Sincerely,

FRANCIS C. H. LUM
State Conservationist

cc: R. M. Davis, Administrator, USDA, SCS, Washington, D. C. 20013
Director, Office of Federal Activities (Mail Code A-104), Environmental Protection Agency, Room 537, West Tower, 401 M Street, S.W., Washington, D. C. 20460

Department of Energy
Washington, D.C. 20545

DEC 4 1978

G. Facer, DP
A. Schoen, EV
J. Swinebroad, EV
R. Stern, EV
S. Miller, OGC
D. Smith, AD
R. Miller, AL
C. Lindeken, LLL (2)
J. Jeutten, SAN
Library, Room 1223, 20 Mass Avenue
G. Dennis, AL
G. Pitchford, CH (2)
R. Blackledge, ID
J. Felton, OR
T. Bauman, RL
D. Cook, SAN
D. Peek, SR
D. Jackson, NV

COMMENTS ON DRAFT ENVIRONMENTAL IMPACT STATEMENT, DOE/EIS-0028-D, LIVERMORE SITE, LIVERMORE, CALIFORNIA, SEPTEMBER 1978

Attached for your information or placement in your respective public document room for public inspection is a copy of comment letter No. 2 received on the subject draft statement from Mr. Francis C. H. Lum, State Conservationist, Soil Conservation Service, Department of Agriculture, dated November 8, 1978.

W. H. Pennington
Division of NEPA Affairs
Office of Environmental Compliance
and Overview/EV

Attachment

Response to Letter 2

DOE RESPONSE TO LETTER FROM THE DEPARTMENT OF AGRICULTURE

We appreciate your concern for erosion control at both the Livermore and Site 300 locations. Suggestions for protecting against erosion control associated with site drainage and building landscaping are being considered.

Cecilie Hoffman
350 Soquel Ave #9
Santa Cruz Ca 95060

SAN JOSE, CA
PM
NOV
1978

DEPARTMENT OF ENERGY
W. H. Pennington
Mail Station E201
GTN
Washington D.C. 20545

[illegible] Laurence Livermore Lab — Nov 27

[illegible] Sirs and Madames of the Dept. of Energy

[illegible] you review the Environmental Impact Report filed by the Laurence Livermore Lab in California, please consider this resident's opinion.

I would prefer to see the plutonium cache put into an underground installation; it has no business in the highly populated area of Northern California.

I urge you to act on behalf maintaining the genetic integrity of the people in Northern California, and preventing the high probability of lung cancer in the population here. — Thank you. Sincerely Cecilie Hoffman

Department of Energy
Washington, D.C. 20545

DEC 8 1978

G. Facer, DP	Library, Room 1223, 20 Mass Avenue
A. Schoen, EV	G. Dennis, AL
J. Swinebroad, EV	G. Pitchford, CH (2)
R. Stern, EV	R. Blackledge, ID
S. Miller, OGC	J. Felton, OR
D. Smith, AD	T. Bauman, RL
R. Miller, AL	D. Cook, SAN
C. Lindeken, LLL (2)	D. Peek, SR
J. Jeutten, SAN	D. Jackson, NV

COMMENTS ON DRAFT ENVIRONMENTAL IMPACT STATEMENT, DOE/EIS-0028-D, LIVERMORE SITE, LIVERMORE, CALIFORNIA, SEPTEMBER 1978

Attached for your information or placement in your respective public document room for public inspection is a copy of comment letter No. 3 received on the subject draft statement from Ms. Cecilie Hoffman, Santa Cruz, California, dated November 27, 1978.

W. H. Pennington
Division of NEPA Affairs
Office of Environmental Compliance
and Overview/EV

Attachment

DOE RESPONSE TO LETTER FROM MS. CECILIE HOFFMAN

As discussed in the DEIS, geographical separation of any of the research projects from Livermore would lose the benefit of proximity to highly unique support activities that is essential for smooth programmatic progress. Consequently, your suggestion of moving plutonium operations to an underground storage area is not practical at this time.

United States Department of the Interior

OFFICE OF THE SECRETARY
WASHINGTON, D.C. 20240

In Reply Refer To:
ER 78/929

DEC 8 1978

Mr. W. H. Pennington
Director
Division of Program Review
and Coordination
Office of NEPA Affairs
Department of Energy
Washington, D.C. 20545

Dear Mr. Pennington:

Thank you for your letter of September 18, 1978, requesting our views and comments on the draft environmental impact statement for continued operation of the Livermore Site, Alameda County, California. We have the following comments arranged by areas of jurisdiction and special expertise.

General

Neither the "summary" nor the "background" chapters seem to give a clear description of the proposed action other than that it is a continuation of current activities. When the reader reaches page 2-20 the concept of future planning is introduced with reference to the Livermore Site Development Plan. What seems to be unclear is whether "continuation of current activities" means at the present level or at an incrementally higher level. The list of alternatives does not shed any further light on this problem.

If the purpose of the statement is to assess only the impacts of continuing present operations at Livermore, then analysis appears to be generally adequate. However, if the statement is intended to assess the impacts of enlarged operations according to the Livermore Site Development Plan, then we have serious reservations concerning the adequacy of the environmental analysis. We suggest that this apparent problem be eliminated by clarifying the proposed action, reassessing the analysis in Chapter 3, and expanding the list of alternatives to include the residual possibility of a higher level of operation (if this is valid).

Cultural Resources

Cultural resources are not adequately addressed. Archeological Consulting and Research Services, under contract to Lawrence Livermore Laboratory, conducted a preliminary archeological reconnaissance of Site 300 which documented seven archeological sites. However, there is no evidence of further efforts by the Department of Energy to follow up on this discovery by evaluating the sites for their significance and potential inclusion in the National Register of Historic Places.

The Federal cultural resource protection guidelines (36 CFR 800) set forth Federal agency responsibilities to identify historic and archeological sites within the area of impact of Livermore Site operations, evaluate them against the National Register Criteria (36 CFR 800.10), and request a determination of eligibility. The agency must coordinate these activities with the appropriate State Historic Preservation Officer.

Apparently damage to archeological sites on Site 300 has already occurred. Continued high explosive testing, as well as planned construction of a 15 MeV linear accelerator on the site, will undoubtedly increase the loss of cultural information. DOE should contact the SHPO immediately to evaluate the significance of the sites known on Site 300, and to develop a mitigation plan incorporating measures recommended by the SHPO and the consulting archeologists.

Fish and Wildlife Resources

Our records show that in December 1975 the GSA deeded approximately 100 acres of surplus AEC property on the east side of Site 300 to the California Department of Fish and Game for use as a wildlife preserve. The statement should discuss any potential effects of continued testing and future construction on the wildlife at the Corral Hollow Ecological Preserve.

Appendix 2D lists the biota found on the Lawrence and Sandia Laboratory sites near Livermore. A similar listing for site 300 would be desirable. The bald eagle is listed in this appendix, but no treatment is given in the text of the statement concerning the effects, if any, of project activities on this endangered species.

The draft statement indicates that an area containing the rare plant amsinckia grandiflora has been roped off. The statement should also explain any existing or planned project activities in or near the area, particularly upgrade from these plants.

Seismicity

The discussion of geology and seismicity (p. 2-47 and 48, sec. 2.3.3) should mention that the Las Positas fault could involve the Livermore site in addition to the Sandia site. Further, the Verona fault could be a continuation of the Las Positas fault and this greater length of fault would have significant implications for the extent of potential displacement. The environmental statement should clearly indicate whether there are critical structures at the Livermore site, and if so, should give their location with respect to faults.

We must disagree with the assertion (p. 2-48, lines 7-8) that "there is no evidence of faulting that would produce surface ground ruptures in close proximity to the TRL." The Las Positas and Verona faults have demonstrated geologically recent relative movement of young deposits and soil of probable Holocene age.

We suggest that a note should be added to the geologic and seismic data in appendix 2A referring to the discussion of more recent information in section 2.3.3 (p. 2-48) based on mapping by the U. S. Geological Survey (reference 2-3).

Groundwater

The discussion of the groundwater monitoring program (p. 2-31, sec. 2.18.3) needs clarification. It appears that monitoring of public supplies involves a mixture of surface water and groundwater, thus lacking the capability to detect sources of contamination. Further, the discussion does not indicate precautionary onsite monitoring of groundwater to detect contamination before it reaches public or domestic supply wells. The statement should also indicate whether monitoring of groundwater occurs downgradient from waste holding, treatment, and disposal facilities. Because low-level radioactive wastes are released to sanitary sewers, the statement should comment on sewer specifications, particularly those related to control of exfiltration.

We hope these comments will be of assistance in preparing the final statement.

Sincerely,

Larry E. Meierotto
Deputy Assistant SECRETARY

Department of Energy
Washington, D.C. 20545

G. Facer, DP	Library, Room 1223, 20 Mass Avenue
A. Schoen, EV	G. Dennis, AL
J. Swinebroad, EV	G. Pitchford, CH (2)
R. Stern, EV	R. Blackledge, ID
S. Miller, OGC	J. Felton, OR
D. Smith, AD	T. Bauman, RL
R. Miller, AL	D. Cook, SAN
C. Lindeken, LLL (2)	D. Peek, SR
J. Jeutten, SAN	D. Jackson, NV

COMMENTS ON DRAFT ENVIRONMENTAL IMPACT STATEMENT, DOE/EIS-0028-D, LIVERMORE SITE, LIVERMORE, CALIFORNIA, SEPTEMBER 1978

Attached for your information or placement in your respective public document room for public inspection is a copy of comment letter No. 4 received on the subject draft statement from Mr. Larry E. Meierotto, Deputy Assistant Secretary, Department of the Interior, dated December 8, 1978.

W. H. Pennington
Division of NEPA Affairs
Office of Environmental Compliance
and Overview/EV

Attachment

Response to Letter 4

DOE RESPONSE TO LETTER FROM THE DEPARTMENT OF THE INTERIOR

The purpose of the DEIS was to assess the environmental impacts associated with current and continuing activities at the Livermore site. Neither the introduction of new programs nor the need to increase the number of employees is expected to raise the level of environmental impact significantly above that discussed.

With respect to cultural resources at Site 300, we have conducted a cultural resource survey in accordance with 36 CFR 64. You will be informed of items qualifying for inclusion in the National Register.

The Staff Statement in Response to Comments Received on the DEIS, which is included in the Hearing Record of the Public Hearing on the Draft Environmental Impact Statement, Livermore Site, Livermore, California, discusses the impact of Site 300 operations on the approximately 100 acres on the eastern side of the site that were recessed to the State as a wildlife reserve.

Appendix 2E of the FEIS contains lists of plants and animals found at Site 300. There are no plans at present for any facility construction in the immediate up-grade area of the rare plant *Amsinckia grandiflora*.

No changes in activities are anticipated that would change our present impact on the bald eagle.

Section 2.3.3, Geology and Seismicity, has been completely written to better address the points raised in your letter.

Appendix 2A of the FEIS describes the Livermore site's environmental monitoring of local groundwater down gradient from the point of release of treated sewage effluent from the City of Livermore's Water Reclamation Plant.

Dec. 4, 1978

Dear Sir,

I am greatly concerned about the Livermore Nuclear power plant. It is my understanding that the poisonous plutonium is being kept at the site and endangering everyone in the Bay Area. I would like to know why that cannot be handled in less populated places; like the deserts!

Thank you,

Sue Creswell
600 Smith Rd.
Watsonville, Ca.
95076

Department of Energy
Washington, D.C. 20545

DEC 1978

G. Facer, DP	Library, Room 1223, 20 Mass Avenue
A. Schoen, EV	G. Dennis, AL
J. Swinebroad, EV	G. Pitchford, CH (2)
R. Stern, EV	R. Blackledge, ID
S. Miller, OGC	J. Felton, OR
D. Smith, AD	T. Bauman, RL
R. Miller, AL	D. Cook, SAN
C. Lindeken, LLL (2)	D. Peek, SR
J. Jeutten, SAN	D. Jackson, NV

COMMENTS ON DRAFT ENVIRONMENTAL IMPACT STATEMENT, DOE/EIS-0028-D, LIVERMORE SITE, LIVERMORE, CALIFORNIA, SEPTEMBER 1978

Attached for your information or placement in your respective public document room for public inspection is a copy of comment letter No. 5 received on the subject draft statement from Ms. Sue Creswell, Watsonville, California, dated December 4, 1978.

W. H. Pennington
Division of NEPA Affairs
Office of Environmental Compliance
and Overview/EV

Attachment

Response to Letter 5

DOE RESPONSE TO LETTER FROM MS. SUE CRESWELL

There are no nuclear power plants at the Livermore site. Until March of 1980, a small pool-type training reactor was operated by the Lawrence Livermore National Laboratory; however, that reactor is now decommissioned.

With respect to relocating the plutonium activities, geographical separation of this research effort from the Livermore site would reduce the activities to those of a satellite operation. As a result, the work would lose the benefit of highly unique support activities available to on-site facilities.

12/6/78

Mr. W.H. Pennington
Mail Station E 201, G.T.N.
Dept. of Energy
Washington DC. 20545

Dear Sir,

I recently received the Draft Environmental Impact Statement for Lawrence Livermore Laboratory at Livermore California. I find it abyssmally inadequate. The imment danger from earthquake is not explored in any depth. The Laboratory is in a high density population area & surrounder by faults. It is imperative that public hearing be held.

Marjorie Bowman
1815 Elm St. El Cerrito, Calif
94530

Department of Energy
Washington, D.C. 20545

1978

G. Facer, DP
A. Schoen, EV
J. Swinebroad, EV
R. Stern, EV
S. Miller, OGC
D. Smith, AD
R. Miller, AL
C. Lindeken, LLL (2)
J. Jeutten, SAN
Library, Room 1223, 20 Mass Avenue
G. Dennis, AL
G. Pitchford, CH (2)
R. Blackledge, ID
J. Felton, OR
T. Bauman, RL
D. Cook, SAN
D. Peek, SR
D. Jackson, NV

COMMENTS ON DRAFT ENVIRONMENTAL IMPACT STATEMENT, DOE/EIS-0028-D, LIVERMORE SITE, LIVERMORE, CALIFORNIA, SEPTEMBER 1978

Attached for your information or placement in your respective public document room for public inspection is a copy of comment letter No. 6 received on the subject draft statement from Ms. Marjorie Bowman, El Cerrito, California, dated December 6, 1978.

W. H. Pennington
Division of NEPA Affairs
Office of Environmental Compliance
and Overview/EV

Attachment

Response to Letter 6

DOE RESPONSE TO LETTER FROM MS. MARJORIE BOWMAN

A public hearing on the draft EIS for the Livermore site was held on April 12, 1979. Based upon review and comment on the document, the seismic and geology portion was rewritten and greatly expanded. In addition, a comprehensive geologic investigation was undertaken to evaluate on-site, and pertinent regional, geologic conditions which might influence the safety of the Livermore site. The findings of this study are scheduled to be published in 1982.

ABAG
Association of Bay Area Governments
Hotel Claremont · Berkeley, California 94705 · (415) 841-9730

December 11, 1978

Mr. W. H. Pennington
Mail Station E-201
GTN
U.S. Department of Energy
Washington, DC 20545

Dear Mr. Pennington:

Thank you for the opportunity to comment on the DEIS for the Livermore Site (DOE/EIS-0028-D). Staff has reviewed this document and is forwarding the following comments. ABAG's Executive Board has not taken a position on this document or the proposed project.

The DEIS, prepared to discuss the impacts of existing and planned activities at the Lawrence Livermore Laboratory and Sandia Laboratories, needs to be supplemented in order to document two significant impacts:

1) As existing and new employees commute to work, air quality conditions (which are already severe in the Livermore-Amador Valley) will continue to deteriorate. The DEIS should discuss the impact of increased vehicle emissions on air quality; the DEIS also should identify measures to mitigate this impact. ABAG's regional policy calls for reduced motor vehicle emissions through transportation actions (transit, carpooling, etc.) to reduce vehicle use. This information should be supplied to determine the consistency between the project and regional policies.

2) The DEIS should be more specific in estimating the housing demand generated by the expansion of the existing facilities. The number, occupational characteristics, and estimated income levels of new employees should be provided along with housing market information about where housing of commensurate rent/price level exists to meet the needs of new employees.

In discussing the relationship of the project to ABAG's Regional Plan (DEIS p.7-1), reference is made to the 1970 plan map. The map was not intended to be interpreted in a site-specific manner. A copy of ABAG's position on growth in development in the Livermore-Amador Valley is included from the Regional Plan 1978, a document issued earlier this year. For your benefit, we are attaching a letter to the Alameda County Water Conservation District, Zone 7, which gives a regional policies history for the Livermore-Amador Valley. Also, the final EIS should include reference to ABAG's most recent population, land use, and employment projections (attached). The text (DEIS p. 2-44) utilizes projections which are no longer used by ABAG and local governments.

Thank you again for the opportunity to comment. If you have any questions about these comments, please contact me.

Sincerely,

Charles Q. Forester,
Director of Planning

Attachments: 2

Department of Energy
Washington, D.C. 20545

'78

G. Facer, DP	Library, Room 1223, 20 Mass Avenue
A. Schoen, EV	G. Dennis, AL
J. Swinebroad, EV	G. Pitchford, CH (2)
R. Stern, EV	R. Blackledge, ID
S. Miller, OGC	J. Felton, OR
D. Smith, AD	T. Bauman, RL
R. Miller, AL	D. Cook, SAN
C. Lindeken, LLL (2)	D. Peek, SR
J. Jeutten, SAN	D. Jackson, NV

COMMENTS ON DRAFT ENVIRONMENTAL IMPACT STATEMENT, DOE/EIS-0028-D, LIVERMORE SITE, LIVERMORE, CALIFORNIA, SEPTEMBER 1978

Attached for your information or placement in your respective public document room for public inspection is a copy of comment letter No. 7 received on the subject draft statement from Mr. Charles Q. Forester, Director of Planning, Association of Bay Area Governments, dated December 11, 1978.

W. H. Pennington
Division of NEPA Affairs
Office of Environmental Compliance
and Overview/EV

Attachment

Note: The enclosures to comment letter No. 7 are being transmitted only to C. Lindeken, LLL.

Response to Letter 7

DOE RESPONSE TO LETTER FROM THE ASSOCIATION OF BAY AREA GOVERNMENTS (ABAG)

Section 3.8.5 of the DEIS has been expanded to include a description of steps taken to reduce commuting by single occupant or auto. Extension of Fig. 3-13 shows that Laboratory growth is similar to town growth. Future population estimates in the FEIS are based in part on the use of data in "Projections 79."

UNITED STATES DEPARTMENT OF COMMERCE
The Assistant Secretary for Science and Technology
Washington, D.C. 20230
(202) 377-~~3XXX~~ 4335

December 8, 1978

Mr. W.H. Pennington, Director
Division of Program Review
and Coordination
Department of Energy
Washington, D.C. 20545

Dear Mr. Pennington:

This is in reference to your draft environmental impact statement entitled " Livermore Site, Livermore, California." The enclosed comment from the National Oceanic and Atmospheric Administration is forwarded for your consideration.

Thank you for giving us an opportunity to provide this comment, which we hope will be of assistance to you. We would appreciate receiving 10 copies of the final statement.

Sincerely,

Sidney R. Galler
Deputy Assistant Secretary
for Environmental Affairs

Enclosure Memo from: Mr. Douglas LeComte
Environmental Data Service
NOAA

UNITED STATES DEPARTMENT OF COMMERCE
National Oceanic and Atmospheric Administration
ENVIRONMENTAL DATA SERVICE
Washington, D.C. 20235

October 30, 1978

TO: A/PP - William Aron

FROM: OA/Dx61 - Douglas LeComte

SUBJECT: DEIS 7809.18 - Livermore Site, CA

Specific Comments

Page 2-58, 1st sentence: It is extremely unlikely that annual rainfall at Site 300 is just 70mm. The precipitation data should be checked.

Department of Energy
Washington, D.C. 20545

DEC 1978

G. Facer, DP
A. Schoen, EV
J. Swinebroad, EV
R. Stern, EV
S. Miller, OGC
D. Smith, AD
R. Miller, AL
C. Lindeken, LLL (2)
J. Jeutten, SAN

Library, Room 1223, 20 Mass Avenue
G. Dennis, AL
G. Pitchford, CH (2)
R. Blackledge, ID
J. Felton, OR
T. Bauman, RL
D. Cook, SAN
D. Peek, SR
D. Jackson, NV

COMMENTS ON DRAFT ENVIRONMENTAL IMPACT STATEMENT, DOE/EIS-0028-D, LIVERMORE SITE, LIVERMORE, CALIFORNIA, SEPTEMBER 1978

Attached for your information or placement in your respective public document room for public inspection is a copy of comment letter No. 8 received on the subject draft statement from Dr. Sidney R. Galler, Deputy Assistant Secretary for Environmental Affairs, Department of Commerce, dated December 8, 1978.

W. H. Pennington
Division of NEPA Affairs
Office of Environmental Compliance
and Overview/EV

Attachment

Response to Letter 8

DOE RESPONSE TO LETTER FROM THE DEPARTMENT OF COMMERCE

The typographical error regarding annual rainfall at Site 300 has been corrected. The correct number is 290 mm.

December 10, 1978

Mr. W. H. Pennington
Mail Station E-201, GTN
Department of Energy
Washington, D. C. 20545

Dear Mr. Pennington:

I have read the Draft Environmental Impact Statement on Lawrence Livermore Labs.

The meager attention given to the Seismologic Evaluation (3 pages) was inadequate in view of the twelve active earthquake faults in the area. The report's assurance that protection is provided and all contingencies covered makes little sense in light of the danger of air, water, and food-chain contamination to nearby large urban areas with a total population of 4,276,000 within 80 km. of the site (your figures).

I was puzzled because so many pages (14) were devoted to the Flora and Fauna of the area and to justifying the taking of agricultural land back in the '50's. I was delighted that there are jackrabbits (lots of them), and gophers, and red-breasted nuthatches, and sowbugs, but that is not addressing the issue. Then I learned that the Statement was written by (or supervised by) the LLL officials. That explained much of its "glossing over" of hazards and the "padding" with all the inconsequential stuff.

I urgently request:

1. An answer to why the report took the "phoney" form it did. What information are you hiding?

2. An adequate public hearing in the Bay Area with time allotted for local citizens to ask questions and receive answers. This necessitates ample public notice of the meeting in an accessible place and an impartial moderator in charge.

I trust I will receive an answer to this letter since public comment was requested.

Yours sincerely,

Evelyn E. Johnson

10-31 Evelyn E. Johnson

Department of Energy
Washington, D.C. 20545

DEC 26 1978

G. Facer, DP
A. Schoen, EV
J. Swinebroad, EV
R. Stern, EV
S. Miller, OGC
D. Smith, AD
R. Miller, AL
C. Lindeken, LLL (2)
J. Jeutten, SAN
Library, Room 1223, 20 Mass Avenue
G. Dennis, AL
G. Pitchford, CH (2)
R. Blackledge, ID
J. Felton, OR
T. Bauman, RL
D. Cook, SAN
D. Peek, SR
D. Jackson, NV

COMMENTS ON DRAFT ENVIRONMENTAL IMPACT STATEMENT, DOE/EIS-0028-D, LIVERMORE SITE, LIVERMORE, CALIFORNIA, SEPTEMBER 1978

Attached for your information or placement in your respective public document room for public inspection is a copy of comment letter No. 9 received on the subject draft statement from Mrs. Evelyn E. Johnson, El Cerrito, California, dated December 10, 1978.

W. H. Pennington
Division of NEPA Affairs
Office of Environmental Compliance
and Overview/EV

Attachment

DOE RESPONSE TO LETTER FROM MS. EVELYN JOHNSON

Based on public review and comment on the Livermore DEIS the seismic and geology section was rewritten and greatly expanded. In addition, a comprehensive field investigation was undertaken to evaluate on-site, and pertinent regional, geologic conditions that might affect the safety of the Livermore site. Results of this study will be reviewed by USGS and an independent geologic consulting company. This company will also impanel a committee of seismic experts to review the adequacy of the study.

A public hearing on the DEIS was held in Livermore on April 12, 1979.

Andy Baltzo
2092 Ahneita Dr.
Pleasant Hill, CA
94523

12-15-78

Mr. W.H. Pennington
Mail station E-201
G-7N, Dept. of Energy
Washington, D.C. 20545

Dear Mr. Pennington,

I most urgently request that public hearings be held on the Draft Environmental Impact Statement on the Lawrence Livermore Lab. I am by no means satisfied with the DEIS of May 1978.

The report of accidental dumping of radioactive materials in a Livermore, CA dump disturbs me greatly. My understanding is that any amount of radiation is harmful to people as well as all other forms of life.

My very highest concern is human life. The products of the work which goes on at these labs very decidedly threatens our species. Nuclear weapons are not researched and developed with the idea that they will never be used. And man being a fallible creature and by no means exempt from irrationality, to state the matter lightly, the odds are heavy that these monstrous weapons will be used in WW III. The environmental impact from that will be world-wide.

Please, lets have some very thorough hearings. Most sincerely,

Andy Baltzo

Department of Energy
Washington, D.C. 20545

G. Facer, DP
A. Schoen, EV
J. Swinebroad, EV
R. Stern, EV
S. Miller, OGC
D. Smith, AD
R. Miller, AL
C. Lindeken, LLL (2)
J. Jeutten, SAN
Library, Room 1223, 20 Mass Avenue
G. Dennis, AL
G. Pitchford, CH (2)
R. Blackledge, ID
J. Felton, OR
T. Bauman, RL
D. Cook, SAN
D. Peek, SR
D. Jackson, NV

COMMENTS ON DRAFT ENVIRONMENTAL IMPACT STATEMENT, DOE/EIS-0028-D, LIVERMORE SITE, LIVERMORE, CALIFORNIA, SEPTEMBER 1978

Attached for your information or placement in your respective public document room for public inspection is a copy of comment letter No. 10 received on the subject draft statement from Mr. Andy Baltzo, Pleasant Hill, California, dated December 15, 1978.

W. H. Pennington
Division of NEPA Affairs
Office of Environmental Compliance
and Overview/EV

Attachment

Response to Letter 10

DOE RESPONSE TO LETTER FROM MR. ANDY BALTZO

A public hearing on the Livermore DEIS was held on April 12, 1979. The americium waste accidently taken to the Eastern Alameda County Disposal Site occurred on August 25, 1978. The material was recovered without incident and no member of the public received a radiation exposure from the material. The reason the incident was not contained in the DEIS was that the DEIS was being printed during that time.

The EIS is restricted to the specific impacts of the Livermore sites. The larger questions of defense posture are national policy issues formulated at the national level.

W.H. Pennington
Mail Station E-201, GTN
Department of Energy
Washington, D.C. 20545

Dear Mr. Pennington;

I am writing in regard to the recently issued Draft Environmental Impact Statement for the Livermore Site (DOE/EIS-0028-D, Livermore Site, September 1978.) Having read this document I now wish to make some critical comments, raise some questions, and call for public hearings.

In addition to my work as a physics teacher and researcher on this campus I have, for a number of years, concerned myself with the activities of the Lawrence Livermore Laboratory: its connection with my university, its use of scientific people and knowledge and, most of all, its contributions to the nuclear arms race which threatens the very survival of humanity. I had not anticipated that the process of drafting and approving an EIS for this laboratory would involve issues as broad as these; but I was mistaken. The DEIS clearly and repeatedly asserts that the main benefit coming from the operation of this Laboratory is its contribution to the National Defense through its primary mission of nuclear weapons research and development. What is totally lacking, however, is any word about the costs or adverse impacts that are likely to follow from this activity. Thus, in a very central manner, the present DEIS is far out of balance and cannot be considered in compliance with the requirements of the law.

There is a large body of opinion and published literature, encompassing both technical and lay people, which holds that the continued development of nuclear weapons is actually increasing the likelihood of nuclear war, thus decreasing the security of the nation and threatening enormous destruction to the human and natural environment. This risk side of the risk-benefit analysis has been totally ignored in the DEIS. Here are a few of the questions which the DOE should answer in order to provide a reasonable beginning for the necessary public review and evaluation of these hazards:
1) What is the probability of nuclear wars, of various sizes, occurring ?
2) What are the likely adverse consequences of such wars, to the population generally and to the LLL area in particular ?
3) How do the above mentioned risks compare with other types of nuclear accident risks that have been much debated - from nuclear power plant accidents, from earthquakes, from sabottage and terrorism, etc. ?

I request that, in addition to providing authoritative government assessments of the questions I have raised, the Department of Energy hold adequate public hearings on this DEIS so that full public input to and scrutiny of such evaluations can be provided.

10-38 Sincerely yours, Charles Schwartz

Charles Schwartz, Professor of Physics (244)

Department of Energy
Washington, D.C. 20545

DEC 26 1978

G. Facer, DP
A. Schoen, EV
J. Swinebroad, EV
R. Stern, EV
S. Miller, OGC
D. Smith, AD
R. Miller, AL
C. Lindeken, LLL (2)
J. Jeutten, SAN
Library, Room 1223, 20 Mass Avenue
G. Dennis, AL
G. Pitchford, CH (2)
R. Blackledge, ID
J. Felton, OR
T. Bauman, RL
D. Cook, SAN
D. Peek, SR
D. Jackson, NV

COMMENTS ON DRAFT ENVIRONMENTAL IMPACT STATEMENT, DOE/EIS-0028-D, LIVERMORE SITE, LIVERMORE, CALIFORNIA, SEPTEMBER 1978

Attached for your information or placement in your respective public document room for public inspection is a copy of comment letter No. 11 received on the subject draft statement from Professor Charles Schwartz, Physics, University of California, dated December 15, 1978.

W. H. Pennington
Division of NEPA Affairs
Office of Environmental Compliance
and Overview/EV

Attachment

Response to Letter 11

DOE RESPONSE TO LETTER FROM MR. CHARLES SCHWARTZ

A public hearing on the Livermore DEIS was held on April 12, 1979. The scope of the DEIS was limited to addressing site-specific environmental impacts of Livermore operations. The scope did not include (1) probabilities of nuclear war, (2) adverse consequences of such wars, or (3) comparison of risks of nuclear war with other types of nuclear accidents.

FRIENDS OF THE EARTH

124 SPEAR SAN FRANCISCO CALIFORNIA 94105

(415) 495-4770

December 18, 1978

W.H. Pennington
Office of NEPA Coordination
Department of Energy
Washington, D.C. 20545

Dear Mr. Pennington,

We have carefully reviewed the Department of Energy's (DOE's) Draft Environmental Impact Statement (DEIS) on the Lawrence Livermore Lab (LLL) and the Sandia Livermore Lab (SLL) published by DOE in September, 1978. The DOE version of this DEIS is essentially, almost verbatim, the same as the DEIS produced by the LLL staff which was first published in October, 1976 by LLL. We have reviewed that document and a companion, the Omnibus Environmental Assessment of the Sandia Livermore Labs (SAND 75-0268) which was printed in October, 1975. Although it is apparently DOE policy not to reveal the names of individuals who work on these DEIS's, we can safely assume that the DOE-DEIS-0028-D published by DOE in September, 1978, was actually written and produced almost entirely by people who work at the labs in Livermore rather than by any DOE staff in Washington. This obvious conflict of interest towards protecting their jobs and workplace has caused the authors of the DEIS to bias the report by underestimating the maximum credible accidents and environmental impacts that could result from operations of these nuclear weapons labs.

Based on a thorough analysis of the DEIS on the Livermore Site, we hereby request the DOE to conduct public hearings on this DEIS because it is inadequate, incomplete, and misleading, from cover to cover, for the reasons explained below. A major inadequacy of the DEIS is that it does not even mention numerous environmental impacts of the operations of the labs, and the ones it does mention are incompletely analyzed.

The text of this DEIS is invalidated because it fails to integrate an appendix that is so significant that every section of the DEIS needs to be reevaluated and revised in detail because of the information presented. That information is in Appendix 2A, "A Geological and Seismological Investigation of the LLL Site."

Although the maps in Appendix 2A (enclosed with these comments) show that there are at least thirteen active earthquake faults that could damage the labs, the DEIS does not analyze the consequences of earthquake damage. It apparently assumes that there will be no damage. Or perhaps the authors of the DEIS realized that earthquake damages could be so devastating to the labs that they should not mention the possibility and in that way suppress discussion. The DEIS should be revised and resubmitted for comments to allow adequate ventilation and discussion of the issues.

There are many critical components in the labs that could be damaged in a quake which would result in the release of radioactive liquids, gases, and solids into the local environment. Several buildings contain hot cells, glove boxes, pipes, filter systems, and radioactive waste retention tanks that are particularly susceptible to earthquake damage. The DEIS must be revised to include an analysis of each of these, including their original design criteria, any modifications made or proposed, and the potential environmental impact if they were damaged during an earthquake. Most of these facilities were built many years before the existence and locations of the nearby faults were known.

In the section of the DEIS on Accidents, the document is supposed to analyze maximum credible accidents, according to NEPA guidelines. However, the handful of accidents analyzed in this DEIS are caused by fires, human errors, and explosions. None are caused by earthquakes. The DEIS should be revised to consider the cumulative effects of an earthquake that damaged several buildings at once or that damaged several glove boxes, hot cells, and filter systems in each building. The fact that the DEIS omits such considerations invalidates the document and makes imperative its reassessment through public hearings. (NOTE: The earthquake hazards to the labs are discussed in more detail in other sections of these comments.)

The DEIS is incomplete because it fails to analyze the environmental impact of routine and accidental releases of radiation being deposited in the reservoirs and aqueducts that border the Livermore Valley. The Hetch Hetchy and South Bay Aqueduct Systems supply drinking water to millions of people in the San Francisco and South Bay areas, and these water supply systems could be contaminated by releases from the labs. The California Aqueduct, which supplies water to people in central and southern California passes east of the labs within range of contamination from radioactive releases. The most vulnerable of these water supply systems is the South Bay Aqueduct which passes within a few hundred feet east of both labs in an open-air concrete lined canal. It is on the eastern border of the labs and is thus downwind most of the time from routine emissions and accidental releases of radioactivity. Associated with this aqueduct are the Patterson Reservoir and the Del Valle reservoir, both within easy contamination distance of the labs. The DEIS fails to analyze the impact of routine and accidental releases of radiation on the water quality in these reservoirs and aqueducts. The DEIS should be revised and resubmitted for comments on these potential environmental impacts. Water quality is a very important issue and it is inexcusable for the DEIS to ignore the impacts of the labs on drinking water and agricultural irragation water.

The considerations of accidents in the DEIS are totally misleading. For example, although the DEIS mentions (in the very last section of the last appendix) that there have been at least 17 serious accidents at the lab since 1960, it only describes these accidents in a brief perfunctory fashion. The accounts of these accidents are so short and incomplete that they do not analyze whether or not water supplies were contaminated, or if agricultural lands downwind in the central valley were affected or even sampled, and it does not describe any methods that may have been used to determine the environmental impacts of these accidents. This list includes releases of 650,000 curies of tritium and spills of various amounts of plutonium into the Livermore sewage system and into soils east of the LLL lab (very near the South Bay Aqueduct). The DEIS does not say what happened to the soils that were contaminated with plutonium (offsite). The DEIS fails to analyze whether or not any attempt was made to determine if the nearby South Bay Aqueduct and Patterson Reservoir were affected or contaminated by the April 1973 Plutonium leaks, or by the large releases of tritium in 1965 and 1970.

The DEIS fails to mention an important piece of relevant research on tritium which was done by L. Dobson, a LLL employee on contract with the EPA. Dobson's research was published in the April-June 1974 issue of Radiation Research and was reprinted in the November 1974 issue of the LLL Newsline. Dobson discovered that surprisingly low levels of tritium in drinking water can kill 90 percent or more of the immature eggs developing in the ovaries of young female mice. Dobson said, "Tritium ... has a strong tendency to form water...Once in the form of tritiated water, the compound gets to human beings just as does any water, primarily as drinking water and as water taken up by crops." He said that his results suggest that for tritium there is no threshold dose below which the mice totally escape the effects. Dobson said subsequent work designed to test his original observations have confirmed them. (A reprint of the report attached to these comments)

Although LLL reprinted this tritium research report in its Newsline, and although the DEIS mentions the fact that huge amounts of tritium could be released from either of the labs in Livermore, and the fact that routine releases of tritium occur, the DEIS fails to mention that there might be adverse health effects from routine or accidental releases of tritium. The DEIS fails to mention the Dobson report or any of the dozens of other scientific research reports available on the health effects of exposure to tritium. The DEIS seems to imply that tritium releases are harmless. This demonstrates how the DEIS is a coverup of realistic environmental impacts.

The most astonishing example of a historic accident listed in the Appendix (3C), states that on March 26, 1963, there was a nuclear excursion during a criticality experiment in the Plutonium Metallurgical Chemistry Building that released 4×10^{17} fissions. The descriptions of the environmental impacts of this accident are totally inadequate, and limited to one sentence which conclude there was nothing to worry about. The releases of radioactivity from this accident may have caused temporary or permanent contamination of agricultural lands and crops in the San Joaquin and Livermore Valleys, but apparently this potential environmental impact was not even considered. This accident description (and its 16 companions) needs to be revised and expanded to include a complete list of any samples or studies that were done to test for contamination, or reasons to explain why such research was not done.

Another inadequacy in the DEIS is its failure to report the facts that fourteen of its employees have contracted multiple melanoma, a rare skin cancer, (at least two of these employees died), and that at least two young children in the Livermore Valley recently died of melanoma. It is almost unheard of in medical history for children under 15 to contract melanoma. Another local child is being treated for a rare tumor called Ewing's sarcoma, and all of these facts have generated significant media coverage (see enclosed articles from the S.F. Chronicle). The newspaper reports say that the rate of increase of malignant melanoma in the Bay Area is 5 to 10 times higher than the national average between 1970 and 1975, and that the overall Bay Area cancer rate rose by about ten percent in those five years. These newspaper reports imply that the increasing cancer rates and deaths in the Bay Area, and especially in the Livermore Valley, may be caused by the operations of the nuclear weapons labs in Livermore. But you would never suspect this kind of environmental impact from reading the DEIS coverup. The DEIS does not mention that its employees are dying of rare cancers that may be caused by exposure to radiation, or that the head of the LLL Biomedical Division, Dr. Bernard Shore, died of malignant melanoma. The DEIS is inadequate and misleading in analyzing the public health impacts of its routine emissions and accidental leaks and emissions. Also it does not analyze the cumulative effects of emissions since 1951.

The DEIS should be revised to include data on cancer incidence and ill health among past and present workers and their families. The discussion should include analysis of cancer rates in the Livermore Valley and in the Bay Area populations whose drinking water quality and air quality and food chains can be affected by the environmental impact of the labs in Livermore. The revision of the DEIS should include discussions of long-term health effects and genetic effects from exposure to various kinds of radioactive materials. It is generally accepted that exposure to radiation can increase the incidence of cancers and leukemias and other health problems including genetic mutations and miscarriages. But there is no mention of this information in the DEIS. The major problems caused by exposure to radiation can be delayed for ten to forty years after exposures. This fact allows nuclear weapons labs to cover up the real environmental impacts that they have on their employees and neighbors in nearby communities. The DEIS should be revised to include any suggestions of epidemilogical studies on long term effects of exposure to radiation. In the revision, the staff should take care to explain how the health effects from radiation can be delayed for years after exposure. The revision should clarify whether or not any attempt is being made by the labs in Livermore to analyze the long term effects of radiation releases into the surrounding regions. Considering the Livermore labs'role in the creation of enormous amounts of radioactive wastes, it is surprising that the DEIS reports no serious biomedical research on the long term health effects.

The DEIS fails to mention pending proposals by the EPA to revise and lower the (1) allowable doses from routine emissions of radioactivity, (2) the allowable occupational exposures to workers in the nuclear industries (including weapons labs), and (3) the allowable exposures to the public from accidental releases of transuranics into the environment. The guideline proposed by EPA in the Federal Register on November 30, 1977, states that the dose to persons offsite from existing or possible future accidental releases of transuranics should not exceed 1 millirad per year to the pulmonary lung or 3 millirad per year to the bone. If contamination of the soils east of the labs from the 1973 accidental releases of plutonium exceed those levels, then that area should be decontaminated if that is possible. The overriding question, however, is did the South Bay Aqueduct and the Patterson Reservoir receive contamination from that and other incidents? Did people in San Jose and elsewhere receive doses of radiation from accidents affecting their water supply? Can the soil east of the lab contain plutonium that gets resuspended and deposited in the water supplies? Does the vegeta ble garden at the lab which used plutonium contaminated sludge allow resuspension of plutonium particles which could deposit in the nearby reservoirs and aqueducts? None of these questions are addressed in the inadequate DEIS. In its proposal, the EPA stated that "Radiation induced risks can be estimated based on a number of different assumptions, but the most prudent is that there is some finite risk to humans no matter how small the amount of absorbed radiation might be, and that the risk at any given low dose level is directly proportional to the damage actually observed at much higher dose levels...On this basis, there is no level of radiation exposure which is absolutely safe and any radiation dose carries with it some degree of risk." The DEIS on the Livermore site does not reflect the EPA's analysis.

The DEIS is inadequate because it does not document the methodologies used to calculate doses from accidents and routine emissions, and it does not describe adequately the postulated pathways used to determine maximum individual dose commitments. Also the dose calculations should be re-examined in terms of source terms, and uptake and transfer coefficients; and all input data should be published with the calculations. Rather than just giving annual doses from routine emissions or one time doses from accidents or potential accidents, the DEIS should be revised to discuss dose commitments over a lifetime. Many of the isotopes released from the labs will be in the biosphere longer than the lifetimes of any person alive today, and for many generations to come. What will the doses be to future generations? What will be the cumulative environmental impacts on them of routine emissions and accidents? The DEIS should be revised, recalculating doses into the future, and thoroughly documenting the calculations of source terms, pathways, assumptions, and equations. Lifetime cumulative dose commitments should be added to the discussion.

For tritium pathways, the skin and lung absorption pathways, and the drinking water ovary pathway should be calculated for routine and accidental emissions. For emissions of Krypton-85, discussions should be added to the revised DEIS concerning recent research which indicates that rising levels of Krypton-85 (from routine emissions from nuclear facilities such as those at Livermore) are reacting in the presence of the sun's ultraviolet rays and causing an increase in skin cancers.

Another inadequacy of the DEIS is that the Emergency Planning and Disaster Control Plan merely deal with on site procedures. There is a general guideline that nuclear facilities are responsible for on site evacuations and planning and that the state and county officials are responsible for dealing with the offsite consequences and evacuation But the DEIS does not state or clarify that guideline in a site-specific manner.

The guidelines do not excuse the Livermore labs from notifying appropriate county and state officials of the potential for offsite releases of radiation and the potential need for evacuations in case of an emergency. The DEIS is entirely deficient in this regard. No mention is made of communications with state and county officials to plan for emergency responses. Apparently the labs can (and do) have disastrous accidnets such as are listed in the Appendix 3C history, without even notifying the county or the state. What about the contamination of land, water and people downwind following those accidents? Was anyone notified? If such an accident occured in the future, would the victims be notified? By whom? Remember that radiation is invisible, and not sensed by humans, so contaminations and exposures could easily be concealed, as they apparently have been in the past at Livermore. Many times in the DEIS, future accidental exposures are calculated in such a questionable manner that they fall within a range that can be interpreted as not requiring evacuations. It seems that the DEIS deliberately manipulates numbers and data to avoid any credible accident that would require evacuations. They just never admit that an accident could occur requiring evacuations. This kind of coverup is used so frequently and pervasively in the DEIS that it avoids entirely the realistic need to evacuate nearby populations in case of maximum credible accidents which are not analyzed. Thus the DEIS in inadequate and misleading and needs to be revised to include the realistic maximum credible accidents, and the realistic emergency responses which would include notifying state and county officials to evacuate people and to declare agricultural lands and crops contaminated. The new DEIS should discuss how long the contamination of soils in the agricultural valleys could last; what types of decontamination procedures exist (describe in detail) or whether large scale decontamination of the central valley would even be remotely possible; and estimates of the economic and sociological impacts of such accidents. It must be noted that the NRC (DOE's sister agency and formerly the same entity in the AEC) commissioned the Rasmussen Report, WASH 1400. Although this report has been criticized by many scientific organizations as being a weak whitewash and coverup of the true potential of nuclear accidents, the Rasmussen Report does give us some guidelines about evacuations and decontamination. It says that following a serious nuclear facility accident, it would be necessary to evacuate the surrounding population within 25 miles downwind, immediately or before the cloud of radiation passed over them. Beyond the 25 mile radius, the radiation might be diluted, but Rasmussen admitted that radioactive contamination of up to 300,000 square miles could result from a single nuclear accident. How would you(DOE) decontaminate that much land in the fertile Central Valley of California which is directly downwind from the labs in Livermore? The DEIS does not deal with this. The revised DEIS should specify in detail who would be notified following a serious accident at LLL or SLL. At what level of release would notification begin? How many counties downwind would be notified? Who would implement necessary evacuations? Who would be financially responsible for contaminated agricultural lands? Who would be financially responsible for contamination of residential property? Who would be financially responsible for contamination of people exposed to the passing cloud? Does the Price-Anderson Act preclude government or DOE responsibility in these situations

The DEIS is extremely misleading because it devotes many pages to glorifying the beneficial financial, economic, and sociological impacts it has on surrounding communities, but it fails to analyze the impacts it would have on the economy and the people if a serious accidents contaminated their property and destroyed their health. Where would all the benefits go after that happened? Are the current benefits worth the risk of future catastrophes? Who decides the risks versus benefits questions? The DOE staff should require the LLL staff to analyze these questions in a realistic manner. And the analysis should be done also by independent objective persons such as insurance agencies and scientific researchers from nearby universities. The DEIS as it now stands is too self-serving and misleading. The DEIS revision should include reports by independent experts whose jobs are not at stake if they admit the truth.

The DEIS is inadequate because it does not even mention or consider the environmental impact of projects designed at LLL butconducted offsite. In other publications by LLL (Newsline, 20th anniversary issue, 25th anniversary issue, annual state of the lab reports) the Lab employees glorify these offsite projects as their most important achievements. These projects were designed and directed by lab employees and should be considered as environmental impacts of lab operations. These offsite projects include over 100 atmospheric nuclear explosions in the South Pacific, 84 atmospheric nuclear explosions in Nevada, hundreds of underground tests in Nevada, and the Plowshare programs in which nuclear explosions were conducted underground in New Mexico, Colorado, and Mississippi. Another relevant project was the tests of the Spartan warhead at Amchitka Alaska in 1971. Another project was the series of enormous megaton range nuclear explosions conducted underground in Nevada in 1975 and 1976 to beat the deadline for the Threshhold Treaty.

The DEIS does not even mention most of these projects and operations. Even though a separate FEIS has been done on the NTS, that is not adequate to analyze the effort put into NTS operations by the LLL staff, and that FEIS does not include bomb tests at other sites. Are DOE and LLL trying to coverup the environmental impact of nuclear explosion tests?

In other publications by LLL (see enclosed reprint "Nuclear Weapons Research") the Labs explain their involvement in these projects much better than they do in the DOE DEIS. A few quotes from the Lab press release will illustrate this point: "Nuclear explosives design remains the largest single program at LLL... Nuclear weapons research and development ... has two general goals: (1) to study nuclear explosives...(2) to design explosives for military weapons...includes advising appropriate agencies on the feasibility and effects of new weapons." The Lab brags that it has designed warheads for most of the nation's strategic nuclear weapons (Polaris, Poseidon, Minuteman, MIRV, Spartan, Trident, and Lance) The most relevant statement to our comments follows: "Evolution of nuclear explosives. A significant change in the design of a nuclear explosive may take ten or more years and ... may include some 10,000 hours on Livermore computers, which make up one of the world's most powerful research computer facilities. Twenty or more underground detonations of different designs may be required; each such experiment typically verifies some predictions, demonstrates something new and raises one or two major questions. <u>A single underground nuclear experiment is apt to require nearly twenty man-years of preparation at Livermore</u>...."

Thus we have to look elsewhere to find information about LLL projects that have significant environmental impacts. The DEIS does not give us this information and thus it is inadequate, incomplete and misleading.

If a single underground nuclear experiment requires 20 man-years of preparation at Livermore, and the design of each new weapon or a change in the design of an explosive takes ten or more years, twenty underground explosions, and some 10,000 hours on Livermore computers, then these activities should definitely be considered in the DEIS on the labs in Livermore. The employees of the Livermore labs shuttle back and forth between Livermore and NTS during the design and implementation of nuclear weapons explosions. Essentially, the Nevada Test Site is a laboratory for the programs developed in research at Livermore.

The DEIS on the labs at Livermore should be revised to reflect and to consider in detail the enormous investment of time and energy (man-years) devoted exclusively to nuclear explosions by the lab staff. If a single underground nuclear explosion requires at least twenty man-years of preparation at Livermore, and there have been over 600 announced (non-classified) explosions, then there have been over 12,000 man-years devoted to exploding nuclear weapons in the environment. It seems that NEPA guidelines would consider these projects by lab staff to be appropriate subjects of an environmental impact assessment to be incorporated in this DEIS or the FEIS. Why does the DEIS not even mention that bombs designed at Livermore have been exploded in Nevada, the South Pacific, Alaska, New Mexico, Mississippi and Colorado? Why does this DEIS not analyze the environmental and health impacts of fallout and long-term contamination from these explosions?

Enclosed is an exerpt from a Scientific American article on the hazards of fallout from nuclear explosions, with a diagram showing the total dose in rems from a single bomb test on Bikini Atoll in 1954. Several thousand rems of radiation were delivered to the islands of Bikini and Rongelap. Hundreds of rems to other islands. Yet, no EIS has been done on the long-term effects of these atmospheric tests in the South Pacific. It is a current issue in American media and in the Congressional Records because some of those South Pacific Islanders would like to return to their original homelands but cannot because the islands are still intensely radioactive and their food chains are contaminated. But the DEIS fails to mention the role of the Livermore labs in these tests and their current role (very evident in other laboratory literature) in assessing the current hazards.

Although the atmospheric tests conducted before 1963 caused the dispersal of over five tons of plutonium, LLL's DEIS does not mention that or consider that the plutonium fallout that it created might have some environmental impact. The only reference to these tests in the Livermore DEIS is the constant comparisons of past or future plutonium releases, spills, and accidents to the "background" levels of plutonium deposited in soils from global fallout. The DEIS implies that the reader should accept the presence of fallout as normal and natural, and that because the fallout levels are so high (in terms of soil contamination) that a little more spilled plutonium would not have much environmental impact. Studies by LLL have shown that certain vegetable crops take up plutonium from the soil more readily than other crops (although the DEIS does not mention this); and other studies have shown that wheat and grain crops take up plutonium from soil contamination. A recent report in Science magazine (a copy is enclosed with these comments) shows that plutonium can easily contaminate drinking water supplies and that it can be readily absorbed from the gastrointestinal tract into other parts of the human body where it can create cancers. These characteristics of plutonium were downplayed and denied for many years by nuclear labs people in such a way that led utilities to tell the public that it is safe to ingest plutonium because it can only hurt you if you breathe aerosol particles of it.

The DEIS does not explain why the labs in Livermore have not led the world in researching the short term and long term health effects of human exposure to fallout from nuclear explosions. Such research should concentrate on the long lived isotopes such as Strontium-90, Cesium-137, tritium and plutonium. These isotopes are now so widespread from Livermore's bomb tests that almost every human on earth and every food chain on earth contains residues of radioactive fallout. THAT IS THE TRUE ENVIRONMENTAL IMPACT OF THE LIVERMORE LABS THAT THE DEIS IGNORES. The DEIS should be revised to correct this deficiency.

It is unfortunate from the point of view of public health and safety concerns that the Livermore labs did not create an Environmental and Biomedical Division until 1963, after all of the atmospheric explosions had been stopped by a treaty. Perhaps, if they had understood the long-term health effects of fallout, they would have never conducted any atmospheric explosions. Unfortunately they contaminated the entire planet, and today (in the DEIS) they act like ostriches with their heads covered up with sand, ignoring reality.

From 1963 to 1969, the first Director of the LLL Biomedical Division was Dr. John Gofman, Professor Emeritus of Medical Physics from the University of California at Berkeley. Dr. Gofman lost his contract and position at the lab because his research showed that their would be large increases in cancer rates as a result of exposure to radioactive materials. The AEC did not want to hear such heresy, and when Dr. Gofman told the Congress and the media of his findings, the AEC tried unsuccessfully to discredit him and his research. Dr. Gofman's research has been published in various books and articles, including an enclosed article from the Journal of the American Medical Association, dated July 19, 1976. Dr. Gofman explains that plutonium is extremely carcinogenic when inhaled and that the hazard is much worse for people who smoke cigarettes. He also notes that 400 kilograms of plutonium was deposited on the United States from weapons fallout. He has calculated that, as a result of weapons-testing fallout, 116,000 lung cancer deaths will occur in the United States and one million deaths in the Northern Hemisphere will result from radiation-induced cancers. It seems appropriate that the DEIS on Livermore should concern itself with this type of environmental impact analysis, even if the current management of LLL and DOE might disagree with Dr. Gofman's statistics. The DEIS should be revised to address the questions raised by the published research of the first, and most famous, Director of the Biomedical Division of LLL.

When you consider that another Director of the Biomedical Division, Dr. Bernard Shore, recently died of a rare skin cancer, and when you consider the statistics published in a recent DOE-contracted study by Thomas Mancuso on the incidence of cancers in workers at DOE nuclear weapons labs, it becomes apparent that the DEIS on Livermore labs is deficient and incomplete because it omits so much important information on the health impact of operations of the labs.

Another health impact that is omitted from the DEIS is the studies of fallout effects on the populations of Nevada, Utah, and Arizona, from atmospheric weapons tests at NTS. Although reports have shown children with thyroid tumors in the downwind communities, and numerous instances of cancer deaths in people of all ages, there is no discussion of these environmental impacts in this inadequate DEIS. The fallout from those tests spread all across the U.S.A., a fact that was detected by college researchers in New York after an atmospheric test in the fifties. But you would never know that from reading this DEIS. Another fact omitted by this DEIS is that Livermore's tests in Nevada left 250,000 square miles of land permanently contaminated with plutonium dust, and left Nevada with one of the highest cancer rates in the world.

However, by far the most dramatic environmental impact of the Livermore lab projects is the fact (see enclosed news reports from recent California papers) over 400,000 military personnel and civilian workers were exposed to direct radiation during the nuclear weapons explosions designed and conducted by lab employees. During one test, "Operation Smokey" on August 31, 1957, over a thousand men were forced to stand just eight miles away from a 44-kiloton atomic explosion. Some of these men were forced to watch the test from 3000 yards away. Unfortunately, or perhaps on purpose, the military lost the records of the names of the soldiers who witnessed "Smokey" and other explosions. Now it is hard to trace them to do the necessary epidemilogical studies, but at least eight cases of leukemia have been discovered among the survivors of "Smokey". Other victims have already died.

It is difficult for the thousands of Americans who were exposed to radiation during atomic explosions designed by the Livermore lab to receive compensation or benefits for their illnesses, cancers and imminent deaths because the government will not admit that such health effects can be delayed for more than twenty years after the initial exposures. The Livermore lab has failed in its analysis of environmental impacts of its projects. The lab has failed in its duty to our nation because it has not been honest about the potential long-term health hazards from exposure to radiation. The DEIS should be revised to reflect these current, ongoing concerns that the American people have about the nuclear weapons explosions designed and conducted by the Livermore labs. Another enclosed news article shows that the Livermore lab (LLL) has been sued for $1.52 million in damages for the death of a man who was exposed to radiation exposure at NTS in 1970 during an underground t explosion that resulted in leakage or venting of radioactive gases. This Baneberry test exposed over 900 people to radiation before they were evacuated. A cloud of radioactive gases passed over them. The suit charges that LLL officials failed to exercise due caution to guard against radioactive leakage, and that they failed to provide adequate evacuations. This incident and consequent lawsuit is not even mentioned as a consequence of the environmental impact in the DEIS.

The DEIS on LLL and SLL needs to be revised and expanded to include analysis of the issues raised in the past few pages of these comments. However, it seems inappropriate for the Livermore employees to do the revision and expansion. They probably feel so much guilt and shame about the environmental and health impacts that their nuclear explosions have created, that they would not be able to honestly admit the full impacts. The DOE should hire independent consultants to undertake this revision. And the DOE staff should take responsibility to see that the DEIS revision is done with integrity and thoroughness.

Another disturbing inadequacy of this DEIS is the way in which it deals with radioactive wastes created by the operations of the labs. The attitude seems to be one of "out of sight, out of mind". Although the DEIS states on page 3-19 that there is "no waste storage" at LLL, it should distinguish between temporary and permanent waste storage because it admits that over 120 cubic meters of solid (compacted) rad-wastes are created annually at the labs, and are shipped out twice a year to DOE burial grounds. Thus radioactive wastes are stored at LLL while they are awaiting the twice annual shipments. Temporary storage of liquid rad-wastes has resulted in accidental spills into the sewers and storm (runoff) pipes, and in plutonium leaks from solar evaporators where liquid wastes were treated.

One important aspect of wastes generated by LLL is the radioactive wastes burial trenches at Site 300. On page 3-33, the DEIS notes that Site 300 explosions result in environmental contamination with depleted uranium, beryllium, some natural uranium, thorium, and tritium. 25% of the depleted uranium is in debris after an explosion, 25 % is in the nearby gravels, and 50 % is dispersed beyond the firing range. The gravel and debris that are contaminated after explosions are buried at Site 300 in disposal pits or trenches. These trenches are each filled with up to 150 kilograms of depleted uranium, covered with 1.2 meters of soil, and spaced 1.8 meters from the next trench. Some wastes are incinerated, although they are not identified as radioactive or non-radioactive. The DEIS does not analyze the long-term effects or potential future environmental impacts of burying hundreds of kilograms of uranium in trenches at Site 300. This section should be expanded to consider such impact analyses. The DEIS is also inadequate here because it does not indicate the quantity and types of wastes that have been buried at Site 300 nor does it estimate the future amounts of wastes to be buried there, nor the total amounts of wastes planned for burial at this site (cumulative).

The DEIS states (3-34) that in past years, solid radioactive wastes from LLL were buried at Site 300 in what is now a fenced-off area. The DEIS describes the wastes as contaminated equipment and contaminated lab animals, but it does not detail the types or amounts of radioactive materials buried in those trenches. The DEIS should be revised to include an environmental impact analysis of the radioactive waste burial trenches located at Site 300.

Another omission from the DEIS has been described elsewhere in another Lab publication, the Annual Environmnetal Monitoring Reports where it was admitted that sampling showed that detectable levels of depleted uranium werediscovered in the soils in the Central Valley near Tracy. Thus it is demonstrated that the 50 % of the depleted uranium that is dispersed beyond the explosion areas at Site 300, can be dispersed into the Central Valley which is downwind (prevailing westerlies) from the site. The DEIS is inadequate because it does not discuss the environmental impact of this dispersal on valuable agricultural lands.

Another important omission from this DEIS involves the radioactive wastes from Livermore labs that were dumped offshore from San Francisco near the Farallon Islands until the practice was stopped in 1966. An enclosed document from the AEC describes the containers (55 gallon barrels and concrete blocks) that were used. The accompanying document notes that "Sea disposal is a convenient method for disposing of certain types of radioactive wastes." Most of these wastes were from laboratory experiments, and were not considered dangerous. Mosts of the barrels used were recycled from prior uses, and many of the drums were without tops. Accurate accounts of numbers of barrels and amounts of radioactivity were not kept. Recently the EPA has discovered

Approximately 60,000 barrels of low-level radioactive wastes were dumped onto the ocean floor, twenty miles west of San Francisco. Hundreds of concrete blocks containing cesium were dumped there also. The EPA recently conducted a special investigation of the environmental impact of these rad-wastes. 25 % of the barrels were broken and leaking. Samples of sediments nearby contained plutonium levels 25 times higher than fallout levels. Since then, the State Department of Health has discovered fish in local markets with high levels of radioactive cesium. And this year, fishermen from Marin pulled up a barrel of radioactive wastes in their nets full of fish.

The DEIS is inadequate because it does not discuss the Livermore labs participation in the dumping of radioactive wastes offshore from San Francisco. It does not take responsibility for the environmental impact of past activities. Again, the DEIS fails to meet credible standards of integrity, perhaps because once again the lab employees are embarrassed to admit mistakes that they have made. The DEIS needs to be revised to include an analysis of rad-wastes from the labs that are offshore leaking and contaminating local fish food chains. The DEIS should also analyze the hazard to these wastes from an earthquake on the San Andreas fault which passes offshore at that point, very close to the wastes.

A final inadequacy concerning radioactive wastes is the DEIS's failure to assess the environmental impact of the rad-wastes that have been created by the labs, and by their projects at other sites, including the mass production of nuclear weapons designed by the LLL. An important question to be considered is why did the Livermore labs spend 25 years creating rad-wastes and designing bombs whose production created more rad-wastes, and yet they never solved the problem of what to do with those wastes for the thousands of years that they will remain radioactive. Cesium and Strontium will endanger global food chains for a 1000 years. Plutonium will be carcinogenic for a half a million years. The problems associated with storing and guarding these wastes have environmental impacts that are not considered by the Livermore DEIS even though Livermore is responsible for the creation of these wastes in huge quantities.

The fact that no solution has been discovered for the problems associated with storing rad-wastes for thousands of years is now a serious national security problem that endangers our nation's future public health and safety. The environmental impact of the enormous quantity of rad-wastes currently existing from the nuclear weapons program could result in the contamination of all the land and waters in the USA. Although LLL often describes extensively in its publications how it has been responsible for the design and development of the nation's nuclear weapons arsenal, LLL never discusses its equal responsibility for creating millions of gallons of high level radioactive wastes that must be guarded and kept out of the environment for many centuries. The DEIS is inadequate because it does not describe any efforts by LLL or SLL to research and solve this problem that they have helped to create. The environmental impact of LLL projects is enormous, extending beyond the boundaries of the fences at the site. The fact that the rad-wastes from LLL are shipped off to some storage site (e.g. Hanford) is no excuse for the DEIS to ignore the problems and environmental impacts of those wastes. The DEIS should be revised to discuss the waste problems and impacts. Obviously Hanford and other sites are discussed in other DOE DEIS's, but the Farallon Islands and Site 300 rad-waste disposal sites are not discussed in any DEIS's and must be included in the Livermore DEIS revision.

Another dramatic inadequacy of this DEIS is the fact that it discusses what are supposed to be maximum credible accidents for single components in certain buildings at LLL. This analysis is limited to accident scenarios involving three facilities at LLL, even though the rest of the DEIS text indicates that there are dozens of locations on the site where extremely serious accidents could occur in which various types of radioactive materials and gases would be released. The DEIS does not even begin to present accident scenarios for these other parts of the facility. The DEIS should be revised to include all credible accident scenarios, especially in light of the earthquake hazards outlined in Appendix 2 A.

1 of the 3 accident scenarios involves a nuclear criticality accident in the Plutonium Metallurgical Chemistry Building # 332. It says that this accident could involve a fission yield of 10^{18} fissions. The DEIS then calculates the dose for the 1,209,000 people in the sector west of LLL. This includes people in the East Bay and Peninsula communities, in densely populated neighborhoods. This accidnet would release over a thousand curies of xenon 138 which decays (half life 17 minutes)into cesium 137 which remains dangerous for hundreds of years and easily enters the food chain (NOTE: the DEIS does not give or analyze this environmental impact potential). And the accident could release over 500 cureies of radioiodine gases which can be inhaled from the passing cloud, or which can be taken up by the food chain from forage to cows to milk to humans. To calculate the dose from these radioactive gases which would be blown by the winds to distant communities, the DEIS diveids the total amounts of radiation by the total number of people downwind, and derives a dose. This methodology has problems but is generally accepted, although other methodologies exist that could be used for comparison. On page 3-64, the DEIS says that the accident in Building 332 could release between 50 and 150 man-rems of gaseous radiation. It dose not say how these numbers were calculated. Doses were calculated for the west site boundary to be between 5.5 rems and 35 rems (from the forage-cow-milk food chain). The DEIS comments that protective measures would have to be taken to replace the milk from cows downwind of the accident. It does not say how this would be carried out or who would do it. Presumably since federal facilities are only responsible for onsite response, this condemnation and confiscation of milk products would be up to local county and state officilas. The DEIS does not explain whether or not these people and the farmers who would be affected have been notified of the possibility of an accident requiring evacuations or the condemnation of agricultural products.

The DEIS does not discuss the longterm contamination of agricultural lands that would be an environmental impact of the release of xenon and cesium. The DEIS does say (page 3-65) that "The forage-cow-milk pathway doses for I^{131} and I^{133} are increased by precipitaion scavenging by factors which increase with distance downwind...Xe^{138} decays to cesium 137; the latter becomes attached to particulates and is available for scavenging...Submersion doses are enhanced by attachment of cesium 137 particles to fog droplets."

Although indications are given, the DEIS is incomplete in this accident scenario because it does not calculate damages downwind in the eastern direction in the central San Joaquin Valley. The winds at LLL are often from west to east and an accident could seriously contaminate the most fertile agricultural lands in the nation. Although this would be a significant environmental impact, the DEIS does not analyze or mention the possibility. What would be the impact of a cloud of radioactive gases passing over the central valley and into the tule fogs which enhanced the deposition of cesium and iodine into the food chain of the valley? Who would estimate the impact on the farmers and ranchers whose land was affected? What would that impact be? What would be the economic losses sustained?

Another accident scenario is for damage to one glove box in Building 251, which in th 1976 version of the DEIS spilled 1600 curies (with only 1.6 curies escaping, thus giving a downwind dose of 9.5 rems). In the 1978 version, the DEIS says that 1251 curies are spilled from a glove box as a result of fire or explosion, but only .006 curies of respirable particles are airborne and released into the room and this amount has to pass through the 95% efficient filters. This accident would give a dose of 5.6 rems to the person breathing while the cloud of gases passed over. The DEIS says that the EPA reccommen ds evacuations be considered if the dose ranges from 1 to 5 rems, but the DEIS says that the DOE guideline (DOE IMD 0524) allows doses to specific organs 3 times higher than whole body doses. Thus evacuations are not considered necessary by these calculations. DOE should explain its use of these guidelines which avoid the need to evacuate.

The third accidnet scenario involves a release of 1.2 M Curies of tritium following the rupture of a pressure vessel in Building 331 at LLL. This results in a dose of 3.8 rems to an offsite resident. This scenario and dose calculation should be contrasted with a Tritium release scenario that was given in the 1975 Sandia document (page 64) in which the new Sandia Tritium Research Lab had an accident releasing 0.12 M curies of tritium. The document says that LLL calculated that a dose from a release of 1.2 M Curies would be 18 rems, and from 0.12 MC would be 1.8 rems. The maximum quantity at Sandia's research lab can be up to 3.0 MCuries and giving a dose of 45 rems. These calculations seem to indicate that the 1978 version is minimizing the dose according to some arbitrary assumptions.

A question to consider in these accident scenarios is what would happen if all of the glove boxes in Building 251 or all of the tritium vessels at LLL or SLL were damaged or destroyed by a severe earthquake on the nearby Tesla Fault with a 6.5 Richter magnitude quake yielding in excess of a 1.0 g ground acceleration. The quake would totally destroy the filters so that all of the curium and tritium spilled would be available for dispersion. The buildings have only been proposed to be modified to a 0.5 g, so what does that earthquake do to the curium oxide powder and the tritium. The aftershocks would resuspend the oxide powder and it would be repeatedly available for dispersion into the environment during aftershocks. All accident scenarios in the DEIS need to be reevaluated in terms of more severe ground motions during earthquakes. Equally important is the fact that the DEIS omits considerations of many likely accident scenarios, and is thus incomplete in the Accident Analysis section.

. The most serious problem in this DEIS as mentioned at the beginning of these comments is its failure to realisticly analyze the earthquake hazards to all components and systems at the labs in light of the information presented in Appendix 2A. There are ten active faults quite near to the labs. Nine of these nearby faults could produce above a 6.1 on the Richter scale. The Livermore, Mocho, Tesla and Las Positas faults could produce a 6.5 on the Richter scale. The Greenville fault could produce a 6.7 on that scale. This data places the potential quakes from these faults in the range of the San Fernando quake of 1971 in Los Angeles. That quake has been significant in the reanalysis of the Vallecitos Nuclear Center which is located about 10 miles from the Livermore Labs. The largest reactor at Vallecitos was shutdown in October 1977 by the NRC because of the earthquake hazard there. Now the continued operations of the plutonium labs there are in question because of these same hazards. In the Vallecitos case (in which Friends of the Earth is legal Intervenors), the NRC Geosciences Branch has conducted a detailed review of the geology and seismology of the region which should be included in the Livermore Site DEIS because of the proximity of the two nuclear research labs and the similarities in seismic potential. The NRC Geosciences Branch published a Safety Evaluation Report Input on August 17, 1978, that should be reviewed by the DOE for the Livermore DEIS revision. That document concludes that the Vallecitos site could experience ground accelerations in excess of 1.0 g from the Verona fault, a thrust fault that was considered inactive at the time Vallecitos was built. This predicted ground motion is based on observations during the San Fernando quake of 1971, in which data was obtained showing several instances of ground accelerations in excess of 1.0 g. Several of the faults near the Livermore site could experience ground accelerations in excess of a 1.0 g. This is based on comparison of their length and potential magnitudes with the San Fernando quake which was a 6.5 magnitude quake on a short thrust fault. Trenching and other geologic investigations should be carried out at the Livermore Site to determine the exact locations and historic motions on the faults near the site.

Serious

The DOE should seriously reevaluate the LLL management's choice of 0.5 g as the ground acceleration level chosen for modifications to the LLL facilities. The 1974 report by Wight in the DEIS Appendix 2 A suggests that a more appropriate value for ground motions would be 0.8 g, but the LLL management chose not to accept their advice, perhaps because it would be more difficult, but safer to modify to that level. Because the Livermore Valley and the lab site were created by tectonic forces related to the San Andreas and Calaveras fault zones, it is necessary to realize that the Livermore labs are located in one of the most seismicly active regions of the world. The geologic history of the region is appropriately detailed in Appendix 2 A and the information there should be taken more seriously by the DOE. When the AEC originally chose the site in 1951, there was little or no seismic evaluation performed. It was just a location conveniently near the Radiation labs in Berkeley where many nuclear physicists were available to work as researchers in AEC programs. It was not until 1974 that a thorough seismic report was completed and by then, most of the buildings had been in operation for many years and it was difficult to change the structural designs. However the environmental impact potential of earthquake damages requires that all of the structures, systems and components at LLL and SLL be reevaluated for ground motions between a 0.8 g and a 1.0 g. A new DEIS needs to be done using these values as input in structural analyses. For this review, the DOE should hire consultants from independent structural engineering firms who do not have a bias or a conflict of interest that would create predetermined outcomes.

Because the Tesla fault passes within 200 feet of crucial structures at LLL, and because the Ramp Thrust fault and the Corral Hollow fault appear to pass beneath the site and near lab structures, DOE needs to carefully analyze the potential structural damages to lab facilities that could result from surface ruptures, ground shearing, and lateral or vertical offset directly beneath the buildings. This type of analysis has not been done. If these types of ground mo motions can take palce beneath the structures, they could be simultaneous with and in addition to the g values previously described, and the structural damage would be increased tremendously.

Structural engineers in California generally recognize that it is difficult to make a structure "earthquake proof" if it is within a zone of possible surface rupture and offset or shearing. For example, the following quotes are from a book titled Peace of Mind in Earthquake Country written by Peter Yanev, an employee of URS/Blume Associates who have done studies of Livermore and Sandia labs.

"Buildings located in fault zones are exposed to the highest possible earthquake risks. This is unequivocally a fact of life in earthquake country, and no measures--whether the most earthquake-resistant bracing and building materials nor the latests and soundest principles of reinforcement--can guarantee or even t tentatively propose that any property astride a fault would survive a moderate quake without severe or total damage... The greatest hazard to structures in fault zones is that they are subject to ground-surface ruptures and displacements during an earthquake, and no building can withstand this faulting beneath it. A ground shift of only a few inches (vertically, horizontally, or , most commonly, both) is sufficient to cause severe structural damage to buildings. A large quake, with its typical displacements in the fault zone of from several inches to several feet, could demolish the most well-engineered building." (page 49)

That quote is sound advise to the DOE in its evaluation the Livermore DEIS. Peter Yanev's employer, URS/ Blume and Associates developed the Seismic Design Criteria for Nuclear REactors in 1973. Unfortunately, most of the structures at Livermore were designed long before any criteria were available and before the information about locations and potential magnitudes of nearby faults was known. Although Blume has done a study of the site, he admits that it does not fulfill the necessary criteria and that if there was the possibility of surface rupture, then a complete reevaluation would be necessary.

In its review of this matter, the DOE should consult with the USGS geologist, Darrell Herd, (in the Menlo Park office of USGS) who has remapped the area near the site, including the Las Positas fault which passes through the Sandia Lab site. Herd's report (USGS Open file report 77-689) should be used in the review.

Friends of the Earth would like the opportunity to present a more detailed analysis of potential ground motions and consequent structural damages to the labs in future communications on this subject. Earthquake hazards to nuclear facilities can cause serious damages that could create the maximum credible accidents in all buildings at Livermore. Because over five million people live within the evacuation and contamination zone radius from the Livermore site, this is a public health and safety question of significant importance. We ask you to please conduct public hearings on this subject of earthquake hazards at the Livermore site.

Enclosed are additional pages of comments on the Livermore DEIS which were written about the original version (virtually a verbatim copy of the current one) which was published by LLL in October, 1976. We believe that these comments are still valid and appropriate. Therefore we submit them to the DOE staff along with the preceeding updated comments.

Also included are some Geological and Seismic Interpretations of the hazards existing in the Livermore Valley region which were submitted as part of our research on the Vallecitos Nuclear Center.

Also included are various clippings, reports, and reproductions that were referred to in the text of the comments.

The Lawrence Livermore Lab is located in a very active earthquake zone. There are thirteen active faults that could potentially damage the structures at the lab. Attached to this report are maps and tables that detail the names, locations, and Richter magnitude potential of these thirteen earthquake faults. Twelve of the thirteen faults could have quakes measuring 6.1 and higher on the Richter Scale. Several of the faults actually intersect the lab property. The potentially most dangerous fault is the Tesla-Fault which has at least three branches near the lab. Many critical structures on the lab site are within 200 feet or less from the Tesla Fault. A significant earthquake occurred in the summer of 1977 on the Tesla Fault. According to the Draft Environmental Impact Statement for LLL and Sandia Lab, published in October, 1976, future quakes could be a hazard to the Labs' operations. The structures at LLL have been designed and upgraded to withstand a quake that would produce a peak ground acceleration of 0.5 g. That DEIS contains an Appendix 2A entitled "A Geological and Seismological Investigation of the LLL Site" published on June 3, 1974. This report discusses the definition of the "Safe Shutdown Earthquake" (SSE) for LLL; "For earthquakes on the nearby Tesla Fault, we calculate that the peak acceleration at the site will be 0.8 g". The report indicates that a 0.5 g peak acceleration would correspond to a 5.5 Richter Magnitude quake, and that the Tesla Fault could have up to a 6.5 Richter Magnitude quake.

But the report states that the LLL management thought that a SSE based on 0.8 g was excessively conservative, even though 2 out of 3 earthquake studies on LLL said that the SSE should be approximately 0.8 g. The Lab management intervened in the definition of SSE and selected the SSE published in a 1972 report entitled "Investigation of Faulting at the LLL", which is also included in the Appendix of the DEIS. That report defines the SSE at LLL as a 5.7 Richter magnitude quake causing a peak ground acceleration of 0.5g. The LLL management reccommended that all Safety Analysis Reports for LLL use that as the SSE. Consequently, since 1974, most of the structures at LLL have been upgraded to withstand a peak ground acceleration of 0.5g. When most of the structures were originally built, the estimated ground acceleration was lower.

It is significant to note that there are many different kinds of buildings, abs, and facilities at LLL that could be damaged by earthquakes. Most of these ere built years before the existence and locations of the nearby earthquake faults ere known. and now, with the new information, some upgrading and modifications are eing undertaken but are not completed. One problem with this process is that because he property legally belongs to the federal government, the AEC and ERDA have tradiionally maintained federal preemption over state, local, and regional government gencies concerning inspections of the facilities at LLL. Thus, the state and county uilding code inspectors and structural engineers investigating earthquake resistance tandards have never been allowed onto the property for investigations to satisfy the tate and county standards. This is a serious mistake that should be corrected. he University of California should demand that ERDA (now the DOE) allow the state nd county inspectors to enter the premises to conduct structural engineering analyses n all the facilities at LLL. The health and safety of the people of California re at stake, because of the serious potential for radioactive contamination.

There are many critical components at LLL that could be damaged in a quake which ould result in the release of radioactive liquids, gases, and solids into the local nvironment. Several buildings contain hot cells, glove boxes, pipes, filter systems, nd retention tanks that are particularly susceptible to earthquake damage and are xtremely difficult to make earthquake proof. The DEIS recognizes that some of the uildings still need "Funding requested to upgrade ventilation and exhaust systems, nd (funding) to incorporate structural modifications to improve seismic resistance."

Several buildings at LLL are involved in the processing, handling, and storing f all levels of radioactive wastes. These buildings often have large quantities of ighly dangerous materials in containers that are not earthquake proof. Especially ılnerable are the liquid radioactive wastes when they are being transported in tanks ıd when they are being processed . The DEIS says that , in Building 514, the Radioactive iquid Waste Treatment Plant, "Equipment failures, could release untreated, highly ıdioactive wastes into the Livermore sewage system.

I reccommend that anyone interested in understanding the full environmental impact of the LLL, should read the DEIS, and

the Annual Environmental Monitoring Reports prepared by LLL. It is interesting to note that LLL is on a Self-Monitoring Program and that no government agency, local, state or federal, conducts independent in-stack monitoring of routine emissions from LLL stacks operations. These routine emissions come from certain facilities at LLL that have been improved during the past few years to reduce the amounts of air and water pollution. However, in 1975, LLL released 3,400 Curies of Tritium into the air, 38 curies of tritium into the sewage system, 600 curies of argon gas into the air, trace amounts of plutonium, Iodine-131, Strontium-90, and Radium-226 into the Livermore sewage system. In the past significant-leaks of plutonium into the sewer caused lab scientists to use the sludge for experiments to discover which vegetables take up plutonium from the soil most rapidly. LLL and Site 300 together have generated over 100,000 pounds of depleted uranium. At Site 50% of the uranium in test explosions is dispersed into the environment and studies of monitoring in the San Joaquin Valley have indicated widespread dispersal in that valle The Sandia Lab, next door to LLL, has 170,000 curies of radioactive cesium which is biologically active and could enter the Central Valley food chain, if dispersed.

The Sandia Lab has a special earthquake problems in that the recently published USGS study by D. Herd shows that the newly discovered Las Positas Fault passes through the Sandia Property. That Fault could endanger weapons test facilities at Sandia.

MAXIMUM CREDIBLE ACCIDENTS

The DEIS discusses maximum credible accidents for single components in certain buildings at LLL. For example, if one glove box in Building 251, was damaged by a fire or explosion, then 1600 curies of curium 244 oxide could be released. If 1.6 curies of this escaped (assuming that filters were not damaged and worked properly) then a person downwind could receive 9.5 rems of radiations. The DEIS does not say what would happen if more than one glove box was damaged or if the filters were damaged.

Another accident analysis in the DEIS postulated a tritium gas release of 1,200,000 curies caused by the rupture of one pressure vessel. The analysis does not consider the rupture of more than one vessel at a time. The postulated tritium release would be from Building 331.

Another postulated accident in the DEIS takes place in Building 332, the Metallurgical Chemistry Building where plutonium is handled in significant quantities. That accident could release 250,000 curies of fission products, including 500 curies of radioactive iodine gases that can produce thyroid cancers. The DEIS does not discuss the evacuations that would be necessary if iodine gas was released. The same accident could release over 1000 curies of xenon that decays into cesium which can contaminate the food chain for 1000 years.

In these postulated accidents, the cause is usually fire, human error or explosions. The DEIS does not consider the cumulative effects of an earthquake that damaged several buildings at once or that damaged several glove boxes, hot cells, filter systems and other components all at the same time. The DEIS also assumes that the filter systems will always work well enought to filter out 95 per cent of the radioactive materials before release to the environment. These assumptions make the DEIS inadequate, incomplete and misleading.

Radioactive Wastes originate in 25 buildings at LLL within over 100 different operations. Five buildings that produce the bulk of the wastes are the Pool Type Reactor, the 100 MeV Linear Accelerator, the Heavy Element Chemistry Building 251, the MetalLurgical Chemistry Building 332, and the Light Isotope Chemistry Building 331. Some of these have hot cells and glove boxes that are vulnerable to earthquake damages. If the filter systems are damaged in a quake, serious contamination of the surrounding areas could occur. If the wind was blowing towards the east or northeast, as is typical during the dry summer season, then the fertile agricultural lands of the San Joaquin Valley would be seriously contaminated and the nation's food supply would be endangered.

If the wind was blowing towards the west or southwest, as is typic.al, during the wet winter season, then San Jose and Palo Alto could be endangered from clouds of radioactive isotopes. Evacuation of metropolitan communities might be necessary, even tho such evacuations have never been rehearsed, and even tho the evacuations might be impossible after a serious earthquake in the area.

An accidental release of radiation from LLL could contaminate several reservoirs and aqueducts that border the Livermore Valley and supply drinking water to millions of people in San Francisco and the South Bay cities. The Hetch Hetchy Aqueduct and the South Bay Aqueduct pass near the Lab site. This type of environmental impact is not analyzed in the DEIS.

A nuclear weapons facility at Rocky Flats, Colorado, has spilled and leaked plutonium and other isotopes into the surrounding area, About 11.000 acres have been contaminated with more plutonium than considered safe by the Colorado Health Department. Rocky Flats operations involve routine emissions of small amounts of radioactive materials leading to measurable doses to people in Denver and Boulder. 500 shipments of radioactive cargo are trucked to and from Rocky Flats each year. leaving measurable amounts of radiation along the roads. ERDA and the Colorado Health Dept. disagree as to how many citizens will suffer health effects from Rocky Flats. The Contamination that has already happened at Rocky Flats represents a fraction of the potential possible at LLL. The GAO has called for an analysis of similar DOE ERDA weapons facilities. The University of Cal. should request that the GAO, EPA, and OES conduct studies of potential contamination at LLL, Sandia, and Los Alamos.

In 1977 it was discovered that Plutonium was being flown in and out of Rocky Flats and Livermore in small turbo prop transport planes, in containers that were not crash proof. The flights had been going on secretly for 25 years or more. When the Congressman from Livermore discovered this he held hearings and pressured ERDA to stop the flights. A crash of one of those planes could have caused serious widespread contamination.

Further information on the Farralon Islands waste sites is contained in the attached report entitled "Radiation and Earthquakes:The Ominous POtential in the Bay Area". The EPA is continuing its investigation and will be issuing further reports in the future.

The University's labs currently use two different methods of disposing of their wastes(1)High level and recyclable wastes are turned over to ERDA, now DOE, for shipment to one of eight federal waste storage sites. These federal radioacitve wastes facilities have a terrible record of leaks and spills that have contaminated the environment. In fact, today a Serious national security problems exists because there has been no adequate solution developed for the radioactive waste disposal problem. Most of the rad wastes are from nuclear weapons facilities.

(2) Low level wastes and non-retrievable wastes are shipped by contract carrier to a privately owned waste storage site near Beatty, Nevada. In 1975, ERDA discovered that the operator there had been illegally recycling radioactive tools and equipment to various local citizens who were found to be inppossession of the items.

The Livermore lab used to bury some radioactive wastes in trenches at Site 300, located 15 miles from the lab in Alameda County, California. That practice has been stopped but the Lab does continue to dump large quantities of radioactive rubble, mostly depleted uranium from Site 300 explosions, into trenches there for burial.

Large quantities of radioactive wastes pass through the Livermore Lab each year. These wastes are transported away from the Lab by contract or common couriers, in containers approved by ERDA. These wastes pass across the fertile Central Valley and through many California communities, without any advance notice to local officials that trucks carrying rad-wastes are passing their way. Earthquakes, accidents, and terrorist attacks or sabotage could cause large-scale contamination of California.

Why has the University of California not reccommended to the weapons labs that they try to solfe the rad-wastes disposal problem before they continue to create longlived radioactive isotopes that will have to be guarded and kept out of the biosphere and food chains for centuries? Plutonium remains hazardous for up to 500,000 years.

Another potential impact to be considered is the fact that the location of the nuclear weapons complex at LLL makes the site a number one target in case of a nuclear or conventional attack on the U.S. by enemy forces. LLL has provided fallout shelters for its employees, with a couple weeks rations of foods, but LLL has not provided for the other 4 or 5 million neighbors who would be affected. Strategic targeting of LLL by enemy missiles is one good reason to remove the LLL to a remote location like NTS.

In its DEIS, LLL recognizes that certain buildings on the site pose extreme hazards potential to the local environment. On page 5-3 of the DEIS, LLL describes the alternative that relocation of these facilities to the Nevada Test Site (NTS) would be feasible and"attractive because NTS is in an area geographically remote from population centers and is owned and operated by ERDA (DOE). Furthermore, many areas within NTS have been exposed to the impact of previous nuclear testing. As a result, the additional radiation impact of the operations listed would be minimal." (DEIS, page 5-3)
The facilities thus categorized as having the most "potential for adverse impact" are the Neutron accelerator in Building 212, the Diagnostic Chemistry Building 251, the Livermore Pool Type Reactor, the Gaseous Chemistry Building R331, and the Plutonium Metallurgy Building 332.

The University of California should make continued operation of LLL contingent on the relocation of these five dangerous facilities to the NTS. This partial relocation would minimize the potential contamination from earthquake damage to the LLL.
The Controversy over structural engineering, Design Basis Earthquakes and SSE's at LLL, make it necessary for new seismic studies to be done independently of LLL management.
The use of several hundred pounds per year of plutonium at LLL creates an enormous and unacceptable health hazard, in light of the dangers of Plutonium and the potential quake damages. All plutonium facilities at LLL should be relocated to NTS, before the Livermore and San Joaquin Valleys become contaminated the way the Rocky Flats area has been contaminated already.

NUCLEAR WEAPONS LABORATORIES AT LIVERMORE

BY GLENN BARLOW,

The environmental impacts of the nuclear weapons labs extend far beyond the boundaries of the labs themselves. Scientists employed by LLL the University of California have conducted over 600 nuclear weapons tests since the Hiroshima and Nagasaki explosions. Over 100 of these tests were in the South Pacific and the other 500 nuclear weapons were exploded in the continental United States. Since the Limited Test Ban Treaty of 1963, all of these tests have been underground, but before that treaty 84 atmospheric tests were conducted at the Nevada Test Site, fifty miles from the California border. Radioactive fallout from those tests has contaminated a large area in Nevada with plutonium and other sources of radiation. Thyroid tumors have been discovered in children in Nevada and Utah where clouds of radioactivity passed over communities. The plutonium contamination of soils in Nevada could last for hundreds of thousands of years. That is environmental impact!

The radioactive fallout from the 100 atmospheric tests in the South Pacific resulted in contamination of the entire planet earth with long-lasting sources of radiation such as strontium-90 and cesium-137 which enter the food chain and deposit in human bones and tissues where they can produce cancers and leukemia.

Unfortunately, the nuclear weapons labs did not begin to study the effects of fallout until after the Test Ban Treaty of 1963. In 1963, the Lawrence Radiation Laboratory established its Biomedical Division to study the health effects of nuclear weapons development. The chief of that Division from 1963 to 1969 was Dr. John Gofman, who in 1969 reported to Congress and the Atomic Energy Commission that previously established radiation standards were inadequate to protect public health, and that the health effects of nuclear weapons development were more serious than previously believed. Dr. Gofman lost his job at Livermore Lab because of his reports. Recently, Dr. Gofman has published a report that indicates that over a million people in the northern hemisphere will die of cancers produced by fallout from atmospheric tests, and that plutonium is much more carcinogenic than what the laboratories have been assuming for many years. Since the cancers produced by exposure to plutonium do not show up until thirty to forty years after exposure, and since most of the plutonium involved in the nuclear weapons labs work has been produced in the past 25 years, the major health impacts may begin to appear in the next 5 to 15 years. A question that we all should ask is, who should be held responsible for the cancers and deaths that are results of nuclear tests? Are the Regents of the University responsible? Are the lab employees responsible? Or the DOE? Should the world's citizens conduct Nuremburg--type trials of the employees to punish them for killing so many people? And if there ever is a nuclear war in the future, would the University of California be held responsible for developing the bombs that caused the death and destruction?

The 400 underground nuclear weapons tests that the has conducted in the U.S. raise another problem that is of special interest to citizens of California. According to a report prepared by the Lawrence Livermore Lab and published by the AEC in April, 1969, "there is concern on the part of some earthquake experts that ... serious earthquakes might be induced by larger yield nuclear tests. This is an area in which further study is necessary."

Another Lab report explains that 'When the Boxcar event (with a yield of 1.2 megatons), conducted in April, 1968, resulted in thousands of small aftershocks (ensuing earth tremors),.. great scientific interest was created and an ad hoc panel of seismic consultants to the Nevada Operations Office was recruited among the foremost seismologists of the U.S. Boxcar was the first U.S. underground test designed for a megaton yield or more."

Because of the Limited Test Ban Treaty, agreed to by Nixon and Breshnev in 1974, and signed by Ford and Breshnev at Vladivostok that same year, all underground nuclear tests were to be limited to 150 kilotons ater March 20, 1976. Because of this impending limitation, both countries increased the size and frequency of underground explosions up to the deadline. During the ten months between May 1975 and March 17, 1976, the U. S. conducted twelve megaton range (a megaton is equivalent to one million tons of TNT) nuclear weapons test and six smaller ones at the Nevada Test Site. Thus the administrators of the University's nuclear weapons labs ignored the advice of the Panel of foremost seismologists who wrote a report published by the Office of Science and Technology, Executive Office of the President, on November 27, 1968, entitled "Report of the Ad Hoc Panel on the Safety of Underground Testing". That report was reprinted in a September, 1969 publication by the Atomic Energy Commission (AEC) entitled "Underground Nuclear Testing". Consider the following quatations from that report: "The Panel is seriously concerned with the problem of earthquakes resulting from large-yield nuclear tests...new and significant evidence demonstrates that small earthquakes do actually occur both immediately after a large-yield test explosion and in the following weeks... a large test explosion might induce, either immediately or after a period of time, a severe earthquake of sufficiently large magnitude to cause serious damage well beyond the limits of the test site...Consideration should also be given to the possibility of establishing a new test site in a non-seismic area...The hazard connected with the triggering of earthquakes is a more serious question because of the potentiality of releasing tectonic energy comparable to, or very much larger than, the energy of the (nuclear) explosion itself... We are now dealing with underground explosions with equivalent earthquake magnitudes in the range 6 to 7... We also know that seismic events in the magnitude range 6 to 7 have been associated in the past as foreshocks to large earthquakes or as components of large earthquakes.

In view of these observations, a risk must be associated with conducting large-yield tests in seismic regions... There is no question that the larger nuclear explosions in Nevada have actually triggered small earthquakes..."

The Nevada Test Site is in a moderately active earthquake zone that joins the Circum-Pacific Seismic Belt which passes through California, and includes the San Andreas Fault System. This belt of fault systems surrounding the Pacific Ocean is responsible for about 80% of the world's earthquakes.

During the megaton range weapons tests, in February, 1976, a major earthquake (measuring 7.5 on the Richter scale) with nearly a hundred aftershocks tremors, struck Central America, inflicting severe damage upon Guatemala, Honduras, and El Salvador. Latin American newspapers accused the U.S. military of causing the disastrous quake by exploding enormous nuclear weapons underground in Nevada. The same reports said that nuclear tests were also responsible for other earthquakes in Mexico and Costa Rica. It is also possible that the San Fernando Quake in Los Angeles in 1971,(measuring 6.6 on the Richter scale) could have been stimulated by nuclear weapons tests 300 miles away at the Nevada Test Site. All of the above locations are in the Circum-Pacific Seismic Belt and earthquake waves can travel deep beneath the surface, causing tremors long distances away from the epicenter.

The nuclear tests in Nevada are carried out under the direction of the University of California's Laboratories. Can the University be held responsible for the damages caused by underground nuclear tests?

The Limited Test Ban Treaty of 1974 has not been ratified by the U.S. Senate. During hearings of the Senate Foreign Relations Committee on September 8, 1977, concerning ratification of the Treaty, the Directors of the University of California's Laboratories at Livermore and Los Alamos, testified against ratification of the treatie because the Labs want to continue to test megaton range bombs in Nevada, regardless of the hazard of stimulating more earthquakes. Why does the University of California not require its employees to present both sides of an issue when they lobby Congress?

December 19, 1978

Mr. W. H. Pennington:

Enclosed you will find additional documents, reports, clippings, and other materials that are referred to in the main text of Friends of the Earth's comments on the Livermore Site DEIS. The main text was sent postal express so as to arrive on or before the deadline for comments. These appendices and addenda are being sent under separate cover. please attach them to the main set of commenhs.

Thank you

Glenn Barlow

Glenn Barlow

Friends of the Earth

FURTHER DOCUMENTATION OF EARTHQUAKE HAZARDS TO THE VALLECITOS NUCLEAR CENTER PLUTONIUM LABS FOR THE DECEMBER 14, 1978, REQUEST FOR ACTION TO THE NRC

PREPARED BY GLENN BARLOW

GEOLOGY AND SEISMOLOGY

In the course of the Vallecitos GETR reactor Show Cause Proceedings (Docket No. 50-70), the NRC Staff published a Preliminary Safety Evaluation Report Input (PSER-GETR), prepared by the Geosciences Branch of the Staff on the geologic and seismic hazards to the site. Although the PSER-GETR was dated August 17, 1978, it was not released to Intervenors until early October, 1978. In the PSER-GETR, the NRC Geosciences Branch makes the following statements:

"The seismic design hazards for the GETR site include vibratory ground motion, fault offset at the surface beneath the unit and vibratory ground motion combined with surface offset caused by postulated movement on the Verona fault. The licensee (GE) has provided an evaluation of these design hazards in reports by EDAC (1976, 1977) and has provided additional supporting discussion in a report by Earth Sciences Associates (ESA, 1978d). The staff has reviewed these reports and has taken account of the analyses and conclusions contained in them in the preparation of this testimony. This testimony is concerned with an evaluation of the nature and magnitude of the hazards of faulting and ground motion at the site... The GETR site is located in a complex fault environment 2.3 kilometers east of the Calaveras fault, directly over the projected surface trace of the postulated Verona fault, and within 3 kilometers of the Las Positas fault... Maximum earthquakes for these faults would have magnitudes of 7 to 7 ½, 6 to 6 ½, and 6 to 6½, respectively... the proposed Verona fault can be presumed to exist beyond the bounds of the area mapped by Herd and to merge with the Calaveras fault... it must be presumed that the Verona fault is structurally connected to larger faults, and that a major portion and possibly all of the 12 kilometers length could rupture during a single earthquake. It is our conclusion, therefore, that the San Fernando earthquake of 1971 could be considered as an earthquake similar in size to a potential event on the proposed Verona fault." (Seismology section)

The section of the PSER-GETR entitled 'Current Staff Position" says: "Geologic data are indicative of a fault (the Verona fault) passing through the GETR site, and this fault should be assumed to exist... The Verona fault should be assumed to be capable within the meaning of Appendix A to 10 CFR Part 100 and, therefore, to pose a potential for surface faulting near or beneath the reactor site... 2.5 meters of net slip at the surface resulting from reverse-oblique movement along a fault plane which could vary in dip angle from 10 to 60 degrees provides a reasonably conservative description of surface slip on the postulated Verona fault during a single event...

"Maximum vibratory ground motion at the GETR site would result from a magnitude 7 to 7 ½ earthquake centered on the sector of the Calaveras fault nearest the site. Acceleration peaks at the free-field surface could be slightly in excess of 1.0 g... The horizontal vibratory ground motion at the GETR site resulting from an earthquake of magnitude 6 to 6 ½ on the Verona fault could contain acceleration peaks as high as 1.0 g."

The following quotes are from the section entitled "Geology":

"The GETR site is located in a highly active tectonic environment (Bolt and others, 1977; Lee and others, 1971)... within the Livermore syncline and the central part of the Coast Ranges structurally related to the San Andreas fault system, a transform fault which forms a major sector of the boundary between the North American and Pacific lithospheric plates...(Anderson, 1971)... We consider the Livermore syncline and the major structural elements therein, including faults, to owe their existence to movement across the Calaveras fault. The faults significant to our review which we consider genetically related to the Calaveras are the Las Positas fault... and the Verona fault which as interpreted is a low angle thrust within the southern flank of the syncline.'

"The existence of a landslide near the site does not in any way preclude the existence of faulting there. As discussed below, evidence for faulting exists in areas away from the landslide are. In fact, landsliding often results from oversteepening of slopes due to fault movement and seismic shaking...

(1)...Areas to the northwest of the GETR show, both in the field and on aerial photographs,the presence of geologic features which are indicative of the existence of faulting. Steeply dipping Livermore gravel beds are truncated along a linear to curvilinear topographic escarpment. Along the base of this escarpment are a number of seeps and springs.
(2)To the southeast of the GETR the geologic log of the La Costa tunnel (California Department of Water Resources, 1966) suggests low angle faulting and folding in an area through which the postulated Verona fault would pass if projected eastward...
(3)The relationship between the Verona fault and the Las Positas fault has not been investigated and the area of the William's fault (Hall, 1958) -La Costa tunnel intersection has not been investigated sufficiently...
AREAS OF INTERSECTION OR MERGING OF FAULTS CAN BE IN A TRANSITIONAL STRESS STATE WHICH USUALLY LEADS TO THE DEVELOPMENT OF FAULT PATTERNS WHICH ARE GEOLOGICALLY COMPLEX SUCH AS EN ECHELON FAULTS RATHER THAN A SINGLE PLANAR FAULT SURFACE. SUCH COMPLEX PATTERNS ARE DIFFICULT TO INTERPRET WITHOUT EXTENSIVE FIELD INVESTIGATIONS. (Emphasis added)
(4)A prominent south-facing scarp and topographic break does exist in the site area.
(5)Existing geologic maps and texts of Vickery (1925), Hall (1958), Prince (1957), URS/Blume Associates (1973) and more recently Herd (1977) support the existence of the Verona fault and other faults in the GETR site area and vicinity. In addition, to the northwest of the GETR site and along the general northwesterly projection of the Verona fault is the northwest trending Pleasanton fault which is identified as a potentially active fault on the California Division of Mines and Geology Special Studies Zones Map, Dublin Quadrangle (Slosson, 1974). Several authors (Burkland, 1975; Judd Hall Associates, 1977; Carpenter, 1977) have assigned various locations to Pleasanton fault. At the present time, it is reasonable to conclude that the Pleasanton fault is a possible continuation of the Verona fault.

(6) Recent seismological studies of earthquake fault plane solutions indicate that the Livermore Valley region is in northeast-southwest compression (Simila and Somerville, 1978) and not extension as argued by the licensee (GE-EDAC, 1978). Moreover, this indirect observation of the stress direction is consistent with the highly active regional tectonic framework. Northeast-southwest compression would support development of, and continued movement along, a northeast-dipping thrust fault such as the Verona.
(8)... The more recent geologic mapping provided by GE contains substantially more geologic structures than the earlier versions, indicating more post-Livermore tectonic deformation than would have been ascertained from GE's earlier mapping.
(9) Photolinears and the cause of seeps and ponds to the south of and in close proximity to the GETR site area have not been trenched or explained. In tectonically active areas photolinears are often due to groundwater barriers or differential erosion due to the presence of a fault."

FRIENDS OF THE EARTH'S COMMENTS AND ANALYSIS

Although the NRC's PSER-GETR report presents interesting information, it is incomplete in analyzing the complex tectonic setting of the Vallecitos Valley and the surrounding fault systems. Several faults that may intersect with the Verona fault are not analyzed. All of these faults seem to intersect with or parallel the Calaveras fault and possibly intersect with the Las Positas fault. These faults include the Pleasanton fault, the Williams fault, the Maguire Peaks fault, and other parallel branches of the Calaveras fault. Also not analyzed by the NRC are the sequence of interactions during an earthquake on the Verona, Las Positas, and Calaveras faults in terms of ground motions and durations, and possible surface ruptures, and how these would affect the operating plutonium labs. All of the above mentioned faults could be branches or subsidiaries of the powerful Calaveras fault which is a branch of the San Andreas. If any of these faults experienced seismic activity simultaneously with the Calaveras, what would be the effects on the reactors and labs at Vallecitos? The NRC seems to have forgotten a memo from one of its geophysicists in the Geosciences Branch concerning the timing of earthquakes on the Calaveras. In his memo to Carl Stepp, John Kelleher states:

"The Calaveras fault zone is a capable fault within the meaning of Appendix A to 10 CFR Part 100 and, at its closest point, is within one or two miles of the GETR site. It is reasonable, in my opinion, to assume that an earthquake of magnitude about 7.0 to 7.5 could occur at any time on this fault and at any location along the fault. Such an earthquake, therefore, could occur at any time within one or two mile of the plant site. The resulting ground motion generated at the plant site by the postulated earthquake would almost certainly be severe and peak ground accelerations would be among the higher observations to date. (emphasis added)
It is unlikely that extensive future investigations will modify this assessment in any significant manner."

That internal NRC Staff memo was written in late October, 1977, and now in December, 1978, the plutonium labs at Vallecitos are still in operation, even though the NRC PSER-GETR admits that the Calaveras could cause in excess of a one g at the site, and GE's structural analysis indicates that a one g could totally destroy the plutonium labs. This situation illustrates the risks that the NRC is willing to take with public health and safety.

Actually it is possible that an earthquake on either the Verona or the Calaveras faults could easily exceed one g. Calculations by a seismologist from Scripps Institute of Geophysics and Planetary Physics (J.N. Brune, Journal of Geophysical Research, 1970, 1978) and by Y. Ida (Bulletin of Seismological Society of America, 1973) indicate that peak acceleration near a surface rupture can easily exceed one g. Also, field evidence from near-epicenter damage studies (N.N. Ambraseys, 1969; C.F. Richter, Elementary Seismology, 1958) indicates that accelerations greater than one g have already been experienced. Furthermore, according to L.H.Wight, there are "data, calculations, and observations (which) clearly indicate that accelerations approaching one g are possible in near-epicentral regions for earthquakes of all magnitudes.

The NRC's PSER-GETR says that the Verona fault could experience an earthquake similar in size to the San Fernando quake of 1971. That quake changed the entire set of seismological theories on relationships between Richter magnitudes and ground acceleration potential. That quake was the first time in history that accurate near-field ground acceleration data was collected. Based on previous records, the maximum ground acceleration possible at San Fernando in 1971 would have been predicted to be 0.1 g to 0.3 g. Instead, the 1971 quake, measuring 6.6 magnitude, caused various ground acceleration measurements in excess of one g including the Pacoima Dam record of 1.25 g, recorded at a distance of 4.4 kilometers from the epicenter. The Vallecitos plutonium labs are less than 1 kilometer from the Verona fault, and less than 3 kilometers from the Las Positas fault, either of which could cause a 6.5 magnitude quake. Thus, it is possible that either of those faults could cause accelerations at Vallecitos in excess of 1 g.

The Calaveras fault can cause a 7.5 magnitude quake with an epicenter one or two miles from the plutonium labs. The way the Richter scale is measured, a quake of magnitude 7.5 could release more than thirty times more destructive energy than a quake of magnitude 6.5. Thus, it is very possible that a Calaveras quake with its epicenter near Vallecitos could cause severe ground accelerations in excess of 2 g. Another relevant quote from the NRC PSER -GETR will help to explain this:

"Numerous complexities are involved in estimating earthquake ground motions at a site. At distances greater than about 20 kilometers from the earthquake source, a fairly large set of observational data exists. At distances closer to the source, however, the observational data set is relatively small. There is,in fact, a virtual absence of records of strong ground motion for locations close to large earthquake sources. Any estimate of free-field ground motion at the GETR site must, therefore, be considered an extrapolation of data rather than supported by direct observations. Simple source theory indicates that peak acceleration near the causative fault may be proportional to the stress conditions and rock physical properties at the source, possibly independent of earthquake magnitude (see for example, Brune, 1970). Limited observational data tend to support these theoretical results (Hanks and Johnson, 1976)."

Following the above statement in the PSER-GETR, the NRC Staff stated that:

"Duration of motion, including duration of high peaks is, however, a function of earthquake magnitude or source size... based on the available data by Page and others (1972)... peak horizontal near-source acceleration for a magnitude 7 to 7 ½ earthquake could exceed 1 g and that the total duration of strong motion could be between 25 and 40 seconds."

Apparently, the NRC may have underestimated the duration, based on recent data from the November 29, 1978 earthquake in Mexico where a quake with its epicenter offshore some 400 miles from Mexico City, had a duration of two minutes and 53 seconds, with a 7.8 magnitude quake. That quake was followed by five more strong aftershocks within twenty four hours. Although that quake had its epicenter about 400 miles from Mexico City, the structural damages in that city were large. This indicates that the Vallecitos site should be reevaluated for damages from quakes on the San Andreas fault system. The November 29 quake and aftershocks were followed on December 7 by another major quake of magnitude 6 to 7 with two large aftershocks, that shook 3 Latin American countries. And then on December 10, 1978, another quake with a 5.9 magnitude shook the Acapulco area. That quake could have been an aftershock of the November 29th quake.
These quakes illustrate the problems that would be experienced at the Vallecitos plutonium labs if a major quake and associated aftershocks damaged the labs, spilled plutonium, and left radioactive materials exposed to resuspension from aftershocks.

Another consideration that the NRC Staff has failed to analyze is the fact that the Calaveras fault zone near Vallecitos is a seismic gap which is defined as any region along an active plate boundary that has not experienced a large thrust or strike slip earthquake for more than 30 years. A seismic gap has the potential to produce a large earthquake in the near future. This is especially relevant now because the earthquake in Mexico last month was predicted by geologists because the area was in a state of seismic gap. When will the next big quake strike the Calaveras fault zone?

The NRC PSER-GETR (August, 1978) failed to analyze in detail the possibility of an *en echelon* series of branch faults in the Livermore and Vallecitos Valleys. *En echelon* faults are very common in northern California because of lateral stresses. If three main faults are located near each other (such as the Verona, Las Positas, and Calaveras) then there will likely be branches, spurs, or parallel offshoots between them. It is probable that several new faults will be discovered if more trenching is done in the Vallecitos Valley.

When discussing potential earthquakes on postulated faults, it is essential to understand that faults are not limited to narrow lines on a map, but are found in zones that range from 100 feet wide to several miles wide. Severe ground motions can occur several miles from the main fault trace, because the actual ground motion originates deep within the earth, not on the surface. The Calaveras and its branches are part of the San Andreas fault system, which is experiencing enormous tectonic stress. According to the plate tectonics theory, the San Andreas is a transform fault that is the dividing line between the North American plate and the Pacific plate, and these two plates are sliding past each other in a right lateral strike slip motion. The San Andreas has had two major quakes in the past 120 years that each caused surface ruptures along 320 kilometers of the fault, with offsets measuring in many meters. The horizontal displacement along that fault system has been over 500 kilometers since Jurassic time (CDMG, 1966). Some of the stress is transferred to the Calaveras branch which is 120 miles long. Hall (1958) estimated a vertical displacement of at least 2,000 feet on the Calaveras fault zone and a right lateral horizontal displacement of at least 3 miles. The Calaveras has had several major earthquakes in historic times; especially notable are the quakes on June 10, 1836 (Intensity IX to X); July 3, 1861 (Intensity IX); May 19, 1889, (Intensity VIII); June 20, 1897 (Intensity IX); March 30, 1898 (VIII), and June 11, 1903 (VIII). Many historic quakes of smaller magnitudes or less intensity have been recorded in the Livermore and Vallecitos Valleys (see epicenters maps in the report by Darrell Herd, USGS Open-file report 77-689). Some of those epicenters seemed to have been located on the Verona fault, especially during the swarm of quakes in 1943. Other epicenters were on the Las Positas fault zone.

It is important to remember that in the San Andreas fault system, surface ruptures usually occur discontinuously across *en echelon* faults. Local stress concentrations can cause a newly created en echelon fault to appear (usually parallel to a known fault zone) and to form a subsidiary fault. The tectonic stresses in the San Francisco Bay Area are particularly conducive to this type of branching. Two branches of the San Andreas, the Hayward and the Calaveras, are among the longest faults in the state, and they each have subsidiary branches. Block faulting between and beside the Hayward and Calaveras faults have created the Sunol Ridge (within sight of the Vallecitos plutonium labs) and the Livermore Valley. The Vallecitos and Livermore Valleys are located adjacent to the Diablo Antiform and the Coastal Range Thrust fault system which is parallel to the San Andreas system. The Diablo Antiform is dissected by many active faults and is seismicly active. Literally hundreds of earthquakes with magnitudes in the 4 to 5 range have been recorded there in recent years. These fault systems have been active for millions of years and tehy will continue to be active long into the future. The Vallecitos Nuclear Center was constructed in one of the most seismicly active regions in the United States.

In the GETR Show Cause Proceedings, GE's structural consultants (EDAC) and the NRC (PSER-GETR) have admitted that the Verona fault could cause surface ruptures, ground shearing, and vertical or lateral offsets directly beneath the GETR reactor. The Verona fault is a thrust fault. Because thrust faults angle diagonally to the surface from deep beneath the surface, they can have a surface rupture zone of up to a half mile wide. The plutonium labs are less than a half mile from the Verona fault. Because two other "apparent thrust faults" have been discovered near the plutonium labs (the Lake Lee and Plutonium faults in trenches B-2 and H), it is necessary and urgent for the NRC and GE to analyze the potential structural damage to the labs from surface rupture, ground shearing, and lateral or vertical offset directly beneath the labs. This type of analysis has not been done. If these types of ground motions can take place beneath the labs, they could be simultaneous with and in addition to the g values previously described, and the structural damage previously analyzed would be increased tremendously.

Structural engineers in California generally recognize that it is virtually impossible to make a structure "earthquake proof" if it is within a zone of possible surface rupture and offset or shearing. For example, the following quotes are from a book titled Peace of Mind in Earthquake Country by Peter Yanev.

> "Buildings located in fault zones are exposed to the highest possible earthquake risk. This is unequivocally a fact of life in earthquake country, and no measures--whether the most earthquake-resistant bracing and building materials nor the latest and soundest principles of reinforcement--can guarantee or even tentatively propose that any property astride a fault would survive a moderate quake without severe or total damage... The greatest hazard to structures in fault zone zones is that they are subject to ground-surface ruptures and displacements during an earthquake, and no building can withstand this faulting beneath it. A ground shift of only a few inches (vertically, horizontally, or, most commonly, both) is sufficient to cause severe structural damage to buildings. A large quake, with its typical displacements in the fault zone of from several inches to several feet, could demolish the most well-engineered building." (page 49)

Yanev's employer is URS/ Blume and Associates who developed the AEC's Seismic Design Criteria for Nuclear Reactors in 1973. Unfortunately, the AEC had inadequate criteria for seismic hazards prior to 1973 (for reactors), and neither the AEC nor the NRC have developed any seismic criteria for the structural design of plutonium labs.

Table 5. Relation of rupture length and magnitude for faults surrounding the LLL site.

Fault	Rupture length (km)	Magnitude (Richter)
San Andreas	670	8.3
Hayward	125	7.5
Calaveras	125	7.5
Livermore	17	6.5
Mocho	17	6.5
Tesla	17	6.5
Ramp Thrust	8.5	6.2
Corral Hollow	12.5	6.4
Doutherty	4.25	5.8
Carnegie	12.5	6.4
Patterson Pass	6.75	6.1
Greenville - Riggs Canyon	21	6.7

most current and comprehensive compilation of data has recently been presented by Schnabel and Seed[33]; their interpretation of the data is summarized in Fig. 12. The accelerations were recorded on rock, and the distance is the shortest distance to the fault rupture.

In Table 6, we summarize the application of these curves to the San Andreas, Hayward, and Calaveras faults. Because the bedrock accelerations at the site are so similar, we will not continue to examine each fault individually, but instead we represent earthquakes on the San

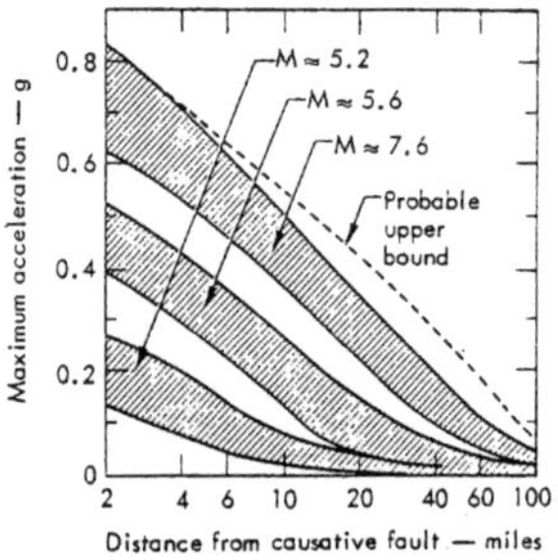

Fig. 12. Earthquake acceleration attenuation (from Ref. 33).

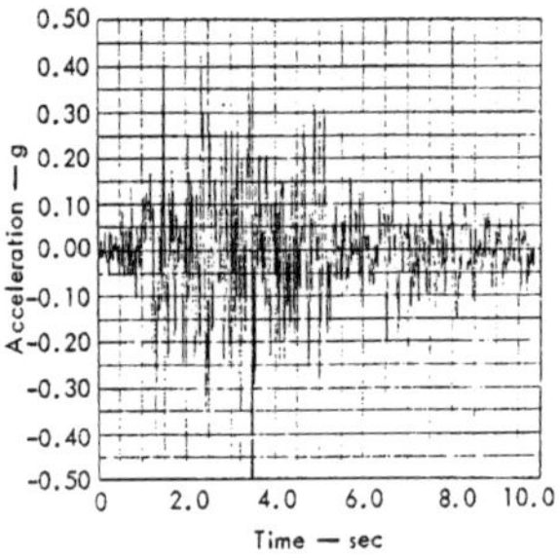

Fig. 13. Taft N21°E accelerogram, scaled to 0.5 g.

Table 6. Relation of attenuation of peak bedrock acceleration to distance as a function of magnitude on three faults.

Fault	Magnitude (Richter)	Distance (km)	Peak bedrock acceleration at site (g)
San Andreas	8.3	58	0.4
Hayward	7.5	42	0.35
Calaveras	7.5	17	0.5

The faults can be conveniently grouped in terms of their proximity to the site: those in the western part of the valley, in the central part and in the eastern part.

In the west is the Calaveras fault; the properties and seismicity of this fault were discussed earlier.

Crossing the center of the valley are the Livermore and the Mocho faults.

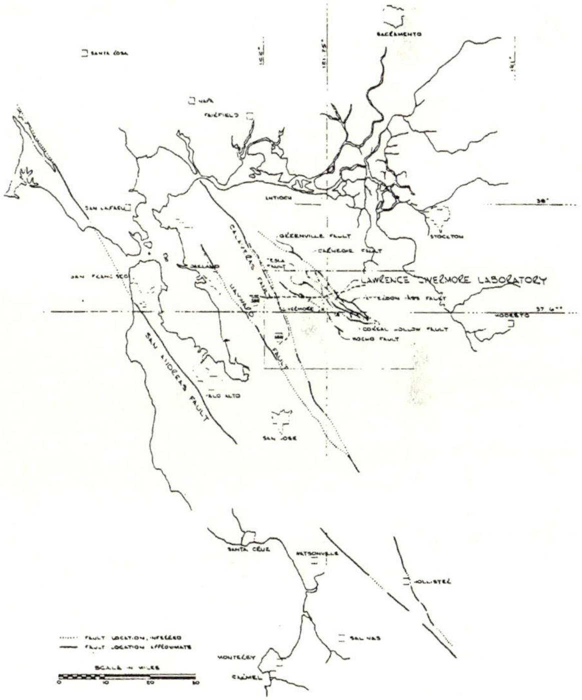

Fig. 9. (a) Faults in Bay Area.

wells.[20,23,24] It is the northernmost segment of the Tesla-Ortigalita fault system. This system, composed of many faults of varying ages, runs along the eastern flank of the Diablo Range from the Livermore Valley to Panoche Valley.[16] The northernmost extent of the fault is not known, but it certainly crosses the Livermore Valley, and may connect with the Stony Creek Fault north of the Delta region.[4,5]

Ramp Thrust Fault

Evidence concerning this fault is scanty, but conclusive. Deep well drilling has revealed displacements on this fault, and there is evidence for surface faulting along its trace.[3] The fault is certainly active although, as far as can be determined, a minor structure. There is no evidence that this fault extends under the site.[3]

Corral Hollow Fault

This fault branches from the Tesla fault 16 km southeast of the site. It has been located by infrared imagery, by gravity surveys, magnetic anomalies, deep drilling, and surface morphology.[3,20] From the nature of the gravity survey, it has been concluded that the fault does not extend to the west beyond Greenville Road. It does not appear to be an active fault.

Doutherty Fault

This is another fault that was located by the comprehensive effort of J. A. Blume and Associates.[3] It was located by infrared imagery, gravimetric and magnetic surveys, geodetic and water table data, and seismic refraction experiments. The gravity data indicate that the block north of the fault is displaced upward relative to the south block. All evidence indicates that the fault is a minor structure which could be significant only in terms of surface faulting.

Carnegie Fault

This fault has been carefully delineated because of its proximity to the Livermore syncline and the oil production. Huey[20] mapped it as a high-angle thrust fault on the basis of surface morphology. It was subsequently better mapped by strong magnetic anomalies, deep well drilling and gravimetric anomalies.[3] Displacement locally on the fault is in the same sense as on the Doutherty. This may represent sympathetic faulting on the relatively minor Doutherty fault. To the southeast, the fault truncates the Tesla fault where the motion is strike slip. This fault may be responding to the same tectonic stresses as the San Andreas system.[16]

Patterson Pass Fault

This fault, which was first recognized by Huey, has many characteristics in common with the Greenville fault. The two faults apparently merge to the northwest, although the Patterson Pass fault appears more like a branch of the Tesla fault.[20]

Greenville-Riggs Canyon Fault

This fault was considered by Clark[19] and Vickery[25] to be a major structural feature of the area. The connection between the Greenville fault on the south and the Riggs Canyon fault on the west flank of Mt. Diablo is not conclusive, but

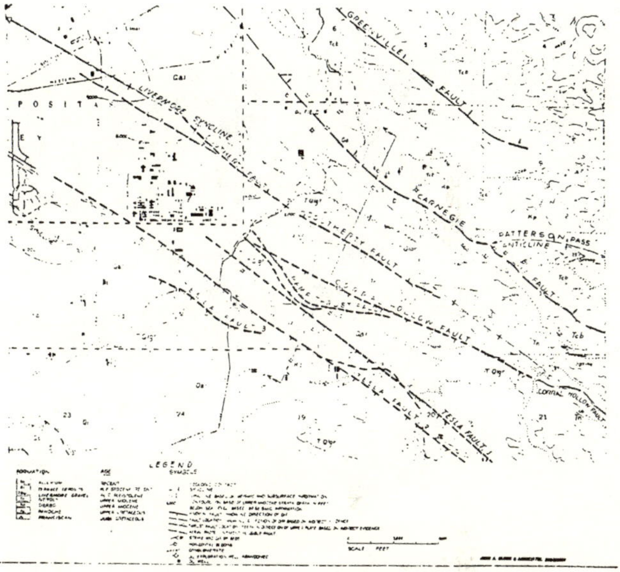

Fig. 9. (b) Faults in the Livermore area (from Ref. 3).

Tesla Fault - 2nd Strand

This fault was located by gravimetric anomalies, breaks in seismic refraction arrival times, and observed soil displacements in trenches.[3] The latter evidence is most persuasive in showing that the fault is still active. The trace of the fault out under the valley is not known, but it probably parallels the Tesla fault for some distance.

Tesla Fault

This well-defined fault is probably a remnant of the ancient Coast Range Thrust fault, although it may have modified during the upper Miocene.[16] It separates Jurassic Franciscan rocks on the west from Cretaceous rocks on the east and has been located by surface morphology, magnetic anomalies, water table data, and logs from deep oil and gas

Observing nuclear blast eight miles away, these GI's were among 1104 whose reactions were being tested in "Operation Smokey" on Aug. 31, 1957. Two men have contracted leukemia, and U.S. wants to check health of all at the blast.

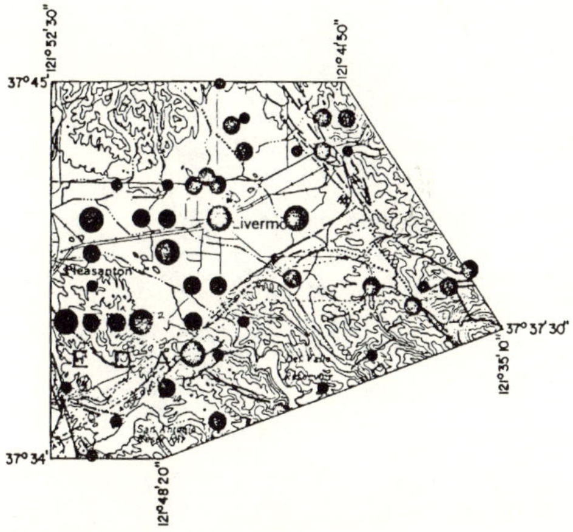

Figure 3.--Epicenters of earthquakes in Livermore Valley, 1942-68 (compiled from University of California, Berkeley, Bulletin of the Seismographic Stations, v. 12, no. 1, 1950--v. 38, no. 2, 1970)

● Magnitude 3.5 and greater	First or largest shock
● Magnitude 2.5 to 3.5	at any specific locality
• Magnitude 1.5 to 2.5	is shown.

All faults in map area are shown.

Livermore oil field

In 1958 a small producing oil field was discovered (California Division Oil and Gas, 1973) in the southeast corner of Livermore Valley. During drilling of the oil field, the Las Positas and Greenville fault zones were found to intersect there, and the precise location of the Greenville-Las Positas fault intersection was established. A number of northeast-trending faults that lie between the Las Positas and Greenville faults were discovered. The blocks north of the northeast-trending faults are predominantly downthrown.

SEISMICITY

Epicenters and magnitudes of eastern Alameda County earthquakes from 1942 through 1968 (fig. 3) were recorded by the University of California, Berkeley Seismographic Station. Since 1969, the area has been monitored by the U.S. Geological Survey seismic network. Microseismicity in eastern Alameda County from 1969 through 1971 recorded during the first 3 years of operation of the Geological Survey seismic network is shown in figure 4. Very few of the earthquakes have been located instrumentally on either the Las Positas, Greenville, or Verona faults. Epicenters occur near the faults, and several at least are astride the faults. Some earthquakes may be associated with the faults, but are yet mislocated as a result of the number and distribution of seismograph stations and the constraints on our ability to correct for the complexities of wave propagation in the earth's crust.

A sequence of earthquakes (five with magnitudes 4.0 or greater) that occurred in Livermore Valley between March 27, 1943, and June 28, 1943 (table 2) may, however, have been generated by movement along the Las Positas fault zone. The sequence was initiated by an earthquake of magnitude 2.8 that occurred shortly before 10 p.m. on the evening of March 27, approximately 3.1 km south of Pleasanton. The earthquake was followed 2 days later by one of the two strongest recorded earthquakes in Livermore Valley (both magnitude 4.2), located at the site of the earthquake of March 27. During the next 3 months, 18 additional earthquakes ranging in magnitude from 2.2 to 4.2 were recorded in Livermore Valley. Although these earthquakes are not well located (the epicenters were determined to within only the nearest minute of latitude and longitude), the epicenters form a northeast-trending band parallel to and about 5 km north of the Las Positas fault zone (fig. 5). The epicenters extend from south of Pleasanton northeastward to the east end of Livermore Valley, roughly approximating the entire length of the Las Positas fault zone. The epicenters could reflect sympathetic motion on a series of unmapped parallel northwest-trending faults in Livermore Valley, but an epicenter pattern wider than the narrow one recorded would have been expected. The areal grouping of the earthquakes and their occurrence in sequence suggests that the quakes were caused by movement along a northeast-trending fault zone like the Las Positas.

High Radioactivity Levels Found In Water

Independent. P. 1, 3/3/78

By ANDREW McGALL

Tests of groundwater and Vallecitos Creek water near the Vallecitos Nuclear Reactor Center have shown levels of radioactive tritium to be much higher than previously reported.

Apparently, the Valelcitos Nuclear Center, which monitors its own radioactive water discharges, has no way of telling how much tritium is getting into downstream waters because its test points are either upstream or near the point of discharge. It has for years reported almost non-existent tritium levels.

Tritium is a low level radioactive particle which occurs naturally and in nuclear reactor cooling waters. It is routinely released into Vallecitos Creek by the General Electric facility and also into the air by Lawrence Livermore Laboratory.

According to Regional Water Qaulity Control Board staff member James Levine, his tests of Vallecitos Creek and well water near the Vallecitos plant showed tritium levels which in one case exceeded the level found downstream from a military tritium production plant on Georgia's Savannah River, previously thought to have the highest level in the nation.

The Environmental Protection Agency tritium standard for drinking water is three million picocuries per liter. However the standard for drinking water will be lowered to 20,000 picocuries in July, 1979.

IN a Vallecitos Creek pond downstream from the Vallecitos Nuclear Center cooling water discharge point, Levine found levels of 10,000 and 11,000 picocuries. In a well supplying water to a ranch in Vallecitos Valley, he found a level of 7000 picocuries.

(A picocurie is an extremeley small amount representing approsimately 2.2 radioactive disintegrations per minute.)

Levine took the water samples while he was a member of the California Public Interest Research Group (CalPIRG) last December. The analysis of the samples was made by the state health department and the EPA and reported back to him.

Levine reported his findings to the Regional Water Quality Control Board which, he said, then hired him to evaluate radiation sampling programs.

He said his intitial report on the Vallecitos sampling program is being reviewed by water board engineers and may soon be reviewed by the board itself.

The tritium levels he found were considerably higher than those reported by Vallecitos, which routinely tests its cooling water discharges. Vallecitos' tests of its own wells showed tritium levels were so low they couldn't be detected, a Vallecitos official reported.

Levine charged that Vallecitos tests wells which are upstream from its discharge point and thus are not an accurate measure of how much tritium is geting into the area's groundwater supply.

In fact, according to Chuck Cain, Vallecitos' environmental quality manager, the cooling water tritium level is measured in retention ponds before the water is discharged.

"For the fourth quarter of 1977, our discharge level was 11,600 picocuries per liter," he reported. He said this was .4% of the maximum permissable concentration for tritium.

Cain was using the federal and state standard of three million picocuries per liter -- the standard for non-drinking water supplies. Levine was using the new drinking water standard of 20,000 picocuries. Valelcitos Creek flows into Alameda Creek which is the source of Hayward's domestic water supply.

Cain said Vallecitos tests four wells, three of them on the Vallecitos property northerly of the discharge point and on across the street. There are no tests of Vallecitos creek or of Alameda Creek water.

Levine said the underground water flows in a southwesterlydirection, which

(See RADIOACTIVE, page 2)

Radioactive . . .

(continued from page one)

means that tests for tritium in north..rly wells will not reflect tritium levels.

Cain also noted that the well across the street had not been tested in the past year because Vallecitos has been unable to obtain access to the private property.

Levine said this well was added to the three GE was already sampling when state water authorities several years ago learned of the southerly flow of the ground water. But even this well, about 1000 feet due east of the Vallecitos discharge point is Inadequate for testing purposes because of the southwest direction of the water; flow, Levine maintained.

Tritium has been classed as one of the less harmful radioactive materials because of its low level of radioactivity and because it cannot penetrate materials such as the h..man skin. However, it does enter the body in water and tends to remain there.

Research at Lawrence Livermore Laboratory has shown that even low levels of tritium damage mice ovaries and increasing levels can destroy their reproductive capacity. Dobson maintains that human ovaries are less sensitive to radioactivity than those of mice.

Other reserachers, notably former LLL medical reseracher Dr. John Goffman have maintained government radiation standards are much too loose and do not reflect the actual dangers of environmental radiation contamination.

NUCLEAR WEAPONS RESEARCH

LAWRENCE LIVERMORE LABORATORY

(Operated for the Energy Research and Development Administration by the University of California)

Lawrence Livermore Laboratory was founded in 1952 for the primary purpose of improving the nation's deterrent posture by providing a competitive base for nuclear weapons development. (The other nuclear weapons design facility is Los Alamos Scientific Laboratory, also operated for ERDA by the University of California.) Nuclear explosives design remains the largest single program at LLL, accounting for about 54 per cent of the Laboratory's budget during the 1977 fiscal year.

NUCLEAR WEAPONS RESEARCH AND DEVELOPMENT

This program has two general goals: (1) to study nuclear explosives, the uses that can be made of them by the U.S. or any other country, and the impact of broadly advancing technologies on potential applications of nuclear explosions; (2) to design explosives for military weapons when responsible agencies of the government decide to deploy a new system or to modify an existing one. This responsibility includes advising appropriate agencies on the feasibility and effects of new weapons.

Both nuclear and non-nuclear experiments are required for this program, as are theoretical calculations utilizing a very powerful computer facility.

Part of the weapons effort is necessarily devoted to unclassified research in a number of fields where further basic and applied knowledge is needed to understand the behavior of nuclear explosives. In addition, research and development capabilities developed under the weapons program have proved invaluable in a number of other efforts at Livermore, such as the search for new energy alternatives.

SOME LLL DEFENSE CONTRIBUTIONS

LLL has designed the warheads for the modern U.S. strategic deterrent missile forces. LLL's leadership in this field began with fundamental advances in nuclear weapons technology at the Laboratory in the 1950s that permitted miniaturization of strategic warheads small enough to fit into missiles. The Laboratory's designs range from the original warheads for the Polaris submarine and the land-based Minuteman I to today's Poseidon and the Minuteman III. LLL achievements made the Multiple, Independently Targetable Re-entry Vehicle (MIRV) possible and provided a foundation for efforts by the U.S. to achieve international arms limitation agreements.

The Laboratory has also provided leadership in the conception and design of ballistic missile defense and tactical warheads. For example, LLL designed the warheads for the Spartan ABM and the LANCE, the Army's most modern missile system.

EVOLUTION OF NUCLEAR EXPLOSIVES

A significant change in the design of a nuclear explosive may take 10 or more years and involve coordinated efforts by tens of thousands of people around the country. The effort may include some 10,000 hours on Livermore computers, which make up one of the world's most powerful research computer facilities. Twenty or more underground nuclear detonations of different designs may be required; each such experiment typically verifies some predictions, demonstrates something new and raises one or two major questions. A single underground nuclear experiment is apt to require nearly 20 man-years of preparation at Livermore and 20 to 100 man-years of work at the Nevada Test Site. When an underground test is to be conducted, necessary components are shipped from around the country to the Nevada Test Site; only there are they assembled into a nuclear explosive. Complete nuclear explosives are never assembled at Lawrence Livermore Laboratory or at its Site 300 (see below).

Nevada Test Site. To test Livermore-designed nuclear explosives, the Laboratory maintains a small permanent staff at the Energy Research and Development Administration's Nevada Test Site north of Las Vegas. All nuclear explosives testing has been performed underground since 1963.

Site 300. Site 300, now occupying about 7,000 acres in the Corral Hollow area about 15 miles east of Livermore, was established as a major chemical explosives and high pressure research facility of the Livermore Laboratory in 1955. Research there has made major contributions to the nuclear design capability.

Discoveries in the East Bay

Quake Faults Near Nuclear Facilities

By David Perlman
Science Correspondent

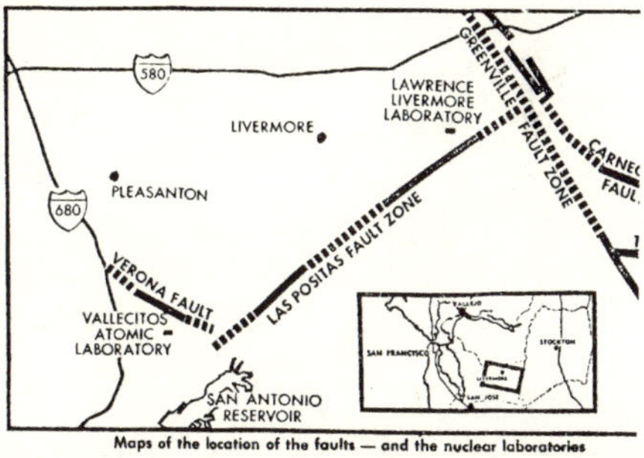

Maps of the location of the faults — and the nuclear laboratories

Government geologists reported yesterday they have mapped a group of previously undetected "young" earthquake faults running through the Livermore valley in the East Bay and passing close to three nuclear research facilities

Traces of the faults lie close to the University of California's Lawrence Livermore Laboratory and the adjacent Sandia Corp plant, where atomic weapons and their hardware are designed and developed, and to the General Electric Co's Vallecitos nuclear research laboratory

But government atomic energy officials say they have already studied the new evidence of earthquake activity in the area and are confident none of the faults poses any health or safety problems to people in the region

The most recently discovered zone of quake activity is called the Las Positas Fault, and it has been mapped for about nine miles by Darrell G Herd of the U S. Geological Survey in Menlo Park

It runs northeastward from the San Antonio reservoir past the city of Livermore, the Lawrence laboratory and the Sandia laboratory to the Livermore oil field

According to Herd the fault zone is highly complex, with three or four parallel strands It has been active within the last 40,000 years, and perhaps much more recently, Herd said

In considering evidence of earthquakes for the siting of atomic power plants, movement within the past 500,000 years is considered "active" by the Nuclear Regulatory Commission For dam-building sites a fault that has moved within the past 100,000 years is considered active by the U S Bureau of Reclamation

Plutonium, the radioactive component of many nuclear weapons and advanced reactors, is used and stored both at Vallecitos and at the Livermore Laboratory.

The G E. plant, which includes two small reactors and a plutonium laboratory, is licensed by the government to handle up to 330 pounds of plutonium and 1000 pounds of fissionable uranium

The quantity of plutonium used and stored at the Livermore laboratory site is classified, but a recent publication of the environmental organization Friends of the Earth put the figure at 600 to 800 pounds

Nuclear scientists and engineers, however, do not consider that an earthquake of even significant magnitude would so disrupt the atomic facilities in the Livermore valley that hazardous radioactivity would be released into the atmosphere.

In recent years, according to Herd, several dozen small earthquakes have been recorded in the Livermore area, and five have registaered 4 on the Richter scale. They may have struck along the Las Positas fault, Herd said, but the evidence is still uncertain

Quakes of up to 6 5 have been recorded on other faults similar in structure to the Las Positas zone, Herd said, and temblors of that size are "not inconceivable" in the Livermore area But he emphasized that Geological Survey scientists have not tried to calculate what the "maximum credible" quake might be in the area There is no evidence that any quakes all are imminent, Herd said

Herd has also mapped in great detail two fault regions that were previously known One is the Verona fault, about six miles southwest of Livermore, which passes the Vallecitos atomic laboratory. The other is the Greenville fault zone, which forms the eastern boundary of the Livermore valley

The Verona fault is geologically young, Herd said, but there is no evidence that it has mov[e]... least the past 40,000 ye[ars]... Greenville zone shows no ... of movement for at lea[st] ... years, Herd said.

Officials at Livermore ... Energy Research & Dev[elopment] Administration said they h[ave been] studying earthquake faul[ts in the] area since 1975.

"We do not anticip[ate] ... ERDA operations would ... health and safety proble[ms] ... significantly affected by ... information" in the geol[ogical re]port, a government statem[ent] ...

The officials did say ... Livermore laboratory has [been un]dergoing a "seismic up[grading"] program since 1974, and th[e] ... protection improvements ... ready been completed at th[e] ... laboratory.

No further changes in ... design at Livermore are ... necessary, officials said.

The Puzzling Jump in Bay Area Cancer Rate

By Charles Petit
Science Correspondent

When a close friend at the Lawrence Livermore Laboratory developed malignant melanoma last year, the laboratory's chief physician, Dr Max Biggs, began to look into the occurrence of the fast-moving, often fatal skin cancer among other employees.

What he found startled him — the rate of melanoma at the sprawling nuclear laboratory appeared to be more than twice that of the general Bay Area population

His discovery has also made the laboratory's cancer data a part of the broader investigation of why Bay Area rates, for several different types of tumors are going up

Biggs' close friend at Livermore was Dr Bernard Shore, 49, who died early last week. His death was followed this week by the disclosure that the State Health Department is actively investigating melanoma incidence at the federal laboratory complex, which is operated by the University of California in southern Alameda county.

The state study resulted from Biggs' request to the California Tumor Registry, operated in Berkeley by the State Health Department, for general statistics with which to compare the 14 diagnosed cases of melanoma among laboratory employees in the past ten years The laboratory employs about 6800 persons

So far, detailed statistical analysis has not been performed to confirm that the lab's experience is significantly out of line with what would be expected, or if working conditions such as possible radiation exposure played a role.

But melanoma at one federal facility is not the only thing about Bay Area cancer statistics that worries state health officials.

Dr. Donald Austin, chief of the tumor registry, said that between 1970 and 1975, the overall Bay Area cancer rate rose by about ten percent, including a doubled melanoma rate.

Melanoma, he said, went from about five reported cases per 100,000 persons in 1970 to ten cases per 100,000 persons in 1975.

Stricken Vet Testifies About A-Blast

Washington

Russell Dann, who as a soldier 21 years ago was ordered to watch a nuclear bomb test, sat in his wheelchair yesterday and told a congressional panel that his teeth have fallen out, he is deaf in one ear, has a blood disease and seems to be sterile.

Testifying at a House hearing on radiation hazards, Dann said he suspects the reason for all his ailments is that, as an Army corporal, he had to march within 300 yards of the Operation Smoky atomic test sight in Nevada in 1957 and endure a "sizzling" blast that knocked him off his feet.

Joseph Califano, the secretary of health, education snd welfare, assured the same House Commerce subcommittee hearing that the government will expedite its search for other soldiers who participated in the 1957 exercise and later developed leukemia.

Califano said eight leukemia victims have been identified among 500 of the 3153 men known to have been present at the test But he declined to make a direct connections between the test and the disease.

The panel is probing possible connections between radiation and leukemia.

Dann, 41, of Albert Lea, Minn., was among the Army troops at Camp Desert Rock, Nev., on the day of the Operation Smoky blast.

As part of the exercise, hundreds of troops were marched into the immediate area of the blast to conduct maneuvers and determine the efficiency of soldiers in a nuclear blast area.

Dann said his group had been moved from a protective trench to an unprotected hillside vantage point, where they felt the effects of a "sizzling" blast that "knocked me and some other troops ten to 15 feet."

Retired Army Colonel Thomas Stedman of Savannah, Ga., who comamanded a unit at the site, testified that in his judgment safety procedures "appeared to be adequate." But he did not discount the ossibility that individuals could have been affected by the radiation.

United Press

AP Wirephoto

RUSSELL DANN AT HEARING
He watched test 21 years ago

In women over the age of 50, the increase is "remarkable," Austin said.

Marin county, he said, "may have more endometrial cancer than any place in the country. Certainly more than anywhere I have heard of."

The Marin incidence rate for this uterine cancer, he said has reached a rate of 341 cases per 100,000 women over the age of 50, more than triple the rate in 1969.

During the same period in five Bay Area counties — Marin, San Francisco, Alameda, Contra Costa, and San Mateo — the combined rate of endometrial cancer increased from 103 to 202 reported cases per 100,000 persons.

For women of all ages, the rate in 1975 stood at 47.5 cases per 100,000 and Austin said "the way things are going, it will overtake breast cancer as the leading cancer among Bay Area women within five years." The present breast cancer rate in these counties is 98 cases per year per 100,000 women.

He said the rising trend here for most tumors is similar to trends nationwide, but the California Tumor Registry data is much firmer [text cut off]

the air. The female Bay Area lung cancer rate stood at 20.6 per 100,000 in 1970, compared to 30.3 in 1975.

The incidence of all cancers rose by 19 percent among Bay Area women, going from 291 cases per 100,000 in 1970 to 346.2 cases in 1975.

The perplexing incidence of melanoma at the Livermore laboratory, while just part of a larger puzzle, illustrates the complexity of finding out what lies behind health statistics.

Biggs' first move was to calculate the melanoma rate at the big nuclear weapons laboratory. Based on the average employment over the past ten years, it came to 26 cases annually per 100,000 persons, more than twice the average Bay Area rate of ten per 100,000.

The disparity remained even with a rough correction for the differences in age, race, and sex between the lab population and that of the general Bay Area. The typical laboratory employee — a middle aged white man — has a statistically higher risk for melanoma that the average, Biggs has found.

tin's tumor registry to permit more precise calculation of what the number of melanoma cases would have been expected to be.

And, if the rate still remains suspiciously high, investigation of working conditions and possible radiation or other carcinogens could follow.

Shore was among two laboratory workers who died of the disease. He was head of the facility's biomedical division, whose workers often undertake studies with radioactive materials.

However, Biggs said, "I don't think that was a factor. Bernie seldom worked with radionuclides. In fact, radiation exposure doesn't seem to have played a role at all in who got it and who didn't."

Plutonium in Drinking Water: Effects of Chlorination on Its Maximum Permissible Concentration

Abstract *Soluble plutonium is oxidized to the Pu(VI) oxidation state by chlorine during water treatment. Under certain conditions Pu(VI) is readily absorbed from the gastrointestinal tract. It appears that due consideration has not been given to the effect that the presence of plutonium in this oxidation state may have on the maximum permissible concentration of plutonium in drinking water.*

We have established that Pu(IV) is oxidized to Pu(VI) by chlorine in water treatment plants and distribution systems. The consequence of this observation is that the present values for the maximum permissible concentration (MPC) of plutonium in drinking water (5 pCi/ml for the general public) (*1*) appear to be too high by several orders of magnitude. The gastrointestinal absorption factor used to calculate the MPC is based on the results of experiments in which solutions of Pu(III) or Pu(VI), or both, were fed or administered intragastrically to animals. It is our view that, in deriving this factor, due consideration was not given to evidence in the literature that the absorption of Pu(VI) is higher by three orders of magnitude than that for Pu(IV) or to the possibility the Pu(VI) could be formed during water treatment (*2*).

The experiments were carried out under the conditions that exist in the water treatment plants and distribution system for the city of Chicago. The water chlorination process begins immediately after intake from Lake Michigan, and the chlorine concentration is maintained at about 1 part per million (ppm) throughout the treatment plant and in the distribution system. The average elapsed time from initial chlorination to consumption is 24 hours. (In other water treatment plants, the average chlorine concentration during treatment is frequently higher, by as much as a factor of 10, and the elapsed time is generally longer.)

We used two kinds of water in the experiments: Chicago drinking water (*3*) and a synthetic Chicago drinking water.

Scoreboard for Reports: The acceptance rate for Reports during the last year has been about 25 percent. The number accepted has exceeded the number published and publication delay has increased to about 4 months. For the next few months, our acceptance rate will be about 15 percent or ten Reports per week.

We prepared the synthetic drinking water by adding sufficient potassium bicarbonate to distilled water to make the bicarbonate ion concentration and the *p*H the same as they are in Chicago drinking water. The plutonium stock (*4*) was a dilute potassium bicarbonate solution with more than 99 percent of the plutonium in the Pu(IV) state. The chlorine stock was a dilute sodium hypochlorite solution. Portions of the plutonium and chlorine stock solutions were added to the waters, and these solutions were analyzed for Pu(IV) and Pu(VI) (see below) immediately and after 24 hours. The ^{239}Pu concentrations were 2.0 and 0.002 pCi/ml, the chlorine concentrations were 1.0 and 9.8 ppm, and the *p*H of the solutions was 8.6.

We used the classical lanthanum fluoride method to determine the amount of plutonium in each oxidation state (*5*, p. 12). In this method, Pu(IV) is coprecipitated with lanthanum fluoride whereas Pu(VI) is not. From measurements of the amount of plutonium in the precipitate and in the supernatant solution, the percentage of plutonium in each oxidation state can be calculated. We confirmed the results by analyzing some of the water samples by a method in which Pu(IV)

Table 1. Oxidation of Pu(IV) to Pu(VI) by chlorine in two types of drinking water

Chlorine concentration (ppm)	Time (days)	Percentage* of Pu(IV)	Percentage* of Pu(VI)
Chicago drinking water			
1.0	0.01	98	1
1.0	1.0	28	69
9.8	1.0	4	92
Synthetic Chicago drinking water			
1.0	0.01	97	1
1.0	1.0	25	72

*The uncertainty in each of these values is ± 3

ples in which the ^{239}Pu concentration was 0.002 pCi/ml (Table 1) it can be seen that the chlorination of drinking water results in the oxidation of Pu(IV) to Pu(VI). The results obtained from the analysis of the water samples in which the ^{239}Pu concentration was 2.0 pCi/ml were not significantly different from those given in Table 1, that is, the oxidation rate is independent of the plutonium concentration in this concentration range.

The use of chlorine in water treatment plants to destroy harmful bacteria, and in water distribution systems to prevent bacterial growth, is standard practice, hence, the effect of chlorine on the oxidation state of plutonium must be considered. Hamaker (*6*) has shown that in acetate-buffered solutions (*p*H 4.5 to 8.4) Pu(IV) is completely oxidized to Pu(VI) by chlorine in 15 minutes at 80°C. However, his data could not be extrapolated to a water treatment and distribution system. The concentrations of plutonium and chlorine in his experiments were higher by orders of magnitude, and the temperature was 80°C rather than 10° to 20°C. These factors are offset by the increase in reaction time, from minutes to days. (In the absence of experimental evidence, oxidation would be predicted from the standard oxidation potentials. In acidic solution the Cl(0)-Cl(−1) and Pu(VI)-Pu(IV) couples are −1.36 and −1.04 V, respectively, whereas in basic solution they are −0.89 and −0.51 V, respectively.)

In 1965, Committee 2 of the International Commission on Radiological Protection (ICRP) established a task group on the metabolism of plutonium and related elements. One of the conclusions drawn by this task group was that the current value for the gastrointestinal absorption factor, 3×10^{-5} appears to be reasonable for soluble plutonium compounds (*7*, p. 49). In drawing this conclusion, the task group either did not consider the possibility that Pu(VI) would be formed during water treatment or, if they did, they concluded either that the data obtained by Weeks *et al.* (*2*) on the absorption of Pu(VI) were invalid or that Pu(VI) would be rapidly reduced to Pu(III) or Pu(IV), or both, in the gastrointestinal tract.

Weeks *et al.* (*2*) studied the effect of oxidation state on the absorption and retention of plutonium by rats after intragastric administration. When all the pluthat Weeks *et al.* carried out appears to be quite definitive.

The gastrointestinal absorptions of Np(VI) by the rat and of U(VI) by man substantiate the absorption of Pu(VI) found by Weeks *et al.* (2). [Both Np(VI) and U(VI) are very close chemical analogs of Pu(VI). The compounds formed when each is precipitated from solution by a particular reagent are isomorphous, they form complexes with the same ligands and to a comparable degree, and they are extremely difficult to separate from each other when they are all in the VI state.] Ballou *et al.* (8) found that the gastrointestinal absorption of Np(VI) by the rat was 2 percent. From measurements of uranium in man and his diet, Hursh and Spoor (9) estimated that the gastrointestinal absorption of U(VI) is between 10 and 30 percent. The absorption of Pu(VI) in man should not differ significantly, that is, by more than a factor of 10, from that of U(VI).

The fact that conditions within the gastrointestinal tract are reducing in nature may lead to the reduction of Pu(VI) to Pu(IV) shortly after water has been consumed. In this case, the gastrointestinal absorption factor for Pu(IV) rather than for Pu(VI) should be used to calculate MPC's. In reviewing the paper of Weeks *et al.* (2) with one of its authors (10), we learned that in their experiments (i) the rats were food-deprived both before and after the administration of the plutonium and (ii) the solutions that contained Pu(VI) were about 0.01*M* in dichromate. Thus, at the time of administration, the

Venus: Further Evidence of Vortex Circulation

Abstract. *A space-time composite of polar stereographic ultraviolet images of Venus from Mariner 10 shows a remarkable circumpolar vortex. The vortex is characterized by a cloud which appears similar to dense terrestrial stratus having an albedo that is 50 percent higher. Spiral streaks converge into it from low latitudes, akin to the spiral bands of a hurricane. The bright visible polar cloud is not axisymmetric but has roughly an elliptical shape. The high brightness of the polar cloud suggests that it has a different origin from the rest of the Venus cloud cover.*

Soon after the Mariner 10 encounter with Venus, the Mariner Venus Mercury-73 imaging team (*1*) presented a preliminary view of the atmospheric circulation on Venus as revealed by the ultraviolet (UV) markings. In particular, Murray *et al.* made the following comments about the polar region (*1*, p. 1312). "Our preliminary impression is that the pole of atmospheric rotation is on the terminator . There is an indication of vortex structure in the streaks emanating from the poleward side of the edge of the polar region. Indeed, the entire polar region may be a vortex fed by meridional flow from the equatorial regions." Subsequently Suomi (2) and Suomi *et al.* (*3*) tracked the motions of UV features of a few Mariner 10 UV frames taken over a small time interval compared to the total Venus encounter. These observations showed highly zonal motion with maximum speeds near ± 50° latitude suggestive of the conservation of angular momentum in the outer zone of the vortex. We have completed another analysis of Mariner 10 images that covers almost the entire period of the Venus encounter, about 7 days, using an extension of the basic technique. The new approach has produced striking evidence of a global circumpolar vortex in the stratosphere of Venus.

First, all of 22 frames spanning 6.85 days were normalized to a standard scattering geometry. The normalization was performed in order to remove shading due to scattering geometry variation over the planet. The images were normalized to a standard sun-planet-observer geometry as described by Limaye and Suomi (*4*). Second, the images were remapped into a polar stereographic projection to give a better view of the high-latitude regions of Venus. Third, several separate polar stereographic projections spanning several days were made into a composite for the whole polar region. This procedure simulates the view that would be obtained from a flight over the pole.

The polar projection has the advantage that it is easier to discern motion patterns in the high latitudes than in the

0036-8075/78/0915-1009$00.50/0

Reprinted from the Journal of the American Medical Association
July 19, 1976, Volume 236

The Plutonium Controversy

John W. Gofman, MD

IF THE world chooses to seek a solution to the energy dilemma through nuclear energy, the element plutonium will become an article of commerce to be handled in quantities of the isands of tonnes annually. Plutonium is a uniquely potent inhalation carcinogen, the potential induction of lung cancer dwarfing other possible toxic effects For reasons to be presented here, it is my opinion that plutonium's carcinogenicity has been very seriously underestimated. If one couples the corrected carcinogenicity with the probable degree of industrial containment of the plutonium, it appears that the commercialization of a plutonium-based energy economy is not an acceptable option for society.

Sagan's statement[1] that "the experience of 30 years supports the contention that plutonium can be used safely" is manifestly indefensible. No meaningful epidemiological study of plutonium-exposed workers for that 30-year period has ever been done Since thousands of those possibly exposed have left the industry and are not even available to follow-up, it is doubtful that any meaningful study of "the experience of 30 years" will ever be accomplished.

Lung Cancer

The important forms of plutonium undergo decay by the emission of α particles That α particles produce bronchogenic cancer in man is now an established medical fact, from the tragic experiences of the US uranium miners.[2] Since the α particles from plutonium are approximately of the same energy as those from the radon daughter products that provoked lung cancer in the miners, it follows that plutonium α particles must necessarily be capable of provoking lung cancer.

The key determinant of *how many* lung cancers will be produced per unit of plutonium deposited will be the length of residence of particles bearing plutonium in or on the cells of the bronchial epithelial lining. In commercial situations, plutonium will be encountered as the extremely insoluble compound plutonium dioxide. As Sagan has pointed out, evidence indicates that plutonium, once deposited, has a residence time in the lung of some few years. During such long residence times, the α particles emitted deliver potentially carcinogenic levels of radiation.

Estimation of the expected number of human lung cancers becomes a problem of knowing how much plutonium will be retained in pulmonary tissues, since this determines .ie α-particle radiation level. There are some crucial voids in our understanding of the behavior of plutonium particulates in the lung, particularly in the lungs of humans who smoke. This makes radiation dose-estimation difficult. As a supplementary approach to estimation of carcinogenic potential, we can first consider the experimental animal evidence.

Cancer in Beagles

Bair and Thomson[1] have induced lung cancer in beagles with plutonium 239. From those experiments, it is possible to estimate only the minimum hazard, because the carcinogenicity of plutonium was initially underestimated, with the result that lung cancer developed in essentially 100% of the beagles, even at the lowest plutonium dose tested. In the beagles, a dose of 0.049μg of plutonium 239 deposited per gram of bloodless lung produced lung cancers in 100% of the dogs.

Assuming man to be equally sensitive, 27.9μg or less of plutonium 239 is a dose sufficient to cause fatal lung cancer. In a nuclear reactor, the plutonium 239 is admixed with several shorter-lived nuclides, so the α radioactivity will be approximately 5.4 times greater than that of pure plutonium 239. Therefore, the carcinogenicity will be enhanced 5.4 times. Thus, based on the saturation experiments in beagles, the extrapolated human dose of 5.2μg or less of reactor-type plutonium will produce one lung cancer. No matter what the distribution of this much plutonium is in people, 5.2μg equates to one lung cancer. Thus, for a specific lung cancer type, 5.2μg deposited into one human causes one lung cancer, 5.2μg distributed into ten people causes lung cancer in one out of ten people, and 5.2μg distributed into 100 people causes lung cancer in one of 100 people. Because of the saturation feature of the beagle experiment, the true required dose is not more than 5.2μg per lung cancer produced, and it

From the Division of Medical Physics, University of California, Berkeley

Reprint requests to Division of Medical Physics, Donner Laboratory, University of California, Berkeley, CA 94720 (Dr Gofman)

may be several times smaller, a result that must await the conclusion of ongoing experiments.

Whether one can extrapolate directly from dog to man is a moot point. The human may be more or less sensitive. Conservatism argues for assumption of at least equal sensitivity. A crucial point is that the beagle lung cancers are almost all bronchioloalveolar in origin, *not* bronchial. Thus, extrapolating to human from dog, we can only predict the occurrence of bronchioloalveolar carcinoma in man. The important question we must now address is whether factors operate in man to supplement such cancers by the far more common human variety, namely, bronchogenic carcinoma.

Bronchogenic Cancer

The International Commission on Radiological Protection (ICRP) suggested a model for the physiologic clearance of plutonium particulates from bronchopulmonary tissues. That model essentially assumes no long-term retention of plutonium in the bronchial epithelium, with all long-term retention occurring in the terminal bronchioles and alveoli. The reasoning presented by the ICRP is that the combination of mucus secretion and ciliary action will propel any plutonium deposited in the bronchi back up to the nasopharynx within a day, with subsequent gastrointestinal excretion. Analogous reasoning suggested to the ICRP that the long residence time (half excretion in 500 days) for the bronchioloalveolar region is caused by the absence of ciliated cells there. All of this may well be applicable for the nonsmoking beagle and be consistent with the occurrence of bronchioloalveolar carcinoma rather than bronchogenic carcinoma in the beagle.

This set of assumptions may be seriously in error for the human, particularly for the approximately 50% of humans who smoke cigarettes. As a result, the occurrence of bronchogenic cancer in man would be seriously underestimated. Numerous studies have demonstrated that serious ciliary injury exists in the cigarette-smoker. Indeed, Ide and co-workers showed 30% of ciliated cells to be denuded of their cilia among smokers. Thus, in the cigarette-smoker, the bronchi will have sizable regions free of cilia, which may result in clearance times for plutonium particulates comparable to the very long times observed for the bronchioloalveolar regions. In the absence of experimental data, this is the most reasonable assumption consistent with the ICRP model. A given quantity of plutonium retained in the bronchial epithelium, rather than being distributed into the entire bronchioloalveolar region, will give approximately 500 times as high a radiation dose, simply because the mass of the bronchial epithelium is so small compared with the entire lung mass. Moreover, the radiation dose is being delivered to the more carcinoma-prone bronchial cells rather than to the less carcinoma-prone bronchioloalveolar cells.

Based on such estimates of impaired clearance of plutonium from the bronchi of smokers and thus its much longer residence time there, I have previously estimated that the cigarette-smoking human would be approximately 125 times more susceptible to bronchogenic cancer induced by plutonium than the nonsmoker. Such susceptibility to bronchogenic cancers would be over and above any occurrence of bronchiolo-alveolar carcinomas predicted from the beagle data. The final calculations of those studies provide the following estimates for bronchogenic carcinoma induction in the human by reactor-grade plutonium in humans: For cigarette smokers, 0.011μg of reactor-grade plutonium produces one lung cancer. For nonsmokers, 1.4μg of reactor-grade plutonium produces one lung cancer.

Implications

Workers in the Plutonium Industry.—Currently "permissible" levels of plutonium 239 lung depositions (derived before the current considerations of the cigarette-smoker problem) are 0.26μg. The lung cancer incidence mentioned previously would indicate that 4.5 lung cancers per lifetime will develop in cigarette-smoking workers exposed to the permissible levels. Lung cancer will develop in one of 30 nonsmoking workers, at this level. Obviously, such "permissible" levels of plutonium 239 are not acceptable.

The Population-at-Large.—For the public-at-large the "permissible" average lung burden is 0.008μg of plutonium 239. My estimate, assuming half of the adult population to be cigarette smokers, is that exposure to the "permissible" level would provoke 235,000 extra lung cancers annually just among the men in the population. This is four times the 1975 fatality rate (63,000 deaths) from lung cancer in men in the United States. Major revisions of acceptable plutonium exposure levels are obviously in order.

The Relevant Human Experience.—One often hears cited as evidence of a lesser carcinogenicity of plutonium the fact that 400 kg of plutonium 239 has been deposited on the United States from weapons fallout and that this has not provoked a lung cancer epidemic. That statement will not stand up under critical examination. Bennett has measured average air concentrations of plutonium from such weapons-test fallout, from which the lung depositions in humans of the United States and the Northern Hemisphere are readily estimated. These estimates, coupled with the lung cancer doses, lead to the following estimates: Approximately 116,000 lung cancer deaths will occur in the United States and 1 million in the Northern Hemisphere as a result of weapons-testing plutonium fallout.

Given the uncertainties in the lung-clearance model, it is probable that these numbers could be low or high by a factor of two or three. Since the expected cancer fatalities will occur over about 30 years, the average annual rate in the United States would be of the order of 4,000 per year. These would be occurring against a background of 81,000 fatalities per year. Obviously, it would be difficult to directly attribute the 4,000 additional fatalities to exposure to plutonium 239 against such a background, but this is a very different matter from the totally unjustified assumption that the 4,000 additional fatalities are not occurring. The only meaningful way to address this question is by calculation. It is public health irresponsibility to equate "no effect observed" with "no meaningful epidemiological study."

Plutonium was inhaled by 25 Manhattan Project workers and, to quote Sagan, "they have shown no significant effects." I have considered the

Perfection, %	Dispersed, kg	per Year
99	9,000	13,900,000
99.9	900	1,390,000
99.99	90	139,000
99.999	9	13,900
99.9999	0.9	1,390
99.99999	0.09	139

*Nine hundred tonnes of plutonium is processed annually

doses to these workers in detail, and based on that analysis, the estimate is that 0.2 of a lung cancer should have occurred by now for this exposure. The occurrence of zero cancers by this time is in accord with this estimate and in no way mitigates the lung carcinogenicity of plutonium. In another group, approximately 25 workers at the Rocky Flats plutonium plant received more than the permissible dose in a 1965 accident. Because of the long latency period for lung-cancer induction, it is really too early to assess the impact in these workers. In another ten years an appreciable yield of lung cancers would be expected in these men (assuming that about half of them were smokers).

Safe Plutonium Energy?

It is self-evident that if plutonium is perfectly contained in a nuclear energy economy, then there is no hazard of plutonium-induced lung cancer. Since industrial human endeavor is never perfect, it behooves us to consider the consequences of less-than-perfection in such an endeavor, especially when we consider not only human and machine fallibility, but also acts of God and malevolent human actions.

A fully developed nuclear energy economy would mean 1,000 or more large nuclear power plants of the breeder variety, based on plutonium. An average breeder reactor would have about three tonnes of plutonium in it, and at least one third of this must be reprocessed and handled annually. The annual handling of one tonne of plutonium per plant means a total annual handling of some 900 tonnes of reactor-grade plutonium in the United States alone.

Since we have estimated that 116,000 lung cancers have developed by inhalation of plutonium from 400 kg of plutonium fallout over the United States, we can estimate the number of cancers that will develop annually for various degrees of containment of this 900 tonnes of plutonium to be handled annually. Presumably, the inhaled plutonium per kilogram dispersed will be comparable to that for weapons fallout. In fact, it may turn out to be equal to, greater, or less than the case for weapons fallout. The real hazard of plutonium releases is not at the nuclear reactor, but rather at the fuel-reprocessing and fuel-fabrication facilities and in the transport between these two facilities. In these steps, plutonium is handled as approximately 1μ particles of plutonium dioxide, the form and size of ultimate toxicity for lung cancer to develop.

In the estimates in the Table, the toxicity of reactor-grade plutonium is taken as 5.4 times that for plutonium 239 because of the 5.4 times greater α radiation from such reactor-grade plutonium, compared with the almost pure plutonium 239 of weapons-grade plutonium.

Proponents of nuclear power argue that planned releases of plutonium will not exceed one part in a billion. In such a technological paradise of only "planned" releases, plutonium-induced lung cancer would not be a serious hazard (about one case per year). But in the real world, with all the fallibilities involved, containment perfection to one part in 10,000 would be a fortunate experience indeed. There is no evidence that even this has been achieved in our 30 years of experience. And yet such containment in a plutonium energy economy would lead to an expectancy of 139,000 additional lung cancer fatalities per year in the United States, which no society should accept.

The problem does not end with the initial inhalation of plutonium particulates released from a nuclear winds and being inhaled, producing additional cancers. One often hears the assertion that such plutonium will rapidly be incorporated into the soil and not be subject to resuspension by the winds. At the Rocky Flats installation, careful air monitoring of a region near the careless spill of about 100 gm of plutonium (from leaky drums) into soil has shown air levels of resuspended plutonium not declining even after five years.[10] The resuspension contribution to additional lung cancers is anticipated to be substantial.

The essence of the concern must center about the expectation of the level of containment perfection. In view of the gross mishandling of plutonium to date,[11] I do not find it credible to expect better than 99.99% containment of plutonium, and such containment is far from acceptable. For this reason, I believe that society should not accept a plutonium-based energy economy.

References

1. Sagan LA: The plutonium controversy. *JAMA* 234:1267-1268, 1975
2. Lundin FE Jr, Wagoner JK, Archer VE: Radon daughter exposure and respiratory cancer: Quantitative and temporal aspects. *Report from the Epidemiological Study of United States Uranium Miners*, NIOSH-NIEHS Joint Monograph No. 1. US Department of Health, Education, and Welfare, 1971
3. Bair WJ, Thomson RC: Plutonium: Biomedical research. *Science* 183:715-722, 1974
4. Task Group on Lung Dynamics (for Committee II of ICRP): Deposition and retention models for internal dosimetry of the human respiratory tract. *Health Phys* 12:1973-2007, 1966
5. Ide G, Suntzeff V, Cowdry EV: A comparison of the histopathology of tracheal and bronchial epithelium in smokers and non-smokers. *Cancer* 12:473-484, 1959
6. Auerbach O, Stout AP, Hammond EC, et al: Changes in the bronchial epithelium in relation to cigarette smoking and in relation to lung cancer. *N Engl J Med* 265:253-267, 1961
7. Gofman J: The cancer hazard from inhaled plutonium. *Congressional Record* 121:S14610-S14616, 1975
8. Gofman J: Estimated production of human lung cancers by plutonium from worldwide fallout. *Congressional Record* 121:S14616-S14619, 1975.
9. Bennett BG: Fallout ^{239}Pu dose to man. *Fallout Program Q Summary Rep.* Health and Safety Laboratory, USAEC Report HSAL-278, 1974, pp 41-66.
10. *US AEC Rocky Flats Plant Surveillance*, monthly reports. Denver, Colorado Department of Health, 1970-1975
11. Gofman J: Nuclear power, no. *Congressional Record* 122:S3319-S3322, 1976

Printed and Published in the United States of America

US SEISMIC ZONE MAP
NUCLEAR POWER PLANT DATA FROM NUCLEAR NEWS, AUG 1975, VOL. 18, NO. 10
SEATTLE
SACRAMENTO
SAN FRANCISCO
LOS ANGELES
DETROIT
NEW YORK
LEGEND
ZONE DAMAGE
GREAT
MAJOR
MODERATE
MINOR
NONE
NUCLEAR POWER PLANTS
▲ OPERATING
■ ORDERED OR UNDER CONSTRUCTION
PREPARED BY
WYLE LABORATORIES

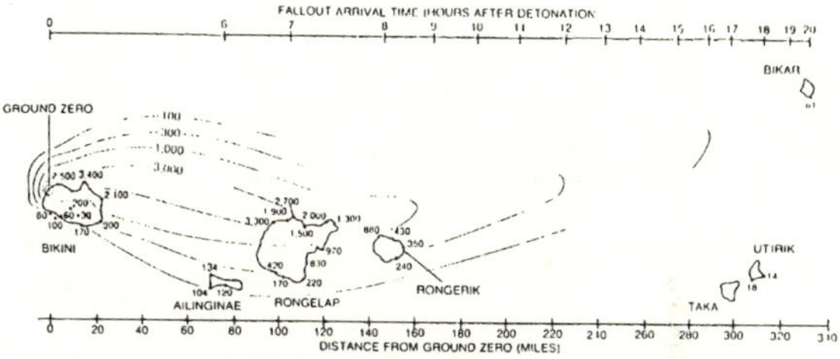

HAZARDS OF LOCAL FALLOUT downwind from a thermonuclear explosion were dramatized by the U.S. test of a 15-megaton fission-fusion-fission bomb on Bikini Atoll on March 1, 1954. The measurements (*black numbers*) give the total dose, in rems, that had accumulated 96 hours after the explosion Contour lines calculated on the basis of those measurements outline the fallout pattern

triggers a fusion explosion involving, for example, the hydrogen isotopes deuterium and tritium The high-energy neutrons emitted by the fusion reactions then fission the nuclei of a large amount of the non-chain-reacting isotope uranium 238, releasing more fission energy [*see illustration on opposite page*] In the Defense Department calculations 50 percent of the energy release was assumed to be due to fission, and that is a representative fraction.

The biological consequences of gamma radiation depend on the total dose received and the time period over which it is delivered The median lethal radiation dose was taken by Defense Department analysts to be 450 rems for doses received within a few days (The rem, standing for "roentgen equivalent man," is a unit of the biological effect of radiation) For doses delivered over a longer time the lethal dose was taken to be somewhat higher because, given time, a biological system can repair a considerable amount of radiation damage. The effective dose suffered by the exposed population when the rate of repair just balances the rate of damage being done by the decaying ambient field of radiation would be the "maximum biological dose" and would determine the lethality of the exposure.

Death from radiation sickness would be neither quick nor painless As described in the Glasstone book, "the initial symptoms are ... nausea, vomiting, diarrhea, loss of appetite and malaise " Beginning two or three weeks after the exposure "there is a tendency to bleed into various organs, and small hemorrhages under the skin ..are observed " Spontaneous bleeding from the mouth and intestinal tract is common. "Loss of hair also starts after about two weeks Ulceration about the lips may spread from the mouth through the entire gastrointestinal tract " Eventually "the decrease in the white cells of the blood and injury to other immune mechanisms of the body .allow an overwhelming infection to develop " One has only to multiply that description by the millions to get a partial picture of the possible consequences of "limited" nuclear attacks on the U S and the U S S R

If the fresh fission products from one megaton of fission were spread uniformly over a perfectly flat area of 1,000 square miles, the gamma-ray dose rate one meter above the ground would be about 250 rems per hour after 10 hours For human beings the median lethal dose at such a high dose rate is about 450 rems The gamma-ray dose rate would decrease about sixteenfold for every tenfold increase in time for the first six months after the explosion and more rapidly thereafter In our example the radiation intensity would be down to about 15 rems per hour after four days and about one rem per hour after 40 days For a person remaining in the radiation zone, however, the cumulative dose would continue to rise significantly for quite a long time. Consider the local fallout beginning about 10 hours after an explosion, which is a typical time for the fallout to reach ground level A full 40 percent of the dose accumulating after that time would remain to be delivered after four days, and 25 percent of it would still remain to be delivered after 40 days

The height of burst of the warheads, which has an important influence on the amount of fallout deposited downwind would be affected by the choice of target In the counterforce attacks envisioned by the Defense Department most of the megatonnage would be directed against underground Minuteman silos The Department reported that the Minuteman-killing effectiveness of surface bursts and of airbursts at the "optimum height of burst" would be about equal (The optimum height of burst is the height that, for a given yield provides a blast pressure exceeding a certain value over the largest area, for a one-megaton yield and an overpressure of 1,000 pounds per square inch it would be about 1,000 feet) The attacker would thus be faced with a trade-off On the one hand a surface burst does not have to be as precisely placed as an airburst (an important consideration, since attacks on hardened targets put a high priority on accuracy) On the other hand Defense Department calculations show that, other things being equal, for an attack on the U S ICBM's fallout fatalities could be four times higher for surface bursts than for airbursts

The fireball from a one-megaton nuclear explosion and the fission products it contains rise rapidly until the top of the cooling fireball cloud enters the stratosphere, about six miles above sea level at middle latitudes At a height of about eight miles the cloud stabilizes, with its fission products spread over an area about four miles in diameter An average settling time for the local fallout from a one-megaton explosion might be about eight hours The settling time and the average speed of the winds between the top of the fireball cloud and the ground determine how far the particles drift downwind For a typical aver-

10-95

SCIENTIFIC AMERICAN

NOV. 1976 "LIMITED NUCLEAR WAR" by DRELL & VON HIPPEL

Assignment Bay Area

The Cancer 'Cluster' In the Suburbs

By Roger Rapoport

"Our doctor here in Livermore wouldn't believe me when I came back from San Francisco and told him little Jimmy had malignant melanoma," says Billie Long with a faint trace of her native Texas drawl "He told me little kids just don't get melanoma He thought the UC Medical Center lab had made a mistake"

Mrs Long is sitting in the Mediterranean-style living room of her Cinnabar Court ranch home just a few steps away from a handsome family portrait taken shortly before Jimmy's death last November Nothing in the picture hints at the pain of those final days for Billie, her husband Stan, and their four children

Even Jimmy, who spent the last four months of his life commuting back and forth to Moffitt Hospital where fluid was painfully suctioned from his lungs, looks happy in the photograph The spitting image of his blonde mother, the seven-year-old sported a healthy tan thanks to endless fishing trips with his father — between visits to the cancer ward

Stan Long, a mustachioed Pacific Telephone man who brought his family to Livermore's vineyard country ten years ago for the healthy climate, tried during the month following Jimmy's death to think of factors that might have contributed to his son's one in a million case.

Talks with doctors indicated medical experts simply don't know what's behind this cancer which typically appears as a dark mole and spreads from the pigmented skin cells to other portions of the body The Longs debated over the kitchen table about the X rays Billie had reluctantly agreed to during her pregnancy with Jimmy They also considered the potentially harmful effects of food additives, and the hateful smog that frequently blows in from cities to the west

But it wasn't until late January, when the nearby Lawrence Livermore Laboratory announced that 14 employees had contracted multiple melanoma that they began worrying about the nuclear weapons design facility

DR DONALD AUSTIN
He's looking for answers

community began swarming in to local surgeons' offices to have moles removed Predictably, most of the tissue removed proved non-malignant

However within weeks a new wave of anxiety was moving through the Livermore-Amador valley's 150,000 residents First came a news report on Jimmy's case Then it was revealed that a 13-year old Dublin child, whose parents did not want his name made public, was also being treated for the same disease In Berkeley, Dr Donald Austin, head of the state health department's tumor registry, voiced concern

"Two cases in that age bracket for an area of this size is certainly more than you would expect by chance Over the past five years a Bay Area study of 15 million person years showed only 7 cases of malignant melanoma under 15 We've never heard of prepubertal clusters like this"

This new development has naturally impelled many Livermore parents to begin poring over their children's bodies searching for moles that might be cause for alarm A number of these residents have also been directing inquiries to the health department's Dr Austin

number worth looking into because of a peculiar situation that developed in the Bay Area between 1970 and 1975 "You see, malignant melanoma has been increasing around the nation by one to two percent a year. But in Alameda, Contra Costa, San Mateo and Marin counties the rate has been going up five to ten percent a year. At the same time the incidence in San Francisco has remained unchanged. The only obvious difference between the city and the suburbs is the amount of sunlight. We wonder if San Francisco's fog screens out enough sunlight to have some effect"

While this data hardly reassures those who abandoned the "polluted" city environment for the relative environmental purity of the suburbs, it does not mean one can expect to avoid multiple melanoma by staying indoors with the blinds closed.

Dr Austin points out that office workers who experience short, intense exposure to sunlight are considered to be running a higher risk than those who regularly work outdoors That's because regular exposure reduces the risk of sunburn, which may add to the chance of getting the disease.

A few miles away, inside the fenced perimeter of the laboratory that Ernest O Lawrence and Edward Teller built to help America break into the nuclear age, employees sound philosophical about the problem At the bio-medical division Dr Virgie Shore, whose husband Bernard became the lab's second victim of malignant melanoma last January, doubts the suggestion that nuclear materials were a factor "We never worked with large quantities of radioactive isotopes," says the slim biochemist with short gray hair

Still surrounded by parts of the vast array of technical literature that they consulted during the two and a half years of her biophysicist husband's illness, Virgie Shore has no qualms about continuing her own work here "As a scientist you accept the fact that there are certain risks that go with your work I don't feel in any particular danger"

Of course, cancer clusters are not unheard of in various communities throughout the world. And the lab was quick to point out that the odds that 14 out of 6800 employees would develop the same type of cancer were unusual but not significantly high. But this was hardly reassuring to many residents of the town of 42,000. As state health officials moved in to study a cancer incidence that appeared to be more than double the Bay Area rate for malignant melanoma, adults in the

"People out there are very anxious to have this thing resolved," Austin says. "We've also gotten some tips from technical people out there. One scientist called and told me about a journal article which suggested that rising levels of radioactive Krypton 85 reacting in the presence of the sun's ultraviolet rays could be causing an increase in skin cancer.

"Melanoma, of course, is the most serious type of skin cancer. And the Krypton theory is one of a

A team throughout their professional lives, the Shores worked together for the Livermore lab on a variety of projects ranging from blood plasma lipoproteins to the impact of radioactive materials in fallout.

After Shore's cancer was diagnosed in 1975 he and his wife began contacting friends throughout the nation for leads on promising therapies. Among those recommended was a new immunotherapy technique being tried at a San Francisco hospital. Unfortunately, the only way to qualify was by agreeing to enter a "blind" study. Shore signed up hoping he would be one of the lucky ones to receive the potentially valuable drug. But when his case worsened Virgie analyzed the medicine in her lab, and determined Bernard was receiving dummy pills — placebos — instead of the real thing. He dropped out of immunotherapy.

Jimmy Long (left) and Dr. Bernard Shore both died of melanoma. Dr. Shore was a biophysicist at Lawrence Livermore Laboratory

From there the Shores visited doctors in Walnut Creek, Napa, Los Angeles and other cities in search of the right therapy. But operations, chemotherapy, and other treatments failed to slow the disease. The 49-year-old scientist was hospitalized on Christmas Day 1977 and died last January 16.

"The thing that was so terribly hard for him," says Dr. Shore looking up from a diary she has kept of the nightmare, "was to be familiar with the literature and know exactly what was happening. We thought we were doing everything, but in the end the treatment didn't make any difference. Now you sit and wonder if he would still be alive had the doctor been quicker about operating, processing lab tests and putting him on chemotherapy."

But like most other relatives of melanoma victims in the Livermore Valley, Virgie Shore suspects that the only long term answer to the problem is identifying whatever environmental pollutants may be responsible.

For its part, the state health department is now planning to publicize the sudden upsurge of cases in suburban Bay Area counties. They will make urgent recommendations about the value of early detection and reduced exposure to intense sunlight.

Over on Cinnabar Court in Livermore, families such as the Longs are interested in this idea. They and their neighbors have become extremely sensitive to new cancer cases such as a local 7-year-old now being treated at Stanford for another rare tumor called Ewing's sarcoma. Although this disease is not related to melanoma, that fact does little to reassure those who originally moved to Livermore for their health.

"My husband and I are thinking about moving to Sacramento now," says the Longs' neighbor, Anita Redding, who was like a grandmother to Jimmy. "We came here from South San Francisco to

Tritium linked with ovary damage in mice

10-58

A [illegible] physician here has shown that surprisingly low levels of tritium can kill 90 percent or more of the immature eggs developing in the ovaries of young female mice.

The researcher, Lary Dobson, reported his findings on tritium toxicity in the April-June 1974 issue of *Radiation Research*.

Tritium is a [illegible]ive form of hydrogen and, when it appears as water, has long been considered among the least toxic of all [illegible]ive substances. That is the position of both the International Commission on Radiological Protection and the National Council on Radiation Protection and Measurements.

But because it is an important [illegible]ct of many nuclear technologies, Dobson said, exposure to trit[illegible] m[illegible] both on the job and in the environment, is certain to increase.

Dobson, who spent 10 years with the World Health Organization as Chief [illegible] [illegible]r, Radiation and Isotopes, emphasized that his findings, while signaling caution, should not be cause for undue alarm.

"There are many [illegible] to believe that the mouse is a particularly sensitive animal," he said.

Monkeys, whose immature eggs more [illegible]ly resemble those of humans, show much greater [illegible] to radiation damage than do mice.

Tritium, Dobson said, enters the body primarily as tritiated water--water with one of its hydrogen atoms in the radioactive form.

"Tritium, just like all hydrogen, has a strong tendency to form [illegible]r," he said. "So as it escapes from gas [illegible]ks of nuclear power plants, most of the tritium son[illegible] ends up as water in general circulation."

Once in the form of tritiated [illegible]r, he said, the compound gets to human beings just as does any water, primarily as drinking water and as water taken up by crops.

But general environmental exposure is not [illegible]

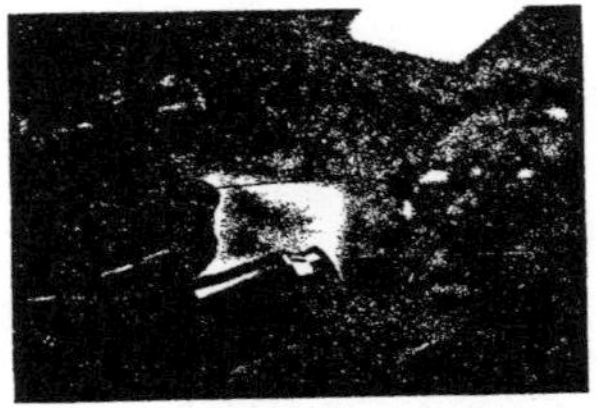

[illegible] : [illegible]re is of much greater concern to me," Dobson [illegible], pointing out that even small amounts of tritiated [illegible] : [illegible] in the [illegible] can pack a powerful [illegible] [illegible] [illegible]se it has not yet had the chance to become diluted in the environment.

Dobson began this work after reading a published PhD thesis on tritium's effect on baby rats. Those data showed [illegible] [illegible] damage at high levels of exposure, but a [illegible] [illegible]ly diminishing impact at lower [illegible].

One effect, [illegible]r, remained at relatively low tritium [illegible] [illegible] dw weight in sex organs, both [illegible] and ovaries.

"It occurred to me," Dobson recalled, "that if the ovary failed to develop properly, it might be left with fewer [illegible], the immature cells destined to become eggs."

They are especially vulnerable to permanent damage, Dobson said, [illegible] their number is set by the time of birth. They are neither [illegible] nor [illegible] after that.

"If our experiments [illegible] that there [illegible] were [illegible] [illegible] in the ovaries of the mice, it [illegible] mean that some cell [illegible] are [illegible]ly sensitive to tritium," he said.

"For our own biological safety," Dobson said, [illegible]

Dobson experim[illegible]ted by giving mother mi[illegible] very small amounts of tritium in their drinki[illegible] [illegible]ter throughout pregnancy. Tritium remained [in] the dr[illegible]king water while the mothers [illegible] their new[illegible]

When the female young [illegible] 1 [illegible] o[illegible] Dobson and his [illegible] looked at their ovari[illegible]

There they found a shortage of [illegible] ranging from 13 percent in mice [illegible] with [illegible] [illegible]st levels of tritium to 93 percent in th[illegible] [illegible] to higher levels.

Dobson p[illegible] out that even the mice t[illegible] had [illegible] the highest [illegible] level got [m]ore than what--for tritium--is a low [illegible].

He said his [illegible] suggest [illegible] for triti[illegible] there is no [illegible] [illegible] which the m[illegible] [illegible]lly escape the effects.

Dobson said subsequent work designed to t[illegible] his original [illegible] has confirmed them.

Those [illegible], he said, have [illegible] that m[illegible] of the [illegible] destruction in mice occurs after bi[illegible] during suckling and not during pregnancy.

Dobson compared the tritium sensitivity [illegible] damage he induced using gamma radiation, [illegible] perennial suspect in [illegible] of damage to the [illegible] structures in cells.

At levels [illegible] in the real world, Dobson s[illegible] trit[illegible] [illegible] effectiveness in destroying m[illegible] [illegible] is between two and three times tha[illegible] gamma rays. Also, tritium's effect relative to [illegible] of gamma radiation seems to [illegible] at lo[illegible] [illegible], he said.

"Experiments on monkeys and clin[illegible] experience with women [illegible] for [illegible] reasons tend to reassure us [illegible] the s[illegible] sensitivity is not [illegible] in man," Dobson s[illegible]

"But whether or not the human female i[illegible] vulnerable to tritium as the mouse," he said, [illegible] have a warning here. We have [illegible] at least [a] population of mammalian cells that is extre[illegible] sensitive to radiation effects at remarkably [illegible]

Department of Energy
Washington, D.C. 20545

DEC 2[illegible] 1978

G. Facer, DP
A. Schoen, EV
J. Swinebroad, EV
R. Stern, EV
S. Miller, OGC
D. Smith, AD
R. Miller, AL
C. Lindeken, LLL (2)
J. Jeutten, SAN
Library, Room 1223, 20 Mass Avenue
G. Dennis, AL
G. Pitchford, CH (2)
R. Blackledge, ID
J. Felton, OR
T. Bauman, RL
D. Cook, SAN
D. Peek, SR
D. Jackson, NV

COMMENTS ON DRAFT ENVIRONMENTAL IMPACT STATEMENT, DOE/EIS-0028-D, LIVERMORE SITE, LIVERMORE, CALIFORNIA, SEPTEMBER 1978

Attached for your information or placement in your respective public document room for public inspection is a copy of comment letter No. 12 received on the subject draft statement from Friends of the Earth, San Francisco, California, dated December 18, 1978.

W. H. Pennington
Division of NEPA Affairs
Office of Environmental Compliance
and Overview/EV

Attachment

Response to Letter 12

DOE RESPONSE TO LETTER FROM FRIENDS OF THE EARTH

Appendix 1B in the FEIS contains a list of the principal preparers of the document. A public hearing on the DEIS was held on April 12, 1979. Based on public review and comment on the DEIS the geology and seismology section was rewritten and greatly expanded. In addition, a comprehensive field investigation was undertaken to evaluate on-site and pertinent regional geological conditions that might affect the safety of the Livermore site. Results of this study will be reviewed by USGS and an independent geological consulting company. This company will also impanel a committee of seismic experts to review the adequacy of the study. Following these reviews, the report of the seismic study will be made public as a separate document, which is scheduled for publication in 1982.

Maximum credible accidents discussed in the DEIS were selected because of their potential impact on the off-site environment. When such an accident involves the release of radioactivity, by definition the release occurs under the worst-case conditions. Accordingly, whether an earthquake or fire destroyed the integrity of a glove box, the environmental impact of the radioactivity released would be the same. Damaging several glove boxes simultaneously would likewise have little additional impact, because the hypothetical accident utilizes the maximum credible amount of material to be handled at LLNL. In the case of Building 968, the tritium involved in the release is the entire building inventory.

The results of the California Department of Health Services epidemiological study concerning the incidence of melanoma among Livermore employees, completed in April 1980, are discussed in section 3.7.2.1.

The Environmental Protection Agency (EPA) has statutory authority to set radiation guidelines and standards to assure protection of the public. This authority extends to federal operations, and the Department of Energy will adopt these EPA standards as they become effective.

Methodologies used to calculate radiation doses from releases of radioactivity at the Livermore site are included as an appendix to the 1980 annual environmental monitoring report. This report is included as Appendix 2A in the FEIS.

As noted in the Staff Statement in Response to Comments Received on the DEIS (included in the Hearing Record of the Public Hearing on the Draft Environmental Impact Statement, Livermore Site, Livermore, California), DOE assesses potential incidents at the Livermore site that might affect the public and coordinates its emergency planning with appropriate agencies having the authority for the protection of the public. The Livermore site has mutual aid agreements with the cities of Livermore,

Pleasanton and Alameda County. Laboratory emergency forces are prepared to notify local and county officials if an emergency requires off-site action.

There are no facilities for long-term storage of radioactive waste at Livermore. The FEIS states that these wastes may be temporarily stored in the waste treatment area until they can be treated. In addition, packaged treated wastes are frequently stored until a shipment is accumulated for movement to a designated DOE waste-storage site.

Somewhat elevated concentrations of uranium have been detected in San Joaquin Valley agricultural soils. However, analysis showed that this uranium had the $^{235}U/^{238}U$ isotopic ratio typical of naturally occurring uranium and not the depleted (depleted in ^{235}U) form used in Site 300 operations. Further investigation demonstrated that the source of the uranium was the phosphate fertilizer applied to these soils. This matter was not discussed in the FEIS because the impact is minimal and not one related to Livermore operations.

Section 3.9.2.3 has been revised to read "the range of 1 to 5 rem (whole body) suggested by the EPA for considering protective action can be increased to 3 to 15 rem by applying the guidance of DOE 0524. Since this latter guidance specifies that allowable doses to specific organs are three times higher than those for the whole body, evacuation is not considered necessary." Protective action does not necessarily mean an action as drastic as evacuation. Protective action can be any action to reduce exposure or the chance of exposure.

The question of multiple glove box damage was discussed in the second paragraph of this response. Simultaneous loss of "all the glove boxes in Building 251" is not believed to be a credible accident.

1605 Milvia St. Apt A
Berkeley, Ca. 94709
December 17, 1978

W. H. Pennington
Department of Energy

Sir

I respectfully request full public hearings on the Draft Environmental Impact Statement on the Lawrence Livermore Lab. I think there is room to doubt the Lab's testing procedures if they have found all radioactive leaks from the site to be only of negligible impact to the area!

Also I can't believe that, as the DEIS earthquake map shows, all faults end at the fence. It seems to me that a major earthquake could do big damage to the "hot" lab buildings, including their filtering and monitoring systems, and leave the results of your "maximum credible accident" as quite an understatement. So I hope we can have a hearing on this because a mere strategic exchange of letters can hardly resolve the issue.

Sincerely,

Lee A. Arnold

Lee A. Arnold.

Department of Energy
Washington, D.C. 20545

JAN 1 1979

G. Facer, DP
A. Schoen, EV
J. Swinebroad, EV
R. Stern, EV
S. Miller, OGC
D. Smith, AD
R. Miller, AL
C. Lindeken, LLL (2)
J. Jeutten, SAN
Library, Room 1223, 20 Mass Avenue
G. Dennis, AL
G. Pitchford, CH (2)
R. Blackledge, ID
J. Felton, OR
T. Bauman, RL
D. Cook, SAN
D. Peek, SR
D. Jackson, NV

COMMENTS ON DRAFT ENVIRONMENTAL IMPACT STATEMENT, DOE/EIS-0028-D, LIVERMORE SITE, LIVERMORE, CALIFORNIA, SEPTEMBER 1978

Attached for your information or placement in your respective public document room for public inspection is a copy of comment letter No. 13 received on the subject draft statement from Mr. Lee Arnold, Berkeley, California, dated December 17, 1978.

W. H. Pennington /gab

W. H. Pennington
Division of NEPA Affairs
Office of Environmental Compliance
and Overview/EV

Attachment

Response to Letter 13

DOE RESPONSE TO LETTER FROM MR. LEE ARNOLD

A public hearing on the DEIS was held in Livermore on April 12, 1979. Based on public review and comment on the Livermore DEIS, the FEIS contains a completely rewritten and greatly expanded section on geology and seismicity. In addition, a comprehensive field investigation was undertaken to evaluate on-site and pertinent regional geological conditions that might affect the safety at the Livermore site. The result of this study will be made public as a separate document, scheduled for publication in 1982.

December 18, 1978

Mr. W. Herbert Pennington
Mail Station E-201, GTN
U.S. Department of Energy
Washington, D.C. 20545

Dear Mr. Pennington:

We are writing to offer our reaction to the Department of Energy's Draft Environmental Impact Statement on its Livermore Site, Livermore California (DOE/EIS-0028-D).

The Draft Statement is glaringly inadequate in its coverage of the central issues of the risks of working with dangerous substances and of spurring on the nuclear aspects of the arms race. It is a self-serving document designed more to conceal than to reveal those risks to both the government and the public. While entertaining few illusions about the possibilities of objectivity in what amounts to an internally prepared review, we were nonetheless dismayed by the results. This process could have been used by the Department as an opportunity to reexamine the entire nuclear weapons development program. Failing that, there are still any number of controversial, intermediate range issues which should have been addressed. Instead, you have produced a document apparently devoted from its inception to supporting the conclusion that <u>nothing</u> is wrong. It demands widespread public challenge.

Please consider this letter a formal request for well-advertised public hearings, as well as a critique.

Below are fourteen major areas in which the Draft Statement is insufficient. Under each of these summary observations are listed the most important unanswered questions on which they are founded.

1. INADEQUATE STANDARDS EMPLOYED FOR DETERMINING MAXIMUM CREDIBLE ACCIDENT, FOR SAMPLING FOR THE PRESENCE OF PLUTONIUM, AND FOR EVALUATING LEVELS OF EXPOSURE TO RADIONUCLIDES

<u>Maximum Credible Accident</u>

A. The scenarios for the postulated release of Tritium and for nuclear criticality are not credible as maximums because accidents have already in fact occured in both cases that were of roughly the same order of magnitude (Appendix 3C). Two previous accidents at the Lab involving Tritium each led to the release of 1/4 the 1.2MCi hypothesized as maximum. The nuclear criticality scenario postulated a maximum yield of 10^{18} fissions. One previous accident yielded about 1/2 this amount (3-47 through 3-65).

B. Maximum credible spill makes the wholly unwarranted assumption that the building air filters continue to work fully (3-65).

Serious accidents occur when there is a multiple failure of several safety precautions. This means the accident is less likely to happen, but the consequences are severe when they do. A proper risk evaluation will consider such cases; why didn't yours?

Responses about improving procedures since earlier accidents are of little relevance because -as you acknowledge (3-52)- human error is the most common origin of an accident. The one major exception is an earthquake, and your faulty analysis of the potential damage from that event is taken up later.

Sampling for Plutonium

C. Why was whole soil sampling rather than respirable dust sampling used to determine plutonium hazards both on-site (2-62 to 2-65) and off-site (Appendix 3C)?

Dr. Carl Johnson, Jefferson County, Colorado (home of Rocky Flats) Health Commissioner has suggested many times to DOE that whole soil sampling is inappropriate for analyzing transuranic wastes. His comparative sampling at Rocky Flats using respirable dust showed effective levels of plutonium as much as 285 times as high as those obtained by whole soil sampling. His criticism is supported by other experts, including the U.S. Environmental Protection Agency. In its Waste Environmental Standards Program Report, "Consideration of Environmental Protection Criteria for Radioactive Waste" (February 1978), it says:

> A greater potential hazard results from inhalation of dust particles containing TRU (transuranic) materials because a significant fraction would be retained in the lung or be absorbed into other tissue. (p.9)

Levels of Exposure

D. There are no Federal guidelines governing exposure to Americium (in all forms), Californium (in all forms), Thorium 230 and Radon 222. Why is there no discussion of how the Lab governs the use of these elements?

E. There is an enormous and growing controversy over exposure guidelines for radioactive and toxic substances in use at the Lab (by which we mean, unless specified, LLL, Sandia and Site 300). In instances where there are guidelines, why does the Draft Statement always choose as its benchmark those guidelines representing the highest exposure level? Why are the controversies never mentioned?

The recent history of this controversy over exposure standards shows that, if anything, extreme conservatism on exposure standards is warranted; all changes in standards have decreased acceptable levels. A case in point are the EPA staff proposed guidelines being submitted to the Federal Interagency Group in January, 1979. Will the DEIS reflect, throughout, any formal guideline changes that result?

F. In several places in the DEIS, analysis of the impact of radiation is dismissed by comparison to background levels. How do you justify, or more correctly, why did you not justify such action, given the fact that any dose is potentially harmful?

In answering, please note that the EPA has stated that simply comparing doses from various activities with background, finding in comparison they are small and therefore justifiable, is a misuse of facts.

G. The DEIS reports (3-36) that in 1976 all levels of radioactivity in the Livermore Valley were below concentration guidelines. What were the various radiation levels? What disputes are there over those particular guidelines?

2. INSUFFICIENT ATTENTION TO EARTHQUAKE DANGERS

The critique of the DEIS submitted by the Friends of the Earth deals at length with the inadequacies of the document on the subject of earthquakes. We support that critique and commend it to your careful attention.

A. Why are the upgraded potentials for the area's faults not included in the DEIS? Will there be further seismological studies as a result?

B. There are several fault lines, including the major Tesla I Fault, which are shown (Fig. 9b, p. 2A-17) as magically ending at the Lab's boundaries. Will you map these faults through the Lab?

C. It is noted at page 2A-30 that the seismological analysis did not include an assessment of the risk of surface faulting to the Lab. This note is followed by the recommendation that, until this risk can be analyzed, no critical structures should be within 330 yards from the surface expression of the Tesla and Dougherty Faults. What is the definition of a critical structure? Are any located within 330 yards of these faults? Are any located within that distance of the Tesla I Fault, should mapping show it to continue, more or less, the direction it is known to follow, through the Lab property?

3. INSUFFICIENT DEMONSTRATION OF REGARD FOR THE HEALTH AND SAFETY OF LAB PERSONNEL

A. In 1977, 1021 Lab workers were exposed to detectable amounts of radiation; 26 of those were "significant" (i.e. .5 rems or greater). This information is not in the DEIS. No information on exposure of Lab workers to radiation or toxic substances appears in the DEIS. Why not?

In order to evaluate in any meaningful way the radiological impact of the Lab on its own people, there must be listed an annual summary of all exposures. Because of the impending change in the maximum acceptable levels, it is essential for this list to differentiate between "detectable" and "significant" and to further differentiate among "detectables" those above and below .05 rems (i.e. 1/10th the new maximum).

B. It is acknowledged in several places (e.g. 3-20, 9-1) that chronic release of radioactive and toxic substances is an unavoidable part of Lab operations. Why, except in one instance (p.3-37 in re. Building 212), is there no analysis of the impact of these releases on Lab personnel?

This analysis is particularly needed because of new information on the dangers of low-level exposure.

Why is "off-site significance" used as the only risk criterion? What about "on-site significance"?

In the analysis of the ARMS flyover (2-66) it is asserted that of the 11 radioactive spots targeted by the flyover, "None of these represent a radiation hazard to workers in the area." Where is the evidence to support that assertion?

In the analysis of dispersal of radionuclides by testing activities at Site 300, the claim is made (2-66) that debris scattering is confined to a radius of 500 yards and thus "..the areas affected are well within Site boundaries and the uranium levels observed constitute no health hazard." Why is no evidence offered to show that the debris is in fact confined to a 500 yard radius of the firing tables? Does this include very small particles? Why is no evidence offered to support the assertion that the uranium debris constitutes no hazard to Site 300 workers? Why is there no mention, given the public controversy caused by Site 300 guard complaints, of other radioactive and toxic substances that may be hazardous to personnel at Site 300? Why is there no analysis of the environmental impact of these substances?

In answering, note that elsewhere in the DEIS (3-36) it is stated without analysis of impact that tritium, beryllium and uranium have been found in amounts exceeding natural occurence in the tissue of plants and animals taken from Site 300.

C. In the section entitled "Accident Analysis" (3-47 et seq. and Appendix 3C) there is neither acknowledgement nor analysis of the dangers to Lab personnel of accidents having "off-site significance". Why not? This includes both hypothetical analyses and the actual history of accidents.

D. Why is there no discussion of accidents at the Lab which had on-site but not off-site significance? Documentation of three such incidents is attached at the end of this letter; they describe accidents never reported publicly. Other such accidents have been made public but none, of either variety, are discussed in the DEIS.

E. Why is there no acknowledgement or discussion of disagreements between managment and workers over health hazards? Management, for example, investigated ways to fire a Site 300 guard in 1976 because he complained about the accumulated beryllium around the firing tables. At about the same time, management refused to relocate an employee who was diagnosed as marginally leukemic from exposure to benzene on the job in Building 345, apparently because to do so would have made legitimate his workmen's compensation claim. It took the intervention of Congressman Fortney Stark to have the man assigned to other work.

F. Why is there no analysis of the possibility of contaminated workers carrying radionuclides and toxic substances out of the Site on their clothing and bodies? At this juncture on and off-site significance blur, particularly in regard to the families of exposed workers.

G. Why has neither DOE nor the Lab pressed the State Office of Health Services to get their stalled study of Melanoma and other cancer incidence among Lab personnel moving again? Can it be that neither DOE nor the Lab is interested in the results? The cancer study is an essential part of the DEIS; health officials say that, given the people they need, they can have the study done in a matter of a few weeks.

H. Has consideration been given to suspending operations in Buildings 251 and 332, noted by the DEIS as requiring upgrading of their effluent control systems, until such time as the improvements are in place?

4. INADEQUATE ANALYSIS OF THE IMPACT OF TRANSPORTATION AND STORAGE OF RADIONUCLIDES AND TOXIC SUBSTANCES

A. There is no approved permanent site for the disposal of plutonium and other transuranic wastes generated at the Lab. What disposition is made of these wastes and under what authority? How long are such wastes kept at the site?

B. How much waste is generated annually?

C. Why is there no analysis of the impact of the solid wastes buried at Site 300? Is the assumption made that because the policy on burying solid wastes now prohibits using Site 300 that there is no continuing impact from the wastes already there? When asnwering, please note the reference made at 3-36 to the discovery of tritium, beryllium and uranium in tissue of plants and animals taken from Site 300.

D. Why is there no listing in the DEIS of all radionuclides and toxic substances currently on the Site? It is impossible to analyze, or to evaluate an analysis of, the radiological impact of the Lab without knowing what dangerous material is on site. The public has a right to know the extent of risk, and that is based in part on amounts of each substance. Please include average annual amounts as well.

E. What are the total amounts of radionuclides unaccounted for? What amounts are unaccounted for in 1977? What are the explanations for all the missing amounts?

F. Why is there no summary of the releases of radionuclides for each of the Lab's years of operation? Such information is essential for evaluating radiological impact.

G. Have there been any security breaches permitting unauthorized access to radionuclides? If so, please list them.

H. Why has there been no search made for evidence of possible low-level emissions from trucks bearing radionuclides to and from the Lab, and on roads used for intra-Lab transfers?

I. Does the Lab plan to resume routine air transport of plutonium if and when the container tests are satisfactorily completed? Will there be tests made of the container by any agency independent of the NRC and DOE? Have there been any non-routine plutonium flights in the past eighteen months?

J. Has there been disclosure to officials in all counties through or over which the Lab ships radionuclides? What is the frequency of different kinds of shipments? Do each of these counties have emergency plans for dealing with an accident involving one of these shipments in the event containment vessels are breached?

5. INSUFFICIENT DESCRIPTION OF THE SAFETY AND MONITORING SYSTEMS

A. Gaseous radioactive elements escape routinely through the stacks; the HEPA filters cannot stop them. At what size particle does a HEPA filter become 50% effective? Why is there no evidence of a particle size analysis of stack effluents in the DEIS?

B. What happens when an earthquake upsets simultaneously the filter balance of each HEPA filter at the site? How much material gathered by the filters could be expected to escape into the atmosphere? What is the maximum credible accident under these conditions? What level of escape of various substances is required before the site is evacuated?

C. If sewer effluent becomes contaminated and is redirected to storage, how many minutes of storage are available before the contaminant must be dumped in the Niles Canyon sewer? If the contaminant is very dangerous, how long can the effluent be stopped before cooling water supplies would be cut off? With the sewer diverted to holding, is the working population evacuated from the site?

D. The Lab's sewer effluent monitoring station, which is located in the southwest area of the site, is in the immediate proximity of the Tesla II Fault. What protections does the station have against disruption by an earthquake? What additional protection do the back-up systems have?

E. How long has it taken to detect and to report to state authorities (and to relevant county authorities) each contamination incident that has had off-site significance?

6. INADEQUATE DESCRIPTION OF THE EMERGENCY RESPONSE PLAN

A. The DEIS does not give enough attention to the emergency response plan (Appendix 3B). Because of the earthquake potential and because of the possibility of maximum credible accidents larger than described in the DEIS it is essential that the Plan include the surrounding communities. What Emergency Response Plan is there for local residents? Are there only the Plans prepared by the local communities themselves? If so, they are hopelessly inadequate. For example, the City of Livermore's Emergency Plan (November 1977) has but two pages in an appendix devoted to "Emergency Actions to be Taken in Incidents Involving Radioactive Materials"; these pages are devoted solely to small incidents involving no consideration of possible evacuations (p.43 and 44).

B. Why has no Emergency Response Plan been given to all local residents within ten miles of the site? Why are potential homebuyers in the area not routinely alerted to the possible risks caused by the presence of the Lab?

C. Why is there no evacuation plan for the area? If, in the event of an earthquake and a major release at the Lab and blocked transportation routes, what contingency plans are there to protect personnel and area residents?

7. INADEQUATE DEMONSTRATION OF REGARD FOR THE HEALTH AND SAFETY OF PEOPLE IN SURROUNDING AND MORE DISTANT COMMUNITIES

A. The DEIS notes at 3-20 that radioactive and toxic liquid wastes are poured into the Livermore municipal sewer system through a process of controlled dilution either at the site or, if that fails, by gradual release from segregation tanks in the municipal system. What are the containment limits for effluents put into the sewer system (3-19 and 20)?

B. Reference is made on the same page (3-20) to options in the event of a large release into the municipal sewer system. What are those options?

C.The DEIS reports confidently at 3-37 that the Livermore Valley makes a negligible input to mans' food chain. The Valley's contribution to California's food chain, however,is not at all negligible. For example, sizable amounts of wine (Wente Brothers and Concannon vineyards are both located within a few hundred yards of the site).The Valley produces a good deal of honey. Bees will roam up to two miles in search of nectar, and those in the area of the Lab have access to the grounds. Have there been analyses of the wine and honey produced in the area?

D. There is no mention or analysis of the impact of Lab activities conducted off-site. Why not? Obvious examples are Lab-sponsored atmospheric tests in the Pacific and the impact of low-level wastes dumped by the Lab off the Farralon Islands.

In a separate category are the Lab's atmospheric tests at the Nevada Test Site. There is an Impact Statement prepared specifically for the Nevada Test Site, but a summary of its findings belongs in the Livermore Statement, since responsibility for the tests lies with Livermore.

8. INSUFFICIENT ACCIDENT ANALYSIS

A. What criteria are used in evaluating accidents (Appendix 3C) to determine whether or not they have off-site signifcance? Why are these criteria not in the DEIS?

B. On page 3C-3 it says, in the description of an accident involving the release of 300,000 Ci of tritium into the atmosphere on August 6, 1970: "No dectable doses were received by the public." On what evidence is this hopeful assertion based?

Analysis of Lab sampling stations (assuming they showed no detectable presence of tritium) is not sufficient for such a statement.

9. INADEQUATE INFORMATION ON PROPOSED ACTIVITIES

Are there plans to undertake transmutation of heavy radionuclides at the Lab? If so, why is this not discussed in the DEIS? Transmutation generates enormous quantities of relatively short-lived radioactive waste which,if conducted on any scale, increases the hazards to personnel and public.

10. INCOMPLETE ANALYSIS OF THE IMPACT OF OTHER LAB ACTIVITIES

Why is there no mention in the discussion of the benefits of laser isotope separation and laser fusion technologies of the centrality of tritium as a plasma (a negative impact) and the production of plutonium as an intermediate step (another negative impact)? Why is there no mention of the weapons applications of laser fusion or the proliferation potential of laser isotope separation?

11. INSUFFICIENT JUSTIFICATION OF CONTINUED NUCLEAR WEAPONS DEVELOPMENT

A.Why is there no discussion in the DEIS of the merits of further nuclear weapons development and of the impacts of that policy?

When answering please attend to the following two points: :

1. It has been held by the Federal courts in a successful suit against then-Secretary of the Interior, Rogers Morton, that, under the National Environmental Policy Act, the absence within an agency of the ability to implement a force of action does not excuse it from an obligation to explore the wisdom of the course of action.

2. The Department of Energy has in the past formulated its own position on nuclear policy, which was at odds with the Administration. For example, Secretary Schlesinger and the Lab Directors (Agnew and Batzel) have openly opposed the proposed five-year Comprehensive Test Ban Treaty. A Washington Post editorial dated September 28, 1978 charged that the Labs have "led" a "brass knuckle bureaucratic" battle to beat down the Administration's position.

B. Why is there no discussion of the effect on the maximum credible nuclear exchange (My God, what a euphemism!) as a consequence of further weapons development? What are the probabilities of such an event? Why have they not been calculated as the probalities of a nuclear accident at a power plant have been?

12. INCOMPLETE ENVIRONMENTAL TRADE-OFF ANALYSIS

A. Under costs:

1. Why is there no mention or discussion of costs stemming from the fact that the Lab, and thus the whole Valley, is a prime target in the event of nuclear war?

2. In calculating the costs of moving the Lab or portions of its operations, why is there no calculation of the potentially offsetting savings from not being sued in the event of a large accident contaminating Livermore area residents?

3.There is a reference to potential job loss but no discussion of the alternative of a job retraining and relocation program. Why not?

4. Why is there not inclusion of the sizable costs to the state and local jurisdictions incurred because of the Lab's presence?

5. Why is there no mention of the adverse impact on commercial and residential development attributable to the Lab's presence in the Valley?

6. Why is there no contingency planning mentioned as a cost and a reality? Is there no contingency planning to address the Lab's future in the event of a large accident, or hopefully more realistically, the passage of a five-year Comprehensive Test Ban Treaty?

7. Why is there no analysis of the opportunity costs to the region of doing military work at the Lab instead of research for civilian purposes? Studies by Chase Econometrics and researchers at MIT and the University of Pennsylvania have shown conclusively that, compared to military investments, almost any kind of investment has greater multiplier effects (i.e. greater income production and more jobs).

B. Under Benefits:

Why is there no analysis of the benefits to personnel, to the surrounding communities and to the rest of the nation of conversion of the Lab to civilian, peaceful research?

13. INADEQUATE CONSIDERATION OF ALTERNATIVE PLANS FOR THE LAB THAT WOULD MINIMIZE OR ELIMINATE EXISTING HAZARDS

A. Chapter Five of the DEIS eloquently testifies to DOE and Lab disinterest in alternatives to the status quo. In it, four alternatives are considered in the space of three and 1/2 pages, four alternatives examined "in" the space of twelve hundred words. Why is the analysis of alternatives so inexcusably scanty?

When answering this question, keep in mind ~~the possibility~~ that the National Environmental Policy Act requires the following of each Impact Statement:

> A rigorous exploration and factual evaluation of the environmental impacts of the full range of reasonable alternatives to the proposed action shall be presented.
> (10 CFR 1021.41 (c)(8))

14. NO OUTLINE AND EXPLANATION OF THE PREPARATION AND REVIEW PROCESS FOR THE DRAFT ENVIRONMENTAL IMPACT STATEMENT

A. Why is there no description of the employers and professional backgrounds of the people who prepared the DEIS? To what extent was the draft prepared by Lab personnel?

B. How was the existence of the DEIS advertised beyond announcement in the Federal Register?

C. On what basis will decisions be made on whether to hold public hearings on this draft? Who besides respondents will be informed of that decision? Who will make this decision? When will it be made?

D. On what basis will decisions be made on whether to heed particular criticisms of this draft in the next?

E. Will the next draft be the final draft? Who decides/ On what basis?

F. What agency actually checks the Lab to determine if the Lab has overlooked the danger of some activity beyond those reported in the DEIS? Will, for expamle, the Occupational Safety and Health Agency be permitted to survey the site if it so desires? If the answer is no, do not rely on national security as a reason; virtually everything except the formulas for constructing weapons are supposed to be unclassified, leaving more than ample opportunity for an independent survey that does not threaten exposure of classified information.

If you require clarification or elaboration on any of our questions and comments, please call.

Sincerely,

Will Riggan

Will Riggan

Steve Ladd

Steve Ladd

for the UC Weapons Labs Conversion Project

10-113

MEMORANDUM

TO: Roy Mullins

FROM: Hazards Control

SUBJECT: Dust Blow-In at Bunker 312

On Friday June 17, 1966 Bunker 312 fired a beryllium-laden shot which blew out a camera port and blew dust into the camera room and the adjoining areas of the bunker. Because it was after 4:30, Bob Anderson and the crew merely closed up shop and went home. The following Monday morning Lee Frahm came to our office and requested Hazards Control assistance in cleaning up the potentially contaminated dust. However, upon arrival at 312 it was found that the custodians had cleaned up the area, without the benefit of being aware of the potential hazard. Leroy Haverty took some swipes at that time.

HAS HAD LUNG • REMOVED SI

As it turned out the custodians, George Saabye and Henry Brewer, did not receive an appreciable beryllium exposure. Analysis of the swipes revealed no beryllium, the custodians noted no excessive amounts of dust, and proper cleanup methods were used. However, this does not negate the fact that the 312 personnel were remiss in not notifying anyone of a condition which must be assumed to be dangerous. Procedure 301 states that any dust "blow-in" should be reported to Hazards Control (which they did at first opportunity). But they should have either posted the area with signs or notified either the olice patrol or the C & M office.

UHR CHECKED BUILDING BEFORE CLEANUP HAD SPLEEN REMOVED LAST YEAR-1976

It is fortunate that this slip-up did not expose anyone to hazardous conditions. I trust that you will remind your men that part of their responsibility is to "think safety".

Stanley L. Dryden
Hazards Control, Site 300

SLD:jms

cc: Bunker Supervisors
Vern Johnson
Joe Lipera
File

[illegible] cleaned bunker at 10:30 PM.

10-114

LRL ACCIDENT INVESTIGATION REPORT

FACTS RELATING TO THE ACCIDENT

Accident Classification	Location of Accident
·pe A ____ Type B ____ Type C X Type D ____	Bldg. 851 Room Firing Table Area ____

: of Accident 6 November 1970 Time 0930 Department Involved B. Div. and P.E. Oper.

ıre of Accident: [Include as appropriate: description of injury, what caused the injury, what caused the damage, what hazardous material or condition was associated with the accident.]

No injury, no property damage incident. Some internal radioactive contamination to personnel not exceeding guide values.

on taken to care for [illegible] person affected.

Rad. Safety directed that nose swipes be taken, whole body counts be made, and urine samples collected.

on taken to prevent further injuries

Area isolated until decontamination complete.

ions Affected

Name	Function in Area	Injury
›ert T. Harris	Facility Supervisor (B-Division)	Possible radioactive contamination
·vin Foster	Facility Laborer (P.E. Oper)	" "

Description of the accident as established through interrogation of those involved, and witnesses; observation of the effects and any pertinent measurements:

See attached statement from A. T. Harris dated Nov. 9 which describes how the incident took place. The HC Area Rep received the call from A. Harris about 9:40 AM on 11-6-70 and requested the Hazards Control Monitor (R. Decker) to respond to the building to examine the situation. After size-up, the Monitor notified Radiation Safety and the HC Area Team Office of the situation. Control and clean-up procedures were initiated. About 10 lbs of D-38 was found (from the original 84 lbs). It was properly packaged and sent to Livermore for handling by the HC decontamination section as programmatic personnel wanted the metal back if possible.

Harris and Foster were sent to the whole body counter about 2:30 P.M. (11/6).

R. Kloepping (Rad Safety) notified the Area Rep about 4:30 that:

(a) Foster showed a nose swipe count of 45 d/m beta and 15 d/m alpha while Harris showed a nose swipe count of zero.

(b) The whole body count results were negative for both men. The limit of sensitivity was 2 mg or 6.6×10^{-4} µCi. One MPB whole body is 0.4 µCi. One MPB for the critical organ (kidney) is 5×10^{-3} µCi.

On Monday morning (11-9), Rad Safety called and requested urine samples be taken from both men. The HC Monitor made arrangements to procure the samples and they were submitted to Medical for analysis. Urinalysis results were negative for both people.

Investigating Committee

Distribution:
Director's Office -Ass't for Tech. Ops.
H.C. Dept. Head (2)
All Area Representatives (1 each)
Individual(s) Involved (1)
Individual's Supervisor (1) (R. Anderson & C. Humphrey)
Field Support Supervisor (1)
Discipline Leaders (1 each)
F. S. Eby

Signed Robert L. Decker Date 11-
Hazards Control, Area Team 5, Monitor

Roger J. Kloepping 11-
Hazards Control Area Team 5, Health Phy.

Robert W. Anderson
B. Div. Senior Supervisor

Released: H.C. Dept. / HP & Sup Grp. / B Grp. / Field Sup Sect. / Area Rep.

RL-2574 (REV.3/70).

November 9, 1970

On November 5 in the early evening, Shot 651-AN was fired at Building 851. The ramrod on the shot was Robert Poor. On November 6 at about 9:30 A.M., M. Foster and I were attempting to locate any pieces of metal from the shot by searching the firing table. Rain was falling at intervals during the night and in the morning. The table was muddy. We noticed a 4" hole in the bank indicating a metal fragment could possibly be buried there. After Foster cleared some of the dirt away we could see a piece of metal. Foster moved it using gloves and we noticed sparks come off the material. Foster stated the metal felt hot when he touched it and he noticed a peculiar odor. At this point we left the table and I called Hazards Control to report some burning uranium on the table.

Albert T. Harris

A. T. Harris, B-Division Facility
Supervisor, Building 851

LRL ACCIDENT INVESTIGATION REPORT

CONCLUSIONS AND RECOMMENDATIONS

,ocation of Accident: Bldg. 851 Room Firing Table Area ____________

)ate of Accident November 6, 1970 Time 0930 Classification-Type C

ature of Accident:

No injury, no property damage incident. Some internal radioactive contamination to personnel not exceeding guide values.

:onclusions:

Was equipment suitable and appropriate? Yes

Were operating instructions adequate?

Did employee fail to follow an establis

Based on the facts established during the investigation of this accident, the conclusions reached regardi the cause are:

By disturbing the wet earth cover, a piece of burning depleted uranium was exposed to the atmosphere. The movement of D-38 caused a release of the oxide previously formed and initiated sparking and further burning and additional oxide release.

RECOMMENDATIONS:

The changes recommended to prevent a recurrence of this accident are:

alf-mask respirators should be carried by personnel during recovery operation after shot involving D-38 or other radioactive material. The respirators should be worn hen the physical condition of the material is unknown and there is possibility of nhalation. Site 300 Procedure 306 will be revised to reflect this change. (B-Division ad Hazards Control)

Investigating Committee

Signed Robert S. Decker Date 11-13-70
Hazards Control Team 5, Monitor

Roger J. Wheeler 11-17-70
Hazards Control Team 5, Health Phy.

Robert W Anderson 11-13-70
B-Division

Released: CEY — H.C.Dept.; BTR — HP & Sup Grp.; [illegible] — 5 Grp.; [illegible] — Field Sup Sect.; [illegible] 11/13 — Area Rep.

Distribution:
Director's Office (Ass't. for Tech. Ops.)
Dept. Head (2)
Area Representatives (1 each)
Individual's Supervisor (1) (R. Anderson &
Support Supervisor (1) C. Humphrey)
Line Leaders (1 each)
· Eby

1-1 (REV.3/70)

[illegible] Septem[illegible] [illegible] ours a rad [illegible] ill occurred on

table of Bunker 351 in conjunction with shot #904D-3. The spill involved

cidental release of approximately 1000 curies of radioactive gas (Xenon 1

Five people were present on the firing table at the time of the spill.

Those people were:

1. W. Meyers - Bunker Supervisor
2. W. Brummond - Mechanical Engineer
3. C. Lewis - Mechanical Technician
4. W. Hilgosen - Hazards Monitor
5. K. Ellis - Hazards Monitor

The gas was brought to the firing table in a special container equip

two squib operated valves in parallel as shown in the picture below.

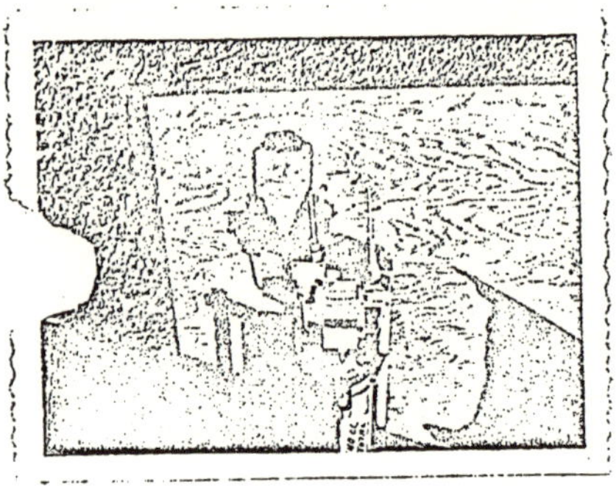

The valves had been installed in Livermore, the squibs removed, and

leak checked prior to filling. This work was done by mechanical technici

the supervision of the project engineer.

The assembly was then sent to__________to be filled with the Xenon

this operation, the holes from which the squibs had been previously remov

erronously fitted with pipe plugs.

The valves consist of a stainless steel body with inlet and outlet p

(marked on valve body); a seat, which consists of a solid portion of the lug.

The xenon and associated gear was shipped to the Site for the shot. When the ime arrived to re-install the squibs in their proper location, the engineer began) remove on of the plugs in order to install the squib. He mistakenly removed ıe wrong plug, so that the opening vented the pressurized gas to atmosphere. ince the squib had been removed and replaced by a plug identical to that on the ther side, the proper location of the squib was not obvious. The engineer made ıe wrong choice.

As soon as they heard gas rushing out, all personnel moved away from the ılve and proceeded immediately into the bunker. All bunker personnel were must-ed inside and the blast dampers closed to assure that the gas would not be awn into the bunker ventillating system. Hazards Control, B Division (L. Erickson), ontrol Point, and Police were notified, and all traffic to and from the building as stopped.

Hazards Control began monitoring the area downwind from the container. At ıe end of about three minutes the activity was found to be about two mr/hr. From ıese measurements, we concluded that there would be no danger to other on-site ersonnel, and certainly no danger at off site locations.

By 1200 hours the activity near the gas valves was measured at 1.5 R. We ecided (Hazards, Meyers, and Erickson) to leave the bunker secured until after unch to allow the activity to decrease further during the lunch period. The area as released for general traffic, but the firing table of Bunker 351 was left sec-red.

At 1300, J. Mayhew and L. Erickson arrived at the bunker. Armed with suitable eters, we proceeded to the firing table with W. Mayers and W. Brummond. The ctivity near the valve was less than 1 R/hr. The plug tightened and the gas ssembly was moved to the border of the firing table area and marked with a "radio-ctive material" sign.

The firing table was then released for normal activity. Note — Film Badges indicated — & [illegible] Meyers - 10 mR 10 mR [illegible] - 30 mR

INCIDENT REPORT

1. DATE: 9-5-62 TIME: 11:15 LOCATION: 351

2. EXPERIMENT NO. 984D3

3. NOTIFIED:

	Date	Time
[X] Hazards Control	9-5-62	11:20
[X] B Division/W. Division	"	11:20
[X] Control Point	"	11:22
[X] Police	X"	11:22
[ ] Medical		
[ ] Maintenance Machinist		

4. DESCRIPTION OF INCIDENT (What Happened): Shot used high pressure vessel of Xenon 133. Two squibs were installed on vessel (as per photo). Project engineer removed wrong plug from valve body allowing the gas to escape. The five persons involved in this operation immediately proceeded to the bunker. All personnel in the bunker were mustered inside, blast dampers closed and above groups notified.

5. WHY DID INCIDENT OCCUR? Project engineer was uncertain as to what plug to remove from valve assembly. Bunker supervisor did not have thorough knowledge of the valve.

L. M. Erickson
SUPERVISOR

FIRING POINT OPERATOR

Distribution: B Division/W. Division Rep.
Hazards Control, Site 300
Project Physicists/Engineer

MEMORANDUM

TO: Jim Dittig

FROM: William Groteguth

SUBJECT: Accidental $Xenon^{133}$ Release

While setting up for Shot 984-D3 at 351 on September 12, 1962 the wrong plug was removed, releasing 25 curies of Xe^{133}. The film badge readings ranged from 30 to 70 mr., part of which may be attributed to the setting up of the shot.

The incident occurred due to a confusion over which of two plugs to remove for the attachment of a Squib (explosive) valve. Normally the one of the two plugs is removed and covered with tape so that the problem of removing a wrong plug hasn't existed in the past.

The plugs in question are in a four outlet junction block which has a diaphragm separating the outlets into pairs. (When connected, the "hot" side has a plug and the inlet tubing; the cold side has the outlet tube and the Squib valve.) The plug had an "O" ring seal which didn't leak until removed and then the gas released with a "whoosh".

Upon hearing the noise the engineer hollered "run" and all did.

To avoid a repetition of this incident it would be wise to consider marking the junction block in pairs as A - A, and B - B so that there is an external visual indication as to the internal configuration of the individual block; or Bill Brummond suggested cementing the hot plug in to prevent accidental removal.

It also has been suggested that the whole thing be hooked up (including the Squib and 25 feet of outlet tubing) before filling the cylinder with gas. This would also prevent exposures while adding these things to the hot cylinder on the table at 300.

W.G.

William Groteguth

WG:cy

cc: Wally Meyers
Le Roy Erickson
Bill Brummond
John Muldoon
John Balanda

10-123

Department of Energy
Washington, D.C. 20545

JAN 1 1979

G. Facer, DP
A. Schoen, EV
J. Swinebroad, EV
R. Stern, EV
S. Miller, OGC
D. Smith, AD
R. Miller, AL
C. Lindeken, LLL (2)
J. Jeutten, SAN

Library, Room 1223, 20 Mass Avenue
G. Dennis, AL
G. Pitchford, CH (2)
R. Blackledge, ID
J. Felton, OR
T. Bauman, RL
D. Cook, SAN
D. Peek, SR
D. Jackson, NV

COMMENTS ON DRAFT ENVIRONMENTAL IMPACT STATEMENT, DOE/EIS-0028-D, LIVERMORE SITE, LIVERMORE, CALIFORNIA, SEPTEMBER 1978

Attached for your information or placement in your respective public document room for public inspection is a copy of comment letter No. 14 received on the subject draft statement from Messrs. William Riggan and Steve Ladd, Nuclear Weapons Labs Conversion Project, dated December 18, 1978.

W. H. Pennington/gab

W. H. Pennington
Division of NEPA Affairs
Office of Environmental Compliance
and Overview/EV

Attachment

DOE RESPONSE TO LETTER FROM THE UC NUCLEAR WEAPONS LABS CONVERSION PROJECT

In a letter of April 16, 1979, from W. Riggan to R. A. Du Val several questions not addressed in the Staff Statement were restated. Responses to these questions were as follows:

1B Maximum Credible Spill

We do not believe that the spill of 15 g of ^{244}Cm and the failure of the filter system, regardless of the cause, are credible simultaneous events. However, the present building filters in Building 251 reduce airborne releases by a factor of about 2.5. Procedures now in effect for this facility limit the quantity of material removed from storage to 30 Ci (0.36 g ^{244}Cm), a quantity that is only about 2% as much as postulated in the maximum credible accident. Due to this operating restriction, even loss of the filters and the release of 30 Ci of ^{244}Cm would not result in radiation doses exceeding those in the DEIS.

1C Soil Sampling

As noted in the Staff Statement, it is difficult to relate respirable particles in the soil to respirable particles in the air. Consequently, we believe the respirable dust hazard is best evaluated by air sampling. It is our opinion that air sampling combined with whole soil sampling provides a better assessment of possible risk to plutonium exposure than measurements of respirable plutonium in the soil.

1D Federal Guidelines

Guidelines for exposure to americium, californium, thorium and radon are found in the Code of Federal Regulation 10, Part 20, "Standards for Protection Against Radiation" and DOE 5480.1A Ch. 11.

3A Radiation Exposure to Personnel

The Staff Statement contained a summary of the 1978 radiation exposure data for LLNL personnel. Additional annual summary data are provided in the FEIS to give the reader a basis for comparison. These data are as follows:

Whole Body Doses*	1978	1977	1976	1975	1974	1973
Not detectable above background	88%	86%	86%	86%	87%	85%
≤100 mrem	10%	12%	11.3%	11%	10%	11%
100 to 499 mrem	1.7%	1.5%	2.2%	2.4%	2.4%	3.2%
500 to 2000 mrem	0.3%	0.5%	0.5%	0.5%	0.5%	0.8%
over 2000 mrem	0.0%	0.0%	0.0%	0.1%	0.1%	0.0%

3B(1) ARMS Flyover

All employees wear radiation dosimeters. None of the personnel working in the areas identified in the ARMS flyover showed elevated exposures.

3B(2) Site 300

The best evidence for the statement that firing table debris is "confined to a radius of 500 meters" is the ARMS aerial survey at Site 300, in which the gamma ray isopleths due to depleted uranium show a maximum diameter of about 200 meters (reference EGG-1183-1693, October 1977). Thus the statement is quite conservative. The ground survey was based upon the dissolution and analysis of whole soil samples and not segregated debris or particle size separations. Consequently, all particle sizes were included. Samples collected in the vicinity of the firing tables showed uranium levels from 10 to over 100 μg/g. At the site perimeter the uranium content of samples is 1-2 μg/g, which is typical of the uranium background in northern California soils. This is the basis for the statement that the areas affected are "well within site boundaries." As noted in the Staff Statement, providing for the health and safety of employees is an important requirement specified in all contracts for operation of DOE facilities. However, the scope of the DEIS was limited to assessing the site-specific impacts of Livermore operations on the surrounding environment. Accordingly, on-site employee safety was considered to be outside the scope of the DEIS.

*The maximum permissible annual whole body dose for radiation workers is 5000 mrem/y.

3C Laboratory Employees

Please see last sentence of 3B(2).

3H Suspending Operations

Based on the analysis of the maximum credible accidents for these facilities, we see no justification for suspending operations in Buildings 251 and 332 while the scheduled upgradings are being completed. As noted in 1B restrictions have been imposed on operations in Building 251.

4D Listing Of All Radionuclides

The varied research work at the Livermore site, which is typical of most university research facilities, employs a wide range of radionuclides and toxic chemicals. Because the majority of these are stocked in such small quantities that they constitute no credible off-site hazard, we believe it would be impractical to attempt to list them all. The maximum credible accidents are based on quantities of those materials that could have significant potential for impact if appropriate controls were not maintained. These quantities often represent the current building inventory.

4E Radionuclides Unaccounted For

The Department of Energy has specified accounting requirements as part of its safeguards system for the protection of special nuclear materials. These involve procedures that provide explanations for the generally small differences between the amount of nuclear material charged to DOE facilities and the amounts that could be physically inventoried.

Inventory differences, previously called Materials Unaccounted For (MUF), are now publicly released semiannually. Reporting periods every 6 months are fiscal (FY) rather than calendar years. The data for FY 76, 77 and 78 are shown below. FY 76 covers a period of 15 months owing to a change from July 1 to October 1 as the FY start date:

Period	Material	Inventory difference
FY 76 (July 1, 75 - Sept. 30, 76)	^{239}Pu	0.3 kg gain
	^{235}U (enriched)	Difference less than 0.1 kg
	^{233}U	0.1 kg gain
FY 77 (Oct. 1, 76 - Sept. 30, 77)	^{239}Pu	0.2 kg loss
	^{235}U (enriched)	None
	^{233}U	Difference less than 0.1 kg
FY 78 (Oct. 1, 77 - Sept. 30, 78)	^{239}Pu	0.4 kg loss
	^{235}U (enriched)	None
	^{233}U	None

The losses in Pu in FY 77 and 78 were found to be due to cumulative differences between measurement uncertainty, recategorization of waste to normal operating loss, and a shipper receiver difference. The gain in Pu shown for FY 76 was due to cumulating differences resulting from material recovered after equipment cleanup.

These inventory difference reports, which include data from a number of DOE contractors, including LLNL, are entitled <u>Semiannual Report on Strategic Special Nuclear Material Inventory Differences</u> and are available from:

National Technical Information Service
U.S. Department of Commerce
5285 Port Royal Road
Springfield, Virginia 22161

4F Summary of Releases of Radionuclides

The FEIS contains summaries of annual atmospheric releases of ^{41}Ar, ^{3}H and ^{13}N - ^{15}O and liquid releases to the sewer of tritium and plutonium.

4J Radioactive Shipments

As noted in the Staff Statement, radioactive shipments must conform to DOT regulations, which specify that containers for large quantities of radioactive materials must be able to withstand credible highway accidents. There is no requirement to notify each county through which shipments are made. Neither DOE nor the Laboratory is in a position to determine the adequacy of local emergency plans. However, the Laboratory will support any efforts by local communities to develop such plans.

5C Sewer Effluent

To clarify the question, it should be pointed out that diversion of sewage occurs at the Livermore Water Reclamation Plant, not at the Laboratories. There is sufficient capacity to divert for about six days under average sewage flow. Cooling-tower blowdown occurs intermittently and neither it nor the use of cooling water is affected by sewage diversion. We cannot see any credible circumstance that would require evacuation of the LWRP personnel.

5D LLNL Sewer Effluent Monitoring System

The initial continuous-operating sewer-effluent monitoring system was installed in 1968. Prior to having on-line continuous readout capability, much of our sewage monitoring was done by collecting samples to be analyzed in the laboratory. In the event an earthquake destroyed the monitoring station we would rely on these earlier procedures.

5E Length of Time to Detect and Report Off-site Contamination

The length of time required to detect a contaminating incident depends on whether monitoring for the contaminant can be performed with continuous readout as is the case with pH and gamma radiation monitoring, or whether reliance must be placed on analysis subsequent to sample collection as presently needed for tritium detection. If it is possible to employ continuous readout, detection can be essentially instantaneous. Longer periods are, of course, required if detection is based on the analysis of a previously collected sample. With respect to the time required for reporting, DOE and the State of California regulations require that appropriate notification be made for different classes of accidents. Notification periods vary depending on the seriousness or expected consequences, from immediate notification to quarterly. In such cases as excursions in the pH of the Livermore site sewage effluent, notification is often limited to authorities at the Livermore Water Reclamation Plant.

7A Discharge Limits to Sewer Systems

Liquid radioactive and toxic waste are treated to reduce the concentration of these materials as low as practicable and well below standards set by DOE IMD 0524 and City of Livermore for discharge to the sanitary sewer systems.

7B Options In Event of Large Release

The options available will depend on the nature of the release. However, one option that has been employed following an acid release was to transfer the material in the diversion pond to tank trucks for subsequent treatment as chemical waste.

9 Transmutation

At present, there are no plans to undertake transmutation of heavy radionuclides at Livermore.

10 Other Laboratory Activities

The FEIS contains updating for several programmatic facilities at the Livermore site. Treatment of these facilities will be in balance with that appearing in the DEIS.

11 Nuclear Policy

Topics raised in this question are not within the scope of the DEIS.

13 Alternatives

Based on comments received on the DEIS, the alternatives represented those that were reasonably available and applicable to the Livermore site. The brevity of treatment was not generally an issue.

14F Agency Checking the Livermore Site

Throughout the year DOE specialists visit the Livermore site to review and evaluate contractor (LLNL and SNLL) performance in such areas as general management and technical program operations, nuclear material controls, waste management, security, health and safety, fire protection, and environmental protection. Several independent safety audits have been performed at LLNL under outside contracts. Operations having a potential for air pollution are covered by permits issued by the Bay Area Air Quality Management District.

In addition, the annual reports of environmental monitoring at the Livermore site, which are prepared for DOE, are also sent to Alameda County, the California Department of Health, and the Environmental Protection Agency for review and comment.

Our responses to the five additional questions in your letter are as follows:

1. Accidents Before 1960

Appendix 3A lists the documented accidents at the Livermore site having off-site impact. The Hazards Control Department whose records were reviewed to compile this list was formed in 1959. Search of available records prior to 1959 did not indicate accidents having off-site significance.

2. Burial Site

The Farallones and Site 300--The Farallones were used as an oceanic radioactive disposal site between 1946 and 1965. Starting in 1963, radioactive wastes from the Livermore site were disposed by land burial in Nevada.

3 thru 5: Cancer Incidence Rates

3. We are responding by letter to Dr. Johnson.

4,5. As you know, Dr. Austin of the California State Health Department has studied data on LLNL employees to determine if the incidence of melanoma experienced by LLNL workers is statistically different from that observed in similar age groups in surrounding counties. A discussion of melanoma at LLNL is included in section 3.7.2.1 of the FEIS.

UC Nuclear Weapons Labs Conversion Project

War Resisters League West
1360 Howard Street
San Francisco, CA 94103
(415) 626-6976

Berkeley Students for Peace
608 Eshleman Hall, UC Berkeley
Berkeley, CA 94720
(415) 642-4136

Ecumenical Peace Institute
944 Market Street, Rm 509
San Francisco CA 94102
(415) 391 5215

ADDENDUM:

Enclosed are petitions containing approximately 700 signatures from students at UC Santa Cruz. Another 400 signatures are being sent in a separate envelope.

Dec. 20, 1978

DOE Form AD-10A
(12-77)

U.S. DEPARTMENT OF ENERGY

memorandum

DATE: JAN 15 1979

REPLY TO
ATTN OF:

SUBJECT: Comments on Draft Environmental Impact Statement, DOE/EIS-0028-D, Livermore Site, Livermore, California, September 1978

TO:

G. Facer, DP	Public Reading Room
A. Schoen, EV	G. Dennis, AL
J. Swinebroad, EV	G. Pitchford, CH (2)
R. Stern, EV	R. Blackledge, ID
S. Miller, OGC	J. Felton, OR
D. Smith, AD	T. Bauman, RL
R. Miller, AL	D. Cook, SAN
C. Lindeken, LLL (2)	D. Peek, SR
J. Jeutten, SAN	D. Jackson, NV

Attached for your information or placement in your respective public document room for public inspection are copies of petitions for public hearings on the subject statement that are supplemental to comment letter #14 from the Nuclear Weapons Labs Conversion Project. The complete petitions which include approximately 1100 signatures are on file in this office.

W. H. Pennington
Acting Deputy Director
Office of Environmental
Compliance and Overview

Attachment

Tuesday December 19, 1978

To: W.H. Pennington
Mail Station E-201
U.S. Department of Energy
Washington, D.C. 20545

Comments on the Draft Environmental
Impact Statement
Livermore Site
Livermore, California
DOE/EIS-0028-D
U.S. Department of Energy

From: Peter Lumsdaine
People for a Nuclear Free Future
870 Linden Lane
Davis, California 95616

Section of DEIS

2.1.3, 2.1.4, and 2.1.5: Although research with high explosives in connection with the nuclear weapons development program (at Site 300) is mentioned, there is no mention of LLL/Sandia/Site 300 development of non-nuclear "conventional" weapons. Yet a former employee of LLL has informed me that the Livermore labs complex has played a significant role in the development of "conventional" weapons such as high explosive cluster bombs. Why has this been omitted from the DEIS?

2.1.4, 2.1.7.2.4, and 2.2.2.1.2: In discussing laser fusion and laser isotope seperation no mention is made by the DEIS of the potential military applications of these technologies. They are put under the non-weapons energy programs heading, yet laser fusion can be (or may be) used to covertly conduct miniture nuclear bomb tests, and enrichment of uranium by laser isotope seperation can clearly be used to produce bomb-grade uranium. Development of laser isotope separation technologies could significantly increase nuclear weapons proliferation.

2.1.8.5, and 2.3.11: The DEIS indicates that plutonium from the labs has been recorded on and off LLL property in the Livermore Valley. However, the Department of Energy's method of testing (taking whole soil samples from 0 to 50 mm depths) has been frequently critiqued and deemed inappropriate. For example, the Health Commissioner of Jefferson County, Colorado (where the Rocky Flats nuclear weapons facility is located) found that testing respirable dust samples showed plutonium levels up to 285 times higher than those indicated by whole soil sampling. This seriously calls into question the DEIS assertion that plutonium contamination of the area (using the whole soil sample method of determination) is not at hazardous levels. Yet this significant, serious controversy and doubt is not even mentioned in the DEIS.

(continued)

2.2.1: It is assumed in this section and in section 9.1 that the development of new nuclear weapons systems is necessarily beneficial. In fact many people, including many distinguished scientists, as well as a substantial number of strategic analysts and public officials, regard the development, testing and deployment of nuclear weapons, especially new systems which escalate the arms race, as massively detrimental to national security, to the health, welfare and security of the American people and the entire population of the Earth. It has been clearly documented that LLL has not only developed many new nuclear weapons but has done so in a manner which clearly has accelerated and is accelerating the international nuclear arms race, and that the LLL officials have agressively lobbied in Washington, D.C. and attempted (quite effectively) to influence national policy, rather than staying in the role of technicians. Thus the DEIS again, in this crucial matter, presents a narrow and biased analysis, assuming that all nuclear weapons development by LLL is, implicitly almost by definition, beneficial, and totally neglecting to even mention other respected analyses. (See also comments later on section 9.1)

2.2.2: No programs for the development of solar-thermal, wind, tidal, photovoltaic, or biomass conversion energy technologies are even mentioned. There are two or three problems with this. First, there is a solar energy program at the Livermore site(s) and so the DEIS is innaccurate in this regard. Also section 9.1 claims solar development programs as a benefit of the labs' continued operation, which is inconsistent with section 2.2.2. Further, the absence of substantial programs in the various promising renewable (and clean - which geothermal generally is not)energy technologies mentioned above shows an extreme negligence and bias in the area of energy source development.

2.2.2.7: The strong and clear implication of the inclusion of the Visitors Center in the list of benefits from the labs, is that it will be an open educational facility for the general public. However i and several people who were with me observed on March 16, 1977 that this is not the case. We were excluded from the Visitors Center because of our personal and political beliefs about nuclear weapons, and our lawful exercise of our Constitutional First Amendment rights to freedom of speech and assembly. Earlier in the day we had participated in a peaceful, legal, and quiet demonstration concerning the work on the labs, on the occasion of Hertz Hall's dedication. Somewhat later in the day we went over to look through the Visitors Center. There were about eight of us. The Visitors Center was open, but we were prevented from entering by LLL security officer Robert D. Robertson who informed us that his superiors had ordered him to "disinvite" us from the Center and make sure that we did not go in. We had no picket signs, literature,

(continued)

or any similar material. Our peaceful and lawful demonstration was over, our signs were packed in our automobiles, and we wished, as concerned and interested members of the public, to see the Visitors Center, but we were prevented by LLL officials. They clearly did not consider us at all prone to violence, since we had been allowed to mingle freely with Dr. Edward Teller and other nuclear luminaries at the reception in Hertz Hall. Yet we were not allowed in the Visitors Center. Why? Because, security officer Robertson explained, the LLL officials were afraid that we would talk with the other visitors in the Center and criticize the activities of LLL. A public "Visitors Center" which claims to be a center of public education about the labs, but which bars people from entry on the sole grounds that they peacefully and quietly express their dissent about the activities of the labs is no benefit. A Visitors Center whose officials are that scared of and determined to exclude dissenting views and open discussion, is a center of propaganda, not education. The Visitors Center, operated in such a manner, far from being beneficial, sets a dangerous precedent of vicariously negating the First Amendment and the public's right of access to nonclassified information, under the hypocritical pretense of public education.

3.5.1.8: In the DEIS discussion of radioactive waste management and disposal (sections 3.5.1.8, 3.5.1.12, and 3.5.1.15) reference is made to "commercial underground storage site(s)" and "an offsite, DOE-approved storage facility" to which the "120 m^3 of packaged solid waste (1976)" was presumably shipped. Such references do not adaquately address the severe environmental impacts and hazards which radioactive wastes pose. The Livermore labs are responsible for the radioactive wastes they produce, but there is no demonstrated method of radioactive waste (especially high level radioactive waste) disposal or even long term storage in the United States or anywhere else in the world. This fact is acknowledged by the California state government and the United States government. In light of the extreme toxicity and longevity of these wastes, and in light of the perilous failures at Lyons, Kansas, at Hanford, Washington, and at the Farallones Islands, California to prevent massive leakage into the soil, rivers, and ocean, any further production of such wastes (including by LLL) must be regarded as an unacceptable adverse environmental impact, an unacceptable danger to human life and health in this and future generations and to the biosphere of our planet. Until such time as there is a demonstrated, workable, safe disposal system for radioactive wastes, further production must be regarded as adding to a highly dangerous and unsolved problem.

3.5.3, 3.5.6.1, 3.5.6.2, and 3.6 and 4.4.2: The DEIS description of toxic chemical waste management and disposal is so general and vague as to be nearly meaningless. There is no information on what toxic chemicals are released into the soil, water, air, and foodchain

(continued)

nor in what quantities. There is no explanation of what "remote and shielded conditions" are (3.5.3), or what containment systems and criteria are used. There is only the most abbreviated and cursory description of "unstable compounds and reagents that have lost their identity". There is no discussion of combustion products [redacted] released into the air from the burning of Site 300 chemical wastes (3.5.6.1). In the last several decades thousands of synthetic chemicals which have not, as far as is known, previously existed in the biosphere of Earth, have been produced and released in very substantial quantities into the air, water, and soil. While some of these substances are relatively harmless, many of them are extremely potent carcinogens, mutagens, and teratogens,or have other highly toxic properties. The vast majority of these chemicals, however, have never been adaquately tested, and most have not undergone even elementary testing. Recent chemical waste disasters (such as that in Niagara, New York) and the rising rates of environmental cancer have given the general public some idea of this enormously hazardous situation. Against the background of this chemical Russian Roulette with the biosphere, the nearly total lack of information in the DEIS on what toxic chemicals are released by the operations of the labs is an indefensable ommission.

3.7: The radiological impact section fails to consider <u>on-site</u> radiation levels, the effect of these levels on lab workers who may be exposed to them for eight hours per day, or the genetic effect on the general population via the children of lab workers or former lab workers. Since some on-site areas have radiation levels higher 893 mrem per year (page 3-37 of the DEIS), a 2000 hour work year (40 hours per week, and 50 weeks per year) would suggest that some workers might receive over 200 mrem/year, well in excess of the NRC's 170mrem/year safety limit for the general public.

3.8.6: The economic analysis fails to consider at least two important factors. First there is no discussion of jobs produced <u>per dollar invested</u> in the labs complex versus other sorts of economic development in which DOE (previously ERDA and AEC) might resonably invest. Further, there is no adaquate treatment of whether the workers at the labs came into the area when LLL did, or whether local residents were actually hired in significant numbers. Second, there is no mention of what, if any, property taxes the labs pay to the local government which must pay for the public roads, municipal sewer system, etc. that the labs use. Also, what percentage of the increased public school costs does the Federal "impact aid" pay for?

3.9.2.3: Assuming that the radioactive release from a spill at LLL would not be significantly larger than the one postulated in the DEIS, this section still has two major problems. First it once more neglects the radiation levels to which workers and visitors on-site would be exposed, and the genetic consequences of this exposure for members of the general public whose parents, as workers, were or may be exposed before the birth of their non-worker decendents.

END OF COMMENTS.

Department of Energy
Washington, D.C. 20545

JAN [illegible] 19[illegible]

G. Facer, DP
A. Schoen, EV
J. Swinebroad, EV
R. Stern, EV
S. Miller, OGC
D. Smith, AD
R. Miller, AL
C. Lindeken, LLL (2)
J. Jeutten, SAN
Library, Room 1223, 20 Mass Avenue
G. Dennis, AL
G. Pitchford, CH (2)
R. Blackledge, ID
J. Felton, OR
T. Bauman, RL
D. Cook, SAN
D. Peek, SR
D. Jackson, NV

COMMENTS ON DRAFT ENVIRONMENTAL IMPACT STATEMENT, DOE/EIS-0028-D, LIVERMORE SITE, LIVERMORE, CALIFORNIA, SEPTEMBER 1978

Attached for your information or placement in your respective public document room for public inspection is a copy of comment letter No. 15 received on the subject draft statement from Mr. Peter Lumsdaine, People for a Nuclear Free Future, dated December 19, 1978.

W. H. Pennington/gab

W. H. Pennington
Division of NEPA Affairs
Office of Environmental Compliance
and Overview/EV

Attachment

DOE RESPONSE TO LETTER FROM PEOPLE FOR A NUCLEAR FREE FUTURE

2.13, 2.14, and 2.15 Nonnuclear weapons program

There is a small nonnuclear weapons development program at the Livermore site, which is here because of local facilities for high-explosive research and access to Livermore computers.

2.1.4, 2.1.7.2.4, and 2.2.2.1.2 Laser fusion and laser isotope separation

Laser fusion and laser isotope separation research at Livermore are presently considered as large-scale physics experiments to demonstrate the feasibility of physics and engineering concepts. Laser applications will depend on the progress of these experiments.

2.1.8.5 and 2.3.11

The Environmental Protection Agency has the responsibility for establishing the maximum permissible concentration of plutonium in soil in off-site areas. The soil sampling method used at the Livermore site is the same as that recommended by the Nuclear Regulatory Commission Regulatory Guide 4.5. Section 2.1.8.5 has been revised to discuss some reservations concerning Dr. Johnson's respirable dust sampling.

2.2.1

The scope of the DEIS is limited to discussing site-specific impacts of continued operation of the Livermore site. It does not include assessing the environmental impacts of U.S. policy to produce or test nuclear weapons.

2.2.2

The FEIS contains a description of solar and other nonnuclear energy development work at the Livermore site.

2.2.2.7

We regret that you were unable to see the LLNL Visitors Center. Should you and your group wish to return, arrangements will be made for you to spend as much time as you wish in the Center during regular visiting hours, which on weekends is 9:30 a.m. to 5 p.m.

3.5.1.8

As noted, the scope of the DEIS was limited to addressing the site-specific environmental impacts of Livermore operations. The methods for radioactive waste disposal employed at Livermore meet all present environmental and safety requirements. There is a need for research and development efforts in the field of waste disposal, but this need applies to the nuclear industry nationwide and is not one specifically required for Livermore operations.

3.5.3

The FEIS contains additional information concerning toxic chemical management at the Livermore site.

3.7

In the FEIS Section 3.7 has been expanded to present data for on-site radiation exposures to Laboratory employees.

3.8.6

Comparing the economies of the Livermore site's mission with alternate DOE investments is beyond the scope of this EIS.

When LLNL was established in 1952 many key personnel were transferred to Livermore from the Radiation Laboratory at Berkeley. Similarly, when Sandia was established at Livermore, personnel were transferred from Albuquerque, New Mexico. As need for staff with specialized training continued, these personnel were necessarily recruited nationwide. Clerical and support personnel were hired locally whenever possible.

Federal property, such as the Livermore site, is not subject to state or local property taxes. DOE pays the City of Livermore an annual fee for maintaining that portion of the sewer line originally installed by the Navy during World War II. DOE also pays the City of Livermore for treating Livermore site sewage.

Even though the percentages of employees living in Livermore has remained fairly constant at about 50%, the Livermore site related school enrollment has been decreasing for the past several years. As a result the Federal funds have decreased. This information is shown graphically in Figure 3-15 in the FEIS.

3.9.2.3

The purpose of the maximum credible accident scenarios was to evaluate the off-site environmental impacts. For these evaluations the environment begins at the site boundary.

December 15, 1978

TO: W.H. Pennington
Department of Energy

FROM: Brent Stuart
Environmental News Service
2207 Shattuck Ave.
Berkeley, CA 94704

The Department of Energy's Draft Environmental Impact Statement, Livermore Site(EIS-0028-D) is totally incomplete and inadequate. Never has such lengthy research produced so little information and analysis with so little exposure for scrutiny(nine years for preparation, two months for comment.) The DoE is like a horse with blinders, unable to see but for straight ahead. Any view outside the blinders might question the present course. The DEIS is the blinder itself, a justification of the current path. It does not explore the environmental impact of Livermore operations. The path, meanwhile, leads to an ever-increasing probability of an unparalled environmental catastrophe.

Of course the actual environmental impact of the AEC-ERDA-DOE weapon's complex began in the 1940s and has already committed millions in the Northern Hemisphere to cancer deaths. But tips of icebergs and cancer epidemics in Nevada, Utah, Colorado, South Carolina, Washington, the Pacific and Livermore are surfacing elsewhere, in the press and scientific literature(including articles by Livermore and other DoE scientists.) Radioactive materials generated by LLL and the DoE are the causes of the cancer.

The Department of Energy lives in a world of safe fence-line doses, standards for radioactive releases, waste disposal and national defense that ignores available data, critical experiments and natural laws.

The basic information is missing from the Livermore DEIS. Nowhere is there an index of chemicals, elements, their ranges of amounts and locations. National security is an unacceptable reason for the exclusion of this information that is necessary to determine "maximum credible accidents."

Lawrence Livermore Laboratory has written an argument of positive influences and legality that is a gross distortion of the spirit if not the letter of NEPA that in the least demands an investigation by the Environmental Protection Agency and the Council on Environmental Quality. History will show an entirely different environmental impact of the Livermore site and the DoE weapons complex.

Sincerely,
[signature]

copies: W.H. Pennington, DoE
Ruth Clusen, DoE
Charles Warren, CEQ
EPA

Department of Energy
Washington, D.C. 20545

JAN 4 1979

G. Facer, DP
A. Schoen, EV
J. Swinebroad, EV
R. Stern, EV
S. Miller, OGC
D. Smith, AD
R. Miller, AL
C. Lindeken, LLL (2)
J. Jeutten, SAN

Library, Room 1223, 20 Mass Avenue
G. Dennis, AL
G. Pitchford, CH (2)
R. Blackledge, ID
J. Felton, OR
T. Bauman, RL
D. Cook, SAN
D. Peek, SR
D. Jackson, NV

COMMENTS ON DRAFT ENVIRONMENTAL IMPACT STATEMENT, DOE/EIS-0028-D, LIVERMORE SITE, LIVERMORE, CALIFORNIA, SEPTEMBER 1978

Attached for your information or placement in your respective public document room for public inspection is a copy of comment letter No. 16 received on the subject draft statement from Mr. Brent Stuart, Environmental News Service, dated December 15, 1978.

W. H. Pennington/gab

W. H. Pennington
Division of NEPA Affairs
Office of Environmental Compliance
and Overview/EV

Attachment

Response to Letter 16

DOE RESPONSE TO LETTER FROM MR. BRENT STUART

The quantities of chemical and radionuclides specified in the maximum credible accident section reflect local inventories, and the rationale in developing these accidents is typical of that used in nuclear reprocessing plants, nuclear power plants and similar nuclear installations.

5531 Renwood Drive
Oakland, CA 94611
December 15, 1978

W. H. Pennington
Mail Station E 201 GTN
Department of Energy
Washington, D.C. 20545

Re: DEIS, Livermore Site, Livermore, California 0028-D

Dear Mr. or Ms Pennington,

I am a resident of Alameda County and am very concerned about the environmental hazards of the Lawrence Livermore and Sandia Laboratories. I have read the DEIS and discussed it at length with other concerned residents. I have questions which are not answered in the DEIS.

Have you notified Alameda and other county officials of the nature of radioactive substances shipped through here? Do we have adequate plans for our safety in the event an accident occurs during shipment? Have you measured the leakage of the trucks carrying these materials through our area? What have been the amounts of past leakages? The effect of leakages is cumulative! What are the total amounts of released radioactive materials for which the DEIS has not accounted? Will you be transporting plutonium by air in the future?

The report tends to dismiss levels of exposure of radiation by comparing to background levels. Any dose is potentially harmful. What concentration guidelines were used in deciding that in 1976 the Livermore Valley was within safe levels? Old guidelines are becoming obsolete.

Soil samples present unrealistic readings of hazards from radionuclides. The inhalation of dust poses a far greater danger to us; we need to know the readings from measuring respirable dust.

The DEIS states that until the risk from large displacements that occur directly on the faults can be appraised, critical structures should be sited at least 330 m. from the surface expression of the Testa and Southerty faults. The Lab's sewer effluent monitoring station is quite close to the Testa # fault. What disruptions to the station might happen in the event of an earthquake?

The report seems to consider worker safety of little importance. As a friend of a number of persons working there, I do not.

Your consideration of the above questions is of utmost importance. Answers to these should be included in further E I S's and or public hearings.

Sincerely,
Susan Dembowski

Department of Energy
Washington, D.C. 20545

JAN 4 1979

G. Facer, DP	Library, Room 1223, 20 Mass Avenue
A. Schoen, EV	G. Dennis, AL
J. Swinebroad, EV	G. Pitchford, CH (2)
R. Stern, EV	R. Blackledge, ID
S. Miller, OGC	J. Felton, OR
D. Smith, AD	T. Bauman, RL
R. Miller, AL	D. Cook, SAN
C. Lindeken, LLL (2)	D. Peek, SR
J. Jeutten, SAN	D. Jackson, NV

COMMENTS ON DRAFT ENVIRONMENTAL IMPACT STATEMENT, DOE/EIS-0028-D, LIVERMORE SITE, LIVERMORE, CALIFORNIA, SEPTEMBER 1978

Attached for your information or placement in your respective public document room for public inspection is a copy of comment letter No. 17 received on the subject draft statement from Ms. Susan Dembowski, Oakland, California, dated December 15, 1978.

W. H. Pennington/gab

W. H. Pennington
Division of NEPA Affairs
Office of Environmental Compliance
and Overview/EV

Attachment

DOE RESPONSE TO LETTER FROM MS. SUSAN DEMBOWSKI

All shipments of radioactive material from the Livermore site are in containers meeting or exceeding the safety design requirements set by the U.S. Department of Transportation.

State and county officials are aware that shipments of radioactive material are being made from Livermore, but no system of notification for each shipment has been considered necessary. DOE and the State are organized to respond to any local accident involving radioactivity.

We are not aware of any "leakage" from trucks hauling radioactivity.

We have no plans for making routine shipments of plutonium via air. The only nonroutine air shipment of plutonium involved several small plutonium sources totaling less than 40 μCi, which were shipped to England to calibrate medical equipment. Approval for this shipment was obtained from DOE-Headquarters.

The environmental report for 1980 is included as Appendix 2A of the FEIS. The relations of measured concentrations to concentration guidelines are given in that Appendix.

The usefulness of any soil-sampling method to indicate the potential inhalation hazard is questionable because the correlation of air and soil concentrations is subject to considerable uncertainty. It should be recognized that soil concentration measurements are a secondary method for estimating airborne hazards. Respirable dust measurements are preferably made by air sampling done in the area of interest.

Seismic evaluation discussed in section 2.3.3 shows that large displacements from earthquakes are not a factor at the Livermore site. The monitoring station is not designated a critical facility, so it is possible that it will not function without repairs following a severe earthquake.

Since the publication of the DEIS, the sewage discharge point and the monitoring station have been moved to the northwest corner of the LLNL site.

The scope of the DEIS was limited to evaluating the site-specific impacts on the environment. Providing for the health and safety of employees is a requirement specified in contracts for operation of all DOE facilities. The Staff Statement in Response to Comments Received on the DEIS (included in the Hearing Record of the Public Hearing on the Draft Environmental Impact Statement, Livermore Site, Livermore, California) contains information specifically related to Livermore employee safety.

Dear Mr. Pennington,

I am writing you in regard to the DOE's DEIS on its Livermore site (DOE/EIS-0028-D). As a concerned resident of Contra Costa County, I am hoping to receive some answers to questions I have after luckily obtained and read the report. I will make my questions brief in hope that they will be understood just by referring to points and, for the sake of speed, will be dealt with soon.

The first question deals with the fact that plutonium and other toxic substances are present at the lab. Recently the question of waste has gained public attention. After reading the report, I found lacking specific information as to how much waste is generated yearly from the lab. The larger qustion is that of storage. Since no safe storage areas have been found, that it remains radioactive for many lifetimes, and that presently some is being stored in Livermore, I feel that the report is lacking in analizing this situation. Transportation of these substances also can have an influence in my community, since I found no discussion of consultation with county officials, of the actual transportation that goes on through or above my county, or of radioactivity that is emitted during this transportation.

Two recent news items concern me with regards to this question of radioactive substances. Last spring, some Americium was misplaced, later to be found in the Livermore dumps. Not only doesn't the report fail to mention how the lab governs the use of this substance, it also fails to analize the fact that there are no federal guidelines governing exposure to Americium and that the Livermore community may have been affected by such accidents as the one I just mentioned. The other news item was concerning Contra Costa's inatiquate preparation for dealing with toxic materials. If the lab is transporting radioactive materials around my community, I would like to see this report analize the possibility for contamination in light of this inability to deal with accidents in this and other communities.

The second area of concern I feel was not presented suficiently is that of the lab's influence on this report and the influence the general public has. I would like to know who wrote it, especially if lab personnel had major influence. I am concerned that the lab has basically total control of information regarding monitoring of itself, setting standards, and constantly fighting any independent agency from investigating public safety as it is related to the lab. With this concern in mind, I am wondering who will have a chance to respond to this report, or possibly get a chance to hear opinions of those who may have additional information. I would hope that public hearings be held that would be publicized well throughout the area effected by the presence of the lab in Livermore. I would like to know how such a decision is made, and by whom. With just the few questions I have about the report, I am sure there must be others. I feel there exists a need to not only publicize this report, but also to hear a broader response to it.

The final question I have is actually the most important to me. I would like to know why there was no discussion about the environmental effects of the kind of work that goes on there. I am referring to the weapons research that the lab is primarily in existance for. The lab is responsible for continually developing new ways of using nuclear science in making weapons. This policy should be analized in relation to the possiblity of nuclear war, or the actual use of these weapons.

I would appreciate a response to these questions. Thank you.

10-150 Gary Dobson

Department of Energy
Washington, D.C. 20545

JAN 4 1979

G. Facer, DP
A. Schoen, EV
J. Swinebroad, EV
R. Stern, EV
S. Miller, OGC
D. Smith, AD
R. Miller, AL
C. Lindeken, LLL (2)
J. Jeutten, SAN
Library, Room 1223, 20 Mass Avenue
G. Dennis, AL
G. Pitchford, CH (2)
R. Blackledge, ID
J. Felton, OR
T. Bauman, RL
D. Cook, SAN
D. Peek, SR
D. Jackson, NV

COMMENTS ON DRAFT ENVIRONMENTAL IMPACT STATEMENT, DOE/EIS-0028-D, LIVERMORE SITE, LIVERMORE, CALIFORNIA, SEPTEMBER 1978

Attached for your information or placement in your respective public document room for public inspection is a copy of comment letter No. 18 received on the subject draft statement from Mr. Gary Dobson, Walnut Creek, California, dated December 20, 1978.

W. H. Pennington/gab

W. H. Pennington
Division of NEPA Affairs
Office of Environmental Compliance
and Overview/EV

Attachment

DOE RESPONSE TO LETTER FROM MR. GARY DOBSON

At the Livermore site radioactive liquid wastes are treated to reduce the activity as far below permissible discharge levels as achievable before release to the sanitary sewer. All solid radioactive wastes are packaged in Department of Transportation approved containers and shipped to DOE approved disposal sites. In 1979, 376 m^3 of radioactive solid waste was shipped from Livermore (Section 3.5.1.15 of FEIS).

Section 3.9.2.7 of the FEIS has been rewritten to include more details on radioactive material shipments and their impacts.

Standards for radiation protection against americium are contained in Title 10 Code of Federal Regulations Part 20 and DOE Order 5480.1A, Chapter XI. Permissible concentrations in air and water are contained in Appendix B of these regulations.

Radioactive wastes in the waste treatment areas are either waiting for treatment, or if packaged for shipment these materials are being held for a scheduled shipment.

State and local officials are aware that shipments of radioactive materials (including packaged wastes) are made from the Livermore site, but specific notification of each shipment has not been considered necessary.

Appendix 1B in the FEIS contains an alphabetical list of the principal preparers of material for he Livermore EIS. The annual Environmental Monitoring Report (Appendix 2A of the FEIS) is sent to several federal, state, and local agencies. The laboratories do not set their own standards, but comply with national, state and local standards.

The scope of the DEIS was limited to evaluating the site-specific impacts on the environment of Livermore operations. It is outside the scope of this document to discuss the testing, use or national policy relating to nuclear weapons.

Mr. W. H. Pennington, Director
Division of Program Review and
  Coordination
Office of NEPA Affairs
U.S. Department of Energy
Washington, D.C. 20545

Dear Mr. Pennington:

This is to acknowledge receipt of the draft environmental statement for the Livermore Site, Livermore, California on September 28, 1978. We regret that we will be unable to review and comment on this document in a timely manner pursuant to Section 102(2)(C) of the National Environmental Policy Act of 1969.

Nevertheless, the Department of Energy is reminded that, if the proposed undertaking will affect properties included in or eligible for inclusion in the National Register of Historic Places, it is required by Section 106 of the National Historic Preservation Act of 1966 (16 U.S.C. 470f, as amended, 90 Stat. 1320) to afford the Council an opportunity to comment on the undertaking prior to the approval of the expenditure of any Federal funds or prior to the issuance of any license. The "Procedures for the Protection of Historic and Cultural Properties" (36 CFR Part 800.4) detail the steps an agency is to follow in requesting Council comment.

Generally, the Council considers environmental evaluations to be adequate when they contain evidence of compliance with Section 106 of the National Historic Preservation Act, as amended. The environmental documentation must demonstrate that either of the following conditions exists:

1. No properties included in or that may be eligible for inclusion in the National Register of Historic Places are located within the area of environmental impact, and the

undertaking will not affect any such property. In making this determination, the Council requires:

--evidence that the agency has consulted the latest edition of the National Register (Federal Register, February 7, 1978, and its monthly supplements);

--evidence of an effort to ensure the identification of properties eligible for inclusion in the National Register, including evidence of contact with the State Historic Preservation Officer, whose comments should be included in the final environmental statement.

2. Properties included in or that may be eligible for inclusion in the National Register are located within the area of environmental impact, and the undertaking will or will not affect any such property. In cases where there will be an effect, the final environmental statement should contain evidence of compliance with Section 106 of the National Historic Preservation Act through the Council's "Procedures for the Protection of Historic and Cultural Properties".

Should you have any questions, please call Michael C. Quinn at (303) 234-4946, an FTS number.

Sincerely,

Louis S. Wall
Assistant Director
Office of Review and Compliance, Denver

Department of Energy
Washington, D.C. 20545

JAN 15 1979

G. Facer, DP
A. Schoen, EV
J. Swinebroad, EV
R. Stern, EV
S. Miller, OGC
D. Smith, AD
R. Miller, AL
C. Lindeken, LLL (2)
J. Jeutten, SAN
Library, Room 1223, 20 Mass Avenue
G. Dennis, AL
G. Pitchford, CH (2)
R. Blackledge, ID
J. Felton, OR
T. Bauman, RL
D. Cook, SAN
D. Peek, SR
D. Jackson, NV

COMMENTS ON DRAFT ENVIRONMENTAL IMPACT STATEMENT, DOE/EIS-0028-D, LIVERMORE SITE, LIVERMORE, CALIFORNIA, SEPTEMBER 1978

Attached for your information or placement in your respective public document room for public inspection is a copy of comment letter No. 19 received on the subject draft statement from Mr. Louis S. Wall, Assistant Director, Office of Review and Compliance, Advisory Council on Historic Preservation, dated December 29, 1978.

W. H. Pennington
Division of NEPA Affairs
Office of Environmental Compliance
and Overview/EV

Attachment

Response to Letter 19

DOE RESPONSE TO LETTER FROM THE ADVISORY COUNCIL ON HISTORICAL PRESERVATION

Since publication of the DEIS, a cultural survey of Livermore's Site 300 has been performed in accordance with 36 CFR Part 64. Section 2.3.10 of the FEIS has been revised to reflect this.

JAN 16 1979

Comments on Draft Environmental Impact Statement, DOE/EIS-0028-D, Livermore Site, Livermore, California, September 1979

G. Facer, DP
A. Schoen, EV
J. Swinebroad, EV
R. Stern, EV
S. Miller, OGC
D. Smith, AD
R. Miller, AL
C. Lindeken, LLL (2)
J. Jeutten, SAN
Public Reading Room
G. Dennis, AL
G. Pitchford, CH (2)
R. Blackledge, ID
J. Felton, OR
T. Bauman, RL
D. Cook, SAN
D. Peek, SR
D. Jackson, NV

Attached for your information or placement in your respective public document room for public inspection is a copy of a petition, containing 102 signatures, for public hearings on the subject statement received from P.A.N.P., 944 Market Street, Room 808, San Francisco, California 94102. This is being distributed as comment #20.

/s/

W. H. Pennington
Acting Deputy Director
Office of Environmental
Compliance and Overview

Attachment

FILE: DOE/EIS-0028-D

DOE/EIS-0028-D Comment Letter #20

DD/OECO

WHPennington:gab

1/15/79

Letter 20

Letter 20 was a list of names petitioning for a public hearing on the DEIS. This hearing was held in Livermore on April 12, 1979.

UNITED STATES ENVIRONMENTAL PROTECTION AGENCY
WASHINGTON, D.C. 20460

12 JAN 1979

Mr. W. H. Pennington
Mail Station E-201
GTN
Department of Energy
Washington, D.C. 20545

Dear Mr. Pennington:

Enclosed are the EPA review comments on the Draft Environmental Impact Statement, DOE/EIS-0028-D, entitled, "Livermore Site, Livermore, California".

Our major concerns with this environmental impact statement (EIS) are the lack of environmental data, the question of whether certain effluents are as low as reasonally achieveable (ALARA) and the incomplete dose assessment presented. There are several areas in the EIS where the data presented is not sufficient to allow independent analyses of the radiation impact of the facility. EPA believes that this data should be incorporated into the final statement. The question of achieving ALARA levels for effluents from several specific facilities are detailed in the enclosed comments. Finally, the failure to present population doses, health effects estimates, food and water pathways considerations, radionuclides considered, and the methods and assumptions employed result in an unacceptably incomplete picture of the laboratory's environmental impact.

In light of our review and in accordance with EPA procedures, we have rated the proposed action LO (Lack of Objectives) and classified the statement as Category 2 (Insufficient Information). If you or your staff have any questions concerning our rating or comments, please do not hesitate to call on us.

Sincerely yours,

for William D. Dickerson

Peter Cook
Acting Director
Office of Federal Activities (A-104)

Enclosure

EPA COMMENTS ON DOE/EIS-0028-D
THE DRAFT ENVIRONMENTAL IMPACT STATEMENT
ON THE LAWRENCE LIVERMORE LABORATORY SITE AT
LIVERMORE, CALIFORNIA

General Comments

1. This draft environmental impact statement (DEIS) relies heavily on referencing other reports, probably in order to minimize the size of the document. However, in some cases there is not enough information to enable a reviewer who does not have access to the references to determine the effect of site operations on the environment. The most significant omissions are in describing the environmental monitoring program and in summarizing data collected over the years to show whether any trend is apparent. There is also a need for better maps of both the site and the surrounding area. More detail is included in specific comments below. The final EIS (FEIS) should address these items.

2. EPA understands that the description of current and proposed activities is not up to date and that current plans are different in some cases. The FEIS should be current in all significant ongoing and proposed activities.

3. More information and discussion are needed to assure that the radioactive effluents that may affect persons off-site are at a level considered to be as low as reasonably achieveable (ALARA). The most significant of these are:

(a) The 14 Mev neutron generator which is projected to deliver a fence line dose of 900 mrem per year. This is a high level of radiation for an unrestricted area and there is a need to more explicitly discuss whether this level is ALARA. Also needing discussion are when (and if) the relocation to Building 292 will occur and what the expected fence-line doses from the new facility will be;

(b) The procedure which is relied upon for the Livermore sewage treatment plant to divert contaminated effluent at the plant rather than providing hold-up capability at the site;

(c) The reasons why tritium releases to air and water cannot be further reduced needs to be explained; and,

(d) The expected radiation exposure to passenger traffic from the LINAC, reactor, and relocated neutron generator operations if the new northwest entrance is still planned.

4. There is a deficiency within the DEIS in the description of the data produced by the off-site environmental sampling program. Although detailed information on the sampling locations, the types of samples (i.e., sewer sludge, water, air), and the radionuclide concentrations are provided in the annual reports, from all we believe the FEIS should include a summary of much of the information contained in these reports to allow a complete, independent assessment of the Lawrence Livermore Laboratory (LLL) impact on the local environment. It would be particularly helpful to have a summary of average annual radionuclide concentratons in effluents and in all media for the past five years to aid in relating the annual effluent releases to present radionuclide concentrations in the immediate environs. The use of several years' data would also reflect the apparent variability of site operations over time and would better indicate the full range of possible environmental effects than could be obtained by choosing a single year.

Further, all radionuclide releases from Sandia Laboratories - Livermore (SLL), including liquid tritum releases, should be included in the annual release data (Table 3-1).

5. More discussion is needed on the environmental effects of site operation as determined from summarized trend data. Two areas of special interest are groundwater contamination at both the Livermore site and Site 300 and the effects of discharge from the Livermore Water Reclamation Plant (LWRP).

The Livermore-Amador Valley Wastewater Management Authority Project (presently under construction) will result in LWRP effluent being transported out of the valley and discharged into San Francisco Bay. This will significantly change the fate of future LLL liquid discharges; it should be addressed in the FEIS.

6. EPA questions the procedure of comparing effects from accidents at LLL with the 10 CFR 100 regulatory limits for accidents, this was done in several places in the DEIS. 10 CFR 100 applies strictly to accidents at reactor sites. If the accident doses from various LLL sources are to be compared with it, there needs to be an explanation of how these regulations relate to the accidents being analyzed. On a related subject, it is stated that DOE guidance may be used to triple the levels provided in the EPA Protective Action Guides (PAGs) before evacuation needs to be considered. This is an inappropriate extrapolation of the PAGs. Currently the PAGs are only Agency guidance and provide action ranges for only the whole body (1-5 rem) and the thyroid (5-25 rem). There is no provision made for further extending these ranges. Further, protective action does not necessarily mean an action as drastic as evacuation. Protective action can be action that will reduce exposure or the chance of exposure.

Specific Comments

1. p. 2-18, section 2.1.6.5, last sentence: Please identify the "accepted standard."

2. p. 3-1 to 3-2: Will the run-off from the area drained by Arroyo Las Positas and the other areas feeding the man-made lake cause any significant accumulations of radionuclides in the lake?

3. p. 3-15: At what frequency are the pre-HEPA filters (glove box filters) changed in building 251? Are they disposed of as transuranic waste (i.e., above 10 nanocuries per gram)?

4. p. 3-17: There is a conspicuous absence of a building drain retention system for building 331. This building is the major source of gaseous tritium releases and it is understood that typical tritium liquid effluents originate from equipment contamination in building 419. The FEIS should clarify the relationship between decontamination of building 331 equipment and building 419. The liquid effluents from building 419 should also be addressed. In the future it is possible that a water fire-protection system would be installed in building 331. The FEIS should discuss briefly the mitigating measures that would accompany this decision.

5. p. 3-36 to 3-37: The radiological impact section on these pages is lacking much significant information. EPA believes that the additional information requested in the following items is necessary for a proper and thorough evaluation of the facility's radiological impacts:

a. With the exception of the few maximum individual dose results reported there is no mention of what radionuclides were considered in the assessment. It is necessary to know the significant impacts from the other radionuclides, along with the definition of what is considered significant, to provide a complete picture of the impact.

b. It is necessary to assess population doses as well as the individual doses discussed in "a" above. From this should come health effects estimates in the form of morbidities, mortalities, and genetic effects.

c. There needs to be a presentation of the assumptions and methods used in preparing the dose assessment. The methods, i.e., models, presentation could simply be a reference to the available literature, if appropriate.

d. From this presentation it appears that only direct and airborne pathways were considered. Food and water pathways must also be considered or adequate reasons given for not considering them. The data associated with them should also be presented to the extent that a reviewer could independently evaluate them.

e. There is currently proposed Federal Radiation Guidance from EPA concerning levels of transuranics in the general environment (EPA/4-77-018). While this Guidance has not yet been signed by the President, DOE should consider presenting a comparison of the expected doses to individuals from alpha radiation from transuranics released from LLL/SLL with the levels provided in the Guidance, viz., one millirad per year to the pulmonary lung or three millirad per year to the bone.

6. Section 3.9: The analysis of both historical and postulated accidents and effects was generally well done. The following items would further strengthen this portion of the EIS:

(a) Provide the X/Q values for specific locations such as the nearest residence, nearest cow and pasture, and nearest school;

(b) Provide estimates of individual doses, population doses, and health effects received from historical accidents, if available;

(c) Provide the age groups being assessed; and,

(d) Provide health effects estimates for postulated accidents.

7. p. 3-47, Section 3.9.1: Specify the "appropriate radiation or concentration guides.

Comments not related to radiation

1. p. 2-59: It is noted that DOE believes that Site 300 is the only known natural location for the wildflower known as Amsinckia grandiflora. The DEIS does not cite this flower as being endangered or threatened; however, EPA expects DOE to consult with the Department of the Interior to ascertain the flower's status and what measures need to be taken to protect its critical habitat.

2. p. 3-71 to p. 3-73: EPA understands the sensitivity regarding the discussion of safeguards and security systems. However, heavy reliance upon electronic detection equipment may leave such systems vulnerable in case of a power failure. The assumption is that LLL has contingency plans for this circumstance but a confirmatory mention of this fact in the FEIS would assure that this possibility has not been overlooked.

3. p. 2A-14, Geologic History section, 23rd line: The term "clay" is incorrect, it should be "alluvium" or "siltstones and sandstones."

Department of Energy
Washington, D.C. 20545

JAN 22 1979

G. Facer, DP	Library, Room 1223, 20 Mass Avenue
A. Schoen, EV	G. Dennis, AL
J. Swinebroad, EV	G. Pitchford, CH (2)
R. Stern, EV	R. Blackledge, ID
S. Miller, OGC	J. Felton, OR
D. Smith, AD	T. Bauman, RL
R. Miller, AL	D. Cook, SAN
C. Lindeken, LLL (2)	D. Peek, SR
J. Jeutten, SAN	D. Jackson, NV

COMMENTS ON DRAFT ENVIRONMENTAL IMPACT STATEMENT, DOE/EIS-0028-D, LIVERMORE SITE, LIVERMORE, CALIFORNIA, SEPTEMBER 1978

Attached for your information or placement in your respective public document room for public inspection is a copy of comment letter No. 21 received on the subject draft statement from Mr. Peter Cook, Acting Director, Office of Federal Activities, Environmental Protection Agency, dated January 12, 1979.

W. H. Pennington
Division of NEPA Affairs
Office of Environmental Compliance
and Overview/EV

Attachment

Response to Letter 21

DOE RESPONSE TO LETTER FROM THE ENVIRONMENTAL PROTECTION AGENCY

Response to general comments:

1. Description of Livermore's environmental monitoring program

Appendix 2A in the FEIS contains a copy of the 1980 annual environmental monitoring report. This latter report also contains a description of the sampling procedures and analytical methods employed by the monitoring program together with more detailed maps showing the location of monitoring points. Section 3.7 of the FEIS contains a 5-year summary of radioactive effluents from the Livermore site.

2. Description of activities should be current

Every attempt is made to have the FEIS reflect the status of all environmentally significant activities and exposures up to and including 1980.

3. Assurance that Effluent Levels and Exposures are As Low As Reasonably Achievable (ALARA)

(a) 14-MeV neutron generator

The projected fenceline radiation dose of 900 mrem (1976) has been reduced to about 166 mrem in 1980. These exposures include a natural background of about 60 mrem. The reduction has been achieved by transferring many of the high-flux experiments to the more centrally located Building 292. Site perimeter dosimeters closest to Building 292 show annual increases within about 10 mrem of natural background.

(b) Diverting procedures at Livermore sewage treatment plant

After detecting an accidental release at the sewage effluent monitoring station, Livermore site personnel have about 3 hrs to evaluate the magnitude of the release, since this is the approximate time required for sewage to flow to the Livermore sewage treatment plant.

If this evaluation appears to justify diversion, the Livermore sewage plant is notified. The decision to divert is made by the sewage plant. Diversion can be placed in two holding basins with a combined capacity of 1.5×10^5 m^3. Based on the experience of past releases requiring diversion, the treatment plant has had little difficulty dealing with treatment of these releases. To duplicate the retention and treatment capability now provided by the Livermore plant does not appear to be cost effective, considering the low frequency with which need for diversion occurs.

(c) Reduction of tritium releases to air and sewer

Funding has been requested for upgrading the ventilation system of Building 331 to provide for collection and retention of the small amounts of tritium released to the atmosphere under routine operations. A second system is planned to retain nonroutine releases, which may occur in event of failure of part of the effluent-handling equipment (Section 2.1.6.6 of FEIS).

Tritium releases to the sanitary sewer have been reduced to less than 10 Ci per year. These releases have had detectable impacts on groundwater in the vicinity of the Livermore sewage plant. During the wet season the treated sewage effluent was discharged to Arroyo Las Positas, which served to recharge downstream aquifers supplying local groundwater.

As part of the Livermore-Amador Valley Wastewater Management program, a pipeline was constructed to transport wastewater out of the valley and into the San Francisco Bay. The Livermore sewage plant was connected to this pipeline in February 1980. Although the effluent will still be used for irrigation, it will no longer be discharged into the Arroyo, thus eliminating the principal means of tritium migration to local and downstream groundwater.

(d) Northwest entrance

Traffic on the planned northwest entrance to LLNL will not be exposed to excessive radiation from either the Linac (Building 194) or the 14-MeV neutron generator (Building 292). The reactor (Building 281) is no longer in operation. During 1979, the annual radiation exposure dose rate at a perimeter location closer to these facilities than this planned entrance was within 10 mrem of the natural background.

4. Need for a multi-year summary of annual effluent releases

Section 3.7 of the FEIS contains a 5-year summary of annual airborne and liquid radioactive effluents. Table 3-1 of the FEIS includes the airborne and liquid effluents from SNLL.

5. Groundwater contamination and effects of discharge from the Livermore Water Reclamation Plant

At the Livermore site, there is no surface discharge of radioactive liquids. At Site 300, tritium-contaminated waste in a land burial area has been detected in a nearby spring. However, an adjacent well shows tritium levels typical of background. Neither well is used as a drinking water source.

As noted in 3(c) above in February of 1980 the Livermore Water Reclamation Plant was connected to the pipeline that transports treated sewage effluent out of the valley. Although about 10% of the effluent is still used for irrigation, it no longer is discharged into Arroyo Las Positas, thus eliminating the principal means of impacting on local and downstream groundwater via recharge.

6. Reference to 10 CFR 100 and protective action guides in the DEIS

In the Accident Analysis section, calculated radiation doses from postulated maximum credible accidents were compared with 10 CFR 100 because these regulatory limits for accidents appeared to be appropriate for purposes of perspective. The DEIS also uses the EPA draft protective action guides to provide perspective. Although EPA has no guidance for protective action against lung exposure, it is the Laboratories' intention to use the extension described for emergency response planning.

Response to specific comments:

1. Section 2.1.6.5--The "accepted standard" is DOE Order 5480.1A.

2. Run-off from the area drained by Arroyo Las Positas will not cause accumulations of radionuclides in the man-made lake. It is not expected that the use of runoff water from the east of the Livermore site will result in any measurable accumulation of radioactivity in the man-made lake.

3. Frequency of HEPA filter changing in Bldg. 251--The changing of HEPA filters in Bldg. 251 is based on measured flow rate as sensed by individual Pitot tubes. When the dust load on the filter reduces the flow below a predetermined rate, the filter is replaced. The frequency of filter change depends on work activity in the glove box. All used filters from Bldg. 251 are disposed of as transuranic waste (retrievable storage). At Livermore, the prefilter & HEPA filter for glove boxes are enclosed together so the prefilter cannot be changed separately.

4. Building 419 operations and Building 331 liquid effluent handling--Through an oversight the description of operation at Building 419 (decontamination) was omitted from the DEIS. The FEIS contains this information and addresses its relationship with Building 331.

5. Section 3.7--Appendix 2A of the FEIS contains a copy of the Annual Environmental Monitoring Report for 1980. This report discusses the monitoring of additional radionuclides to those described in Section 3.7. Estimated population doses are presented for significant radioactive effluents and the methodology of dose assessments is described. The monitoring of foodstuff originating in the area is also included in the annual report.

6. Section 3.9--

(a) χ/Q values for specific locations were addressed in the Staff Statement in Response to Comments on the DEIS (included in the Hearing Record of the Public Hearing on the Draft Environmental Impact Statement, Livermore Site, Livermore, California).

(b) Off-site concentrations of radionuclides following accidental releases have been too small to warrant individual or population dose estimates.

(c) and (d) Age groups and health effects for postulated accidents: estimates of these effects can be obtained from the data presented and standard health-effect conversion terms.

7. Appropriate radiation or concentration guide refers to DOE Order 5480.1A.

Response to comments not related to radiation:

1. *Amsinckia grandiflora*--The Fish and Wildlife Service of the Department of the Interior is proposing Endangered Species status for this plant and that 160 acres of Site 300 be declared its critical habitat.

2. Both LLNL and SNLL have contingency plans for dealing with safeguard and security problems.

3. The reference quoted in Appendix 2A in the DEIS is a LLNL published report, which is widely distributed. It is therefore impractical to make the correction suggested.

ENVIRONMENTAL COALITION ON NUCLEAR POWER

Executive Directors: George Boomsma – R D #1 Peach Bottom Pa 17563 717.548 2836 Judith Johnsrud – 433 Orlando Avenue State College Pa 16801 814.237.3900

119 E. Aaron Dr.
State College, Pa.
16801

31 December 1978

Mr. W.H. Pennington
Mail Station E-201
U.S. Department of Energy
Washington, D.C., 20545

Dear Mr Pennington:

In its draft "Environmental Impact Statement, Livermore Site, Livermore, California" (DOE/EIS-0028-D) the department of Energy claims to assess the continued operation of the Lawrence Livermore and Sandia Laboratories at Livermore Cal., for environmental impact as required by the National Environmental Policy Act of 1969 (NEPA). The draft report also proports to compare the costs and benefits of continued operation. The draft report does not fulfill this NEPA requirement.

The very long term health consequences of continued or past operations is completely ignored. In particular, in 1976 Pohl ("Health Effects of Radon-222 from Uranium Mining" in Search, 7(5),345-350 ,August 1976) pointed out that the thorium - 230 in uranium mill tailings decays to radium -226 and then to radon-222, with a time scale determined by the 80,000 year half life of thorium - 230. Kepford (testimony in Three Mile Island Unit 2 operating license hearings before NRC ASLP) has pointed out that uranium - 238 in mill tailings and enrichment tailings (depleted uranium) decays by several steps thru thorium -230 to radon - 222, and should also be considered. This position has been supported by the 21 Sept. 1977 memorandum of Dr. Walter H. Jordan of the NRC ASLBP to James R. Yore, ASLBP Chairman. These matters have also been reviewed by Dr. R.L. Gotchy of the NRC Staff. The NRC is currently trying to deal with this radon issue.

It is stated in section 3.5.1.12 that no radioactive waste remains on site. However, section 3.5.6.1 describes the burial of depleted uranium in pits each of which contains the equivalent of 150 kg of uranium. This IS radioactive waste on site. The total quantity of this depleted uranium at present should be stated, along with the amounts expected to be added during future operations. This uranium - 238 will decay to radon -222. Since the uranium is buried under a few feet of soil, erosion is certain to occur, and expose it at some future time. All radon emissions - covered or exposed, - should be considered for their very serious health consequences. The total burden of such consequences lies with the operation of this facility.

In particular, consider just one such pit containing 150 kg of uranium - 238. The ultimate decay of this material will produce 2.15×10^{10} curies of radon - 222. In light of the EPA estimate I shall suggest that 1/20 of this escapes to the air ("Environmental analysis of the uranium fuel Cycle, Part I - Fuel Supply" EPA, 1973). The NRC estimate (R.L. Gotchy, NRC Staff in Three Mile Island Unit 2 operating license hearings.) of the consequences of release of one curie of radon - 222 from a western state with a U.S. population of 300 million to be 0.56 Person - rem to the bronchial epithelium. This estimate used in this case results in total of 6×10^8 person - rem. The NRC estimate of cancer risk (Same reference) is 22.2 deaths per million person-rem. This leads to a total of 13,000 deaths from a single burial pit containing 150 kg of uranium. Such long - term impacts should not be ignored in the final EIS.

Plutonium and americium levels are discussed in section 2.3.11. These are given as concentrations. It would be useful to have estimates of the total quantities. Radioactive solid waste is discussed in section 3.5.1. Again, it would be useful to have a measure of the total quantities of radioactivity, by isotope, contained therein. The draft EIS takes no impact from the disposal of this material, therefore assuming perfect management, which is not the case. The environmental impact of the Livermore operation includes the impacts from all the wastes generated there. To ignore these impacts would not be entirely candid. NEPA requires that this be considered. In Calvert Cliffs Coordinating Committee v. USAEC, 449 F. 2nd 1109 (D.C. Cir.,1971) the court stated:

> We conclude, then, that Section 102 of NEPA mandates a particular sort of careful and informed decision-making process and creates judicially enforcable duties .... But if the decision was reached procedurally without individualized consideration and balancing of environmental factors--conducted fully and in good faith -- it is the responsibility of the courts to reverse. (emphasis added)

Thus, all environmental costs must be considered fully. Furthermore, the radioactive materials must be considered for the full period of their radioactive decay, as footnote 12 of NRDC v. USNRC, 547 F. 2nd 633 (D.C. Cir. 1976) states in part:

> We note at the outset that this standard is misleading because the toxic life of the wastes under discussion far exceeds the life of the plant being licensed. The environmental effects to be considered are those flowing from the reprocessing and passive storage for the full detoxification period.

Thus the estimates of health consequences must be extended over several half lives of the species under consideration.

The accomplishments of LLL are considered in section 2.1.3.2, including the testing of the Spartan warhead at Amchitka. It should be noted that there are other environmental costs associated with these operations including production of the warhead materials, and the impacts of the Amchitka test which are not discussed. Similarly, section 9.1 discusses the benefits of continued operations, including increased national security from nuclear weapons development. It should be noted that the security arises if the weapons are in fact manufactured, and this process has large environmental costs associated with materials production, and other activities. These other costs are associated with this benefit which is listed here as if that benefit were solely due to LLL operations. This may be difficult to address, but must not be ignored.

I hope these concerns can be addressed in the final EIS.

Sincerely,

William A. Lochstet

Wm. A. Lochstet

Department of Energy
Washington, D.C. 20545

JAN 24 1979

G. Facer, DP	Library, Room 1223, 20 Mass Avenue
A. Schoen, EV	G. Dennis, AL
J. Swinebroad, EV	G. Pitchford, CH (2)
R. Stern, EV	R. Blackledge, ID
S. Miller, OGC	J. Felton, OR
D. Smith, AD	T. Bauman, RL
R. Miller, AL	D. Cook, SAN
C. Lindeken, LLL (2)	D. Peek, SR
J. Jeutten, SAN	D. Jackson, NV

COMMENTS ON DRAFT ENVIRONMENTAL IMPACT STATEMENT, DOE/EIS-0028-D, LIVERMORE SITE, LIVERMORE, CALIFORNIA, SEPTEMBER 1978

Attached for your information or placement in your respective public document room for public inspection is a copy of comment letter No. 22 received on the subject draft statement from Mr. William A. Lochstet, Environmental Coalition on Nuclear Power, dated December 31, 1978.

W. H. Pennington/gab

W. H. Pennington
Division of NEPA Affairs
Office of Environmental Compliance
and Overview/EV

Attachment

Response to Letter 22

DOE RESPONSE TO LETTER FROM THE ENVIRONMENTAL COALITION ON NUCLEAR POWER

Waste storage

Section 3.5.1.12 of the DEIS refers to the Livermore site, while 3.5.6.1 refers to Site 300 operations. Depleted uranium debris from high-explosives tests at Site 300 has been buried there in accordance with land burial regulations contained in 10CFR20.304.

Radon hazard from depleted uranium

Prior to isotopic separation of ^{235}U from ^{238}U by gaseous diffusion, the uranium is chemically separated from its radioactive decay products. As a result, the depleted uranium used at Site 300 is essentially free of radium-226, the parent of radon 222.

Testing the Spartan Warhead at Amchitka

The scope of the DEIS was limited to assessing the site-specific environmental impacts of Livermore operations. The scope does not include environmental impacts of nuclear weapons testing or the impacts associated with nuclear weapons production.

OFFICE OF THE SECRETARY
RESOURCES BUILDING
1416 NINTH STREET
95814

(916) 445-5656

Department of Conservation
Department of Fish and Game
Department of Forestry
Department of Navigation and
Ocean Development
Department of Parks and Recreation
Department of Water Resources

EDMUND G. BROWN JR.
GOVERNOR OF
CALIFORNIA

Air Resources Board
California Coastal Commission
California Conservation Corps
Colorado River Board
Energy Resources Conservation and
Development Commission
Regional Water Quality Control Boards
San Francisco Bay Conservation and
Development Commission
Solid Waste Management Board
State Coastal Conservancy
State Lands Commission
State Reclamation Board
State Water Resources Control Board

THE RESOURCES AGENCY OF CALIFORNIA
SACRAMENTO, CALIFORNIA

JAN 17 1979

U. S. Department of Energy
Washington, D. C. 20545

Gentlemen:

The State of California has reviewed the "Draft Environmental Impact Statement Livermore Site" which was submitted to the Office of Planning and Research in the Governor's Office.

The State's review was coordinated with the Departments of Water Resources, Fish and Game, Food and Agriculture, Health Services, Conservation and Transportation; the Air Resources and State Water Resources Control Boards; and the Public Utilities and Energy Commissions.

The DEIS has been reviewed by the Department of Health Services with particular emphasis on the radiological impacts. It was concluded, based on information provided in the DEIS, that the existence and continuing operation of the Livermore Site does not present a radiological health hazard to members of the public in the vicinity of the facility. However, the statement itself does not provide sufficient information for an independent assessment to be made regarding the adequacy of the Lawrence Livermore Laboratory (LLL) Environmental Radiological Program. Similarly, essentially no information is provided regarding LLL emergency procedures in the event of accidental release of radioactive material that could potentially affect members of the public.

The document should provide a comprehensive summary of information relating to the conduct of operations at the laboratory in order that the public and health protection specialists can be adequately informed about the impact of the laboratory and the implications of the laboratory's existence in areas of their purview. Obviously, there is a trade-off between providing excessive detail and the manageability of the document. The DEIS could be improved in the area of radiological impact assessment through the strengthening of reference documentation and with the addition of some discussion. Specific comments on these points follow, with references to the sections in the document.

Section 2.1.8 Environmental Monitoring

The presentation of the LLL Environmental Monitoring Program could be strengthened by the addition of a discussion of the legal, administrative and technical bases for the program. For example, the legal-administrative requirements should be summarized with reference to appropriate DOE manual chapters. Documents should be cited which explain the technical design of the environmental monitoring program; i.e., sampling and measurement frequency and location specification and criteria. Documentation should be provided for sampling, analysis and quality assurance procedures.

Additional information should be provided on results of the radiological monitoring program, including those data that support the conclusion that no environmental buildup of radioactivity has occurred as a result of the laboratory's continuing operation.

Information provided in this DEIS is inadequate, as it stands, to provide support for independent conclusions to be made by public health professionals in other agencies concerning the environmental effects of the laboratory. The additional information requested should be provided to assist in developing this independent assessment.

Section 3.5.1.7 Light Isotopes Chemistry - Building 331

Some discussion would be desirable in Section 3.5.1.7.3 concerning stack effluent monitor alarm trip points and associated emergency control actions. This should include a summary of LLL internal notification and response procedures in the event of a monitoring alarm trip, similar to the information provided regarding liquid effluent monitoring in Section 3.5.1.13 (pg. 3-20).

Section 3.5.1.15 Radioactive Waste Releases

This section states that "During 1976, 120 m^3 of packaged solid waste was shipped from Livermore". Does this include both transuranium contaminated waste and waste which does not contain transuranium isotopes? It would be desirable to have a summary of waste volumes and the number of shipments in terms of category and disposal site designation. That is, identification in terms of shipments to DOE facilities and to commercial burial sites.

Table 3-1 (pg. 3-22)

This table should include the identification of release points if possible, to aid in the assessment of potential impacts. For example, are the tritium and argon each released from a single stack or vent? Are all the isotopes in liquid effluents released to the sanitary sewer?

Section 3.5.2.2 Sewer System

It is observed that the combined outflow from the Sandia and Livermore Laboratories leaves the site through a vitrified clay sewer line built by the Navy in 1942. Are regular tests for the continuing integrity of this line performed in the offsite monitoring program? If so what are the results?

Section 3.5.2.3 Livermore Water Reclamation Plant

It would be appropriate in this discussion of environmental effects of LLL, to have included in this section a discussion of plans for ultimate disposal of waste water. The DEIS should note that the Livermore-Amador Valley Water Management Agency Project currently scheduled for completion late in 1979, will intercept most of the Livermore treated waste discharge and transport it out of the valley for ultimate disposal into San Francisco Bay via the East Bay Discharge Authority System's outfall. The city of Livermore will, we understand, still continue to "reclaim" about 20 percent of its effluent via local irrigation.

Section 3.5.6 Waste Management at Site 300

The surface and ground water monitoring program in the environment of the 300 site should be described in better detail, particularly in view of the proximity of the State Water Project California Aqueduct. It is not apparent whether a program exists to measure potential movement of nuclides from radioactive waste buried on the site. This could occur through overland and near-surface flow into intermittent streams, or through down gradient flow into the regional groundwater systems, for example. The relation between sampling points, points of water use (if any) in this vicinity, and the burial sites, in the context of the 300 site vicinity hydrology should be discussed. If this analysis has been conducted elsewhere, the findings should be summarized and referenced.

Section 3.7 Radiological Impact

This section summarizes estimated annual individual offsite radiation exposures attributable to LLL routine radioactivity releases. It would be desirable to provide a reference to the actual analyses performed, which would include a more detailed discussion of the assumptions used in the development of the model. A statement should be made about the population dose, in addition to the data presented for individual members of the public in the area potentially affected by LLL operations.

Section 3.9 Accident Analysis

This section is deficient in that essentially no information is provided regarding emergency procedures and planning activities in the event of potential offsite impacts. This section and Appendix 3-B (Disaster Control Plan) tend to project the view of LLL as a self-contained and essentially self-sufficient organization.

No mention is made of procedures for notifying responsible individuals offsite in the event of an incident. Certainly, local, state, and various Federal agencies may play a part in the event of an accident having offsite consequences at LLL as they did in the August 6, 1970 tritium incident.

Existing notification procedures should be summarized for the organizations with whom emergency action agreements exist. This should include police, fire, medical, public health, and transportation agencies and other organizations as appropriate. In particular, notification and emergency procedures involving radioactive material releases and spills which could concernably affect members of the public should be summarized. This should include incidents involving radioactive materials shipments to and from LLL. The public notification criteria should be documented.

Section 3.9.2 Analysis of Postulated Accidents

The potential offsite effects of fault movement at the Sandia Laboratory is not discussed in the maximum credible accident analysis listed in this section. Is the inventory of tritium in Building 331 in fact the maximum that can occur at this site, and do larger quantities ever exist at Sandia?

The following brief questions or comments are arranged by page number appearing in the DEIS.

The document discusses possible site expansions and a new entrance (page 1-3, Section 1.2. third paragraph), yet the impact of these is not discussed in Sec. 3.8.5, Traffic and Transportation. Figure 2.10 shows the new entrance schematic oriented toward Vasco Road. The last sentence in Sec. 3.8.5 states that additional use of the Greenville Road entrance should be encouraged. The two appear to be in conflict. If traffic is to be encouraged to use Greenville Road, such added use of this street may impact the operations of the Greenville Road/Interstate 580 Interchange. This should be discussed, as should the impact, if the proposed Vasco Road entrance is built.

Page 2-27, Line 17

Does this mean that there are no offsite tritium monitors at the Sandia Research Laboratory, so that that facility depends upon LLL's ambient tritium monitoring capability?

If any action level exists based on environmental monitoring results, then they should be published in the DEIS. If not, please explain.

Page 2-29, Table 2-1

The inference is that grab samples are obtained daily. If samples are collected continuously out of the waste streams, then this should be indicated.

Page 2-58

The value of 70 mm for average annual rainfall at site 300 appears to be in error, as does the reference to San Francisco University on the next page.

Pages 2-60 and 2-62

The reference citations are apparently in error, should be rechecked.

Page 3-20, Line 1

Is any attempt to make the alarm system, which activates when a tank is full, redundant or otherwise fail-safe? If so, it should be described.

Page 3-20, Line 15

Are the drinking water standards referred to the ones promulgated by the Public Health Service in 1962, or the current EPA standards?

Page 3-21

The fate of the solid waste which collects as sludge in the cooling towers is not discussed in the DEIS, and should be if any leaves the site.

Page 3-27 Line 28

The sewage monitoring system referred to does not include analysis for tritium. The monitoring program in existence for this radionuclide should be described separately.

Page 3-65, Lines 22 and 23

A reference to the basis for this conclusion should be given.

In general, review of the DEIS was hampered by the fact that maps and photographs were not always provided with a compass direction, that building numbers were not provided on layout maps, and that a map showing the relative locations of LLL, Sandia, and Site 300 in somewhat better detail was not provided.

Thank you for the opportunity to review this document.

Sincerely,

L. Frank Goodson
Assistant Secretary for Resources

cc: Director of Management Systems
Office of Planning and Research
1400 Tenth Street
Sacramento, CA 95814

Department of Energy
Washington, D.C. 20545

JAN 29 1979

G. Facer, DP	Library, Room 1223, 20 Mass Avenue
A. Schoen, EV	G. Dennis, AL
J. Swinebroad, EV	G. Pitchford, CH (2)
R. Stern, EV	R. Blackledge, ID
S. Miller, OGC	J. Felton, OR
D. Smith, AD	T. Bauman, RL
R. Miller, AL	D. Cook, SAN
C. Lindeken, LLL (2)	D. Peek, SR
J. Jeutten, SAN	D. Jackson, NV

COMMENTS ON DRAFT ENVIRONMENTAL IMPACT STATEMENT, DOE/EIS-0028-D, LIVERMORE SITE, LIVERMORE, CALIFORNIA, SEPTEMBER 1978

Attached for your information or placement in your respective public document room for public inspection is a copy of comment letter No. 23 received on the subject draft statement from Mr. L. Frank Goodson, Assistant Secretary for Resources, The Resources Agency of California, dated January 19, 1979.

W. H. Pennington/gab

W. H. Pennington
Division of NEPA Affairs
Office of Environmental Compliance
and Overview/EV

Attachment

DOE RESPONSE TO LETTER FROM THE RESOURCES AGENCY OF CALIFORNIA

Section 2.1.8, Environmental Monitoring

Appendix 2A of the FEIS contains a copy of the 1980 annual environmental monitoring report. An appendix of the annual report contains a description of sampling methods and analytical procedures used in the Livermore environmental monitoring program. These appendices will provide the detailed information requested.

Section 3.5.1.7

The Building 331 stack effluent monitoring system monitoring alarm settings are primarily intended for alerting building personnel, who investigate any such alarm and take corrective action. Although site management are informed, action by outside agencies is not required.

In contrast, release of radioactivity or toxic chemicals to the Livermore sanitary sewer system may require flow division at the treatment plant. Here the action of an outside agency is required and this is the reason why the notification procedure was mentioned in the DEIS.

Section 3.5.1.15, Radioactive Wastes

During 1979 376 m^3 of packaged radioactive solid waste was shipped from Livermore. Of this total 33 m^3 was transuranic (TRU) waste. Three shipments of TRU waste were made to NTS during 1979.

Table 3-1

The identification of effluent release points are clarified in the FEIS. Appendix 2A of the FEIS contains a table (Table 32), which identifies the source of the radioactive effluents released to the atmosphere. The Livermore reactor (Building 281) was shut down in 1980, so this release point no longer exists. All radioactive liquid effluents released at Livermore are released to the Livermore sanitary sewer.

3.5.2.2

Two wells along and adjacent to the section of the sewer line built by the Navy have been monitored annually for tritium activity as a means of assuring the integrity of this line.

In 1980 use of the line was discontinued. The Livermore sewage effluent is now discharged at the northwest corner of LLNL into a new section of sewer that runs north to the Western Pacific Railroad on DOE-owned land and then west along the railroad's right-of-way crossing Vasco Road to the City of Livermore's industrial sewer line.

3.5.2.3

The Livermore-Amador Valley Water Management Agency pipeline is discussed in Appendix 2A and section 2.1.8.3 of the FEIS.

3.5.6

The surface and groundwater monitoring program at Site 300 is described in Appendix 2A.

3.7

Appendix E of the 1980 annual environmental monitoring report (Appendix 2A of the FEIS) describes the methodology used for calculating off-site radiation doses due to routine radioactive releases. These methods are based on the U.S. Nuclear Regulatory Commission's Regulatory Guide 1.1.09.

3.9

The Staff Statement in Response to Comments on the DEIS (included in the Hearing Record of the Public Hearing on the Draft Environmental Impact Statement, Livermore Site, Livermore, California) discusses the DOE role in emergency planning in the public sector as well as the notification channels that have been established.

3.9.2

The discussion of seismic movement on the Livermore site appears in Section 2.3.3 of the FEIS.

In the FEIS the maximum credible accident involving tritium is based on a hypothetical accident at SNLL's Tritium Research Facility (Building 968). Here the accident does involve the entire building inventory.

A separate environmental assessment is being written to address the environmental impact of the new entrance to LLNL.

Page 2-27 Line 17

LLNL has established and maintains 2 tritiated-water-vapor samplers in the off-site vicinity of SNLL. The approximate locations for these samplers are shown in Figure 4 of Appendix 2A in the FEIS. These are historical samples and not real-time tritium monitors. Typical concentrations observed are 10^{-11} $\mu Ci/m^3$ compared with the Concentration Guide of 2×10^{-7} $\mu Ci/m^3$ for uncontrolled areas.

Page 2-29 Table 2-1

Samples of sewage effluent are collected continuously by an automatic sampler. Daily aliquots are collected from this sampler for certain analyses. For some analyses these aliquots are composited for monthly analyses.

Page 2-58

The errors in Sections 2.3.7.6 and 2.3.10 have been corrected in the FEIS.

Page 2-60 - 2-62

The reference to Beck et al. has been corrected in the FEIS.

Page 3-20

Radioactive liquid effluents discharged to the sanitary sewer are treated to reduce radioactivity to as low as reasonably achievable (ALARA) and well below the standards of DOE Order 5480.1A.

Page 3-21

Cooling tower blowdown is discharged to the Livermore sanitary sewer. Sludge is handled as hazardous waste according to the provisions of the Resource Conservation and Recovery Act.

Page 3-27 Line 28

An aliquot of the daily sewage sample is analyzed for tritium. The results for 1980 are discussed in Appendix 2A of the FEIS.

Page 3-65 Lines 22 and 23

In the FEIS these lines have been changed to read "Radioiodine inhalation doses are not increased by the presence of fog since the droplets, which typically have diameters of 8 to 20 μm, are too large to be readily inhaled." References are given for both the size range of fog droplets and their inability to be inhaled.

Your comments have been considered in upgrading the figures in the FEIS.

ALAMEDA COUNTY PLANNING DEPARTMENT

399 Elmhurst Street, Hayward, California 94544 (415) 881-6401

April 2, 1979

Mr. Calvin Jackson
United States Department of Energy
1333 Broadway
Oakland, CA 94612

Dear Mr. Jackson:

The Alameda County Planning Commission has the responsibility of planning for lands in Alameda County which may be impacted by the operation of the Lawrence Livermore Laboratory. The Commission considered a staff report on the Draft Environmental Impact Statement Livermore Site, Livermore, California, September, 1978, prepared by the U.S. Department of Energy at their meeting of Monday, March 19, 1979 to become familiar with potential impacts.

The comments which follow are submitted to you for review and response in the Final Environmental Impact Statement.

1. The distribution of the DEIS to this Commission did not occur with sufficient time available to respond under the original schedule. This did not permit the time necessary to review the total document fully. The Commission had only one copy of the DEIS for its use.

2. The summary contained in the DEIS is brief to the point of being inadequate, and seemed to treat the substance of the report rather superficially.

3. There appears to be minimal correlation of the County General Plan and its elements with the evaluation made in the DEIS. It is questionable whether the County planning elements were reviewed as part of the preparation of the base document.

4. The DEIS appears deficient in its consideration of the impacts on the water resources in the Valley to the extent that the DEIS is judged to be inadequate for use in assessing the impacts the Lab may have on the surrounding community. This is particularly evident in the apparent lack of attention given to the impacts of any accident on the surface and ground water resources. The volume of liquid containing radio nuclides located at the laboratories is not identified nor is the direction of accidential spill addressed. In addition, air borne contamination that may be deposited on the surrounding properties with subsequent surface water runoff directly affecting the health and safety of the public and ultimately carrying the material back into the surface and underground water system has not been addressed.

5. The impacts of a potential nuclear contamination entering the municipal waste disposal system should be assessed.

Mr. Calvin Jackson
April 2, 1979
Page 2

6. There is lack of agreement by geological authorities regarding the location and potential effects of the Las Positas fault. Additional geologic studies should be made and included in the final DEIS to resolve all questions on this matter.

It is requested that the additional studies suggested above to bring the report into conformance with the Federal Guidelines for the preparation of a DEIS be completed and that the new information be distributed to those receiving this DEIS so that comments on the new information may be included in the final DEIS to be certified by the Department of Energy.

Thank you for your assistance and attention.

Very truly yours,

William H. Fraley
Secretary

WHF:rr

cc: Board of Supervisors
Director of Public Works

Department of Energy
Washington, D.C. 20545

APR 26 1979

G. Facer, DP
A. Schoen, EV
J. Swinebroad, EV
R. Stern, EV
S. Miller, OGC
D. Smith, AD
R. Miller, AL
C. Lindeken, LLL (2)
J. Jeutten, SAN
Library, Room 1223, 20 Mass Avenue
G. Dennis, AL
G. Pitchford, CH (2)
R. Blackledge, ID
J. Felton, OR
T. Bauman, RL
D. Cook, SAN
D. Peek, SR
D. Jackson, NV

COMMENTS ON DRAFT ENVIRONMENTAL IMPACT STATEMENT, DOE/EIS-0028-D, LIVERMORE SITE, LIVERMORE, CALIFORNIA, SEPTEMBER 1978

Attached for your information or placement in your respective public document room for public inspection is a copy of comment letter No. 24 received on the subject draft statement from Mr. William H. Fraley, Secretary, Alameda County Planning Department, Hayward, California, dated April 2, 1979.

W. H. Pennington/gab

W. H. Pennington
Office of Environmental
Compliance and Overview, EV

Attachment

1. Distribution of DEIS

Notice of the publication of the Livermore DEIS in September 1979 was contained in the Federal Register. Copies were distributed to State and local government organizations and private citizens indicating an interest in Livermore Site operations. We regret that your copies were delivered too late to prepare comments during the specified comment period.

2. Brevity of DEIS summary

The DEIS summary was prepared in the format of a linear abstract using, wherever possible, topical sentences. An attempt was made to avoid including details that could better be obtained by reading the body of the statement.

3. Alameda County General Plan

The DEIS has been revised so as to more clearly reflect the objectives of such local plans as the Alameda County General Plan (Section 2.1.8 of the FEIS). In addition, the Alameda County Planning Department was contacted for information on land-use plans for property west of the LLNL site and the Alameda County Road Department was contacted for traffic data at the East Avenue and Vasco Road intersection.

4. Water Resources

An adjunct of the Site Seismic Safety Program's effort to evaluate geologic hazards at the LLNL site is the site hydrogeologic study. The goal of this study is to determine the likelihood of a potentially hazardous liquid spill on site traveling through the unsaturated zone and reaching the groundwater. Acquiring data for a detailed characterization of the LLNL subsurface geology and hydrology, together with laboratory and field experimentation and flow modeling, is necessary for evaluating this potential groundwater contamination. This study will detemine whether there are any groundwater barriers to such contamination. The results of this study will be published as a separate report and will be used in evaluating the potential for contamination of groundwater in the LLNL environs.

5. <u>Municipal Waste Disposal System</u>

Radionuclides entering the municipal waste disposal system are typically removed in the waste treatment process and retained in the sewage sludge. With the continuous monitoring capability now in use at the LLNL point of effluent release, an accident of the magnitude discussed in Section 3.9 was not considered credible.

6. <u>Las Positas Fault</u>

Based on the letters received during the comment period for the Livermore DEIS and the questions raised at the Public Hearing on the DEIS, an extensive Livermore Geologic and Seismic field test program was undertaken. Questions raised concerning the Las Positas fault are being addressed in this study. Results of this work will be reported as a separate report scheduled for publication in 1982.

BAY CHAPTER
SIERRA CLUB
WE MOVED. OUR NEW ADDRESS IS
6014 College Ave.
Oakland, Ca. 94618

~~5008~~ 6014 COLLEGE AVENUE / OAKLAND, CALIFORNIA 94618 / (415) 658-7470

April 12, 1979

Mr. W.H. Pennington
Department of Energy
Washington, D.C. 20545

Re: Draft EIS Livermore Site, California

Mr. Pennington,

The Sierra Club San Francisco Bay Chapter area includes the Livermore Valley in its coverage of Alameda, Contra Costa, Marin and San Francisco Counties. Sierra Club members in the valley and bay area communities have an ongoing interest in and commitment to a policy on nuclear research which reflects a concern over public health and safety questions involving exposure to radiation and contingency planning.

In discussion of the Livermore Site and review of the Environmental Impact Statement with other local citizens groups, the Bay Chapter found the EIS lacking information on several important points.

We believe the public has a vital interest in solid information on the risks of exposure to radioactive materials. Therefore, we lay particular stress on the value of completing the epidemiological study begun at the Livermore Lab, including study of subpopulations of employees working at Site 300 and those with a record of exposure to radiation. The study should be completed and its results made public.

Also, the Environmental Statement should contain an outline of a thorough emergency response plan for the Labs and surrounding communities.

Again, along that same line of public information/public assurance, we would wish to see in the EIS a complete presentation of information on the amounts of plutonium handled at the Labs and its transport and disposal. Recognizing that certain information is sensitive and may be classified, we suggest that s statement could be made about limits of maximum amounts of plutonium used.

Finally, the seismic information published in the Draft EIS appears unfinished, unquantified, and spotted with unanswered questions. We would like to see the seismic analysis complete soon by an independent agency such as the US Goelogical Survey.

Thank you for this opportunity to express our concerns.

John Holtzclaw 10-190 Conservation Committee Chair

Department of Energy
Washington, D.C. 20545

APR 26 1979

G. Facer, DP
A. Schoen, EV
J. Swinebroad, EV
R. Stern, EV
S. Miller, OGC
D. Smith, AD
R. Miller, AL
C. Lindeken, LLL (2)
J. Jeutten, SAN

Library, Room 1223, 20 Mass Avenue
G. Dennis, AL
G. Pitchford, CH (2)
R. Blackledge, ID
J. Felton, OR
T. Bauman, RL
D. Cook, SAN
D. Peek, SR
D. Jackson, NV

COMMENTS ON DRAFT ENVIRONMENTAL IMPACT STATEMENT, DOE/EIS-0028-D, LIVERMORE SITE, LIVERMORE, CALIFORNIA, SEPTEMBER 1978

Attached for your information or placement in your respective public document room for public inspection is a copy of comment letter No. 25 received on the subject draft statement from the San Francisco Bay Chapter Sierra Club, dated April 12, 1979.

W. H. Pennington /gab

W. H. Pennington
Office of Environmental
Compliance and Overview, EV

Attachment

Response to Comment Letter 25

DOE RESPONSE TO LETTER FROM THE SIERRA CLUB

Epidemiological Study

Section 3.7.2.1 of the FEIS addresses the status of epidemiological studies.

Emergency Response

Section 3.4.3 of the FEIS discusses emergency response plans.

Plutonium

As you suggest actual movement of plutonium within the site is sensitive information due to safeguards and security considerations. The quantity of plutonium permitted in Building 332 at any time is limited to 225 kg. Transportation impacts are discussed in section 3.9.2.7.

Geology and Seismicity

Based on review and comment in the Livermore DEIS, the seismic and geology portion of the document was rewritten and greatly expanded. In addition, a comprehensive geologic investigation which will include review by the USGS and independent consulting groups was undertaken to evaluate on-site and pertinent regional geologic conditions that might influence the safety of the Livermore site. The findings of this study will be made public as a separate publication, scheduled for publication in 1982.

UNIVERSITY OF CALIFORNIA, DAVIS

BERKELEY • DAVIS • IRVINE • LOS ANGELES • RIVERSIDE • SAN DIEGO • SAN FRANCISCO SANTA BARBARA • SANTA CRUZ

COLLEGE OF ENGINEERING
DEPARTMENT OF APPLIED SCIENCE DAVIS-LIVERMORE

HERTZ HALL
POST OFFICE BOX 808, L-794
LIVERMORE, CALIFORNIA 94550

April 13, 1979

Mr. W. H. Pennington
Department of Energy
Washington, D. C. 20545

Dear Mr. Pennington:

Re: Draft EIS, Livermore Site September 1978

The Draft EIS is obviously of a different character than the majority of EIS's: it reports on a program that has a quarter-century history. Thus the program stands on its history of protecting the public health and welfare. One result of this is that the report can be much briefer than a document which must speculate about future environmental impacts. Nevertheless, there are some omissions.

The first is that there is no discussion of the effect of an earthquake on the LPTR. Is there no chance of loss of water from the pool? If such an event occurs, what will be the result?

The second concerns the LLL program in in-situ gasification. If successful, will the coal-gas be free of the ring-compounds known to be carcinogenic? Is the program even considering the variety of secondary reactions that can take place in-situ?

The third is an omission which could assist the public in evaluating the effectiveness of the perimeter and off-site monitoring program--the employee monitoring program. I recognize the law and tradition focuses EIS's "outward." However, the previously uninformed reader of the EIS is left with the impression that monitoring takes place at the permeter outward. In fact, there are 7000 mobile monitoring stations constantly sampling the environment within the perimeter. This may seem a trivial point, but such internal systems could have prevented several recent industrial tragedies. The one with which I'm most familiar is the Kepone episode in Hopewell, Virginia. There the employees brought the neutrotoxin into their homes, exposing their families. Such a situation could have been prevented had an internal monitoring program been in effect. That LLL has such a program should be part of the EIS.

Finally, two nit-picks: The Department of Applied Science building is closer to 1000 m^2 than the 30,000 m^2 listed. Your entymologists missed vespus occidentalis, the common yellowjacket.

Sincerely,

Wilson K. Talley, Professor
Department of Applied Science

WKT:khs

Att:

Department of Energy
Washington, D.C. 20545

APR 26 1979

G. Facer, DP	Library, Room 1223, 20 Mass Avenue
A. Schoen, EV	G. Dennis, AL
J. Swinebroad, EV	G. Pitchford, CH (2)
R. Stern, EV	R. Blackledge, ID
S. Miller, OGC	J. Felton, OR
D. Smith, AD	T. Bauman, RL
R. Miller, AL	D. Cook, SAN
C. Lindeken, LLL (2)	D. Peek, SR
J. Jeutten, SAN	D. Jackson, NV

COMMENTS ON DRAFT ENVIRONMENTAL IMPACT STATEMENT, DOE/EIS-0028-D, LIVERMORE SITE, LIVERMORE, CALIFORNIA, SEPTEMBER 1978

Attached for your information or placement in your respective public document room for public inspection is a copy of comment letter No. 26 received on the subject draft statement from Professor Wilson K. Talley, University of California, dated April 13, 1979.

W. H. Pennington/gab

W. H. Pennington
Office of Environmental
Compliance and Overview, EV

Attachment

Response to Comment Letter 26

DOE RESPONSE TO LETTER FROM MR. WILSON TALLEY

Seismic Safety of the Livermore Pool-Type Training Reactor (LPTR)

According to the analyses made in the Safety Analysis Report (SAR) for the LPTR, the reactor was capable of withstanding a peak horizontal acceleration of 0.5 g. This SAR also states that even with loss of coolant core meltdown would not occur.

The LPTR was shut down in 1980 and the fuel elements have been removed.

In-situ gasification

The scope of the in-situ gasification program is limited to determining the engineering feasibility of fuel recovery by in-situ processing.

Employee monitoring

Section 3.7 of the FEIS describes "employee monitoring" which is conducted as part of the program designed to provide for the health and safety of employees at the Livermore site.

Department of Applied Science

The error in listing the area of this building has been corrected in the FEIS.

We have included the yellowjacket in our list of insects under the heading of wasps.

APPENDIX 1A

GLOSSARY OF TERMS

The definitions of terms used in the LLNL and SNLL Environmental Impact Statement follow the usages developed during operations on the Livermore site and are in general agreement with established standards.

accelerator: an apparatus for imparting high velocities to charged particles.

activation: the induction of radioactivity in material by irradiation with neutrons, radioactive material, a radiation generating machine, or a nuclear reactor.

activity: a measure of the rate at which a material is emitting nuclear radiations, usually given in terms of the number of nuclear disintegrations occurring in a given quantity of material over a unit of time. The standard unit of activity is the curie (Ci).

alpha radiation: an emission of particles (helium nuclei) from a material undergoing nuclear transformation; the particles have a nuclear mass number of four and a charge of plus two.

aquifer: a subsurface formation containing sufficient saturated permeable material to yield significant quantities of water.

AEC: Atomic Energy Commission, established by the Atomic Energy Act of 1946 and succeeded in 1975 by the Energy Research and Development Administration and the Nuclear Regulatory Commission. In accordance with the Department of Energy Organization Act, the Energy Research and Development Administration became part of the Department of Energy on October 1, 1977.

atomic number: the number of protons in the nucleus of a chemical element.

B

background radiation: the level of radioactivity in an area, which is produced by sources other than the one of specific interest; the natural background radiation is produced by naturally occurring radioactive materials in the crust of the earth, cosmic radiations, and the fallout from nuclear weapons tests.

beta radiation: essentially weightless charged particles (electrons and positrons) emitted from the nucleus of an atom undergoing nuclear transformation.

biological oxygen demand (BOD): a measure of the organic pollution of water determined by the extent to which bacteria and other organisms in a water sample will use dissolved oxygen in a given period of time; therefore, a measure of the residual oxygen in the water available for use by other organisms such as fish.

biotic: caused by living organisms.

chemical oxygen demand (COD): a measure of the extent to which all chemicals in a water sample use dissolved oxygen in a given period of time.

coliform (count, number): a measure of the bacterial content of water. (A high coliform count may indicate contamination of a water supply by human waste.)

concentration guide: the average concentration of a radionuclide in air or water to which a worker or member of the general population may be continuously exposed without exceeding acceptable radiation dose standards (see maximum permissible concentration).

confined aquifer: a subsurface water-bearing region having defined, relatively impermeable, upper and lower boundaries and a pressure that is significantly greater than atmospheric throughout.

contamination (contaminated material): the deposition, solvation, or infiltration of radionuclides on or into an object, material, or area, which is then considered to be "contaminated."

counts per minute (cpm): the number of events per unit time recorded by an instrument designed to detect radioactive particles; often used to indicate the relative amount of radioactive contamination.

critical: the condition of a material that is undergoing nuclear fission at a rate that is self-sustaining. The critical mass of a material is the amount that will sustain nuclear fission when the material in its present form is placed in a specified arrangement. The minimum critical mass is the amount of a fissile isotope that will just sustain nuclear fission when placed under optimum conditions.

critical facilities: Those facilities containing sufficient quantities of radioactive or toxic material such that a failure of containment could result in significant distribution of the material to onsite personnel, the public, or the environment.

CTR: Controlled thermonuclear research.

curie (Ci): a unit of radioactivity defined as the amount of a radioactive material that has an activity of 3.7×10^{10} disintegrations per second (dis/s). Millicurie (mCi) = 10^{-3} curie; microcurie (μCi) = 10^{-6} curie; nanocurie (nCi) = 10^{-9} curie; picocurie (pCi) = 10^{-12} curie; femtocurie (fCi) = 10^{15} curie.

D

daughter products: the nuclides formed in the radioactive disintegration of a first nuclide (parent).

decay chain: the sequence of radioactive disintegrations from one nuclide to another until a stable daughter is reached.

decontamination: the removal of radioactive or toxic material from a surface or from within another material.

decommissioning: the execution of a planned and orderly program of complete or partial decontamination, dismantling, demolition, or entombment of excess radioactively contaminated facilities.

disintegrations per minute (dpm): the number of radioactive decay events occurring per minute.

disposal: the planned release or placement of waste in a manner that precludes recovery.

dose: a general term indicating the amount of energy absorbed from incident radiation by a specified mass.

dose commitment: the integrated dose that results from an intake of radioactive material, evaluated from the beginning of intake to a later time (usually 50 years); also used for a longer term integrated dose to which people are considered committed because radioactive material has been released to the environment.

E

ecology: the branch of biological science that deals with the relationships between organisms and their environment.

ecosystem: a habitat and its biota.

electron-volt: the energy acquired by any charged particle carrying unit electronic charge when it moves through a potential difference of 1 volt.

environmental surveillance: a program to monitor the impact on the surrounding region of the discharges from industrial operations.

excursion: a sudden, rapid increase of power produced when a reactor or other system of fissile material undergoes a sudden increase in reactivity.

exposure: the condition of being made subject to the action of radiation.

fallout: the radioactive materials that descend through the atmosphere and are deposited on the earth's surface following the detonation of nuclear weapons.

FIDLER: an acronym for Field Instrument for the Detection of Low Energy Radiation.

fissile material: material capable of undergoing fission by any process.

fission (nuclear): the division of a nucleus into two or more nuclides of lower mass, usually accompanied by the expulsion of gamma rays and neutrons.

fission products: the nuclides formed by the division of a heavier nucleus, usually in a nuclear reactor.

food-chain: a linear sequence of successive utilizations of nutrient energy by a series of species.

food-web: the concept of nutrient energy transfers (including decomposition) between species in an ecosystem.

fusion: combination of two lighter nuclei with the accompanying release of binding energy.

G

gamma radiation: electromagnetic energy emitted during a nuclear transition.

groundwater: water that exists or flows below the surface (within the zone of saturation).

H

habitat: the characteristics of the place where biota live.

half-life: the time required for the activity of a radionuclide to decay to half its value. It is used as a measure of the persistence of radioactive materials. Each radionuclide has a characteristic constant half-life.

HEPA: high-efficiency particulate air filter.

Hetch Hetchy: The San Francisco Water Department's system of aqueducts extending from reservoirs in the Sierra Nevada mountains to the San Francisco peninsula. The system provides water to San Francisco,the Peninsula, and certain East Bay communities.

high-efficiency particulate air filter (HEPA): an air filter capable of removing at least 99.97% of a test aerosol composed of 0.3-μm-diam di-octylphthalate (DOP).

hood: a canopy and exhaust duct used to confine hazardous materials and thus reduce the exposure of industrial workers.

inversion: a condition existing when temperature increases with height in the atmosphere.

ion exchange: process by which ions of a given species are displaced from an insoluble exchange material by ions of a different species in solution. In water softening, sodium ions from a resin are exchanged for calcium ions from the water.

irradiation: exposure to radiation by material placed near a radioactive source usually in an operating nuclear reactor.

isotope: nuclides with the same atomic number (i.e., the same chemical element) but with different atomic masses. Although chemical properties are the same, radioactive and nuclear properties may be quite different for each isotope of an element.

L

long-lived isotope: a radioactive nuclide that decays at such a slow rate that a quantity of it will exist for an extended period.

M

man-rem: a unit of population dose, calculated by adding together the individual doses (expressed in rems) of a given population.

maximum permissible concentration (MPC): the average concentration of a radionuclide in air or water to which a worker or member of the general population may be continuously exposed without exceeding an established standard of radiation dose limitation.

N

neutron: a particle existing in or emitted from the atomic nucleus; it is electrically neutral and has a mass approximately equal to that of a stable hydrogen atom.

neutron activation: the process of irradiating a material with neutrons so that the material itself is transformed into a radioactive nuclide.

nuclear fission: see <u>fission</u>.

nuclear radiation: particles and electromagnetic energy given off during transformations occurring in the nucleus of an atom.

nuclear reactor: an apparatus in which a chain reaction of fissionable material is initiated and controlled.

nucleon: particles within the atomic nucleus.

nuclide: a species of atom having a specific mass, atomic number, and nuclear energy state.

nucleus: the positively charged center of an atom.

penetrating radiation: forms of radiant energy capable of passing through significant thicknesses of solid material; these usually include gamma rays, x rays, and neutrons.

permissible dose: the dose of ionizing radiation that, in the light of present knowledge, carries negligible probability of causing somatic injury or genetic effect.

pH: a measure of the relative acidity or alkalinity of a solution. A neutral solution has a pH of 7, acids have pH's less than 7, and bases have pH's greater than 7.

population dose (population exposure): the summation of individual radiation doses received by all those exposed to the source or event being considered (see man-rem).

power reactor: a nuclear reactor designed to produce heat for conversion to electrical energy or mechanical propulsion.

proton: a particle existing in or emitted from the atomic nucleus; it is electrically positive and has a mass approximately equal to that of a hydrogen atom.

R

rad: a unit of measure for the absorbed dose of radiation; one rad equals 100 ergs absorbed per gram of material.

radiation (ionizing): particles and electromagnetic energy emitted by atomic and nuclear transitions which are capable of producing ions on interacting with matter. Gamma rays and alpha and beta particles are primary examples.

radiation survey: evaluation of an area or object with instruments in order to detect, identify, and quantify radioactive materials and radiation fields.

radioactive (decay): property of undergoing spontaneous nuclear transformation in which nuclear particles or electromagnetic energy are emitted.

radioiodines: radioactive isotopes of iodine.

radionuclide: a radioactive nuclide.

radiotoxicity: the property that allows a material to adversely affect biological organisms through nuclear radiation.

radwaste: radioactive waste materials.

reactor: a nuclear reactor.

release limit (release guide): a control number that regulates the concentration or amount of radioactive material released to the environment in an industrial situation.

rem: a unit of measure for the dose of ionizing radiation that has the same biological effect as one rad of x rays. One rem is approximately equal to one rad for gamma or beta radiation.

roentgen: a unit of measure of ionizing electromagnetic radiation (x and gamma). One roentgen corresponds to the release by ionization of 86.9 ergs of energy per gram of air.

S

sanitary sewage: human wastes and other nonradioactive material that must be disposed of to preserve public health.

scintillation (count): light flashes produced in crystalline material by ionizing radiation; measurement of the level of activity of the source.

seismicity: the relative frequency and distribution of earthquakes.

shielding: material used to absorb radiation and thus protect personnel or equipment.

short-lived isotope: a radioactive nuclide that decays so rapidly that a given quantity is transformed into its daughter products within a short period (usually one with a half-life of days or less).

skyshine: radiation scattered back to the earth by the atmosphere.

solid wastes (radioactive): either solid radioactive material or solid objects that contain radioactive material or bear radioactive surface contamination.

source term: the quantity of radioactive material, released in an accident or during operation, that subsequently causes exposure after being subjected to some mechanisms of transmission or deposition.

stability (atmospheric): a description of the effect of atmospheric forces on a parcel of air following vertical displacement in an atmosphere otherwise in hydrostatic equilibrium. If the forces tend to return the parcel to its original level, the atmosphere is stable; if the forces tend to move the parcel further in the direction of displacement, the atmosphere is unstable; and if the air parcel tends to remain at its new level the atmosphere has neutral stability.

swipe: a means of measuring loose surface contamination on an object by wiping it with paper, gauze, etc., and then measuring the amount of contaminant on the wipe with an instrument.

TJ: Terajoule (10^{12} joule) 1 TJ = 3.6×10^6 kWh.

tracer: a radionuclide(s) or chemical introduced in minute quantities into a system or process. Radiation or chemical detection techniques are then used to follow the behavior of the process or system.

transuranium: nuclides having an atomic number greater than that of uranium (i.e., greater than 92).

turbidity: a measure of the degree to which sediments and other foreign matter are suspended in water (cloudiness).

U

unconfined aquifer: an aquifer that has a water table or surface at atmospheric pressure.

W

water table: upper boundary of an unconfined aquifer surface below which saturated groundwater occurs.

wind rose: a diagram showing the distribution of prevailing wind directions at a given location; some variations include wind speed groupings by direction.

The principal preparers of the Livermore EIS are listed alphabetically together with a brief tabulation of their qualifications as follows:

Marjorie Auyong, M.S., 4 years' experience in environmental engineering

David W. Carpenter, M.S., Registered Geologist, Certified Engineering Geologist, 20 years' experience in field and geologic hazards investigations

Donald O. Emerson, Ph.D., Registered Geologist, 24 years' teaching and resource geology experience

Thomas A. Gibson, Jr., M.S., Certified Health Physicist, 30 years' experience in safety engineering and environmental science

Carl L. Lindeken, B.S., 28 years' experience in environmental science

Perry K. Lovell, B.S., 26 years' experience in health physics

David R. McIntyre, M.S., 18 years' experience in biological sciences

David S. Myers, M.S., Certified Health Physicist, 15 years' experience in health physics

Byron N. Odell, B.S., 6 years' experience in safety and environmental science

Kendall R. Peterson, M.S., 26 years' experience in meteorology

Harold E. Pfeifer, M.S., 5 years' experience in engineering and environmental science

Russell S. Roberts, M.S., 3 years' experience in health physics and waste management

James F. Scheimer, Ph.D., 7 years' experience in seismology, investigating earthquake sources and wave front propagation

William J. Silver, M.S., Certified Health Physicist, 24 years' experience in safety, health physics and environmental science

Randolph Stone, Ph.D., Registered Geologist, 12 years' experience in petroleum and ground water geology

Frank J. Tokarz, Ph.D., 20 years' experience in structural engineering

Arthur J. Toy, Ph.D., 18 years' experience in safety, health physics and environmental science

Joel H. White, M.S., 7 years' experience in environmental science

Donn A. Wright, M.S., 5 years' experience in health physics

UCRL-50027-80

Environmental Monitoring at the Lawrence Livermore National Laboratory: 1980 Annual Report

A. J. Toy
C. L. Lindeken
K. S. Griggs
R. W. Buddemeier

April 15, 1981

Environmental Monitoring at the Lawrence Livermore National Laboratory: 1980 Annual Report

A. J. Toy
C. L. Lindeken
K. S. Griggs
R. W. Buddemeier

Manuscript date: April 15, 1981

LAWRENCE LIVERMORE LABORATORY
University of California • Livermore, California • 94550

Available from National Technical Information Service • U S Department of Commerce
5285 Port Royal Road • Springfield, VA 22161 • $7.00 per copy • (Microfiche $3.50)

FOREWORD

This report is prepared for the U.S. Department of Energy by the Environmental Evaluations Group of the Hazards Control Department, Lawrence Livermore National Laboratory. Data are obtained through the combined efforts of the Nuclear Chemistry Division and the Hazards Control Department. In addition to the authors listed, the following personnel made significant contributions to this report.

V. E. Arganbright	J. D. Lum
M. Auyong	F. M. McMillen
J. M. Bazan	K. R. Peterson
H. C. Capwell	D. E. Reed
A. Conover	N. H. Rogers
K. J. Davidson	M. R. Ruggieri
R. J. Dupzyk	G. L. Seibel
A. L. Gazlay	C. W. Sundbeck
D. W. Hosmer	R. D. Szidon
Y. M. Kwok	C. R. Veith
M. A. Loquist	M. A. Waterman

CONTENTS

Frontispiece. **Lawrence Livermore National Laboratory (view from southeast).**

(1) LLNL
(2) Sandia
(3) South Bay Aqueduct
(4) Arroyo Seco
(5) Arroyo Las Positas
(6) Nearest residential area
(7) Vasco Road
(8) East Avenue
(9) Greenville Road
(10) Lupin Way
(11) Interstate 580

Environmental Monitoring at the Lawrence Livermore National Laboratory: 1980 Annual Report

INTRODUCTION

The Lawrence Livermore National Laboratory (LLNL) is located about 64 km east of San Francisco, California, in the Livermore Valley of southern Alameda County, approximately 5 km east of the city of Livermore. The site, which occupies an area of 2.54 km^2, is surrounded by open agricultural areas on the north, east, west, and part of the south side. Sandia Laboratories, Livermore, occupies a portion of the adjoining property on the south, and the nearest residential area is 0.8 km from the Laboratory's west perimeter. Of the nearly 4.8 million people who live within 80 km of the Laboratory (Fig. 1), 50,000 live in Livermore.

Established in 1952, the Laboratory is operated for the U.S. Department of Energy (DOE) by the University of California and currently employs approximately 7400 people. Although nuclear weapons research and development has always been the primary mission of LLNL, additional programs include biomedical, magnetic fusion, nonnuclear energy, and laser-fusion research.

Much of the Laboratory's materials testing and high-explosives diagnostic work is conducted at Site 300, 16 km southeast of Livermore. Located in the sparsely populated hills of the Diablo Range, Site 300 covers an area of 27 km^2. Figure 2 shows the location of LLNL and Site 300 with respect to the city of Livermore and surrounding areas.

The Livermore Valley has a climate characterized by mild, rainy winters and warm, dry summers. Annual rainfall averages about 360 mm, and rains occur predominantly between November and April, usually in connection with Pacific storms. Rainfall for the 1979–80 season (July 1, 1979, through June 30, 1980) was 378 mm. By comparison, during two drought periods, 1975–76 and 1976–77, rainfall totals were 138 and 196 mm, respectively. Surface water drainage from the Valley is from east to west through various arroyos, with the outfall near Sunol in the southwest corner of the Valley. Prevailing winds are from the west and southwest during April through September. During the remainder of the year, wind directions are variable, as shown by the wind rose in Fig. 3.

The Livermore site is on a northwest-sloping alluvial flood plain bordering the low hills of the Livermore Uplands to the south. The lithology of the area consists of a series of unconsolidated marine and continental sedimentary units such as sandstones, gravels, silts, and clays overlying the interbedded sandstones of the Franciscan Formation. The hilly terrain surrounding the Valley is used for cattle and sheep pasture, and the principal agricultural products in the vicinity of LLNL are grapes and wine, cattle, and poultry.

Water bodies adjacent to the Laboratory include the South Bay Aqueduct, which runs from northeast to southwest, 1.8 km to the southeast; the Patterson Pass water treatment facility, about 2 km east of LLNL; and Frick Lake, 4 km north of LLNL, a sag pond that is dry most of the year. Aquatic recreation (boating, fishing, and swimming) is available at Lake Del Valle, about 8 km south of LLNL, and at the Shadow Cliffs Recreation Area, 11 km to the west.

The Laboratory normally receives all its treated water from the Hetch Hetchy Aqueduct (which supplies San Francisco) located 11 km southwest of Livermore. Laboratory storm water is channeled through storm sewers designed to accommodate a 10-year flow. Open ditches are used in undeveloped areas of the site. Arroyo Seco crosses LLNL at the southwest corner. Arroyo Las Positas originally crossed the northeast section of the site. However, in 1965, as part of an erosion control program, Arroyo Las Positas was channeled north to the northeast corner of the site, and then west along the north perimeter to an outlet at the northwest corner. This outlet, which also constitutes the main pathway for the Laboratory's surface drainage (storm and irrigation), runs north to the Western Pacific tracks, then west where it joins

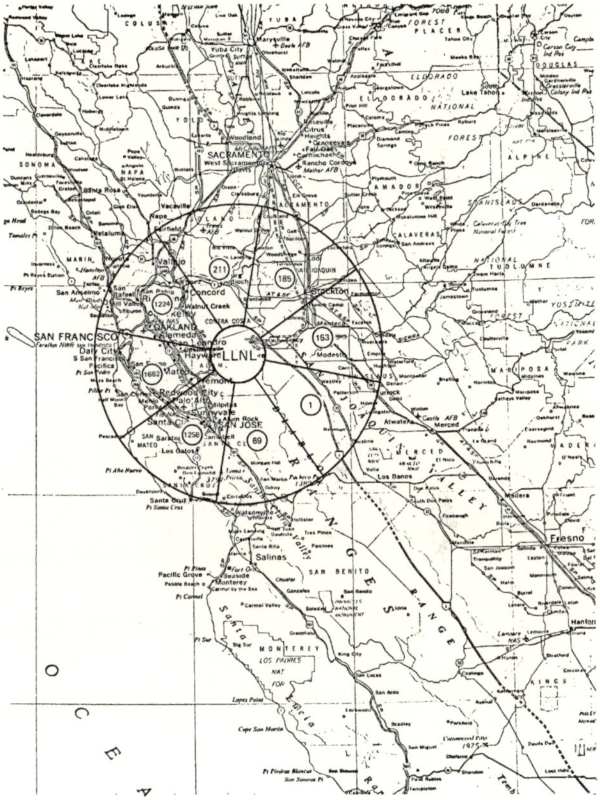

FIG. 1. Estimated population distribution (×1000) within 80 km of Livermore, by sectors.

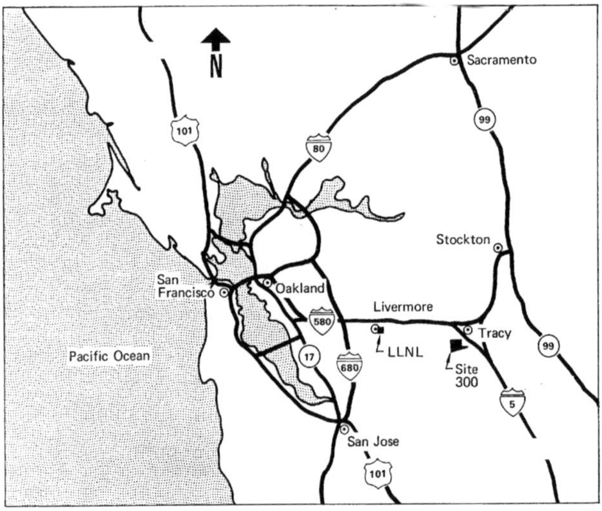

FIG. 2. Locations of LLNL and Site 300.

Arroyo Seco. The LLNL Master Site Plan calls for a small lake to be established in the center of the project. Provisions have been made for rerouting on-site water drainage and the Arroyo Las Positas to fill this lake during the rainy season.

Groundwater is found at depths of 15 to 30 m below the LLNL site with a gradient indicating a generally westward flow. Because stream runoff may be a significant source of groundwater recharge, considerable attention is given to radiological monitoring of the arroyos draining the valley and to the groundwater wells west of the Laboratory. Laboratory sewage is discharged into the City of Livermore's sanitary sewer system and processed at the Livermore Water Reclamation Plant (LWRP).

As part of the Livermore-Amador Valley Wastewater Management program, treated sanitary wastewater is now transported out of the valley via a pipeline and discharged into the San Francisco Bay. The LWRP was connected to this pipeline on February 8, 1980. While the LWRP effluent is still used for summer irrigation of nearby Livermore City property, it is no longer discharged to Arroyo Las Positas, as was done during the wet season before construction of the pipeline.

A strict effluent-control program that emphasizes controlling effluents at the source has been in effect since the Laboratory began operation. The environmental monitoring program is maintained to evaluate the effectiveness of these control measures, to document whether effluents from the

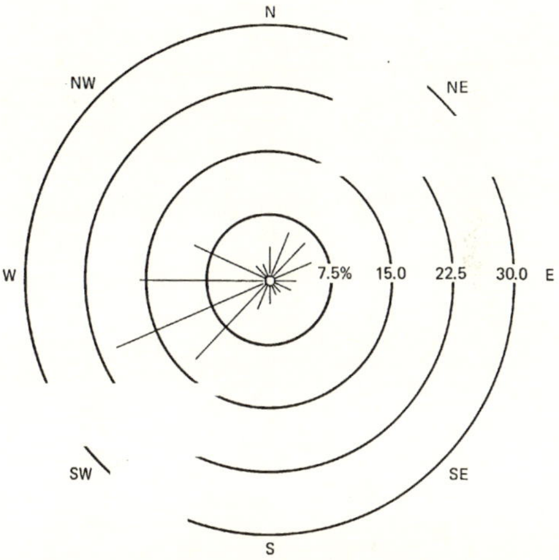

Average annual percent frequency of wind direction vs wind speed

	Speed (m/s)										
Direction	0-2	2-3	3-5	5-7	7-9	9-11	11-16	16-20	>20	Total	Av. speed
N	2.0	0.3	0.3	0.2	0.3	0.1	0.3	0	0	3.6	3.8
NNE	1.9	0.7	1.2	0.6	0.5	0.3	0.3	0	0	5.5	4.2
NE	1.5	0.7	2.4	1.0	0.2	0	0	0	0	5.9	3.6
ENE	1.2	0.7	1.6	1.0	0.4	0	0	0	0	4.8	3.8
E	1.5	0.5	0.5	0.3	0.1	0	0	0	0	2.8	2.5
ESE	1.2	0.2	0.2	0	0	0	0	0	0	1.7	1.8
SE	1.0	0.1	0	0	0	0	0	0	0	1.2	1.5
SSE	1.0	0.2	0.1	0	0	0	0	0	0	1.3	1.5
S	1.3	0.5	0.2	0.1	0	0	0	0	0	2.1	2.0
SSW	1.5	0.7	0.8	0.2	0.1	0	0.1	0	0	3.4	2.9
SW	2.4	2.2	3.8	2.4	1.1	0.5	0.2	0	0	12.7	4.4
WSW	3.2	4.1	6.6	4.1	1.5	0.7	0.1	0	0	20.4	4.2
W	2.6	3.5	5.4	2.7	0.9	0.3	0.1	0	0	15.6	4.0
WNW	1.5	1.0	3.1	3.1	1.1	0.2	0	0	0	10.0	4.6
NW	1.2	0.3	0.3	0.2	0.1	0	0	0	0	2.1	2.5
NNW	1.3	0.2	0.1	0	0	0	0	0	0	1.7	1.9
Calm										5.1	
Total	26.4	16.1	26.8	16.0	6.2	2.3	1.2	0	0	100.0	3.7

FIG. 3. Average annual wind direction and speed pattern at Livermore during 1980. (Measurements are made at 40 m above ground.)

Laboratory and Site 300 operations are within applicable standards, and to estimate the impact of these operations on the environment. Sensitive monitoring equipment is used that can detect radioactive and nonradioactive pollutants at well below environmental background levels. The program includes the collection and analysis of air, soil, water, sewer effluent, vegetation, foodstuff, and milk samples. Environmental background radiation is measured at numerous locations in the vicinity of the Laboratory using gamma and neutron dosimeters.

Each spring, the Laboratory reports the results of environmental monitoring for the previous year. This report is prepared in compliance with ERDA Manual 0513, *Effluent and Environmental Monitoring and Reporting*. Significant changes in either the scope of the program or the levels of effluents are noted.

Appendix A is a tabulation of 1980 environmental monitoring data. Graphics have been used in the body of the report to aid in interpretation. When appropriate, the tabulated data contain maximum, minimum, and average values. Radioactivity values are tabulated with the associated counting uncertainties at the 2σ (95% confidence) level. Unless otherwise stated, the minimum detection limit of these measurements is assumed to have been reached when the 2σ error is $\pm 100\%$. In the case of radioactivity measurements, an attempt has been made to assess the potential impact on man of the observed environmental levels of artificially produced radionuclides. This assessment is made by calculating the whole-body or critical-organ doses delivered to man and comparing these with the much larger radiation dose received locally from natural sources.

SUMMARY

In 1980, the annual average airborne gross beta activity in Livermore Valley air samples was 3.0×10^{-14} μCi/ml, which was greater than the level observed in 1979. This was the result of an increase which occurred during the fourth quarter due to fallout from a nuclear test by the People's Republic of China on October 16, 1980. Airborne ^{238}U concentrations at Site 300 were higher than those at Livermore because of the "depleted" uranium (a byproduct of ^{235}U enrichment) used in high-explosive tests at the Site. However, these concentrations were well below the standards set by DOE. The average annual beryllium concentrations were less than 1% of the appropriate standard at both the Laboratory perimeter and Site 300. The beryllium concentrations can be accounted for by natural beryllium in typical airborne dust.

Water samples collected in the Livermore Valley and at Site 300 exhibit gross beta and tritium activities within the ranges previously observed in these areas. One well-water sample from Site 300 shows an above-average level of gross alpha activity. This activity has been found to be naturally occurring uranium at concentrations well within those specified in ERDA Manual 0524.

Tritium analyses were made on well-water samples collected near the LWRP. These analyses, begun in 1977, were made to determine the extent to which low levels of tritium in the LWRP effluent may be migrating into groundwater. As was found during earlier surveys, the highest tritium values were detected in test wells west of the plant near Arroyo Las Positas. Since the LWRP effluent is no longer discharged to the arroyo, the primary means of tritium movement to nearby groundwater has been eliminated. Consequently, tritium concentrations observed in local wells in 1980 were lower than previous annual measurements. Tritium levels found in Livermore Valley and Site 300 vegetation were comparable to those observed in 1979. As a means of evaluating the possible impact of Laboratory effluents on locally grown foodstuff, the tritium content of Livermore Valley wines was compared with that of other California and European wines. The tritium levels in Valley wines are within the range found to be present in European wines and in surface waters throughout the world, but are somewhat higher than those in other California wines. Honey produced in the Livermore Valley contained tritium levels comparable to those found in honey from neighboring areas.

The decommissioning of a major portion of the LLNL Tritium Facility and reduced activity at the Bldg. 212 14-MeV neutron generator lowered the

Laboratory's atmospheric tritium release from 4517 Ci (1979) to 2305 Ci (1980). During 1980, 5 Ci of tritium (HTO) were released to the municipal sewer system This is the third consecutive year that the quantity of tritium released has been reduced.

For 1980, the median annual gamma-radiation dose at the Laboratory perimeter was 63 mrem, and the median off-site background dose was 59 mrem. The 4-mrem difference between off-site and perimeter is consistent with past years' differences. A 14-MeV neutron generator (Bldg. 212) near the south perimeter continued to be a source of elevated radiation. However, the annual radiation dose at the Laboratory's south perimeter is well below DOE standards.

Due to reduced programmatic need, the Livermore Pool-Type Reactor (LPTR) was permanently shut down on March 31, 1980 The closure of this facility removes the local source of ^{41}Ar and eliminates about 1/5 of the site's radiation dose to the public.

In October 1980, the Laboratory's sewage discharge point and sewage monitoring station were relocated from a connection on East Avenue to a new larger sewer line at the northwest corner of the site. Since the northwest corner is the lowest elevation, the Laboratory sewer system is now completely gravity-flow and the need for lift pumps has been eliminated.

MONITORING DATA—COLLECTION, ANALYSIS, AND EVALUATION

RADIOACTIVE MONITORING

Airborne Radioactivity

Concentrations of various airborne radionuclides are measured at Laboratory perimeters, at off-site locations near the Laboratory, and at Site 300. Sampling locations are shown in Figs. 4 through 7. The 6 samplers on the Laboratory perimeter and the 10 samplers at Site 300 use Whatman-41 cellulose filters (5.2×10^{-2} m^2). These samplers are operated at an average flow rate of 700 liters/min. The filters are cut in half, and half of each is retained for beryllium analysis (see "Nonradioactive Monitoring"). An easily dissolved filter and a low trace-metal background are requirements for these analyses; Whatman-41 represents a balance between such requirements and particulate collection efficiency.[1] Off-site samplers throughout the Livermore Valley use glass-fiber filters (4.56×10^{-3} m^2 Flanders F-700) and are operated at a flow rate of 80 liters/min. All air filters are changed weekly.

After a 4-day delay for decay of the radon-thoron daughters, gross alpha and beta activities on the filters are determined with an automatic gas-flow proportional counter. Monthly composites of Laboratory perimeter and Site 300 filters are also counted for specific gamma-emitting radionuclides using low-background Ge(Li) detectors. Following gamma counting, the Laboratory perimeter filters from individual locations and the Site 300 composites are analyzed for the presence of ^{239}Pu, ^{238}Pu, ^{137}Cs, ^{235}U, and ^{238}U.

Tables 1 and 2 in Appendix A show airborne gross alpha and gross beta activities for the Livermore Valley samples, and Tables 3 and 4 show corresponding activities for Site 300. Average annual gross beta activity in both Livermore and Site 300 air samples was about 15% higher than that observed during 1979.[2] This increase occurred during the fourth quarter and was due to fallout from a nuclear test by the People's Republic of China on October 16, 1980.

Tables 5 and 6 list the activities of the principal radionuclides that contribute to the gross beta activity in Livermore and Site 300 samples These activities are determined by gamma-spectra analysis. The fission products seen on the November and December air filters are a result of successive passes of debris from the Chinese test. Table 7 shows the concentration of plutonium on air filter samples collected in the Livermore Valley. Tables 8 and 9 show the concentrations of airborne ^{239}Pu, ^{137}Cs, ^{235}U, and ^{238}U in Livermore perimeter and Site 300 air samples. The higher concentration of ^{238}U at Site 300 is a result of the "depleted" uranium (a

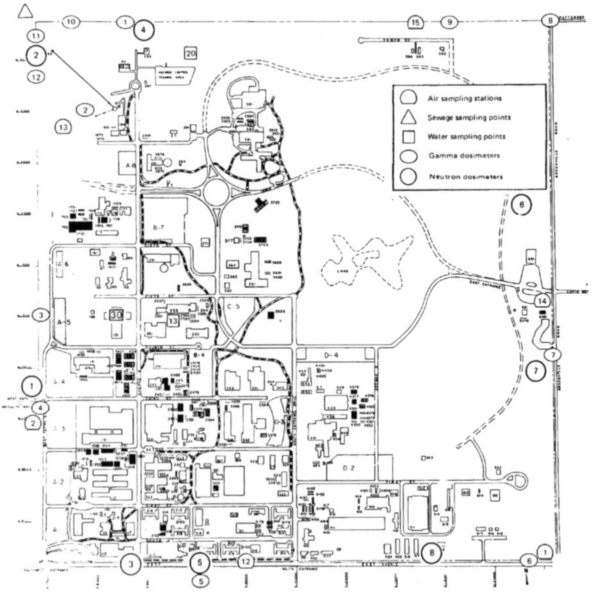

FIG. 4. LLNL on-site environmental sampling locations.

byproduct of ^{235}U enrichment) used at the Site. The uranium concentrations are well below the concentration guides (CG) in ERDA Manual 0524 (see Appendix B).

Concentrations of airborne tritiated water (HTO) were determined for each of the LLNL perimeter air-sampling locations (Fig. 4) and at off-site locations S1 and S2 (Fig. 5). Water vapor was collected on silica-gel samplers that operated at a flow rate of about 0.5 liters/min for a 2-week period. The collected water was recovered by vacuum-drying the silica gel at 150°C, and the HTO was measured by liquid-scintillation counting. Table 10 shows average monthly HTO concentrations observed at each sampling location; the overall annual average concentration is 4.0×10^{-11} μCi/ml. The highest HTO concentration was observed at the west site boundary, Location 2, during October. That concentration (1.3×10^{-10} μCi/ml) is less than 0.1% of the appropriate standard. Location 12 shows the highest annual average concentration, probably because this location is so close to

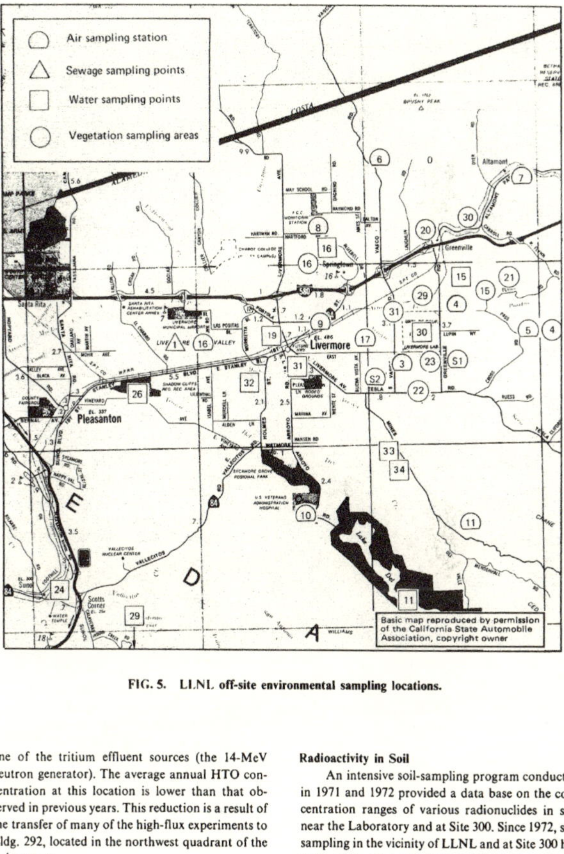

FIG. 5. LLNL off-site environmental sampling locations.

one of the tritium effluent sources (the 14-MeV neutron generator). The average annual HTO concentration at this location is lower than that observed in previous years. This reduction is a result of the transfer of many of the high-flux experiments to Bldg. 292, located in the northwest quadrant of the Laboratory.

Radioactivity in Soil

An intensive soil-sampling program conducted in 1971 and 1972 provided a data base on the concentration ranges of various radionuclides in soil near the Laboratory and at Site 300. Since 1972, soil sampling in the vicinity of LLNL and at Site 300 has been part of a continuing LLNL surveillance

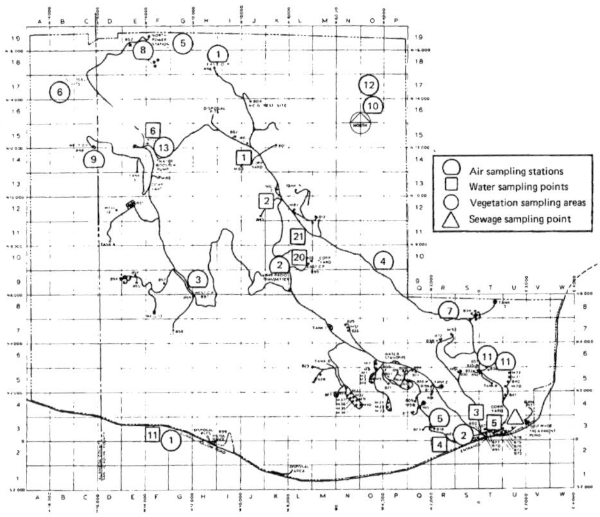

FIG. 6. Site 300 on-site environmental sampling locations.

program to document any changes in environmental levels of radioactivity that may have occurred and to evaluate any increase in radioactivity that might have resulted from Laboratory operations. As in previous years, a group of soil samples was collected at random from the listing of locations sampled in the 1971–72 study. In addition, as an independent survey, the California Department of Health Services collected 18 samples in an area east of Greenville Road along three radials normally downwind from the Laboratory. LLNL received and analyzed aliquots of each of these latter samples. Figure 8 shows the 1980 soil-sampling locations in the Livermore Valley and Fig. 9 indicates the locations at Site 300 where annual samples have been collected since 1973.

All samples were collected to a depth of 5 cm. After collection, the samples were dried, ground, and blended. Plutonium-239 content was determined in each sample following the HASL acid-leaching procedure.[3] For gamma-spectra analysis, approximately 300-g aliquots of soil were sealed in 200-cm^3 thin-walled cans of aluminum and counted with a Ge(Li) detector. Table 11 lists the results. Samples 817 through 834 represent those samples collected by the State. Sample 834 showed an anomalously high plutonium concentration, and the location could not be resampled because the area had been graded since the initial collection; however, check samples taken on either side indicated plutonium levels in the range attributable to global fallout.

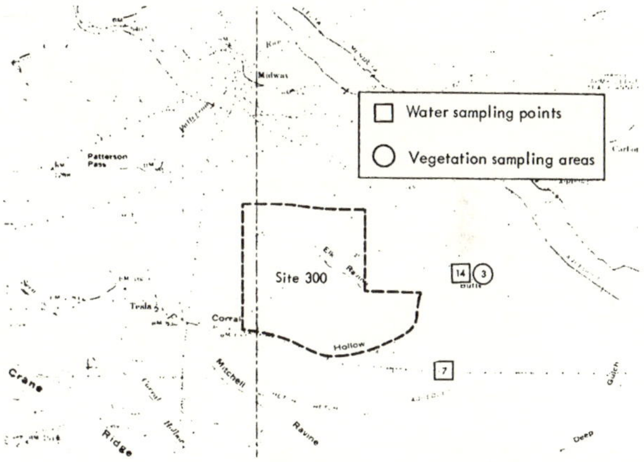

FIG. 7. Site 300 off-site environmental sampling locations.

The data in Table 11 are in the range of those reported in previous years.[2] Samples collected near the east perimeter of the Laboratory reflect the influence of the solar evaporators, which are no longer in use.[4,5] There was close agreement between plutonium measurements made by LLNL and the State laboratories.[6] Figure 10 is a distribution plot of these activities. The three lowest data points in Fig. 10 do not fit the plot as drawn; we have compared these results with analyses of previous samples from the same location. The previous samples showed plutonium levels in the usual range and we can find no reason to expect such a decrease. Therefore, the samples are treated as statistical outliers.

Table 12 shows the plutonium and ^{137}Cs activities in the Site 300 samples. There were negligible changes from activities observed in previous samples collected in the same locations.[2]

High-explosive tests at Site 300 often involve the use of depleted uranium. Accordingly, soil samples are taken annually to determine how these tests perturb the $^{235}U/^{238}U$ ratio of the soil. Isotopic uranium measurements were made with isotopic-dilution mass spectrometry. As in the past, the analyses indicated that isotopic perturbation is essentially limited to areas adjacent to the firing bunkers.[5,7] The isotopic uranium data shown in Table 12 are comparable to those observed during 1979.

Radioactivity in Sewage

Liquid radioactive wastes are treated to reduce activity levels to the lowest levels practicable and to well below the standards in ERDA Manual 0524. After treatment and analysis, the liquid wastes are released into the City of Livermore's sanitary sewer system at the LLNL outfall shown in Fig. 4. The effluent is continuously monitored at the outfall for pH, radioactivity, and transition metals, such as copper and chromium.[8]

Liquid wastes from Livermore's sanitary sewer system are treated at the LWRP, a 200-liter/s tertiary sewage-treatment plant that serves residential, commercial, and industrial water users in Livermore. The salt content of the LWRP effluent

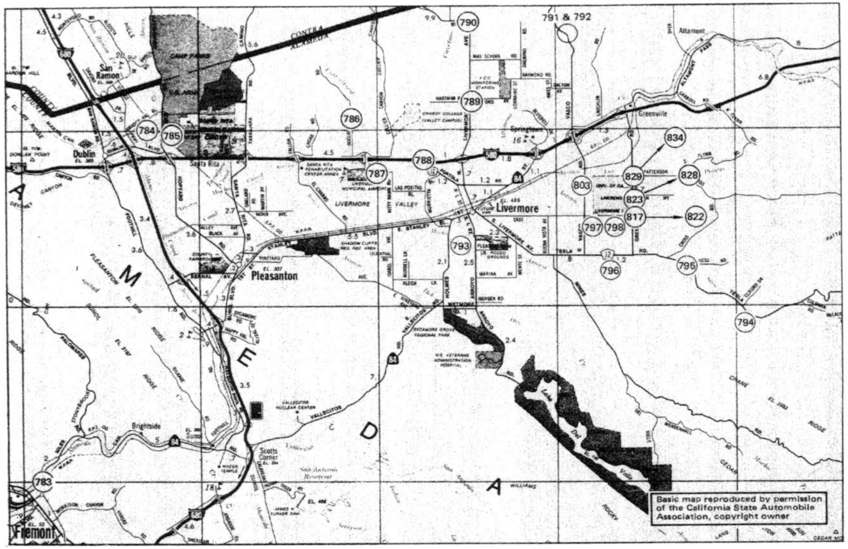

FIG. 8. Locations of soil samples collected in the Livermore Valley during 1980. (Samples 817 through 834 were collected in three sets along the directions of the arrows shown.)

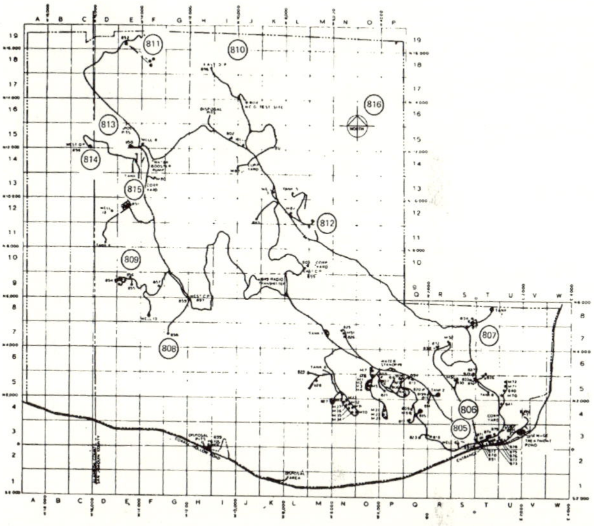

FIG. 9. Locations of soil samples collected inside the Site 300 boundary.

presented a problem for groundwater quality locally and in the Niles Cone aquifers. Accordingly, as part of the Livermore–Amador Valley Wastewater Management program, a pipeline was constructed to transport wastewater out of the valley for discharge into the San Francisco Bay. The LWRP was connected to this pipeline on February, 8, 1980. Although the effluent will still be used for irrigation of municipal property, it will no longer be discharged into the arroyo, thus eliminating the primary means of tritium migration to local and downstream groundwater.

Representative San Francisco Bay water samples were collected before and after connection to the pipeline. Preliminary results of tritium analysis of these samples indicate no significant difference between the two sample sets. The final results of this study will appear in a separate report.

Samples of the LLNL and LWRP liquid effluents are collected daily. Table 13 compares the monthly composite activity levels of certain radionuclides in the LLNL effluent with those in the effluent from the LWRP. All concentrations are well below DOE standards for discharge into the sanitary sewer system.

Radioactivity in Water

Water samples are collected from the various Livermore Valley and Site 300 locations shown in

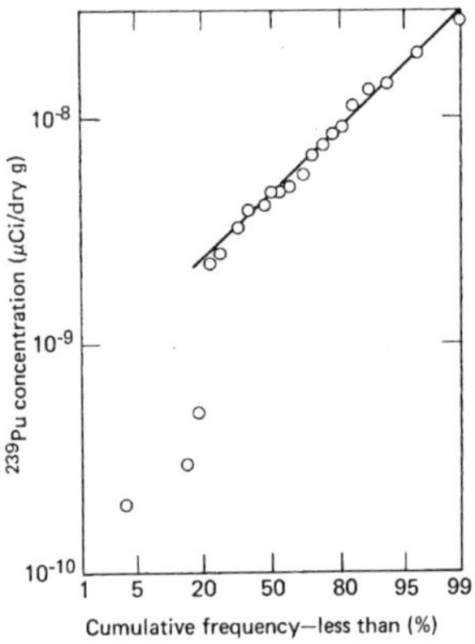

FIG. 10. Distribution plot of ^{239}Pu in soil samples collected in the Livermore Valley during 1980.

Figs. 4 through 7. These samples are analyzed for gross alpha and gross beta activity. Tables 14 and 15 show the gross alpha activities in Livermore Valley and Site 300 samples, respectively. Gross beta activities for Livermore and Site 300 samples are shown in Tables 16 and 17.

Livermore sampling locations 11, 16, and 24 (Fig. 5) are surface water sources (ponds, creeks, and reservoirs), and Location 20 (Fig. 4) is the collection site of Livermore rainfall. The other locations are domestic water sources. Gross alpha and beta activities in Livermore water samples collected in 1980 were below EPA standards for drinking water.[9]

Site 300 water samples are collected from on-site wells (Fig. 6, Locations 1-6), an off-site creek (Fig. 7, Location 14), and off-site wells (Fig. 7, Locations 7 and 11). Location 20 is Site 300 rainwater, and Location 21 is a spring-fed pond near Bunker 812.

Location 4, a well near the Site 300 entrance, had a high gross alpha level (see Table 15). Specific analyses were performed which identified the source of the radioactivity as naturally occurring uranium.[2] Neither the EPA[9] nor the State of California[10] specifies a limit for natural uranium in drinking water. In their limits for gross alpha activity, uranium is specifically excluded from the total. The uranium concentration was well within that specified in ERDA Manual 0524 (2×10^{-5} μCi/ml). A ^{226}Ra measurement based on radon emanation showed the ^{226}Ra concentration to be less than 3×10^{-10} μCi/ml. The low ^{226}Ra activity probably results from the relatively high pH of this well water. Under this condition radium would be expected to coprecipitate with calcium in caliche, coating the grain surfaces within the aquifer.

The water samples from the Livermore Valley and Site 300 are also analyzed for tritium activity. Because of the low tritium activities, it is necessary to distill and electrolytically enrich the samples before liquid-scintillation counting. Tables 18 and 19 show the data for the Livermore and Site 300 samples, respectively. The samples have concentrations that are well below recommended CG values. Tables 18 and 19 also include an estimate of the annual dose that may be delivered to an adult who consumes water containing the listed tritium concentrations. These doses, which are all less than 0.1 mrem, are based on a water consumption of 2 liters/d and the dose conversion factors contained in NRC Reg. Guide 1.109[11] (see Appendix C).

As noted previously, treated effluent from the LWRP is used to irrigate nearby municipal property. This effluent contains low levels of tritium which come from normal LLNL operational releases to the sanitary sewer system. As part of a study begun in 1977,[12] tritium measurements are now made annually on water samples collected from neighboring wells to determine the extent of tritium migration into groundwater. Many of the wells were in the immediate vicinity of the LWRP; however, additional samples were also collected from areas at some distance. Locations sampled during 1980 are indicated in Fig. 11, and the tritium data are shown in Table 20. The highest tritium values appear in wells west of the LWRP. Tritium activities in all samples were well below the guidelines for water in uncontrolled areas as stated in ERDA Manual 0524. The tritium levels in these wells are also lower than those observed in the 1979 samples, which is to be expected with diversion of effluent to the pipeline.

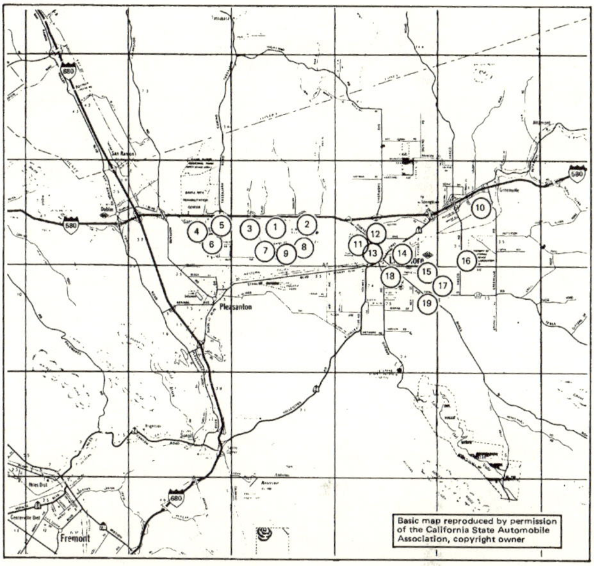

FIG. 11. Locations of groundwater samples collected in the Livermore Valley during 1980.

Radioactivity in Vegetation and Foodstuffs

Each month, vegetation samples (usually native grasses) are collected at locations in the Livermore Valley, at Site 300, and at off-site locations near Site 300, as shown in Figs. 5 through 7. These samples are freeze-dried, and the tritium activity in the recovered water is determined by liquid-scintillation counting. Table 21 shows the tritium data for vegetation collected in the Livermore Valley. The whole-body radiation doses shown in Table 21 were derived using the dose conversion factors in NRC Reg. Guide 1.109,[11] conservatively assuming that all vegetables consumed by an adult have the tritium concentrations found in these unirrigated grasses. These potential doses are all less than 1 mrem/y.

Table 22 shows the 1980 tritium data for Site 300 vegetation. Location 6 is adjacent to an area that contains tritium-contaminated debris from a firing table. As a result of the seasonal rains, the tritium apparently entered an aquifer whose outflow is in the area where Location 13 samples are routinely collected.

Beginning in 1977, as a means of evaluating the possible impact of Laboratory effluents on locally grown foodstuff, the tritium content of Livermore

Valley wines was measured and compared with that found in other California wines and European wines.[12] Wine samples collected in 1980 were catalytically oxidized to carbon dioxide and water, and the tritium content of the recovered water was measured by gas-proportional counting. The data in Table 23 represent the analysis of 11 samples purchased from retail outlets in 1980. As found in 1977, the tritium levels of the Valley wines were somewhat higher than those California wines produced from grapes grown outside the Valley, but lower than that of the European wine sampled. The same European wine source has been sampled in previous years.

Samples of honey produced from a variety of flower sources both in and outside the Livermore Valley were analyzed for tritium content. Following the oxidation of the samples in a Parr oxygen bomb, the tritium content of the water produced was determined by gas-proportional counting. The data in Table 24 show that the tritium content of Livermore Valley honey samples is comparable to that of honey from neighboring areas.

Radioactivity in Milk

During 1980, goat milk samples were obtained from several farms within about 5 km of the Laboratory. A portion of each sample was vacuum-distilled and then analyzed for tritium activity by liquid-scintillation counting. The samples were then oven-dried, and the resultant solid matter was ground and gamma-counted in a Ge(Li) system. The activities of the ^{137}Cs, ^{40}K, and HTO in the samples are shown in Table 25. Also shown are the calculated annual whole-body or critical-organ radiation doses that could be received from consuming this milk. These calculations are based on a milk intake of 310 liters/y and on the models previously referenced. The only dose above 1 mrem to an individual is from naturally occurring ^{40}K.

Environmental Radiation Measurements

Quarterly, environmental gamma radiation is measured at 12 LLNL perimeter locations (Fig. 4) and at 41 off-site locations (Fig. 12). These measurements are obtained with thermoluminescence dosimeters (TLD's) using a previously published procedure.[13] Based on past measurements,[14] environmental terrestrial exposure rates in the Livermore Valley vary from 30 to 60 mR/y. Cosmic radiation, calculated from the local elevation and geomagnetic latitude according to the data of Lowder and Beck,[15] is approximately 35 mR/y.

Table 26 shows quarterly and annual radiation doses (in millirem) derived from measurements at perimeter locations. The operation of a 14-MeV neutron generator adjacent to the south boundary fence was responsible for the elevated doses at Location 5 on the south site boundary directly opposite this facility. However, these doses are lower than those observed during 1979 because many high-flux experiments normally performed at this location are now being performed in Bldg. 292 in the northwest quadrant of the Laboratory.

The median annual off-site dose of 59 mrem is identical to that observed in 1979. Although the median annual perimeter dose of 63 mrem is slightly higher than the 61 mrem of 1979, this difference is not statistically significant. The 4-mrem difference between perimeter and off-site median doses is consistent with the difference seen in previous years. Perimeter locations 10, 11, and 12 are near a linear accelerator facility. Figure 13 shows the 1980 annual frequency distribution of environmental dose rates observed at the 41 off-site locations. The dosimeter that recorded the highest dose (140 mrem) was near an off-site industrial plant where radiography is frequently performed. The second highest off-site exposure (92 mrem) was due to a 52-mrem third-quarter response from a dosimeter located about 2 km southeast of LLNL. Prior measurements and the fourth-quarter measurement were somewhat below the average for the Livermore Valley. No explanation is presently available for this anomaly. Figure 14 is a dose-distribution plot combining Laboratory perimeter and off-site measurements. The three doses above those typical of environmental background have been identified above and in the previous paragraph.

Environmental neutron dose rate measurements are also made at eight locations on the LLNL site perimeter using ^{235}U track-etch detectors (Fig. 4). A detailed description of the detector and the spark-counting procedure has been published.[16] The 1980 quarterly measurements are shown in Table 27. With the exception of Locations 3 and 5, which monitor the 14-MeV neutron generator in Bldg. 212, all levels are within the range typical of natural background.

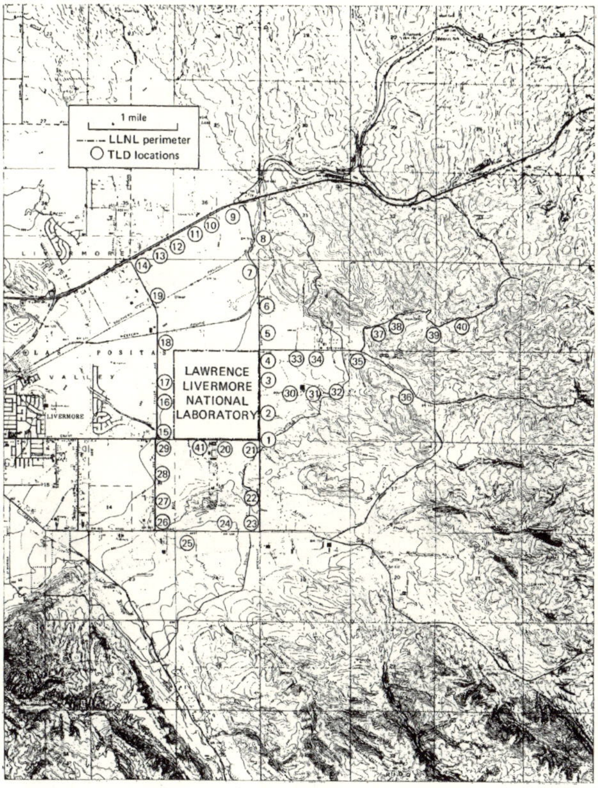

FIG. 12. Locations of TLD's in the vicinity of LLNL.

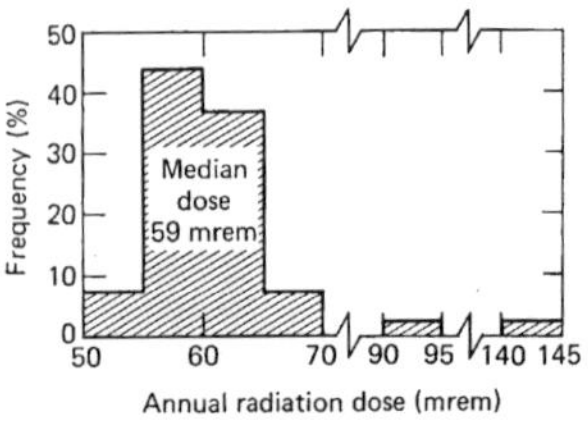

FIG. 13. Annual off-site gamma radiation background for 1980.

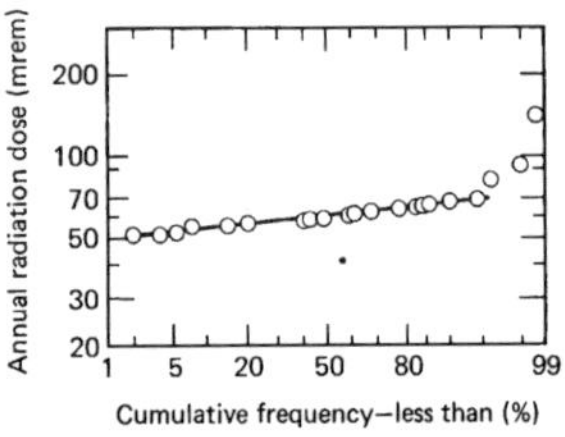

FIG. 14. TLD dose-distribution plot for the LLNL perimeter and Livermore Valley during 1980.

NONRADIOACTIVE MONITORING

Airborne Beryllium

Beryllium monitoring of air, both in-plant and at or near LLNL property boundaries, has always been a part of the Laboratory's safety program. Monthly, half of every filter from the LLNL perimeter and Site 300 is composited by sampling location and wet-digested. Then the beryllium content of the solutions is determined by atomic absorption analysis.

Tables 28 and 29 show average monthly concentrations of airborne beryllium for LLNL perimeter and Site 300 sampling locations, respectively. There appear to be no differences between the levels at Site 300, where beryllium is frequently expended in high-explosive experiments, and those observed at Livermore. The concentrations, which are two to three orders of magnitude below the emission standard, can be accounted for by resuspension of surface soil containing naturally occurring beryllium. Local soils contain approximately 1 ppm of beryllium, and Livermore's air typically contains 10–100 μg of particulates per cubic meter. By using a value of 50 $\mu g/m^3$ for an average dust load and 1 ppm for beryllium content of this dust an airborne beryllium concentration of 5.0×10^{-5} $\mu g/m^3$ can be calculated. This value is in good agreement with the data in Tables 28 and 29. These concentrations are plotted in Figs. 15 and 16. Average annual concentrations are less than 1% of the appropriate standard.

Heavy Metals Released to Livermore Sanitary Sewer

As noted previously, sanitary sewage from the Laboratory is treated at the LWRP, a 200-liter/s tertiary sewage-treatment plant serving residential, commercial, and industrial users in Livermore. This effluent is continuously monitored for pH, radioactivity, and transition metals before it enters the Livermore sewer system.[8] Sewage samples representative of daily flow are collected and composited monthly, and the composites are analyzed for the metals shown in Table 30.

Physical and Chemical Analysis of LLNL Sewage

Samples of Laboratory sewage effluent are collected quarterly. These samples are subjected to a variety of analyses, including biochemical oxygen demand, ammonia, nitrate, total nitrogen content, alkalinity, and total solids. Table 31 shows the data for 1980. All data demonstrate compliance with the City of Livermore's discharge limits (listed in Appendix D).

Noise Pollution

As noted earlier, the Laboratory's high-explosive diagnostic work is conducted at Site 300. Because Site 300 is so remote, these experiments can be performed with minimal off-site impact from annoying noises or damaging overpressures. On the basis of meteorological measurements made twice

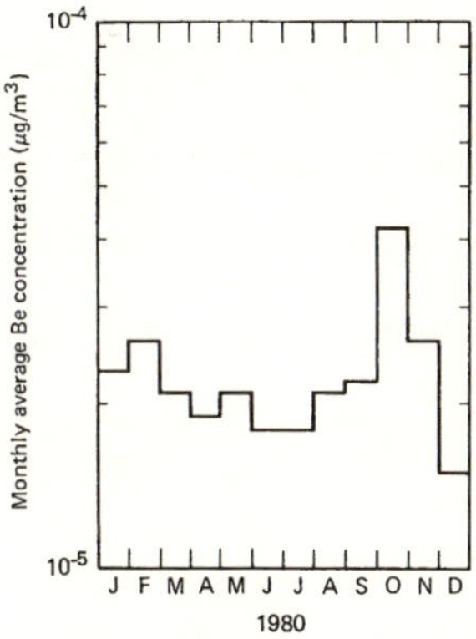

FIG. 15. Beryllium concentration in LLNL perimeter air filters during 1980.

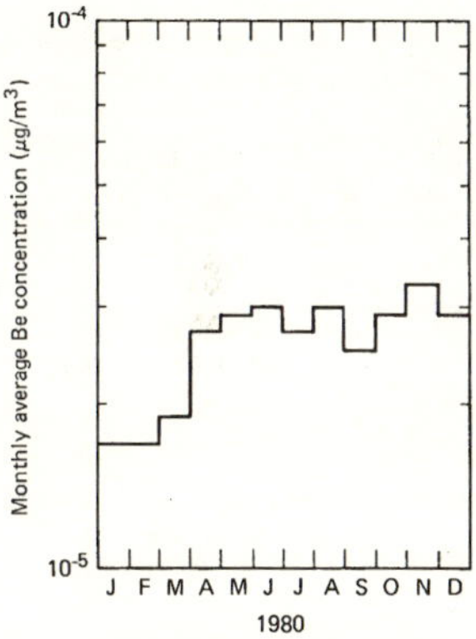

FIG. 16. Beryllium concentration in Site 300 air filters during 1980.

each day, a limit is set on the weight of high explosives that can be detonated without impact in populated areas. To monitor these limits, four microbarograph sensors are maintained in or near the city of Tracy. The probability of overpressure is greatest in the Tracy area because of the direction of the prevailing winds. The Laboratory received no complaints regarding possible overpressures associated with Site 300 operations during 1980.

Pesticide Monitoring

Beginning in 1975, the Laboratory's environmental surveillance program was expanded to include pesticide monitoring. Pesticides used at LLNL include herbicides, fungicides, and insecticides. The most probable way pesticides used at LLNL could be transported to the off-site environment is by entrainment in surface runoff water. Most of this surface drainage leaves the Laboratory via a ditch at the northwest corner of the property. A sample was collected from the ditch following the first major storm.

This sample was extracted with organic solvents, and the extracts were analyzed by gas-liquid chromatography (GLC) using a variety of detectors. Data obtained from these analyses were compared with the pesticides listed in Title 22 of the California Health and Safety Code.[10] No materials were detected in the samples at concentrations exceeding the State-adopted standards for these organic chemicals.

ENVIRONMENTAL IMPACT OF LLNL OPERATIONS

Radioactive Airborne Effluents

In 1980 (see Table 32), radioactive airborne effluents consisted of an estimated 165 Ci of ^{41}Ar from Bldg. 281 (reactor), a total of 2305 Ci of tritium from Bldg. 212 (14-MeV neutron generator) and Bldg. 331 (tritium facility), and 1656 Ci of ^{15}O-^{13}N from Bldg. 194 (electron-positron linear accelerator). All radionuclides, with the exception of tritium, are short-lived. Comparative releases of radioactive effluents at Livermore during the 5-year period from 1976 through 1980 are shown in Table 33. The Livermore reactor was shut down on

March 31, 1980, due to a lack of programmatic need. Closure of this facility removes the local source of ^{41}Ar and eliminates a major contributor to the site's radiation dose to the public. Decommissioning of a major portion of the LLNL tritium facility and reduced activity of the 14-MeV neutron generator in Bldg. 212 are responsible for a nearly 50% reduction in the quantity of tritium released to the atmosphere in 1980. The quantity of ^{15}O-^{13}N released from Bldg. 194 in 1980 is higher than that released in 1979, since this facility was shut down for major maintenance and modification during 1979; activity released during 1980 was comparable to that released in 1978.

Table 32 also contains estimated radiation doses to the public from these radioactive airborne effluents. Three dose-reference points were used: (1) the "fence-post" dose at that location on the site boundary where maximum exposure rates exist, (2) the dose to the nearest resident, and (3) the man-rem dose within a radius of 80 km.

Dose calculations were made using a continuous-point-source computer code based on the Gaussian plume model.[17] This code provides ratios of concentration to release rate (χ/Q) through 16, 22.5° compass sectors, and distances from 0.1 to 100 km from potential release points. The average annual χ/Q values have been calculated using local meteorological data from an instrumented tower. This tower, located near the Laboratory's north site boundary, is equipped with sensors mounted at 10- and 40-m levels that measure wind direction, wind speed, and temperature. From records of these data, wind speed, wind direction, and atmospheric stability estimates were tabulated at 1/4-h intervals over the calendar year. Variance in the horizontal wind direction was used to estimate Pasquill-Gifford stability categories based on the method described by Slade.[18] Lateral and vertical standard deviations, σ_y and σ_z, are entered in the computer code as functions of these stability categories and the respective distances. From annual effluent data the release rate Q (in Curies per second) was calculated for each of the principal radionuclides released to the atmosphere, and the concentrations at the site boundary and for the nearest resident were calculated from appropriate χ/Q values. (The nearest resident means that resident receiving the highest dose from each radioactivity release point, not necessarily the resident nearest to the site boundary.) Dose estimates were based on the dose conversion factor in the NRC Regulatory Guide 1.109.[11] The results indicate that the maximum estimated dose to the nearest resident was less than 1 mrem.

Table 32 shows a combined population dose of less than 2 man-rem from ^{41}Ar, ^{3}H, and neutron activation products in Laboratory airborne effluents. This dose is based on a population of 4.8×10^6 within 80 km of the Laboratory. Using 100 mrem/y as a typical average radiation dose from natural sources, the comparable natural radiation dose received by the same group is 4.8×10^5 man-rem. By comparison, the population dose from Laboratory operations is negligible.

Radioactive Liquid Effluents

Low-level radioactive liquid wastes are treated to reduce their radioactivity to levels as low as reasonably achievable and are well within applicable health and safety standards. These wastes are then discharged into Livermore's sanitary sewer system. During 1980, the principal radionuclides released into the sewer system were 2.8×10^{-4} Ci of ^{239}Pu and 5 Ci of HTO. Table 13 shows that the average annual concentrations of these radionuclides represent 9.3×10^{-4}% and 2.4×10^{-2}% of the relevant standards, respectively.

Quality Assurance

During 1980, the Laboratory participated in the Environmental Protection Agency's interlaboratory Cross Check program and DOE's Sample Analysis Intercomparison program conducted for DOE by the Environmental Measurements Laboratory (EML). The Laboratory also participated in the 5th International Intercomparison of Environmental Dosimeters and continued its quarterly intercomparison of thermoluminescence dosimetry measurements with EML.

A statistical summary published annually by EML compares the analytical performance of participating DOE contractors with measurements made by EML.[19] Table 34 shows the comparison of LLNL's and EML's analyses, indicating the ratio of LLNL's data to EML's and the ratio of LLNL's data to the respective mean of all analyses reported.

A description of the sampling and analytical procedures used at LLNL is included as Appendix E in this report.

REFERENCES

1. C. L. Lindeken, R. L. Morgan, and K. F. Petrock, "Collection Efficiency of Whatman 41 Filter Paper for Submicron Aerosols," *Health Phys* **9**, 305 (1963).
2. W. J. Silver, C. L. Lindeken, J. H. White, and R. W. Buddemeier, *Environmental Monitoring at the Lawrence Livermore Laboratory, 1979 Annual Report*, Lawrence Livermore National Laboratory, Livermore, CA, UCRL-50027-79 (1980).
3. "Radiochemical Determination of Plutonium in Soil by Leaching," *HASL Procedure Manual, Procedure E-Pu-06*, Energy Research and Development Administration, HASL-300 (1972).
4. W. J. Silver, C. L. Lindeken, J. W. Meadows, W. H. Hutchin, and D. R. McIntyre, *Environmental Levels of Radioactivity in the Vicinity of the Lawrence Livermore Laboratory, 1973 Annual Report*, Lawrence Livermore National Laboratory, Livermore, CA, UCRL-51574 (1974).
5. P. H. Gudiksen, C. L. Lindeken, J. W. Meadows, and K. O. Hamby, *Environmental Levels of Radioactivity in the Vicinity of the LLL, 1972 Annual Report*, Lawrence Livermore National Laboratory, Livermore, CA, UCRL-51333 (1973).
6. B. R. Tamplin, California Department of Health Services, private communication (1980)
7. W. J. Tipton, *An Aerial Radiological Survey of the Lawrence Livermore Laboratory*, EG&G, Las Vegas, NV, EGG-1183-1693 (1975).
8. M. Auyong, J. L. Cate, Jr., and D. W. Rueppel, *On-Line Monitoring of Toxic Materials in Sewage at the Lawrence Livermore Laboratory*, Lawrence Livermore National Laboratory, Livermore, CA, UCRL-83664 (1980).
9. *National Interim Primary Drinking Water Regulations*, Environmental Protection Agency, EPA-570/9-76-003 (June 24, 1977).
10. *California Domestic Water Quality and Monitoring Regulations, California Administrative Title Code 22*, State of California (1977).
11. *Calculation of Annual Doses to Man from Routine Releases of Reactor Effluent for the Purpose of Evaluating Compliance with 10CFR Part 50, Appendix I*, U. S. Nuclear Regulatory Commission, Regulatory Guide 1.109 (October 1977).
12. W. J. Silver, C. L. Lindeken, K. M. Wong, E. H. Willes, and J. H. White, *Environmental Monitoring at the Lawrence Livermore Laboratory, 1977 Annual Report*, Lawrence Livermore National Laboratory, Livermore, CA, UCRL-50027-77 (1978).
13. C. L. Lindeken, J. H. White, A. J. Toy, and C. W. Sundbeck, *Ambient Environmental Radiation Monitoring at the Lawrence Livermore Laboratory*, UCRL-77106 (1975).
14. C. L. Lindeken, P. H. Gudiksen, J. W. Meadows, K. O. Hamby, and L. R. Anspaugh, *Environmental Levels of Radioactivity in Livermore Valley Soils*, Lawrence Livermore National Laboratory, Livermore, CA, UCRL-74414 (1973).
15. W. M. Lowder and H. L. Beck, "Cosmic Ray Ionization in the Lower Atmosphere," *J. Geo. Phys. Rev.* **71**, 4611 (1966).
16. J. C. Fisher, Jr., "Calibration of Anderson-Braun Remmeters with Track Etch Detectors," in *Hazards Control Progress Report No. 52*, Lawrence Livermore National Laboratory, Livermore, CA, UCRL-50007-76-1 (1976), p. 37.
17. K. R. Peterson, T. W. Crawford, and L. A. Lawson, *CPS: A Continuous-Point-Source Computer Code for Plume Dispersion and Deposition Calculations*, Lawrence Livermore National Laboratory, Livermore, CA, UCRL-52049 (1976).
18. D. H. Slade, Ed., *Meteorology and Atomic Energy* (U. S. Atomic Energy Commission, 1968).
19. G. A. Welford, I. M. Fisenne, and C. Sanderson, *Summary Report of the Department of Energy, Division of Operational and Environmental Safety—Quality Assurance Programs 9 through 12*, Environmental Measurements Laboratory, New York, NY, EML-369 (February 1, 1980).

CJT/jp

APPENDIX A. TABLES

The statistical values (2σ estimates) that accompany individual measurements of radioactivity in the following tables are the result of counting statistics. The minimum detection limit is assumed reached when the 2σ estimate is $\pm 100\%$. Statistical values for groups of data like annual averages are calculated standard deviations of the mean (average). Standard deviations of the mean are reported at the 95% confidence level.

TABLE 1. Gross alpha activity on air filters—LLNL perimeter and Livermore Valley.

	10^{-15} μCi/ml														
Location[a]	Jan.	Feb.	Mar.	Apr.	May	June	July	Aug.	Sept.	Oct.	Nov.	Dec.	Average	% SDM[b]	% CG[c]
Perimeter															
01	0.4	0.4	0.6	0.6	0.4	0.5	0.4	1.2	0.7	0.8	0.6	1.7	0.7	57	3.5
02	0.6	0.6	0.8	0.8	0.5	0.5	0.5	0.6	0.7	1.5	1.0	2.0	0.8	63	4.0
12	0.6	0.5	0.7	0.6	0.6	0.6	0.3	0.4	1.1	0.7	0.7	3.3	0.8	100	4.0
13	0.4	0.4	0.5	0.4	0.4	0.3	0.3	0.4	0.6	0.8	0.8	1.6	0.6	67	3.0
14	0.5	0.5	0.6	0.7	0.5	0.5	0.5	0.7	0.7	0.8	1.0	2.9	0.8	88	4.0
15	0.4	0.4	0.6	0.5	0.6	0.5	0.4	0.4	0.7	0.8	1.1	1.9	0.7	57	3.5
Valley															
03	0.8	1.1	1.1	0.9	0.8	0.8	0.7	0.5	0.9	0.9	0.8	1.9	0.9	37	4.0
04	1.4	1.3	3.1	1.7	0.9	0.6	0.5	0.5	1.1	1.6	1.8	1.7	1.4	50	7.0
05	1.6	0.8	1.6	1.3	0.9	1.1	0.7	0.6	0.7	0.8	0.7	1.0	1.0	36	5.0
06	2.0	—	1.1	1.0	0.9	0.8	0.8	0.6	0.8	1.1	1.0	1.9	1.1	41	5.5
07	1.1	0.6	1.1	1.1	0.8	0.8	0.6	0.7	0.8	0.9	1.0	1.8	0.9	35	4.5
08	1.1	0.9	0.8	0.9	0.8	1.0	0.7	0.7	0.8	1.0	1.1	1.6	1.0	26	5.0
09	0.8	0.8	1.3	1.2	0.8	1.1	0.9	0.8	0.7	0.8	1.3	1.8	1.0	32	5.0
10	—	0.5	0.9	0.5	0.5	0.4	0.4	0.4	0.5	0.6	0.6	0.9	0.6	33	3.0
11	1.2	0.7	1.2	1.3	1.0	1.1	0.8	0.8	1.0	1.2	1.1	1.7	1.1	25	5.5
16	0.8	1.0	0.8	0.6	0.8	0.7	0.6	0.6	0.6	0.6	0.7	1.6	0.8	78	4.0
17										1.9	1.1	1.8	1.6	28	8.0
Annual average													0.9	29	4.5

[a]See Figs. 4 and 5 for sampling locations.

[b]% SDM = % standard deviation of mean at 1σ.

[c]Concentration guide (CG) = 2.0×10^{-14} μCi/ml.

TABLE 2. Gross beta activity on air filters—LLNL perimeter and Livermore Valley.

	10^{-14} μCi/ml														
Location[a]	Jan.	Feb.	Mar.	Apr.	May	June	July	Aug.	Sept.	Oct.	Nov.	Dec.	Average	% SDM	% CG[b]
Perimeter															
01	1.8	1.8	0.8	1.1	1.0	0.6	0.9	1.3	1.7	1.6	5.8	10.2	2.4	117	2.4
02	2.3	2.6	1.0	1.4	1.2	0.8	1.3	1.4	1.6	3.0	7.4	11.9	3.0	110	3.0
12	2.0	2.2	0.8	1.1	0.7	0.7	0.7	0.8	1.2	2.9	7.1	11.1	2.6	123	2.6
13	1.8	1.7	0.8	1.1	1.0	0.7	1.0	1.0	1.2	2.4	5.2	10.2	2.3	122	2.3
14	2.3	2.6	0.9	1.2	1.1	0.8	1.2	1.3	1.4	2.7	7.0	20.5	3.6	156	3.6
15	1.7	1.8	0.8	1.2	1.0	0.6	1.1	1.1	1.2	2.2	7.0	9.9	2.5	116	2.5
Valley															
03	3.1	2.6	1.9	2.1	2.2	1.9	2.1	1.9	2.1	3.0	6.0	8.2	2.9	73	2.9
04	6.0	4.9	2.2	3.0	1.9	0.8	1.2	1.1	2.0	5.4	6.1	11.5	3.8	81	3.8
05	4.0	3.0	2.3	2.6	2.5	2.2	1.9	1.5	1.6	2.2	3.9	4.9	2.7	38	2.7
06	4.6	—	2.1	2.1	2.3	2.2	1.8	2.2	1.9	3.0	5.7	9.5	3.4	70	3.4
07	3.4	2.2	2.1	2.3	2.5	1.8	2.2	2.3	2.4	3.0	5.4	12.6	3.5	86	3.5
08	3.2	3.8	2.2	2.1	2.0	1.9	2.1	2.1	2.2	3.0	5.6	9.2	3.3	65	3.3
09	2.0	3.4	2.2	2.6	2.5	2.0	2.6	2.6	2.5	3.7	7.7	10.7	3.7	73	3.7
10	—	1.0	0.4	0.6	0.5	0.3	0.5	0.5	0.8	1.0	3.9	6.4	1.4	133	1.4
11	3.5	2.7	2.4	2.5	2.5	2.1	2.3	2.4	2.6	4.1	8.1	11.2	3.9	73	3.9
16	2.9	2.3	0.8	1.2	0.9	0.6	1.1	1.6	1.4	1.9	4.0	8.2	2.2	94	2.2
Annual average													3.0	24	3.0

[a]See Figs. 4 and 5 for sampling locations.
[b]CG = 1.0×10^{-12} μCi/ml.

TABLE 3. Gross alpha activity on air filters—Site 300.

Location[a]	Jan.	Feb.	Mar.	Apr.	May	June	July	Aug.	Sept.	Oct.	Nov.	Dec.	Average	% SDM	% CG[b]
	10^{-15} μCi/ml														
01	0.5	0.4	0.6	0.7	1.0	0.8	0.4	1.0	0.6	—	1.3	1.3	0.8	38	4.0
02	0.5	0.5	0.7	0.6	0.6	0.5	0.5	0.6	0.6	0.7	0.8	0.8	0.6	17	3.0
03	0.5	0.6	0.7	0.6	0.6	0.6	0.5	0.9	0.8	0.9	1.1	0.8	0.7	29	3.5
04	0.5	0.5	0.6	0.8	0.7	0.5	0.5	0.6	0.6	1.1	0.7	1.1	0.7	29	3.5
05	0.4	0.9	0.7	0.5	0.7	0.6	0.6	0.7	0.7	0.8	1.5	4.5	1.1	100	5.5
06	—	—	—	0.6	1.0	1.0	0.7	2.2	—	1.7	2.6	3.0	1.6	56	8.0
07	0.5	0.4	0.6	0.6	0.7	0.6	0.6	0.8	0.7	0.7	0.9	1.0	0.7	29	3.5
08	0.5	0.5	0.6	0.6	0.5	0.6	0.7	0.6	0.9	0.8	0.7	0.9	0.7	14	3.7
09	0.5	0.6	2.4	0.7	0.5	0.5	0.4	0.9	0.5	1.3	1.0	1.3	0.9	67	4.5
10	0.4	0.4	0.6	0.7	0.8	0.5	0.9	1.0	0.7	0.9	1.2	1.2	0.8	38	4.0
11	0.6	0.6	0.7	0.6	0.7	0.5	0.4	1.1	0.7	1.0	0.7	1.6	0.8	38	4.0
Annual average													0.9	33	4.5

[a]See Fig. 6 for sampling locations.
[b]CG = 2.0×10^{-14} μCi/ml.

TABLE 4. Gross beta activity on air filters—Site 300.

Location[a]	Jan.	Feb.	Mar.	Apr.	May	June	July	Aug.	Sept.	Oct.	Nov.	Dec.	Average	% SDM	% CG[b]
	10^{-14} μCi/ml														
01	1.8	1.8	1.3	1.4	1.4	1.3	1.3	2.4	1.8	—	4.5	12.1	2.8	114	2.8
02	1.8	2.3	1.3	1.4	2.0	1.4	1.4	2.1	1.7	3.1	5.5	12.1	3.0	103	3.0
03	1.9	2.2	1.1	1.2	1.4	1.2	1.3	2.7	2.0	2.7	7.5	10.6	3.0	100	3.0
04	1.9	2.7	1.3	1.3	1.6	0.9	0.9	1.3	1.4	2.7	6.3	10.5	2.7	107	2.7
05	1.5	2.5	1.0	0.9	1.5	1.0	1.3	1.9	1.7	3.2	8.6	28.3	4.5	173	4.5
06	—	—	—	1.3	1.4	0.8	1.0	1.7	—	5.4	7.7	20.1	4.9	135	4.9
07	1.5	1.8	0.9	1.3	1.5	1.0	1.6	2.2	1.7	2.1	6.9	9.3	2.7	96	2.7
08	1.7	1.9	1.0	1.3	1.6	1.1	0.7	2.0	1.7	2.3	5.8	9.5	2.6	100	2.6
09	1.4	2.0	1.4	1.4	1.6	1.2	1.5	2.9	1.9	3.8	9.7	15.5	3.7	119	3.7
10	1.5	2.0	1.7	1.4	1.4	1.1	2.0	2.8	2.1	2.6	10.1	12.0	3.4	106	3.4
11	1.9	2.3	1.2	1.2	1.4	1.0	1.3	2.7	1.9	2.2	6.1	12.8	3.0	113	3.0
Annual average													3.3	23	3.3

[a]See Fig. 6 for sampling locations.
[b]CG = 1.0×10^{-12} μCi/ml.

TABLE 5. Gamma activity on air filters—LLNL perimeter.

Month	10^{-13} μCi/ml ± 2σ(%)	10^{-16} μCi/ml ± 2σ(%)				
	^{7}Be	^{40}K	^{106}Ru	^{125}Sb	^{137}Cs	^{144}Ce
Jan.	0.8 ± 2	7.8 ± 33	5.1 ± 42	0.9 ± 41	2.3 ± 9	3.8 ± 20
Feb.	0.9 ± 2	10. ± 25	7.6 ± 35	1.5 ± 37	3.3 ± 11	6.0 ± 23
Mar.	0.8 ± 2	7. ± 23	5.9 ± 29	1.3 ± 24	3.3 ± 6	5.1 ± 33
Apr.	1.0 ± 2	1.1 ± 100	9.1 ± 10	2.5 ± 15	5.7 ± 5	7.4 ± 14
May	0.8 ± 2	1.1 ± 100	7.4 ± 29	2.3 ± 22	5.8 ± 6	6.5 ± 26
June	0.5 ± 3	0.7 ± 100	0.7 ± 100	0.3 ± 100	3.9 ± 8	3.9 ± 34
July	0.7 ± 2	0.9 ± 100	4.7 ± 15	1.6 ± 15	4.6 ± 4	5.0 ± 12
Aug.	0.7 ± 2	4.5 ± 67	2.6 ± 50	1.0 ± 31	2.9 ± 9	2.5 ± 31
Sept.	1.0 ± 2	5.9 ± 36	1.2 ± 63	0.8 ± 43	2.1 ± 11	2.0 ± 55
Oct.	1.0 ± 2	5.7 ± 78	1.5 ± 57	0.7 ± 64	1.7 ± 11	1.7 ± 45
Nov.	0.8 ± 2	10. ± 56	8.9 ± 31	0.5 ± 100	1.9 ± 20	16. ± 21
Dec.	1.0 ± 2	6.2 ± 44	31. ± 10	2.3 ± 49	4.1 ± 12	75. ± 100
Annual average	0.83×10^{-13}	5.1×10^{-16}	7.1×10^{-16}	1.3×10^{-16}	3.5×10^{-16}	11.2×10^{-16}
% SDM	19	68	113	57	40	182
CG	4.0×10^{-8}	4.0×10^{-9}	2.0×10^{-10}	9.0×10^{-10}	5.0×10^{-10}	2.0×10^{-10}
% CG	2.1×10^{-4}	1.3×10^{-5}	3.6×10^{-4}	1.4×10^{-5}	7.0×10^{-5}	5.6×10^{-4}

TABLE 6. Gamma activity on air filters—Site 300.

Month	10^{-13} μCi/ml ± 2σ(%)	10^{-16} μCi/ml ± 2σ(%)				
	^{7}Be	^{40}K	^{106}Ru	^{125}Sb	^{137}Cs	^{144}Ce
Jan.	0.8 ± 2	3.1 ± 33	4.5 ± 20	1.0 ± 24	2.2 ± 7	3.9 ± 16
Feb.	0.8 ± 2	3.9 ± 22	5.5 ± 27	1.2 ± 20	3.1 ± 7	0.5 ± 11
Mar.	0.9 ± 2	3.8 ± 23	6.6 ± 24	2.0 ± 11	4.2 ± 4	7.8 ± 18
Apr.	1.1 ± 2	0.9 ± 100	10. ± 32	2.9 ± 12	6.0 ± 5	8.5 ± 12
May	1.0 ± 2	0.9 ± 100	9.4 ± 13	2.8 ± 22	6.9 ± 5	8.4 ± 34
June	0.7 ± 2	0.3 ± 100	0.5 ± 100	1.5 ± 65	5.3 ± 5	7.5 ± 27
July	1.1 ± 2	4.8 ± 46	7.5 ± 13	2.0 ± 17	6.6 ± 3	7.8 ± 20
Aug.	1.5 ± 2	5.8 ± 54	5.9 ± 17	2.1 ± 18	6.3 ± 4	6.8 ± 16
Sept.	1.2 ± 3	3.7 ± 57	3.5 ± 32	1.1 ± 26	3.2 ± 5	2.5 ± 18
Oct.	1.3 ± 3	4.4 ± 63	2.2 ± 27	0.9 ± 34	2.0 ± 7	1.9 ± 26
Nov.	0.9 ± 2	6.5 ± 40	6.7 ± 23	0.6 ± 154	1.8 ± 12	13. ± 30
Dec.	1.2 ± 2	2.4 ± 106	35. ± 9	3.3 ± 28	4.9 ± 9	86. ± 5
Annual average	1.0×10^{-13}	3.4×10^{-16}	8.1×10^{-16}	1.8×10^{-16}	4.4×10^{-16}	12.9×10^{-16}
% SDM	23	58	110	49	43	181
CG	4.0×10^{-8}	4.0×10^{-9}	2.0×10^{-10}	9.0×10^{-10}	5.0×10^{-10}	2.0×10^{-10}
% CG	2.5×10^{-4}	8.5×10^{-6}	4.1×10^{-4}	2.0×10^{-5}	8.8×10^{-5}	6.5×10^{-4}

TABLE 7. Plutonium-239 on air filters—Livermore Valley.

Location[a]	Jan.	Feb.	Mar.	Apr.	May	June	July	Aug.	Sept.	Oct.	Nov.	Dec.	Average	% SDM	% CG[b]
	10^{-17} μCi/ml ± 2σ(%)														
04	0.6 ± 15	0.9 ± 12	1.3 ± 18	1.8 ± 15	1.4 ± 8	0.6 ± 12	0.6 ± 20	0.4 ± 30	0.5 ± 30	0.3 ± 40	0.5 ± 58	0.6 ± 20	0.8	58	1.3×10^{-2}
10	—	0.3 ± 19	0.4 ± 22	0.5 ± 10	0.4 ± 12	0.2 ± 21	0.4 ± 22	0.2 ± 22	0.1 ± 38	0.4 ± 26	0.1 ± 48	0.4 ± 21	0.3	45	0.5×10^{-2}
16	0.3 ± 28	0.4 ± 18	0.5 ± 14	0.7 ± 10	0.7 ± 14	0.5 ± 22	0.4 ± 56	0.4 ± 34	0.4 ± 28	0.2 ± 30	0.3 ± 29	0.5 ± 22	0.4	34	0.7×10^{-2}

[a]See Fig. 5 for sampling locations.
[b]CG = 6.0×10^{-14} μCi/ml.

TABLE 8. Plutonium, cesium, and uranium on air filters—LLNL perimeter.

		10^{-17} μCi/ml ± 2σ(%)	10^{-2}	10^{-15} μCi/ml ± 2σ(%)	10^{-2}	10^{-7} μg/m^3 ± 2σ(%)	10^{-5} μg/m^3 ± 2σ(%)	10^{-3}
Month	Location[a]	^{239}Pu[b]	^{238}Pu/^{239}Pu	^{137}Cs	^{239}Pu/^{137}Cs	^{235}U	^{238}U	^{235}U/^{238}U
Jan.	01	0.4 ± 18	6.0	0.2 ± 6	2.0	1.3 ± 2	2.0 ± 1	6.5
	02	0.4 ± 18	2.0	0.2 ± 7	2.0	1.8 ± 1	2.9 ± 1	6.4
	12	0.5 ± 20	9.0	0.2 ± 10	2.5	3.0 ± 2	4.6 ± 2	6.5
	13	0.3 ± 22	1.2	0.2 ± 7	1.5	1.4 ± 1	2.1 ± 1	6.7
	14	0.5 ± 20	13.	0.2 ± 7	2.5	1.3 ± 1	2.1 ± 1	6.4
	15	0.3 ± 24	8.	0.2 ± 9	1.5	1.7 ± 1	2.6 ± 1	6.7
Feb.	01	0.5 ± 28	0.3	0.4 ± 7	1.2	2.3 ± 1	5.0 ± 1	4.6
	02	0.6 ± 12	5.0	0.4 ± 6	1.5	3.5 ± 1	7.8 ± 1	4.5
	12	0.7 ± 20	7.0	0.4 ± 14	1.8	4.7 ± 2	16. ± 1	2.9
	13	0.4 ± 14	3.0	0.3 ± 8	1.3	2.3 ± 2	5.0 ± 1	4.7
	14	1.1 ± 12	7.0	0.5 ± 8	2.2	2.0 ± 4	3.7 ± 1	5.5
	15	0.4 ± 12	3.0	0.3 ± 7	1.3	2.9 ± 2	7.7 ± 1	3.8
Mar.	01	0.6 ± 14	0.9	0.4 ± 6	1.5	1.8 ± 2	2.6 ± 1	7.1
	02	0.5 ± 14	0.7	0.4 ± 8	1.2	1.9 ± 2	2.8 ± 1	7.0
	12	0.4 ± 14	0.9	0.4 ± 11	1.0	1.5 ± 2	2.1 ± 1	7.1
	13	0.8 ± 10	4.1	0.4 ± 8	2.0	3.0 ± 2	4.6 ± 1	6.7
	14	0.8 ± 12	1.3	0.4 ± 8	2.0	2.1 ± 1	3.1 ± 1	6.9
	15	0.6 ± 12	2.6	0.4 ± 10	1.5	2.5 ± 2	3.6 ± 1	7.1
Apr.	01	0.8 ± 10	1.0	0.6 ± 4	1.3	2.4 ± 1	3.3 ± 1	7.1
	02	0.9 ± 8	0.8	0.7 ± 3	1.3	2.7 ± 2	3.8 ± 1	7.1
	12	0.7 ± 8	0.1	0.6 ± 3	1.2	3.0 ± 2	4.3 ± 1	7.0
	13	0.9 ± 8	2.3	0.5 ± 4	1.8	1.9 ± 2	2.7 ± 1	7.1
	14	1.1 ± 8	2.9	0.7 ± 4	1.6	2.4 ± 1	3.4 ± 1	7.2
	15	0.8 ± 8	2.1	0.6 ± 4	1.3	3.5 ± 1	4.9 ± 1	7.2
May	01	0.7 ± 10	0.02	0.6 ± 4	1.2	2.7 ± 2	4.0 ± 1	7.0
	02	0.8 ± 24	2.7	0.7 ± 3	1.1	2.7 ± 2	3.9 ± 1	7.1
	12	0.6 ± 14	1.3	0.4 ± 7	1.5	4.0 ± 1	5.9 ± 1	6.9
	13	0.6 ± 12	3.8	0.5 ± 4	1.2	2.0 ± 1	2.8 ± 1	7.4
	14	4.9 ± 6	32.	0.6 ± 7	8.2	5.5 ± 2	7.8 ± 1	7.1
	15	0.7 ± 10	1.9	0.6 ± 4	1.2	5.8 ± 2	7.9 ± 1	7.5
June	01	0.5 ± 11	4.2	0.4 ± 7	1.2	3.6 ± 1	5.2 ± 1	7.2
	02	0.6 ± 13	0.7	0.5 ± 5	1.2	2.6 ± 1	3.6 ± 1	7.3
	12	0.6 ± 13	4.7	0.4 ± 6	1.5	3.6 ± 1	5.1 ± 1	7.2
	13	0.4 ± 16	1.2	0.4 ± 8	0.8	2.2 ± 1	3.0 ± 1	7.2
	14	3.4 ± 9	13.5	0.4 ± 6	8.5	6.4 ± 1	9.1 ± 1	7.1
	15	0.5 ± 17	3.2	0.4 ± 5	1.2	5.1 ± 1	7.1 ± 1	7.3
July	01	0.7 ± 23	1.0	0.5 ± 6	1.4	3.5 ± 4	4.8 ± 2	7.4
	02	0.7 ± 20	3.0	0.6 ± 5	1.2	3.6 ± 9	5.1 ± 5	7.1
	12	0.7 ± 32	4.0	0.4 ± 8	1.8	2.3 ± 9	3.2 ± 3	7.1
	13	0.4 ± 34	3.0	0.5 ± 6	0.8	3.0 ± 6	3.8 ± 4	8.0
	14	1.1 ± 22	19.	0.5 ± 6	2.2	5.5 ± 7	6.9 ± 4	8.1
	15	0.6 ± 26	1.0	0.5 ± 6	1.2	5.0 ± 3	6.9 ± 2	7.3

TABLE 8. Continued.

		10^{-17} μCi/ml ± 2σ(%)	10^{-2}	10^{-15} μCi/ml ± 2σ(%)	10^{-2}	10^{-7} μg/m³ ± 2σ(%)	10^{-5} μg/m³ 2σ(%)	10^{-3}
Month	Location[a]	^{239}Pu[b]	$^{238}Pu/^{239}Pu$	^{137}Cs	$^{239}Pu/^{137}Cs$	^{235}U	^{238}U	$^{235}U/^{238}U$
Aug.	01	0.7 ± 22	8.0	0.4 ± 7	1.8	6.5 ± 1	9.4 ± 1	7.0
	02	0.4 ± 29	1.0	0.3 ± 6	1.3	4.0 ± 7	5.6 ± 4	7.3
	12	0.3 ± 28	9.0	0.2 ± 14	1.5	3.2 ± 13	4.4 ± 6	7.4
	13	0.3 ± 24	2.0	0.3 ± 13	1.0	2.9 ± 13	4.3 ± 6	6.9
	14	0.7 ± 20	11.	0.3 ± 9	2.3	4.9 ± 31	7.2 ± 16	6.9
	15	0.4 ± 20	15.	0.3 ± 8	1.3	5.0 ± 5	6.9 ± 3	7.3
Sept.	01	0.2 ± 42	28.	0.3 ± 10	0.7	6.1 ± 1	8.8 ± 1	7.0
	02	0.3 ± 29	3.0	0.2 ± 8	1.5	4.8 ± 1	6.8 ± 1	7.1
	12	0.1 ± 60	46.	0.2 ± 20	0.5	3.6 ± 1	5.1 ± 1	7.2
	13	0.2 ± 39	8.0	0.2 ± 10	1.0	3.7 ± 1	5.2 ± 1	7.2
	14	1.2 ± 18	18.	0.2 ± 10	6.0	6.3 ± 2	8.8 ± 1	7.2
	15	0.3 ± 32	2.0	0.3 ± 7	1.0	7.8 ± 1	11. ± 1	7.2
Oct.	01	0.8 ± 26	6.0	0.3 ± 12	2.7	6.7 ± 1	9.6 ± 1	7.1
	02	0.2 ± 44	4.0	0.4 ± 13	0.5	7.6 ± 1	10.8 ± 1	7.1
	12	0.3 ± 35	1.0	0.6 ± 6	0.5	4.8 ± 2	8.0 ± 1	6.1
	13	0.1 ± 46	48.	0.1 ± 13	1.0		Not analyzed	
	14	0.4 ± 34	10.	0.4 ± 11	1.0	5.6 ± 1	8.1 ± 1	7.0
	15	0.2 ± 42	28.	0.4 ± 6	0.5	8.9 ± 2	12.7 ± 1	7.1
Nov.	01	0.2 ± 30	6.0	0.2 ± 12	1.0	8.1 ± 1	11.2 ± 1	7.3
	02	0.4 ± 20	3.0	0.2 ± 9	2.0	7.8 ± 1	10.9 ± 1	7.2
	12	0.4 ± 22	10.	0.2 ± 11	2.0	5.8 ± 1	8.2 ± 1	7.2
	13	0.2 ± 28	5.0	0.2 ± 11	1.0	5.8 ± 2	8.2 ± 1	7.2
	14	0.4 ± 22	6.0	0.2 ± 10	2.0	7.7 ± 2	10.7 ± 1	7.3
	15	0.3 ± 28	9.0	0.2 ± 11	1.5	12.1 ± 2	16.8 ± 1	7.3
Dec.	01	0.5 ± 23	0.5	0.4 ± 5	1.3	2.4 ± 2	3.5 ± 1	7.0
	02	0.6 ± 23	10.	0.5 ± 5	1.2	3.2 ± 2	4.4 ± 1	7.4
	12	0.7 ± 25	20.	0.5 ± 6	1.4	3.4 ± 2	4.8 ± 1	7.0
	13	0.4 ± 27	-3.	0.4 ± 8	1.0	2.1 ± 1	2.9 ± 1	7.1
	14	0.8 ± 18	2.	0.6 ± 6	1.3	2.9 ± 1	4.2 ± 1	7.0
	15	0.5 ± 20	7.	0.5 ± 8	1.0	3.5 ± 2	4.8 ± 1	7.3

Annual averages:

	10^{-17} μCi/ml			10^{-15} μCi/ml			10^{-7} μg/m³			10^{-5} μg/m³		
Location	^{239}Pu	% SDM	% CG[c]	^{137}Cs	% SDM	% CG[d]	^{235}U	% SDM	% CG[e]	^{238}U	% SDM	% CG[f]
01	0.6	±38	1.0×10^{-2}	0.4	±33	8.0×10^{-5}	4.0	±58	2.1×10^{-5}	5.8	±54	3.9×10^{-4}
02	0.5	±39	0.8×10^{-2}	0.4	±42	8.0×10^{-5}	3.9	±52	2.1×10^{-5}	5.7	±50	3.8×10^{-4}
12	0.5	±40	0.8×10^{-2}	0.4	±40	8.0×10^{-5}	3.6	±32	1.9×10^{-5}	6.0	±60	4.0×10^{-4}
13	0.4	±58	0.7×10^{-2}	0.3	±42	6.0×10^{-5}	2.8	±44	1.5×10^{-5}	4.1	±42	2.7×10^{-4}
14	1.4	±100	2.3×10^{-2}	0.4	±41	8.0×10^{-5}	4.4	±48	2.3×10^{-5}	6.4	±48	4.3×10^{-4}
15	0.5	±39	0.8×10^{-2}	0.4	±36	8.0×10^{-5}	5.3	±57	2.8×10^{-5}	7.7	±52	5.1×10^{-4}

[a]See Fig. 4 for sampling locations.

[b]In all tables activity listed as ^{239}Pu includes activity due to the ^{240}Pu isotope.

[c]CG = 6.0×10^{-14} μCi/ml for ^{239}Pu (soluble) activity in air.

[d]CG = 5.0×10^{-10} μCi/ml for ^{137}Cs (insoluble) activity in air.

[e]CG = 1.9 μg/m³ for ^{235}U (insoluble) activity in air.

[f]CG = 15 μg/m³ for ^{238}U (insoluble) activity in air.

TABLE 9. Plutonium, cesium, and uranium on air filters—Site 300.

Month	10^{-17} μCi/ml ± 2σ(%) ^{239}Pu	10^{-2} $^{238}Pu/^{239}Pu$	10^{-15} μCi/ml ± 2σ(%) ^{137}Cs	10^{-2} $^{239}Pu/^{137}Cs$	10^{-7} μg/m^3 ± 2σ(%) ^{235}U	10^{-5} μg/m^3 ± 2σ(%) ^{238}U	10^{-3} $^{235}U/^{238}U$
Jan.	0.8 ± 4	3	0.3 ± 2	2.7	2.3 ± 3	8.6 ± 2	2.8
Feb.	2.3 ± 3	3	0.4 ± 2	5.8	11.6 ± 4	55.6 ± 4	2.1
Mar.	1.8 ± 4	3	0.5 ± 2	3.6	1.7 ± 1	4.7 ± 1	3.6
Apr.	1.0 ± 6	4	0.6 ± 1	1.7	3.2 ± 1	6.7 ± 2	4.9
May	1.3 ± 4	2	0.9 ± 2	1.4	3.2 ± 1	6.5 ± 1	5.1
June	1.4 ± 5	3	0.7 ± 1	2.0	4.4 ± 1	7.6 ± 1	5.9
July	1.3 ± 7	4	0.6 ± 2	2.2	4.0 ± 4	6.4 ± 4	6.4
Aug.	1.0 ± 8	4	0.5 ± 2	2.0	7.6 ± 1	15.2 ± 2	5.1
Sept.	0.5 ± 8	3	0.3 ± 2	1.7	5.9 ± 3	9.4 ± 3	6.4
Oct.	0.4 ± 11	4	0.2 ± 5	2.0	6.9 ± 3	13.2 ± 3	5.2
Nov.	0.5 ± 8	4	0.2 ± 3	2.5	5.6 ± 12	8.4 ± 11	6.7
Dec.	0.8 ± 8	3	0.5 ± 3	1.6	3.4 ± 3	10.1 ± 2	3.4
Annual average	1.1×10^{-17}		0.5×10^{-15}		5.0×10^{-7}	12.7×10^{-5}	
% SDM	56		44		55	109	
CG	6.0×10^{-14}		5.0×10^{-10}		1.9	15	
% CG	1.8×10^{-2}		1.0×10^{-4}		2.6×10^{-5}	8.5×10^{-4}	

TABLE 10. Tritium (HTO) in air—LLNL perimeter and Livermore Valley.

	10^{-11} μCi/ml															Calculated[c] adult whole body dose, mrem
Location[a]	Jan.	Feb.	Mar.	Apr.	May	June	July	Aug.	Sept.	Oct.	Nov.	Dec.	Average	% SDM	% CG[b]	
Perimeter																
01	4.2	1.7	2.5	2.8	2.4	1.6	2.7	—	1.6	2.3	3.5	4.2	2.7	35	1.4×10^{-2}	3.6×10^{-2}
02	3.8	3.8	3.0	3.1	1.5	1.0	1.7	1.9	0.9	12.7	11.5	11.0	4.7	94	2.4×10^{-2}	6.1×10^{-2}
12	5.9	4.6	4.3	5.9	3.6	2.4	5.6	7.5	4.6	8.9	6.8	6.3	5.5	32	2.8×10^{-2}	7.1×10^{-2}
13	3.5	2.2	3.1	2.1	2.3	1.0	0.7	1.3	1.4	3.7	4.5	4.5	2.5	52	1.3×10^{-2}	3.3×10^{-2}
14	4.3	2.5	3.1	5.9	4.9	4.3	8.5	6.7	5.2	3.3	3.7	3.9	4.7	36	2.4×10^{-2}	6.1×10^{-2}
15	6.1	3.0	2.9	4.1	3.2	3.4	4.9	3.3	2.3	2.3	2.4	3.4	3.4	33	1.7×10^{-2}	4.3×10^{-2}
Valley																
S1	2.9	2.0	2.2	2.2	1.7	1.5	2.0	1.5	1.8	1.9	4.8	4.6	2.4	47	1.2×10^{-2}	3.0×10^{-2}
S2	2.8	2.6	1.6	—	1.2	0.9	1.7	0.5	0.8	3.3	2.5	2.5	1.9	51	1.0×10^{-2}	2.5×10^{-2}

[a]See Figs. 4 and 5 for sampling locations.
[b]CG = 2.0×10^{-7} μCi/ml for tritium (HTO) in air.
[c]Doses are calculated using the methods in U.S. NRC Regulatory Guide 1.109 unless otherwise stated.

TABLE 11. Various radionuclides in soil—Livermore Valley.

Location[a]	Sampling depth, cm	μCi/dry g ± 2 σ(%)			μg/dry g ± 2σ(%)	
		^{239}Pu (10^{-9})	^{40}K (10^{-5})	^{137}Cs (10^{-7})	^{232}Th	^{238}U
783	0–5	0.5 ± 10	0.7 ± 4	0.3 ± 26	0.4 ± 7	0.9 ± 30
784	0–5	0.3 ± 14	0.8 ± 6	0.2 ± 28	0.3 ± 12	0.6 ± 32
785[b]	0–5	0.2 ± 16	0.9 ± 4	0.2 ± 40	0.3 ± 9	0.8 ± 16
786	0–5	0.3 ± 14	1.0 ± 8	0.2 ± 44	0.6 ± 12	0.6 ± 54
787	0–5	0.3 ± 30	1.3 ± 4	0.1 ± 68	0.7 ± 4	1.4 ± 16
788	0–5	2.3 ± 12	1.0 ± 4	0.3 ± 42	0.5 ± 10	1.1 ± 25
789	0–5	5.6 ± 8	1.0 ± 4	0.3 ± 6	0.6 ± 6	1.4 ± 16
790	0–5	3.3 ± 10	1.0 ± 4	2.0 ± 6	0.6 ± 6	1.1 ± 22
791	0–5	2.3 ± 16	1.2 ± 4	1.3 ± 10	0.6 ± 8	0.6 ± 56
792[c]	0–5	1.8 ± 17	1.1 ± 4	0.7 ± 14	0.5 ± 6	0.6 ± 80
793	0–5	0.6 ± 20	0.7 ± 6	0.5 ± 14	0.5 ± 6	1.0 ± 23
794	0–5	3.4 ± 11	1.2 ± 3	2.4 ± 5	0.6 ± 5	1.4 ± 14
795	0–5	4.6 ± 15	1.4 ± 4	3.2 ± 4	0.6 ± 7	1.0 ± 27
796	0–5	3.5 ± 15	1.1 ± 6	2.0 ± 6	0.6 ± 7	1.2 ± 17
797	0–5	2.7 ± 10	1.6 ± 2	1.6 ± 8	0.7 ± 4	1.3 ± 22
798	0–5	7.6 ± 13	1.0 ± 4	2.7 ± 6	0.5 ± 8	0.8 ± 20
803	0–5	6.4 ± 8	1.5 ± 4	3.9 ± 4	0.7 ± 8	1.5 ± 12
817	0–5	2.7 ± 4	1.0 ± 10	6.3 ± 6	0.6 ± 12	0.9 ± 30
818	0–5	8.9 ± 8	1.2 ± 18	3.5 ± 8	0.8 ± 14	0.8 ± 28
819	0–5	3.3 ± 10	1.2 ± 16	1.3 ± 16	1.0 ± 12	0.8 ± 30
820	0–5	8.3 ± 8	1.1 ± 14	3.2 ± 8	0.7 ± 16	0.9 ± 24
821	0–5	4.7 ± 6	1.3 ± 14	2.1 ± 12	0.8 ± 16	0.8 ± 60
822	0–5	2.5 ± 8	1.5 ± 16	1.2 ± 14	0.7 ± 14	0.8 ± 30
823	0–5	19. ± 6	1.4 ± 8	2.2 ± 10	0.7 ± 12	1.1 ± 54
824	0–5	13 ± 6	1.3 ± 14	1.6 ± 12	0.8 ± 12	1.0 ± 32
825	0–5	11 ± 6	1.3 ± 16	1.8 ± 10	0.9 ± 14	1.0 ± 22
826	0–5	4.9 ± 6	1.2 ± 10	1.3 ± 12	0.9 ± 16	0.4 ± 34
827	0–5	5.6 ± 8	1.6 ± 4	2.1 ± 12	0.7 ± 14	0.8 ± 42
828	0–5	7.2 ± 6	1.5 ± 10	3.4 ± 6	0.7 ± 6	0.7 ± 102
829	0–5	6.7 ± 6	1.5 ± 14	2.9 ± 10	0.6 ± 12	0.6 ± 30
830	0–5	4.6 ± 6	1.4 ± 14	2.5 ± 8	0.7 ± 10	0.8 ± 30
831	0–5	4.1 ± 6	1.4 ± 14	1.9 ± 12	0.8 ± 14	0.6 ± 46
832	0–5	3.9 ± 6	1.4 ± 8	1.6 ± 14	0.8 ± 12	0.8 ± 38
833	0–5	4.1 ± 8	1.3 ± 10	2.0 ± 12	0.7 ± 20	0.7 ± 60
834	0–5	14. ± 4	1.2 ± 2	4.1 ± 6	0.8 ± 18	0.8 ± 26

[a]See Fig. 8 for sampling locations.

[b]Replicate of 784.

[c]Replicate of 791.

TABLE 12. Plutonium, cesium, and uranium in soil—Site 300.

Location[a]	Sampling depth, cm	µCi/dry g ± 2σ(%) ^{239}Pu (10^{-9})	µCi/dry g ± 2σ(%) ^{137}Cs (10^{-7})	µg/dry g ± 2σ(%) ^{238}U
805	0–5	4.0 ± 8	0.2 ± 6	1.2 ± 63
806[b]	0–5	3.7 ± 19	0.2 ± 34	0.7 ± 28
807	0–5	8.9 ± 8	0.5 ± 4	1.3 ± 22
808	0–5	1.9 ± 14	0.1 ± 10	0.04 ± 64
809	0–5	3.3 ± 10	0.2 ± 8	1.5 ± 16
810	0–5	4.2 ± 10	0.2 ± 8	1.8 ± 24
811	0–5	4.3 ± 10	0.3 ± 7	1.4 ± 35
812	0–5	3.7 ± 11	0.2 ± 8	73. ± 6
813	0–5	0.4 ± 33	0.03 ± 34	1.9 ± 14
814	0–5	5.8 ± 8	0.3 ± 8	1.4 ± 48
815	0–5	2.5 ± 11	0.1 ± 16	4.8 ± 4
816	0–5	6.2 ± 8	0.3 ± 5	1.7 ± 23

[a]See Fig. 9 for sampling locations.
[b]Replicate of 805.

TABLE 13. Various radionuclides in effluents—LLNL and Livermore Water Reclamation Plant.

Month	10^{-6} µCi/ml ± 2σ(%) HTO LLNL	10^{-6} µCi/ml ± 2σ(%) HTO LWRP	10^{-11} µCi/ml ± 2σ(%) ^{137}Cs LLNL	10^{-11} µCi/ml ± 2σ(%) ^{137}Cs LWRP	10^{-12} µCi/ml ± 2σ(%) ^{239}Pu LLNL	10^{-12} µCi/ml ± 2σ(%) ^{239}Pu LWRP
Jan.	12.0 ± 49	3.9 ± 70	40.7 ± 7	5.3 ± 26	250 ± 4	1.3 ± 30
Feb.	4.7 ± 59	1.0 ± 61	66. ± 5	4.5 ± 36	217 ± 6	1.4 ± 34
Mar.	2.2 ± 72	5.9 ± 25	30. ± 9	5.6 ± 30	139 ± 6	1.4 ± 34
Apr.	31.8 ± 20	21.2 ± 18	76.9 ± 4	4.9 ± 39	700 ± 4	1.1 ± 24
May	6.1 ± 44	1.7 ± 62	20. ± 11	5.6 ± 42	74 ± 4	1.2 ± 30
June	5.8 ± 64	0.7 ± 62	91. ± 4	4.3 ± 36	2.3 ± 46	1.2 ± 22
July	42.1 ± 39	3.82 ± 30	67.6 ± 5	4.0 ± 37	1.3 ± 46	1.5 ± 58
Aug.	53.8 ± 24	3.7 ± 42	65.7 ± 5	5.2 ± 30	376 ± 8	2.8 ± 38
Sept.	23.2 ± 40	1.7 ± 51	123. ± 3	4.2 ± 42	93 ± 8	0.2 ± 124
Oct.	101. ± 20	4.2 ± 50	253. ± 3	7.2 ± 39	6470 ± 6	1.1 ± 62
Nov.	4.8 ± 50	4.9 ± 50	26.1 ± 8	5.6 ± 46	1010 ± 7	1.7 ± 46
Dec.	5.3 ± 41	1.1 ± 74	29. ± 8	20. ± 11	1810 ± 7	1.4 ± 34
Annual average	24.4×10^{-6}	4.5×10^{-6}	74.0×10^{-11}	6.4×10^{-11}	929×10^{-12}	1.4×10^{-12}
% SDM	121	123	86	69	196	43
CG	0.1	3.0×10^{-3}	4.0×10^{-4}	2.0×10^{-5}	1.0×10^{-4}	5.0×10^{-6}
% CG	2.4×10^{-2}	15×10^{-2}	1.9×10^{-4}	3.2×10^{-4}	9.3×10^{-4}	2.8×10^{-5}

TABLE 14. Gross alpha activity in water—Livermore Valley.

Location[a]	Number of samples	10^{-9} μCi/ml Maximum	Minimum	Average	% SDM	% CG[b]
11	4	≤3.3	≤2.6	≤2.9	10	≤10
15		≤2.4	≤1.8	≤2.1	13	≤7
16		15.0 ± 16.7	2.6 ± 2.4	≤7.3	91	≤24
19		≤3.4	≤2.4	≤2.8	18	≤9
20		≤2.5	≤0.9	≤1.8	32	≤6
24		≤3.8	≤2.9	≤3.4	11	≤11
26		≤4.5	≤3.3	≤3.8	14	≤13
29		≤3.5	2.4 ± 1.6	≤2.8	19	≤9
31		≤3.9	≤2.4	≤3.2	22	≤11
32		≤3.3	≤1.9	≤2.7	24	≤9
33		4.4 ± 12.1	0.3 ± 3.7	≤2.7	73	≤9
34		8.1 ± 5.6	3.7 ± 4.1	≤5.9	34	≤20

[a]See Fig. 5 for sampling locations.
[b]CG = 3.0×10^{-8} μCi/ml.

TABLE 15. Gross alpha activity in water—Site 300.

Location[a]	Number of samples	10^{-9} μCi/ml Maximum	Minimum	Average	% SDM	% CG[b]
01	3	≤3.7	≤2.8	≤3.2	15	≤11
02		8.4 ± 3.0	2.8 ± 2.7	≤5.2	56	≤17
03		≤4.9	≤2.3	≤3.3	24	≤11
04		46.3 ± 8.4	29.1 ± 8.8	≤35.	29	≤0.2[c]
05		≤5.0	≤3.6	≤4.4	16	≤15
06		≤4.2	≤4.0	≤4.1	3	≤14
07		≤4.3	-2.2 ± 4.6	≤0.9	375	3
11		≤4	-1.3 ± 8.4	≤2.5	102	≤8
14		16.4 ± 6.1	4.3 ± 3.1	≤8.2	75	≤27
20		≤1.6	≤0.8	≤1.4	36	≤5
21		16.8 ± 8.9	≤3.0	≤6.9	95	≤23

[a]See Figs. 6 and 7 for sampling locations.
[b]CG = 3.0×10^{-8} μCi/ml.
[c]Specific analyses of these samples demonstrate that all the activity is due to naturally occurring uranium, for which the concentration guide value is 2.0×10^{-5} μCi/ml.

TABLE 16. Gross beta activity in water—Livermore Valley.

Location[a]	Number of samples	10^{-9} μCi/ml			% SDM	% CG[b]
		Maximum	Minimum	Average		
11	4	<8.2	2.1 ± 2.0	<6.1	57	<2.0
15		<8.6	4.7 ± 2.4	<5.9	31	<2.0
16		<39.8	6.5 ± 2.2	<18.5	100	<6.0
19		<5.7	2.8 ± 1.7	<4.6	31	<1.5
20		<13.3	<3.3	<5.9	58	<2.0
24		8.4 ± 1.8	<3.3	<5.5	39	<1.8
26		6.5 ± 3.9	3.8 ± 1.8	<4.9	24	<1.6
29		<5.1	2.7 ± 2.2	<4.0	30	<1.3
31		<4.0	2.8 ± 2.7	<3.6	16	<1.2
32		<8.0	<2.4	<4.9	49	<1.6
33		7.4 ± 4.5	5.2 ± 2.8	<6.1	16	<2.0
34		12.4 ± 2.1	10.1 ± 2.4	<11.3	14	<3.8

[a]See Fig. 5 for sampling locations.
[b]CG = 3.0×10^{-7} μCi/ml.

TABLE 17. Gross beta activity in water—Site 300.

Location[a]	Number of samples	10^{-9} μCi/ml			% SDM	% CG[b]
		Maximum	Minimum	Average		
01	3	<8.7	5.3 ± 1.9	<7.4	25	<2.5
02	3	<37.2	5.1 ± 3.1	<17.3	100	<5.8
03	9	9.7 ± 2.3	4.6 ± 3.8	<8.0	22	<2.7
04		<47.4	14.9 ± 1.8	<27.7	63	<9.2
05		<32.5	8.1 ± 1.8	<16.7	82	<5.6
06		<8.4	4.0 ± 2.6	<6.2	35	<2.1
07		12.9 ± 3.3	10.9 ± 3.7	12.0	9	3.6
11		<75.5	4.7 ± 4.4	<24.4	140	<8.1
14		21.2 ± 3.2	7.5 ± 3.2	<12.3	49	<4.1
20		<11.8	<2.4	<6.0	71	<2.0
21		16.5 ± 2.9	6.2 ± 3.7	<11.6	37	<3.9

[a]See Figs. 6 and 7 for sampling locations.
[b]CG = 3.0×10^{-7} μCi/ml.

TABLE 18. Tritium (HTO) in water—Livermore Valley.

Location[a]	Number of samples	10^{-7} μCi/ml ± 2σ(%)			% SDM	% CG[b]	Calculated adult whole body dose, mrem
		Maximum	Minimum	Average			
11	4	1.3 ± 6	0.9 ± 9	1.1	20	3.7×10^{-3}	1.1×10^{-2}
15	4	1.2 ± 7	1.0 ± 7	1.1	9	3.7×10^{-3}	1.1×10^{-2}
16	3	2.7 ± 5	1.5 ± 5	2.2	27	7.3×10^{-3}	2.2×10^{-2}
19	4	1.6 ± 6	0.5 ± 15	0.9	52	3.0×10^{-3}	0.9×10^{-2}
20	7	16.8 ± 3	1.5 ± 20	9.8	50	$33. \times 10^{-3}$	9.6×10^{-2}
24	4	2.0 ± 5	1.0 ± 8	1.4	32	4.7×10^{-3}	1.4×10^{-2}
26	4	2.4 ± 6	2.2 ± 5	2.3	4	7.7×10^{-3}	2.2×10^{-2}
29	4	1.1 ± 9	0.7 ± 9	0.9	19	3.0×10^{-3}	0.9×10^{-2}
30	12	1.0 ± 15	0.4 ± 55	0.8	24	2.6×10^{-3}	0.8×10^{-2}
31	4	0.9 ± 10	0.8 ± 8	0.8	4	2.7×10^{-3}	0.8×10^{-2}
32	3	1.4 ± 14	0.7 ± 9	1.0	28	3.4×10^{-3}	1.0×10^{-2}
33	4	1.3 ± 15	0.8 ± 10	1.1	21	3.7×10^{-3}	1.1×10^{-2}
34	2	0.9 ± 7	0.8 ± 9	0.9	7	3.0×10^{-3}	0.9×10^{-2}

[a]See Fig. 5 for sampling locations.
[b]CG = 3.0×10^{-3} μCi/ml.

TABLE 19. Tritium (HTO) in water—Site 300.

Location[a]	Number of samples	10^{-8} μCi/ml ± 2σ(%)			% SDM	% CG[b]	Calculated adult whole body dose, mrem
		Maximum	Minimum	Average			
01	4	9.0 ± 8	2.1 ± 30	4.0	84	1.3×10^{-3}	3.9×10^{-3}
02	4	3.2 ± 22	2.0 ± 27	2.3	24	0.8×10^{-3}	2.2×10^{-3}
03	4	9.0 ± 8	0.7 ± 84	3.6	104	1.2×10^{-3}	3.5×10^{-3}
04	3	2.5 ± 23	0.9 ± 79	1.6	53	0.5×10^{-3}	1.6×10^{-3}
05	4	5.8 ± 16	2.9 ± 23	4.1	30	1.4×10^{-3}	4.0×10^{-3}
06	4	6.8 ± 14	2.1 ± 28	3.6	59	1.2×10^{-3}	3.5×10^{-3}
07	3	7.8 ± 12	2.4 ± 24	4.3	69	1.4×10^{-3}	4.2×10^{-3}
11	4	10.1 ± 20	6.4 ± 11	8.2	19	2.7×10^{-3}	8.0×10^{-3}
14	4	9.1 ± 9	6.6 ± 26	7.7	13	2.6×10^{-3}	7.5×10^{-3}
20	8	12.9 ± 17	3.6 ± 16	8.1	37	2.7×10^{-3}	7.9×10^{-3}
21	4	4.8 ± 14	2.8 ± 22	3.7	26	1.2×10^{-3}	3.6×10^{-3}

[a]See Figs. 6 and 7 for sampling locations.
[b]CG = 3.0×10^{-3} μCi/ml.

TABLE 20. Tritium (HTO) in groundwater—Livermore Valley.

Location[a]	Well identification	Well depth, m	Activity, 10^{-6} μCi/ml $\pm$ 2σ(%)	% CG[b]
1	3S1E-02N2	24	0.329 ± 4	1.1×10^{-2}
2	3S1E-02R1	10	1.53 ± 3	5.1×10^{-2}
	3S1E-03Q1	107	0.475 ± 3	1.6×10^{-2}
4	3S1E-08H4	61	0.097 ± 8	0.3×10^{-2}
5	3S1E-09A1	44	0.020 ± 38	0.07×10^{-2}
	3S1E-09G1	49	0.506 ± 3	1.7×10^{-2}
	3S1E-10A2	27	0.513 ± 3	1.7×10^{-2}
	3S1E-12D2	14	1.31 ± 3	4.4×10^{-2}
9	3S1E-12G1	27	1.57 ± 3	5.2×10^{-2}
10	3S2E-01P2	44	0.033 ± 46	0.1×10^{-2}
11	3S2E-07C2	15	0.256 ± 15	0.9×10^{-2}
12	3S2E-08H2	14	0.078 ± 10	0.3×10^{-2}
13	3S2E-08K2	23	0.135 ± 6	0.5×10^{-2}
14	3S2E-09Q4	24	0.189 ± 5	0.6×10^{-2}
15	3S2E-10Q1	13	0.216 ± 8	0.7×10^{-2}
16	3S2E-14A3	34	0.071 ± 9	0.2×10^{-2}
17	3S2E-15J2	57	0.165 ± 5	0.6×10^{-2}
18	3S2E-16E4	15	0.141 ± 6	0.5×10^{-2}
19	3S2E-22B1	17	0.219 ± 5	0.7×10^{-2}

[a]See Fig. 11 for sampling locations.
[b]CG = 3.0×10^{-3} μCi/ml.

TABLE 21. Tritium (HTO) in vegetation—Livermore Valley.

Location[a]	Number of samples	10^{-7} μCi/ml $\pm$ 2σ(%), water recovered			% SDM	Calculated adult whole body dose, mrem
		Maximum	Minimum	Average		
04	8	11.3 ± 14	3.7 ± 26	5.8	41	5.2×10^{-2}
15	[illegible]	21.3 ± 5	8.0 ± 15	12.1	41	10.8×10^{-2}
16		7.6 ± 16	3.8 ± 27	6.0	23	5.3×10^{-2}
20		19.1 ± 6	6.2 ± 17	12.4	32	11.0×10^{-2}
21		22.3 ± 5	7.9 ± 13	12.8	44	11.4×10^{-2}
22		31.8 ± 4	2.6 ± 44	12.2	80	10.9×10^{-2}
23		40.7 ± 4	9.1 ± 14	22.2	50	19.8×10^{-2}
29	[illegible]	38.5 ± 4	15.3 ± 8	22.9	34	20.4×10^{-2}
30	[illegible]	21.7 ± 7	5.2 ± 19	10.7	55	9.5×10^{-2}
31	8	34.8 ± 5	6.8 ± 18	16.2	67	14.4×10^{-2}

[a]See Fig. 5 for sampling locations.

TABLE 22. Tritium (HTO) in vegetation—Site 300.

Location[a]	Number of samples	10^{-7} μCi/ml ± 2σ(%), water recovered			% SDM	Calculated adult whole body dose, mrem
		Maximum	Minimum	Average		
01	9	7.7 ± 16	0.98 ± 100	4.3	61	3.8×10^{-2}
02	10	7.4 ± 17	1.1 ± 100	4.8	42	4.3×10^{-2}
03	8	6.6 ± 18	1.1 ± 100	3.9	60	3.5×10^{-2}
05		7.4 ± 23	1.9 ± 53	4.8	38	4.3×10^{-2}
06		60.3 ± 3	3.4 ± 30	17.9	118	15.9×10^{-2}
11		8.0 ± 15	1.4 ± 71	4.3	48	3.8×10^{-2}
12		8.9 ± 15	6.8 ± 18	7.7	14	6.9×10^{-2}
13	6	13.8 ± 10	3.2 ± 30	8.6	48	7.7×10^{-2}

[a]See Figs. 6 and 7 for sampling locations.

TABLE 23. Tritium (HTO) in wine.[a]

Location	Number of samples	10^{-6} μCi/ml ± 2σ(%), water recovered			% SDM
		Maximum	Minimum	Average	
Livermore Valley	8	0.41 ± 8	0.10 ± 21	0.24	45
Other California areas	2	0.13 ± 15	0.08 ± 20	0.11	35
Europe	1	2.46 ± 5			

[a]Samples represent vintages ranging from 1977 to 1979.

TABLE 24. Tritium (HTO) in honey.

Location	Number of samples	10^{-6} μCi/ml ± 2σ(%), water recovered			% SDM
		Maximum	Minimum	Average	
Livermore Valley	4	0.510 ± 6	0.195 ± 12	0.30	46
Other California areas	4	0.411 ± 5	0.342 ± 7	0.38	8

TABLE 25. Various radionuclides in milk—Livermore Valley.

	10^{-7} μCi/ml ± 2σ(%)	10^{-6} μCi/ml ± 2σ(%)	10^{-9} μCi/ml ± 2σ(%)
	HTO	^{40}K	^{137}Cs
Number of samples	25	16	16
Maximum	13.0 ± 7	2.3 ± 3	4.9 ± 18
Minimum	1.1 ± 100	1.2 ± 3	1.8 ± 54
Average	4.7	1.6	3.4
% SDM	64	19	29
Calculated adult whole body dose, mrem	2.0×10^{-2}	20.3	7.5×10^{-2}

TABLE 26. Environmental radiation measurements (TLD)—LLNL perimeter.

Location[a]	mrem				
	Jan.-Mar.	Apr.-June	July-Sept.	Oct.-Dec.	Annual[b]
1	15	17	18	14	64
	13	14	17	11	55
	14	18	17	14	63
4	12	15	19	13	59
5[c]	16	19	28	18	81
6	13	16	18	—	63
	10	14	16	12	52
8	12	15	17	13	57
9	11	15	17	13	56
10	15	19	20	15	69
11	15	19	19	15	68
12	15	17	19	15	66
Average	13	17	19	14	63

[a]See Fig. 4 for dosimeter locations.

[b]TLD measurements in the off-site vicinity of the Laboratory (Fig. 12) have a median annual background of 59 mrem. However, subtracting this value from the data above to estimate the contribution from Laboratory operations yields several negative contributions, thus demonstrating that background levels at various perimeter locations cannot be represented by a single value.

[c]As shown in Table 27, neutron dose measurements at Location 5 indicate an additional dose of 85 mrem. A public transportation bus stop on East Avenue is located about 90 m west of Location 5. Neutron measurements at the site perimeter nearest this bus stop (Location 3 in Fig. 4) showed an annual neutron exposure dose of 46 mrem.

TABLE 27. Environmental neutron monitoring—LLNL perimeter.

Location[a]	mrem				
	Jan.-Mar.	Apr.-June	July-Sept.	Oct.-Dec.	Annual
1	5	2	1	8	16
[illegible]	5	[illegible]	[illegible]	4	13
	15			26	46
	5	1	2	2	10
	27	10	26	22	85
	4	1	1	5	11
	7				15
	13				18
Average	10	3	5	9	27

[a]See Fig. 4 for dosimeter locations.

TABLE 28. Beryllium on air filters—LLNL perimeter.

Location[a]	10^{-5} μg/m^3													
	Jan.	Feb.	Mar.	Apr.	May	June	July	Aug.	Sept.	Oct.	Nov.	Dec.	Average	% SDM
01	<2.1	<1.6	<2.2	1.3	1.7	1.6	<1.3	<2.7	<2.2	5.2	2.7	<1.5	<2.2	49
02	<2.3	<1.7	<2.1	1.2	1.4	1.3	<1.1	1.4	1.2	5.5	2.2	1.3	<1.9	64
12	<3.3	<5.7	<2.1	2.3	<2.8	1.4	<2.8	<1.8	<2.8	<2.8	2.8	1.9	<2.7	40
13	<2.0	<1.5	<2.0	1.2	1.4	1.4	<1.2	<1.5	1.2	3.4	<2.3	<1.4	<1.7	37
14	<2.2	<3.4	<2.3	1.8	2.2	2.0	<1.7	<2.1	3.4	2.2	<2.9	<1.8	<2.3	25
15	<2.0	<1.4	<2.0	3.6	3.1	2.9	2.4	2.9	2.4	5.9	2.8	<1.3	<2.7	44
Average	<2.3	<2.6	<2.1	1.9	<2.1	1.8	<1.8	<2.1	<2.2	<4.2	<2.6	<1.5	<2.3	
% SDM	21	67	6	49	35	34	40	30	40	37	11	17		
% Standard[b]	0.2	0.3	0.2	0.2	0.2	0.2	0.2	0.2	0.2	0.4	0.3	0.2	0.2	

[a]See Fig. 4 for sampling locations.
[b]Emission standard is 0.01 μg/m^3.

TABLE 29. Beryllium on air filters—Site 300.

Location[a]	10⁻⁵ μg/m³												Average	% SDM
	Jan.	Feb.	Mar.	Apr.	May	June	July	Aug.	Sept.	Oct.	Nov.	Dec.		
01	<1.4	<1.3	<1.3	1.2	2.7	8.2	<1.6	<2.2	<3.6	—	<7.0	<1.3	<2.9	86
02	<1.4	<1.3	<1.4	2.7	5.0	3.8	<1.5	<1.5	1.2	3.0	<2.9	<8.2	<2.8	75
03	<1.9	<1.7	<2.0	3.5	2.4	2.6	<2.3	<3.6	<2.0	2.3	<2.5	<2.0	<2.4	25
04	<2.5	<3.0	<2.9	4.2	3.2	1.4	<1.9	<2.3	<1.9	<3.0	2.1	<4.7	<2.8	36
05	<1.6	<1.6	<2.0	2.6	3.9	3.7	1.6	5.0	5.0	4.9	7.1	3.5	<3.5	49
07	<0.7	<1.7	<1.6	1.7	2.6	1.2	<2.3	<3.2	<1.9	<2.0	2.2	<1.5	<1.9	37
08	<1.7	<1.6	<1.6	3.4	2.4	1.4	<3.3	<2.6	<1.9	<2.1	2.0	<1.6	<2.1	33
09	<1.7	<1.8	<1.5	1.4	2.2	2.0	<1.6	<2.5	<1.4	4.1	2.0	<1.6	<2.0	40
10	<1.8	<0.7	<2.6	3.8	2.5	4.3	<3.5	3.5	<2.6	2.4	2.8	<2.1	<2.7	37
11	<2.2	<2.1	<2.3	2.2	<2.1	1.2	<7.1	<3.4	<2.1	<2.0	<2.2	<2.2	<2.6	58
Average	<1.7	<1.7	<1.9	2.7	<2.9	3.0	<2.7	<3.0	<2.5	<2.9	<3.3	<2.9	<2.6	
% SDM	29	35	26	37	31	73	63	33	48	34	61	76		
% Standard[b]	0.2	0.2	0.2	0.3	0.3	0.3	0.3	0.3	0.3	0.3	0.3	0.3	0.3	

[a]See Fig. 6 for sampling locations.

[b]Emission standard is 0.01 $\mu g/m^3$.

TABLE 30. Various elements in LLNL liquid effluent.

Month	ppm							
	Cd	Cr	Cu	Fe	Pb	Ni	Ag	Zn
Jan.	0.01	0.39	2.3	0.19	0.08	0.12	0.10	0.61
Feb.	0.01	0.35	1.4	4.3	0.06	0.07	0.09	2.07
Mar.	0.01	0.28	1.5	2.3	0.07	0.90	0.12	1.16
Apr.	0.01	0.27	0.67	2.0	0.03	0.05	0.02	0.41
May	0.01	0.35	1.6	3.1	0.07	0.05	0.11	0.53
June	0.01	0.34	0.26	2.7	0.15	0.07	0.16	0.53
July	0.01	0.23	2.0	2.0	0.11	0.06	0.10	0.57
Aug.	0.01	0.27	1.3	1.9	0.07	0.06	0.03	0.53
Sept.	0.01	0.21	1.1	2.5	0.04	0.06	0.01	0.55
Oct.	<0.01	0.24	0.93	3.3	0.05	0.03	0.01	0.45
Nov.	<0.01	0.22	0.09	0.80	0.02	0.01	0.03	0.27
Dec.	<0.01	0.21	0.08	0.55	0.01	0.01	0.02	0.24
Average	<0.01	0.28	1.10	2.14	0.06	0.12	0.07	0.66
% SDM	0	21	65	56	67	208	71	76

TABLE 31. Physical and chemical examinations of LLNL liquid effluent.

	mg/l					
Analysis	Jan.-Mar.	Apr.-June	July-Sept.	Oct.-Dec.	Average	% SDM
BOD	90	120	78	46	84	37
COD	203	470	220	135	257	57
Total nitrogen (as N)	33	39	33	29	34	12
Ammonia nitrogen (as N)	24	23	31	23	25	15
Nitrate nitrogen (as N)	<0.01	<0.01	<0.01	<0.01	<0.01	
Nitrite nitrogen (as N)	<0.014	0.039	0.03	<0.01	<0.02	58
Oil and grease (FEM)	<5	24	17	8	14	64
Sulfate	49	49	70	44	53	22
Arsenic	0.0014	0.0025	0.0034	0.0011	0.0021	50
Boron	0.66	0.76	0.87	0.47	0.69	25
Cyanide	0.20	0.16	<0.01	<0.02	0.10	99
Mercury	0.0040	0.0069	0.0024	0.0011	0.0036	69
Selenium	<0.0005	<0.0005	<0.0005	<0.0005	<0.0005	
Total alkalinity	126	121	105	107	115	9
Total phosphorus (as P)	5.4	6.5	4.5	4.5	5.2	18
Chloride	32	21	35	31	30	20
Phenols	0.031	0.018	0.036	0.017	0.026	37
Calcium	11	9.9	13	9.6	11	14
Magnesium	3.2	1.6	2.1	2.9	2.5	30
Sodium	33	30	28	29	30	7
Potassium	20	19	22	15	19	15
Sodium (as % of cations)	52	54	49	63	55	11
Total solids	290	362	300	248	300	16
Dissolved solids	208	202	217	190	204	6
Suspended solids	56	225	92	43	104	80
Volatile solids	119	179	103	127	132	25
Settleable solids (ml/l/hr)	2.0	7.5	2.5	<0.1	3.0	104
Identifiable chlorinated hydrocarbons	<LOS[a]	<LOS[b]	<LOS	<LOS		
PCB(ppb)	0.2 (1254)	<LOS	<LOS	<LOS		

[a]Exception is 0.2 ppb of technical chlordane (LOS = 0.10 ppb).

[b]Exceptions are 0.48 ppb of Aldrin (LOS = 0.05 ppb) and 0.36 ppb Heptachlor epoxide (LOS = 0.05 ppb).

TABLE 32. Estimated radiation dose to the public from LLNL airborne effluents during 1980.

Nuclide	Facility	Curies	Dose at site boundary, mrem	Dose to nearest resident, mrem	Dose within 80-km radius of LLNL, man-rem
^{41}Ar	Livermore pool-type reactor	165	1.3	0.26	0.31
^{3}H	Tritium facility	2218	0.39	0.31	1.3
^{3}H	Insulating core accelerator	70	0.06	0.05	0.04
^{3}H	Rotating target neutron source	17	0.009	0.004	0.01
^{13}N-^{15}O	Linear accelerator	1656	2.10	0.56	0.16

TABLE 33. Radioactive effluent releases from LLNL from 1976 through 1980.

Year	Airborne effluents, Ci			Liquid effluents, Ci	
	^{41}Ar	^{3}H	^{13}N-^{15}O	HTO	^{239}Pu
1976	470	3991	1035	10	1.5×10^{-4}
1977	380	5210	990	13	3.6×10^{-4}
1978	766	5362	1445	9	8.6×10^{-4}
1979	383	4517	829	7	9.8×10^{-4}
1980	165	2305	1656	5	2.8×10^{-4}

TABLE 34. Summary of analyses for the Quality Assurance Program.[a]

Isotope	Media	Period[b]	LLL	EML	All	LLNL/EML	LLNL/All
^{137}Cs	Air		0.312	0.257	0.271	1.21	1.15
^{134}Cs	Air		0.313	0.247	0.258	1.27	1.21
^{239}Pu	Air	1	0.128	0.120	0.128	1.07	1.00
		2	0.212	0.246	0.228	0.86	0.93
^{239}Pu	Soil	1	0.510	0.563	0.529	0.91	0.96
		2	0.950	0.900	0.984	1.06	0.97
^{3}H	Water	1	0.946	1.03	1.04	0.92	0.91
		2	0.132	0.149	0.147	0.89	0.90
^{239}Pu	Water		0.410	0.577	0.417	0.71	0.98
^{238}Pu	Water		0.680	0.830	0.689	0.82	0.99
Non-radioactive elements[c]							
Cu	Air		0.600	0.600	0.564	1.00	1.06
Zn	Air		0.605	0.600	0.611	1.01	0.99
Mg	Air		0.263	0.240	0.255	1.09	1.03
Cu	Water		0.120	0.120	0.123	1.00	0.98
Zn	Water		0.120	0.120	0.122	1.00	0.98
Mg	Water		0.210	0.200	0.199	1.05	1.06

[a]All of the values shown are relative; i.e., the exponents are not included, and therefore do not indicate total activity or concentration levels.

[b]Sampling frequency decreased from quarterly to semiannually during 1980.

[c]Analytical results for second set of non-radioactive elements were lost.

APPENDIX B. ENVIRONMENTAL ACTIVITY CONCENTRATION—GUIDE LEVELS

The standards for Radiation Protection (ERDA Manual Chapter 0524, issued March 3, 1977) state that the average activity of a mixture of radionuclides (whose identities and concentrations are unknown) in air and water should not exceed the following values:

1. Air (controlled area)	6×10^{-12} μCi/ml
2. Air (uncontrolled area)	2×10^{-14} μCi/ml
3. Water (controlled area)	4×10^{-7} μCi/ml
4. Water (uncontrolled area)	3×10^{-8} μCi/ml

If alpha emitters and ^{227}Ac are definitely not present, the following values may be used to determine permissible average activity:

5. Air (controlled area)	3×10^{-11} μCi/ml
6. Air (uncontrolled area)	1×10^{-12} μCi/ml

If ^{129}I, ^{226}Ra, and ^{228}Ra are definitely not present, the following values may be used:

7. Water (controlled area)	3×10^{-6} μCi/ml
8. Water (uncontrolled area)	1×10^{-7} μCi/ml

Both air and water samples are subjected to gross alpha and gross beta measurements. The average annual alpha activities of samples may not exceed the activity values listed as 1–4 above. Since the alpha emitters have been accounted for in the gross alpha measurements and the assumption is made that ^{129}I, ^{227}Ac, ^{226}Ra, and ^{228}Ra are not present in the samples, the average annual gross beta activities of the samples may not exceed the activities listed as 5–8 above. The assumption that ^{129}I, ^{227}Ac, ^{226}Ra, and ^{228}Ra are not present in air and water samples is reasonable in view of the minute quantities of these radionuclides available at the Laboratory. Chapter 0524 of the ERDA Manual also states that average tritium activities in off-site water samples may not exceed 3×10^{-3} μCi/ml.

The external whole-body radiation dose to workers in controlled areas may not exceed 5 rem/y, and the dose to an individual in an uncontrolled area may not exceed 500 mrem/y. Also, a group of individuals in an uncontrolled area may not receive an average annual dose of more than 170 mrem.

APPENDIX C. METHOD OF DOSE CALCULATIONS

The doses shown in this report have been calculated using the models and methods in the Nuclear Regulatory Commission Regulatory Guide 1.109, "Calculating Annual Doses to Man from Routine Releases of Reactor Effluent." Examples of these calculations and assumptions are shown in this appendix.

ANNUAL DOSE FROM POTABLE WATER

Assuming that all water sampled is available as drinking water, the annual whole body dose for tritium has been calculated using the following equation:

$$R_{total\ body} = C_w U_w D_w \quad . \tag{1}$$

where

C_w = concentration in pCi/l,
U_w = intake rate, l/yr,
= 730 l/yr for maximum exposed individual,
D_w = dose factor, mrem/pCi,
= 1.05×10^{-7} mrem/pCi for the whole body ingestion pathway for an adult.

$R_{total\ body}$ = annual dose in mrem to the total body from ingestion of 730 litres of potable water with concentration C_w.

ANNUAL DOSE FROM FORAGE–COW–MILK PATHWAY FOR TRITIUM IN VEGETATION

Assuming that all the feed for the cattle was pasture grass, the annual whole body dose per μCi/ml HTO for the maximum exposed individual has been calculated using the following equation:

$$D_{total\ body} = D_{veg} + D_{meat} + D_{milk} \quad . \tag{2}$$

$$D_{veg}\ \text{(leafy vegetables)} = U_{veg} \times C_{veg} \times D_{HTO} \ , \tag{2a}$$

where

U_{veg} = intake rate, kg/yr, = 64 kg/yr, for maximum exposed individual,

C_{veg} = concentration in pCi/kg = $\dfrac{\text{pCi/kg}}{\mu\text{Ci/ml}} \times C_{veg}\ \mu$Ci/ml (measured),

D_{HTO} = dose factor, mrem/pCi = 1.05×10^{-17} mrem/pCi for ^3H for the adult whole body ingestion pathway.

$$D_{meat} = U_{meat} \times C_{meat} \times D_{HTO} \quad , \qquad (2b)$$

where

U_{meat} = 110 kg/yr,

D_{HTO} = 1.05 X 10^{-7} mrem/pCi,

C_{meat} = $(F_f)(Q_f)(C_{veg}) \exp(-\lambda_i t_s)$,

F_f = fraction of daily intake of nuclide per kg of animal/fish, days/kg,

Q_f = amount of feed consumed, kg/day,

$$C_{meat} = \left(1.2 \times 10^{-2} \frac{day}{kg}\right)\left(50 \frac{kg}{day}\right)\left(3 \times 10^{9} \frac{pCi/kg}{\mu Ci/ml}\right)$$

$$\times \exp[-4.5 \times 10^{-3}(20)] \quad , \quad = 1.8 \times 10^{9} \frac{pCi/kg}{\mu Ci/ml} \times C_{veg} \frac{\mu Ci}{ml} \text{ (measured)},$$

C_{veg} = same as above,

λ_i = radiological decay constant, day^{-1},

t_s = time between slaughter to consumption, days

$$D_{milk} = U_{milk} \times C_{milk} \times D_{HTO} \quad , \qquad (2c)$$

where

U_{milk} = 310 l/yr,

D_{HTO} = 1.05 X 10^{-7} mrem/pCi,

C_{milk} = $F_m Q_f C_{veg} \exp(-\lambda_i tf)$,

F_m = fraction of daily intake of nuclide per litre of milk, day/litre),

Q_f = amount of feed consumed, kg/day,

C_{veg} = same as above,

λ_i = radiological decay constant, $days^{-1}$,

t_f = transport time from the feed to milk receptor,

$$C_{milk} = \left(1.0 \times 10^{-2} \frac{day}{l}\right)\left(50 \frac{kg}{d}\right)\left(3 \times 10^{9} \frac{pCi/kg}{\mu Ci/ml}\right)$$

$$\times \exp[-4.5 \times 10^{3}(2)] = 1.5 \times 10^{9} \frac{pCi/l}{\mu Ci/ml} \times C_{veg} \frac{\mu Ci}{ml} \text{ (measured)}.$$

$$D_{total} = \left(2.04 \times 10^{4} \frac{mrem}{\mu Ci/ml}\right) veg + \left(2.07 \times 10^{4} \frac{mrem}{\mu Ci/ml}\right) meat$$

$$+ \left(4.88 \times 10^{4} \frac{mrem}{\mu Ci/ml}\right) milk = 8.96 \times 10^{4} \frac{mrem}{\mu Ci/ml} \times C_{veg} \frac{\mu Ci}{ml} \text{ (measured)}.$$

ANNUAL POPULATION DOSE

To calculate the "fence-line" site boundary, nearest resident, and population doses, a continuous point source computer code based on the Gaussian plume model was used.

$$C_{downwind} = 3.17 \times 10^4 (\chi/Q)(Q) , \quad (3)$$

where

χ/Q = diffusion parameter, sec/m^3 ,

Q = release rate , Ci/yr,

$3.17 \times 10^4 = 1 \times 10^{12} \frac{pCi}{Ci} \Big/ 3.15 \times 10^7 \frac{sec}{yr}$,

$C_{downwind}$ = concentration downwind, pCi/m^3.

$$D_{max\ individual} = U \times C_{downwind} \times D , \quad (4)$$

where

U = intake rate, m^3/yr = 8000 m^3/yr, inhalation rate for adult maximum exposed individual ,

$C_{downwind}$ = $3.17 \times 10^4 (\chi/Q)(Q)$,

D = dose factor, mrem/pCi ,

for ^3H, $D = 1.58 \times 10^{-7} \frac{mrem}{pCi}$,

for ^{41}Ar, $D = 8.84 \times 10^{-3} \frac{mrem - m^3}{pCi - yr}$,

(Inhalation rate is included in the dose factor.)

for ^{15}O, $D = D(^{41}Ar) \times \frac{1.74}{1.2}$

for ^{13}N, $D = D(^{41}Ar)$

$D_{max\ individual}$ = mrem/yr .

For population dose, the diffusion factors and population figures for an area within 80 km of the Laboratory were summed over all directions.

$$\text{Dose (man-rem)} = 3.17 \times 10^4 \left[\sum_i^n (\chi/Q)_i P_i\right] Q\, U\, D , \quad (5)$$

where

$\left[\sum_i^n (\chi/Q)_i P_i\right]$ = Summation of the (χ/Q) for region i times the population in region i for all regions n, $\frac{man\text{-}sec}{m^3}$,

Q = release rate, Ci/yr ,

U = inhalation rate, average individual (adult) ,

D = dose factor, rem/pCi ,

Dose = man-rem .

APPENDIX D. DISCHARGE LIMITS TO THE SANITARY SEWER SYSTEM OF THE CITY OF LIVERMORE

Sections 18.63 and 18.66 of the Code of the City of Livermore (1959) state the discharge limits for Livermore's sanitary sewer system. These limits are as follows:

Section 18.63

No person shall discharge, or cause to be discharged, except for salt waste discharge from water softener units of any kind or description installed and in operation on or before January 31, 1966, which are regenerated by the owner thereof at the place of use of such units, any of the following described water or wastes to any public sewer unless the customer obtains a permit from the city in accordance with Section 18.65.

(a) Any liquor or vapor having a temperature higher than one hundred fifty degrees Fahrenheit.

(b) Any waters or wastes which contain more than two hundred ppm of fat, oil or grease that is petroleum ether soluble.

(c) Any gasoline, benzene, naphtha, fuel oil or other inflammable or explosive liquid, solid or gas.

(d) Any garbage, except properly ground with a mechanical garbage grinder. Specifically excluded from the sewers are waste products resulting from the handling, storage and sale of fruits and vegetables from other than retail produce establishments, or other foods not intended primarily for immediate consumption.

(e) Any ashes, cinders, sand, mud, straw, shavings, metal, glass, rags, feathers, tar, coal tar, asphalt, cement, plastics, woods, paunch manure or any other solid viscous substance capable of causing obstruction to the flow in sewers or other interferences with the proper economical operation of the sewage works.

(f) Any wastes or water with a pH lower than six and eight-tenths or higher than eight.

(g) Any waters or wastes containing total dissolved solid increments greater than three hundred and twenty-five ppm, nor chloride increments greater than seventy-five ppm, increase during a single cycle use of the water supply.

(h) Any water or wastes having a B.O.D. greater than three hundred ppm (the average B.O.D. for residential users).

(i) Any waters or wastes containing more than three hundred ppm of suspended solids (the average suspended solids for residential users).

(j) Any waters intended to be used or used to dilute waste discharge to avoid violation of the above limitation (Order No. 586, paragraph 1).

Section 18.66

No person shall discharge or cause to be discharged any radioactive wastes into any public sewers, except where:

A. The waste is discharged in strict conformity with current Atomic Energy Commission recommendations for safe disposal of radioactive wastes.

B. The discharging of radioactive waste will not cause injury to personnel or damage to the sewer works. Any person discharging a radioactive waste to a public sewer in accordance with the provisions of the preceding paragraph shall submit to the council such report as the council may deem necessary.

In the event of an accidental spill of any radioactive material into the public sewer, the person responsible shall (a) immediately notify the plant superintendent, and (b) render such technical or other assistance to the department of public works within his power to prevent the sewage works from becoming contaminated with radioactivity.

APPENDIX E

UCID- 17853

Lawrence Livermore Laboratory

SAMPLING AND ANALYTICAL PROCEDURES FOR ENVIRONMENTAL MONITORING AT LAWRENCE LIVERMORE LABORATORY

C. L. Lindeken, K. M. Wong, G. L. Seibel, and K. S. Griggs

July 14, 1978

This is an informal report intended primarily for internal or limited external distribution The opinions and conclusions stated are those of the author and may or may not be those of the laboratory
Prepared for U S Department of Energy under contract No W-7405-Eng-48

SAMPLING AND ANALYTICAL PROCEDURES FOR ENVIRONMENTAL MONITORING AT LAWRENCE LIVERMORE LABORATORY

ABSTRACT

Described herein are sample collection and analysis procedures employed in environmental monitoring at the Lawrence Livermore Laboratory. An integral part of the quality assurance program developed for environmental monitoring at Livermore, these procedures provide a basis for verifying that sampling and analytical activities are being performed as specified.

INTRODUCTION

Written procedures have been prepared for each environmental montoring activity at Livermore as part of the quality assurance program developed for environmental monitoring at Lawrence Livermore Laboratory (LLL). The sample collection and analysis procedures described herein have been reviewed and approved by those responsible for managing the monitoring program. During a program audit, such written documentation can be used to verify that sampling and analytical procedures meet program specifications.

The "Sampling" sections of this report describe the sampling procedures used for each sample medium monitored. A general description of each medium is usually provided. This is followed by the collection procedure used, provisions for sample identification, and a schedule for sample replication.

The "Analysis" sections of this report cover sample analysis. General comments on each sample medium analyzed are followed by specific descriptions of standards and calibrations, analytical procedures, and/or counting procedures as applicable for each medium.

AIR SAMPLING

Continuously operating air samplers are used at LLL to measure the concentration of airborne particulate radioactivity, beryllium, and tritiated water. Samplers placed at 6 perimeter locations at LLL and at 10 locations at Site 300 measure particulate radioactivity and beryllium. Particulate radioactivity is also measured at 10 off-site locations near the

Laboratory. Tritiated water samplers are operated at the six LLL perimeter locations and at two off-site locations. In all cases, samplers are so placed as to provide reasonable assurance that any significant concentration of effluents from Laboratory operations would be detected regardless of local meteorology.

Collection

Particulates

LLL perimeter and Site 300 particulate samples are collected on 5.2- x 10^{-2} -m^2 Whatman filters, using average flow rates of 700 ℓ/min. Off-site samplers in the Livermore Valley use 4.6- x 10^{-3}-m^2 Flanders F-700 glassfiber filters operated at a flow rate of 80 ℓ/min. Particulate sample flow rates are calibrated with a spirometer that has been calibrated against an immersion unit certified by the National Bureau of Standards. Flow rates of Hi-vol air samplers are verified at monthly intervals with a portable field-calibration unit.

Tritiated Water

Samples of tritiated water vapor are collected by drawing air through silica-gel-packed columns at flow rates of about 0.5 ℓ/min. Columns are exchanged weekly.

Identification

Particulates

Particulate samplers are run continuously, and sample filters are exchanged weekly. Each filter is identified by location, date on, date off, elapsed sampling time, and flow rate. Filter samples are placed in glassine envelopes and are transported to the laboratory, where this information is transferred to log sheets and each sample is given a serial number that accompanies it during analysis. Half of each LLL perimeter and Site 300 filter is used for beryllium analysis; the other half is retained for radioactivity measurements.

Tritiated Water

Tritiated water vapor samplers are run continuously, and silica-gel holders are exchanged biweekly. Each sample is identified by location, date on, date off, elapsed sampling time, and flow rate. This information is transferred to log sheets in the laboratory, and each sample is given a serial number that accompanies it during analysis.

Replication

Particulates

At bimonthly intervals, a particulate air sampler is operated in parallel with the permanent sampler at one of the six LLL perimeter locations. This parallel operation is continued for one month, filters are changed weekly, and both filters are submitted for analysis in the usual manner. Bimonthly rotation of the extra sampler among the six locations ensures samplers are checked annually. The replicate samples are then compared with respect to gross alpha and beta activities and to ^{239}Pu content.

Tritiated Water

Parallel samples of tritiated water vapor are collected at LLL perimeter locations during alternate months from those locations in which particulate replicates are being collected.

SOIL SAMPLING

Soil samples are collected annually within the Livermore Valley and at Site 300. Radiochemical analysis of these samples serves to document any changes that may have occurred during the year. Increases in radioactivity that may result from Laboratory operations are brought to the public's attention through annual monitoring reports.

Collection

Sampling sites are selected in reasonably level areas that represent undisturbed soil. A 2-m square is marked off with each such area, and an 8.25-cm-diam coring tool designed at LLL is used to collect 5-cm-deep samples at the corners and center of the square.[1]

Identification

The five samples of soil collected from each 2-m square are placed in plastic bags and are identified by number. This number is entered in a log book, together with the sampling data and a description of the sample location. The number is used to identify the sample throughout the laboratory analysis and in the annual monitoring report.

Replication

During each annual collection of soil samples, at least 10% of the sites are sampled in duplicate. In such collections, two adjacent 5-cm-deep cores are taken from the corners and center of each 2-m square. Separate composites of the five cores are then made, and the composites are identified by successive numbers.

WATER SAMPLING

At quarterly intervals, water samples from various sources in the Livermore Valley and at Site 300 are analyzed for gross alpha and beta radioactivity and for tritium content. These analyses are performed to determine if detectable changes in radioactivity have occurred.

Collection

Grab samples of such surface sources as ponds, creeks, and reservoirs are obtained with a tethered plastic pail. The samples are transferred to 4-l plastic containers to which 6.5 mℓ of concentrated HCl has been added. For tritium analyses, a 1-ℓ sample is collected in an argon-flushed glass container fitted with a ground-glass stopper.

Identification

As samples are collected in the field, they are tagged with sampling location and date. In the laboratory, each sample is assigned the number that accompanies it during analysis.

Replication

During each sample collection period, at least 10% of the water samples are duplicates.

SEWAGE SAMPLING

Sewage from the Laboratory is discharged into the City of Livermore's sanitary sewer system. Radioactive or otherwise hazardous liquid wastes are first treated to reduce concentration levels to within applicable standards before they are released into the sanitary sewer. Sewage samples are collected from LLL effluent and from the treated effluent of the Livermore Water Reclamation Plant (LWRP). Quarterly samples are also collected from the Site 300 sewage-oxidation pond.

Collection

LLL Effluent

A 24-hr composite of LLL sewage effluent is collected daily by a motorized proportional sampler. Aliquots of this composite are transported to the laboratory in 500-mℓ, wide-mouth polyethylene bottles.

LWRP Effluent

Daily composites of treated effluent from the LWRP are also collected by a proportional sampler. Aliquots of these composites are placed in 500-mℓ polyethylene bottles and are retained for weekly collection by LLL.

Site 300 Sewage-Oxidation Pond

Grab samples of the Site 300 sewage-oxidation pond are collected quarterly in 3.78-ℓ polyethylene containers.

Identification

As each sewage sample is collected in the field, it is tagged with the sampling location and date of sampling. In the laboratory, each sample is assigned a number that accompanies it during analysis.

Replication

LLL Effluent

Every Wednesday, one replicate sample of LLL effluent is taken for gross alpha, beta, and tritium. For one month each year, duplicate samples of LLL effluent are taken each day to permit preparation of duplicate monthly composites.

LWRP Effluent

One replicate sample of LWRP effluent is taken every Wednesday and is analyzed for gross alpha, beta, and tritium. For one month each year, duplicate samples are taken each day to permit preparation of duplicate monthly composites.

VEGETATION SAMPLING

At monthly intervals, samples of vegetation (usually native grasses) are collected throughout the Livermore Valley, at Site 300, and at the off-site locations near Site 300. After these samples are freeze dried, the tritium content of the recovered water is determined with liquid scintillation counting.

Collection

Samples of vegetation are routinely collected from the same locations each sampling period. Grass samples are pulled up or cut close to the ground, and any soil is discarded. The bulk volume of these samples is usually between 0.5 and 1 ℓ. As each sample is collected, it is placed in a plastic bag and frozen in a dry-ice chest to minimize water loss on the bag surface. The duplicate samples collected at each location are later transferred to a freezer in the laboratory.

Identification

Samples of vegetation collected in the field are tagged according to sample type and location. In the laboratory, each sample is assigned a number that accompanies it until the measurement is reported. Measurement data are permanently retained on computer cards.

Replication

Two samples of vegetation are collected at each location in case the first sample is lost during analysis or the measurement is in question. At least one set of each group of samples collected is analyzed in duplicate to furnish replicate measurement data.

MILK SAMPLING

Milk samples are obtained at monthly intervals from two goat farms located about 5 km south and 5 southeast of the Laboratory. A 3-ℓ portion of each milk sample is vacuum distilled, and the tritium content of the distilled water is determined by liquid scintillation. Each 3-ℓ sample is then concentrated by evaporation and gamma counted.

AIR ANALYSIS

Environmental air samples are analyzed for gross alpha and beta activity and for various gamma-emitting radionuclides, plutonium isotopes, uranium isotopes and beryllium.

Gross Alpha and Beta Counting

After a four-day delay to allow for decay of the radon-thoron daughters, all environmental-radioactivity air filters are counted for alpha and beta activity. Counting is done in a Sharp gas-proportional counter using 20-min counting periods. Normally, this counter is used only for environmental samples since a duplicate counting system is provided for routine samples.

Standards and Calibration

Separate ^{239}Pu and ^{90}Sr standards on 5-cm-diam stainless steel convoluted planchets are used for determining alpha and beta counting efficiencies, respectively. These standards are traceable to NBS or to equivalent certified sources. Counting efficiency measurements are made with each set of filters counted, and a background count is taken at the beginning of each run and between each set of 10 samples. Records are kept of background and counting efficiency variations in the Sharp counter.

Gamma Counting

Monthly composites of Laboratory perimeter and Site 300 filters are analyzed for specific gamma-emitting radionuclides. These filters are sealed in 210-cm^3, thin-walled aluminum cans and are counted for nominal 1000-min periods. Counting is done with an 80-cm^3, low-background Ge(Li) spectrometer that is equipped with a background-suppression system.[2]

Standards and Calibration

Low-level uranium-ore (New Brunswick) and NBS river-sediment standards are used periodically to check counting system response. Efficiency calibration checks are made with calibrated sources supplied by the International Association of Environmental Analysts (LAEA), the Environmental Monitoring Laboratory (EML), or NBS.

^{238}Pu, ^{239}Pu

Following gamma counting, the monthly composite of Laboratory perimeter filters is divided according to sampling location. This composite and that from Site 300 are dry ashed in a 450°C muffle furnace. Ashed samples are then dissolved with a HNO_3-HF-H_2O_2 mixture and are equilibrated with a standardized cesium carrier and tracer amounts of ^{242}Pu and ^{233}U. This solution is made 8N with HNO_3, the plutonium is oxidized to PU^{+4} with $NaNO_2$, and the plutonium, cesium, and uranium radionuclides are separated by anion-exchange techniques.

The ^{137}Cs is collected first in the 8N fraction. Then the plutonium is eluted with a mixture of concentrated HCl-NH_4I, and the uranium fraction is eluted with 0.1N HCl.

The plutonium fraction is purified by a second anion-exchange separation and is electrodeposited on a platinum disc. Then, ^{238}Pu and ^{239}Pu are determined by alpha spectrometry.

Standards and Calibration

The LLL Heavy Element Group purifies and calibrates internal tracer ^{242}Pu by means of mass spectrometry.[3] Alpha spectrometry is also used to periodically calibrate ^{242}Pu against ^{236}Pu and ^{239}Pu standards from EML.

^{137}Cs

The cesium fraction collected in the plutonium separation is heated to evaporate excess acid. After it is diluted with water, sodium hydroxide (NaOH) is added to bring the pH to 2-3 and the cesium is extracted with ammonium molybdophosphate. The cesium is further purified by ion exchange with a Bio-Rex 40 cation-exchange resin and is then precipitated as Cs_2PtCl_6 for yield correction. The precipitate is mounted for ^{137}Cs determination and is counted in a low-background beta counter.

Standards and Calibration

Standard solutions of ^{137}Cs from EML, LLL, and commercial laboratories are used to prepare efficiency and self-absorption counting standards to calibrate low-background beta detectors.

^{235}U, ^{238}U

The uranium fraction from plutonium separation is converted to sulfate by evaporating to dryness and by fuming with H_2SO_4. Further purification is obtained with anion exchange in sulfate form. Then ^{235}U and ^{238}U are determined with isotopic-dilution mass spectrometry.[4]

Standards and Calibration

The mass spectrometer is calibrated with NBS uranium sources containing certified quantities of ^{235}U, the balance being ^{238}U. Mass values are, as noted, based on the use, of ^{233}U, and semiannual alpha spectrometry measurements are employed to verify its purity.

HTO

Water vapor samples are collected biweekly at LLL perimeter locations by silica-gel samplers operated at flow rates of about 0.5 ℓ/min. The collected water is recovered by vacuum drying at 150°C, and the HTO is measured by liquid scintillation counting.

Standards and Calibration

A primary HTO standard is obtained from NBS. The calibration curve for each counting set is made from eight replicate measurements of a dilution of this primary standard, and the background is determined from eight replicate measurements of a deep-well water sample.

Beryllium

Every month, half of each weekly LLL perimeter and Site 300 paper air filter is composited by sampling location. Two paper filters at a time are wet ashed with a mixture of 80% nitric and 20% perchloric acid. The solutions are then evaporated to 1-2 ml, taking care not to allow samples to bake dry. After the samples are diluted with water, they are filtered, any residues are discarded, and the filtrates are diluted to 25 ml with demineralized water.

Standards and Calibration

Beryllium standards are prepared with 0.5 and 1-μg of beryllium per 25 ml of solution. The recorder readout of the Model 306 Perkin Elmer atomic absorption spectrophotometer is set at 30× absorbance expansion, and the spectrophotometer is zeroed while aspirating deionized water into the flame. Instrument responses from the 0.5- and 1-μg beryllium standards are then recorded. Following these calculations, the response of each monthly composite is recorded and its beryllium content is calculated from the calibration data.

SOIL ANALYSIS

Each soil sample collected in accordance with the "Gamma Counting" section below is dried to constant weight at 110°C, is pulverized in a mechanical grinder, and is screened through a 32-mesh screen to remove pebbles and dry vegetation. The sample is then blended, and aliquots are taken for various analyses.

Gamma Counting

Approximately 300 g of the pulverized and blended soil sample is sealed in a 210-cm^3, thin-walled aluminum can. It is then counted for a nominal 1000 min in the low-background gamma counter for gamma emitters and ^{238}U.[2]

Standards and Calibration

Low-level uranium-ore (New Brunswick) and NBS river-sediment standards are used periodically to check counting system response. Efficiency calibration checks are made with calibrated sources supplied by IAEA, EML, or NBS.

^{238}Pu, ^{239}Pu

Tracer ^{242}Pu is added to a 100- to 500-g aliquot of soil sample prepared as previously indicated in the first paragraph of the "Soil Analysis" section of this paper. The sample is then acid leached with HNO_3-HCl acid, using the EML soil-leach method.[5] Plutonium isotopes are separated, purified, and analyzed in accordance with the "Air Analysis" section on ^{238}Pu and ^{239}Pu.

^{235}U, ^{238}U

In addition to the ^{238}U data obtained from gamma measurement ("Soil Analysis" section on gamma counting), natural isotopic content and depleted uranium concentration are also determined by isotopic-dilution mass spectrometry in certain selected samples. These samples are analyzed in a manner similar to the procedure given in the "Air Analysis" section on ^{238}Pu and ^{239}Pu and on ^{235}U and ^{238}U.

WATER ANALYSIS

Environmental water samples are analyzed for gross alpha and beta activity and for tritium content.

Gross Alpha and Beta Activity

Each 500-mℓ water sample is acidified with HNO_3. Then 30% H_2O_2 is added, and the sample is evaporated to near dryness and transferred to 5-cm-diam planchets of convoluted stainless steel. After drying and flaming, the sample is counted for 30 min in a Nuclear-Chicago proportional counter.

Standards and Calibration

The ^{239}Pu and ^{90}Sr standards are used with every sample set (see the "Soil Analysis" section on standards and calibration). Instrument background measurements are made between evey 10 sample-counting measurements.

HTO

Samples collected in argon-flushed glass bottles are distilled under argon. A 250-mℓ aliquot of sample is electrolytically enriched, using the enrichment technique described by Ostlund.[6] Following enrichment, the HTO content of the sample is determined with either liquid-scintillation or internal gas-proportional counting.

Standards and Calibration

Each enrichment set contains duplicate aliquots of the secondary HTO standard to verify the enrichment factors. See the "Standards and Calibration" section of "Air Analysis' on HTO for scintillation counter standards and calibration. For internal gas-proportional counter standardization, replicate samples of a secondary HTO standard are reduced to HT and are counted after 10 unknown samples are run.

SEWAGE ANALYSIS

Except for tritium analyses, all sewage samples are wet digested with a mixture of 20% $HClO_4$ and 80% HNO_3. Those sewage samples for tritium analysis are distilled to reduce self absorption before counting.

Gross Alpha and Beta Radioactivity

A 100-mℓ quantity of LWRP effluent is wet digested, and the residue is transferred to 5-cm-diam planchets and is counted in accordance with the procedures in the "Water Analysis" section on HTO. Aliquots of 500 mℓ are taken for all other gross alpha and beta measurements.

Tritium

A 1-mℓ aliquot of sewage sample is added to 10 mℓ of Packard Insta-Gel in a 25-mℓ screw-cap glass bottle. Then, 1 mℓ of tap water is used to prepare a background for the sample, and both are placed in the refrigerated detection chamber of the Packard scintillation counter for a 2-hr temperature-equilibration period prior to counting. The sample and background are each counted for 100 min.

^{239}Pu, ^{137}Cs, and ^{90}Sr

Nuclear Chemistry analyzes monthly composites of Laboratory sewage effluent and treated effluent from LWRP for ^{239}Pu and ^{137}Cs. Duplicate composites are prepared by Hazards Control and are analyzed for ^{239}Pu and ^{90}Sr.

Procedure

Daily samples of sewage effluent are combined for the monthly composite, are acidified with 3N HCl, and ^{242}Pu and cesium carrier are added. Ten milliliters of saturated $KMnO_4$ are added to the mixture, and the pH is adjusted to 8-10 with 3N NaOH. Then, 150 mℓ of $MnCl_2$ are added, and the plutonium coprecipitates with the MnO_2.[7] Each sample is later filtered through a 1-μm cotton filter cartridge, which is then dried and ashed at 475°C. The filtrate is acidified to pH 1-3 with 3N HCl, and the cesium is extracted with 5 g of AMP. The sample is then refiltered, and the cartridge is dried and ashed.

The plutonium filter is heated with 100 mℓ of concentrated HNO_3, and the MnO_2 is dissolved with 30% H_2O_2. The volume of solution is then reduced to about 50 mℓ, and the sample is filtered through 934-AH glass-fiber filter paper. The plutonium is oxidized with $NaNO_2$ purified by anion exchange, is electroplated, and is counted by solid-state alpha spectrometry.

The ashed cesium filter is dissolved in acid, excess ammonia is evaporated with NaOH, and the cesium is reextracted with 1 g of AMP. Further purification is carried out as outlined in the "Air Analysis" section on ^{137}Cs.

Radiochemical Separations

The procedure outlined in the "Air Analysis" section on ^{238}Pu and ^{239}Pu is used to purify ^{239}Pu. The purified ^{239}Pu is then electro-deposited and is counted by solid-state alpha spectrometry.

The Sr-Y is washed from the anion column (used in plutonium separation) with 8N HNO_3. The combined washings are then evaporated and are converted to chloride by repeated HCl additions followed by evaporation. Residue is taken up in 8N HCL, transferred to a freshly prepared Dowex 1 column, and the column is washed with 8N HCl. The washings are later collected and evaporated to near dryness. Water is added, and the solution is adjusted to pH 1.5 with NH_4OH. This solution is extracted twice with 20% 2,2-diethyl hexyl phosphoric acid, and the organic phase is washed twice with 0.5N HCl and 1N HCl. The Y is then back extracted with three 20-mℓ portions of HCl, the solution is evaporated to about 10 mℓ, and the Y is precipitated by adding HF. The YF_3 is dissolved and precipitated as hydroxide; then it is redissolved with HCl. The Y is then precipitated as oxalate and is filtered and converted to oxide in a muffler furnace set at 900°C for 1 hr. The ash is weighed, dissolved in HNO_3, transferred to a 5-cm-diam planchet, and dried. After drying, the ash is beta counted.

Nonradioactive Metals and Fluorides

Monthly composites of LLL sewage effluent are analyzed for copper and chromium with a Model 306 Perkin Elmer atomic-absorption spectrophotometer. Aliquots of these composites are also analyzed for cadmium, iron, lead, nickel, silver, zinc, and fluoride.

A monthly composite of Laboratory sewage effluent is prepared by combining 500-mℓ daily samples. Following each 500-mℓ addition, the solution is evaporated with HNO_3 to approximately 100 mℓ. After compositing is complete and organic matter has been destroyed by $HClO_4$ and HNO_3 treatments, the sample is evaporated to near dryness. The residue is taken up in about 30 mℓ of deionized water, is filtered through a sintered glass funnel, and any filter residue is discarded. The filtrate is made up to 100 mℓ in a volumetric flask.

Standards and Calibration

The atomic-absorption spectrophotometer is calibrated with solutions of the metals or compounds of the metal of interest. This spectrophotometer is zeroed with deionized water and is calibrated with standards. Dilution of stock solutions and the monthly composite may be necessary to obtain readings within the spectrophotometer's linear response region. Following calibration, the monthly composite sample is aspirated into the flame, and concentrations are read out directly.

Precision Checks. The monthly composite sample is used to prepare four dilutions. The first dilution provides a concentration near the limit of sensitivity; two dilutions provide intermediate concentrations; and the fourth provides a concentration near the upper limit of the spectrophotometer's linear response region. To reflect maximum interference, they are analyzed in order of highest concentration, lowest concentration, and then by the two intermediate concentrations. This set of measurements is repeated seven times, and the average and standard deviation for each concentration are recorded.

Accuracy Checks. Using the monthly composite, accurace checks are performed by adding known amounts of the metal of interest to the low and intermediate concentrations. The amount of metal added to the low concentration is designed to double in concentration, and the amount of metal added to the intermediate concentrations is sufficient to result in concentrations that are within 25% of the upper limit of the spectrophotometer's linear response region. As in the precision measurements, seven replicate determinations are made at each concentration, and accuracy is expressed as percent recovery based on the average recovery of the seven replicates.

Fluoride Measurements

Fluorides in LLL sewage effluent are determined with a specific ion-electrode measurement. Daily additions of 100-mℓ aliquots of sewage effluent are used to prepare a monthly composite sample. This composite sample is stored in a plastic bottle, and no chemical treatment or evaporation is employed. At the end of the month, an aliquot of the composite sample is analyzed for fluorides with an Orion Model 401 specific ion meter equipped with a lanthanum fluoride electrode. Precision and accuracy measurements are conducted quarterly in a manner similar to those described for metals in the "Nonradioactive Metals and Fluorides" section on precision and accuracy checks above.

VEGETATION ANALYSIS

Frozen vegetation is transferred to freeze-drying equipment, and a 10-μm vacuum is established. Recovered water is collected in a receiver chilled with dry ice and Dowanol (dipropylene methyl ether). The vacuum is checked periodically, and dry ice is added as needed over a four-day period. Liquid scintillation counting is then used to analyze an aliquot of the recovered water for tritium content.

Standards and Calibration

See the "Air Analysis" section on standards and calibration for HTO.

REFERENCES

1. C. L. Lindeken, P. H. Gudiksen, J. W. Meadows, K. O. Hamby, and L. R. Anspaugh, *Environmental Levels of Radioactivity in Livermore Valley Soils*, Lawrence Livermore Laboratory, Rept. UCRL-74424 (1973).
2. D. C. Camp, C. Gatrousis, and L. A. Maynard, "Low Background Ge(Li) Detector Systems for Radioenvironmental Studies," *Nucl. Instrum. Meth.* 117, 189 (1974).
3. P. G. Johnson, R. D. Carver, and R. J. Dupzyk, *Preparation of ^{242}Pu for Use as an Alpha Spectrometry and Mass Spectrometry Tracer*, Lawrence Livermore Laboratory, Rept. UCRL-78596 (1976).
4. R. J. Dupzyk, R. D. Carver, and I. A. Dupzyk, *Isotope Analysis of Plutonium Samples by Isotope Dilution Mass Spectrometer*, Technical Report Series 169 - STI/DOC 10, 2nd Panel on Reference Methods for Marine Radioactivity Studies, International Association of Environmental Analysts (1972).
5. "Radiochemical Determination of Plutonium in Soil Leaching," *ERDA Health and Safety Laboratory Procedures Manual*, E-Pu-06-01, HASL-300 (1972).
6 H. G. Ostlund and E. Werner, "The Electrolytic Enrichment of Tritium and Deuterium for Natural Tritium Measurements," *Tritium in the Phys. and Biol. Sci.* 1 (1962).
7. K. M. Wong, G. S. Brown, and V. E. Noshkin, "A Rapid Procedure for Pu Separation in Large Volumes of Fresh and Saline Water using MnO_2 Co-precipitation," *J. Radioanal. Chem.* 42, 7-15 (1978).

JAC

DISTRIBUTION

External Distribution

T. V. Crawford
W. C. Reinig
E. I. duPont de Nemours and Co.
Savannah River Plant
Aiken, SC 29801

A. P. Hull (2)
Brookhaven National Laboratory
Upton, NY 11973

J. O. Ward
Department of Health Services
Radiologic Health Section
714 P Street
Sacramento, CA 95814

C. D. Jackson (15)
U.S. Department of Energy
San Francisco Operations Office
1333 Broadway
Oakland, CA 94612

H. F. Anderson (2)
Monsanto Research Corporation
Mound Laboratory
Miamisburg, OH 45342

W. R. Hansen
Los Alamos Scientific Laboratory
Los Alamos, NM 87544

R. E. Yoder (2)
Rockwell International
Rocky Flats Plant
Golden, CO 80401

J. A. Auxier
Oak Ridge National Laboratory
Oak Ridge, TN 37830

P. Lovell (4)
Sandia Laboratories
Livermore, CA 94550

D. Duncan, A-3
Environmental Protection Agency
215 Fremont Street
San Francisco, CA 94105

H. Brinkley
Bay Area Air Quality Management District
939 Ellis Street
San Francisco, CA 94109

H. J. Naftzger
ABAG
Claremont Hotel
Ashby Ave. and Domingo Ave.
Oakland, CA 94705

P. E. Bramson
Battelle Northwest
P.O. 999
Richland, WA 99352

Fred Moss
Alameda County Flood Control Dist., Zone 7
1404 Concannon Blvd.
Livermore, CA 94550

R. E. Broz
Vallecitos Nuclear Center
Pleasanton, CA 94566

S. Morse
California Regional Water Quality Control Board
1111 Jackson Street
Oakland, CA 94612

G. Facer
A. Pressesky
J. Miller
C. Sherman
USDOE Headquarters
Washington, DC 20545

E. L. Lenahan
Alameda County Water District
38050 Fremont Blvd.
Fremont, CA 94537

V. V. Williams
San Joaquin Local Health District
P.O. Box 2009
Stockton, CA 95201

W. Adams
Livermore Water Reclamation Plant
1250 Kitty Hawk Road
Livermore, CA 94550

J. Robertson
California Regional Water Quality Control Board
3201 S Street
Sacramento, CA 95816

Tak Shirasawa
Environmental Health Planning
Alameda County Health Care Services Agency
470 27th Street
Oakland, CA 96412

M. Williamson
Director of Radiological
and Environmental
Sciences Laboratory
DOE-IDO
550 2nd Street
Idaho Falls, ID 83401

Distribution Category
UC-11 (250)

U. S. Government Printing Office: 1981/6-789-002/5534

SITE SEISMIC SAFETY PROGRAM

INTRODUCTION

The mission of the Site Seismic Safety Program (SSSP), which began in January 1979, is to identify and characterize geologic hazards at the Lawrence Livermore National Laboratory (LLNL) site. Primary emphasis is placed on earthquake hazards in the Livermore Valley. In addition to characterizing the hazards, a specific objective of the SSSP has become to provide input to the Geology, Seismology, and Groundwater Hydrology sections of the final Environmental Impact Statement (EIS) for the LLNL site. Specific questions about some of these sections of the draft EIS were raised during public hearings in April 1979.

The Hearing Board Statement discussed those critical issues requiring more attention. It identified five major areas that need to be considered by the Site Seismic Safety Program:

1. Re-evaluation of the surface-rupture potential.
2. Re-evaluation of surface and subsurface geology (including definition of bedrock).
3. Improved seismotectonic model.
4. Determination of design-basis earthquake.
5. Independent review.

Areas 1, 2, 3 and 4 require both a review of all currently available geological and seismological information pertinent to the site and the generation of new information. The tasks necessary to generate the information in each of these four areas will be outlined in the Program Plan. Each of the individual tasks will contribute information pertinent to more than one of the areas of concern. The Program is divided into three phases:

Phase I. Preliminary Data Collection.

Phase II. Hazard Characterization and Parameterization.

Phase III. Seismic Hazard Exposure Assessment.

Each of the areas 1-4 has specific criteria which need to be considered within the three-part framework of the work plan.

INVESTIGATIONS RELATING TO AREA #1:

RE-EVALUATION OF THE SURFACE-RUPTURE POTENTIAL

The re-evaluation of surface rupture potential will require thorough investigations of faults hypothesized to pass through the LLNL site. It will be necessary to determine, first, whether faults are in fact present, second, whether any detected faults are active, and third, the age of activity on any faults which are identified. Direct geological observations, trenching, drilling, and geophysical studies may be used to evaluate whether a fault exists or is active.

Although the on-site investigation may verify the existence or absence of specific postulated faults, it will not provide a general framework. Regional investigations will contribute to identifying and understanding those features that were previously identified as faults. The actual evaluation of earthquake hazard will also require the classification of regional fault activity.

INVESTIGATIONS RELATING TO AREA #2:

RE-EVALUATION OF SURFACE AND SUBSURFACE

GEOLOGY (INCLUDING DEFINITION OF BEDROCK)

The objectives of this portion of the SSSP should be:

1. Documentation of surface geologic data pertinent to areas containing faults which may cause surface rupture or significant ground motion.

2. Identification of areas where subsurface methods (i.e. geophysical, hydrologic, trenching, drilling) can be applied to supplement surface data.

3. Formulate spatial and temporal tectonic models of the region and test the models using seismic information and data acquired from 1 and 2.

4. Review step 2 (iterative process) to determine if more data can be obtained to further support or refine the models.

5. Data from 1-4 serve as input to the design-basis earthquake decision.

The tectonic models will result in a detailed characterization of the structural character (and hence physical character) of the valley which will serve as input to site foundation-stability determination and ground-motion characterization.

INVESTIGATIONS RELATING TO AREA #3:

IMPROVED SEISMOTECTONIC MODEL

The formulation of an improved seismotectonic model requires estimates of current and historic seismic activity in and near the Livermore Valley, accurate location of earthquakes, and accurate determination of the source mechanisms. Geologic studies will provide a list of potential faults which may be identified as associated with the seismic activity, and geodetic information will indicate on-going deformation. Conceptual models will be evaluated computationally or by comparison with analogous locations.

INVESTIGATIONS RELATING TO AREA #4:

DETERMINATION OF DESIGN-BASIS EARTHQUAKE

The improved seismotectonic model, accurate regional geologic mapping, and the classification of fault activity will be inputs to the determination of the design-basis earthquake (DBE). The definition of bedrock is also needed for this area of investigation.

SITE HYDROGEOLOGIC STUDY

An adjunct of the Site Seismic Safety Program's effort to evaluate geologic hazards at the LLNL site is the site hydrogeologic study. The goal of this study is to determine the likelihood that a potentially hazardous liquid spill on site will travel through the unsaturated zone and reach the saturated groundwater system. Acquiring data for a detailed characterization of the hydrology of the LLNL site, together with laboratory and field experimentation and flow modeling, is necessary for evaluating the potential for groundwater contamination. This study will determine whether there are any groundwater barriers to such contamination. Hydrogeologic tasks will be coordinated with the SSSP's evaluation of faulting and subsurface characterization in the LLNL environs since both require extensive drilling.

WORK PLAN

In the following discussion we will describe the scope of work for each of the three phases of the work plan, relate the work to the areas identified by the hearing board, and outline the schedule for completion of the program. Since certain tasks in the hydrology project will be directed toward SSSP goals, they will be discussed in the scope of work for Phase I of the SSSP.

It should be noted that many of the tasks have been partially or fully completed. The work schedule in Table 1 will clarify the current status of the program.

PHASE I: PRELIMINARY DATA COLLECTION

Deliverables

The major products of Phase I will be: (1) evaluation of existing geological, geophysical, and seismological data; (2) development of a preliminary seismotectonic model of the Livermore Valley; (3) a listing of faults requiring further study, ranked in order of decreasing possible hazard to the LLNL site according to their potential for (a) ground failure or rupture on site and (b) possible strong ground shaking at the LLNL site; (4) development of specific investigations that will be needed for further study of the most likely hazardous faults; (5) establishment of an operating seismic observatory. Documentation of our work will be provided via memoranda to the Site Survey Library and Status Reports.

Scope of Work

During Phase I it will be necessary to lay the ground work for a comprehensive geological, geophysical, and seismological investigation evaluating on-site and regional geologic conditions which might influence the safety of the LLNL site. These investigations will include surface and near-surface geologic studies, geophysical exploration, and studies of local seismology.

Task 1: Collection and Interpretation of Existing Data for All Areas

Substantial work in geology, geophysics, and seismology has been done in the Livermore Valley and on the LLNL site. Documentation and interpretation of the existing work is a primary goal of Phase I. A bibliography of available reports will be prepared and copies of original reports will be

Table 1. Work schedule.

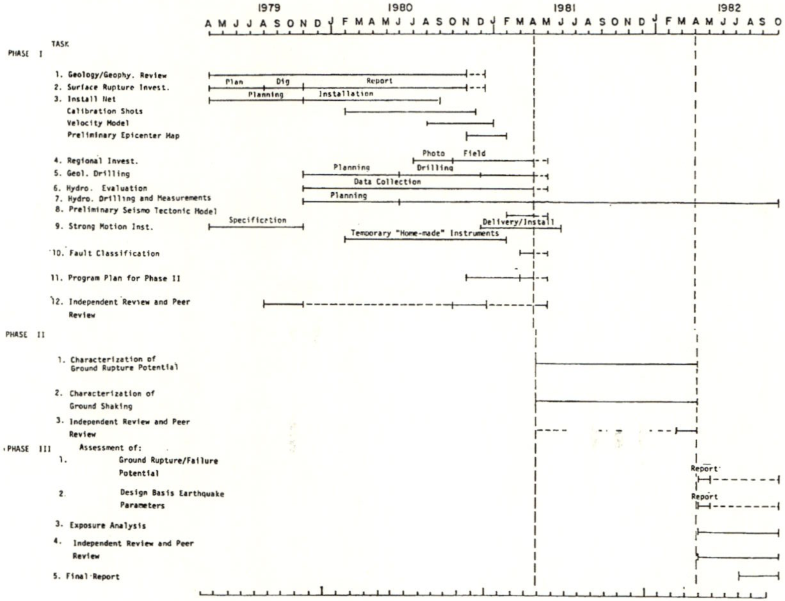

acquired whenever possible. A site reference library of this work will be established and maintained at LLNL. Re-evaluation and re-interpretation of available original data are being conducted and will be reported on at the conclusion of Phase I.

Additionally, existing hydrogeologic information compiled by the Alameda County Flood Control and Water Conservation District Zone 7 will be gathered and evaluated (e.g., driller's logs, well-monitoring records, and hydrographs). Local private wells, in addition to county observation wells, will be considered. Wells involved with the Hazards Control Water Quality Monitoring Program will receive special attention to enable further interpretation of later LLNL well-monitoring results. Evaluation will result in the construction of geologic cross-sections and potentiometric surface maps in areas of concern.

Task 2: Initial Data Collection Relating to Surface Rupture Potential

A first priority in the site survey is the determination of the possible hazard due to surface rupture on the Laboratory site. Therefore, the first stage of surface geological and geophysical exploration will be investigation of faults which prior researchers have postulated and/or extrapolated onto the LLNL site. Surface and near-surface geologic investigations will include trenching of projected traces of the Las Positas, the Corral Hollow, the Doutherty, and Tesla faults. Geophysical investigations will include the evaluation of a possible intersection of Las Positas and Tesla faults using resistivity, self-potential (SP), small-scale-seismic refraction, and magnetic methods.

This Task will also include the completion and joint interpretations of LLNL and prior investigators' magnetic data, and the evaluation of the diagnostic capability of various geophysical tools for on-site faults and for regional mapping. Upon completion of this work, a report will be prepared.

Task 3: Development of Seismological Database

This task requires the establishment of a seismic observatory capable of accurate, rapid location and analysis of earthquakes within 20-30 km of LLNL. During Phase I we are installing 3-component seismic stations in the Livermore Valley and augmenting this with data from nearby U.S. Geological Survey (USGS) single-component stations. Initially, 7 stations are being installed by the USGS under contract to LLNL. In exchange for access to data from these stations, the USGS will provide LLNL with telemetered links to 12 of their nearby stations. Both sets of telemetered data (LLNL and USGS) will be digitized in real time, and seismic events will be recorded directly onto digital tapes allowing for sophisticated post-event processing. Combining the data from both LLNL and USGS stations with the digital analysis capabilities of the seismic monitoring group will allow us to determine the locations and mechanisms of local earthquakes with significantly higher accuracy than has heretofore been obtained. Location accuracy in critical areas should be on the order of ±0.5 km as opposed to ±2-5 km before the establishment of the observatory. This will allow us to assign the activity to specific fault traces and thus delineate them and determine their status.

Following the installation of all stations, a number of high-explosive calibration shots will be conducted to determine the time corrections for each station. The execution of the calibration shots will be handled by the USGS under contract to LLNL. These calibration results will be applied to Task 8, relocation of USGS-determined epicenters for the time period 1969 to the present.

Task 4: Regional Investigations

Upon completion of initial on-site geological and geophysical investigations, field work will be extended to include interpretation of remote-sensing and aerial photo imagery, field reconnaissance, and analysis of existing geophysical data on a regional scale. The existing geodetic data will be evaluated and extended to help determine strain rates in the local area. Another major element of these investigations will be establishing age relationships of the Quaternary units. This work will be limited to the areas that are necessary to characterize the geologic hazards to LLNL operations and will be coordinated with the initial analyses of the seismic data. Studies necessary to accomplish these tasks are:

(1) Detailed field mapping will be carried out in areas south and east of the laboratory where relatively good control of the locations of the Greenville, Carnegie, Tesla, Las Positas, Corral Hollow, and other faults can be obtained. Mapping will include documentation of outcrop locations, structural information, and inferences based upon remote sensing and aerial photo imagery. Preliminary fault locations will be determined based upon these data.

(2) Existing geophysical data will be compiled and analyzed to evaluate the potential of various geophysical methods for identifying fault locations. Pertinent methods will be employed to extend fault locations defined in 1, beneath the valley alluvium.

(3) Other available regional data, including drilling data and hydrologic data, will be incorporated with 1 and 2 to help formulate the regional tectonic characterization.

(4) Data acquired in 1, 2, and 3 will be compared with seismic evidence to identify locations of active faults.

Task 5: On-Site Geologic Drilling

The on-site drilling portion of the geological field investigations is an exploratory program and will be integrated with the drilling for the site hydrogeological investigations. The drilling program will seek possible marker horizons which might be used to trace subsurface structures across the Laboratory site and obtain geotechnical data bearing on the potential for ground failure at LLNL during a major earthquake.

Task 6: Hydrogeologic Data Assembly and Evaluation

An important part of the task is the determination of a hazardous spill potential from the evaluation of data on (1) credible accident estimates, (2) annual environmental monitoring at LLNL, (3) actual release occurrences, (4) past, present, and future locations of contaminated waste-holding tanks, pipelines, and transportation routes, and (5) chemical and radiochemical characteristics of liquid wastes and experimental materials. The data, to be obtained from the Hazards Control Department, should establish the possible locations, estimated volumes, times of release, and chemical makeup of potential contaminating liquid spills.

In addition, hydrologic characteristics of local soils, including ion-retardation factors and solute-migration characteristics for radionuclides or contaminants, will be reviewed. Locations of natural, enhanced (arroyo or storm sewer), and retarded (paved or otherwise protected) recharge areas will be determined.

Task 7: Site Hydrogeologic Drilling Program

In conjunction with Task 5, on-site geologic drilling, wells will be completed on site to a depth of about 25 feet below the water table (estimated to be between 55 and 90 feet). Drilling locations will be selected to represent enhanced as well as natural recharge areas. Locations will also reflect probable spill sites determined as outlined in Task 6. At appropriate intervals samples will be taken for subsequent testing, stratigraphic control, and soil moisture and tritium analyses. Geophysical logs of the wells will complement stratigraphic analysis. Hydraulic head fluctuations in selected wells will be monitored for several years. Water table configurations will be drawn from resulting data.

To investigate the saturated zone one or more water wells, approximately 300 feet deep, will be completed on site and tested to determine the effective porosity, hydraulic conductivity, and dispersivity. Water-quality monitoring of these wells will be added to the study of the shallower wells. All water-quality monitoring will eventually be incorporated into Hazard Control's continuing environmental monitoring program. Due to the time necessary for these measurements, this task will continue beyond Phase I. If it is determined that movement of contaminants to the saturated zone is likely, a simulation of contaminant transport would be undertaken.

Task 8: Preliminary Seismotectonic Model

By the end of Phase I, a preliminary velocity structure for the Valley will be determined, daily seismicity will be recorded and located using this model, and a preliminary seismicity map will be prepared for the period 1969 to the present. Focal mechanisms will be determined for selected events and will be combined with preliminary results of the regional field investigations to produce a preliminary seismotectonic model.

Task 9: Strong Motion Instrumentation

Phase I will also include the planning, procurement, and installation of equipment for a strong-motion accelerograph network. This accelerograph network is intended to augment the seismic network to provide site-specific free-field and building acceleration response information that can be used in engineering studies. The proposed system is a digital recording system with a "pre-event memory" to provide complete acceleration records that include the first arrivals. The combination of such acceleration records with information on seismic activity from the Seismic Network should provide as complete a basis as is possible for predicting future ground motion at the LLNL site.

Task 10: Classification of Fault Activity

To complete Phase I, all features that have been identified as being tectonic faults must also be classified according to their degree of potential activity. This classification is only intended to provide guidelines for setting priorities for further studies in Phase II.

For the purposes of setting Phase II priorities, we have defined three activity classes for faults. In Phase II, faults in the different classes will require different levels of field investigation as input for the complete characterization of potentially damaging earthquakes. The three classes are active, indeterminate, and inactive. The indeterminate classification is further divided into potentially active and uncertain activity subclassifications. The activity classifications, their definitions, and projected further studies for Phase II are outlined in Table 2.

Two criteria dominate the classification scheme. For rupture, only faults crossing the site need detailed study; for shaking, only the most hazardous faults or fault zones need be investigated in detail.

Figure 1 outlines a decision tree for determining whether or not a feature requires further study in the assessment of ground-shaking potential; and, if so, what observables are needed. This tree is based on the classifications and criteria in Table 2.

Task 11: Phase II Program Plan

During the completion of Phase I studies for each of the tasks, a program plan will be developed for Phase II. This plan will outline the specific investigative tasks needed for characterization of the faults classified in Task 10.

Task 12: Independent and Peer Review

During the completion of each of the above tasks, informal independent review will be obtained by conducting the work in an open manner and inviting qualified representatives of local, state, and federal agencies to inspect field sites such as exploratory trenches. Formal peer review is provided for by contractual arrangement with Woodward-Clyde Consultants (WCC). In addition to inspection of field sites, WCC will formally review all LLNL Phase I studies and document these inspections and reviews.

In order to establish an additional independent review, WCC will prepare a list of possible members of a broad-based independent review panel. This list will be submitted by WCC to the California State Seismic Safety Commission (CSSSC). The CSSSC will be requested to make additions and deletions and return to WCC a list of approved independent reviewers. From this approved list, WCC will empanel an independent review board, following the guidelines of the Independent Review Committee of the CSSSC.

Table 2. Classification of fault activity on available data (modified from Cluff et al.)

Activity Classification and Definition		Criteria: Historic	Criteria: Geologic	Criteria: Seismologic	Further Studies If Characterization of Hazard not Sufficient	Alternative to Further Studies
Active	A tectonic fault with a history of strong earthquakes or surface faulting, or a fault with a short recurrence interval relative to the life of the planned project. The recurrence interval used to define activity rate may vary according to the consequence of activity.	(1) Surface faulting and associated strong earthquakes. (2) Tectonic fault creep, or geodetic evidence of fault displacement or deformation	(1) Geologically young deposits cut by fault <50,000 years. (2) Youthful geomorphological features that are characteristic of geologically young displacements along the fault trace. (3) Groundwater barriers in geologially young or unconsolidated deposits.	Earthquake epicenters can be assigned with confidence to the fault (±1 km or better).	Additional investigation and exploration are needed to define: (1) Exact location of individual fault traces. (2) Recurrence interval. (3) Probable magnitude of future events. (4) Type of surface deformation associated with the surface faulting. (5) Probable epicenter of future earthquakes.	Hazard deemed already sufficiently documented and characterized.
Indeterminate	Potentially Active--a tectonic fault without historic surface offset, but with a recurrence interval that could be sufficiently short to be significant to the particular project.	No reliable report of historic surface faulting.	(1) Geomorphic features that are characteristic of active faults, but with subdued, eroded, and discontinuous form (2) Faults not known to cut or displace youngest alluvial deposits, but offset older quaternary deposits. (3) Water barriers in older deposits. (4) Geological setting in which the geometry in relation to active or potentially active faults suggests similar degree of activity. (5) Mapped by previous investigators but as yet unconfirmed by direct investigation.	Alignment of some earthquake epicenters along or near fault but assigned locations have low degree of confidence in location.	Additional investigations are needed to resolve: (1) Time since previous activity. (2) Recurrence interval. (3) Location of possible fault traces.	Completion of classification is less important if fault does not cross the project site and a known active fault that is capable of more frequent or higher magnitude earthquakes is closer to the site.*
	Activity Uncertain--a fault with insufficient evidence to define past activity of recurrence interval. The following classifications can be used until the results of additional studies provide definitive evidence.	Available information is insufficient to provide criteria that are sufficiently definitive to establish fault activity This lack of information may be due to the inactivity of the fault or to lack of investigations needed to provide definitive criteria.			This classification indicates that additional studies are necessary if the fault is found to be critical to the project. The importance of a fault with this classification depends upon the type of structure involved, the location of the fault in respect to the structure, and the consequences of movement.	

*Thus, an indeterminate fault presenting less hazard to the site may be simply classified as indeterminate (assumed active), and further direct study may then be reduced in priority.

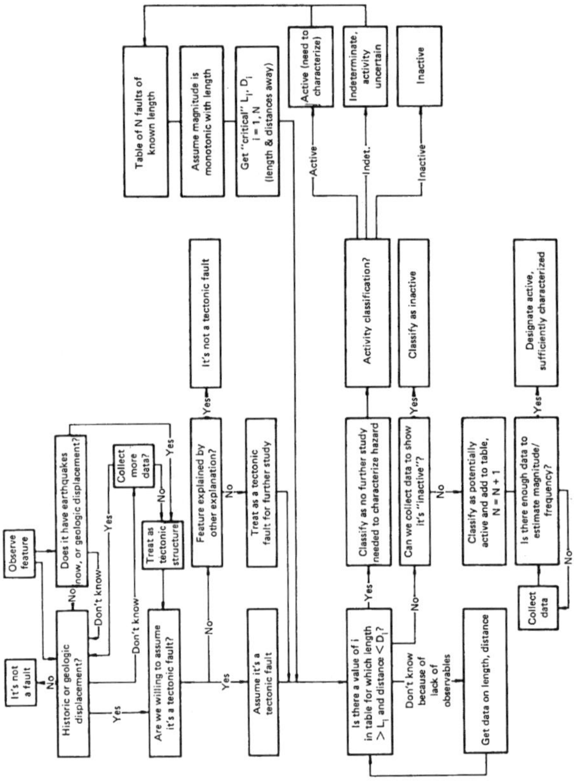

Observe feature
It's not a fault
Historic or geologic displacement?
Does it have earthquakes now, or geologic displacement?
Collect more data?
Treat as tectonic structure
Are we willing to assume it's a tectonic fault?
Feature explained by other explanation?
It's not a tectonic fault
Treat as a tectonic fault for further study
Assume it's a tectonic fault
Table of N faults of known length
Assume magnitude is monotonic with length
Get "critical" Li, Di i = 1, N (length & distances away)
Is there a value of i in table for which length > Li and distance < Di?
Don't know because of lack of observables
Get data on length, distance
Classify as no further study needed to characterize hazard
Activity classification?
Active (need to characterize)
Indeterminate, activity uncertain
Inactive
Can we collect data to show it's "inactive"?
Classify as inactive
Classify as potentially active and add to table, N = N + 1
Is there enough data to estimate magnitude/frequency?
Collect data
Designate active, sufficiently characterized
Yes
No
Don't know
Active
Indet.

Figure 1.

Deliverables

Phase II is intended to supplement Phase I data as needed to determine the seismic hazard exposure at the LLNL site. The products of this Phase are the final data base and analyses needed for the characterization of potential ground failure and rupture, and the characterization of potential ground shaking as a function of earthquake magnitude on the most significant faults. Each of these characterizations proceeds from a set of observable quantities or directly inferred characteristics (such as fault length or recurrence rate) through a characterization methodology to the final parameterization of the hazard. These procedures are outlined below.

Task 1: Characterization of Potential Ground Rupture

The characterization of potential ground rupture involves investigations which are confined to an area on the LLNL site or very nearby. This is the area in which the occurrence of such an event could affect LLNL facilities either as a result of ground displacement or permanent changes in ground level. The methodology is outlined below.

Observables: Geomorphic features associated with active faults; e.g., disrupted drainages; enclosed depressions; spring lines; mole tracks; "lineaments"; disruption of young strata as revealed by trenching, mapping, or geophysical surveys; historic surface faulting or creep; associated seismicity; changes in geodetic measurements.

Seismic Source: Amount and sense of movement.

Characterization of Possible
Potential Ground Rupture: Locations of possible rupture, offsets, recurrence intervals.

Although in favorable circumstances it may be possible to estimate recurrence intervals for a given fault segment, success cannot be assumed. Therefore, probabilities will most likely only be determined in general terms, such as high, moderate, or low.

Scope of Work. At the end of Phase I, mapped faults will have been classified according to their probable activity and will have been prioritized for further study under this task. Any faults identified in Phase I that cross the site will be evaluated in more detail by the examination of young geologic strata for evidence of faulting. This examination may include additional trenching, drilling, surface mapping, or geophysical surveys.

Task 2: Characterization of Ground Shaking

The flow chart in Fig. 1 highlights the methodology used in characterizing strong ground shaking at the site.

Observables: Some or all of the following: time and size of last motion, recurrence rate, slip rate, fault length, seismicity, location.

Seismic Source: Magnitude, moment, radiation pattern.

Path Effects/Site Response: Soil damping, attenuation.

Characterization of Ground Shaking: Amplitude, duration, frequency content.

Scope of Work. The input needed for the characterization of the DBE depends upon the choice of the specific methodology used to assess the earthquake ground-motion parameters. The parameters that are generally construed to be of engineering significance include peak values of ground motion (acceleration, velocity or displacement), spectral content, and duration of strong ground shaking. However, it is generally agreed that earthquake ground motion parameters are affected by source factors, path effects and local conditions as outlined above. Thus, the observables are, in the main, similar for all methodologies. To evaluate the characterization of the DBE, we will initially use a deterministic, empirical attenuation approach, which is suitably site-specific. Determination of empirical attenuation approaches involve the estimation of the maximum credible earthquake via the use of observed rupture-length (L_{max}) versus Magnitude (M) relations. The ground motion at the site is then determined using the maximum magnitude (M_{max}), the distance (R) of the causative fault, and typical observed attenuation relations which estimate peak ground motion values depending on M_{max} and R. For conservatism, the maximum credible ground motion is taken to be the mean value of this relation plus one standard deviation. This approach has been the traditional means of determining DBE's and is the approach reported on in the EIS. This approach will be used for consistency, both to assess the relative significance of sources and as an element of the final design process.

However, new "near-source" observations have prompted a rapid evolution in the state of the art with respect to estimating strong-ground-motion parameters. Considerable controversy surrounds the determination of $_{Lmax}$ and its relation to M_{max}. Probablistic analyses of both the probable source characteristics and the probable ground motions are gaining wider acceptance, and will be incorporated into the determination of the DBE. The completion of Phase II will require both empirical and computational estimates of the strong-motion parameters of the DBE.

PHASE III: SEISMIC HAZARD EXPOSURE ASSESSMENT

Deliverables

The deliverables for the final seismic hazard exposure assessment will be: (1) report on assessment of surface rupture and ground failure potential on site, (2) report on assessment of DBE parameters, (3) report on assessment of seismic exposure, and (4) geologic, seismologic and hydrogeologic reports.

Scope of Work

Phase II is essentially an interactive process and may require the acquisition of data beyond that developed during Phase I. When the characterization is deemed sufficient, the hazard assessments can be made. Phase III will consist of the completion and documentation of these final assessments, the final review, and the preparation of the reports.

Surface Rupture Potential

The evaluation of surface rupture potential will be reported on in Phase III. This evaluation will be assessed by the review panel and their critique will be included in the final project report. An initial assessment of existing geotechnical data for alluvial deposits underlying LLNL indicates that the ground-failure potential is low to negligible. However, the final program report will include an assessment of the potential for liquefaction and related ground failures at LLNL based on criteria such as those developed by the USGS. With the exceptions of landscaping areas, the banks of open drainage ditches, and the Arroyo Seco stream channel, slopes within the LLNL site do not exceed three percent. Slope-stability problems have not been experienced at LLNL. The final program report will include a brief assessment of any potential hazard of on-site slope stability.

Determination of Design-Basis Earthquake Parameters

The final determination of the parameters describing the DBE will be reported on in Phase III. This determination will also be submitted to the review panel and their critique will be included in the final program report.

Seismic Exposure Analysis

Based on the parameters obtained, a Seismic Exposure Analysis will be undertaken and reported on in Phase III.

Reviews

Phase III will also include the final technical review by WCC of the overall program, and a comprehensive technical review of the program by the Independent Review Panel. The content of these reviews will be included in the final program report.

Preparation and Publication of Reports

Following the review procedures mentioned above, the pertinent results and interpretations of the SSSP will be published as a separate report.

SURFACE WATER HYDROLOGY

1. INTRODUCTION

The Lawrence Livermore National Laboratory occupies 2.6 km^2 at the eastern end of the Livermore Valley. The site slopes southeast to northwest from an elevation of 200 to 170 m MSL. Figure 1 shows the location of the Site, plus the topography and local natural drainage channels.

2. HYDROLOGIC DESCRIPTION

Four water systems should be considered because of their potential hydrological effect on the Laboratory site. These are: (1) treated water, (2) storm water, (3) the South Bay aqueduct, and (4) the Del Valle Reservoir.

2.1. TREATED WATER

The Zone 7 water treatment plant, which provides water for the City of Livermore, is located just east of the Laboratory. The 0.68-m pipeline (welded steel pipe) from the treatment plant crosses the northern boundary of the Laboratory and runs parallel to the Arroyo Las Positas on its way to Livermore. A 0.3-m water line has been tapped into the Zone 7 pipeline to provide an emergency water supply.

The Hetch Hetchy Aqueduct, which provides treated water for the City of San Francisco, is located approximately 11 km southwest of the Laboratory. LLNL receives all of its treated water from this source. Water is pumped from the aqueduct (elevation 110 m) to two steel holding tanks (elevation 373 m) that each have a storage capacity of 79.5 m^3. Water from the storage tanks then flows 11 km down the Arroyo Mocho Canyon to storage tanks at the LLNL site. The first 9.6 km of pipeline are 0.25-m, class 250 cast iron pipe, while the last mile is 0.4-m ductile steel pipe.

2.2. STORM WATER

Laboratory storm water is channeled through storm sewers and open ditches that are designed to accommodate a 10-yr flow. Open ditches are used in undeveloped areas of the Laboratory site. Most of

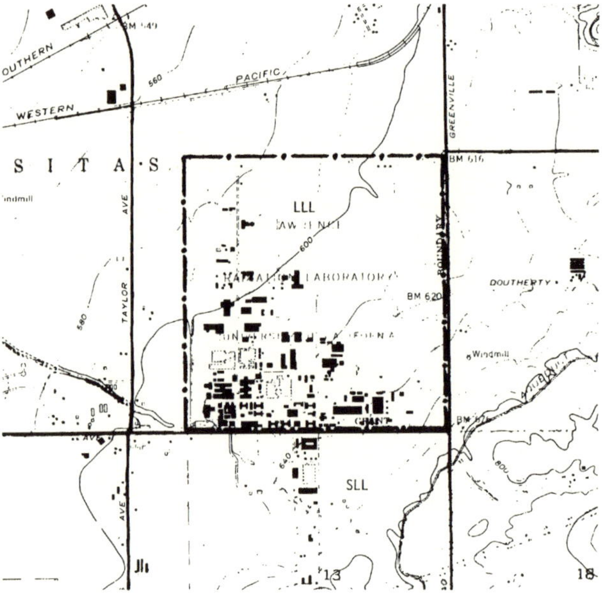

Figure 1. DOE Livermore site topography.

The South Bay Aqueduct begins at the Bethany Reservoir near Byron, California. Water is pumped from Bethany Reservoir to an elevation of about 240 m MSL. From there, the water flows through the aqueduct by gravity to Santa Clara County through a series of pipelines and open canals. The aqueduct is an open channel as it crosses the eastern edge of the Livermore Valley at just about the 210-m contour line. Maximum flow in the aqueduct is 8.5 m^3/s with the average running 7.1 m^3/s. Siphons were used in crossing the major streams in the Valley, i.e., Arroyo Seco and Arroyo Mocho.

Users of the South Bay Aqueduct include the Alameda County portion of Zone 7, Alameda County, and Santa Clara County. Zone 7 is the only user of the water in the Livermore Valley. The water is used to recharge groundwater by releasing it directly from the canal to the Altamont Creek, from where it flows into the Arroyo Las Positas. Groundwater recharging is also obtained by releasing water from the Del Valle Reservoir to the Arroyo Del Valle. Water is also used to supply the Zone 7 treatment plant located northeast of the Laboratory.

2.4. DEL VALLE RESERVOIR

Del Valle Reservoir is located on the Arroyo Del Valle just above and southeast of the U.S. Veterans Administration Hospital, and is approximately 600 m upstream from the South Bay Aqueduct. The dam is an earthfill embankment rising 68 m above the stream bed. Total capacity of the reservoir behind the dam is approximately 9.5×10^7 m^3. The reservoir is a multipurpose facility providing water conservation, flood control, and recreation. Normally, Del Valle Reservoir has about 2.5×10^7 m^3 of water in the winter and 4.9×10^7 m^3 in the summer, leaving room for at least an additional 4.6×10^7 m^3 for flood control. Drainage area above the dam is about 381 km^2. Surface areas of the reservoir for two different volumes are:

Volume	Surface Area
9.5×10^7 m^3	4.3 km^2
4.9×10^7 m^3	2.9 km^2

A 1.5-m pipeline carries water from the aqueduct to the pump house at the bottom of the dam. Water is then pumped into the reservoir and held until needed. Tunnels through the dam are used to release water for conservation and flood control. The conservation tunnel is also used to pump water into the reservoir. Five valves are located at varying elevations on the dam to release water. The flood control tunnel has two gates and a morning-glory spillway.

3. HYDROSPHERE

Alameda Creek drains a portion of the coastal mountains, located on the eastern side of the southern arm of the San Francisco Bay, for a total watershed area of 1800 km^2. The two main tributaries to Alameda Creek are Arroyo de la Laguna and Calaveras Creek which drain approximately 1100 km^2 and 260 km^2, respectively.

The main drainage streams for the Livermore Valley are Arroyo del Valle, Arroyo Las Positas, Arroyo Mocho, Arroyo Seco, Cottonwood Creek, and Tassajara Creek. All streams flow west with the exception of Cottonwood and Tassajara Creeks, which drain the hills north of the Valley and flow south. Cottonwood Creek and Arroyo Seco converge with Arroyo Las Positas which flows into Arroyo Mocho at the western end of the Valley along with Tassajara Creek. Arroyo del Valle and Arroyo Mocho converge with Arroyo de la Laguna at the extreme western end of the Valley. Until recent geological times, all drainage from the Valley flowed north through San Ramon Valley to Suisun Bay. Now the drainage flows through Niles Canyon via Alameda Creek.

All the arroyos and creeks in Livermore Valley are dry during most of the year and have water flow in them from October to April, which constitutes the typical rainy season. Arroyo del Valle and Arroyo Mocho have the largest drainage basins in the Valley and have caused more flooding than have other streams. Consequently, more data exists on these two streams than on others. However, since only Arroyo Las Positas and Arroyo Seco could directly affect the Laboratory, comments will be directed at these two arroyos.

3.1. ARROYO LAS POSITAS

The Arroyo Las Positas watershed is in the northeastern and eastern hills above the Valley floor. The only part of this basin that directly affects the Laboratory is the hills directly to the east. This basin is about 13 km^2 in area and 5.6 km long. Several smaller streams converge in the hills and on the flood plain east of the Laboratory. All semblance of streams is lost until a channel is formed along the eastern and northern boundary of the Laboratory.

In December 1971, the USGS installed a gauging station at the northwest corner of the Laboratory. This is the first to be installed on Arroyo Las Positas.

3.2. ARROYO SECO

The hills southwest of the Laboratory form the basin for the Arroyo Seco. This basin is about 41 km in area and 19 km long. The channel is well defined, and cuts across Sandia Laboratory just to the south of the Laboratory. Arroyo Seco then cuts across the southwest corner of the Laboratory on its way to Arroyo Las Positas.

. FLOODS

4.1. HISTORY

Numerous floods have occurred on Alameda Creek since records of stream flow were started in the 1890s. Flood years with the associated peak discharges as measured on Alameda Creek near Niles are listed below. The flood of 1955 would have been the largest in recorded history, surpassing the flood of 1911, had not Calaveras Reservoir impounded all the flood water from Calaveras Creek.

Date	Peak Discharge m^3/s
November - 1892	382
January - 1895	419
March - 1907	462
January - 1909	354
March - 1911	807
January - 1914	208
February - 1938	297
November - 1950	428
January - 1952	580
December - 1955	657
April - 1958	558

Since the floods of 1955 and 1958 were so completely documented by the Corps of Engineers, data on these two floods were used in developing much of the material for this section. During the 1955 and 1958 floods, damage in the Livermore-Amador Valley was mostly at the western end where the Arroyo de la Laguna went over its banks and caused extensive agricultural damage. Water depth in the flooded area was 0.3 to 1 m. Damage at the upper end of the Valley was due primarily to the Arroyo del

Valle cutting into an existing road alongside the stream. The Corps of Engineers makes no mention in their documents of either the Arroyo Las Positas or Arroyo Seco leaving their banks.

4.2. FLOOD DESIGN CONSIDERATIONS

Since the floods of the fifties, much of the Valley has changed from agriculture to residential. During this time, the stream channels have been enlarged to handle flood water at the lower end of the Valley. A reservoir with a capacity of 9.5×10^7 m^3 was built during the sixties to control flooding caused by the Arroyo del Valle in the western end of the Valley. Of the 9.5×10^7 m^3 holding capacity, 4.6×10^7 m^3 is for flood control.

4.3. FLOODING AT THE SITE

Flooding of the Laboratory site could occur only if the Arroyo Las Positas and Arroyo Seco overflowed during a severe storm. For this study, this is assumed to be caused by the probable maximum precipitation for the two basins that is developed below.

Actually, Arroyo Las Positas flow and overflow would have no effect on the Site, affecting only the eastern corner and northern portion of LLNL. However, assuming the Arroyo Seco left its banks south of the Laboratory during the postulated storm, this would give the overflow water an elevation of 189 to 198 m. The flooding would be a sheet flow moving north across the Laboratory, using the existing streets as channels. Water depth would not exceed 15 mm, and would flow fairly fast. This would last only until the peak of the storm had passed. Since there is about an 18-m drop from south to north across the Laboratory, the water would not pond until it met the Western Pacific Railroad bank, where it would then flow to the west.

5. PROBABLE MAXIMUM PRECIPITATION

This section presents data and assumptions used in developing the probable maximum precipitation (PMP) for the Arroyo Las Positas and Arroyo Seco. The PMP for the Arroyo del Valle can be taken directly from data used by the Corps of Engineers in their study of Alameda Creek. This is found to be 0.612 m over a 72-h rainfall period for the area above the dam which has a drainage area of 386 km^2. The data were prepared by the Hydrometeorological Section of the U.S. Weather Bureau for the Corps of Engineers during 1957.

5.1. PRECIPITATION STATION AND RECORDS

There are two U.S. Weather Bureau precipitation stations in the vicinity of Livermore Valley. These include the one on Mt. Hamilton (Lick Observatory) and the one in the City of Livermore. Continuous records have been kept at these two sites since 1870 (Mt. Hamilton) and 1881 (Livermore). Rainfall extremes for the two areas vary from 1.47 m at Mt. Hamilton in 1883-1884 to 138 mm at Livermore during 1975-1976.

5.2. MAJOR STORMS

The U.S. Weather Bureau indicates that for this area effective rainfall contribution to a flood during a storm occurs within a 72-h period. The three most severe storms on record listed in Table 1 illustrate the maximum rainfall that has occurred during approximate 72-h periods.

5.3. PROBABLE MAXIMUM STORM

Probable maximum precipitation was developed for the Arroyo Las Positas and Arroyo Seco above the Laboratory using "Hydrometerological Report No. 36"[1] which presents criteria for estimating PMP over basins above prospective flood control structures in the Pacific drainage of California. The PMP was prepared for orographic and restricted convergence storms separately and then combined for comparison with an unrestricted convergence storm. Because of the small area of the basins and small amount of rainfall resulting from the orographic storm, PMP was also prepared for an unrestricted convergence storm (see Tables 2 and 3 and Figs. 2 and 3). Snow melt would have no effect on PMP for this area.

6. FACTORS AFFECTING PRECIPITATION LOSS

6.1. ANTECEDENT PRECIPITATION

Since PMP was developed for the wet season, antecedent precipitation would be high. Before the storm of April 1958, the antecedent preciptiation at the Laboratory site was 114 mm during March. Total precipitation at the U.S. Weather Bureau Station in Livermore five days before the December storm of 1955 was 33 mm.

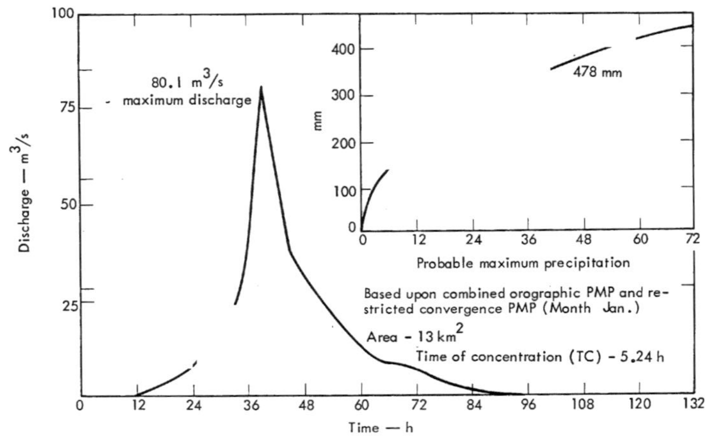

Figure 2. Hydrograph for Arroyo Las Positas.

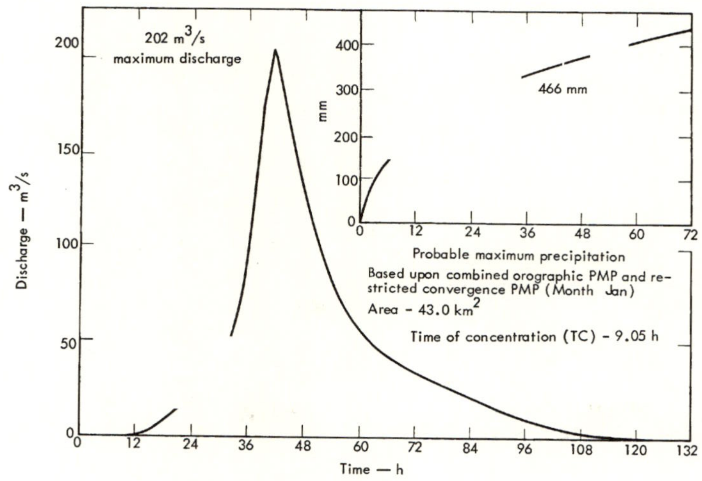

Figure 3. Hydrograph for Arroyo Seco.

Table 1. Major storms.

Date	Station	Rainfall per day (mm)				
		Day 1	Day 2	Day 3	Day 4	Total
11-14 January 1911	Mt. Hamilton	58.2	65.5	33.0	36.1	192.8
	Livermore	17.8	63.5	45.5	65.8	191.3
21-24 December 1955	Mt. Hamilton	5.3	104.1	174.5	6.6	290.6
	Livermore	0.8	19.0	82.8	49.0	151.6
1-3 April 1958	Mt. Hamilton	25.4	38.1	30.5	0.0	94.5
	Livermore	17.8	3.0	45.7	0.0	66.5
	LLNL Site[a]	19.3	2.3	42.9	0.0	64.5

[a] The LLNL site rain gauge was installed on February 28, 1958.

Table 2. Probable maximum precipitation Arroyo Las Positas accumulated unrestricted PMP in mm.

Duration (H)	1	3	6	12	18	24	30	36	42	48	54	60	66	72
Oct.	95.0	157.5	205.7	253.5	284.2	306.3	324.4	339.9	354.1	368.3	379.7	391.2	401.3	411.5
Nov.	86.4	140.5	186.2	240.3	275.1	300.7	321.3	339.3	355.9	370.1	383.0	396.0	408.9	421.9
Dec.	75.7	128.5	169.4	224.8	263.4	290.3	313.4	334.0	350.5	366.0	380.2	394.5	407.4	420.4
Jan.	70.9	119.4	160.3	219.2	259.1	286.0	309.9	330.5	348.5	365.0	380.5	394.5	408.4	422.4
Feb.	70.9	119.4	160.3	219.2	259.1	286.0	309.9	330.5	348.5	365.0	380.5	394.5	408.4	422.4
Mar.	73.4	120.6	163.1	223.5	262.1	291.6	315.5	336.0	352.6	366.8	379.7	392.7	404.1	415.5
Apr.	74.7	127.5	167.1	225.0	263.7	293.1	316.2	334.3	349.8	362.7	374.1	385.6	395.7	405.9

Table 2. (cont'd). Combined orographic PPM and restricted convergence PPM (mm).

Duration (H)	1	3	6	12	18	24	30	36	42	48	54	60	66	72
Oct.	75.9	131.3	178.1	233.9	274.6	306.3	333.0	356.4	377.4	397.0	413.3	428.8	442.0	454.9
Nov.	69.6	118.4	164.1	223.8	269.5	304.3	333.2	358.6	381.5	401.3	418.8	435.4	450.8	465.8
Dec.	62.0	110.0	152.4	215.4	263.1	299.7	331.0	358.9	382.5	403.6	422.4	440.2	455.9	470.9
Jan.	58.2	103.4	146.3	212.3	261.4	300.0	332.2	360.4	385.1	407.2	427.2	445.0	461.8	477.8
Feb.	58.2	103.4	146.0	212.3	261.4	300.0	332.2	360.4	385.1	407.2	427.2	445.0	461.8	477.8
Mar.	59.9	103.6	146.8	213.1	260.1	297.9	329.4	357.1	380.2	400.3	417.8	434.6	449.3	463.3
Apr.	60.2	107.4	147.6	210.1	255.5	292.1	321.8	346.2	367.5	385.6	401.6	416.6	429.8	442.2

Table 3. Probable maximum precipitation Arroyo Seco accumulated unrestricted PMP (mm).

Duration (H)	1	3	6	12	18	24	30	36	42	48	54	60	66	72
Oct.	92.5	153.4	201.9	248.2	278.9	300.7	318.5	334.0	348.2	361.2	372.6	384.0	394.2	404.4
Nov.	83.1	135.9	181.9	235.5	270.3	295.9	316.5	334.3	350.8	365.0	378.0	390.9	403.9	416.8
Dec.	73.2	124.2	166.9	221.7	260.1	287.0	309.9	330.5	347.0	362.5	376.7	390.9	403.9	416.8
Jan.	68.8	116.1	158.2	217.2	257.0	286.5	310.9	331.5	349.2	365.8	381.3	395.5	409.7	423.9
Feb.	68.8	116.1	158.2	217.2	257.0	286.5	310.9	331.5	349.2	365.8	381.3	395.5	409.7	423.9
Mar.	68.8	118.4	160.5	221.0	259.6	289.1	313.4	334.0	350.5	366.8	379.7	392.7	404.1	415.5
Apr.	71.9	99.6	169.7	227.3	265.9	295.4	318.3	336.0	351.5	364.5	375.9	387.3	397.5	407.7

Table 3. (cont'd). Combined orographic PMP and restricted convergence PMP in mm.

Duration (H)	1	3	6	12	18	24	30	36	42	48	54	60	66	72
Oct.	74.2	128.0	174.2	229.1	269.7	301.5	328.2	351.5	372.6	391.2	407.4	422.9	436.4	449.1
Nov.	67.3	115.3	161.0	222.2	259.6	294.4	323.3	348.7	371.6	391.4	408.9	425.5	440.9	455.9
Dec.	59.9	106.9	150.4	213.1	260.9	297.4	328.7	356.6	380.2	401.3	420.1	437.9	453.6	468.6
Jan.	56.4	98.6	144.3	210.6	252.6	298.2	333.2	358.1	382.8	404.9	417.6	435.6	452.1	469.6
Feb.	56.4	98.6	144.3	210.6	259.6	298.2	333.2	358.1	382.8	404.9	417.6	435.6	452.1	469.6
Mar.	56.4	101.9	144.8	211.1	258.1	295.9	327.7	355.3	378.5	400.0	417.6	436.9	451.6	465.6
Apr.	58.7	105.9	149.6	212.1	257.6	294.1	323.8	348.2	369.6	387.6	401.1	414.8	428.0	440.4

6.2. INFILTRATION RATE

The soils in both basins have been classified as to type by the U.S. Soil Conservation Service.[2] Since they are either type C or D, infiltration rates would be very slow. Ground cover in the area is annual grass with about 1% of perennial grass. In the Arroyo Seco basin at the higher elevations, there is brush and California Live Oak.

7. POTENTIAL DAM FAILURE (SEISMICALLY INDUCED)

If it is assumed that the Del Valle Dam failed due to an earthquake and that at the same time Arroyo de la Laguna Canyon was closed by a seismically induced landslide, water would flow to and collect in the west end of the Valley. This is due to the difference in elevation between the Valley entrance point of Arroyo Del Valle (122 m MSL) and the elevation at the lower end of the Valley floor (98 m MSL). Total surface area of the Valley below the 122-m contour line is 65 km^2, more than adequate to collect the maximum assumed storage in Del Valle Reservoir of 4.9×10^7 m^3. Also, in prehistory, all water from the Valley flowed north through San Ramon Valley. Elevation at the head end of San Ramon Valley is currently 140 m MSL. Since the elevation of the Laboratory is between 150 and 180 m MSL, there would be no danger to the Laboratory from failure of the Del Valle Dam.

REFERENCES

1. Interim Report, Probable Maximum Precipitation in California, prepared by Hydrometeorology Branch Office of Hydrology (rev. October 1969).
2. Soil Survey - Alameda Area, California, prepared by the U.S. Department of Agriculture (March 1966).

APPENDIX 2D

GROUNDWATER HYDROLOGY

. INTRODUCTION

The Lawrence Livermore National Laboratory is located about 40 km east of San Francisco Bay at the east end of the Livermore Valley. The Laboratory property occupies all of Section 12, T 3S, R 2E. This report is designed to provide a concise description of the occurrence and movement of groundwater near LLNL in the eastern Livermore Valley. The hydrogeologic description is based principally on the results of previous investigations, from which information has been freely drawn.[1,2]

2. PHYSIOGRAPHY AND DRAINAGE

The Livermore Valley is a prominent east-west structural depression within the California Coast Range. At the surface, the Valley forms an irregularly shaped lowland area about 5 km wide and 22 km long. The floor of the Valley slopes to the west at about 4 mm/m from an elevation of 182 m on the eastern end to about 91 m near the southwestern corner. The Diablo Range and foothills border the Valley on the south. Elevations of this fairly rugged mountain range average 1 km and from it issue the intermittent flows of Arroyo del Valle, Arroyo Mocho, and Arroyo Seco (see Fig. 1). The hills east of the Valley reach to elevations of about 500 m and give rise to the intermittent flows of Arroyo Las Positas and Altamont Creek. Mount Diablo and its foothills provide the northern boundary of the Livermore Valley, and from them a number of intermittent streams drain. The intermittent streams that flow into the eastern Livermore Valley from the surrounding uplands ultimately merge on the valley floor and drain to the west where they flow into Arroyo de la Laguna. Arroyo de la Laguna empties through the southwestern outlet of Livermore Valley into Alameda Creek which finally finds its way to San Francisco Bay. The streams draining into the Livermore Valley have been transporting debris into it since late Pliocene time, and have deposited a complex body of sediment in the depression including alluvial fan, terrace, and floodplain morphologies.[2]

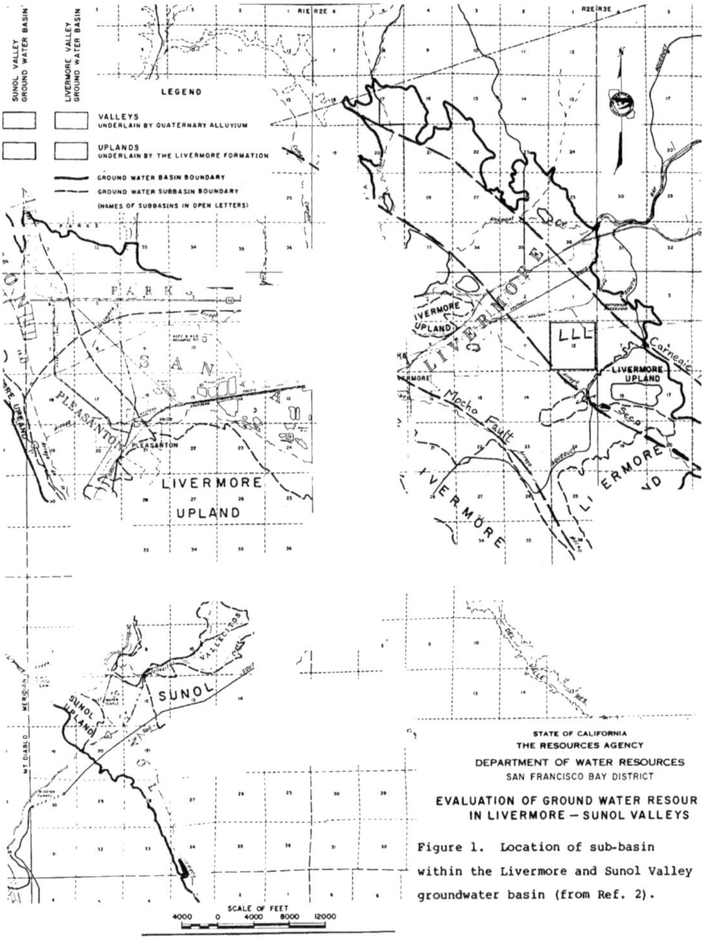

Figure 1. Location of sub-basin within the Livermore and Sunol Valley groundwater basin (from Ref. 2).

The climate of Livermore Valley is characterized by a marked seasonal rainfall distribution. Most of the precipitation falls between the months of October and April; very little falls during the warmer months of the year. Most rainfall occurs during general winter storms that move inland from the coast. The average annual precipitation at Livermore is 367 mm. The actual annual evapotranspiration calculated by soil scientists of the U.S. Department of Agriculture[3] for the same station is 293 mm. Therefore, on the average, an excess of precipitation exists to form surface runoff and to infiltrate the soils of the region. In some areas, this infiltration apparently proceeds to the extent that groundwater recharge is affected.

4. BASIN WATFR BALANCE

Before 1962, the water needs of Livermore Valley were supplied almost entirely from groundwater. Since 1945, recharge of groundwater has been less than total withdrawals, resulting in a general decline in groundwater levels.[2] The water level in a 214-m well on the LLNL site has dropped about 10 m since 1942. The lowered water levels have caused cessation of subsurface outflow from the southwestern outlet of the Livermore Valley groundwater basin. This condition, coupled with reuse of water, has served to increase the salt content of groundwater, particularly in the central portion of the Livermore Valley.[2] In 1962, the first deliveries of imported water were made to the Valley through the South Bay Aqueduct. This water importation continues as part of the effort to balance groundwater withdrawal with recharge. The Laboratory originally derived its water supply from two wells on the Laboratory site.[4] The water for the Laboratory now comes from the Sierra Nevada via the Hetch Hetchy Aqueduct, built in 1934 by the City of San Francisco. A standby water supply is provided through the South Bay Aqueduct. Groundwater is no longer withdrawn by Lawrence Livermore National Laboratory.

5. STRATIGRAPHY: GEOLOGIC FORMATIONS AND THEIR WATER-BEARING PROPERTIES

The Livermore Valley has two major sources of groundwater: the alluvial deposits that lie immediately beneath the valley floor, and the older Livermore Formation that generally is found beneath the alluvium. The Livermore Valley groundwater basin, as it is defined by Finlayson et al,[2] encompasses the surface exposure of the alluvium and the Livermore Formation, and is shown in part in

Fig. 1. It is suggested that a better definition of the Livermore Valley groundwater basin would be based on topographic considerations and could include all the area with surface drainage to the Valley. A third water-producing material, the Tassajara Formation, underlies the northern portion of the Livermore Valley and has a large area of surface exposure in the hills immediately north of the valley. The Tassajara Formation is substantially less important as a source of groundwater because of its lower transmissivities relative to those of the alluvium and the Livermore Formation.

The stratigraphy of the eastern Livermore Valley area will be discussed in order of decreasing age of formations. The units are classified as being either water-bearing or nonwater-bearing. The nonwater-bearing group includes formations that yield water to wells in quantities so low as to be useful only for stock watering and limited domestic supplies. Figure 2 portrays the surface exposures of some of the formations in the eastern Livermore Valley.[5]

6. NONWATER-BEARING FORMATIONS

Descriptions of these strata are primarily from Ref. 6. Rocks of the nonwater-bearing group crop out on all sides of the Livermore Valley. They also underlie the Valley and form the effective hydrologic basement at depths of as much as 300 m near the axis of the Valley. The rocks of this group were all deposited under marine conditions.

6.1. FRANCISCAN GROUP (JURA-CRETACEOUS)

The geologic basement in the area is composed everywhere of rocks of the Franciscan assemblage. These rocks are exposed throughout the entire Diablo range south of Livermore Valley, and at Mount Diablo to the north. The Livermore Formation laps onto the Franciscan rocks about 5 km southeast of the Lawrence Livermore National Laboratory site. The Franciscan surface dips about 20 degrees to the northwest beneath Livermore Valley.

The Franciscan Group is composed primarily of sandstone with smaller amounts of interbedded siltstone and shale. Minor rock types include conglomerate, various colored chert, altered igneous rocks, and small bodies of serpentine.

6.2. PANOCHE FORMATION (UPPER CRETACEOUS)

The Panoche Formation overlies the Franciscan and is widely exposed in the Altamont anticline northeast of the Valley. The Panoche, which attains a thickness of about 3000 m, consists of a series

Figure 2. Plan view of site geology (from Ref. 5).

of interbedded shales and sandstones that are hard and fairly well indurated. The density of the Panoche Formation is close to that of the Franciscan Group, in contrast to the less dense younger tertiary strata.

6.3. TESLA FORMATION (MIDDLE EOCENE)

The oldest tertiary rocks in the area are found in the Tesla Formation that has limited exposure in a narrow band along Tesla Road, some 6 km southeast of the Laboratory site. The Formation has a reported thickness of up to 600 m and is composed of sandstone, clay, and shale with occasional coal seams and conglomerate beds.

6.4. CIERBO FORMATION (UPPER MIOCENE)

The poorly exposed Cierbo Formation overlies the Tesla Formation. It is known principally from deep drilling, and has been proven as a minor oil reservoir. The Cierbo is about 300 m thick and is composed of poorly consolidated sandstone, shale, and tuff.

6.5. NEROLY FORMATION (UPPER MIOCENE)

The Upper Miocene is also represented in the eastern Livermore Valley area by the Neroly Formation that attains a thickness of up to 800 m. The Neroly Formation is typically a hard, pale bluish-gray sandstone, but also contains conglomerate, shale, and tuff. It crops out locally in the hills east of the Lawrence Livermore National Laboratory.

7. WATER-BEARING FORMATIONS

Rocks of the water-bearing group underlie the entire valley floor of the Livermore Valley. Under most conditions, these units yield large quantities of groundwater to wells. The quality of this groundwater is mostly in the good to excellent range.

7.1. TASSAJARA FORMATION (PLIOCENE)

The rocks of the Tassajara Formation[1] unconformably overlie the Upper Miocene strata, and include the oldest continental sediments in the Livermore Valley area. These rocks, which previously have been considered as part of the Orinda Formation, consist of fresh- to brackish-water sandstone, tuffaceous sandstone, siltstone, conglomerate, shale, and limestone. The Tassajara Formation is exposed over a large area immediately north of the Livermore Valley. It occurs beneath the floor of the Valley at a depth of less than 60 m in the northern portion of the City of Livermore, and is believed to occur at depths greater than 230 m beneath the City of Livermore.

Groundwater in the Tassajara Formation is a sodium bicarbonate type of moderate quality.

7.2. LIVERMORE FORMATION (PLIO-PLEISTOCENE)

The Livermore Formation[1,2] is exposed in low hills to the south and southeast of the Livermore Valley in the Livermore Upland (see Fig. 1). Limited exposure of the Formation also occurs in a hill mass northeast of the City of Livermore. Throughout its outcrop area, the Livermore Formation consistently dips to the north or northwest at from 5 to 30 degrees. These stratal attitudes are likely a combination of initial sedimentary dip and inclination imposed by the continued structural development of the Livermore Valley. These dips carry the Livermore Formation beneath the younger alluvium of the Valley where it is found nearly everywhere at depths ranging from a few meters to over 120 m.

The Livermore Formation was deposited by streams draining the highlands surrounding the Valley, and in ephemeral lakes within the Valley. It is composed of various proportions of siltstone, claystone, sand, and "gravel." The "gravel" facies predominates and is composed of gravel, cobbles, and boulders derived largely from the highland Franciscan terrain south of Livermore Valley. The rock fragments of the "gravel" facies are contained in a reddish-brown sandy clay matrix.

The Formation rests with angular unconformity on all older rocks, and attains maximum thicknesses of about 1200 m. A tuff bed near the base of the Livermore Formation has been dated at 4.5 million years.[7] This age confirms the Mid-Pliocene age of the basal Livermore Formation.

The Livermore Formation is one of the principal water-bearing formations in the Livermore Valley. All of the deep wells (wells deeper than about 45 m) in the eastern half of the Valley produce from this unit. Yields to wells are adequate for most irrigation, industrial, or municipal purposes. Transmissivitiy of the Livermore Formation is estimated to be in the range from 124 to 806 m^2/d which is considerably less than the corresponding values for the overlying, younger alluvium.[1]

Groundwater from the Livermore Formation is a sodium bicarbonate water of generally good quality. Chemical analyses of water from two presently unused deep wells on the Lawrence Livermore National Laboratory site are presented in Table 1, taken from Ref. 4. Both wells are completed in gravel beds, presumably of the Livermore Formation. The analyses in Table 1 were made prior to March

Table 1. Chemical analyses of water from deep wells at Lawrence Livermore National Laboratory (concentrations given in parts per million).

Determination	Well No. 1	Well No. 2
Sodium plus potassium (Na + K)	166	254
Calcium (Ca)	31	59
Magnesium (Mg)	34	31
Nitrate (NO_3)	0	0
Sulfate (SO_4)	16	2.6
Chloride (Cl)	166	200
Bicarbonate (HCO_3)	400	661
Carbonate (CO_3)	-	-
Free carbon dioxide (CO_2)	16	53
Total Hardness ($CaCO_3$)	217	275
Silica (SiO_2)	16	20
Iron (Fe)	0.17	0.28
Manganese (Mn)	0	0
Total solids (on evaporation)	623	902
pH	7.6	7.3
Dissolved oxygen	0	0

1955. Water from both wells exhibited faint iron and noticeable saline taste. Water from Well 1 had a definite sulfide odor, and water from both wells had substantial amounts of methane gas entrained.

The important aspects of the chemical character of the groundwater from the Livermore Formation are the predominance of sodium and potassium over other cations, the predominance of bicarbonate over other anions, and the substantial chloride concentration.

7.3. ALLUVIUM AND LACUSTRINE DEPOSITS (PLEISTOCENE-RECENT)

Alluvium and lacustrine deposits[2] of Pleistocene to Recent age are grouped together, for the purpose at hand, as Quaternary alluvium. The Quaternary alluvium consists of stream and lake sediments including various mixtures of gravel, sand, silt, and clay. The alluvium is largely unconsolidated, and overlies the Livermore Formation in most of the Livermore Valley and the Tassajara Formation in the northern portion of the Valley.

The exact thickness of the Quaternary alluvium is difficult to determine because of its similarity to underlying formations, especially the Livermore Formation. Some well logs vaguely suggest a decrease in grain size within intervals known to contain both Quaternary alluvium and the Livermore Formation. The decrease is apparently gradational, and may describe the contact between the two formations. The thickness of the alluvium in Livermore Valley increases gradually from east to west. It reaches thicknesses of about 60 m in the vicinity of the City of Livermore. Elongated zones of high sand and gravel content in alluvium closely follow the present courses of Arroyo Mocho and Arroyo del Valle (see Fig. 3). The alluvium along the north side of Livermore Valley is thinner than elsewhere, and is much finer-grained than that along the southern portion of the Valley. In the east portion of the Livermore Valley, the alluvium is revealed in well logs to be composed of overlapping, interfingering lenses and sheets of gravel, sand, silt, and clay. Individual layers are not extensive enough to be traced between well logs, because they change in physical nature over very short distances.

The Quaternary alluvium, especially in the western half of Livermore Valley, is the most prolific aquifer in the area. Water yields to properly designed wells are sufficient for any type of use. Transmissivities of the alluvium range from 930 to 4650 m^2/d.[1] Groundwater quality ranges from poor to excellent.

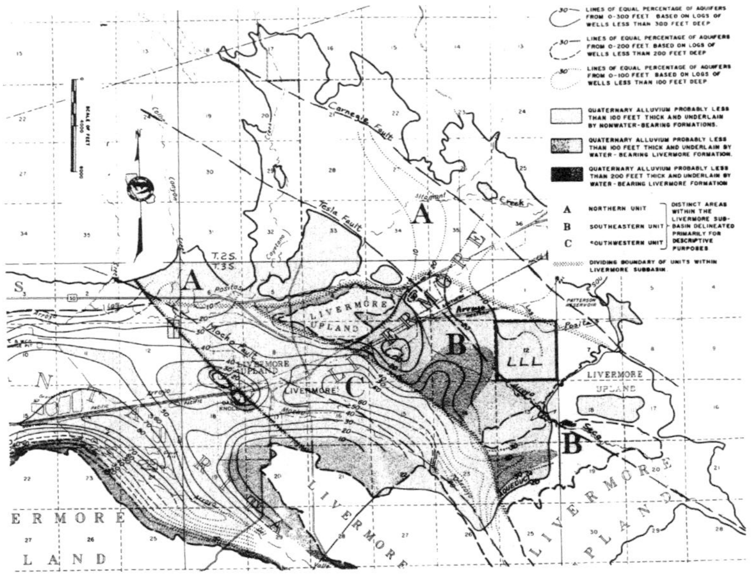

Figure 3. Lines of equal precentage of aquifers within the interval 0 to 91 m (0 to 300 ft) beneath the Livermore Valley (from Ref. 2).

8. STRUCTURES AFFECTING GROUNDWATER MOVEMENT

Faults within the Livermore Valley are the major structural features known to have marked effect on the movement of groundwater.[1] Faults in the Valley tend to act as barriers to groundwater flow. This barrier effect is commonly manifest in differences in hydraulic head, as measured in wells, across faults.

The Livermore Valley is cut by six major faults. These faults compartmentalize the Livermore Valley groundwater basin into a number of sub-basins. Study of groundwater flow in any one sub-basin is obviously made easier by knowledge of the extent of the sub-basin, which is defined in part by its fault borders. Determining the flow pattern in the whole groundwater basin then becomes a matter of linking the flow between sub-basins. Much work remains to be done in determining the nature of the flow linkage between sub-basins in the Livermore Valley groundwater basin.

Of the six major faults in the Livermore Valley, only those in the eastern portion of the valley will be discussed here. The locations of the faults are shown in Fig. 4.

8.1. CARNEGIE FAULT

The Carnegie fault runs along the eastern edge of the Livermore Valley. South of the Valley it brings Cretaceous rocks into juxtaposition with beds of the Livermore Formation. Recent oil exploration drilling in the eastern part of the Valley has shown that beneath the valley floor the Carnegie fault is a reverse fault, with older rocks from the east being moved over younger rocks on the west. Water level data along a portion of the length of the Carnegie fault indicate that it acts as a barrier to westward movement of groundwater. The water table drops some 45 m in step-wise fashion across the fault, with higher water table position on its northeast side.

The Carnegie fault appears to affect a contribution of fluoride to groundwater. Six wells located along the fault yield water with 1 part per million or more of fluoride.

8.2. TESLA FAULT

The Tesla fault enters the Livermore Valley along the canyon of Arroyo Seco. Movement on the Tesla fault appears to be primarily strike-slip with left-lateral sense. The Tesla fault presents a barrier to the flow of groundwater through much of its length in the Valley. Water levels in wells are about 9 m lower on the northeastern side of the fault than on the southwestern side. Groundwater is probably unimpeded in its southerly movement across the Tesla fault in the thin alluvium along Altamont and Cayetano Creeks.

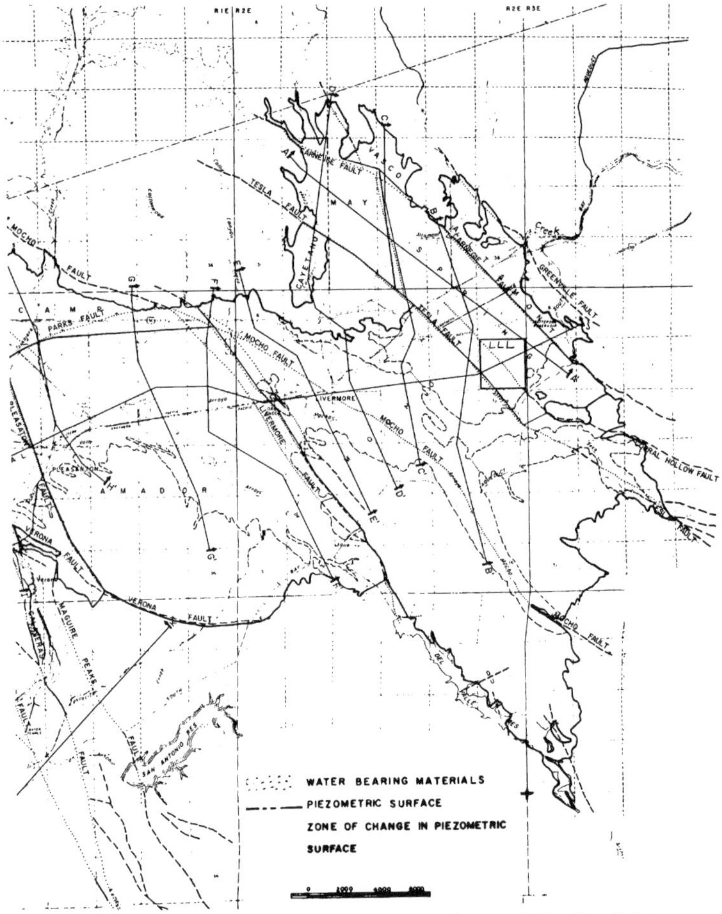

Figure 4. Geological sections and faults in eastern Livermore Valley (from Ref. 1).

The Tesla fault is a minor contributor of fluoride to groundwater. Three wells near the fault yield water containing fluoride in excess of 0.5 part per million.

8.3. MOCHO FAULT

The Mocho fault is part of one of the major zones of crustal weakness of the Diablo Range. The direction and magnitude of movement along the Mocho fault in the Livermore Valley is uncertain. The fault has an effect on groundwater flow through much of its length in the Livermore Valley as evidenced by well water levels that are depressed by 9 to 15 m on the northeast side.

9. GROUNDWATER MOVEMENT NEAR LAWRENCE LIVERMORE NATIONAL LABORATORY

Groundwater flow patterns are influenced by the configuration of the water table surface, and by variations in permeability of the saturated media. Permeability contrasts are found that result from original sedimentary processes and subsequent structural deformation. Some of these contrasts in the Pliocene to Recent materials of Livermore Valley have been described.

The configuration of the water table surface in the eastern Livermore Valley has not been defined. Potentiometric maps of hydraulic head distribution in confined aquifers of the eastern Livermore Valley are unavailable. It is known, however, that the water table is located at depths of from 20 to 30 m beneath the surface in the Lawrence Livermore National Laboratory area.[5]

The experience of groundwater hydrology has shown that the water table surface generally follows surface topography in alluvial materials. Using this premise and knowledge of the topography, structure, and stratigraphy of the eastern Livermore Valley, a description of the most likely general groundwater flow pattern can be assembled.

The effective lower boundary of the groundwater flow system in most of the Livermore Valley is found at the base of the Livermore Formation. Groundwater recharged to the Livermore Formation on the slopes south and southeast of the Valley moves northward under the younger alluvium of the Valley. Groundwater that enters the Quaternary alluvium along the northern and southern edges of the Valley moves generally toward the course of Arroyo Las Positas, and thence westward.[2] This westward movement is postulated on the basis of the surface gradient to the west and on the fact that the lowest groundwater levels occur in the western Livermore Valley, near the City of Pleasanton, where the heaviest groundwater withdrawals take place.

Hydraulic head potential is generally a decreasing function of depth in the eastern Livermore Valley.[2] Therefore, a substantial vertical downward component of groundwater flow from surface recharge in permeable soils and arroyo beds is inferred for much of the area.

Groundwater in the two compartments of the eastern Livermore Valley defined by the Mocho, Tesla, and Carnegie faults is thought to move from recharge areas along the margins of the Valley in the southeastern and northwestern ends of the compartments, down the topographic gradient, parallel to the faults, toward the low areas of the compartments along the courses of Arroyo Las Positas and Altamont Creek. Some recharge to the groundwater system within the compartments probably occurs along the course of the upper reaches of Arroyo Las Positas, along Arroyo Seco, and along Cayetano Creek.[2] Recharge from Arroyo Mocho certainly occurs along the southeastern portion of the Mocho fault in the Valley.[2] Some groundwater flow from the northeastern side of the Carnegie fault must occur because water levels are higher on the northeast side of the fault. Movement of groundwater from the Carnegie-Tesla fault compartment certainly occurs in the alluvium of Altamont Creek. Other flow-linkage between these compartments or sub-basins is possible, but difficult to predict without mapping the water table and other potential surfaces. Water levels along the southwest side of a large portion of the length of the Mocho fault in the Valley are higher than on the northeast side of the fault. It would seem, therefore, that flow into the Tesla-Mocho fault compartment comes along from the southwest. This contradicts the generalization that groundwater flow in the Valley is from east to west. A major question that must presently go unanswered is whether or not the Tesla-Mocho fault compartment is outflowing to the southwest or receiving groundwater inflow from that direction. Groundwater withdrawals in the Tesla-Mocho fault compartment may be great enough to cause flow across the Mocho fault to be from the southwest.

Section A-A' in Fig. 5 illustrates the relation between land surface topography and the hydraulic head potential surface of the shallow aquifers in the Carnegie-Tesla fault compartment.[1] Groundwater flow from the uplands near Cayetano Creek in the northwest, and from near Greenville Road in the southeast, moves toward the course of Altamont Creek, where the hydraulic head is least. The quality of groundwater in the compartment near Altamont Creek is poor, with total dissolved solids content averaging 2150 parts per million. The groundwater is a sodium chloride-sulfate type, high in boron. The surface soil in the area near Altamont Creek is rich in sodium sulfate and sodium chloride salts.[2] The area coincides with a low topographic basin, inefficiently drained by Altamont Creek. Finlayson et al.[2] state in discussing the area that "the high groundwater levels, salt-rich soil, and poor groundwater quality all suggest that groundwater in most of the northern unit does not readily move into the southeastern unit." The northern unit refers to an area generally north of Highway 50. The southeastern unit is south of Highway 50. Finlayson et al.[2] recognized all the

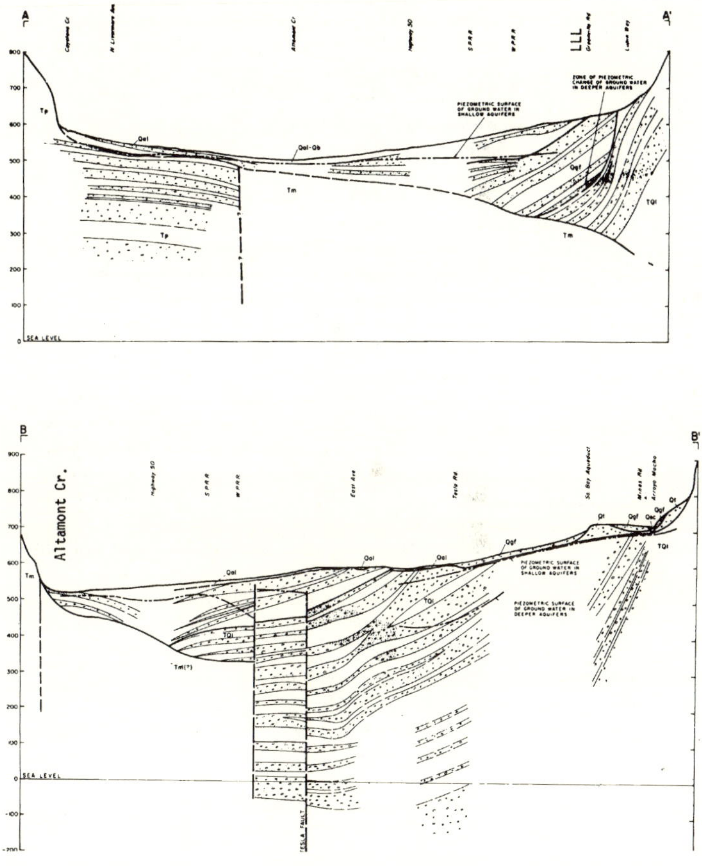

Figure 5. Geologic sections (from Ref. 1).

characteristics of the area along Altamont Creek that identify it as a groundwater discharge area, yet never quite came to that conclusion. All of the characteristics of the area can be explained by the movement of groundwater towards the surface along Altamont Creek in the compartment. Topographic influences and the thinning of water-bearing rocks beneath Altamont Creek, cause the vertical upward movement of groundwater, and force its discharge as diffuse seepage. Groundwater probably does not "readily move into the southeastern unit" because the gradient for flow is in the opposite direction.

The overall pattern of groundwater flow in the Tesla-Mocho fault compartment is likely similar to that in the Carnegie-Tesla fault compartment. More complex topography in the Tesla-Mocho compartment and greater groundwater withdrawal from it complicate its hydrology enough that generalizations concerning the groundwater flow pattern will be fraught with errors of detail. Again, water table and hydraulic head maps are needed for accurate flow description. Section B-B' of Fig. 5 shows that a northerly slope of the shallow aquifer potential surface exists in the Tesla-Mocho fault compartment. Section C-C' of Fig. 6 indicates the same slope. Section D-D' of Fig. 7 illustrates a southerly water table gradient from the north toward Arroyo Las Positas.

Groundwater recharge takes place by infiltration of precipitation in the low hills of the Livermore Formation east and southeast of the Lawrence Livermore National Laboratory site. Recharge is affected by flow losses during the rainy season from the channels of Arroyo Seco and Arroyo Las Positas above the mouth of Arroyo Seco. Water thus input to the underground system moves between the Mocho and Carnegie faults toward the northwest where a part of it is discharged as diffuse seepage in the low areas near Altamont Creek and Arroyo Las Positas below Altamont Creek. The remainder of groundwater flow moves an undetermined distance west by flow-linkage between sub-basins (fault compartments). A major question that remains to be answered revolves about the groundwater balance in the Tesla-Mocho fault compartment. It is not known that groundwater flow to the southwest out of the compartment occurs. There is some reason to believe that it does not. Hydraulic head potential mapping and other studies will be necessary to resolve the question.

10. SUMMARY OF GROUNDWATER HYDROLOGY

The eastern Livermore Valley, including the Lawrence Livermore National Laboratory site, is underlain by water-bearing strata, mostly of alluvial origin, that contain and transport groundwater. The Pliocene to Recent water-bearing materials are underlain by nonwater-bearing rocks of Miocene and older age. The water-bearing rocks contain aquifers at various depths that are used as groundwater supply sources. Most wells in the eastern Livermore Valley tap aquifers at depths of at least 30 m; many wells in the area produced from depths of 115 to 215 m.

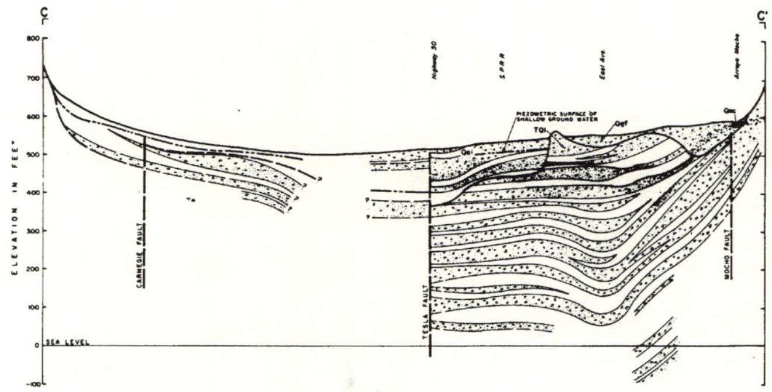

Figure 6. Geologic section (from Ref. 1).

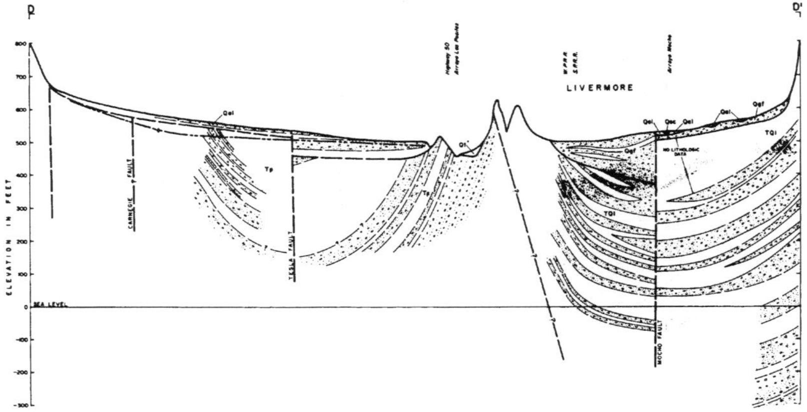

Figure 7. Geologic section (from Ref. 1).

Faults are the major structural features known to have a marked effect on the movement of groundwater in the eastern Livermore Valley. They tend to act as barriers to groundwater flow and divide the Livermore Valley groundwater basin into sub-basins or compartments.

The configuration of the water table surface in the eastern Livermore Valley has not been defined. Potentiometric maps of hydraulic head distribution in confined aquifers of the eastern Livermore Valley are unavailable. The water table is known to be located at depths from 9 to 30 m beneath the surface in the area of Lawrence Livermore National Laboratory. The general pattern of groundwater flow near Lawrence Livermore National Laboratory is inferred using topographic considerations and hydrologic profiles prepared by the California Department of Water Resources. The pattern inferred shows groundwater recharge entering the two compartments, formed by the Carnegie, Tesla, and Mocho faults, in areas southeast and east of the Laboratory site. Flow in the compartments is to the northwest, beneath the Site. Some of the groundwater ultimately is discharged by diffuse seepage to Altamont Creek and Arroyo Las Positas some 3.5 km northwest of the Laboratory site. The remaining groundwater moves an undetermined distance west, generally along Arroyo Las Positas. The direction of net groundwater flow across the Mocho fault has not been demonstrated. The surface gradient of Arroyo Las Positas is to the west, across the Mocho fault. On the other hand, groundwater pumpage from the Tesla-Mocho fault compartment may make it a closed groundwater sub-basin. Water levels in wells stand 9 to 15 m higher along much of the Mocho fault, on its southwest side. The determination of the nature of the groundwater flow-linkage between the Tesla-Mocho fault compartment and the next compartment to the southwest awaits further study.

REFERENCES

1. California Department of Water Resources, Evaluation of Ground Water Resources: Livermore and Sunol Valleys, Bulletin 118-2 (1974).
2. D. J. Finlayson, W. R. Hansen, and J. V. Vantine, Livermore and Sunol Valleys, Evaluation of Ground Water Resources, Appendix A: Geology, California Department of Water Resources Bulletin 118-2 (1966).
3. U.S. Department of Agriculture, Soil Conservation Service, Soil Survey--Alameda Area, California, Series 1961, No. 41 (1966).
4. K. W. Brown and B. P. Haskell, Water Supply Survey--Livermore Radiation Laboratory, Report, Brown and Caldwell, Civil and Chemical Engineers, San Francisco (1955).
5. D. L. Bernreuter and F. J. Tokarz, Design-Basis Earthquakes for the Lawrence Livermore Laboratory Site, Lawrence Livermore National Laboratory, Rept. UCRL-51193 (1972).
6. J. A. Blume and Associates, Engineers, Investigation of Faulting at the Lawrence Livermore Laboratory, Lawrence Livermore National Laboratory, Rept. UCRL-13568 (1972).
7. Andrei M. Sarna-Wojcicki, Correlation of Late Cenozoic Pyroclastic Deposits in the Central Coast Ranges of California, thesis, University of California, Berkeley, California (1971).

APPENDIX 2E

ECOLOGY

FLORA AND FAUNA OF THE LIVERMORE SITE

The biological features of the area occupied by DOE's Livermore sites have been examined at length. Plants and animals identified are listed in the following tables. At least one example of each listing has been observed. The plants identified are shown in Table 1; plants considered to be native to the area are accompanied by an asterisk. Mammals identified are listed in Table 2. Of the mammals present, jackrabbits are the most numerous. Gophers, snakes, and field mice are observed in the undeveloped portions of the sites. Birds, which are quite numerous, are listed in Table 3. Table 4 shows two reptiles and five amphibians observed on the Livermore sites. Although not observed, it is probable that there are more than one species of lizard and one species of snake on the Livermore sites. Tables 5 and 6 list the insects, arachnids, and crustaceans on the Livermore sites.

Altogether these listings include 114 species of vascular plants; 16 mammals, including man; 43 birds; 2 reptiles; 5 amphibians; 45 insects; 5 arachnids; and 3 others.

Tables 7, 8, and 9 list species observed at Site 300. This essentially grassland community is discussed in section 2.3.9. Site 300 is thought to be the only natural location for a rare and endangered species of wildflower, Amsinckia grandiflora; a report on its status there is included as the second part of this Appendix.

Table 1. Plants of the LLNL and SNLL sites.

Cupressaceae (Cypress Family)	
Juniper	Juniperus sp.
Golden cypress	Chamaecyparis obtusa
Salicaceae (Willow Family)	
Golden weeping willow	Salix babalonia
Sandbar willow*	Salix exigua
Moraceae (Mulberry Family)	
Fruitless mulberry	Morus alba
Ulmaceae (Elm Family)	
Chinese elm	Ulmus pumila
Zelkova	Zelkova sp.
Polygonaceae (Buckwheat Family)	
Curly dock *	Rumex crispus
Chenopodiaceae (Goosefoot Family)	
Nettleleaf goosefoot	Chenopodium murale
Lambsquarters	Chenopodium album
Russian thistle (tumbleweed)	Salsola kali
Portulacaceae (Purselane Family)	
Miner's-lettuce *	Montia perfoliate
Common purslane	Portulaca oleraceae
Rhamnaceae (Buckthorn Family)	
Ceanothus	Ceanothus sp.
Cruciferaceae (Mustard Family)	
Shepherd's purse *	Capsella bursa-pastoris
Black mustard	Brassica nigra
Wild radish	Raphanus sativus
Wild turnip	Brassica campestris
Juglandaceae (Walnut Family)	
English walnut	Juglans sp.

Table 1. (continued)

Leguminosaceae (Pea Family)	
Vetch	Vicia americana
Lupine *	Lupinus sp.
Alfalfa	Medicago sativa
California burclover	Medicago polymorpha
Locust (black)	Robinia sp.
Geraniaceae (Geranium Family)	
Filaree (Heronbill) *	Erodium cicutarium
Zygophyllaceae (Caltrop Family)	
Puncture-vine	Tribulus terrestris
Malvaceae (Mallow Family)	
Cheeseweed	Malva parviflora
Rose of sharon	Althaea sp.
Hypericaceae (St. Johnswort Family)	
St. Johnswort	Hypericum perforatum
Hydrophyllaceae (Waterleaf Family)	
Great valley phacelia*	Phacelia ciliata
Labiataceae (Mint Family)	
White Horehound	Marrubium vulgare
Purple sage*	Salvia dirrii
Rosemary	Rosmarinus officinalis
Compositaceae (Thistle Family)	
Prickly lettuce	Lactuca serriola
Common groundsel*	Senecio vulgaris
Annual sowthistle	Sonchus oleraceus
Milk thistle	Silybum marianum
Smooth cats-ear	Hypochoeris glabra
Pineapple weed	Matricarica matricarioides
Yellow starthistle	Centaurea solstitialis
Mayweed	Anthemis cotula
Dandelion	Taraxacum officinale
Coyote bush*	Baccharis pilularis
Spiny clotbur	Xanthium spinosum

Table 1. (continued)

Boraginaceae (Borage Family)	
Common fiddleneck*	Amsinckia intermedia
Polygonaceae (Buckwheat Family)	
Common knotweed	Polygonum aviculare
Onagraceae (Evening-Primrose Family)	
Panicled willow-herb	Epilobium paniculatum
Evening primrose*	Oenothera sp.
Proteacea (Protea Family)	
Silk oak	Grevillea robusta
Liliaceae (Lily Family)	
Grass nut*	Brodiaea laxa
Amoryllidaceae (Amaryllis Family)	
Lily of the Nile	Agapanthus africanus
Urticaceae (Nettle Family)	
Burning nettle	Urtica urens
Typhaceae (Cattail Family)	
Cattail*	Typha latifolia
Graminaceae (Grass Family)	
Large crabgrass	Digitaria sanguinalis
Rye	Secale cereale
Barnyardgrass	Echinochloa crusgalli
Littleseed canary grass	Phalaris minor
Wild barley	Hordeum californicum
Squirrel tail grass (Foxtail barley)	Hordeum jubatum
Wild oats	Avena barbata
Rabbitfoot grass	Polypogon monspeliensis
Annual bluegrass	Poa annua
Italian ryegrass	Lolium multiflorum
Ripgut brome	Bromus rigidus
Bermuda grass	Cynodon dactylon
Bluegrass	Poa sp.
Perla grass (Timothy)	Phleum pratense
Wheat grass	Agropyron sp.
Field oats	Avena sp.
Barley	Hordeum sp.

Table 1. (continued)

Primulaceae (Primrose Family)	
Scarlet Pimpernel	Anagallis aryensis
Amaranthaceae (Amaranth Family)	
Redroot pigweed (Green amaranth)	Amaranthus retroflexus
Tumble pigweed	Amaranthus albus
Euphorbiaeae (Spurge Family)	
Turkey mullein	Eremocarpus setigerus
Convolvulaceae (Morning-Glory Family)	
Field bindweed	Convolvulus arvensis
Hopseed bush	Dodonea sp.
Rosaceae (Rose Family)	
Tea rose	Rosa sp.
Firethorn	Pyracantha sp.
India hawthorn	Phaphiolepsis indica
Toyon*	Heteromeles arbutifolia
Stone fruits	
Apricot	Prunus sp.
Green-gage plum	Prunus sp.
Pear	Pyrus sp.
Quince	Chaenomeles sp.
Apple	Malus sp.
Hawthorn	Crataegus sp.
Punicaceae (Pomegranate Family)	
Pomegranate	Punica sp.
Anacardiaceae (Cashew Family)	
Pistachio	Pistacia sp.
Pinaceae (Pine Family)	
Aleppo pine	Pinus halepensis
Monterey pine	Pinus radiata
Mugho pine	Pinus sp.
Fagaceae (Beech Family)	
Black oak	Quercus sp.
Cork oak	Quercus sp.

Table 1. (continued)

Oleaceae (Olive Family)	
Ash	Fraxinus sp.
Taxodiaceae (Taxodium Family)	
Coast redwood	Sequoia sempervirens
Giant redwood	Sequoia gigantea
Casuarinaceae (Casuarina Family)	
Beefwood or she-oak	Casuarina stricta
Myrtaceae (Myrtle Family)	
Gum-tree	Eucalyptus sp.
Bottle brush	Calistemon sp.
Apocynaceae (Dogbane Family)	
Oleander	Nerium oleander
Gorylaceae (Hazelnut Family)	
Alder*	Alnus sp.
Hamamelidaceae (Witch-Hazel Family)	
Liquidambar sweet-gun	Liquidambar sp.
Platanaceae (Plane-Tree Family)	
Sycamore *	Platanus sp.
Iridiaceae (Iris Family)	
Blue eyed grass *	Sisyrinchium bellum
Araliaceae (Ginseng Family)	
Ground ivy	Hedera sp.
Acanthaceae (Acanthus Family)	
Bears-breech	Acanthus latifolius
Leguminosaceae (Pea Family)	
Mimosa	Albizzia sp.
Red Bud *	Cercis occidentalis
Elaeagnaceae (Oleaster Family)	
Russian olive	Elaeagnus angustifolia

Table 1. (continued)

Cyperaceae (Sedge Family)	
Yellow Nutgrass	Cyperus esculentus
Scrophulariaceae (Figwort Family)	
Owl clover *	Orthocarpus purpurascens
Ericaceae (Heath Family)	
Strawberry tree	Arbutus unedo
Papaveraceae (Poppy Family)	
California poppy *	Eschscholzia californica
Solanaceae (Nightshade Family)	
False tobacco	Nicotiana glauca

Table 2. Mammals of the LLNL and SNLL sites.

Marsupialia (pouched)	
Opossum	Didelphis marsupialis
Chiroptera (Bats)	
Little brown bat	Myotis lucifugus
Carnivora (Meat-eaters)	
Spotted skunk	Spilogale putorius
Rodentia (Gnawing)	
Muskrat	Ondatra zibethica
Pocket gopher	Thomomys bottae
Deer mouse	Peromyscus maniculatus
House mouse	Mus musculus
Meadow vole	Microtus californicus
Norway rat	Rattus norvegicus
Lagomorpha	
Black-tailed jackrabbit	Lepus californicus
Brush rabbit	Sylvilagus auduboni
Domestic Animals	
Cows	Bos sp.
Goats	Capra sp.
Sheep	Ovis sp.
Cats	Felis domestica
Dogs	Canis familiaris
Horses	Equus caballus
Chickens	Gallus gallus

Table 3. Birds of the LLNL and SNLL sites.

Turkey vulture	Cathartes aura
White-tail kite	Elanus leucurus
Red-tailed hawk	Buteo jamaicensis
Sparrow hawk (American kestrel)	Falco sparverius
Golden eagle	Aquila chrysaetos
Bald eagle	Haliaeetus leucocephalus
California quail	Lophortyx californicus
Ring-necked pheasant	Phasianus colchicus
Chukar	Alectoris graeca
Killdeer	Charadrius vociferus
Ring-billed gull	Larus delawarensis
California gull	Larus californicus
Rock dove (Domestic pigeon)	Columba livia
Mourning dove	Zenaidura macroura
Barn owl	Tyto alba
White-throated swift	Aeronautes saxatalis
Anna's hummingbird	Calypte anna
Red-shafted flicker	Colaptes cafer
Western kingbird	Tyrannus verticalis
Cliff swallow	Petrochelidon pyrrhonota
Scrub jay	Aphelocoma coerulescens
Yellow-billed magpie	Pica nuttalli
Raven	Corvus corax
Crow	Corvus brachyrhynchos
Red-breasted nuthatch	Sitta canadensis
Mockingbird	Mimus polyglottos
Robin	Turdus migratorius
Cedar waxwing	Bombycilla cedrorum
Loggerhead shrike	Lanius ludovicianus
Starling	Sturnus vulgaris
Yellow warbler	Dendroica petechia
House sparrow (English sparrow)	Passer domesticus
Western meadowlark	Sturnella neglecta
Redwinged blackbird	Agelaius phoeniceus
Bullock's oriole	Icterus bullockii
Brewer's blackbird	Euphagus cyanocephalus

Table 3. (continued) L and SLL sites. (continued)

House finch (Linnet)	*Carpodacus mexicanus*
Pine siskin	*Spinus pinus*
American goldfinch (Common goldfinch)	*Spinus tristis*
Lesser goldfinch	*Spinus psaltria*
Savannah sparrow	*Passerculus sandwichensis*
White-crowned sparrow	*Zonotrichia leucophrys*
Golden-crowned sparrow	*Zonotrichia atricapilla*

Table 4. Amphibians and reptiles of the LLNL and SNLL sites.

Toad and Frog	
Pacific treefrog	*Hyla regilla*
Western toad	*Bufo boreas*
Lizard	
Western fence lizard	*Sceloporus occidentalis*
Salamanders	
Eschscholtz's salamander	*Ensatina eschscholtzii*
California slender salamander	*Batrachoseps attenuatus*
Pacific giant salamander	*Dicamptodon ensatus*
Snake	
Gopher snake	*Pituophis catenifer*

Table 5. Insects of the LLNL and SNLL sites.

Diptera	
House fly	Musca domestica
Syrphid fly	Syrphus ribesii
Mosquito	Culex
Crane fly	Tipula
Horse fly	Tabanus
Horse bot fly	Gasterophilus intestinalis
Vinegar flies	Drosophila melanogaster
Sun fly	Pseudoleria
Green bottle fly	Lucilia
Thysanura	
Machilids	Machilis
Silverfish	Thermobia
Ephemeroptera	
May fly	Caenis
Odonata	
Dragon fly	Anax
Dragon fly	Libellula
Damsel fly	Argia
Orthoptera	
Katydids	Microcentrum
Field crickets	Gryllus
Grasshoppers	Melanoplus
Dermaptera	
Earwig	Forficula auricularia
Coleoptera	
Whirligig beetles	Dineutes
Grain beetles	Tenebroides
Click beetles	Monocerpidius
Lady beetle	Hippodamia convergens

Table 5. (continued)

Hemiptera	
Stink bug	Chlorochroa
Water strider	Gerris
Squash bug	Anasa
Back swimmers	Notonecta
Homoptera	
Cicadas	Magicicada
Leaf-hoppers	Platymetopius
San Jose scale	Asphidiotus perniciosus
Whiteflies	Trialeurodes
Plant lice	Aphis
Ants	Formica
Neuroptera	
Snakeflies	Mantisapa
Aphis lions	Chrysopa oculata
Lepidoptera	
Swallowtail butterfly	
Cabbageworm	Pieris rapae
Monarch butterfly	Danaus plexippus
Fritillary	Euptoieta
Tobacco hornworm (Sphinx)	Protoparce sexta
Measuring worms	Cleora
Hymenoptera	
Wasps	Polistes
Mud-dauber wasp	Sceliphron
Bumble bee	Bombus
Honey bee	Apis mellifera

Table 6. Arachnids and crustaceans of the LLNL and SNLL sites.

Arachnida	
Spiders and mites	
Red Spider mite	Paratetranychus pilosus
Garden spider	Argiope
Black widow	Latrodectus mactans
Scorpion	
Harvestman spider	
Chilopoda	
Centipede	
Crustacea	
Sow-bug	Cylisticus convexus
Diplopoda	
Millipede	Spirobolus

Table 7. Plants of Site 300.[a]

Common name (blossom color, if noted)	Scientific name
Annual bluegrass	Poa annua
Ash	Fraxinus velutina
Blue dick	Brodiaea pulchella
Bluegum	Eucalyptus globulus
Burr clover	Medicago polymorpha
California pepper	Schinus molle
California poppy	Eschscholtzia californica
Cattail	Typha latifolia
Coast beefwood	Casuarina stricta
Common groundsel (yellow)	Senecio vulgaris
Coyote bush	Baccharis pilularis
Cream cup	Platystemon californicus
Deer weed	Lotus rigidus
Deodar cedar	Cedrus deodara
Fiddleneck (orange)	Amsinckia intermedia
	Amsinckia grandiflora
Fillaree (blue)	Erodium cicutarium
Firethorn	Pyrocantha fortuncana
Forget-me-not (white)	Myosotis sylvatica
Goldfield (yellow)	Baeria chrysostoma
Grape	Vitis vinifera
Grass nut	Brediaca laxa
Great valley phacelia	Phacelia ciliata
Hollywood juniper	Juniperus chinersis
Juniper tam	Juniper sabina
Larkspur	Delphinium decorum
Lovegrass sunflower (white)	Eragrostis diffusa
Lupine (blue), perennial	Lupinus arboreus

Table 7. (continued)

Common name (blossom color, if noted)	Scientific name
Lupine (white)	*Lupinus densiflorus*
Lupine (blue and white)	*Lupinus nanus*
Lupine (blue), annual	*Lupinus polyphyllus*
Manzanita	*Arctostaphylos glauca*
Milkthistle	*Silybum marianum*
Miner's lettuce (light yellow)	*Montia perfoliata*
Monterey pine	*Pinus radiata*
Mulberry	*Morus alba*
Oleander	*Nerium oleander*
Owl clover (white)	*Orthocarpus*
Owl clover (blue)	*Orthocarpus purparascens*
Panicled willow-herb	*Epilobium paniculatum*
Plane-tree	*Platanus acerifolia*
Red ironbark	*Eucalyptus sideroxylon*
Ripgut brome	*Bromus rigidus*
Rosemary	*Rosmarinus officinalis*
Ryegrass	*Lolium multiflorum*
Sagebrush	*Artemisia tridentata*
Shepherd's purse	*Capsella bursa-pastoris*
Shooting star (dark blue)	*Dodecatheon*
Soap plant (white)	*Chlorogalum pomeridianum*
Tidytip (yellow center, white tips)	*Layia platyglossa*
Turkey mullein	*Eremocarpus setigerus*
Valley oak	*Quercus lobata*
White ironbark	*Eucalyptus leucoxylon*
Wild barley	*Hordeum leporinum*
Wild cucumber	*Marah fabaceus*
Wild heliotrope	*Heliotropium*

Table 7. (continued)

Common name (blossom color, if noted)	Scientific name
Wild oat	*Avena fatua*
Yarrow (white)	*Achillea borealis*
Yellow starthistle	*Centaurea solstitialis*

[a]This list is as complete as possible for areas around Buildings 850 and 851 and the east power station and includes plants introduced as weeds and landscaping. Other areas of Site 300 were not as extensively surveyed.

Table 8. Mammals of Site 300.[a]

Audubon cottontail	Sylvilagus auduboni
Badger	Taxidea taxus
Big brown bat	Eptesicus fuscus
Black-tailed deer	Odocoileus hemionus
Bobcat	Lynx rufus
Brush mouse	Peromyscus boylei
Brush rabbit	Sylvilagus bachmani
California ground squirrel	Citellus beecheyi
California jackrabbit	Lepus californicus
California meadow mouse	Mycrotus californicus
Coyote	Canis latrans
Deer mouse	Peromyscus maniculatus
Feral cat	Felis domesticus
Feral dog	Canis domesticus
Grey fox	Urocyon cinereoargenteus
Heermann kangaroo rat	Dipodomys heermanni
Kit fox	Vulpes macrotis
Long-tailed weasel	Mustela frenata
Man	Homo sapien
Mountain lion	Felis concolor
Opossum	Didelphis marsupialis
Pinyon mouse	Peromyscus truei
Pocket gopher	Thomomys bottae
Raccoon	Procyon lotor
San Joaquin pocket mouse	Perognathus inornatus
Spotted skunk	Spilogale putoris
Striped skunk	Mephitis mephitis
Western harvest mouse	Reithrodontomys megalotis

[a]Most mammals were positively identified. Observations were substantiated by duplicate sightings and by checking the range of various animals.

Table 9. Crustacea, spiders, and insects of Site 300.

Ant	Formica
Black widow spider	Latrodecius mactans
Bumblebee	Bombus
Centipede	Solopendra morsitans
Dragon fly	Libellula
Earwig	Forficula auricularia
Field cricket	Gryllus
Garden spider	Argiope
Grasshopper	Melanoplus
Honeybee	Apis mellifera
House fly	Musca domestica
Jerusalem cricket	Stenopelmatus
Lady beetle	Hippodamia convergens
Leaf-hopper	Platymetopius
Millipede	Spribolus
Scorpion	Centruroides
Snakefly	Mantisapa
Sow bug	Cylisticus convexus
Sulfur butterfly	Euremia
Tarantula	Tarantula
Tarantula hawk	Pepsis

EG&G

Energy Measurements Group

EGG 1183-2425

OCCURRENCE AND STATUS OF ENDANGERED SPECIES, SAN JOAQUIN KIT FOX, Vulpes macrotis mutica, AND LARGE-FLOWERED FIDDLENECK, Amsinckia grandiflora, ON LAWRENCE LIVERMORE NATIONAL LABORATORY, SITE 300, CALIFORNIA

APRIL 1981

PREPARED FOR THE LAWRENCE LIVERMORE NATIONAL LABORATORY THROUGH THE
U.S. DEPARTMENT OF ENERGY, NEVADA OPERATIONS OFFICE
UNDER CONTRACT NO. DE-AC08-76NV01183

2E-21

SANTA BARBARA OPERATIONS
EG&G INC 130 ROBIN HILL RD., GOLETA, CALIF 93017

EG&G
Energy Measurements Group

EGG 1183-2425
S-715-R

OCCURRENCE AND STATUS OF ENDANGERED SPECIES, SAN JOAQUIN KIT FOX, *Vulpes macrotis mutica*, AND LARGE-FLOWERED FIDDLENECK, *Amsinckia grandiflora*, ON LAWRENCE LIVERMORE NATIONAL LABORATORY, SITE 300, CALIFORNIA

by
William A. Rhoads, Thomas P. O'Farrell, and Mary L. Sauls

APRIL 1981

This report is unclassified: Henry M. Borella
Classification Officer

PREPARED FOR THE LAWRENCE LIVERMORE NATIONAL LABORATORY THROUGH THE
U.S. DEPARTMENT OF ENERGY, NEVADA OPERATIONS OFFICE
UNDER CONTRACT NO. DE-AC08-76NV01183

2E-23

SANTA BARBARA OPERATIONS
EG&G INC 130 ROBIN HILL RD., GOLETA, CALIF 93017

SUMMARY

The purpose of this project was to provide Lawrence Livermore National Laboratory (LLNL) with information to assist it in complying with the Endangered Species Act of 1973 (ESA).

Field work was conducted at Site 300 between 17 March and 22 August 1980 in a search to determine whether the endangered San Joaquin kit fox, *Vulpes macrotis mutica*, occurred there, to survey the Site for additional populations of the rare plant species *Amsinckia grandiflora*, and to determine whether LLNL activities might be impacting on that plant species.

No evidence was found to suggest that the San Joaquin kit fox is present on Site 300.

No new populations of *A. grandiflora* were found. The known population of *A. grandiflora* below Drop Tower 858 consisted of 28 individuals. Evidence of a recent burn on a part of the knoll where *A. grandiflora* occurs was the only indication of habitat disturbance. There was no evidence that LLNL activities are impacting adversely on the species.

It is likely that *A. grandiflora* will be listed as endangered (it is now listed under Category 1 in a candidacy package). If so, a consultation with Fish and Wildlife Service is required, and an impact assessment statement will be needed. This study should satisfy most of the requirements for the impact statement.

ACKNOWLEDGEMENTS

Our thanks to our colleague, Patrick McCue, who assisted during ground and aerial surveys for the kit fox. We most gratefully acknowledge the cooperation and assistance of the many Site 300 personnel who provided escort, information, and in many cases, extra eyes during the surveys. Without these people, the field work would have been difficult. Roy Mullins, Site 300 Manager, and Owen Van Dyke provided us with much of the information necessary to coordinate our work on Site 300, as well as personnel, office space, and vehicles.

We are especially thankful for the warm and gracious assistance of Dr. Carl Lindeken, whose personal interest in our work and in the welfare of the animals and plants of Site 300, made this project possible.

CONTENTS (continued)

ILLUSTRATIONS

TABLES

1. INTRODUCTION

1.1 BACKGROUND

This investigation was undertaken to provide the managers of Lawrence Livermore National Laboratory (LLNL) with information to assist it in complying with the Endangered Species Act (ESA) of 1973, as amended in 1978 and 1979. Section 2 of the Act states the policy that ... all federal departments and agencies shall seek to conserve endangered species and threatened species and shall utilize their authorities in furtherance of the purposes of the Act. Further, the purpose of the Act is to conserve the ecosystems upon which the species depend and, when needed, to provide a program for recovery of such. species. Section 7 of the ESA requires all federal agencies to determine the distribution and status of any federally listed or candidate endangered or threatened species which occur on lands under their jurisdiction; and in consultation with the U.S. Fish and Wildlife Service (FWS) to determine whether any of the agency's actions will jeopardize the continued existence of the species or adversely impact the habitat of such species which is determined by the Secretary of the Interior to be critical.

The presence of two species, one animal and one plant, on or adjacent to Site 300 has led LLNL to investigate its responsibilities under the terms of the Act. The San Joaquin kit fox, *Vulpes macrotis mutica*, is a federally listed endangered species whose range is reported to extend along the western foothills of the San Joaquin Valley north to Contra Costa County (Laughrin, 1970; Morrell, 1975; Swick, 1973). Kit fox have been observed denning 3 to 4 miles north and east of Site 300 (Swick, 1973), and unverified sightings of kit fox have been reported for Site 300 (McIntyre and Johnson, 1980).

The last known population of a rare plant, *Amsinckia grandiflora* Kleeberger (Boraginaceae), the large-flowered fiddleneck, occurs on Site 300 (Ornduff, 1977; Hanson, 1978). The FWS is preparing to list this plant as a candidate endangered species. With this announcement the ESA requires that the species be treated as endangered, and requires LLNL to determine whether its activities will negatively impact the species or its essential habitat, and to develop reasonable management plans to conserve both.

1.2 OBJECTIVES

The primary goal of this project was to provide LLNL with additional information to assist it in complying with the Act. Specific objectives were to: 1) determine whether Site 300 is being used for denning or hunting by the San Joaquin kit fox, 2) search for additional populations of *Amsinckia grandiflora*, 3) determine abundance and distribution of the known population in 1980, and 4) suggest protective measures for the plant and its habitat if appropriate.

2. METHODS

2.1 SAN JOAQUIN KIT FOX

Kit fox are primarily nocturnal but night spotlight surveys to observe them may not be effective in areas with low population densities. Therefore, a combination of survey methods was employed. Daytime surveys to find dens, tracks, and scats were combined with night spotlight surveys and live-trapping to determine whether the kit fox was present on Site 300.

2.1.1 Field Surveys

Road surveys were used to observe as much of Site 300 as possible to determine presence of kit fox dens. Numerous roads and fire trails were driven slowly to allow observers to scan terrain for possible signs of kit fox. Frequent stops were made to allow observations of areas not visible from the vehicle. Potential den sites were investigated to determine whether they were made by kit fox. Most dens can be positively identified by a combination of characteristics, including size and shape of entrances, presence of fox tracks, scats, or prey remains.

Personnel also walked portions of almost every drainage on Site 300 looking for less obvious kit fox sign, such as tracks and scats along game trails. Animal tracks, scats, prey remains, and game trails were observed in areas that would normally be frequented by kit fox duirng hunting or territorial wanderings. Special efforts were made to look for evidence of fox at major game trail crossings, along fire roads, in drainages, along ridgelines, and adjacent to springs and other water sources. Scats were collected for later identification.

Ground searches were also conducted on private lands in two areas near Site 300: west of Corral Hollow Road and south of where it intersects Highway 580 on lands where dens were observed from the air; and on land southeast of the junction of Corral Hollow Road and Highway 580, at the end of Jefferson Road where kit fox and their dens had been observed previously (Swick, 1973).

2.1.2 Spotlight Surveys

Night spotlight surveys were conducted along the roads and fire trails on Site 300 to obtain information on presence of nocturnal animals, including kit fox. A vehicle was driven 5 to 8 mph with high beams on, while observers used spotlights to observe animals in areas perpendicular to the path. When eye-shines were observed the vehicle was stopped; the animal was identified; and records of species, time, and mileage were made. A flashlight was used to approach unknown animals to obtain positive identification, but when this failed the approximate size of the animal and color of eye shine were recorded.

2.1.3 Aerial Surveys

Aerial surveys were flown to find kit fox dens in areas remote from road systems. High-wing aircraft were used because 1) their configuration permitted an unobstructed view of the ground, 2) they could carry at least two passengers which increased effectiveness of search patterns, 3) their speed permitted rapid coverage of long transects, and 4) their maneuverability allowed safe searches along steep ridges and canyons. Surveys were flown at an altitude of 200 to 400 ft above ground level and an airspeed of 70 to 90 mph. Observations were made out of both sides of the aircraft along transects.

When a possible den site was noted, the aircraft circled to allow further observations with binoculars to insure that the den probably was a kit fox den and warranted ground searching. Potential locations were plotted on topographic maps.

2.1.4 Live-Trapping*

Live-traps were operated in an attempt to capture kit fox that might have been hunting on the area without leaving conspicuous signs along our field survey routes. Collapsible, double-door, National live-traps measuring 15 by 15 by 40 inches were placed in locations normally expected to be frequented by fox, such as along game trails, ridge lines, and in washes. Each trap was opened in late afternoon and baited with chicken parts. Traps were checked for captured animals the following morning shortly after sunrise. Traps were shut during the heat of the day to prevent accidental captures.

2.1.5 Interviews

People familiar with Site 300 and the surrounding lands and animals were interviewed to obtain information on presence of kit fox over past years. We were particularly interested in interviewing night security personnel who have driven around Site 300 for several years, firefighters stationed at the nearby Castle Rock State Forestry Station, neighboring sheep ranchers, and highway patrolmen.

2.2 *Amsinckia grandiflora*

Field methods used to search for additional populations of *Amsinckia grandiflora* were limited by the rugged terrain and the need to verify species identifications in the field. Walking surveys were conducted with priority for areas near the known location for the species, and to habitats elsewhere that appeared to be similar to that around Drop Tower 858.

Six species of *Amsinckia* occur on Site 300. Some resemble each other superficially, but the most common, widely distributed species, *A. tessellata*,

---

*Permission to live-trap this endangered species was granted by the State of California in a 9 April 1980 Memorandum of Understanding between the Department of Fish and Game and EG&G, and by the U.S. Fish and Wildlife Service through permit PRT.2-4573.

is not distinguishable from *A. grandiflora* at more than a few meters. Thus positive identification of the species required examination of floral parts of each prospective clump of plants, and scanning large areas for likely habitats from a distance had to be supplemented by close examination of each suspected population.

2.2.1 Drop Tower 858

During April, observations were made of the known population of *A. grandiflora* near Drop Tower 858. Plants were counted, examined for seed set, observed for evidence of disease or predation, and the number of both floral morphs were counted. Plants growing in association with *A. grandiflora* were collected for identification. Observations were made of its site characteristics such as aspect, slope angle, soil type, elevation, density, and height of vegetation. Locations of individual *A. grandiflora* were drawn on a map. Evidence of erosion, surface disturbances, or signs of recent burning that might be related to Site 300 activities were noted.

2.2.2 Other Site 300 Surveys

Road surveys were used to locate both the occurrence of *A. grandiflora* and habitats resembling that below Drop Tower 858. Graded fire trails provided access to most of the ridges and drainages. We drove slowly along them while observating plants and potential suitable habitats. Frequent stops allowed us to walk across slopes to observe areas not visible from roads and trails.

Promising areas seen during road surveys were observed more closely on foot. Generally, these were locations having west to northwest-facing slopes, loose soils on gully banks, and plant species known to occur with *A. grandiflora*. The entire drainage around Drop Tower 858 was surveyed intensively on foot. Barren, rocky, south-facing slopes with shallow soils or exposed rock outcrops, and slopes covered by a dense sward of wild oats, *Avena barbata*, are not considered to be likely habitats for *A. grandiflora* and were not surveyed on foot.

3. RESULTS

3.1 SAN JOAQUIN KIT FOX

3.1.1 Field Surveys

Field surveys to find evidence of San Joaquin kit fox on Site 300 were conducted in March and April (during the survey for *Amsinckia grandiflora*) and in June and July, 1980 (Table 1). Intensively searched areas are indicated in Figure 1. No kit fox dens, tracks, or scats were observed. A fresh lagomorph gastrointestinal tract, often evidence of kit fox predation, was found on the bare ground in the eastern-perimeter fire break, but this was not unequivocal evidence of the presence of kit fox since other carnivores and raptorial birds also leave this portion of their prey.

Ground surveys of private lands near Site 300 were conducted on 17 July and 19 August. Those areas surveyed off Site 300 are shown in Figure 2. No kit fox dens, tracks, scats, or remains of prey were observed. Appendix B list the vertebrates observed during these surveys.

3.1.2 Spotlight Surveys

Seven spotlight surveys were conducted during the periods 2-4 June, 14-15 July, and 20 August, a total of 12 hours of observations for nocturnal animals along a 55-mile transect on Site 300 roads and trails. Although a number of mammals and birds were observed (Table 2), no San Joaquin kit fox were seen.

3.1.3 Aerial Surveys

On 16 July a 2-hour aerial survey was conducted along the northern boundary of Site 300 over the gentle foothills and valley floor from the north perimeter of Site 300 to Highway 580, and from the area of Patterson Pass to just east of Corral Hollow Road. Although kit fox and their dens had been reported from these areas in the past (Swick, 1973), none were seen during these aerial searches.

Many large burrow systems were visible in pastures north of the Site, but numerous California ground squirrels, *Spermophilus beecheyi*, were observed on them, and the burrows were tentatively identified as ground squirrel colonies. Subsequent ground surveys confirmed the aerial identification. The similarity in appearance between aerial observations of San Joaquin kit fox natal dens and large California ground squirrel colonies convinced us that aerial surveys to find kit fox dens were ineffective around Site 300.

Table 1. San Joaquin kit fox survey, LLNL, Site 300, 1980

Date	Type of Survey	Location*
17 March- 18 April	Observations made for kit fox sign during driving and walking surveys for *Amsinckia grandiflora*	See Table 4
2 June	Night spotlight survey	NW, N, NE, E sectors
3 June	Driving/walking survey Night spotlight survey (Interviews with night security personnel)	NW, N sectors NW, N sectors ---
4 June	Walking survey Driving/walking survey Night spotlight survey	Near Facility 831 E, NE sectors and near 852 NW, N, Cent sectors
5 June	Walking survey Driving/walking survey	NW sector SW sector
6 June	Walking survey Driving/walking survey	SE sector SE, S, SW, NW, N, NE, E sectors
14 July	Driving survey Night spotlight survey	S, SW, W, N, NW sectors SE, E, N, NW, W sectors
15 July	Walking survey Driving/walking survey (Interviews with personnel, Division of Forestry) Live-traps set Night spotlight survey	East perimeter of SE sector E, NE, N sectors Castle Rock Fire Station Trap locations 1-10 (Figure 1) NW, W, SW, Cent sectors
16 July	Aerial survey Live-traps set Night spotlight survey	North of Site 300 to Hwy 580, from Patterson Pass east to 2 mi E of Corral Hollow Rd. Trap locations 1-10 E, Cent, N, NW sectors
17 July	Walking survey (Interview with ranch owner) Live-traps set	Private land, ranch NW of Corral Hollow Rd., E of Site 300 (Figure 2) --- Trap locations 1-10
18 July	Driving/walking survey	NW, W, Cent sectors
18 August	Driving survey Live-traps set	E, NE, N sectors Trap locations 1, 3-7, 10-13
19 August	Walking survey Live-traps set	Private land S of Jefferson Rd., ca. 2 mi SE of jn Corral Hollow Rd. and Hwy 580 (Figure 2) Trap locations 1, 3-7, 10-13
20 August	Live-traps set Night spotlight survey	Trap locations 1, 3-5, 10, 12-16 NW, Cent, N, NE sectors
21 August	Live-traps set	Trap locations 1, 3-5, 10, 12-16

*General locations, "sectors" referred to in this table, correspond to areas of Site 300 as shown here:

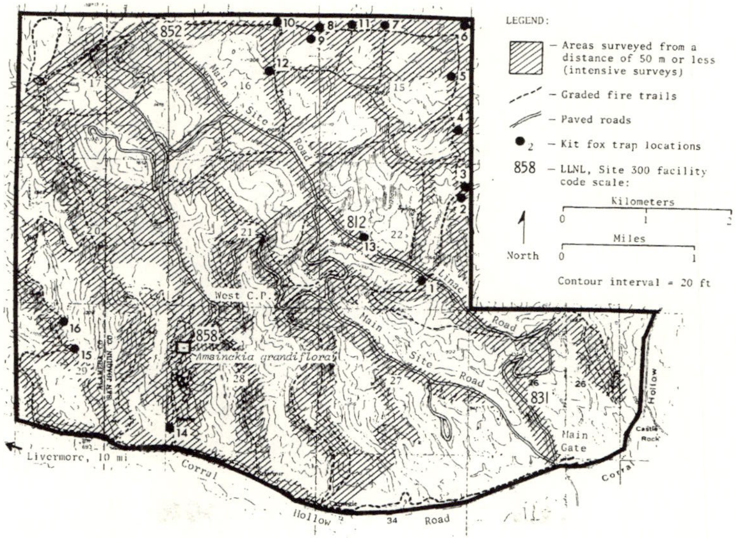

Figure 1. Location of 1980 field surveys for San Joaquin kit fox and *Amsinckia grandiflora*, LLNL, Site 300, 1980

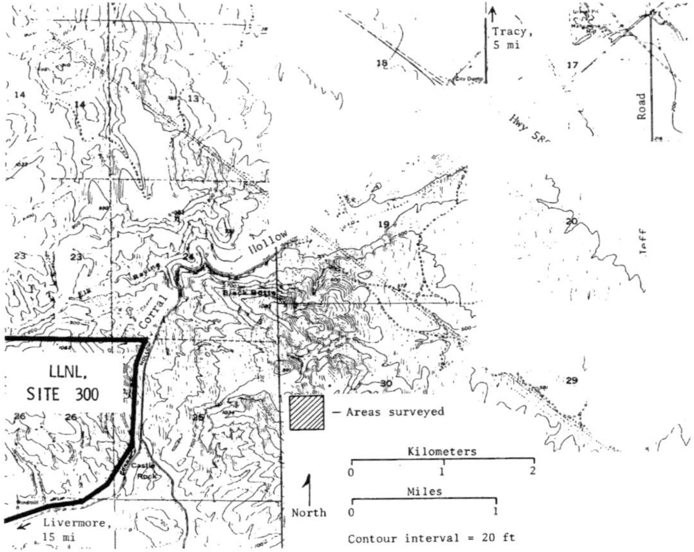

Figure 2. Locations of ground surveys for San Joaquin kit fox on private land adjacen LLNL, Site 300, 1980

Table 2. Vertebrates observed during night spotlight surveys on LLNL, Site 300, 1980

Table 2

Date Length (mi) Duration (hr/min)	2 June 7.5 2/35	3 June 4.8 1/20	4 June 12.8 1/20	14 July 9.2 2/0	15 July 6.1 1/40	16 July 6.9 1/30	20 August 7.9 1/30
MAMMALS							
Lepus californicus Black-tailed Jackrabbit	8	1	16	27	8	27	8
Sylvilagus audubonii Audubon's Cottontail	1	--	17	18	2	21	3
Dipodomys heermanni Heermann's Kangaroo Rat	~20	6	7	30	24	15	--
Peromyscus sp. Deer Mouse and allies	2	--	--	--	2	--	--
Taxidea taxa Badger	3	1	5	2	1	3	--
Odocoileus hemionus Mule Deer	--	--	--	2	7	--	--
Canis latrans Coyote	--	--	--	1	--	--	--
BIRDS							
Athene cunicularia Burrowing Owl	5	3	7	28	10	32	9
Tyto alba Barn Owl	4	--	--	2	--	--	1
Bubo virginianus Great Horned Owl	1	--	1	--	--	--	--
Asio flammeus Short-eared Owl	--	--	1	4	1	--	1
Eremophila alpestris Horned Lark	--	--	2	--	--	--	1
REPTILES							
Pituophis melanoleucus Gopher Snake	1	--	--	--	--	--	1

3.1.4 Live-Trapping

Between 15 July and 21 August, 70 trap nights (one live-trap set for one night) of effort were expended trapping for kit fox at trap locations 1-16 (Figure 1). No kit fox were live-trapped; however, four desert cottontails, *Sylvilagus audubonii*, a raccoon, *Procyon lotor*, and a striped skunk, *Mephitis mephitis*, were captured and released unharmed (Table 3).

3.1.5 Interviews

Several guards insisted that two "families" of kit fox had been observed, one recently and often in a culvert below Facility 831, and another on a hill

Table 3. Dates and results of live-trapping on LLNL, Site 300, 1980 at locations shown in Figure 1

Table 3

Date	Trap Location																
	1	2	3	4	5	6	7	8	9	10	11	12	13	14	15	16	
15 July	S	0	0	0	0	0	0	0	0	0	--	--	--	--	--	--	
16 July	0	Syau	0	0	0	0	0	0	Syau	0	--	--	--	--	--	--	
17 July	0	0	0	0	0	0	0	0	0	0	--	--	--	--	--	--	
19 August	0	--	0	0	0	0	0	--	--	0	0	0	Syau	--	--	--	
20 August	0	--	0	0	0	0	0	--	--	0	0	Syau	0	--	--	--	
21 August	0	--	0	0	0	--	--	--	--	0	--	0	0	Prlo	0	0	
22 August	0	--	0	0	0	--	--	--	--	0	--	0	0	0	Meme	0	
Number of Trap-Nights	7	3	7	7	7	5	5	3	3	7	2	4	4	2	2	2	= 70

* S = trap sprung
0 = trap open
Syau = *Sylvilagus audubonii*
Prlo = *Procyon lotor*
Meme = *Mephitis mephitis*

near Facility 852. Their descriptions did not mention key characteristics of the species which might have helped us to verify their identifications. Our doubts were substantiated when we visited the culvert and areas around the facilities, because no kit fox dens, scats, tracks, or prey remains were found. We did find holes dug by foraging badgers near 831.

A sheep rancher claimed to have seen a kit fox denning on his property east of Site 300 several years ago, but he had not seen any this year. None of the other persons interviewed had seen San Joaquin kit fox on or near Site 300.

3.2 *Amsinckia grandiflora*

Of the March, April, and June surveys (Table 4) only on the April survey were flowering plants observed, and these were at the site of the previously known location at Drop Tower 858. Although a large proportion of Site 300 was searched (Figure 1), no additional populations of *A. grandiflora* were found.

The single population was distributed along the north- and northwest-facing slopes of a knoll at an average elevation of 960 ft (293 m) (Figure 3 and 4). Aspect ranged between 265° and 320°; slope varied between 10° and 40°.

Soils supporting *A. grandiflora* appeared lighter in color and texture than the heavy-textured, dark gray soils typical of much of Site 300. Cole, et al (1943), classified soils of that drainage as "Linne clay loam, rock-outcrop phase," but this classification may be too general to allow application to that particular hillside where *A. grandiflora* was found.

Table 4. Field surveys for *Amsinckia grandiflora* on LLNL, Site 300, 1980

Table 4

Date	Type of Survey	Location*	Observation of *Amsinckia grandiflora*
17 March	Observations at *A. grandiflora* population	Drop Tower 858	*A. grandiflora;* not in bloom.
	(plant collections)	Drop Tower 858	---
18 March	Driving survey	Fire trails, SW sector	---
	Walking survey	Drainage 1 mi N of 858, W sector	---
	(plant collections)	Drainage 1 mi N of 858, W sector	---
3 April	Observations at *A. grandiflora* population	Drop Tower 858	*A. grandiflora;* starting to bloom, 21 counted
	(plant collections)	Drop Tower 858	---
	Walking survey	Drainage S of 858 to Corral Hollow Rd.	---
	(plant collections)	Drainage S of 858 to Corral Hollow Rd.	---
4 April	Walking survey	Drainage 1 mi N of 858 through W sector	---
	(plant collections)	Drainage 1 mi N of 858 through W sector	---
	Driving/walking survey	SW sector	---
	Walking survey	Slopes east of Tower 858, S sector	---
16 April	Observations at *A. grandiflora* population	Drop Tower 858	---
	Driving/walking surveys	SW, W sectors	---
	(plant collections)	SW, W sectors	---
17 April	Driving/walking survey	S sector	---
	(plant collections)	S sector	---
	Observations at *A. grandiflora* population, drawing of schematic diagram (Figure 4)	Drop Tower 858	28 individuals of *A. grandiflora* counted in peak bloom
18 April	Driving/walking surveys	E and N sectors	---
5 June	Observations at *A. grandiflora* population during kit fox survey	Drop Tower 858	*A. grandiflora* dead and dried, nutlets still attached

*General locations, "sectors" referred to in this table, correspond to areas of Site 300 shown here:

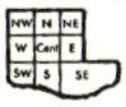

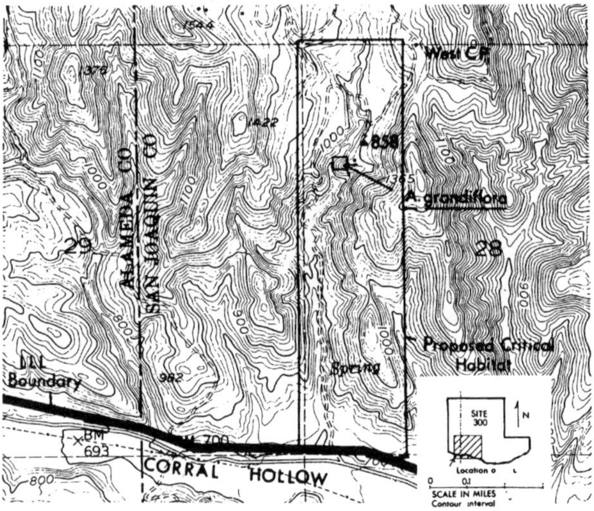

Figure 3. Location of *Amsinckia grandiflora* population below Drop Tower 858 on LLNL, Site 300, showing area of proposed critical habitat for this species

Vegetation on the knoll was typical of that on steep north-facing slopes in the southwestern portion of Site 300. Annual grasses, *Festuca megalura, Bromus rubens, Bromus tectorum,* were dominant, but there were diverse annuals and perennials including *Achillea borealis, Silene antirrhina, Stylomecon heterophylla, Trifolium variegatum, Montia perfoliata,* and *Allium amplectans*. These and others (Appendix A) were searched for as "indicator species" during surveys to find other populations of *A. grandiflora*.

Grasses, notably *Festuca*, growing to a height of 2 decimeters (dm) were dominant on north-facing slope where the larger individuals of *A. grandiflora* grew in 1980. On the west and northwest-facing slopes with smaller *A. grandiflora* there was a sparse grass cover, and the soil was looser and lighter in color than on the north. Western and southern slopes supported dense stands of *Monolopia, Phacelia, Streptanthus,* and *A. tessellata*.

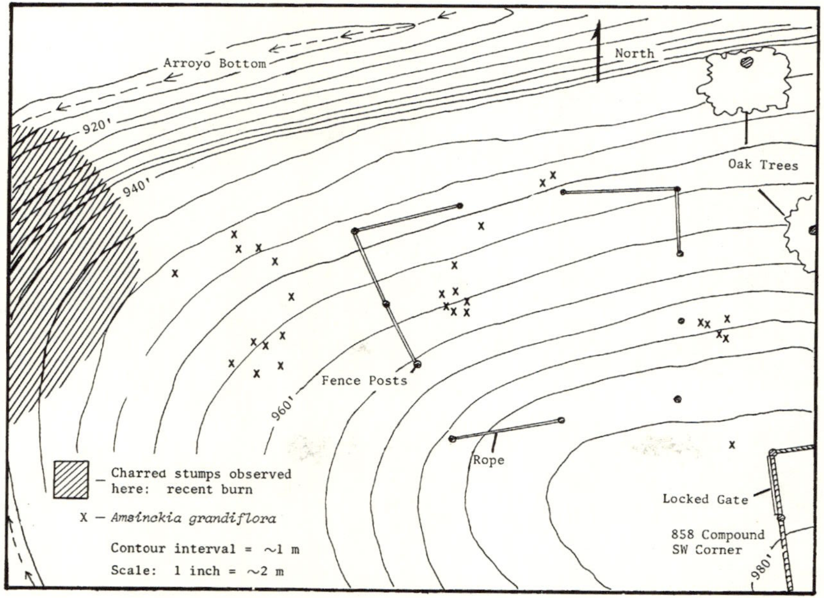

Figure 4. Locations of individual *Amsinckia grandiflora* in 1980 at population site below Drop Tower 858, LLNL, Site 300

On 3 April, 21 plants were counted, including 12 "pins" (plants whose flowers have exserted styles), "thrums" (plants whose flowers have exserted anthers), and two immature plants still in bud stage. On 17 April, 28 *A. grandiflora* were counted. Twenty individuals germinated outside the roped enclosure presumably delineating distribution of the population in earlier years. Five individuals were large plants about 7 dm in height, having branching stems and 5 to 10 inflorescences. The remaining individuals were smaller, 3 to 4 dm tall, and had only one or two inflorescences. All *A. grandiflora* appeared to be free of disease, and there was no evidence they were being eaten by animals.

A cursory examination to determine seed set was made on 2 June when plants had dried. Most flowers had only 1 to 2 nutlets (maximum is four), a proportion observed previously (Ornduff, 1976).

Charred stumps of shrubs south of Drop Tower 858 and also west of *A. grandiflora* (Figure 4) indicated a recent burn, but the north and northwest faces of the knoll were free of charred material. No evidence of either recent surface disturbances or excessive erosion was observed.

4. DISCUSSION AND CONCLUSIONS

No evidence was found that the San Joaquin kit fox either visits or makes dens on Site 300, even though it has been observed in the past within three to five miles of the area. Based on this information, it is reasonable to conclude that Site 300 activities do not impact on the kit fox.

No populations of *Amsinckia grandiflora* other than that one already known at Drop Tower 858 were found. Searches outside Site 300 in Contra Costa County have also been unsuccessful (Hanson, 1978). All available information suggests that the small population on Site 300 is the only one in existence. Because of this and the species' recent history, to be discussed subsequently, there is little doubt that *A. grandiflora* fulfills the legal description of an endangered species: "... any species which is in danger of extinction throughout all or a significant portion of its range ..."

Historical records suggest that *A. grandiflora* has always been a rare plant and that it has become rarer in this century. It was first described by Gray in 1876 and was known only from locations in the vicinity of Antioch, Contra Costa County (Ornduff, 1977). There is a collection from 1889 by O.L. Green "collected in Livermore Valley" as *A. spectabilis* and subsequently annotated as *A. grandiflora* by W.N. Suksdorf in 1931. In the California Academy of Sciences Herbarium there are numerous sheets of *A. grandiflora* from a locality "one mile north of Corral Hollow near Alameda County line, San Joaquin County," also several labelled "Corral Hollow, Alameda County," and one "central part of Corral Hollow, Alameda County." All of the latter were dated in the 1930's (Alva Day, Associate Curator, personal communication).

Ornduff (1976) has reported on the population at Drop Tower 858. There were several thousand plants present in a dense population at the tower in 1966 and also in 1967. In 1974 the same area contained a relatively few individuals that occurred in small, widely scattered groups.

In 1980 we counted 28 plants in the Drop Tower 858 population.

Because the area adjacent to Drop Tower 858 now appears to be the sole site known for *A. grandiflora*, some history of the area and conditions around it seem appropriate. The drop tower was built in 1958, and its control room in 1978, which required no additional clearing (Roy K. Mullins, Jr., personal communication). A heavy chain link fence surrounds the tower facility and associated parking area. A gate leading to *Amsinckia* population is kept locked. There is little evidence of human disturbances outside the chain fence with two exceptions.

1. On the south side of the drop tower (the side away from the *Amsinckia* population), heavy concrete blocks have been left near the bottom of the drainage channel.
2. East of the population, we noted some erosion below a drain pipe from the fenced enclosure.

Some time in the last few years, steel posts and ropes were used to show the location of *A. grandiflora*. Although the stakes were in place in the spring of 1980, only a portion of area is still enclosed behind the deteriorated ropes.

If there were overburdens of soil taken from the top of the knoll when the drop tower was constructed, no evidence remained in 1980. All slopes in the immediate vicinity of the *A. grandiflora* population are richly vegetated, as noted earlier.

We observed no evidence of other conditions that might have affected *A. grandiflora*, but there is little natural history and no certain knowledge of specific requirements against which causes could be identified. Traditional causes to which loss of species might be attributed were not present: recent construction of roads or buildings, vehicle traffic, foot traffic, field collection of plants, grazing by live stock, or land clearing for agriculture.

Absence of obvious physical causes for the decline of *A. grandiflora* has been indirectly acknowledged by others by the introduction of hypotheses citing other possible causes.

Ray and Chisaki (1957) suggested a hypothesis based on evolutionary principles. They pointed out that *A. tessellata*, a homostylic species, (abundant on Site 300) probably evolved from *A. grandiflora*, a heterostylic species. They suggested that when homostylic populations arise from heterostylic, the latter may be crowded out and thereby replaced. Ornduff (1976) followed this same reasoning and suggested "It is possible that the greater reproductive success of these weedy species has allowed them to displace *A. grandiflora* over much of the latter's former range." He suggests that the restricted distribution is perhaps associated with its "archaic and relatively inefficient reproductive system."

As a speculation of how *A. grandiflora* persists on Site 300 after its disappearance elsewhere, two conditions are evident. First, grazing by livestock is absent. Second, the area is still subject to controlled burning, whereas fires on agriculturally developed lands are strongly suppressed. That the burning on Site 300 is a factor in altering species composition was apparent in the spring of 1980. On many hills, especially on the north end of Site 300, there were herbaceous annual species that produced massive displays of color, unlike similar slopes and exposures on the agricultural lands surrounding Site 300 where flowering annuals were relatively rare.

The report by Ornduff (1976) concerning numbers of plants from year to year suggested another possible unknown concerning the occurrence of *A. grandiflora*, viz., year-to-year oscillations in population size and area extent. Many annual populations of herbaceous species are known to fluctuate, generally attributed to particular environmental conditions such as temperature regimes, times and amounts of precipitation, and other factors. But little is known about these fluctuations except that they occur.

It is also possible that the Ray and Chisaki hypothesis is correct; that we are witnessing the final stages of an evolutionary process by which *A. grandiflora* is being displayed by its descendants, abetted by competition from introductions of exotic species of grasses.

It is apparent that broader studies are needed to assist in understanding not only what has occurred but also for assistance in maintaining *Amsinckia grandiflora* in its present habitat, or establishing it elsewhere.

4.1 ENDANGERED SPECIES ON SITE 300 AND THE ENDANGERED SPECIES ACT OF 1973

4.1.1 San Joaquin Kit Fox

This study appears to fulfill LLNL obligation under terms of the ESA. Since the kit fox does not occur on Site 300, LLNL activities obviously do not impact on the species, and LLNL has no further responsibilities under implementing regulations of the Act. An informal consultation with U.S. Fish and Wildlife Service (FWS) in Sacramento would appear to be in order to report this conclusion. This report might be submitted to support this position.

4.1.2 *Amsinckia grandiflora*

We already noted that this species appears to qualify as endangered under ESA. On 15 December 1980, the Department of the Interior published a list of native plant taxa being considered for listing as Endangered or Threatened under ESA (Federal Register, 45(242):82480-82569). *Amsinckia grandiflora* was listed under Category 1, "Taxa for which the Service presently has sufficient information on hand to support the biological appropriateness of their being listed as Endangered or Threatened species." The FWS in Sacramento has compiled a candidacy package, including designation of a proposed critical habitat, required for a formal proposal for listing the species as Endangered (Monty Knudsen, FWS, Sacramento, 1980, personal communication), and publication of its candidacy appears imminent. Once candidacy intent is published, ESA amendments require that *A. grandiflora* be given the same protection as if it were already listed. ESA then requires a review of possible impacts of nonconstruction projects to determine whether those actions may affect the species or its designated critical habitat — tentatively proposed as the western quarter of Section 28, T3S; R4E.

If LLNL activities are considered to have a negative impact, then LLNL is required to request a conference with FWS, while *A. grandiflora* is a candidate, or a formal consultation after it is formally listed. The purpose of either meeting is to allow the Department of Interior to evaluate the seriousness of impact of the proposed activities and to resolve potential conflicts through mitigation. For construction in the area, ESA regulations stipulate informing the Regional Director, FWS, of the proposed activities prior to initiation. LLNL is responsible for providing both the biological information needed to conduct either a consultation or conference, and the preparation of a Biological Assessment before formal consultations are initiated. Information needed includes: 1) on-site inspection to determine presence of the species, 2) reviews of scientific literature and data, 3) interviews with recognized experts, 4) a review and analysis of the effects of the proposed activities on the species and its habitat, including cumulative effects, and 5) an analysis of how possible impacts might be mitigated. With this study, LLNL has completed items 1) and 2). Information for assessment of impacts will of course be specific to the actions contemplated, and item 5) will depend in part on the action contemplated, or may not be possible considering the state of knowledge about the species.

If *A. grandiflora* becomes a candidate for endangerment or is declared Endangered, regardless of the reason for its decline and because it occurs on Site 300, LLNL, with the assistance of the Secretary of the Interior, must carry out a program to conserve the species.

In anticipating FWS questions, we have speculated as to Site 300 activities that might be considered as impacting on the species based on Appendix 3B, Environmental Assessment, Site 300, originally included in the draft Environmental Impact Statement for LLNL (DOE EIS-0028-D). These impacts may be harmful or beneficial, or both, with the balance lying somewhere between. Activities include explosives testing, controlled burning, application of herbicides, grading and maintaining fire trails, and construction or modification of drop tower facilities. High explosive tests may produce 1) blast, 2) shrapnel and fires from the hot fragments, 3) low-level radioactive debris, and 4) possibly toxic or beneficial nitrogenous materials or gases. Cumulative effects are even more speculative.

Since FWS already has informally expressed concern about possible negative effects of burning (Monty Knudsen, FWS, Sacramento, 1980, personal communication), LLNL can expect the FWS will request information in an attempt to determine whether controlled burning poses a threat to species or habitat. We note that current management calls for avoidance of burning on the knoll supporting *A. grandiflora* (Roy Mullins, 1980, personal communication).

Although use of herbicides has been curtailed since preparation of the Draft EIS, LLNL can expect to be questioned about the use of herbicides for weed control along roads, telephone poles, parking lots, or firing tables in the area.

Grading of fire trails and construction activities for parking facilities that might affect runoff into the critical habitat will be questioned. We note that Ornduff (1977) speculated that changes in the local runoff due to construction of Drop Tower 858 might have contributed to the decline of *A. grandiflora*.

In discussions with FWS, LLNL might note that despite the possibility of adverse impacts of LLNL activities, *A. grandiflora* probably exists only because of the protection within a security area, even though the factors responsible for its disappearance elsewhere are speculative. As mentioned above, Ornduff (1977) linked its extirpation to the introduction of domestic livestock. He also suggested that introduction of alien winter annual grasses (principally of *Bromus* on Site 300) may affect the welfare of *A. grandiflora*.

Once the species is listed, LLNL can expect that FWS will likely suggest adopting a management plan, like they did at Elk Hills Naval Petroleum Reserve. Successful application of such a plan implies an understanding of the species' life cycles, ecological requirements, and habitat interactions. Much of this information does not exist, but other investigations ought to produce sufficient information for a management plan that will conserve and benefit *A. grandiflora* without interfering with Site 300 activities. Objectives of such investigations might include the following:

1. Determination of the ecological or life history characteristics responsible for its past and present distribution pattern
2. Assessment of the species reproductive capacity with regard to the following parameters:

    a. With chronic burning

b. In the presence of dense winter annual grasses

c. In competition with other species of *Amsinckia*

d. In the absence of domestic herbivores or with grazing by them

e. On soils containing products of explosive testing

3. Development of management strategies that would contribute to conservation of the species might include:

   a. Curtailment of testing at Drop Tower 858 if information develops that *A. grandiflora* might be vulnerable to impacts of testing

   b. Implementation of controlled burning that might have proven useful in 2a above

   c. Provide supplemental irrigation in dry years, if evidence indicates that reproduction would be aided

4. Exploration of ways in which *A. grandiflora* might be established or re-established in other, more remote areas of Site 300, or to portions of its former range

Such studies should be based on cultivated populations of *A. grandiflora*. Ray and Chisaki (1957) raised this species under glass at Berkeley, and this appears to be the best way to accumulate seed for experimentation or particularly for planting elsewhere. Subjecting the wild population to manipulation would be very unwise, since the risk of extinction to such a small population is too great. Some of these suggested activities are certainly idealized and may not be possible. The highest priority appears to be increasing the numbers of the population in its present habitat, and research can be planned around that priority.

5. RECOMMENDATIONS

An informal consultation with FWS will satisfy LLNL obligations under ESA for the San Joaquin kit fox, since LLNL activities do not impact on that endangered species.

An informal consultation with FWS, as a continuation of those already held, should be initiated in anticipation of the probability that *Amsinckia grandiflora* is likely to be listed as Endangered. Since a conservation and management plan for execution by LLNL management to protect *Amsinckia grandiflora* appears likely, LLNL might consider what such a plan might entail, perhaps with the following priorities:

1. It should provide for an annual survey of the population on Site 300 and elsewhere, based on joint funding with FWS, or their cooperation.
2. Its primary objective should be to increase the size of the present population.
3. If the population increases or remains stable, emphasis in the management plan should turn to other objectives, such as:
   a. Investigation of its natural history, its development, pollinators, and seed production
   b. Understanding the following effects:
      (1) Competition from exotic grasses
      (2) Competition from other *Amsinckia*
      (3) Grazing by livestock
      (4) Burning
      (5) Other effects, possibly those from test activities
4. Until the population can be increased, or if it cannot be increased, it should not be manipulated, with the possible exception of removal of a small number of seeds for the purpose of growing elsewhere, possibly under glass or in a lath house. (We note that Prof. Robert Ornduff, University of California, Berkeley offered a seed supply in the spring of 1980.)

LITERATURE CITED

Anonymous. 1978. Draft Environmental Impact Statement, Livermore Site, Livermore, California. U.S. Department of Energy DOE/EIS 0028-D.

Anonymous. 1974. (unpublished) Appendix 3B: Environmental Assessment, Site 300, Lawrence Livermore National Laboratory, Livermore, California. Revised August, 1974. 37 pp.

Cole, R.C., L.F. Koehler, F.C. Eggers, and A.M. Goff. 1943. Soil survey of the Tracy Area, California. U.S. Department of Agriculture and University of California Experiment Station, Soil Survey Series 1938, No. 5.

Gray. A. 1876. *Botany of California* 1:525 in California Geological Survey. University of California Press, Cambridge, Massachusetts.

Hanson, L. 1978. Status report for *Amsinckia grandiflora*. Unpublished document, Endangered Plant Program, California Department of Fish and Game, Sacramento. 4 pp.

Laughrin, L. 1970. San Joaquin kit fox, its distribution and abundance. Wildlife Management Branch Administrative Report No. 70-2, California Department of Fish and Game, Sacramento. 20 pp.

McIntyre, D.R. and J.S. Johnson. 1980. A naturalist's view of Site 300 in Corral Hollow Valley. Unpublished LLNL Pre-print, UCRL-84300. 34 pp.

Morrell, S.H. 1975. San Joaquin kit fox distribution and abundance in 1975. Wildlife Management Branch Administrative Report No. 75-3, California Department of Fish and Game, Sacramento. 27 pp.

Ornduff, R. 1976. The reproductive system of *Amsinckia grandiflora*, a distylous species. Systematic Botany, 1:57-66.

Ornduff, R. 1977. Rare plant status report, *Amsinckia grandiflora*. Unpublished document compiled for the California Native Plant Society, Sacramento. 4 pp.

Ray, P.M. and H.F. Chisaki. Studies on *Amsinckia*. I: A Synopsis of the genus with a study of heterostyly in it. *American Journal of Botany*, *44*:529-536.

Swick, C.D. 1973. Determination of San Joaquin kit fox range in Contra Costs, Alameda, San Joaquin and Tulare Counties, 1973. Special Wildlife Investigations Report, Project W-54-R-4, California Department of Fish and Game, Sacramento. 15 pp.

APPENDIX A: PLANTS OBSERVED ON LAWRENCE LIVERMORE NATIONAL LABORATORY, SITE 300, 1980

Cupressaceae	
Juniperus californica	
Amaranthaceae	
Amaranthus sp.	
Asteraceae	
Achillea borealis ssp. *californica*	*C
Artemisia californica	
Baeria chrysostoma ssp.	C
gracilis	C
Coreopsis callipsida	C
Evax sp.	
Gutierrezia bracteate	
Haplopappus sp.	
Hemizonia kelloggii	C
Hemizonia ssp.	
Holocarpha obconica	
Layia platyglossa	*C
Monolopia lanceolata	*C
Boraginaceae	
Amsinckia grandiflora	
Amsinckia intermedia	*C
Amsinckia lycopsoides	C
Amsinckia menziesii	C
Amsinckia tessellata	*C
Amsinckia vernicosa	C
Cryptantha intermedia	*C
Plagiobothrys sp.	C
Brassicaceae	
Streptanthus sp.	*C
Thysanocarpus curvipes	C

Campanulaceae	
Downingia bella	C
Caprifoliaceae	
Sambucus mexicana	
Caryophyllaceae	
Silene antirrhina	
Cucurbitaceae	
Murah macrocarpus	
Ericaceae	
Arctostaphylos sp.	
Fabaceae	
Lotus subpinnatus	*C
Lupinus albifrons	*C
Lupinus bicolor	*C
Lupinus densiflorus	*C
Trifolium variegatum	*C
Fagaceae	
Quercus douglasii	
Geraniaceae	
Erodium cicutarium	
Hippocastanaceae	
Aesculus californica	
Hydrophyllaceae	
Eriodictyon sp.	
Phacelia tanacetifolia	*C

* — Plant species that occur with *Amsinckia grandiflora* on the slope below Drop Tower 858, used as indicator species in our searches for potential *A. grandiflora* habitat.

C — Plant species that were collected during the course of the 1980 field surveys.

Lamiaceae	
Marrubium vulgare	
Salvia mellifera	
Loasaceae	
Mentzelia affinis	*C
Onagraceae	
Camissonia boothii ssp. *decorticans*	
Camissonia micrantha	*
Camissonia strigulosa	
Clarkia purpurea	
Clarkia unguiculata	
Papaveraceae	
Eschscholzia californica	
Platystemon californicus	*C
Stylomecon heterophylla	*C
Polemoniaceae	
Gilia capitata ssp. *staminea*	C
Gilia clivorum	C
Gilia tricolor	C
Polygonaceae	
Eriogonum fasciculatum	
Eriogonum sp.	
Portulacaceae	
Calandrinia ciliata var. *menziesii*	C
Montia perfoliata	*C
Ranunculaceae	
Delphinium hesperium	C
Delphinium sp.	
Ranunculus canus	C

Rosaceae	
Prunus sp.	
Rubiaceae	
Galium aparine	C
Salicaceae	
Populus fremontii	
Salix sp.	
Saxifragaceae	
Ribes sp.	
Scrophulariaceae	
Castilleja foliolosa	C
Collinsia heterophylla	C
Mimulus sp.	
Orthocarpus purpurascens	*C
Scrophularia californica	
Urticaceae	
Urtica holoseriacea	
Hesperocnide tenella	
Amaryllidaceae	
Allium amplectans	*C
Dichelostemma pulchella	*C
Tritelia laxa	*C
Poaceae	
Bromus mollis	*C
Bromus rubens	*C
Bromus tectorum	*C
Festuca megalura	*C
Mellica californica	C
Poa scabrella	*C
Sitanion sp.	*
Stipa cernua	C

* — Plant species that occur with *Amsinckia grandiflora* on the slope below Drop Tower 858, used as indicator species in our searches for potential *A. grandiflora* habitat.

C — Plant species that were collected during the course of the 1980 field survey.

APPENDIX B: VERTEBRATES OBSERVED ON LAWRENCE LIVERMORE NATIONAL LABORATORY, SITE 300, 1980

MAMMALS	
Didelphis marsupialis Opossum	T
Lepus californicus Black-tailed Jackrabbit	
Sylvilagus audubonii Desert Cottontail	T
Spermophilus beecheyi California Ground Squirrel	
Thomomys bottae Southern Pocket Gopher	
Perognathus californicus California Pocket Mouse	T
Dipodomys heermanni Heermann's Kangaroo Rat	T
Peromyscus maniculatus Deer Mouse	T
Neotoma fuscipes Dusky-footed Wood Rat	T
Mus musculus House Mouse	T
Canis latrans Coyote	
Procyon lotor Raccoon	T
Taxidea taxus Badger	
Mephitis mephitis Striped Skunk	T
Lynx rufus Bobcat	
Odocoileus hemionus Mule Deer	

T — Live-trapped 1980

APPENDIX 2F

A Cultural Resource Inventory of
Lawrence Livermore National Laboratory's
Site 300, Alameda and San Joaquin
Counties, California

Purchase Order No. 2628801

May, 1981

A Cultural Resource Inventory of Lawrence Livermore National Laboratory's Site 300, Alameda and San Joaquin Counties, California

University of California
Purchase Order No. 2628801
For Contract No. W-7405-ENG. 48
With the Department of Energy

PRINCIPAL INVESTIGATOR
Colin I. Busby

BY

Colin I. Busby, Donna M. Garaventa and Larry S. Kobori
With the Technical Assistance of
P.E. Endzweig, D.J. Fee, R.M. Harmon, A.C. Oetting and F.M. Oglesby

BASIN RESEARCH ASSOCIATES, INC.
31162 San Clemente Street
Suite 110
Hayward, California 94544

May, 1981

EXECUTIVE SUMMARY

A Class III cultural resources inventory was undertaken of ca. 7000 acres of Lawrence Livermore National Laboratory's Site 300 property. Twenty-four cultural resource properties and twenty-five site types were located and recorded. Of the properties, three are prehistoric, twenty historic and one is a multicomponent site. Historic cultural resources comprise 83% of the total site assemblage. In terms of defined site types, historic petroglyphs and structures are the most representative of the recorded cultural resources.

A brief site locale analysis, utilizing the inventory data, indicates that cultural resources occurrence is associated more strongly with the canyon-gully landforms than the foothills. Based on this analysis, it is probable that there is a greater probability of impacting cultural resources when projects occur in and around canyon-gully areas.

The majority of the sites are either of CRES S3 or S4 significance ("low significance") and while they merit consideration by Lawrence Livermore National Laboratory, that consideration should be mostly of a defensive nature. Only four of the cultural resource properties are either potential or eligible resources for the National Register of Historic Places and merit a high degree of consideration by Lawrence Livermore National Laboratory. No Native American or other ethnic cultural locales were noted during the inventory.

Management recommendations for both general and specific cultural resources indicate a variety of options ranging from patrolling/surveillance to their designation as "Spec.›l Management Areas." Several sites are recommended for selective subsurface testing to fully evaluate their National Register significance. One site, the habitation/residence area of the former town of Carnegie, is recommended for nomination to the National Register after a limited testing/archival research program.

TABLE OF CONTENTS

LIST OF FIGURES

LIST OF TABLES

ACKNOWLEDGEMENTS

The cultural resources inventory of Lawrence Livermore National Laboratory's Site 300 were contracted for by the University of California and the Department of Energy. To Ms. Violet Churchill, Mr. Carl Lindekin, Mr. Art Toy, Mr. Roy K. Mullins, Mr. Owen Van Dyke and the Security Officers of Site 300 we express our thanks for their field assistance and advice.

Numerous people contributed their support and expertise to the project and helped make it a success. To those who we have not mentioned below, please accept our apologies and thanks.

The authors are indebted to our dedicated field crew who worked under extremely trying conditions and tolerated all of the hardships of an early spring field project: Pamela Endzweig, David Fee, Bob Harmon, Chip Oetting and Fred Oglesby.

A special note of thanks is due to the members of Basin Research Associates Technical Staff for their assistance in preparing the report: Chip Oetting, forms processing and site summaries; Pamela Endzweig, vegetation, climate and fauna research; Fred Oglesby, geology and geomorphology; Pat Ogrey and Melody Tannam, maps and report production; Bob Harmon, photography; and, Melissa Eizenberg, graphics.

A note of thanks is due to the staffs of the Bancroft Library and the Stockton San Joaquin County Public Library for their generous assistance.

Dr. James C. Bard, Basin Research Associates is thanked for his general advice and comments on the report.

INTRODUCTION

This report presents the results of a literature/archive search and a Class III cultural resource field inventory of the Lawrence Livermore National Laboratory's Site 300. This study was commissioned for inclusion in a Lawrence Livermore National Laboratory environmental impact statement and is specifically directed towards determining the eligibility of specific sites or areas for inclusion as historical properties on the National Register of Historic Places.

The intent of this study, completed during the months of April and May, is to provide Lawrence Livermore National Laboratory with a brief overview and synthesis of the existing cultural record, including historic, prehistoric, and ethnographic data available for the project area as well detail the results of an intensive cultural resources field inventory of the LLNL Site 300 area. Lawrence Livermore National Laboratory, in cooperation with the United States Department of Energy, is mandated by the Antiquities Act of 1906, the Reservoir Salvage Act of 1960 (as amended by Public Law 93-291), the National Historic Preservation Act of 1966 (as amended), the National Environmental Policy Act of 1969 (NEPA), Executive Order 11593, the Federal Land Policy and Management Act of 1976, the Archaeological Protection Act of 1979 (among other Federal legislation) and the California Environmental Quality Act (CEQA) to identify, evaluate and protect prehistoric, historic and ethnic cultural resources on lands under its jurisdiction. The purpose of this study is to provide data on the cultural resources within the project boundaries and in the immediate vicinity that can contribute material for informed management decisions that will minimize any present or future impacts to the resources and encourage long-term planning that may result in the conservation and protection of a non-renewable portion of America's heritage.

The area of this investigation is the present Lawrence Livermore National Laboratory's Site 300 located in the region north of Corral Hollow, approximately 8.5 miles northwest of Tracy, San Joaquin County, California (Fig. 1). The project area is included within Township 3 South, Range 4 East (Mount Diablo Meridian), and Sections 15-17, 20-22, 26-29, and portions of 8-10, 25, 33-35 of the Tracy and Midway USGS 7.5 minute topographic quadrangles (1968 edition) (Fig. 2). The majority of the approximate 7000 acres of the project lies within San Joaquin County with a small portion of the western area within Alameda County (Fig. 2).

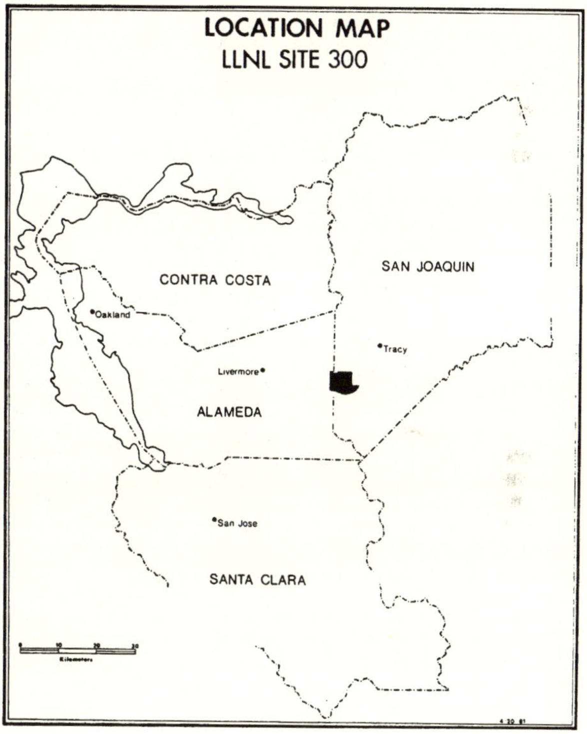
LOCATION MAP
LLNL SITE 300
CONTRA COSTA
SAN JOAQUIN
Oakland
Tracy
Livermore
ALAMEDA
San Jose
SANTA CLARA
Kilometers

Figure 1

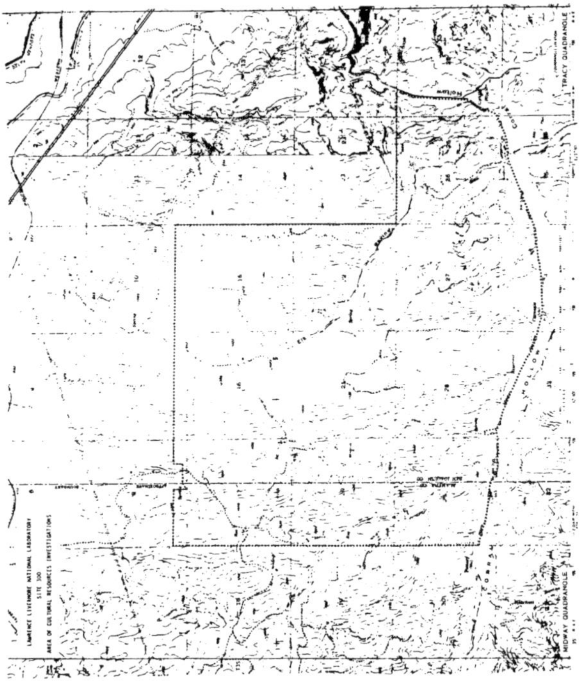

Figure 2 - Project Area

NATURAL SETTING

The Lawrence Livermore National Laboratory's Site 300 is located in an area of rolling hills immediately to the north of Corral Hollow, a pass in the Diablo Range of central California. The hill slopes vary from gentle to extremely steep with elevations ranging from 600 feet on the floodplain of Corral Hollow Creek to approximately 1722 feet at the West Observation Point within the site. Drainages separate the larger hills with deep, near vertical walled canyons. The drainages have no floodplains or terraces present.

The specific regional geology has been described by Huey (1948) who has noted a three formation geologic sequence ranging in age from upper Cretaceous to Mio-Pliocene.

The upper Cretaceous Panoche formation is the oldest present on Site 300. This formation is divided into two general groups: (1) sands and sandstones; and, (2) conglomerate. The massive sandstones, grey weathering to tan or buff and with fine to medium grains, characterize 60% of this formation. The grains are angular and the sorting is fair (Huey 1948).

Conglomerates are very uncommon among rocks of upper Cretaceous age in the area and are only prominent on Rocky Ridge (Huey 1948). No conglomerates of the Panoche formation were observed during the survey of LLNL Site 300.

The Cierbo formation is a transgressive formation of upper Miocene age. Several different types of lithologies, including beds of quartzose sand and conglomerate, are present. Beds of quartzose sand are very common in the mapping unit (cf. Huey 1948) and can be seen in the canyons south of the West Observation Point. The sands are poorly sorted, coarse grained, massive and cross-bedded, friable, steaked with limonite and carry round pebbles of quartz and black chert (Huey 1948). The black chert was not observed at Site 300. The conglomerate carries rounded pebbles and cobbles of quartz, varicolored chert, lavendar quartzite and sandstone. Northwest of this area the conglomerate carries angular pebbles and cobbles of Franciscan chert and sandstone characteristic of the base of the Cierbo formation (Huey 1948).

The Neroly formation is of transitional Mio-Pliocene age and like the Panoche and Cierbo formations has sandstones and conglomerates present. The sandstones of this formation are a distinctive blue color. Neroly conglomerates consist of round andesitic pebbles and cobbles, 5 to 13 cm in diameter, set in a matrix of blue sandstone (Huey 1948). This formation is found throughout the Site 300 area and a number of rockshelters have been formed in the sandstone by wind and water.

The depositional history of the area is that of a shallow sea and coast line. The Panoche formation was deposited in a shallow sea during the upper Cretaceous. This deposition was followed by a period of folding and erosion until the upper Miocene. During this period, the Cierbo formation was formed during a sea expansion. It rests with angular unconformity upon Panoche rock. Environmental change marked the transition from the Miocene to Pliocene and the formation of the Neroly group. In most places the Neroly overlies the Cierbo unconformably and there are slight angular discordances between the attitudes of bedding in the two formations. This break marks a change from a marine environment to a broad floodplain or coastal plain as a local site of deposition for the Neroly (Huey 1948).

Folding took place after the deposition of the Neroly formation. Two major synclines and one anticline are present within the boundaries of Site 300 (cf. Huey 1948). Faulting occurred concurrent with this folding with the combination creating the ridge which traverses Site 300.

Stream down cutting and modern soil formation began with the faulting and folding actions. The streams drain into two major drainages both of which follow synclines and faults. Elk Ravine follows the Patterson Pass syncline and fault while Corral Hollow Creek follows the Corral Hollow syncline and fault. Elk Ravine drains the northernmost portion of Site 300 and south to the ridge top. Corral Hollow Creek drains the remainder south of the ridge top. Small alluvial fans have developed in the southern part of Site 300 just north of Corral Hollow Road and Corral Hollow Creek has a well developed flood plain and terrace on the northside just south of Site 300. No flood-plain or terraces are present for Elk Ravine. Soil creep and slumping were observed in the field only on the steepest slopes.

The soils for Site 300 and vicinity have been mapped and described by Welch et al. (1966). All of the soils are either clay or clay loam on moderate to steep slopes (cf. Welch et al. 1966). The soils formed under a mesothermal climate of cool, moist winters and hot, dry summers. They contain relatively large amounts of organic matter and are suggestive of thick stands of perennial grasses and scattered oak woodland. The parent material was weathered, fine-grained sandstone with environmental conditions similar to the present.

Floristically the project area is transitional between a Coastal Prairie ecotype and the somewhat more arid Valley Grassland of interior California (Munz and Keck 1959, Plant Communities 24 and 25). Annual grasses such as wild oats (Avena fatua), rye (Secale sp.), soft chess and foxtail brome (Bromus mollis; B. rubens) and fescue (Festuca spp.; e.g., foxtail fescue, F. megalura) predominate with overgrazing having reduced the native cover of perennial bunchgrasses such as threeawn (Aristida spp.), needlegrasses (Stipa spp.) and bluegrasses (Poa spp.). During the first three weeks of the survey, large numbers of blooming forbs could be identified (Table 1) most of which had died by mid-May when the field work was completed. Trees and shrubs are isolated and infrequent and generally confined to the better soil and moisture conditions provided by springs and the lower slopes of ephemeral drainage channels. They include valley oak (Quercus lobata), Fremont cottonwood (Populus fremontii), California buckeye (Aesculus californica), poison oak (Rhus diversiloba), willow (Salix sp.), and chamise (Adenostoma fasciculatum). A number of scattered arborescent shrubs with small scale-like leaves were observed, probably representing a species of juniper (Juniperus californica ?). Spring areas of shallow sub-surface water exhibit marshy vegetation including cattail (Typha sp.), tule (Scirpus sp.) and sedges (Carex spp.).

Jimsonweed (Datura meteloides) was noted in close proximity to and possibly associated with Site 26.1. As the project area is situated well to the north of the biogeographical range of this plant (cf. Jaeger 1941:229), its presence may suggest introduction during historic times. Additional detailed information on the Corral Hollow region may be found in Sharsmith (1965), Smith (1959), Crampton (1974), Bakker (1971) and Ornduff (1974).

Wildlife is abundant and could be observed frequently during the survey. Most numerous are small rodents, of which ground squirrels (Citellus beecheyi) were particularly visible. Other members of the Rodentia order present include chipmunk (Eutamias sp.), California vole (Microtus californicus), mouse (Peromyscus spp.), pack rat (Neotoma fuscipes), pocket mouse (Perognathus inornatus) among others. Rabbits are common with black-tailed rabbit (Lepus californicus) somewhat more visible than the brush rabbit (Sylvilagus auduboni)

The availability of this large population of small mammals and the protected nature of the Site 300 area have allowed for the establishment of numerous predator species. Observed carnivores included coyote (Canis latrans), bobcat (Lynx rufus), skunk (Mephites mephites or Spilogale putoris), badger (Taxidea taxus), buteos, turkey vultures and several owl species). Lizards and snakes were observed (cf. Stebbins 1959 for additional information).

Adult and juvenile mule deer (Odocoileus hemionus) were spotted throughout the duration of the project. Detailed information on the local fauna can be found in Berry and Berry (1959).

Table 1

Observed Common Forbs of the Project Area

Lupine	Lupinus sp.
Purple sanicle, snake root	Sanicula bipinnatifida
Fiddleneck	Amsinckia spp.
Morning glory	Convolvulus sp.
Tidy tips	Layia platyglossa
Buckwheat	Eriogonum sp.
Soap plant	Chloragalum pomeridianum
Yarrow	Achillea millefolium
Wild cucumber	Marah fabaceus
Filaree	Erodium sp.
Owl's clover	Orthocarpus densiflorus
Indian paintbrush	Castilleja affinis
California poppy	Eschscholzia californica
Grass nut	Brodiaea laxa
Blue dick	B. pulchella
White mariposa lily	Calochortus venustus
California mustard	Thelypodium lasiophyllum
Miner's lettuce	Montia perfoliata
Iris	Iris sp.
Blue-eyed grass	Sisyrinchium bellum
Wild onion	Allium sp.
Black sage	Salvia mellifera

With regard to climate, California exhibits the Mediterranean pattern of summer drought and winter rainfall caused by the seasonal north-south migration of a high pressure center over the Pacific Northwest. Situated within the eastern ridges and canyons of the Diablo Range, the project area itself is subject to a rainshadow effect that inhibit the precipitation of coastally derived moisture over this region. These conditions result in the low average annual precipitation of 14.4 inches for the Town of Livermore (Elford 1970) and even less for the more sheltered project area. While the interior location of Site 300 accounts for lower precipitation figures, it is at the same time responsible for the more continental aspect of its seasonal temperature variation. Though snow is infrequent, the area does experience a short frost-free period, with 100-150 frost-free days for the Livermore area. Seasonal temperatures average 71.7^{O}F in July and 46.1^{O}F in January, spanning a broader range than in the coastal region to the west (Elford 1970). Greater detail on the general area is available in Gilliam (1962).

PREHISTORY[1]

Direct archaeological data for the inland project area are sorely lacking although basic comparative information for the greater Bay Area and central California in general is available.

The San Francisco Bay Area was first regarded as an archeological unit by N.C. Nelson in 1909 who observed that:

> ". . . enough is known to warrant the statement that a general similarity in culture obtains for the entire region; but the differences, if any, remain to be brought clearly (to light) (Nelson 1909:327)."

Uhle (1907) and Nelson (1909, 1910) contributed to the earliest studies of the regional prehistory. In specific, Uhle (1907) was responsible for the first published report on a Bay Area shellmound in Emeryville. Using stratigraphy for chronological control, he reported change through time in burial customs, in the frequency of certain artifact forms, and in the relative proportions of oyster and clam shells in the midden. Nelson (1909) later suggested a general similarity in culture among Bay Area shellmounds. He reported on his excavation at the Ellis Landing site and argued for the general cultural unity of all inhabitants of the site. Nelson did note a change from a preponderance of mussel shell in lower levels to that of clam in higher levels and suggested that this was an involuntary adaptation to environmental change on the Bay bottom.

Kroeber (1925) believed that the San Francisco Bay region was a culture zone that remained spatially and temporally homogenous. Bickel (1976:10) notes that Kroeber based his early summary of California prehistory on archeological data from the Bay Area. Based on his analysis, Kroeber (1925: 926) concluded that

> ". . . the upshot of the correlation of the findings of archaeology and ethnology is that not only the general California culture area, but even its subdivisions or provinces, were determined a long time ago and have ever since maintained themselves with relatively little change."

By 1929, local and regional sequences of culture change were developed elsewhere in the state. Theodoratus et al. (1979:35) have suggested that studies by Schenck and Dawson (1929), M.J. Rogers (1929) and D.B. Rogers (1929) established chronologies in the Lodi area of the San Joaquin Valley, the Yuman area of southern California and along the Santa Barbara Coast, respectively.

Lillard, Heizer and Fenenga (1939) proposed the first significant chronological sequence to document cultural change in prehistoric Central California. Evidence from mortuary practices and decorative artifacts indicated that variation in modes of burial of the dead and differences in the relative abundances of associated artifacts were the result of cultural change. A three part classification scheme was developed and was comprised of an Early, Transitional and Late Horizon. Beardsley (1948, 1954) later refined this sequence into what is now known as the Central California Taxonomic System with his Transitional Horizon being named the Middle Horizon (Table 2).

Heizer and Fenenga's (1939) Delta scheme provided an example of cultural change which typified the prehistory of California and suggested a similar and parallel development in the Bay Area. However, there are difficulties in the extension of one regional sequence to another area (cf. Bickel 1976).

Wallace (1978) and Elsasser (1978) provide the most current synthesis of post-Pleistocene archaeology and later prehistoric cultures in California. While a great deal is now known regarding central California cultural chronology, there are still unresolved problems with respect to the Middle Horizon, Transitional Phase and the Late Horizon (cf. Table 2). With respect to the Middle Horizon, its terminal dates are estimated to be between A.D. 700 and A.D. 900 (cf. Fredrickson 1974a, b), yet Bennyhoff (1977) places the inception of the Early Phase I of the Late Horizon at A.D. 300 - well within the Late Phase or Terminal Phase of the Middle Horizon as noted by Fredrickson (1974a, b). The term "Transitional Phase" (A.D. 700 - A.D. 900) has been used by some archaeologists for this disputed time period.

Archaeologists do agree that the Early Horizon is the most poorly known of the periods after 2000 B.C. Intersite comparison is complicated by apparent widespread variations. Gerow with Force (1968) note that great cultural divergence was present during Early Horizon times and that diagnostic traits utilized to characterize the Early Horizon from the Windmiller Facies are limited in how they can be applied to other regions of central California. Archaeologists are agreed that basic Early Horizon traits include dolichocephalic and platyrrhine physical types, hunting and fishing for subsistence and the presence of millingstones for vegetal food processing. Other traits are the use of the atlatl, a relative absence of fire-altered rock, greasy midden, organic soil, charcoal and ash in the middens. Early Horizon cultures practiced elaborate burial rituals and placed a wealth of grave goods with the dead. Well developed trade networks with other areas of the Pacific Coast and the Sierra were also developed by this time.

Archaeologists are also in agreement that Middle Horizon sites are more common and are relatively better known. These sites usually have deep deposits containing large quantities of ash and charcoal, fire-altered rock, faunal remains of fish, bird and mammal species, and evidence suggestive of a growing reliance upon plant foods as opposed to hunted animal foods. The aboriginal populations were generally dolichocephalic and platyrrhine.

The Late Horizon emerges from the Middle Horizon with many earlier traits continuing and the introduction of new traits. Late Horizon sites are the most numerous and are composed of rich, greasy midden with bone and fire-altered rock. The use of the bow and arrow, flexed interments, "killed" grave offerings, and occasional cremation of the dead were known traits. A dietary emphasis on acorn and seed gathering is evident for this horizon. Physical types change to mostly brachycephalic, mesorrhine types who were short in stature with a finer bone structure than the earlier peoples.

Bay Area archaeologists of the 1970s have recognized and attempted to address a number of crucial questions regarding archaeological site location, the nature of subsistence and settlement systems, the driving or motivating forces which may have influenced the direction of prehistoric economies and the kinds of cultural adaptations necessary to cope with long-term changes in the productivity of past ecosystems. It is hoped that the inventory data gathered during the LLNL Site 300 survey may provide additional material for the current data bases and future analyses with a view towards answering some of the still current questions of contemporary archaeology.

Notes

1. An archival site record search was performed by the State of California Regional Site Survey Offices located at CSU-Stanislaus and CSU-Sonoma for the LLNL Site 300 area. No prehistoric or historic sites are on file at these two institutions for the project area (Appendix I).

Table 2

GENERALIZED CENTRAL CALIFORNIA PREHISTORIC CULTURE SEQUENCE

San Francisco Bay, Delta, and Sacramento and San Joaquin Valleys

(after Bennyhoff 1977, Elsasser 1978, Fredrickson 1974a and Wallace 1978)

PERIOD I	9000 B.C. - 6000 B.C.	PaleoIndian. Hunting/Fluted Point (?)
PERIOD II	6000 B.C. - 3000 B.C.	Lower Archaic. Collecting/ Millingstone
PERIOD III	3000 B.C. - 2000 B.C.	Middle Archaic-Windmiller-West Berkeley. Hunting/Fishing/ Collecting

\- -

EARLY HORIZON	2000 B.C. - 1000 B.C	Windmiller-West Berkeley.
MIDDLE HORIZON	1000 B.C. - 700 A.D.	(or 1000 B.C. - 900 A.D.)
Early Phase		1000 B.C. - 100 A.D.
Intermediate Phase		100 A.D. - 300 A.D.
Late Phase.		300 A.D. - 500 A.D.
Terminal Phase.		500 A.D. - 700 A.D.
TRANSITIONAL PHASE	700 A.D. - 900 A.D.	
LATE HORIZON	300 A.D. - 1850 A.D.	(or 700 A.D. - 1850 A.D., or 900 A.D. - 1850 A.D.)
Early Phase I		300 A.D. - 700 A.D.
Middle Phase I		700 A.D. - 1100 A.D.
Late Phase I		1100 A.D. - 1500 A.D.
Early Phase II		1500 A.D. - 1700 A.D.
Late Phase II		1700 A.D. - 1850 A.D.

ETHNOGRAPHY

Introduction

The location of the Lawrence Livermore National Laboratory's Site 300 falls within the tribal boundaries of two different California Native American groups - the Costanoans or Ohlone and the Northern Valley Yokuts (cf. Levy 1978; Wallace 1978; Bennyhoff 1977; Heizer 1966; Kroeber 1925). Researchers are in some doubt as to the group(s) present in the Corral Hollow region with the general consensus that the area was probably utilized on a sporadic basis by both groups for marginal hunting and gathering (cf. Levy 1978; Wallace 1978; Cook 1955, 1957; Cutter 1950; Bennyhoff 1977 among others).

Costanoans

One of the aboriginal groups belonged to a group of tribes known as the Costanoans (from the Spanish Costanos or "coastal people") (Fig. 3). The group believed to have utilized the Site 300 area is thought to be the Chochenyo Costanoans (or East Bay Costanoans) with a pre-contact estimated population of 2000 individuals (cf. Levy 1978; Thompson 1957; cf. Galvan 1968: 12).

Costanoan is a language of the Penutian language family (cf. Broadbent 1972:55) with seven to eight known dialect areas (cf. Krober 1925:463-465; Levy 1978) (Fig. 3). Pre-contact ethnographic data on this group is sorely lacking due to the effects of missionization, disease and subsequent alteration of the traditional lifeway. Survivors from this period often left their home territories, undergoing extreme and organized pressure to assimilate into the larger society, and in general experiencing the discrimination and deprivation of a dispossessed people. Anthropologists place present estimates for persons of Costanoan descent in the Bay Area at over 200 (cf. Galvan 1968; Levy 1978).

With respect to ethnographic information on the contact-period Costanoans, Levy (1978) has presented the most thorough synthesis of the presently available data. The brief ethnographic sketch below relies heavily on his synthesis. Theodoratus et al. (1979) and Bickel (1976) present other reviews of Costanoan ethnography while King (1977, 1978) details additional ethnohistoric information on the Costanoan groups of the Santa Clara Valley.

Linguistic evidence points to A.D. 500 as the date when the Costanoans moved into the area replacing earlier Hokan (?) speakers. This apparent move roughly coincides with the appearance of the Late Horizon artifact assem-

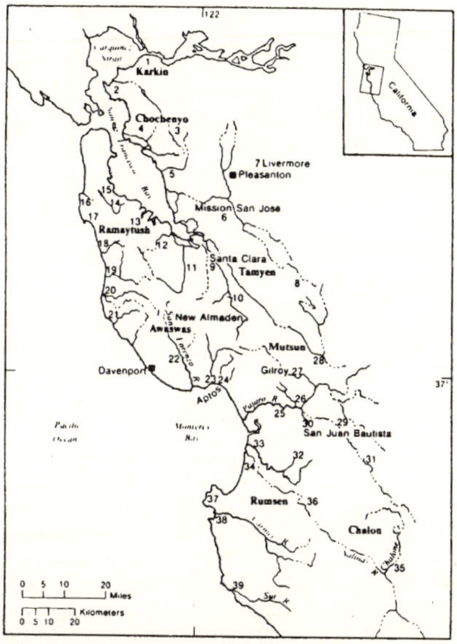

Fig I Ethnic groups and tribelets (Late 18th century) Tribelets. 1. *karkin* (Los Carquines). 2. *xučvun*. 3. (Palos Colorados). 4. (San Antonio); 5. *lisvan*. 6. *ʔorovšom* (San Francisco Solano). 7. *šewnen* (El Valle). 8. (Santa Ysabel). 9. (Santa Clara). 10. (San Juan Bautista). 11. (San Jose Cupertino). 12. *puyšon* (Arroyo de San Francisco). 13. *lamšin* (Las Pulgas). 14. *salson* (San Matheo). 15. *šipliškin* (San Bruno). 16. *ramay* (Cañada de las Almejas). 17. *ṣatunumno* (San Egidio). 18. *kotxen* (La Purisima). 19. *ʔolxon*. 20. *kuxasta* (San Antonio); 21. *čitaktak* (San Juan). 22. *sayant* (San Juan Capistrano); 23. *ʔuypi* (San Daniel). 24. *ʔaptos* (San Lucas); 25. *ʔawsaymu*. 26. *xuristak*. 27. *kulu·listak* (San Bernardino). 28. *ʔorestak*. 29. *kotetak*. 30. *xumontwaš*. 31. *paxšin*. 32. *mutsun* (La Natividad); 33. *wačron*. 34. *kalenta ruk*. 35. *čalon*. 36. *ʔensen* (Los Sanjones). 37. *ʔačista* (San Carlos); 38. *ʔičxenta* (San Jose). 39. *sarxenta ruk* (R del Sur) Names in parentheses are Spanish designations (From Levy 1978)

Figure 3

blages. In 1770, the Costanoans were living in 50 separate politically autonomous nations or tribelets - each of which had one or more permanent village sites. During various time of the year, groups left the villages for temporary camps at scattered locations in the triblet's territory to engage in fishing, hunting and the collection of seasonal plant foods. The average tribelet number some 200 individuals with a range of 50 to 500 persons. The large triblets usually had several permanent villages located close to one another (Levy 1978).

The territorial boundaries were clearly defined by physiographic features and hostile neighbors kept each tribelet confined. Chiefdomships were inherited patrilineally by the son (or in rare cases daughter or sister) with the approval of the community. The chief was the leader of a council of elders and his main function was as advisor to the community and as host to visitors. The Costanoan individual was free to pursue life without interference except in time of war (Levy 1978:487-488).

Costanoan kinship and social organization differed to some degree from those of other Penutian groups. Households were larger comprising ten to fifteen individuals. Ethnographic evidence indicates some occurrence of sororal polygnous marriages with co-wives sharing the same residence with the children. Patrilineally extended families are also noted with clan groupings within deer and bear moieties. Kinship terminology indicates possible cross-cousin marriage and appears to be a practice due to the heavy influence by the Salinan to the south (Levy 1978:488).

Warfare was a practice among the Costanoans and was commonly caused by territorial infringements. Captives were killed (excluding young females), heads taken as trophies and enemy villages burned. The chief weapon was the bow and arrow. Trade relations are revealed indirectly by linguistic evidence in the use of borrowed words for items not available locally by Costanoan, Miwok, Yokut and Salinan groups. Mussels, dried abalone shells, salt and cinnabar were commonly exported, while pinon nuts, obsidian and clam shell disk beads from the east are the only known imports (Levy 1978:487-488;Davis 1961).

In religious practice the Costanoan regarded prayers and offerings to the sun as important. Meal and smoke were common offerings. Dreams and omens aided and guided future personal actions, while shamans controlled natural events by dancing and cured serious illness and injury by sucking and the use of herbs. Witchcraft was practiced by the grizzly bear doctors (Levy 1978:489-

490).

Music for the Costanoan was closely connected with ritual and myth. The musical form is described as relaxed, non-pulsating with the "rise" type of form and movemen and closely resembles Yuman style. Instruments included bird bone whistles, alder flutes, split stick rattles of laurel wood, cocoon rattles and a stringed instrument plucked with the fingers.

At puberty girls observed the menstrual avoidances similar to those of post-partum and were removed from male contact while boys were initiated into a datura society where they were given a hallucinogen to induce visions necessary for entrance into manhood (Levy 1978:490).

Marriage was informally marked by a gift exchange to the bride's kin and followed by patrilocal residency. Divorce occurred not infrequently but the children remained with the mother. The death of a member was observed by the mourning of the widow and other female kin by cutting of the hair, smearing of the face with ash or asphalt and self mortification of their bodies with a pestle. Cremation was common with inhumation less common as a result of a lack of kinsmen to gather firewood for the pyre. The personal belongings of the dead were either destroyed in the cremation or buried. The widow observed a period of mourning for one year. The Costanoan had a belief in the hereafter as the dead were thought "to go to a land across the sea." The name of the deceased was taboo until given to another. A special suffix was added to the name when reference to the deceased was desired. Levy (1978:490) postulates that annual mourning ceremonies were probably observed for all the individuals who had died the previous year.

The subsistence of the Costanoan was that of a hunter/gatherer. Annual controlled burnings insured an abundant regrowth of seed-bearing annuals and increased the forage areas of larger game. The acorn ranked high among plant foods. Harvesting was done by long poles to knock them to the ground. They were gathered, ground and leached of tannin. Bread and mush were the favored food forms. Other nuts included California laurel, hazel nuts, and buckeyes. The seeds of numerous plants were gathered and parched in trays. Other seeds were crushed to make meal. Berries and wild grapes were dried. Roots of various plants were eaten along with green shoots, sprouts and pollens. Nearly all mammals of every size were trapped or shot by bow and arrow. Hides and skins were preserved and used for mats, blankets and robes. Waterfowl were lured by decoys and were captured in nets and snares. Bolas and cagelike traps of twigs were used to capture smaller birds. Eagles, owls, ravens and buzzards were not killed or eaten. Fish and shellfish comprised an important part of the diet with steelhead, salmon and sturgeon the major portion. Spearing and dip netting were the main methods of capture. Mussels, abalone, and octopus were among the common shellfish collected. Reptiles were eaten although toads and frogs were excluded. Insects included yellow jacket larvae, grasshoppers and caterpillars (Levy 1978:491-492).

Costanoan structures included domed thatched houses, wickiups, sweathouses or temescals, dance houses, and storage structures. The houses ranged from 6-10 feet across with a square doorway and a hearth in the center of the floor. The covering was described as a thatch of tule, alfalfa or fern over a bent willow framework. The temescal was an excavated pit in the middle of a stream with the superstructure laid against the bank. Wickiups were pole, brush and plaster wind or sunshelters (Theodoratus et al. 1979:21). Dance enclosures were circular or oval fence-like structures with a door and an opposing opening in the rear and usually located in the village proper (Levy 1978:492).

Costanoan technology included numerous woven items such as baskets, fish nets, mats, cradles, balsas, traps and snares. Stone tools included manos, metates, mortars, pestles, net sinkers, projectile points, bifaces and other items manufactured from either locally available or imported materials. Cinnabar and hematite were used a pigments. Bone items included awls, scrapers and whistles. Wood was used for the manufacture of paddles, cooking utensils and decorative items. Shell was used for ornaments and spoons (Levy 1978:492).

The Costanoan male usually went naked while the female wore a small front apron of braided grasses and rear one of buckskin. Both sexes wore robes of woven rabbitskin or buckskin for protection in cold weather. Hair styles were long or cropped, women wore bangs. Males had beards or were clean shaven. Shell tweezers or hot coals were used to remove facial hair. Tatooing was favored as were pierced ears and septums. Jewelry consisted of shell pendants and feather and bead ornaments (Levy 1978:493).

Social amusements consisted of gambling and athletic games. Ball race, played by kicking a wooden ball along a course, and shinny, played with a wooden puck, were favorites. Gambling games included "toussi" where four players try to guess which hand conceals a small wooden tube and "takersia" a a game using a five foot cane and a small hoop, the object being to keep the hoop spinning (Culin 1902-1903:248, 282, 472).

Northern Valley Yokuts

The other aboriginal group present within the Lawrence Livermore National Laboratory Site 300 region is the Northern Valley Yokuts whose westernmost boundary was the crest of the Diablo Range (cf. Wallace 1978; Bennyhoff 1977; Latta 1977) (Fig. 4). Little is known ethnographically of this northern San Joaquin Valley group due to their rapid disappearance as the result of disease, missionization and colonization of the Gold Rush. Wallace (1978) has presented a cogent summary of this group.

The extant linguistic data for the group suggests that the Yokuts are relatively recent arrivals in the northern Valley possibly having displaced the earlier Costanoans, Miwok or both, who had previously occupied the country (cf. Kroeber 1959:269-277; Wallace 1978). Pre-contact population estimates vary with recent estimates ranginf from 25,000 to 31,000 (Cook 1955; Baumhoff 1963). The native population was not evenly distributed with the highest densities present on the lands bordering the San Joaquin River and its main tributaries (10+ per square mile). The plains density has been estimated at 2-3 inhabitants per square mile while to the west, the population, concentrated on semipermanent watercourses well within the foothills, was much sparser (Wallace 1978:463).

Northern Valley Yokut's subsistence was oriented around a gathering/hunting lifeway directed towards the seasonal exploitation of plant, animal, and fish resources. Fish and water fowl were important dietary items and were taken by variety of capture methods. Big-game hunting of deer, elk and antelope was probably a marginal subsistence activity (cf. Wallace 1978:464). The harvesting of wild plant foods, especially the acorn, was of prime importance. Seeds of various types were also collected as were tule roots. The Yokuts also practiced the regular firing of native vegetation to improve and promote the following year's seed crop (cf. Cook 1960; Wallace 1978).

Clothing was simple, probably similar to the Costanoans, and personal adornment consisted of marine shell necklaces probably secured through trade (Wallace 1978:464). Facial tatooing was practiced.

The usual dwellings consisted of small, lightly built structures covered with tule stalks, apparently woven into mats. Two other specialized structures are also known - the sweathouse and ceremonial assembly chamber

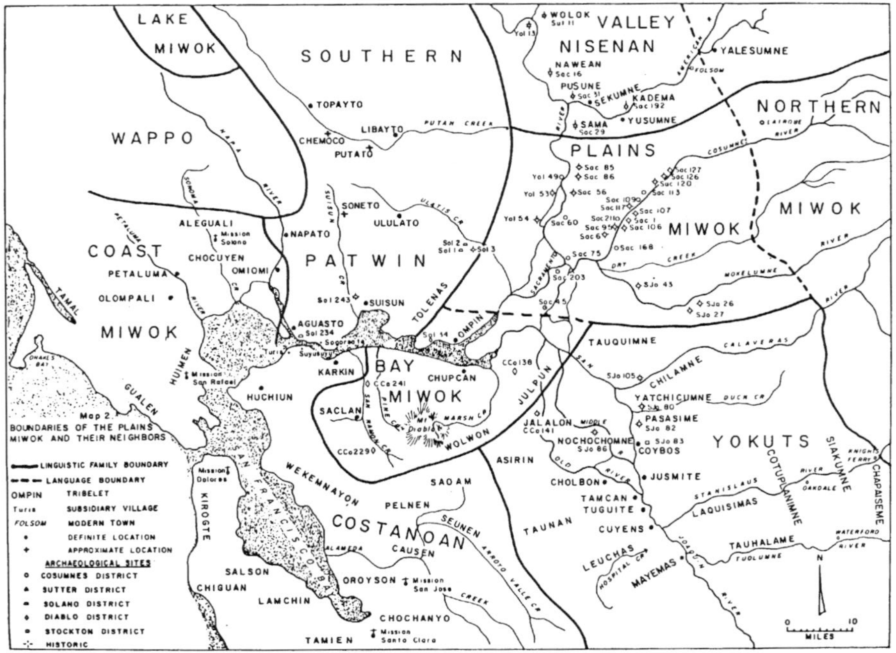

Map 2.
BOUNDARIES OF THE PLAINS MIWOK AND THEIR NEIGHBORS

(Wallace 1978:465).

Twined and coiled basketry was made from local plant materials. Stone mortars, pestles and chipped stone tools were manufactured from both local and imported stone. Both bone and wood tools and implements were fabricated for a number of uses. Light watercraft of tules were manufacturing for fishing use (Wallace 1978:465).

Trade relations were maintained with a number of groups including the Miwok and Costanoans (cf. Davis 1961).

Social organization is very poorly known. It is probable that the family unit was dominant. Kroeber (1925:493) has suggested that a totemic moiety system based on patrilineal descent prevailed among this Yokut group based on their association with the southern Yokuts and upland Miwok. The Northern Valley Yokuts were divided into tribes of approximately 300 or so individuals. Most members of the tribe lived in one principal settlement under the direction of a headman. Smaller communities of varying sizes existed within each group's territory (Wallace 1978:466). Seasonal excursions for gathering and hunting were made from the principal village by the family units.

Warfare, usually on the level of petty hotilities, did occur between neighboring groups although this was the exception rather than the rule (cf. Wallace 1978:466-467).

Very little is known concerning the religious beliefs and practices of the lower San Joaquin Indians. Ethnographic data gathered from the bordering tribes suggests participation in the datura and Kuksu ritual systems although the evidence for the Kuksu cult is open to some question (cf. Wallace 1978 467-468 and the references therein). Shamanism was undoubtedly practiced although little data are available for this or other ceremonies concerned with birth, puberty and death. Death was followed by either cremation or inhumation in a flexed position (Wallace 1978:468).

HISTORIC OVERVIEW

Introduction

Corral Hollow and Lawrence Livermore National Laboratory's Site 300 project in particular straddle both Murray and Tulare Townships of Alameda and San Joaquin Counties respectively. The regional transportation corridor, Corral Hollow Road, is located along the southern boundary of LLNL Site 300.

During the Hispanic Period, the road, creek and canyon were known as "Buenos Ayres" or "Buenos Aires" ("Good Winds") with the present name of Corral Hollow apparently due to the influx of Euro-American influence during the American Period of settlement. At present the flow of water through Corral Hollow Creek has been reduced considerably on account of the Hetch-Hetchy Reservoir system and no longer poses a flood threat during times of heavy rainfall as in the past (cf. Williams 1956-58/1975).

Various county histories have viewed the mountainous terrain of Corral Hollow as only suited to stock raising (Wood 1883:457; Gilbert 1968:128). The area was so devoid of population during the late 19th century that Robert Livermore, of the historic Livermore clan, apparently allowed his cattle to roam from the Amador Valley into the San Joaquin River (Wood 1883:461). In addition to stock raising, minerals and timber were also recognized as significant resources in Corral Hollow. Though few trees remain today, steam powered wagon trains were used to harvest timber in Corral Hollow circa. 1888 (San Joaquin County Historical Society 1973:14).

Prior to the extension of the railroad system to the area in the 1890s, the residents of the Corral Hollow region depended upon the single main road now known as "Corral Hollow Road." The expansion of the railroad was not due to the ranching activities but was the result of mineral exploitation. In time three town sites were established in Corral Hollow - the mining town of Tesla, and the manufacturing facilities of Pottery at Walden Spur and Carnegie in the vicinity of LLNL Site 300. The initial dependence on coal, the sole resource at Tesla, was later supplemented by the mining of clay and the production of pottery and fired bricks at Pottery and Carnegie. This marriage of mining and manufacturing was responsible for the explosive growth of the western area adjoining LLNL Site 300.

Ultimately this dependency on a single resource and product was responsible for the demise of the towns. As company towns the towns were planned, flourished and died within the remarkably short time span of 1892 to 1912. The prior pattern of stock raising and isolated on-site residence pattern continued throughout the industrial period. This same pattern, with the exception of Site 300 and the state recreational park, is still viable within Corral Hollow today.

Compilation Sources

The historical portion of this report has relied on the resources of the Bancroft Library of the University of California, Berkeley and the manuscripts on file in the Stockton and Tracy branches of the the Stockton San Joaquin Public Library. Additional materials were consulted from the files of the LLNL Site 300 library.

The manuscripts of Earle E. Williams form the single most important set of documents on the Corral Hollow area from the Hispanic to the Late American Period. A more intensive historical review of the Corral Hollow District would include consulting the collections of the Historical Societies of both Alameda and San Joaquin Counties as well as the personal collections of Earle E. Williams (Tracy) and Louis L. Stein (Berkeley). Further library research on the mines and ceramic industry in the Bay Area should also be undertaken along with a detailed county records search. No photographs of the Corral Hollow area are presently available aside from several early views of Carnegie in various publications. Undoubtedly early photographs of this area are extant but the scope of this project did not allow for their location.

Hispanic Period (ca. 1750-1850)

The Hispanic Period was an era of both exploration and nationalistic expansion undertaken first by Spain and then continued by Mexico. For the most part, the emphasis of these programs was upon the assessment of geographical resources. None of the exploratory parties entered the Corral Hollow region although the expedition led by Pedro Fages reached the southern rim of the San Joquin Valley in 1772. The party of Captain Juan Bautista de Anza, commissioned by the Viceroy of Mexico, Antonio Maria Bucareli y Ursua, was the first group to actually enter the San Joaquin Valley in April of 1776 (Williams 1956:10). Captain Bautista was accompanied by Father Pedro Font and

Lieutenant Jose Moraga who were seeking to find a route from "El Rio Grande de San Francisco" to the Sierra Nevada. Their trek began after Christmas in 1775 and ended rather abruptly on account of the combination of impassable tule patches and tule burning along El Rio Viejo by the Native American inhabitants of the region (Williams 1956:10). In returning to Monterey, the de Anza party camped just west of Corral Hollow in Callagham Gulch on April 4, 1776 (Anonymous 1976:2; Williams 1956:10)[1]. Callaghan Gulch is located 5 or 6 miles to the west of Corral Hollow in a region characterized by Font as, "It appeared to me that the country is so bad that it could not easily be inhabited by human beings. At least I was left with no desire to return to travel through it, for besides the smarting of the eyes which I brought from there, and the fever in my mouth which I had corrected but which today returned to assail me, I have never seen an uglier country" (Williams 1956:11 (from Bolton 1930)).

The next Spanish party under the leadership of Gabriel Moraga was sent by Governor Jose Joaquin de Arillaga in 1805 from Mission San Jose into the "Valle de los Tulares" or the San Joaquin Valley to review the Indian problems and locate sites appropriate for missionization (Williams 1956-58;2,5). Although Moraga did not explore even the periphery of the Corral Hollow area, he did ford the San Joaquin River just south of present-day Stockton and explored the entire length of the Calaveras River. Fortunately for the Native Americans located in the interior Moraga failed to locate sites suitable for the construction and support of a mission(s) (Williams 1956-57:5).

In 1810 Father Jose Viades accompanied Gabriel Moraga on his second reconnaissance through the area of Pescadero (Bethany) to the north of Corral Hollow (Beck and Hasse 1974:No. 21). The Mexican wars for independence from Spain curtailed the expeditions and settlement throughout Alta California (Beck and Hasse 1974:No. 41). With the transfer of Alta California to Mexico in 1822, the military concentrated on the recovery of stolen animals and limiting attacks by Indians on towns, missions and ranchos. Further, no major expeditions were commissioned but rather, the policy was toward private settlement (Beck and Hasse 1974:No. 22). As a result of this policy, land grants were made to individuals during the latter part of the Mexican Period (1828-1846) in contrast to the Spanish Period practice of granting only the rights of settlement and grazing privileges (Beck and Hasse 1974:No. 24).

Corral Hollow Road was part of the El Camino Viejo, the "Old Road" of the Hispanic Period from about 1795. At this time the road was known as the "Camino del las Buenos Ayres" or "Aires." The road originated in the south at San Pedro and continued through the San Joaquin Valley along the eastern slope of the Coast Range foothills (the El Diablo range) until reaching Corral Hollow in San Joaquin County. The route then proceeded westerly over the summit and down Arroyo Seco (Dry Gulch) to the Las Positas (Livermore) Valley, over Vallecitos and through the Sunol Valley. It continued over Mission Pass to Mission San Jose de Guadalupe and then west to its terminus at Yerba Buena (San Francisco) (Williams 1965:11). It should be noted that the Corral Hollow road was not a major road such as a Camino Real[2].

According the E.E. Williams, a local historian, the old Spanish trails followed the valley rims, that is, along high ground, not along creeks and canyons as used by the game and aboriginal groups. The justification for this upland placement was supposedly for the better footing provided throughout the year and the access to fresh water every 10 to 15 miles at springs and pools (Williams 1965:3). The position of the Corral Hollow Road contradicts the traditional upland road location but it must be noted that Corral Hollow is the most southerly exit through the Diablo Mountains, a spur of the Coast Range. As part of the El Camino Viejo, the road served as a conduit for the movement of travelers and settlers as well as for the annual spring cattle drives which occured from 1808 to 1849 as part of the annual Matanza cycle (cf. Bente 1980). The hides and tallow recovered as part of this cattle raising cycle formed the economic basis of the economy of western North America as well as constituting a major foreign export product during the Hispanic and Early American Periods (Williams 1965:10).

The noted historian Jacob Bowman studied the disenos (maps) of land grants for the period ca. 1835 to 1846 and includes some information on Corral Hollow Road (Bowman 1946). He concluded that the topographic features of Corral Hollow Canyon, Creek and Road found on contemporary maps, first appeared as the Portezuela (pass) de Buenos Ayres on the diseno of Las Positas (Gudde 1969:75). The Mexican land grant of Las Positas was located to the northwest of the Corral Hollow region (Beck and Hasse 1974:No. 30). By the 1850s the name of "Corall" replaced the Arroyo Buenos Ayres on the map as drawn by Trask and Goddard (Gudde 1969:76). The name change may be attributed to presence of a large corral used for wild horses which was located at the mouth of the canyon (Gudde 1969:76). Conversely the local oral and written tradition ascribes the present name of Corral Hollow to the misspelling of the surname of Edward B. Carrell, one of the owners of a road house located on the eastern end of the hollow (Gudde 1969:76; Williams 1961:1). Apparently confusion was minimal because as even as late as 1879, Thompson and West illustrate a transition with both "Arroyo Buenos Ayres or, Carral Hollow" (Fig. 7).

The location of ranchos/land grants and their relationship with the Corral Hollow area as outlined by Beck and Hasse indicate that Corral Hollow Road was not a major route between ranchos or even missions or a presidio (Beck and Hasse 1974:Nos. 28, 30; Bowman 1946:5). As far as can be determined, there were no adobe structures within the Corral Hollow region - a factor which would have fostered a road network to the east and west (Bowman 1951; Hendry and Bowman 1940).

The lack of Hispanic settlement in the Corral Hollow region is related to two major environmental factors - the hilly terrain and the lack of potable water. The lack of abundant water and by extension navigable waterways, prevented easy access with the other economic centers in the state. Thus, the original residents arrived gradually and concentrated on enterprises demanding minimal capitalization such as ranching. The area was not directly explored during the Spanish period of discovery or exploration. Nonetheless, it did reflect the transition from Spanish to Mexican rule in that the region was part of a road network related to ranching but was considered inappropriate for missionization or land grants which were characteristic of the Hispanic cultural pattern.

American Period

Toward the end of the Hispanic Period, isolated forays were made into Alta California by Canadian and American frontiersmen. To the east of Corral Hollow, in the San Joaquin Valley, the earliest Americans were trappers and include such notables as Jedediah S. Smith, 1925-1827 and John M. Leod, 1827-1828 (Gilbert 1968:10-11). The arrival of French-Canadian trappers in the valley in 1828 was associated with the Hudson Bay Company and with the California-Oregon trail which extended from Fort Vancouver to French Camp. Trappers and their families returned to this area, known as "Castoria" repeatedly until about 1845 (Williams 1958:1). Other less established trappers who ventured into the San Joaquin Valley were Ewing Young in 1829, 1830 and 1832 and Michel La Framboise in 1832-1833 (Gilbert 1968:20).

Proceeding closer to the Site 300 study area, the first American residents within San Joaquin County settled along the Upper Sacramento Road while the second concentration was located at the mouth of Corral Hollow. The Corral Hollow contingent arrived early in November of 1846 in four covered wagons under the command of Captain Charles Imas (Williams 1965:8). The party members consisted of Captain Imas, his brother (Christian name unknown), John W. Laird, his brother William Laird and brothers John F. and Thomas Pyle (Williams 1965:9). These men and presumably their families pitched their tents on the high ground of the fork of the El Camino Viejo near the future site of "Wright's Zink House" (Williams 1965:8-9). The placement of the Zinc House in 1850 was approximately 500 yards north of the California Registered Landmark No. 755 located to the east side of Site 300 (San Joaquin County Historical Society 1966). The Laird Brothers continued to live in their tents near the Zink House after its construction in an area known to have been an Indian village (Williams 1965:9-10).

The year 1847 brought problems between the new settlers of Corral Hollow and the Indians. The conflict was rumored to have been initiated by a "renegade Mexican" who disputed the "possesion of California with the American." As a result of this turmoil, which had a great impact on the San Joaquin Valley, Captain Charles Weber of Stockton reportedly returned to San Jose via Corral Hollow Road " . . . leaving four thousand head of cattle and his possessions to the mercy of the Indians . . . " (Williams 1965:17).

After the discovery of gold January 19, 1848 at Sutter's Mill, some of the first gold rush horde of Spaniards, Mexicans and Americans travelled through Corral Hollow. These fortune seekers went east and north to the southern part of the Mother Lode traversing either the expanse of the San Joaquin River or via the more indirect, but less arduous route of the experienced traveler along the El Camino Viejo south (Gilbert 1968:20; Williams 1965:21-22).

In the 1850s, the wealth of the San Joaquin Valley continued to be exploited by hunting parties. Migrating honker geese were killed and processed so that the feathers were shipped for sale in San Francisco; fat rendered for the Jewish trade; and, the meaty thigh and breast meat dried and exported to China (Williams 1956:2-3). This massive "harvesting" helped to hasten the demise of the native fauna and in combination with the drought of 1864 irreparably altered the ecology. The general trend from ~~wildlife~~ hunting and trapping to ranching, wheat growing and other such sedentary pursuits was then repeated in the San Joaquin Valley (Gilbert 1968:130).

The increasing traffic between the west to the eastern side of the Coast Ranges was accomplished by travelling through one of three passes. In addition to Corral Hollow, Patterson Pass to the north was used as was Altamont Pass still further to the north (Williams 1975:1). A tavern was built along Corral Hollow Road to take advantage of the movement through Corral Hollow. The builders of the only American tavern along the El Camino Viejo arrived in Corral Hollow in 1849 when they returned from mining in the Tuolumne area (Williams 1960:1). Horatio P. Wright, William H. Brayton and John A. Stockholm erected this building, known as the "Zink House", from materials purchased in Stockton and hauled by wagon to the site. This tavern, on the mail route, served both Americans and Mexicans. It provided alcoholic beverages, food and supplies for both Corral Hollow residents and transients (Williams 1960:4). Upon the murder of Brayton on October 24, 1850, reportedly for the gold accumulated for services provided to the miners, Edward B. Carrell became a part owner of the "Zink House" (Williams 1960:4).

In addition to the tavern several other establishments were set up in Corral Hollow to serve the road traffic. One of these was a combination gambling and entertainment tent which had been moved from Sonora to Tuolume City to Corral Hollow. The relocation was superb since Corral Hollow was a major access road between the coast region and the southern mines. The enterprise lasted only two months from its initial arrival in December 1850 on account of the murder of four men in the tent (Williams 1973b:20). In addition to the road traffic, the Henry C. Lee Little South American Circus (later the Lee and Marshall's Great National Circus, 1852; and Lee and Bennett's Circus, 1857) was one of the annual trekkers through the Corral Hollow Pass from 1850 to 1859 (Williams 1975:1-2, 6). Each year the circus travelled from its headquarters in San Francisco to Howard's Circus Ranch in Stockton and on to the Mother Lode towns as part of its annual tour (Williams 1975:7).

Hittel (1861) in his account of James Capen Adams, better known as Grizzly Adams, states that Corral Hollow Pass was used intensively by the "mountain men." While Grizzly Adams was hunting and capturing grizzly bear, cougars and the like in the Corral Hollow area, he noted three hunters from the "Redwoods" along with another group of adventurers from Kern River. Adams also recognized the presence of coal and sulphur springs in the Corral Hollow area (Hittel 1861:311-312). Adams built three bear traps in 1855 (Williams 1975:8) and with Charley Foster built a hunter's cabin at the mouth of Mitchell Ravine (located to the west and south of Pottery) in 1856 (Williams 1956-58/1975:9). Horatio P. Wright's diary of the Zinc House includes the supplies furnished for Grizzly Adams among which were "2 bottles of cologne, large quantities of sugar and syrup, shot and powder, sheet iron, lumber, nails" and cash loans to the "bear man" totalling $124.56 (Williams 1960:5).

Between 1854 and 1857 California was in a depression. This apparently led to the excavation of a prospect tunnel in Corral Hollow (Williams 1975:7). This event began in 1856 with sheepman John O'Brien developing a coal outcrop which had originally been discovered by a man known only as "Baker." The O'Brien Ranch was situated on the extreme western part of the "gulch of Corral Hallow in Alameda County adjoining the San Joaquin County line" (that is, within LLNL Site 300) (Ward and Williams 1971:3). With Edward Carrell of Zinc House fame as both a friend and business partner, O'Brien succeeded in the development of what was known as the "Eureka" seam which was later to be incorporated into the Tesla Mines. The mining activities of O'Brien and Carrell at Baker's Ravine started on January 1, 1857.

Henry C. Lee and David Howard of the Great National Ci us also played a part in the early development of the coal deposits in Corral Hollow (Williams 1975:6-7, 10). O'Brien secured a loan for the mining operation from Lee in March of 1857. David Howard, who was the third partner in the initial organization of the Pacific Coal Mine, helped to finish the prospect tunnel using circus equipment (Williams 1975:6, 8, 10). The financial arrangement between O'Brien, Carrell and Lee resulted in a one quarter ownership of the mine for Lee. O'Brien hired a Dr. McClintok at $40 per month to cook and a blacksmith in San Francisco at the rate of $50 per month (Williams 1975:8). Charley Foster, a compatriot of Grizzly Adams and who lived in the cabin built by the two, also labored in the prospect tunnel in 1857 and 1858 (Williams 1956-1958/1975:9). Work on this tunnel was finished on Saturday, August 7, 1858. During these operations, Carrel continued his search for additional capital in San Francisco. When the Pacific Coal Mining Company was formally constituted, Carrell reportedly took a "note for $6000" (Williams 1960:6). The Eureka Mining Company came into existence after Carrell, unable to meet the note, transferred his share to F. Griffings on May 21, 1860. This company later became the Commercial Coal Mining Company with Carrell as the principal (Williams 1961:2). Historic maps place the Commercial Coal Mining Company in Sections 29, 30 and 32 (T 4S, R 3E) (Figs. 5-6).

Coal transportation was via a wagon road to Mohr's Landing located some 14 miles from the Zinc House. This road was "put in service" at the estimated cost of $500 (Williams 1960:6). All coal was transported on the completed road running eastward from Elkhorn Ravine past the Zinc House and northward to Mohr's Landing on the Old River at which point the coal was loaded on barges (Williams 1960:6-7). Wheat grown in the San Joaquin Valley was also shipped to San Francisco in the same manner. While the coal mining was not especially successful, approximately 1800 tons were shipped via this route to San Francisco and San Antonio (East Oakland) between 1857 and 1861 (Williams 1974:1).

Teamsters hauling the coal were furnished room and board at Carrell's "White House Corral Hollow." This "White House" was a two story house of re-sawed siding built beside the creek about midway between the Zinc House and Hog's Back to the east. Built in 1861, "White House Corral Hollow" was situated upon an Indian village/cemetary site (Williams 1960:6-7).[3] Thus, O'Brien and various backers of the mine were responsible for the second phase of economic development within Corral Hollow. The traditional pattern of stock-raising still continued while the era of coal mining was initiated.

In 1861 the Whitney Geologic Survey, lead by William H. Brewer, actually sought out the Corral Hollow area in order to view the traces of coal which had been found by "some forgotten prospector named Baker" (Williams 1956-1958/1975:25).[4] Brewer and his three assistants arrived in Corral Hollow on October 10, 1861 and took advantage of the recently built "White House." The tavern was situated at a spring and apparently had the only trees in a "dozen miles." Brewer also noted that at this time there was no water in Corral Hollow Creek though water was present in Mitchell Ravine (Williams 1956-1958/1975:3, 25). While leading this geological exploring party, William Brewer sent letters from Corral Hollow on October 3rd and 12th of 1861, and again on June 3rd of 1862. In this correspondence there is no reservation as to the rigors of the Corral Hollow environment " . . . we find it a most

Godforsaken, cheerless, inhospitable, comfortless region" and " . . . few trees grow in the bottom of this Canyon (Brewer 1930:205)." The lack of water was a problem for the only water consisted of " . . . some alkaline springs which neither mule or I could drink (Brewer 1930:200)." At this time, water was secured from a deep well located at the O'Brien House some three miles up the canyon. This source was inadequate in amount and taste, and known "to spils (spoil) tea" (Williams 1956-1958/1975:3). The original Spanish name of Arroyo de los Buenos Ayres, that is, "good winds" appears to be linked to the fierce winds described carrying dust, grass, sticks and other such debris which contributed to the discomfort of the Brewer party (Brewer 1930:206).

As a geologist, Brewer was the first to comment upon the inferior quality of the coal found in Corral Hollow. The position of the coal beds was a complicating factor as well for the bedswere found discontinuously and generally only encountered at a 45 degree angle (Brewer 1930:107). During the years of 1861-1862, Brewer noted that only one mine in Corral Hollow was of any consequence and that it had sold not over 300 to 400 tons.[5] As a portent of the future, Brewer continued, "I question if any mine here will ever prove profitable (Brewer 1930:206)." The great deluge of 1861-1862 began in November of 1861 and subjected Corral Hollow to such flooding that the road was destroyed. As a consequence, all coal mining stopped and only a few men opted to stay (Williams 1956-1958/1975:12).

On the death of Edward B. Carrel, September 5, 1880, his estate became the principal stock holder of the then inoperative coal properties in Corral Hollow (Williams 1961:2). According to the research of Earle E. Williams, Carrell spent part of each year in San Francisco where he projected the image of a coal baron. Needless to say, the coal mine was not equal to the myth (Williams 1961:3).

From the Hispanic Period through to the Twentieh Century, stock raising was a traditional pattern in the Corral Hollow area. In fact, the diary of Edward Carrell discusses the purchase of a "beef" from Joe Livermore, son of the original settler John Livermore who married an heir to a Mexican land grant (Williams 1975:7). At the time of the purchase in 1857, just after the infusion of capital from Henry C. Lee for the coal mine, Carrell lived in a tent "on the ledge in the upper gulch." The steer (presumably) was brought by Livermore and two of his vaqueros, butchered on site, and hung to age. For his effort Livermore received payment of $25, plus $5 for a previous debt (Williams 1975:7). The mention of this debt provides the only evidence for continuous or at the very least prior relationships between the residents of Corral Hollow and Livermore. Further, the interaction with Livermore suggests that the stock raising in Corral (Carrel) Hollow was confined to sheep.

If the maps of Wallace, Thompson and West and their accompanying data are correct, there was no building or mining structures within the boundaries of LLNL Site 300 in 1870-1878 (Wallace 1870; Thompson and West 1878; Gilbert 1968; Figs. 5-7). Further, the occupations of the men listed in Thompson and West are primarily farmers and stock-raisers, although the Murray township does include a miner and a farmer and a miner/farmer combination. This roster of names is on further indication of the importance of ranching within the Corral Hollow region which was ongoing during the initial portion of the mining era. There is no doubt that a number of great sheepdrives began in Corral Hollow proper (Rickman 1976:2) and that life in the region was extremely precarious. The short biographical sketch of sheepherder Henry Comes Banta catalogs the vagaries of nature - dry years in 1877, 1898, interspersed with floods in 1881, 1883, 1890 and the complication of market price fluctuations for meat and wool in 1894 and 1895 (Banta 1954:4).

The importance of the ranching pattern within LLNL Site 300 is best summarized in the short biography of Michael Mulqueeney published in 1883. Within this sketch, Mulqueeney is identified as a native of Ireland; an emigree to Canada; and, a Canadian resident for four years. Upon his arrival in San Francisco on April 23, 1868, he moved to Alameda County. The next year, 1869, he purchased the first part of his holdings, which by 1882 were to reach "four thousand acres located about two miles from Midway", that is, Corral Hollow and environs. The succeeding year Mulqueeney doubled his acreage and he was acknowledged " . . . king of that industry in this section of the state, having from five to eight thousand head of sheep on his range (Wood 1883:950)." This emphasis on stock raising continues in Corral Hollow though a portion of the Mulqueeney property, 1202 acres to be exact, was to form a part of LLNL Site 300 in the 1950s (R. Mullins, personal communication, 1981).

Late American Period (c. 1880-1930)

During the winter of 1888 coal was scarce. This scarcity and the resultant high cost was the consequence of strikes in the mines of British Columbia as well as a reduced export market for wheat. Wheat was important in that English coal was shipped to the United States only as ballast and was then exchanged in California for wheat (Mosier 1978:114). Though the coal obtained from the Mount Diablo and Livermore regions was extremely high in sulphur, it was considered appropriate for generating steam and used in " . . . locomotives, ferryboats, factories and mills (Mosier 1978:115; cf. Tesla Coal Co. 1900)."

Corral Hollow, with its minimal resources, was a backwater which seems to have escaped the railroad building trend prevalent from 1865 through 1880 (Sandoval n.d.a.:4). The building of a rail line to and through Corral Hollow had to await capitilization of the mining resources. The apparent scarcity of coal in 1888 led to a reassessment of the coal deposits within the region. If coal was to be profitably exploited, a more efficient market transportation system was necessary. Toward this end a preliminary railroad survey through Corral Hollow to the Livermore coal mines was made in January of 1888 (Mosier 1978:115-116). Thus, the original plan for the transport of coal by rail was to proceed from Livermore to and through Corral Hollow. As projected, this road/line would have veered off of the Western Pacific Railroad at George May's crossing, 2.5 miles south of Livermore, and run east following the foothills (Mosier 1978:116). This line was not built.

In the early 1890s, the noted San Francisco financiers, the Treadwell brothers, initiated a move to purchase all the outstanding shares of the Commercial Coal Company. At this time, share values were as low as $2 - a marked contrast to the earlier par value of $10 per share (Williams 1961:3). As stated earlier, the predecessors of the Tesla Coal Mines of the Treadwell brothers were the Commercial Coal Company, the Eureka Coal Mine and the Pacific Coal Mines (Williams 1956-1958/1975:3). The Commerical Coal Mine, located midway along Corral Hollow Road, is not within the southwestern boundaries of LLNL Site 300 (Thompson and West 1878; Gilbert 1968; Wallace 1870; Figs. 5-7). In addition, the Livermore Coal Company, probably active in the 1870s, was located in the mid-Corral Hollow area as indicated by the 1878 map of Thompson and West (1878) of Alameda County (Fig. 6). The Tesla Mine system incorporated all of the individual mines as illustrated in the 1907 map by Barzellotti (Fig. 11).

The Treadwells and their associates proceeded to develop the mines at Tesla named in honor or the inventor Nicolai Tesla. The improvements, of reportedly a million dollars, included the building of a railroad to the tidewater in Stockton. In time, two pottery manufacturing plants were built - one at "Pottery" located at Walden Spur in the middle of Corral Hollow, and the other, Carnegie, further to the east (Williams 1961:3). The impact of the branch railroad on Corral Hollow was immense. The spur ran along Corral Hollow Road from the east along the southern border of LLNL Site 300. The original Western Pacific Railroad attempted to build the rail branch following the coal wagon route from Corral Hollow crossing the railroad at Ellis Coaling Station which was located three miles west of Tracy. This railroad spur was abandoned after only four miles had been laid, stopping quite conveniently across the creek from the old "Zink House."

The construction of the Alameda and San Joaquin Railroad line, between Stockton and Tesla, began in earnest in 1891. In keeping with the expansion of the Treadwell empire, John Treadwell held the position of General Manager, while his brother had the title of Director of the Alameda and San Joaquin Railroad (Ward and Williams 1971:16). This rail line was built by more than 200 men, mostly Chinese laborers, along with White laborers who were engaged as teamsters, mule skinners and bridge builders. Five bridges or trestles were necessary as the line crossed and recrossed Corral Hollow Creek (Williams 1962:32). The "Zink House" of H.P. White and E.B. Carrell was reopened on account of the construction of the railroad line. Prior to the construction, the tavern had been closed for approximately 25 years. The rebuilt house functioned as both a saloon and tavern catering to the railroad workers (Williams 1962:32).

When completed, the Alameda and San Joaquin Railroad Company line was only 36.6 miles in length connecting the mines at Tesla with the coal bunkers in Stockton (Ward and Williams 1971:3). Designated stops on the route proceeding from the turntable at Tesla were Harrietville, equidistant between Tesla and the next stop at Pottery at Walden Spur, followed by Carnegie and Manganese. The latter two stops were in or near the southern border of LLNL Site 300. Further east the stops included River Rock and Kerlinger, Carbona and then Lyoth which was the junction and crossing of the Southern Pacific line (from the San Joaquin Valley to Fresno) and on to Lathrop and Stockton (Denny 1913; Ward and Williams 1971:Map 2, 3, 6).

The daily railroad schedule consisted of moving empty cars from Stockton to Tesla in the morning, exchanging the rolling stock for filled cars and the proceeding back to Stockton with a noon stop for lunch at the Company boarding house (Williams 1961:33). Local transportation between Tesla and Pottery at Walden Spur was supplied by a large, four-wheel flat car, gravity operated, which could carry some fifty to sixty persons to work or school. "In the late afternoon the return trip was made with the aid of a white horse. The boy from the livery stable in Tesla rode the animal down and hitched onto the car loaded with workers for Harrietville and Tesla, plus any other wayside stops." The same procedure was followed when a dance took place in Carnegie (Ward and Williams 1971:10).

The Tesla quadrangle map, based on the survey data of 1905, has the most extensive record of the placement of buildings in the Corral Hollow area (Fig. 9 ; Ward and Williams 1971:17). In addition to the structures, the map also has the exact route of the railroad line in relation to Corral Hollow road. In combination with the adjacent Carbona quadrangle map (1922 edition) a number of observations can be made (cf. Figs. 10). With only one minor exception, the railroad line is to the north of the road. The town of Carnegie is bounded by the two rail lines so as to enclose the portion of the town located directly opposite LLNL Site 300. The southern portion of this rail spur was definitely outside of the LLNL Site 300 boundary (Fig.11 ; Barzellotti 1907). Only when the line turns norths in Section 25 (T 3S, R 4E) does the rail line cross the road twice - moving to the east and back again. Still later, in Section 24 (T 3S, R 4E), outside of the eastern boundary of LLNL Site 300 the rail line crosses again. In brief, the railroad line is always north of the road except when enclosing Carnegie and when the road and rail line move sharply northward. The relative position of the line is important for industrial debris was often loaded on railroad cars and hooked behind the caboose. During the trip back to Stockton, the cars would be "cūt off" and two Chinese laborers would unload the debris before the arrival of the next Tesla bound train (Williams 1961:33). In addition, dumping of the debris often occurred on the grade along the Hog's Back and old Carrell House. At this point the discards would be shovelled directly into the creek and would await the "yearly freshnets" (Williams 1963:

30).

The railroad adjusted to the limited and hard water by erecting a 15,000 gallon holding tank at the west side of a bridge leading into the Stockton Channel. This tank was used to pump soft water into the locomotive and tank cars which were used to haul this water to Tesla for mine machinery use. The water problem was so severe that condensors were employed by both the railroad and mining company to recover the desperately needed soft water (Ward and Williams 1971:6). The problems with the boilers and subsequent explosions in Corral Hollow were directly related to the mineralization associated with hard water use.

In keeping with the rise and fall of the Treadwell empire, the railroad was ordered to terminate at Carnegie in 1918 by the United States Railroad Administration. However, the railroad continued in operation to Tesla until 1922. In 1922 the railroad was moved from Tesla to Moy located four miles west of Carbona (Ward and Williams 1971:16).

There were three major residential clusters within the Corral Hollow area in addition to scattered residences. Tesla at the far west along Corral Hollow Road was the most important with mines for coal and clay. The second cluster was Pottery at Walden Spur, a sewer pipe and tile plant fabrication center. The town of Carnegie and its associated industrial facility produced firebrick, face brick and miscellaneous terra cotta wares. Each town or locus was approximately two to two and half miles from the others (Fig. 9). Carnegie, directly opposite and present on a portion of LLNL Site 300 is commerated as California Registered Landmark 740 (San Joaquin Historical Society 1966).

The Treadwell businesses in Corral Hollow were known as "The San Francisco and San Joaquin Coal Company" in contrast to "The Alameda and San Joaquin Railroad." Undoubtedly San Francisco was much more prestigous than "Alameda" as well as being the final destination for the Tesla coal. As discussed previously, the coal was transported from Corral Hollow eastward to Stockton and then shipped via barge to San Francisco (Williams 1961:3).

During the heyday of mining, the daily output reached 500 tons while the annual productionfor the years of 1897 to 1902 hovered around 90,000 tons (Ward and Williams 1971:12). At Tesla, electric power was generated by the boiler plant and used to operate the electric mine locomotive as well as to run the plant sawmill. Electricity was also used for mine illumination as well as for street lighting (Ward and Williams 1971:12).

The mineral resources in Corral Hollow were not confined to coal alone. Both shale and clay were known as a result of the exploitation of the coal deposits. The quality of the clay was excellent and led to the development of another Treadwell Company, the "Carnegie Brick and Pottery Company." The clays ranged in quality from high grade plastic fire clay to red burning clays and shales used in the manufacture of sewer pipe and paving bricks. Further, large amounts of high grade quartz were available from the Tesla Mine. The quartz, when combined with the non-calcareous white or light cream color clay, resulted in the famous Carnegie "firebrick." In fact the term "Carnegie" for this brick type eventually became the generic name applied to the highest grade of fire brick (Williams 1961:6).

In addition to the local clays and quartz, lime was produced locally from 1900 to 1911. The lime was a necessary ingredient for the mortar used in the construction of the kilns and smokestakes at Pottery and Carnegie. The limestone was mined from a ravine in the rear of the Carnegie Hotel (Williams 1961:5) and from the crest of a hill about a quarter of a mile from the plant at Carnegie (i.e., the southeast corner of Section 33, T 3S, R 4E) (Ward and Williams 1971:10). The limestone was then concentrated in the lime-burning kilns located to the south of Carnegie (Williams 1961:5). Production at the hill quarry averaged approximately 75 barrels a day (Ward and Williams 1971:10; cf. also Clark 1959:39). Another lime source was located in the southwestern corner of Section 32, T 3S, R 4E to the south of Corral Hollow Road between Carnegie and Pottery (Huey 1948:62).

Deposits of cinnabar were also mined in Corral Hollow and processed to provide the mercury necessary in some mining operations. It is possible that both the Phoenix Quicksilver Mining Company and possibly the Marsel Mining Company were the only cinnabar producers in Corral Hollow (Alameda County, California 1904:50; Ward and Williams 1971:10). The rail stop of Manganese appears to be named on account of the manganese deposits within Mitchell Ravine located to the south of Corral Hollow Road (i.e., T 3S, R 4E, (Denny 1913)). The Ladd Mine reportedly shipped 5000 tons to England between 1867 and 1875 depending on the wagon drayage to Mohr's Landing at Old River (Clark 1955:39; Ward and Williams 1971:6). The mine, in the southeast quarter of Section 2, T 4S, R 4E, continued production until 1902 and reopened during World War I (Huey 1948:62-63). It is currently inactive.

Gravel and sand deposits were also mined. A pit was located to the east of Carnegie and the material was shipped by train to Stockton and beyond (Leary 1962:5). The gravel deposits were exploited until 1911 when the flood of Corral Hollow Creek destroyed five railroad trestles (Ward and Williams 1971:8). These gravel pits were the last segment of the Treadwell industrial complex to be abandoned in 1911 on account of both the collapse of the trestles and the bank failure of the California Safe Deposit Bank in San Francisco (Williams 1961:6; Ward and Williams 1971:8).

The pattern of urbanization in Corral Hollow during this Late American Period was essentially that of planned company towns with scattered, affiliated residential clusters. Tesla and Carnegie had both a public and residential section, with the residential sections divided and ranked according to the position of the worker within the plant hierarchy. On the other hand, Pottery had no residential section. Residences were nearby and scattered.

The plant at Pottery consisted of three brick smokestacks with 12 beehive kilns clustered around them (Williams 1961:4).[6] Four kilns were arranged with each smokestack with brick-lined tunnels running from the stack to each kiln (cf. Lowell 1916:608). When not in use, a kiln was blocked up. To facilitate transportation of the finished products a spur track of the railroad entered the plant (Williams 1961:4). Among the many specialities manufactured were glazed porcelain headrests for Chinese as well as cornices and store fronts for Chinatowns (Williams 1962:12). The plant at Pottery was so successful that a larger plant, known as "Carnegie", was constructed along Corral Hollow Creek about two miles east of Pottery (Williams 1961:4).

From 1895, the Carnegie Brick and Pottery Company operated both the Pottery and Carnegie plants as a single entity with clay supplied from the Tesla deposit (Ward and Williams 1971:10). The machinery and plant equipment was estimated to have approached one half of a million dollars (Lowell 1916:608).

The first stage of development at Carnegie consisted of the building of several kilns and making brick on site (Stewart 1964:14). Initially the first four kilns at Carnegie were located around a low smokestake. The bricks manufactured in these kilns were then used to construct the other kilns and smokestacks with a final total of 13 stacks and 45 kilns (Williams 1961:4). When the Carnegie plant was enlarged in 1904, the number of kilns increased from 3 to 8 bee-hive shaped kilns; 3 additional small kilns and another four muffle type kilns. Shortly after the initial building phase, the hotel, general store and "everything" of Tesla was moved to Carnegie (Stewart 1964:12). The official post office, however, remained at Tesla along with apparently a number of buildings (cf. Frickstad 1955:2; Fig. 9). In its heyday, Carnegie had churches, schools, company stores, a hotel, saloons, pool halls, laundries, ice cream parlors, barber and beauty shops, bunk house for the single men and company housing for married men and their families (Williams 1961:7; Stewart 1964:11).

The approximately 2500 inhabitants of Carnegie were not entirely of European ancestry. Japanese bakers, pantrymen and vegetable "peelers", Chinese cooks, dishwashers and laundrymen, one black family and one Mexican family were also present (Williams 1961:7, 13, 21; Stewart 1964:11, figures pp. 12-15).

The transition from Tesla to Carnegie for many of the Corral Hollow residents consisted of residing in Tesla and commuting the five miles to Carnegie by foot, horse or by railroad hand car (Stewart 1964:14). The livery stable and lumberyard appear to have remained in Tesla but the fate of the "residential" suburbs is unknown. The exact placement of the various "towns" or "suburbs" is currently not possible. The personal accounts of residents of Corral Hollow such as Josephine Leary (1962) and Marie Cordelia Stewart (later Mrs. Charles Dewalt (1964)) provide some insight but often describe the residential concentrations by name or physical characteristics rather than by geographical location. For example, 25 or more houses were scattered on the hills between Carnegie and Tesla and many of these structures were built of brick with "beautiful yards which were enclosed with fences and shaded with buckeye and pepper trees" (Williams 1961:21). At present, it is not possible to correlate this description with the Tesla quadrangle map (Fig. 9) or the approximate locations for the "suburbs" of "Treadwell Row", "Fry Town", "Jimtown", and "Harrietville." "Jimtown", named in honor of James Treadwell, was associated with Tesla and located on a "hill at the end of Treadwell Row." Treadwell Row consisted of about 16 to 20 rows of five small houses per row, each of four rooms each, while the Treadwell House was first and larger than the others. Another concentration was found, "On the right, if you were in Jimtown, and down a hill, was a small flat, or meadow, with three big tents." Further, "Across a small creek and nestled into the hill was Frytown, named after Bob Fry" (Williams 1961:19). "Harrietville" named in honor of James

Treadwell's daughter Harriet, was located about one mile from Tesla and consisted of about 48 houses, a school, slaughterhouse and a diary (Williams 1961: 20). The houses at Harrietville were arranged so that the "the quadruple row of four-room houses on the lower flat was known as "Silk Stocking Row" by the people who lived in a double row of smaller houses higher on the hill" (Williams 1961:30).

In addition to these named suburbs, there was "more than a dozen neat brick homes for workmen who worked in Carnegie" located on the hills between Pottery and Carnegie (Ward and Williams 1971:9-10). Cultural material associated with this series of houses is still probably present on Lawrence Livermore National Laboratory's Site 300. The density and stratification within and between residential districts is quite evident in the manuscripts presently available. This differential social stratification may be reflected in the number, types and quality of archaeological surface material present at these locales.

While the town of Carnegie flourished, some of the sheep and cattle raised in the area were butchered in Carnegie. The meat was processed for the hotel and sold in the butcher shop for individuals (Williams 1961:8). The "industrial revolution" in Corral Hollow obviously did not replace the traditional pattern of stock raising to any great degree. One of the more vivid events of informant Marie Stewart involved watching Italian and Basque sheep herders shear sheep at the shearing sheds located one mile south of Carnegie (Stewart 1964: 15-16).

The quality of the coal mined at Tesla was poor, so poor that a briquette plant was built in Stockton as a means of compressing the soft coal and dust into a more "useful" product. These briquettes were used by the locomotives of the Alameda and San Joaquin Railroad Company but fired so poorly that the firebox grates had to be cleaned halfway up to Tesla (Ward and Williams 1971:4). Further, the instantaneous combustability of the briquettes must have been another factor which may have discouraged the mining of the Tesla deposits (Eugence R. Prince, personal communication, 1981).

The April 6th, 1906 earthquake was such that, in the words of Marie Stewart, " . . . our beds skidded across the rooms hitting first one wall and then back to the other, all furniture doing the same. The broken dishes and windows crashing added to the din. We looked over at the brick plant and the tall smoke stacks were toppled to the ground, and most all the bricks and building (sic) were in shambles" (Stewart 1964:20). The Tesla Coal Mine closed in 1906 as a result of the April 6 earthquake and the failure of the California Safe Deposit Bank of San Francisco (Williams 1961:6). Carnegie continued in operation utilizing oil-fired kilns (Ward and Williams 1971:10) even though the earthquake had damaged the facilities.

The intensive use of the Tesla clay deposit had exhausted the clay near the surface of the mine by 1911 or 1912 (Williams 1960:4; 1961:6). The wet winter of 1911 and related flooding down the gulch had a devastating effect. The mine was closed below the 250 foot level. The floods destroyed five railroad testles and caused widespread damage along the entire line as well as destroying the John O'Brien and Edward Carrell ranches (Williams 1961:6).

Carnegie continued operations until ca. 1911 although production had been declining since 1902. The lack of quality water and an adequate supply, the poor quality of the Tesla coal and the earthquake of 1906 coupled with the failure of the financial foundations of the Treadwell empire all conspired against Carnegie. The earthquake of 1906 led to a switch from clay sewer pipe to reinforced concrete in both Oakland and San Francisco lessening the demand for Carnegie products. Floods caused extensive damage in 1907 and 1911 (or 1912). By 1916 "the era was over," the Carnegie plant was sold to Gladding, McBean and Company who dismantled it to keep out competion. Tesla was purchased by the Beckman-Linden Corporation in 1919, while the Pottery at Walden Spur and the gravel operation were dismantled (Ward and Williams 1971: 14). Carnegie was abandoned by 1912 and by 1919 only the mine tailings, plant foundation and miscellaneous depressions marked the former Treadwell operations in Corral Hollow (Williams 1961:9). The order to terminate the railroad was issued in 1918 although it continued in operation until 1922 (Ward and Williams 1971:6).

Thus, Corral Hollow shared in the "Industrial Revolution" during the waning years of the 19th century and opening years of the twentieth. The revolution included a railroad, a commercial coal mine and a ceramic manufacturing facility. In contrast to the initial migration into Corral Hollow, a population explosion occurred. However, the lack of profitability, due to both natural and cultural causes, resulted in the failure of the industrial enterprises and the reversion to the original patterns of growth native to Corral Hollow.

At present, the Corral Hollow region has reverted to its traditional pattern of livestock grazing and scattered residences coexisting with a State Recreation Area and the Lawrence Livermore National Laboratory's research facility of Site 300.

Notes

1. In early California, a camino was understood to be a horse or pedestrian trail, while at the latter part of the Mexican Period, a camino referred to a cart road.

2. The program of the Stockton San Joaquin County Public Library places Callaghan Gulch to the west of Corral Hollow. If this gulch is "Callahan Gulch" as drawn on the Tesla Quadrangle of 1907, the location is directly south of Corral Hollow. Of course, the exact route of the de Anza party through this region is problematic.

3. Both the prehistoric and historic remains of the site appear to have been destroyed during the construction of a modern bridge (Williams 1960:6-7).

4. Bakers Ravine is not labelled on any historic or contemporary maps.

5. The mine referred to by Brewer may be the O'Brien and Carrell Mine.

6. Unfortunately the number of smokestacks and kilns is in dispute. The total ranges from 3-12 (Williams 1961:4) to 2-8 (Ward and Williams 1971: 11-12). Note that the photograph of the Carnegie plant in Lowell (1916) exhibits eight smokestacks.

HISTORIC EVENTS

Statewide

Gold Rush	1848
Statehood	1850

Corral Hollow

Hunting/Capture	ca. 1820s
First American Period Occupation	Nov. 1846, Capt. Imas Group
Stock Raising	ca. 1840s - Present
First Commercial Building	1850 - Zinc House
Second Commercial Building	1861 - White House Corral Hollow (Carrell)
Railroad - From Stockton	ca. 1870 - abandoned across from Zinc House
- From Livermore	1888 - Surveyed, not built
- From Stockton	1891-1922 - Alameda and San Joaquin RR
Industrialization	
Company Towns - Tesla	ca. 1896 - 1912
- Pottery	ca. 1895 - 1912
- Carnegie	ca. 1904 - 1912
General Corral Hollow	ca. 1892 - 1912

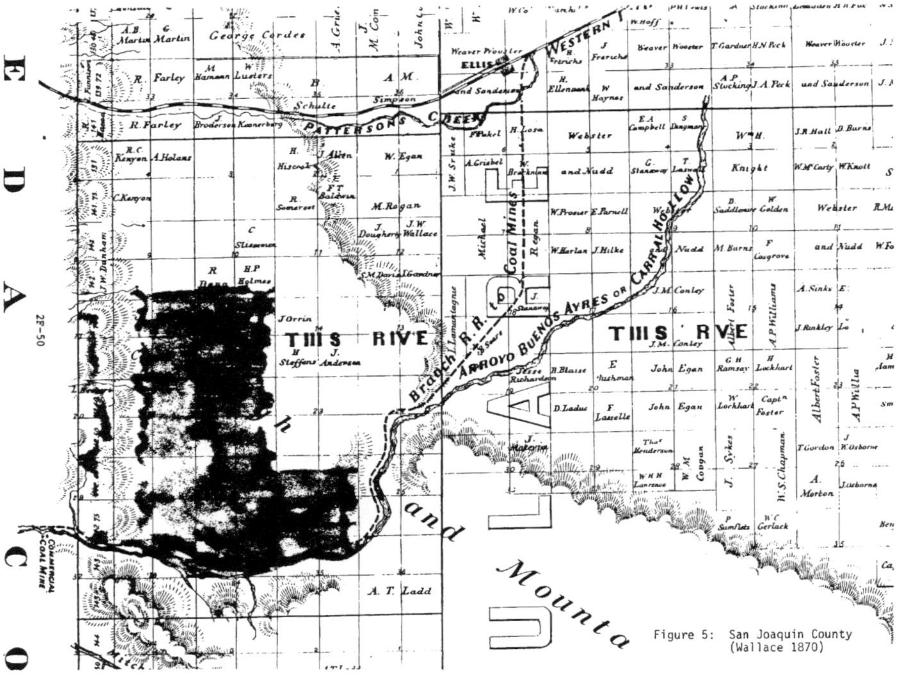

Figure 5: San Joaquin County (Wallace 1870)

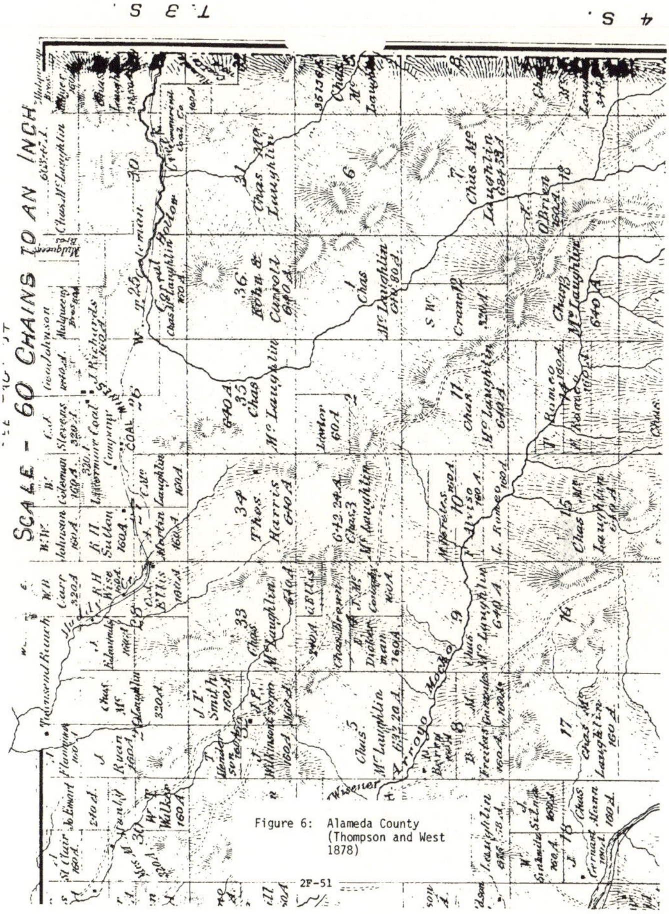

Figure 6: Alameda County (Thompson and West 1878)

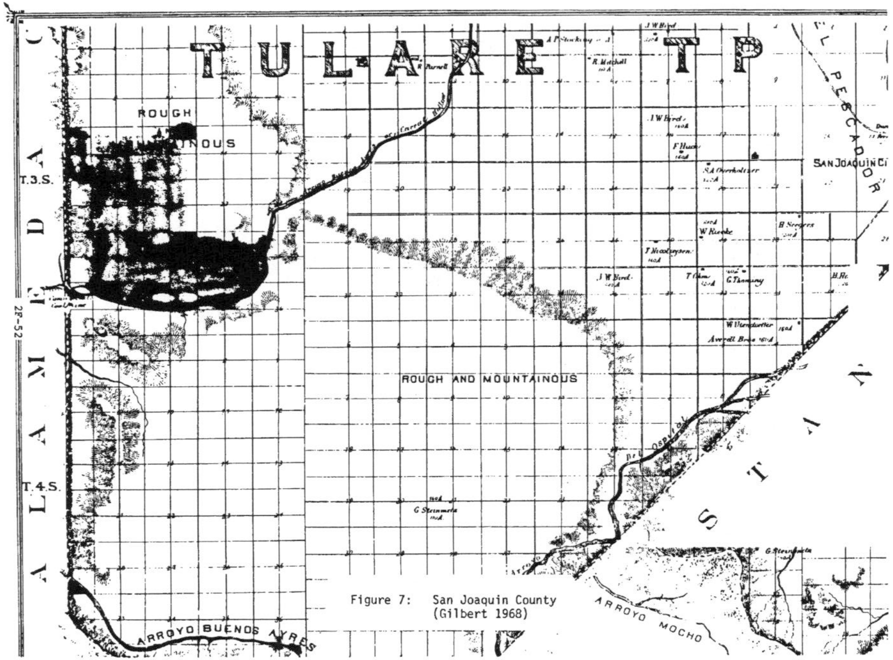

Figure 7: San Joaquin County (Gilbert 1968)

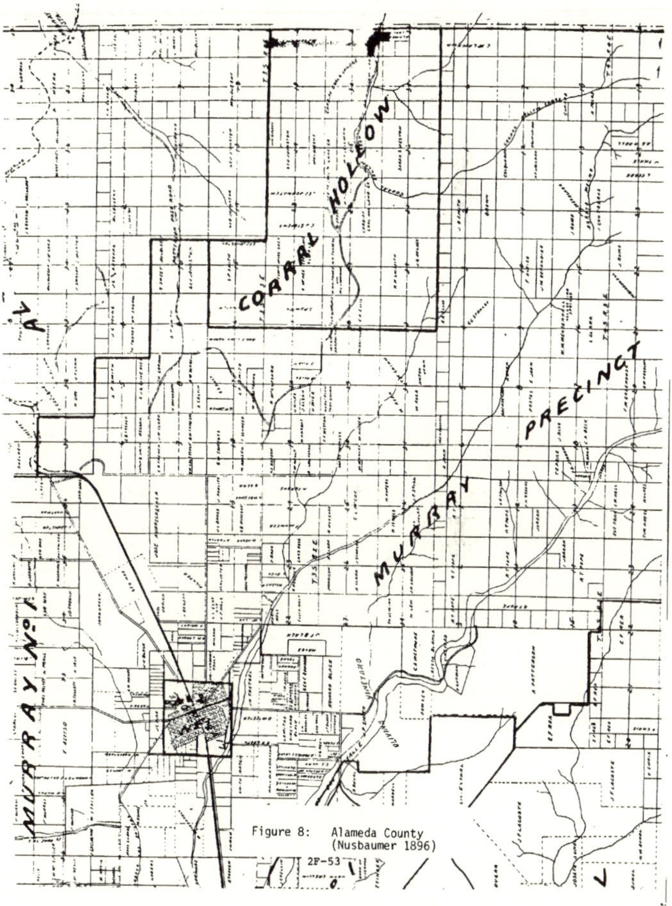

Figure 8: Alameda County (Nusbaumer 1896)

This page of the original report is an envelope containing foldout maps for Figures 9, 10, 11, and 12; economy precludes reproducing them here.

FIELD RECONNAISSANCE

Field Methodology

An intensive Class III field reconnaissance conforming to Bureau of Land Management specifications was conducted for all accessible areas of the Lawrence Livermore National Laboratory Site 300.

> "The objective of a Class III inventory is to identify and record, from surface and exposed profile indications, all cultural resources within a specified and defined area. The Class III inventory results in a total inventory of cultural resource sites observable within a specified area. Upon completion of a Class III inventory within a specified area, no further cultural resource inventory work will usually be needed. However, further cultural resource data studies may be carried out, as necessary (Bureau of Land Management, Manual, Release 8-3, 8111.14)."

The survey was conducted systematically on a section by section basis by a three to five member field team utilizing straight line transects spaced on 25 meter intervals and averaging one mile in length. The orientation of the individual transects varied (Table 3) but in general they were oriented either north-south or east-west. In several sections the topography was too rugged to attempt compass-oriented transects effectively or safely. Transects oriented along the contours of the major topographical features were utilized in this situation. To ensure full coverage using this approach, flagging tape was left at intervals to use as a guide in subsequent transects. This procedure allowed the survey crew to walk the canyon sides, bottoms and ridgetops rather than attempting to keep straight line transects while surveying the steep slopes. Intervals of 25 meters were maintained on these transects.

Table 3

Transect Orientation

North-South	East-West	Contour Orientation
15	22	21
16	26	27
17	33	28
20	34	29
26	35	26

(Note: Mixed strategy in several cases)

Survey progress and ground inspection were hampered by the thick grass ground cover present throughout the project area. The ankle to waist high grasses and forbs obscured the ground surface in many areas making inspection difficult. Some ground visibility and subsurface soil exposures were provided by rodent burrows, animal trails and rocky areas.

Several small areas of LLNL Site 300 were not surveyed due to disturbance impacts (e.g., parking lots, administration areas, golf course); safety considerations (e.g., designated disposal areas); and, security requirements (e.g., "Process Area")(Table 4). In addition, some of the extremely steep hill and canyon sides in Sections 21, 27, 28 and 29 were not inspected due to their hazardous nature.

Table 4

Non-Surveyed Areas

"No Access Policy"	Disturbed/Impacted
"Process Area"	Administration Area
Test Areas 801, 818, 823, 825-828, 832-838, 840, 841, 851, and 854	Parking Lots - Main and Contractors
Disposal Pits - Sections 16, 17 and 23	Golf Course

For the purposes of the project, a site was defined as an area with five or more cultural objects occurring within a 20 meter diameter circle. Locations of fewer than five cultural objects were treated as isolated finds. Site loci were identified utilizing standard Bureau of Land Management - Department of the Interior site definitions (cf. Appendix II). Rock art and rockshelter sites were identified by the presence of one or more permanent cultural features (i.e., bedrock mortars, incised/pecked petroglyph panel, etc.) as well as by the presence of any portable cultural objects. Prehistoric and historic sites were recorded on separate forms - the BLM Cultural Resources Inventory Form (Fig.13) and the Basin Research Associates' Historic Site Survey Form (Fig.14). Individual isolated finds and small sites were recorded on the Basin Research Associates' Short Form, Cultural Resource Inventory Record (Fig. 15). Rock art sites were recorded using another special form (Fig.16) in addition to the standard site record. All sites and isolated finds were photographed using both color print and black and white film. Photographic logs (Appendix VI) were maintained for each exposed roll. All sites were flagged and sketch mapped from a datum point. Historic sites were normally recorded in English measurements while prehistoric sites used the metric system. All petroglyph panels and design elements were measured and sketched. Each cultural resource was plotted on the appropriate USGS topographic map and the existing Site 300 blueline topographic map. Isolated finds of a portable nature were collected since field relocation would be difficult. Otherwise, a no-collection policy was followed.

Each crew chief kept a field notebook to record data pertaining to the dialy fieldwork. Topics of interest included local topography, vegetation, observed fauna, geologic data and other relevant information not recorded on the site forms. In addition to the field notebook and site form information, a Basin Research Associates' Sample Unit Record Form was completed for each surveyed half section (Fig.17) (cf. Appendix IV for forms).

All cultural resource sites were field evaluated according to the criteria set forth in the Bureau of Land Management Cultural Resource Evaluation System (BLM-CRES) (Appendix III).

Inventory Results (Fig. 18)

The seven-hundred and twelve man-hours of field effort resulted in the location of 24 cultural resource properties. Of these, three are prehistoric, twenty historic and one is a multicomponent site consisting of both aboriginal and historic materials (Table 5).

Overall, historic materials dominate the cultural resource inventory. Historic cultural resources, both sites and isolated combined, comprise 83% of the total compared to 13% for prehistoric materials and 4% for multicomponent sites (Table 6).

In terms of the defined site types, historic petroglyphs and structures are most representative of the types recorded during the inventory.

Site Summaries (cf. Appendix V)

16.5 - T 3S, R 4E, Section 16, NW¼ of NW¼ (CRES S3)

Prehistoric, small, light lithic scatter. Raw material is small chunks of chert and chalcedony-like material which may be opalized petrified wood. Five to six "waste" flakes were identified but whether or not they are culturally produced objects could not be reliably determined. No worked flakes were noted. Area is 7.5m x 5.0 m on a north facing hillside overlooking

Table 5

General Site Inventory Results

Site Category	% of Total Sites
Prehistoric (3)	13%
Prehistoric Isolate (Ø)	-
Historic Site (18)	75%
Historic Isolate (2)	8%
Multicomponent (1) (Prehistoric and Historic)	4%

Table 6

LLNL Site 300 - Site Types

Site Type (Aboriginal)	#
Lithic Scatter	1
Rockshelter with Bedrock Mortar(s)	2
Rockshelter/Milling Station	1

Site Type (Historic)	#
Petroglyph	7
Structure	6
Trash Dump/Rubble	4
Isolated Find	2
Town	1
Mine	

the northern boundary of Site 300.

17.1 - T 3S, R 4E, Section 17, SE¼ of NE¼ (CRES S3)

Historic petroglyph panel. Located on a single vertical sandstone panel, three-quarters of the way up a steep hillside. It consists of historic graffiti incised in the soft sandstone. There are no reliably discernible dates or cultural associations.

20.1 - T 3S, R 4E, Section 20, SE¼ of NE¼ (CRES S3)

Historic trash scatter, small and localized. Found on a flat grassy area south of small ravine. Scatter consists of rusted metal, broken white porcelain, buff crockery and broken bottle glass (various colors). Artifacts were clustered around a weathered wooden stake suggesting a secondary deposition of materials.

22.1 - T 3S, R 4E, Section 22, SW¼ of NW¼ (CRES S2/S3)

Prehistoric rockshelter. Originally recorded by Dietz and Jackson (n.d.). The rockshelter faces NNE, near the base of a large hill. A spring is found about 150m ESE. The rockshelter is 2m high, 8m wide and 2.8m deep. The shelter contains three bedrock mortars with one possible incipient mortar on a step of bedrock along the rear wall. There is a tan-gray midden deposit within the rockshelter and extending a short way beyond it. A mano-pestle and a worked obsidian flake were present on the surface within the shelter. The ceiling is partially fire-blackened and some fire affected rock is present.

22.2 - T 3S, R 4E, Section 22, NE¼ of SE¼ (CRES S2/S3)

Prehistoric Rockshelter with one bedrock mortar. A shallow, narrow rockshelter facing NW. It is high on a steep slope above a N-S trending canyon. The shelter is 9.2m wide, 2.8m high and 3.4m deep. One shallow bedrock mortar (9cm x 15-17cm deep) is present in the back of the shelter. No other cultural material or midden was present. Recent (1957-1960) graffiti was found on the soft sandstone at the rear of the shelter.

25.1 - T 3S, R 4E, Section 25, NW¼ of SW¼ (CRES S3)

Isolated find, historic. Partially buried, rusted metal band. Probably the outer binding for a wooden wagon wheel. Band is 1 5/8" wide. Diameter of wheel not known. Item not collected.

26.1 - T 3S, R 4E, Section 26, SW¼ of SE¼ (CRES S3)

Historic, pile of weathered wood on surface of alluvial fan. Several pieces are connected with wire and nails. Several other metal artifacts are also present.

26.2 - T 3S, R 4E, Section 26, SE¼ of SW¼ (CRES S3)

Historic rubble, mainly wood, just SW of an intermittent stream. The rubble pile contains mainly wooden boards and standard guage railroad ties with spikes still embedded. Other metal, concrete and recent ceramic debris is scattered to the NW, 20m up the drainage.

27.1 - T 3S, R 4E, Section 27, SE¼ of NE¼ (CRES S3)

Historic structure, partially collapsed. Found straddling the drainage of a deep NW-SE trending canyon. Large weathered beams cross the drainage while boards criss-cross on top of this. Standing portion held together by wire nails. No other artifacts associated with this structure.

27.2 - T 3S, R 4E, Section 27, NW¼ of NW¼ (CRES S3)

Historic trash scatter. Scatter spread down small drainage on steep east side of a large N-S trending canyon. The scatter includes historic to recent material including metal, glass (broken and jars), metal pots and cans, wood, a socket wrench, and the frame/chassis of a Ford Model-T.

28.1 - T 3S, R 4E, Section 28, SW¼ of SW¼ (CRES S3)

Historic, portion of a pipeline and concrete foundations. Sections of a rusted metal pipeline and a parallel ceramic pipeline in a N-S drainage. Both go underground to the north and small stretches are exposed intermittently beyond this. The metal pipe terminates on the south at a concrete foundation of four concrete posts, later found to be for a water trough. The ceramic pipe continues 13.7 feet further south before it ends.

28.2 - T 3S, R 4E, Section 28, SW¼ of NW¼ (CRES S3)

Historic structure. Two room cabin standing, with a surrounding barbed wire fence in the bottom of a large N-S canyon. The building has square-cut nails in some of the wall boards but are not part of the building structure indicating that the boards were scavenged from elsewhere. Some historic debris was scattered around the building, including parts of a wood burning stove. "Oral testimony" indicates that the site was once a sheep station.

28.3 - T 3S, R 4E, Section 28, SE¼ of NW¼ (CRES S3)

Historic trash scatter. Wood, metal, ceramics and glass scattered over approximately 125 x 100 feet, with a concentrated dump near the center of this scatter which is at the confluence of two drainages. The site may have contained a building judging from the plate glass and amount of wood present. Purpled bottle glass is present along with some square cut nails. There are the metal head boards of a bed upright in the ground just northeast of the main dump.

28.4 - T 3S, R 4E, Section 28, NE¼ of NW¼ (CRES S3)

Historic petroglyph in rockshelter. A sandstone rockshelter on a gently sloping hill with a single date, Mar. 11, 39, incised in the rock. No artifacts are associated with the site.

28.5 - T 3S, R 4E, Section 28, NW¼ of N½ (CRES S2/3)

Multi-component rockshelter, historic petroglyphs and prehistoric milling features. Originally recorded by Dietz and Jackson (n.d.) as 28.1, a prehistoric site only. Large rockshelter with smaller alcove part way up the east side of a large, deep north-south canyon. Historic graffiti found throughout; names and initials with dates ranging from 1922 to 1976 incised in the soft sandstone. Three bedrock mortars and four depressions that may be incipient mortars are found beneath the sandy floor cover in the smaller alcove/shelter. Chunks of opalized petrified wood are found in and near the large shelter but only one flake noted. No midden deposit discernible.

29.1 - T 3S, R 4E, Section 29, NW¼ of NW¼, (CRES S4)

Isolated historic find. Weathered hammer found hanging on northern section fence on side of steep canyon. Collected by survey crew.

29.2 - T 3S, R 4E, Section 29, NE¼ of SW¼ (CRES S3 - ?)

Historic power/telegraph pole line. A line of wooden poles, some upright, some fallen, extending an unknown distance across the hills and canyons, approximately east-west (?). Wire is still present, running from pole to pole. Poles have glass insulators present. One insulator collected by survey crew.

29.3 - T 3S, R 4E, Section 29, SW¼ of SW¼ (CRES S3 - ?)

Historic mine addit with nearby foundation rubble along drainage of N-S canyon. The addit has support timbers and continues an unknown distance into the hillside. Standing water present within the addit. On the slope above were several metal pipes coming vertically out of the ground, possibly for ventilation. Three discrete possible foundation sites with concrete and Carnegie bricks. Historic debris also present.

*33.1 - T 3S, R 4E, Section 33, NW and SE¼'s of NE¼ (CRES S1)
Section 34, SW¼ of NW¼

Historic townsite. This appears to be a major residential area for the factory town of Carnegie. The brick and pottery plant was located in Corral

natural rather than cultural.

34.2 - T 3S, R 4E, Section 34, NW¼ of NE¼ (CRES S3)

Rockshelter with historic petroglyphs. Shelter is midway up the steep western slope of a N-S trending canyon. Graffiti is incised in sandstone and consists of initials and the number 14 (representing 1914 ??). No artifacts were noted.

34.3 - T 3S, R 4E, Section 34, SW¼ of NE¼ (CRES S3)

Historic petroglyph. Two vertical sandstone panels, 20m apart, on the eastern slope of a N-S trending canyon. Only elements present are initials, no dates. The panels face west and northwest. No artifacts were noted.

34.4 - T 3S, R 4E, Section 34, SW¼ of NE¼ (CRES S3)

Rockshelter with historic petroglyphs in and near it. Shelter is 60m north of Corral Hollow in a N-S trending canyon, 300m east of the townsite of Carnegie. The shelter and nearby panels contain historic graffiti. These are initials and dates (1913 and 1939) incised in the sandstone. No associated artifacts were noted.

35.1 - T 3S, R 4E, Section 35, NE¼ of NW¼ (CRES S3)

Historic foundation. Found on southern slope of ridge terminus above two drainages. The foundations consist of a rectangular concrete platform with five oblong concrete slabs set on it. The concrete extends into the hillside. Three of the slabs have bolted on boards. The USGS map indicates a windmill at this site. This may have been the foundation for it. No other cultural material was associated with this site.

UNITED STATES
DEPARTMENT OF THE INTERIOR
BUREAU OF LAND MANAGEMENT

Cultural Resources Inventory Record

☐ Aboriginal ☐ Non-Aboriginal ☐ Both

1. CRES rating (complete item 31, and enter here): ☐

2. Fieldsite number:

3. CA site number:

4. BLM CR report number (if applicable):

5. Project:

6. State:

County:

District

Resource area:

Planning unit:

7. Map reference:

8. Township:

Range:

Section (to nearest ¼ of ¼):

Elevation:

9. UTM (always complete if S1 rated):

10. Location (proximity to roads, bldgs., towns, major topographical features):

11. Land ownership status:

12. Other site numbers/designations/names:

13. Site types:

14. Cultural affiliation(s), dates of use:

15. Site description (use continuation sheet if necessary):

16. Area of occupation:

17. Depth (tested?):

18. Artifacts, materials (collected? observed?):

19. Storage (if collection was made):

20. Site disturbance (Man caused and/or natural causes - erosional state, previous excavations, collections, etc.):

21. Possibility of destruction:

22. Site marked? How?

1. CRES rating:

2. BLM site number:

(continued on reverse)

Figure 13

23. Hydrological data (nearest water, types of drainage patterns, ephemeral sources, possible former water sources, rain gauge data, etc.):

24. Geomorphic context (geographical situation - landform type, slope, exposure, etc.):

25. Soil & substrate on site:	26. Surrounding soil & substrate:

27. Vegetation on site (major community, species composition, and % of cover):

28. Vegetation off site (major community, species composition, and % of cover):

29. Faunal observations:

30. Potentially exploitable resources (Your opinion, what resources did the occupants of this site possibly exploit - minerals? fauna? flora? water? soil? etc.):

31. CRES Classification, only to be completed by a CR Professional. Circle one and enter in item 1.: S1 S2 S3 S4 S0

Explanation:

Evaluator : Title: Date:

32. Other evaluation & remarks:

33. Informants & references (published & unpublished references, National Register properties in general area):

34. Photos:	35. Xerox of topo. sheet: Yes No
36. Locational sketch, site sketch: Yes No	37. Continuation Sheet: Yes No
38. Artifact illustrations: Yes No	
39. Recorded by:	40. Date recorded:

1. Site Number ____________ 2. CRES Rating ____________________

3. Other (numbers/names) ______________ 4. County ______________

5. Location: T ______ R ______ Section ______, _____ of ______

6. Map Ref __________________________ 7. Elevation ____________

8. Verbal Location ______________________________________

____

9. UTM Grid Location: Zone __________ N __________ E __________

10. Ownership: Federal __________ State _____ Private _____ Unk _____

11. NR Status: Candidate ______ Potential ______ Not Eligible ______

No Determination ______

12. Disturbance: Animal _____ Burning _____ Vandalism _____ ORV ________

Other ____________ Explain __________________

____

13. Present Condition: Good _____ Fair _____ Poor _____ Explain ________

____

14. Activity: Mining _____ Railroad _____ Military _____ Homesteading _____
Exploration/Traveling _____ Settlement _____ Ranching _____
Other _____ Explain ________________________

15. Site Type: Town _____ Camp _____ Homestead _____ Road _____ Trail _____
Mine _____ Railroad _____ Graveyard _____ Trashdump _____
Military _____ Other ________________________

16. Features: Structure _____ Dugout _____ Fire Hearth _____ Cairn _____
Rock Alignment _____ Trashdump _____ Irrigation _____
Trail _____ Road _____ Corral _____ Burial _____ Well _____
Spring _____ R&R Grade (berm) _____ Tram (road/way) _____
Mine Tailings _____ Other _____ Explain _____

____

17. Artifacts: Wood (size, type) _____ Glass (color) _____ Metal (type) _____
_____ Bone (species) _____ Ceramic (color) _____
Adobe (condition) _____ Nails (size, type) _____
Cans (size, type) _____ Ordnance _____ Other _____

____

18. Temporal Period: Circa ______________ Era ______________

19. Recorder ______________ 20. Date ____________ 21. Photos ___

Figure 14

1. Recorder(s):_______

____

2. Date:_______________

BASIN RESEARCH ASSOCIATES

Short Form, Cultural Resources Inventory Record

3. BLM Rating:__________

4. Field #:_______________

5. CA #:_______________

USE: For the recording of isolated finds and extremely small cultural resource properties (less than 20 items) as defined by current government practices and/or Basin Research Associates internal guidelines (06/79).

7. Project:____

8. State:_______________ 9. County:____________ 10. Elevation:__________

11. Map Reference:_______________________________________

12. T.__________ R.__________, Section _______, ¼ of_______ of ¼ ___________

13. Site Type:____

14. Geological/Geographical Situation and Brief Description: _______________

____

____

15. Nearest Water:_______________________________________

16. Vegetation (Major community and flora at site or in immediate vicinity):

____

17. Artifacts, Materials (If all observed materials were not collected, so note):

____

____

____

____

18. BLM Classification (Note one and enter in No. 3): S1 S2 S3 S4

Date:__________________ Explanation:______________________________

____

Evaluator:______________________ Title:___________________________

19. Remarks (Photos (?), sketches (?), etc.):_________________________

____

20. Site Marked (staked (?), flagged (?), describe):__________________

____

Use Reverse If Necessary

Figure 15

ROCK ART RECORDING FORM

BASIN RESEARCH ASSOCIATES

IDENTIFICATION

Type of Site (petroglyph, pictograph, combination)______________________

Name of site______________________ Site Designation______________

Recorded by (name/address)__________ Previous Designation(s)______________

______________________ ______________________

______________________ Date______________________

LOCATION

Geographic Coordinates________ ________ ________ ________ ________ ________

Section__________ Lot__________ Plan__________ Marine Chart______________

UTM Grid Reference______________________ Map______________________

Elevation (metric units above sea level)______________Airphoto No.__________

Location and Access (describe in detail)______________________

____

____

____

____

____

____

Historic Band Territory______________________

Band Address______________________

____

____

Linguistic Group______________________

____

Figure 16

PROXIMITY TO KNOWN ARCHAEOLOGICAL SITES (be explicit)

____

____

MAP OF SITE (indicate access routes, orientation, topographic features, etc.)

SCALE________________

Indicate North by the use of an arrow.

ESCRIPTION

Method of Manufacture (pecked, incised, painted with brush, etc.)__________________

____

Type of Rock____

Direction the panel(s) face, use cardinal, quadrant or azimuth notation (eg. Northeast; N45E, 450):

Panel 1____

Panel 2____

Etc.____

Angle of Inclination of panel(s) to ground surface:__________________________

Panel 1__________________________

Panel 2__________________________

Etc._____________________________

Estimated insolation: (the number of hours of éxposure per day for each season)

1) Spring______________________hrs./day
2) Summer______________________ "
3) Fall ______________________ "
4) Winter______________________ "

FLORA OF AREA (be as specific as possible)

____

____

____

DESIGN MEASUREMENTS AND CLASSIFICATION

"Panel" refers to significantly separated design groups and are indicated by a capital letter eg., Panel A, Panel B, etc. "Designs" refers to individual figures and are indicated by consecutive, non-repeated numbers, eg., Designs 1,2, etc. "Designs" refers to individual figures and are indicated by consecutive, non-repeated numbers, eg., Designs 1,2, etc. "Type" may be either anthropomorphic, zoomorphic, geometric, or unknown. Dimensions of panels and individual designs are given in metric units.

for example:

PANEL	PANEL DIMENSIONS	DESIGN	DESIGN TYPE	DESIGN DIMENSIONS
A	30m x 20m	1	anthropomorphic	20cm x 9cm
A	" "	2	geometric	30cm x 30cm
B	10m x 4m	3	?	10cm x 6cm
B	" x "	4	zoomorphic	12cm x 2cm

PANEL	PANEL DIMENSIONS	DESIGN	DESIGN TYPE	DESIGN DIMENSIONS

2F-70 (continued on reverse if necessary)

SIGN COLOUR (Preferably from standard chart such as Munsell Soil Charts)

DESIGN #__________ COLOUR__________

(continue on reverse if necessary)

TERPRETATION (give source of information, book, informant, personal, etc.)

DESIGN #__________ INTERPRETATION__________ SOURCE__________

NDITION

Lichen Present on Designs__________ Nearby__________ Type(s)__________

Details (include diameter of lichen)__________

Mineral Layer on Designs__________ Nearby__________ Type(s)__________

Details__________

Vandalism (description, location)__________

Natural Damage (description, location)__________

Recommendations/Conservation____

RECORDING

Rubbings/Tracings (list method, materials, place of storage) and label each rubbing or tracing with panel letter and design number(s).

Number made________Method/Materials_____________Storage Location__________________

Details____

Moulds/Casts (list method, date and place of storage. A Casting Sheet fic details of each moulding operation should be attached to this form

Number made_______Method/Materials____________Storage Location_______

Details

Field Sketch of Panels/Designs (each panel and design should be assigned its correct letter and number).

SCALE________________________

PHOTOGRAPHY ("Subject" refers to panel and individual design or group being photographed It should also indicate distance from rock face. All sites should be photo graphed from a distance to show location, then closer to show entire site a finally each group and individual design should be photographed close up.)

ROLL	FRAME	FILM TYPE	TIME OF DAY	SUBJECT

Additional Comments Regarding Photography______________________________

Other Photographs (if privately owned give owner's names, addresses, and date when photographs were taken)

ADDITIONAL COMMENTS CONCERNING SITE______________________________

BASIN RESEARCH ASSOCIATES, INC.

SAMPLE UNIT RECORD FORM

1. Sample Unit Number ____________________ 2. Photo Number(s) ____________

3. Type of Unit (Circle One Only) Original Altered Discretionary

4. Map ______________________________ Location of Unit Within Section

5. Township ____________

6. Range ______________

7. Section ____________

9. Date ________________ 10. Other Units Today ________________

11. Field Supervisor (Name) ______________________________________

12. Crew Members (Names) ____

____

13. Prehistoric Loci Recorded (Sites/Isolated Finds) ____________/____ ______

14. Historic Loci Recorded (Sites/Isolated Finds) _______________/__________

15. Describe (the suitability of this area for past human activity) __________

____

____

____

16. General Survey Conditions (Circle One Only) Good Average Poor

17. Describe (General Survey Conditions) ___________________________________

____

____

____

18. Describe (Method and Accuracy of Locating Sample Unit) ________________

____

____

____

Figure 17

BASIN RESEARCH ASSOCIATES UNIT ________________

19. Vegetation (Describe)

____

20. Drainage (rank at least one)

- [ ] Converging
- [ ] Diverging
- [ ] Braided
- [ ] Other (Describe)

21. Distance to Nearest Permanent Water ______________________________ meters

22. Type (Circle One Only) Spring Seep Lake Stream Other

23. Water Resources (Describe)

24.

25. Slope (rank at least one)

- [ ] Level (0-3°)
- [ ] Gentle (3-8°)
- [ ] Moderate (8-16°)
- [ ] Steep (16-26°)
- [ ] Very Steep/Prec. (26°+)

26. Aspect (rank at least one)

- [ ] North
- [ ] Northeast
- [ ] East
- [ ] Southeast
- [ ] South
- [ ] Southwest
- [ ] West
- [ ] Northwest
- [ ] None

25/26. Comments/Remarks

27. Surficial Deposts (rank at least one)

- [ ] Extrusive Igneous
- [ ] Intrusive Igneous
- [ ] Metamorphic
- [ ] Consolidated Sediments
- [ ] Desert Pavement
- [ ] Alluvium
- [ ] Colluvium
- [ ] Aeolian Deposits
- [ ] Other (Describe)

28. Geology (Describe)

29.

30. Disturbance (rank at least one)

- [ ] Off-Road Vehicles (ORV)
- [ ] Mining
- [ ] Other Construction
- [ ] Erosion
- [ ] Grazing
- [ ] Other Animal Disturbances
- [ ] Cultivated Agriculture
- [ ] Other

31. Intensity of Disturbance

High Moderate Low

31. Disturbance (Describe)

32.

This page of the original report is an envelope containing a foldout map for Figure 18; economy precludes reproducing it here.

SITE LOCALE ANALYSIS

A total of 25 sample units were intensively surveyed. Nine of these units were devoid of cultural material. 16 units had prehistoric or historic cultural remains present. Of these, 13 possessed historic remains while four units contained prehistoric sites (one sample unit had a multi-compnent site--a site exhibiting both prehistoric and historic material--thus was counted twice). Though the sample size of units is small, a key question to ask is 'what distinguishes those units with sites from those without sites?' Site locale analysis, besides being a major topic in anthropology (Bettinger 1975; Busby and Kobori 1980; Thomas and Bettinger 1976; among others), can assist land managers by providing summary statements regarding the probability of site occurrence on land under their direct jurisdiction. To determine the pattern of site occurrence within Site 300, elementary summary statistics of central tendency plus non-parametric tests of comparison were computed. These are described below.

Table 7 summarizes the total number of sample units with cultural resources present. 64% of all units contained cultural material remains. Table 8 details the occurrence of historic sites and prehistoric sites. This table lists the total number of units, total number of sites, the mean number of sites per unit, the range of sites per unit, the standard deviation about the mean number of sites per unit, and the Coefficient of Dispersion (CD). The Coefficient of Dispersion is an elementary variance-mean ratio that examines the degree of clustering of cultural resources. A CD value equal to or less than 1.0 indicates a uniform distribution of sites whereas a value greater than 1.0 points to a nonrandom, clustered pattern of site occurrence. The table shows that units with historic sites possess a greater mean number of sites per unit, greater than 1 per unit. The units with prehistoric sites averaged only 1 site per unit in a uniform distribution. Meanwhile, the units with historic sites ranged from one to four sites per unit. However, the CD value is still below 1.0. Based on this data the occurrence of sites on Site 300 could be interpreted as being almost random. Yet by examining the maps, the sample unit forms, and the actual land, it is obvious that some sample units were situated on rolling foothills while others crossed steep-walled canyons or gullies.

Sample units were divided up by landform. Numerous units (20) crossed a canyon or gully at some point in their 320 acres. Of these units, 15 contained archaeologic or historic sites. Units located strictly within the foothill area of Site 300 (i.e., those units that did not cross canyons or gullies) had one unit with cultural resources present. Despite the low Coefficient of Dispersion values, it would appear that an association between site occurrence and landform exists. To test this possible association, the Chi-Square test was performed on the data. Due to the small values in expected and observed frequencies for the Chi-Square test, this test was re-computed utilizing Yates' Correction for Continuity (Siegel 1956; Blalock 1972; Johnson 1976). Chi-Square is indicated by X^2, while Chi-Square utilizing Yates' Correction is indicated by X_c^2. Table 9 tests the null hypothesis, H_0, that regardless of associated landform, all units have an equal probability of cultural resource occurrence. The alternative hypothesis, H_1, is that all surveyed units do not possess equal probability of cultural resource occurrence. The value of .1 is considered adequate to test for statistical significance when dealing with limited archaeological data (Plog 1978). The results comparing sample units with and without sites depending upon associated landoform, are statistically significant. The value for X_c^2 is regarded as more accurate. The null hypothesis is rejected, the alternative hypothesis, H_1, is accepted.

Since the sample size of units is so small, a more reliable statistical test is the Fisher's Exact Probability Test. The Fisher's Exact Probability Test does not approximate probability as the Chi-Square test. The tested null hypothesis is, again, all units have an equal probability of cultural resource occurrence regardless of associated landform. The alternative hypothesis is directional, units that exhibit greater variety in landform will have a greater probability of cultural resource occurrence. The level of significance is .1 but since this is a directional test, the correct α is .1/2 = .05. Table 10 lists the probability figures for the Fisher's Exact Probability Test. The probability figure is significant. The null hypothesis is rejected.

The number of surveyed units and the actual number of sites and isolated finds recorded is very low. However, these elementary statistical tests indicate that cultural resource occurrence is associated more strongly with the canyon-gully landforms than the foothills. That is, activities on the Site 300 stand a much greater probability of impacting cultural resources when those tasks take place in and around canyon-gully areas. However, the occurrence of cultural resources does not appear to be clustered.

Table 7

Summary of Survey Units with Cultural Resources Present
(isolated finds included)

units with historic sites	units with prehistoric sites	total units with sites	total units w/out sites	total units surveyed
13*	4	16 (64%)	9 (36%)	25

* a single multicomponent site (prehistoric and historic) counted twice

Table 8

Site 300 Lawrence National Livermore Laboratory
Summary - Cultural Resource Occurrence

Survey Unit	n units	n sites	$\bar{X}$ per unit	range-sites per unit	s	CD
Units with historic sites*	13	21^{+}	1.62	1 - 4	1.19	0.89
Units with prehistoric sites	4	4^{+}	1.00		0.00	0.00
Units without sites	9					

* two isolated finds included

+ a single multicomponent site (prehistoric and historic) counted twice

n = number

$\bar{X}$ = mean

s = standard deviation

CD = Coefficient of Dispersion

Table 9

Chi-Square Test
Landform and Cultural Resource Occurrence

	units with sites	units without sites	Total
Units with gullies, ravines, canyons	15 (12.8)	5 (7.2)	20
Foothill units	1 (3.2)	4 (1.8)	5
	16	9	25

( ) = expected frequencies

df = 1

α = .1 level

H_o = Regardless of associated landform, all units have an equal probability of cultural resource occurrence.

H_1 = All surveyed units do not possess equal probability of cultural resource occurrence.

$$X^2 = 5.25$$

$$X_c^2 = 3.13$$

Reject the H_o, results are significant.

Table 10

Fisher's Exact Probability Test
Landform and Cultural Resource Occurrence

For the Fisher's Exact Probability Test the H_1 will be directional.

$$p = \frac{(A + B)!(C + D)!(A + C)!(B + D)!}{N!A!B!C!D!}$$

(for a 2 x 2 table)

(Siegel 1956:97)

H_0 = Regardless of associated landform, all units have an equal probability of cultural resource occurrence.

H_1 = Units with gullies, ravines, canyons have a greater probability of cultural resource occurrence.

$\alpha = .1/2 = .05$

Fisher's Exact Probability Test, $p = .0379 + .0016 = .0395$

Reject the H_0, results are significant

Units that exhibit greater variety in landform will have a greater probability of cultural resource occurrence.

SITE SIGNIFICANCE

It is the implicit purpose of both the federal and state environmental legislation and cultural resource mandates that all cultural resources found on federally and/or state owned or managed lands or adjacent to these lands are considered of importance and merit consideration. Not all cultural resources are of equal value nor do they all merit National Register of Historic Places listing. In order to assess relative importance for management purposes and to identify those properties on the Lawrence Livermore National Laboratory's Site 300 that should be nominated to the National Register, Basin Research Associates used a Cultural Resources Evaluation System (CRES) devised by the Bureau of Land Management for its large scale inventories (Appendix III).

Of the 24 cultural resource properties identified during the inventory, only four are either potential or eligible resources for the National Register of Historic Places (Table 11). The majority of the sites are either of S3 or S4 significance ("low significance") and while they merit consideration by Lawrence Livermore National Laboratory, that consideration should be mostly of a defensive nature. That is, the Site 300 management should only institute measures (other than normal protection from vandalism) to actively preserve such sites only when they are threatened by a proposed activity or undertaking.

The S1 and S2 sites (National Register significance to "mid-significance") merit a high and active degree of consideration by the management of Lawrence Livermore National Laboratory. Both the Department of Energy and Lawrence Livermore National Laboratory must work aggresively to insure the physical preservation of S1 rated properties. These cultural resources must be nominated to the National Register of Historic Places. The "mid-significance" level sites (S2) also merit a high degree of consideration. Properties rated as S2 are such that with minor informational changes they would be classified as S1. Management recommendations for specific cultural resources are discussed in the following chapter.

Table 11

SITE SIGNIFICANCE RATINGS

Site Number	Site Type	CRES Rating	National Register Rating
16.5	Lithic Scatter	S3	No
17.1	Petroglyph (Historic)	S3	No
20.1	Trash Scatter (Historic)	S3	No
22.1	Rockshelter - Prehistoric	S2/S3	Potential
22.2	Rockshelter - Prehistoric	S2/S3	Potential
25.1	Isolated Find - Historic	S3	No
26.1	Trash (Historic)	S3	No
26.2	Rubble (Historic)	S3	No
27.1	Structure (Historic)	S3	No
27.2	Trash Scatter (Historic)	S3	No
28.1	Pipeline (Historic)	S3	No
28.2	Structure (Historic)	S3	No
28.3	Trash Scatter (Historic)	S3	No
28.4	Petroglyph (Historic)	S3	No
28.5	Rockshelter - Multicomponent	S2/S3	Potential
29.1	Isolated Find - Historic	S4	No
29.2	Power/Telegraph Line	S3 (?)	Possible
29.3	Mine Addit	S3 (?)	Possible
33.1	Townsite - Historic	S1	Eligible
34.1	Petroglyph (Historic)	S3	No
34.2	Petroglyph (Historic)	S3	No
34.3	Petroglyph (Historic)	S3	No
34.4	Petroglyph (Historic)	S3	No
35.1	Foundation (Historic)	S3	No

SITE PROTECTION MEASURES

The identification of site specific protection needs must be accomplished through the consideration of the regional archaeological and historical record. The protection measures employed must also be appropriate to the particular "use" identified for the resource. Such a committment is generally best determined where research and management objectives for an area have been developed. In general, the development of protection measures must be based on an understanding of the values associated with the resource, it's potential uses, and the nature of the threats to the resource (cf. Table 12). Clearly, the manipulation of the resource may not be appropriate in cases where socio-cultural values are concerned with religious matters or formal social activities of a ceremonial nature. Such uses can frequently be impacted by modern intrusions out of character with the site values. The intrusions may not even need to leave physical evidence to contaminate the sacred character.

Table 12

Selected Types of Impacts
Applicable to Site 300

Vandalism	Materials Sites
Casual Off-Road Use	Rights of Way/Access Roads
Range Fires/Fire Control	Construction

The following table includes the major categories of protection measures that may be applicable to the cultural resources located within the boundaries of Site 300.

Table 13

Protection Measures

1. Patrolling/Surveillance - to monitor natural deterioration, direct and indirect effects of development projects, and prevent vandalism and other unauthorized uses. This measure is appropriate for all site types, particularly those most accessible to human traffic.

2. Public Awareness - accomplished through signing, interpretive trails, brochures and publications. This measure is most effective for curbing vandalism and building popular support for archaeological/historical programs.

3. Project Avoidance - the preferred action when dealing with all site types, but particularly in cases where sites are of such substantial nature (e.g., rockshelters, extensive historic sites, etc.) that adequate data recovery procedures could not be implemented due to funding deficiencies and, particularly short time deadlines.

4. Fencing - restricts access to sites. Should be used only in areas where surveillance and maintenance is feasible.

5. Erosion Control - to protect sites from lake or river water levels, runoff areas, movement of sands by wind action, and other potential problems. Drainages may be modified, stream and lakeshore banks reinforced, and construction of catch basins, diversions or windbreaks.

6. Systematic Data Recovery - for situations where sites cannot be preserved in place. This option is more applicable to scientific values than socio-cultural values, and is more accomplished by detailed recordation, surface collection and excavation.

7. Special Management Area Designations - this action is intended to provide long term <u>in-situ</u> preservation. In regard to scientific values, the resource is set aside in some cases so that future generations of scholars may be able to pursue field research with more sophisticated analytical methods and techniques than are currently available.

The selection of the most appropriate measures is dictated by research objectives in addition to other factors. Research objectives can only be refined as the knowledge of the data base. Major data gaps presently exist for the LLNL Site 300 area especially in terms of aboriginal use and certain historic activity-use areas. These gaps may be corrected through future research.

CULTURAL RESOURCES MANAGEMENT RECOMMENDATIONS

A number of cultural resource protection/management options are available to the management of Lawrence Livermore National Laboratory for Site 300 in order to fulfill the requirements of the various federal and state mandates. For the CRES rated S3 and S4 sites, it is recommended that a strategy of passive/defensive protection (i.e., patrolling/surveillance) be instituted with active measures considered only when the resources are threatened by a proposed activity or undertaking (cf. Table 14).

Table 14

Passive Protection Measures

Site Number	Site Type
16.5	Lithic Scatter
17.1	Petroglyph (Historic)
20.1	Trash Scatter (Historic)
25.1	Isolated Find - Historic
26.1	Trash (Historic)
26.2	Rubble (Historic)
27.1	Structure (Historic)
27.2	Trash Scatter (Historic)
28.1	Pipeline (Historic)
28.2	Structure (Historic)
28.3	Trash Scatter (Historic)
28.4	Petroglyph (Historic)
29.1	Isolated Find - Historic
34.1	Petroglyph (Historic)
34.2	Petroglyph (Historic)
34.3	Petroglyph (Historic)
34.4	Petroglyph (Historic)
35.1	Foundation (Historic)

The following recommendations are directed at specific sites inventoried during the survey.

Prehistoric Cultural Resources

Site 22.1 - This prehistoric rockshelter with three bedrock mortars and a midden deposit has potential for contributing data of scientific/educational value based on the evaluation of its surface component. A true assessment of its "significance" can only be determined through the implementation of a limited subsurface tesing program. It is recommended that the site be tested to provide the necessary data for determining its National Register of Historic Places significance. Patrolling, project avoidance and fencing are suggested as protection measures prior to the testing program. If testing is rejected, it is suggested that the site be designated as a "Special Management Area."

Site 22.2 - One bedrock mortar and no discernible midden characterize this rockshelter. This site may have a potential subsurface desposit which should be determined through a limited testing program. It is recommended that the site be tested to provide the necessary informational data for determining its National Register significance. Until the advent of the testing program, it is recommended that patrolling, project avoidance and fencing be utilised as protection measures. If the testing option is rejected, it is suggested that the site be designated as a "Special Management Area."

Multicomponent Cultural Resources

Site 28.5 - This site contains both a prehistoric and historic component. Three bedrock mortars and four depressions, that may be incipient mortars, characterize the prehistoric features of the rockshelter. No midden deposit was discernible by the archaeological field team although all of the prehistoric features were found slightly below the present ground surface. Historic grafitti, ranging in date from ca. 1922 to 1976, are found incised on the rockshelter walls. In terms of National Register significance, it is recommended that the site be tested to determine if any significant subsurface prehistoric component is present. If the testing option is rejected, it is recommended that patrolling, project avoidance and fencing be considered as protective measures. In addition, it is recommended that the site be considered as part of a "Special Management Area" if no immediate determination of its significance can be made.

Historic Cultural Resources

Site 29.2 - This historic power or telegraph line requires additional archival information to establish its significance in the overall historic record of Corral Hollow. It is recommended that a passive program of avoidance be followed for the line. Additional archival research is recommended to determine its origin, use and significance.

Site 29.3 - This mine addit with a S3 rating should be further investigated through archival research to determine its use and historical significance. It is recommended that a program of passive protection and unobtrusive signing be undertaken to warn personnel of the dangers of abandoned mine shafts.

Site 33. 1 - This cultural resource locale appears to be a major residential area for the town of Carnegie. As such, it must be S1 rated due to the significance of Carnegie in the overall historic records of Corral Hollow. It is recommended that this area be nominated to the National Register of Historic Places or, in cooperation with the State of California, that this area and the current site of Carnegie be nominated as a Historic District. Prior to the nomination process, it is recommended, if sufficient funds are available, that a selective subsurface testing program be instituted in Sections 33 and 34 to determine the locational boundaries, variety of material culture debris and integrity of the existing site. If funds are not available to adequately test the areas within the jurisdiction of Lawrence Livermore National Laboratory's Site 300, it is recommended that the area be placed in a "Special Management Area" designation and subjected to active protection including but not limited to patrolling/surveillance, public awareness and fencing due to its exposed location. It is further recommended that a selective "systematic data recovery program be given the highest priority to determine the significance of the scientific values currently extant at the site.

Areas of Probable Historic Archaeological Impact

In addition to the above specific sites, a number of areas within the Site 300 boundaries may be of potential archaeological significance.

Mining - Section 29 (SW portion) is known to have principal shafts, addits and/or tunnels present (Sites 29.3; Barzellotti 1907). The San Francisco and San Joaquin Coal Company owned property all along the Corral Hollow Road including Section 29; the southern half of Section 28; Section 34 (which contains Carnegie); and the SW¼ of the SW¼ of Section 27. The Lorraine Mining Company owned and worked within the NW¼ of Section 26.

Habitation - Sections 33 and 34. These sections had residential structures present which included houses occupied by management families, along with other residential row houses and probably bunkhouses assigned to the Italian artisans. In addition to the houses, there should be numerous out-buildings such as privies and trash pits (cf. Site 33.1).

Ranching - On the basis of personal interviews with Messrs. James E. McFarland and Roy F. Mullins of LLNL Site 300 coupled with archival research, a number of ranching related structures are known to have existed on the property. The O'Brien Ranch, destroyed in 1911-1912, was probably located in Sections 20 or 29. Other ranching related structures may be found in Sections 15, 16, 28 and 35. Section 15 had a ranching residence which on-site grading has buried. Section 16 was occupied by a number of separate, but family related buildings, which included a home, corral, barn and windmill. Section 28 has part of a sheepherder shack present (Site 28.2). The last section, 35, had a house, barn, corral and windmill (Site 35.1) present prior to condemnation.

Native American Considerations

No sites or locales of a sacred or utilitarian nature to local Native American groups were noted during the literature survey of the ethnographic data. Inquiries to the State of California Native American Heritage Commission revealed no known "sacred places" on their current inventory although their reply letter requested such information if any were located during our survey. Considering the transitional location of the property between two different tribal groups (cf. Ethnography, this report), it is unlikely that specific traditional gathering locales or religious areas would have been located in a zone utilized intermittently by two tribal groups.

It is recommended however, that Lawrence Livermore National Laboratory cooperate with the Native American Heritage Commission if positive information or data are located that may support the presence of sacred locales within the boundaries of Site 300 as per Public Law 95-341 (American Indian Religious Freedom Act).

Summary

A number of management options have been offered for the cultural resource properties located during the site inventory. It is recommended that the site testing and analysis option be seriously considered, where applicable, to further determine specific cultural resources properties significance. Passive protection measures are suggested for all sites to insure their preservation. An active program of site protection is recommended for Carnegie due to its accesibility and close proximity to a well travelled road.

REFERENCES CITED

Alameda County, California
1904 Commissioner to the Louisiana Purchase Exposition. Copyright, Roosevelt Johnson, Alameda County.

Allardt, G.F.
1874 Official Map of Alameda County, California. Compiled from Official Surveys and Records and Private Surveys. Board of Supervisors of Alameda County. Britton Rey & Co., Lith, San Francisco.

Anonymous
1976 de Anza Dedication. A program printed by the Stockton San Joaquin County Public Library, Tracy.

Baker, J.E. (ed.)
1914 Past and Present of Alameda County, California. The S.J. Clarke Publishing Company, Chicago.

Bakker, E.
1971 An Island Called California. University of California Press, Berkeley.

Banta, H.C.
1954 Ups and Dowens of Ole Calafornen: A Biographical Sketch by Henry Comes Banta, 1835-1919. San Joaquin Pioneer and Historical Society, Publication No. 4, Stockton.

Barzellotti, C.E.
1907 Map of Land Owned by the San Francisco and San Joaquin Coal Company. Location and Strike of Principal Veins of Tesla Coal Beds, Alameda-San Joaquin Counties, California. On file, Bancroft Library.

Baumhoff, M.A.
1963 Ecological Determinants of Aboriginal California Populations. University of California Publications in American Archaeology and Ethnology 49(2):155-236.

Beardsley, R.K.
1948 Cultural Sequences in Central California Archaeology. American Antiquity 14:1-29.

1954 Temporal and Areal Relationships in Central California Archaeology. University of California Archaeological Survey Reports Nos. 24 and 25.

Beck, W.A. and Y.D. Haase
1974 Historical Atlas of California. University of Oklahoma Press, Norman.

Bennyhoff, J.A.
1977 Ethnogeography of the Plains Miwok. Center for Archaeological Research at Davis, Publication No. 5.

Bente, V. et al.
1980 Test Excavation of LAn-106a-H: The Ontiveros Adobe, Santa Fe Springs, California. Redevelopment Agency, City of Santa Fe Springs, Greenwood and Associates, Pacific Palisades.

Berry, W.D. and E. Berry
1959 Mammals of the San Francisco Bay Region. University of California Press, Berkeley.

Bettinger, R.L.
1975 The Surface Archaeology of Owens Valley, Eastern California: Prehistoric Man-Land Relationships in the Great Basin. Unpublished Ph.D. dissertation, University of California, Riverside.

Bickel, P.M.
1976 Toward a Prehistory of the San Francisco Bay Area: The Archaeology of Sites Ala-328, Ala-13 and Ala-12. Unpublished Ph.D. dissertation, Department of Anthropology, Harvard University.

Blalock, H.M.
1972 Social Statistics. Mc-Graw-Hill, New York.

Bolton, H.E.
1930 Anza's California Expeditions, Vol. 4. University of California Press, Berkeley.

Bowman, J.N.
1946 The Roads of Provincial California. MS on file, Bancroft Library.

1951 Adobe Houses in the San Francisco Bay Region. IN O.P. Jenkins (prep.), Geologic Guidebook of the San Francisco Bay Counties. California Division of Mines Bulletin 154, pp. 57-64.

Brewer, W.H.
1930 Up and Down California in 1860-1864 (ed. by F.P. Farquhar) Yale University Press, New Haven.

Brown, V. and G. Lawrence
1965 The California Wildlife Region. Naturegraph Publishers, Healdsburg.

Busby, C.I., and L.S. Kobori
1980 Draft Report, A Cultural Resource Inventory of the MX Missile System in Nevada: Phase I, 1980. Submitted to HDR Sciences, Inc., Santa Barbara.

Clark, W.B.
1955 Mines and Mineral Resources of San Joaquin County, California. California Journal of Mines and Geology 51(1):22-104.

Compton, H.T.
1895 Map of San Joaquin . . . H.T. Compton Co. Surveyor. R.T. Andrews, Del. Britton and Rey, San Francisco (c. 1894, 1895). On file, Bancroft Library.

Cook, S.F.
1955 The Aboriginal Population of the San Joaquin Valley, California. University of California Anthropological Records 16:2.

1957 The Aboriginal Population of Alameda and Contra Costa Counties, California. University of California Anthropological Records 16(4).

1960 Colonial Expeditions to the Interior of California: Central Valley. University of California Anthropological Records 16(6).

Crampton, B.
1974 Grasses in California. University of California Press, Berkeley.

Culin, S.
1902-03 Games of the North American Indians. Twenty-fourth Annual Report of the Bureau of American Ethnology. GPO, Washington.

Cutter, D.C.
1950 Spanish Exploration of California's Central Valley. Unpublished Ph.D. dissertation, University of California, Berkeley.

Davis, J.T.
1961 Trade Routes and Economic Exchange Among the Indians of California. University of California Archaeological Survey Reports No. 54.

Denny, E.
1913 Denny's Pocket Map of San Joaquin County, California Showing Wagon Roads, Railroads, Trails, etc.. Denny & Co., San Francisco.

Dietz, S.A. and R. Jackson
n.d. Report of the Preliminary Archaeological Reconnaissance of the Lawrence Livermore Laboratory Site 300, San Joaquin County, California. MS on file, Lawrence Livermore National Laboratory Site 300.

Elford, C.R.
1970 Climate of California. Climatography of the United States, No. 60-4. U.S. Department of Commerce Environmental Data Service.

Elsasser, A.B.
1978 Development of Regional Prehistoric Cultures. IN R.F. Heizer (ed.), Handbook of North American Indians, Vol. 8, California, pp. 37-57. Smithsonian Institution Press, Washington.

Fredrickson, D.A.
1974a Social Change in Prehistory: A Central California Example. IN L.J. Bean and T.F. King (eds.), ?Antap, California Indian Political and Economic Organization. Ballena Press Anthropological Papers 2:55-74, Ramona.

1974b Cultural Diversity in Early California: A View from the North Coast Ranges. Journal of California Anthropology 1(1):41-53.

Frickstad, W.N.
1955 A Century of California Post Offices 1848 to 1954. A Philatelic Research Society Publication. Pacific Rota-printing Company, Oakland.

Galvan, P.M.
1968 People of the West: The Ohlone Story. Indian Historian 1(2):9-13.

Gerow, B.A. with R.W. Force
1968 An Analysis of the University Village Complex with a Reappraisal of Central California Archaeology. Stanford University Press, Stanford.

Gilbert, F.
1968 Reproduction of Thompson and West's History of San Joaquin County, California with Illustrations (1879). Howell-North Books, Berkeley.

Gilliam, H.
1962 Weather of the San Francisco Bay Region. University of California Press, Berkeley.

Gudde, E.G.
1969 California Place Names: The Origin and Etymology of Current Geographical Names (3rd Edition). University of California Press, Berkeley.

Handy, H.P.
1862 Index Map of San Joaquin County Showing All Traces of Land Purchased or Located Upon in the County. Drawn and published by H.P. Handy, Britton and Co., San Francisco. On file, Bancroft Library.

Haviland, R.A.
1915 Map of Murrary Township, Alameda County, California. Tribune Publishing Company, Oakland.

Heizer, R.F. and F. Fenenga
1939 Archaeological Horizons in Central California. American Anthropologist 41:378-399.

Hendry, G.W. and J.N. Bowman
1940 The Spanish and Mexican Adobe and Other Buildings in the Nine San Francisco Bay Counties, 1776 to about 1850. MS on file, Bancroft Library.

Hittell, T.H.
1861 The Adventures of James Capen Adams, Mountaineer and Grizzly Bear Hunter of California. Towne and Bacon, San Francisco.

Hoover, M.B., H.E. Rensch and E.G. Rensch
1966 Historic Spots in California (3rd Edition, revised by W.N. Abeloe). Stanford University Press, Stanford.

Huey, A.S.
1948 Geology of the Tesla Quadrangle, California. California Division of Mines, Bulletin No. 140.

Johnson, R.
1976 Elementary Statistics (2nd Edition). Duxbury Press, North Scituate.

King, C.D.
1977 Matalan Ethnohistory. IN S.A. Dietz (ed.), Final Report of Archaeological Test Excavations for Construction of Freeway 04-SCl-101, Post Mile 17.2/29.4, Cochran Road to Ford Road. MS on file, California Archaeological Site Survey, Cabrillo College.

1978 Historic Indian Settlements in the Vicinity of the Holiday Inn Site. IN J.C. Winter (ed.), Archaeological Investigations at CA-SCl-128, the Holiday Inn Site, pp. 436-469. MS on file, California Archaeological Site Survey, Cabrillo College.

Kroeber, A.L.
1925 Handbook of the Indians of California. Bureau of American Ethnology Bulletin No. 78. GPO, Washington.

1959 Ethnographic Interpretations 7-11. University of California Publications in American Archaeology and Ethnology 47(3): 235-310.

Latta, F.F.
1977 Handbook of Yokuts Indians. 2nd Edition. Bear State Books, Santa Cruz.

Levy, R.
1978 Costanoan. IN R.F. Heizer (ed.), Handbook of North American Indians, Vol. 8, California, pp. 485-497. Smithsonian Institution Press, Washington.

Lillard, J.B., R.F. Heizer and F. Fenenga
1939 An Introduction to the Archaeology of Central California. Sacramento Junior College, Department of Anthropology Bulletin No. 2.

Lowell, F.L.
1916 San Joaquin County. IN Report XIV of the State Mineralologist, pp. 607-608. Mines and Mineral Resources of Portions of California. Biennial Period 1913-1914. California State Printing Office, Sacramento.

Mosier, D.
1978 Harrisville and the Livermore Coal Mines. Mines Road Books, San Leandro.

Munz, P.A. and D.D. Keck
1973 A California Flora and Supplement. University of California Press, Berkeley.

Nelson, N.C.
1909 Shellmounds of the San Francisco Bay Region. University of California Publications in American Archaeology and Ethnology 7:309-356.

1910 The Ellis Landing Shellmound. University of California Publications in American Archaeology and Ethnology 7:357-426.

Nusbaumer Co.
1896? Map of Murray Township. Surveyor's Office, Oakland. On file, Bancroft Library.

Nusbaumer, G.L. and W.F. Boardman
1889 Official Map of Alameda County, California. Drawn by J.C. Henkenius. Oakland Tribune Publishing Company. Adopted 1888, issued 1889. Lith. H.S. Crocker & Co., San Francisco. On file, Bancroft Library.

Ornduff, R.
1974 Introduction to California Plant Life. University of California Press, Berkeley.

Plog, F. (ed.)
1978 An Analytical Approach to Cultural Resource Management: The Little Colorado Planning Unit. Anthropological Research Papers No. 13, Arizona State University, Tempe.

Quail, F.C.
1905 Official Map of San Joaquin County, California. Compiled from Official Records and Surveys. Drawn by D.C. Carlton. On file, Bancroft Library.

1912 Official Map of San Joaquin County, California. Compiled from Official Records and Surveys by F.C. Quail, County Surveyor. Drawn by A.B. Massey. Britton & Rey, San Francisco. On file, Bancroft Library.

Rickman, J.
1976 Corral Hollow. MS on file, Stockton San Joaquin County Public Library, Tracy.

Rogers, D.B.
1929 Prehistoric Man of the Santa Barbara Coast, California. Santa Barbar Museum of Natural History Special Publication No. 1.

Rogers, M.J.
1929 Stone Art of the San Diequito Plateau. American Anthropologist 31(3):454-467.

Sandoval, J.
n.d.a. A Century of . . . Transportation in the East Bay. Chapel of the Chimes: No.5, Hayward.

n.d.b. A Century of . . . Sheriffdom in the East Bay. Chapel of the Chimes: No. 8, Hayward.

San Joaquin County Historical Society
1966 Bulletin No. 2(2). San Joaquin County Historical Society, Lodi.

1973 San Joaquin Historian XI(2). San Joaquin County Historical Society, Lodi.

Schenck, W.E. and E.J. Dawson
1929 Archaeology of the Northern San Joaquin Valley. University of California Publications in American Archaeology and Ethnology 25(4):289-413.

Sharsmith, H.K.
1965 Spring Wildflowers of the San Francisco Bay Region. University of California Press, Berkeley.

Siegel, S.
1956 Nonparametric Statistics for the Behavioural Sciences. McGraw-Hill, New York.

Smith, A.C.
1959 Introduction to the Natural History of the San Francisco Bay Region. University of California Press, Berkeley.

Stebbins, R.C.
1959 Reptiles and Amphibians of the San Francisco Bay Region. University of California Press, Berkeley.

Stewart, M.C. (Mrs. C. DeWelt)
1964 After Fifty Years . . . My Happy Childhood Days. MS on file, Stockton San Joaquin County Library, Tracy.

Tesla Coal Company
1900 California Can Produce Good Coal, Jan. 16, San Francisco.

Theodoratus, D., et al.
1979 Cultural Resources Evaluation: Edenvale Redevelopment Project Area Expansion. MS on file, California Archaeological Site Survey, Cabrillo College.

Thomas, D.H. and R.L. Bettinger
1976 Prehistoric Pinon Ecotone Settlements of the Upper Reese River Valley, Central Nevada. Anthropological Papers, American Museum of Natural History 53(3).

Thompson, L.
1957 Costanoan Survey, October 1956-September 1957. (MS in William F. Shipley's Possession).

Thompson and West
1878 Official Historical Atlas Map of Alameda County, California. Thompson and West, Oakland.

Tinkham, G.H.
1923 History of San Joaquin County, California with Biographical Sketches. Historic Record Company, Los Angeles.

Turner, M.D.
1951 Clay and Ceramic Industry of the San Francisco Bay Counties. IN O.P. Jenkins (prep.), Geologic Guidebook of the San Francisco Bay Counties, pp. 57-64. California Division of Mines, Bulletin No. 154.

Wallace, J.W.
1870 Map of the county of San Joaquin. Compiled from the United States Surveys, the Maps and Records of the County Surveyor and County Assessor. Map approved and declared official, Supervisors, July 6, 1870. On file, Bancroft Library.

Wallace, W.J.
1978a Post-Pleistocene Archaeology, 9000 to 2000 B.C. IN R.F. Heizer (ed.), Handbook of North American Indians, Vol. 8, California, pp. 25-36. Smithsonian Institution Press, Washington.

Williams, E.E.
1973b Tales of Old San Joaquin City. San Joaquin Historian 9(3). San Joaquin Historical Society, Inc., Lodi.

1973c Tales of Old San Joaquin City. San Joaquin Historian 9(4). San Joaquin Historical Society, Inc., Lodi.

1974 Tales of Old San Joaquin City. San Joaquin Historian 10(1). San Joaquin Historical Society, Inc., Lodi.

1975 Pauline Lee and Mazeppa of the Henry C. Lee Little South American Circus. IN Writings by Earle E. Williams, MS on file, Stockton San Joaquin County Public Libraries, Stockton and Tracy.

Wood, M.W.
1883 History of Alameda County, California: Including its Geology, Topography, Soil and Productions. M.W. Wood, Oakland.

Uhle, M.
1907 The Emeryville Shellmound. University of California Publications in American Archaeology and Ethnology 7:1-106.

APPENDIX 3A

ACCIDENT EXPERIENCE AT THE DOE LIVERMORE LABORATORIES

This appendix lists the accidents at the DOE Livermore Laboratories which either had off-site impact or the potential for such impact. Accidents are listed in chronological order. A search of available records prior to 1960 indicated that none of the accidents listed had off-site impacts. Following each accident, an investigation was conducted to determine its cause, prevent reoccurrence, and decide if the potential existed for similar accidents. For those accidents not due solely to human error, some of the corrective actions are presented.

Fire in a Curium-Processing Cave--Nov. 8, 1960

The fire started, apparently, as a result of an overheated oil bath. The fire, spread by the coating on the interior of the glove box, destroyed the contents of the room containing the cave. The fire was out in 12 min due to the rapid and effective response of the Fire Department. The total cost of the fire was estimated at $194,000. Fortunately, the cave contained only a few μCi of curium so that contamination was restricted to the immediate area.

The following changes were made in the facility to prevent and mitigate a reoccurrence:

- Overhead sprinklers were installed.
- A research program on coatings and their flammability was started.
- A drain and sump system was installed to retain contaminated runoff water from fire fighting.

Nuclear Excursion--March 26, 1963

The excursion occurred in Building 261, during a criticality experiment, in a room designed for such experiments. The excursion of 4×10^{17} fissions was attributed to mechanical failure during the experiment.

Sampling undertaken immediately after the incident showed that only small amounts of short-lived gaseous fission products were released from the experiment room. Equipment was redesigned to minimize reoccurrence.

Release of Tritium to Atmosphere--January 20, 1965

350,000 Ci of tritium were released from Building 331 and vented to the atmosphere through a 30-m stack. The accident was the result of human error while working on a system containing ^{3}H gas under pressure. Most of the ^{3}H remained as $^{3}H_2$ gas rather than oxidizing to tritiated water. Thus, no significant exposures or deposition occurred, either on site or off site. Administrative controls were adopted to provide greater safety in gas transfers.

Plutonium Fire in Building 332--September 13, 1965

A plastic bag containing some plutonium and plutonium-plated pieces caught fire as it was being moved for placement in a metal can. It was immediately extinguished. No detectable plutonium escaped the building. The cost of $30,000 for the incident was for decontamination.

Handling procedures were changed to prevent a reoccurrence.

Release of Acid to the Livermore Sanitary Sewer--March, 1967

An acid discharge from LLNL's Building 321 Plating Shop caused the pH at the Livermore City treatment plant to drop to 3.2. This resulted in a reduction in the anerobic bacteria colony necessary for function of the sludge digesters. Plating Shop personnel were informed of the effects of such acid releases in the Treatment Plant's operation.

Release of ^{239}Pu to Sewer--May 25 to June 15, 1967

During the above interval, 32 mCi of ^{239}Pu was accidentally released by LLNL to the sanitary sewer. No samples taken during the release had concentrations greater than the maximum permissible concentration in water as specified by ERDA Manual Chapter 0524. The ^{239}Pu followed the sludge through the sewer plant and was deposited principally in the bottom of the sludge lagoons.

The dried sludge, which is used mainly as a soil conditioner, contained 2-3 pCi/g of ^{239}Pu. LLNL has tilled samples of this dried sludge into a vegetable garden on the Livermore site. Air samples taken downwind during tilling showed concentrations up to 2.5% of the permissible concentration specified for the general public by ERDA Manual Chapter 0524. Samples of the vegetables grown in the test garden were analyzed for plutonium. Calculated radiation doses to an individual tilling the sludge and eating the vegetables were negligible compared with that received from natural sources. Details of this study are reported in IAEA-SM-199/42.

Corrective action consisted of closer surveillance of tank discharges and installation of a continuously operating, highly sensitive effluent monitorial system.

Release of Chromium to the Livermore Sanitary Sewer--September 6 & 20, 1967

Chromium was found in the influent stream in concentrations up to 50 ppm. The activity of the bacteria colony in one digester was reduced. LLNL paid for cleanup costs. Release due to "bright dip" cleaning operations. During investigation of the first release there was a second release of approximately 150 liters of chromic acid solution containing copper residue also from "bright dip" operations. Corrective action for these releases consisted of written procedures covering disposal of spent chromic acid and safety talks to shop personnel.

Release of Radioactivity to the Storm Sewer--February 1, 1968

A liquid waste retention tank at Building 281 overflowed and released 380 μCi ^{131}I and 2 μCi ^{90}Sr, which eventually ran into the storm sewer. The 24-h average concentration, in water, for the two nuclides combined was 50 times the maximum permissible concentration in water specified by the ERDA Manual Chapter 0524 at the point where it left the site. However, dilution and deposition reduced the concentration to below detectable limits at the point where the Las Positas Creek (into which the storm sewer empties) crosses Vasco Road. Improved procedures for retention tank operation were adopted to minimize reoccurrence.

Release of Copper-Cyanide to Sewer--April 1968

A tank containing copper-cyanide in the LLNL Building 321 Plating Shop failed. About 210 liters were released to the sewer. About 50% of the bacteria in the trickle filter (aeration tank) were killed. Routine inspections of tankage integrity were adopted.

Release of Radioactivity to the Storm Sewer--April 13, 1970

Liquid waste was being transferred between tanks at LLNL Building 281 with two valves in the wrong position. About 1640 liters of water containing 6.6 μCi of ^{60}Co, ^{58}Co, ^{65}Zn, and ^{51}Cr were released to the storm sewer. Rain water, mixed with the liquid waste, reduced the 24 h average concentration at the site boundary to 1/2 the maximum permissible concentration in water as specified by ERDA Manual Chapter 0524. Initial concentrations in Las Positas Creek, at Vasco Road, were 1% of the maximum permissible concentration. Samples taken at the same point two days later were below detectable limits.

Two corrective measures were taken as a result of this incident: (1) the valve that allowed the contaminated water to escape was padlocked closed and (2) a berm was constructed to retain future spills from the waste tank area on site.

Release of Tritium to the Atmosphere--August 6, 1970

The failure of a component in a pressurized gas system containing tritium resulted in the loss of 300,000 Ci of $^{3}H2$ to the atmosphere through the 30-m stack at Building 331. As a result of this release, the design criteria for $^{3}H_2$ pressure systems have been strengthened. Secondary vessels to contain the gas were included, where possible, to reduce the probability of another incident. No detectable doses were received by the public.

Release of Acid to Sewer--February 10, 1971

A low pH led to diversion of flow at Livermore Water Reclamation Plant. Corrective action consisted of administrative controls in the form of written procedures governing discharge of acids to sanitary sewer.

Release of Acid to Sewer--October 20, 1971

A low-pH alarm was caused by a leaking acid tank at LLNL's Building 321 Plating Shop. No diversion was required. Tankage repaired and routine surveillance of chemical tankage adopted.

Plutonium in Off-Site Soil--April 1973

On December 10, 1973, ERDA-SAN was notified by LLNL that several annual off-site soil samples collected in 1973 at locations east of Greenville Road contained ^{239}Pu levels above those typical of global fallout. The plutonium content of these samples ranged from 30 to 200 fCi per gram, whereas global fallout ^{239}Pu in soils within the Livermore Valley ranges from 3 to 30 fCi/g. The elevated ^{239}Pu levels are believed to be due to an April 1973 release of activity during transfer of dry material from one of the solar evaporators located upwind from the Greenville Road locations.

As a corrective measure, a closed evaporator is now used for volume reduction of radioactive liquid wastes and the solar evaporators are no longer employed for these wastes.

Fuel Oil Tank Leak--January 1975

On January 14 or 16, 1975, a construction contractor working at SNLL unknowingly drove a grounding rod through the feed line connecting the fuel oil storage tank to the central boilers. On the 31st, natural gas service to SNLL was interrupted and oil was let into the line so that oil could be pumped from the fuel oil storage tank into the day tanks serving the central boilers. A gross leak resulted, which was discovered on February 11 after rain displaced oil to the surface. About 227 m^3 of fuel oil of the 655 m^3 stored there had seeped into the ground. A continuously reading fuel-level meter was placed on the tank.

Release of Acid to Sewer--March 10, 1975

A low-pH alarm led to diversion at the Livermore Water Reclamation Plant. The release was due to nitric acid from SNLL Building 913 Plating Laboratory. Administrative controls were instituted to regulate disposal of chemicals and an improved design of pH meter was installed at sewage outfall.

Americium to County Disposal Site--August 25, 1978

Twenty-one waste sacks containing approximately 43 μCi of americium were mistakenly placed in an LLNL Dempster Dumpster and delivered to the Eastern Alameda County Disposal Site. The material was located and recovered. Decontamination of the area was completed on August 29, 1978. A program of training and improved supervision was adopted to prevent a recurrence of misplaced radioactive waste.

Gasoline Tankage Loss--March 11, 1979

On March 11, 1979, gaging showed that 33 m^3 of gasoline had been lost at the LLNL motor pool due to probable rupture of old Navy tankage. Samples from a nearby off-site water well located down gradient (to the west) showed no hydrocarbon contamination of the groundwater. Operations were transferred to new tankage and old tankage was not repaired. No correction action taken.

Plutonium Incidents-April 8 and 16, 1980

On April 8, 1980, a length of plastic tubing, used as part of an argon supply line inside a glove box in Building 332, popped off a hose-barb connection and overpressurized the glove box. The pressure burst a glove and contaminated the laboratory room with plutonium; approximately 3 µg of plutonium was released to the environment outside Building 332.

On April 16, 1980, a flash fire involving ethanol from an ultrasonic cleaner occurred in a sample-preparation glovebox in Building 332. The pressure generated during the fire was sufficient to force the top of the glove box out of its retaining clips, thus allowing a small amount of plutonium to escape and contaminate the laboratory room. No plutonium was released to the outside environment.

On the first incident, release of plutonium to the outside environment was determined to be due to improper installation of high-efficiency particulate air (HEPA) filters and failure to perform the required filter tests. Because such failures might apply to the entire building, routine operations in the Plutonium Facility were stopped until similar glove boxes were inspected for adequate pressure-relief mechanisms and all filters were tested for proper installation and performance.

The second incident was caused by failure to turn off the ultrasonic cleaner, which resulted in evaporation of the ethanol and eventual electrical breakdown of the cleaning unit. A contributory cause of this accident was failure to flush the glove box sufficiently with an inert gas to reduce the oxygen content below that which will support combustion.

Corrective action for both incidents included intensive training of all personnel in the technique of safety surveillance. A quality assurance program was instituted for filter installation and testing. Particular emphasis was placed on assuring that those responsible for facility management also recognized their safety responsibilities.

M-014
Rev. 3

APPENDIX 3B

DISASTER CONTROL PLAN

University of California

Rev. 3

LLNL DISASTER CONTROL PLAN

October 1, 1981

If any changes or corrections are necessary, please contact Rice Trolan, Hazards Control, Ext. 2-5123

CONTENTS

LLNL DISASTER CONTROL PLAN

INTRODUCTION

Lawrence Livermore National Laboratory (LLNL), in its continuing effort to ensure safe and continuous operation, care for its employees, safeguard laboratory property and records, and minimize any off-site effects of incidents which may occur at the laboratory, hereby sets forth its Disaster Control Plan.

The disaster response and mitigation philosophy of LLNL is one of maximum reliance upon and use of on-site organizational capabilities and resources. This is based upon the realization that during a major disaster, such as an earthquake or nuclear attack, outside help may not be available.

The Laboratory Emergency Services, and other human and mechanical resources throughout the laboratory, shall strive for the common goal of incident mitigation, continuity of operations, and recovery. LLNL also stands ready to assist the surrounding community in time of disaster.

The LLNL Disaster Control Plan describes how the integrated Matrix system, common to all laboratory operations, functions in an emergency. This plan includes the following components: 1) the overall disaster control plan; 2) the Emergency Operations Guides; 3) supplements; and 4) the Organization Activation Matrix. The key is simplicity. The Disaster Control Organization must expand upon existing emergency service units which routinely cope with small and moderate accidents (Fig. 1). The basic emergency service support elements include the Fire Department, Security, Plant Engineering and Safety Team units. The plan outlined in this document is concerned with major emergencies or disasters that involve the total Disaster Control Organization. The Disaster Control Organization is divided into an Administrative Group and a Field Group. The Field Group is subordinate to the Administrative Group and is responsible for performing the field operations necessary to alleviate the effects of a disaster.

The Field Group usually operates out of a field command post. The Adminstrative Group generally operates out of the Emergency Operations Center (EOC), which is currently located in Bldg. 271; the Administrative Group develops policy guidelines governing the operations of the Disaster Control Organization. In the event of a disaster, the Administrative Group in the EOC

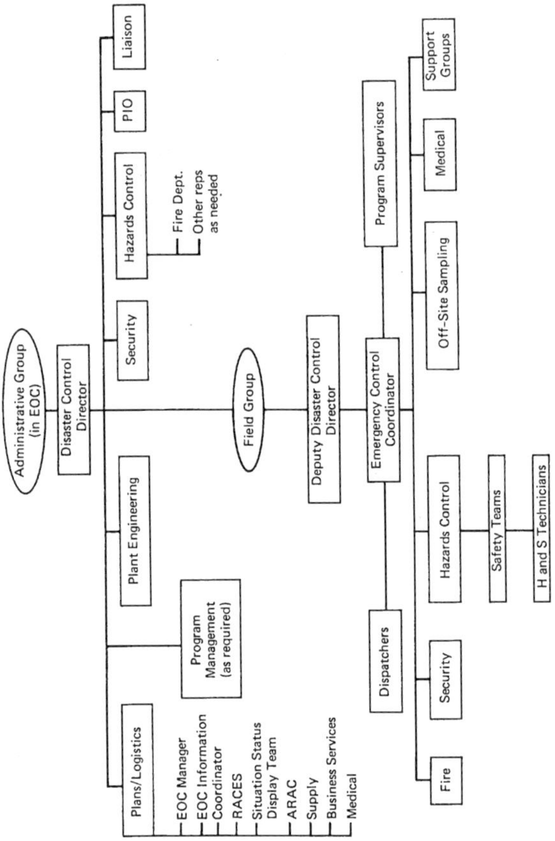

FIG. 1. Disaster Control Organization.

also provides overall control and administrative support, and notifies concerned individuals and off-site agencies, including the media. All Laboratory scientific and technical departments are required to assist when requested by the Disaster Control Director.

In general, most emergencies do not interrupt wide segments of laboratory operations, and the general public or the local community does not become involved. Emergencies are reported to the Fire Department and are referred, in turn, to the person(s) responsible for controlling that particular type of accident. Examples of such emergencies are hazardous spills or water, flammable material, toxic materials or radionuclides releases, accidental explosions, fires or suspected fires, and injuries requiring first aid. Major emergenices are accidents that endanger life and property.

Disasters are defined as serious accidents that cause injuries or extensive damage and threaten to cause additional injuries and damage; disasters result from natural or man-made causes. Generally, accidents that can cause serious off-site effects and create public relations problems with the community are classified as disasters. The entire Disaster Control Organization is available to the community during disasters to control the extent of injuries and property damage.

Disasters of natural origin are earthquakes, floods, severe weather, and hurricanes. Of these, earthquakes are the most likely to affect overall laboratory operations by damaging buildings, spilling hazardous materials, and starting fires from short-circuited electrical equipment. Man-made disasters are caused by explosions, nuclear criticality excursions, widespread fire, terrorism and nuclear attack. Conceivably, natural and man-made causes can combine to create disastrous conditions. Lightning, for example, could strike a large explosive mixture. High winds at an off-site fire could carry firebrands to many laboratory buildings where they could start additional fires.

PURPOSE OF THE LLNL DISASTER CONTROL PLAN

- To provide for the mobilization and direction of LLNL's Disaster Control Organization under major emergency or disaster conditions (see Fig. 1).

- To establish and define the operational organizations, define tasks to be performed, identify who performs these tasks and provide coordination between emergency service personnel and Laboratory departments and divisions.
- To identify who is in command, thus maintaining unity of command.

SCOPE

The LLNL Disaster Control Plan sets forth the emergency organization structure, response procedures and roles, for all major emergencies and disasters occurring on LLNL properties, or occurring off-site with a potential or actual impact upon LLNL. These disasters include, but are not limited to, the following potential incidents:

1. Earthquake
2. Hazardous materials spill or release, criticality, etc.
3. Major fire
4. Explosion
5. Off-site incident exposing LLNL
6. Severe weather
7. Civil disturbance (Security Classified Supplement 12 applies here)
8. Terrorism (Security Classified Supplement 12 applies here)

This plan outlines the Disaster Control Organization which utilizes or may utilize any and all laboratory employees as disaster workers. All employees and units of the Laboratory are hereby subject to disaster duties under this plan.

AUTHORITY AND PROMULGATION

This plan shall be the official Disaster Control Plan. It may be activated by any authorized individual serving in one of the following Disaster Control Organization positions, in concert with the activation matrix:

1. Emergency Control Coordinator (ECC);
2. Deputy Disaster Control Director (DDCD); or
3. Disaster Control Director (DCD).

When this plan is in effect, it and the Disaster Control Organization operates with the full authority of the Laboratory Director.

Basic Authorization for this plan is set forth in Section 3.00 (Emergency Control) of the LLNL Health and Safety Manual.

The plan represents LLNL's formal response to disasters. This plan is approved by the State of California's Office of Emergency Services. All members of the Disaster Control Organization are qualified disaster workers and are granted authority under the California Disaster Act of 1943, as amended, and Chapter 6 of the Alameda County Administrative Code.

This plan and its supplements shall be reviewed annually by the originators to establish that its contents are appropriate and adequate for current operations. The LLNL Fire Chief has the responsibility to ensure that the review is accomplished, changes coordinated, and revisions published. The Emergency Operations Management Group (EOMG) has the oversight responsibility to ensure that the Disaster Control Organization is capable of performing the functions described in this plan.

EMERGENCY OPERATIONS GUIDE

In order to facilitate implementation of the tasks that must be carried out in order to mitigate a disaster, a simple checklist booklet, called the Emergency Operations Guide (EOG), has been developed for each position in the Disaster Control Organization. Each booklet includes the checklists necessary to perform the duties of that position in all potential disasters. The checklists are guides. They assume that the person in the position is a qualified individual who is performing tasks which closely resemble his day-to-day job.

The EOG also includes an organization chart of the Disaster Control Organization, Position Duty Statements of each position, a copy of the Disaster Organization Activation Matrix, and a "Yellow Pages" or Resource Listing Section. This should be referred to when ordering needed resources, human or hardware.

The EOG is all that is needed by the individual in order to understand his role and what is to be done. Master sets of these guides are kept in the EOC, Dispatch Centers, Fire Department Command Vehicle, and Command Post Trailer.

MISSION OF DISASTER ORGANIZATION

In the event of any major emergency or disaster occurring on Laboratory property, or off-site exposing the Laboratory facilities, the Disaster Control Organization will initiate all appropriate action to protect life and property in the Laboratory and vicinity, and restore operational integrity as soon as possible. Duties will be simply an expansion of routine duties with a vastly increased workload to be accomplished in a compressed time frame.

ROLE OF LABORATORY ORGANIZATIONS

Fire Department

The Fire Department responds promptly to an emergency to evaluate the nature and severity and assumes initial control of the scene. At security or terrorist incidents, the senior Police Department Officer on-scene assumes initial control. The Emergency Dispatcher handles activation of the Disaster Control Organization unless the function is given to the Police Department by the Emergency Dispatcher.

Security Department

The Security Department responds to an emergency in order to assist in pedestrian and vehicular traffic control and to provide protection of classified material. Security personnel may establish access control to buildings when so directed. The Security Department representative is the initial on-scene commander in a terrorist or a security incident. All requirements pertaining to security/police operations in an emergency will be coordinated through the Police Command Center (Bldg. 271).

Plant Engineering Department

Plant Engineering provides maintenance machinists and electricians on initial emergency calls. These basic units can be supplemented by other support groups such as welders, plumbers, carpenters, etc., depending upon the nature and extent of the emergency. The Plant Engineering Field Team is available to advise upon the operation of facilities' support functions in an emergency. All requirements pertaining to Plant Engineering operations are processed and controlled by the Plant Engineering Operations Center in Bldg. 511.

Hazards Control Department

The Hazards Control Safety Team assigned to specific buildings will be available to advise upon the control of hazardous conditions. When the EOC is operational, the Safety Team Leaders will provide information on hazardous conditions to the Hazards Control representative at that location.

Medical Department

The Medical Department advises the Disaster Control Director on medical matters. It also provides assistance to the Field Group.

LLNL Departments and Divisions

The line management of the Laboratory will implement, when necessary, their self-help plans to provide information and assistance to employees in a disaster situation in which Laboratory emergency services are extended beyond their capabilities to adequately respond. Assistance should also be provided to contractors, consultants, and visitors who are in a facility or performing work for a responsible Laboratory organization. LLNL departments and divisions will also provide advice and assistance to the Disaster Control Organization. Additionally, Laboratory management has the authority to direct the actions of all contractors and consultants on-site during a major emergency.

POSITION DUTY STATEMENTS

LLNL Director

The Director of the Laboratory is responsible for the overall direction of all laboratory operations, including disaster control. However, the responsibility for directing disaster control operations at any time has been delegated to the "Disaster Control Director."

Disaster Control Director (Administrative Group)

The Disaster Control Director (DCD) is responsible for directing people, equipment, and operations either directly or indirectly involved in any disaster or disaster exercise. He also coordinates the activities between the EOC and the Field Groups. He may delegate or assign this authority as he believes appropriate during any emergency or exercise. The Manager of Plant Services or his designated alternate (see Supplement 2) is the Disaster Control Director.

Deputy Disaster Control Director (Field Group)

The Deputy Disaster Control Director (DDCD) takes charge in the field and acts to control the disaster in accordance with the Disaster Control Plan. He implements the directions given by the Disaster Control Director and commands the field operations. He informs the DCD of the progress made to control the disaster. He also coordinates the return to work of disaster control personnel after control has been established. (In emergencies falling primarily within the purview of the Security Department, the Head of the Security Department or his designated alternate is the DDCD; otherwise, the Head of the Hazards Control Department or his designated alternate is the DDCD. At Site 300, the Site Manager is the DDCD.)

Emergency Control Coordinator (Field Group)

The Emergency Control Coordinator (ECC) assumes command of the incident from the initial on-scene commander, until he is relieved by the Deputy Disaster Control Director. In carrying out these responsibilities, the Emergency Control Coordinator directs the activities of the various emergency groups, decides the general course of field operations, and establishes a command post. Once relieved, the ECC assists the Deputy Disaster Control Director as necessary. (In emergencies falling primarily within the purview of the Security Department, the Chief of the Protective Service Division or the Security Emergency Response Team Commander is the ECC; otherwise, the Fire Chief is the ECC). The Emergency Control Coordinator has the authority to expand activation of the Disaster Control Organization in concert with this plan.

Other duties of the ECC include the responsibility for the development of training programs and exercises to maintain the proficiency of emergency response personnel and maintenance of the Disaster Control Organization in a state of constant preparedness. The Emergency Control Coordinator also assists program personnel, Hazards Control Safety Team leaders, fire officers, security personnel and others in preparation of pre-emergency plans for each critical facility.

Plant Engineering Department Representative

As the senior representative of the Plant Engineering Department, he advises the Disaster Control Director on general operations of the Laboratory and support requirements of Laboratory programs and departments. He also provides administrative support for the Plant Engineering personnel in the Field Group. He coordinates EOC requirements with the Head of the Plant Engineering Department located in the Plant Engineering Operations Center (Bldg. 511).

Security Department Representative

He advises the Disaster Control Director on general security and police operations during a disaster. He coordinates EOC requirements with the Security/Police Command Center (Bldg. 271), and provides administrative support for the Security/Police field units. As previously noted, the Head of the Security Department or his designated alternate will perform the function of DDCD in hostage or terrorist situations.

Senior Fire Officer (Field Group)

In any major emergency not within the purview of the Security Department, the Senior Fire Officer present at the disaster scene assumes command until the Emergency Control Coordinator arrives. He supervises all fire-fighting, rescue, and first-aid operations. He also directs operations required to contain and control hazardous spills of flammable materials and water. At the scene of an emergency, the Senior Fire Officer directs the salvage operations necessary for immediate control of an emergency until he is relieved. He requests assistance from the Emergency Control Organization if necessary, and coordinates the activities of mutual-aid fire companies. He performs other emergency activities as directed by the ECC. He is also responsible for assisting the Emergency Control Coordinator and the Hazards Control Safety Team Leader with formulation of plans for controlling emergencies.

Plans/Logistics Section (Administrative Group)

The Plans/Logistics Section in the EOC is responsible for the compilation, evaluation and display of information regarding the status of the emergency. It is also responsible for predictions of future problems and considerations in the emergency. The Plans/Logistics Section makes provisions for needed resources, both human and hardware, from on-site or off-site in support of the emergency. They order the resources and notify the assembly points regarding the availability of said resources. The Section also arranges for medical advice, field medical assistance and triage, ambulance, and selections and notification of receiving hospitals. This Section includes the following personnel:

EOC Manager. The EOC Manager activates and directs the Plans/Logistics Section in the EOC. He is responsible for activating the EOC facilities and overseeing the facility operation; he oversees the operation of the Information Coordinator and insures EOC security. He also oversees the RACES operation and is the interface with ARAC operation. The LLNL Emergency Preparedness Program Leader or his designated alternate is the EOC Manager.

EOC Information Coordinator. The Information Coordinator activates and oversees the operation of the Situation/Status Display Team and supervises the receipt, validation, flow and display of necessary information in EOC.

Situation/Status Display Team. This team is part of the Plans/Logistics Section in the EOC. They are under direction of the Information Coordinator and have the responsibility for receiving incoming information regarding situation status and damage assessment, elimination of redundant messages, validation of information and the posting of the information on proper displays in EOC, and distribution of messages to various individuals in EOC.

RACES (Radio Amateur Civil Emergency Service--Administrative Group). This is a federally authorized, volunteer, amateur radio operators group. The members are LLNL employees. RACES will establish a communications net between Laboratory departments and divisions and the EOC under direction of the EOC Manager. They will relay damage assessment information and situation status information to the Plans/Logistics Section in EOC. They also provide a radio communications net throughout the Laboratory and will serve as a communications link for the Disaster Control Organization.

ARAC (Atmospheric Release Advisory Capability--Administrative Group). ARAC provides for the collection of real-time meteorological, observational, and forecast data which is used to calculate air concentrations and ground deposition estimates that can be expected from the release of toxic and radioactive materials.

Supply Operations Representative (Administrative Group). As a member of the Administrative Group, assigned to Plans/Logistics, this individual provides administrative support to supply operations division personnel engaged in disaster control activities.

Business Services Representative (Administrative Group). As a member of the Administrative Group assigned to Plans/Logistics, this individual provides administrative support to the Disaster Control Director. This includes advice on legal matters, procurement of off-site supplies and equipment from outside sources, activation of cafeterias, and the housing and feeding of disaster workers.

Medical Department Representative. The Medical Department representative advises the Disaster Control Director and Emergency Control Coordinator about medical problems, cares for the injured, conducts triage, assists with the establishment of emergency medical-aid facilities, and arranges for transportation to hospitals. Medical personnel respond to the Field Command Post as needed and are under the direction of the Field Group Commander.

Liaison (Administrative Group)

The Liaison Officer is responsible for all inter-agency interface, under the direction of the Disaster Control Director. Liaison maintains contact as necessary with FEMA, DOE, OES, Red Cross, NRC, FBI, Livermore City, Pleasanton, ALCO, and any other involved entities.

PIO (Administrative Group)

The Public Information Officer writes and disseminates all releases to the media and public. He is under direction of DCD and all media releases shall be approved by DCD prior to release. PIO functions as contact point and host for on-scene media and other concerned groups from the private sector.

Off-Site Sampling Team (Field Group)

The Off-Site Sampling Team is responsible for field measurements, sample collection and preparation, and analysis of contamination during a disaster, and will inform the Disaster Control Organization of the extent of the contamination. They also work outside the Laboratory perimeter to establish contamination levels beyond the Laboratory. The team may be given other assignments by the person in charge of the Field Group.

Support Groups (Field Group)

Various support groups are integrated into the Disaster Control Organization. These groups are under direction of the Plant Engineering Department and are assigned to the Field Group. They include riggers, welders, plumbers, electricians, carpenters, laborers, truck drivers, and other labor-type positions.

TRANSITION OF OPERATIONS

Any response to a major emergency or disaster must be appropriate to manage the scope of the incident. Transition must be automatic and keyed to certain incident criteria. A disaster can be classified into various operational levels. Figure 2 describes these levels relating to potential Laboratory disasters. Figure 2 shows 3 levels: the incident builds from Level 0 to Level 3. This does not preclude going into a Level 3 mode

INCIDENT LEVEL	CLASSIFICATION	INCIDENT COMMAND CRITERIA	INCIDENT COMMAND TRANSITION	FIELD OPERATIONS COMMAND
Level Three Activator: Deputy Disaster Control Director	Disaster: Serious incidents that cause extensive injury, or threaten to cause additional injury/death, incidents causing extensive damage, incidents involving major security problems, incidents with off-site implications. High level lab-wide managerial efforts required for mitigation. Intensified interagency interface.	Severe earthquake Severe weather Major fire Criticality Hostage incident Terrorism Nuclear war Severe hazard Materials incident Severe radioactive release with off-site impacts Off-site incident which exposes lab. (Hazardous materials leak, etc.)	Disaster Control Director in charge of overall incident.	Deputy Disaster Control Director in charge of field operations.
Level Two Activator: Emergency Control	Major Emergency: Incident requires intensified lab-wide commitment and management of lab-wide resources towards mitigation.	Minor earthquake (gentle) Hostile pickets, bomb found, multiple fires, serious hazardous material spill or leak, explosion, radioactive release to atmosphere on-site, threat of terrorism, utility/water supply failure lab-wide, sanitation system failure lab-wide.	Deputy Disaster Control Director in charge of overall incident at Livermore. Site 300 incident = Site 300 Manager.	Deputy Disaster Control Director
Level One Activator: Senior Fire or Police Officer	"Minor Emergency" Incident limited in scope requiring relatively minimal management/coordination	Bomb threat, single fire alarm, small hazardous material spill, injury requiring first-aid, pickets outside lab, minor security problem.	Emergency Control Coordinator Senior Fire or Police Officer Program or Facility Supervisor.	Emergency Control Coordinator Senior Fire or Police Officer Program or Facility Supervisor.
Level Zero	Minor Problem incident "in house". Does not actively involve emergency response units.	Minor injury, minor spill physical plant problem.	Program or Facility Supervisor.	Program or Facility Supervisor.

FIG. 2. Organization transition matrix (continued on next page).

EOC STATUS	FIELD COMMAND POST STATUS	ENTITIES INVOLVED	DISASTER CONTROL ORGANIZATION ACTIVATION	NOTIFY
Activated by Emergency D spatchers on orders of Deputy Disaster Control Director (Severe earthquake - automatic activation)	Activated	Admin. Group, Field Group, Tri-Valley Mutual-Aid, OES FBI Sandia Reps. FEMA DOE Programs. Local Law Enforcement	Admin. Group, Field Group, Call-up by Sierra Dispatchers.	Admin. Group, Field Group, FBI DOE OES Alameda County, Livermore, FEMA
Optional activation by Deputy Disaster Control Director. Call up by Emergency Dispatchers. (Prepare for Level Three activation)	Activated	Programs Fire Security Hazards Control Plant Engineering, Tri-Valley Mutual Aid, Safety Teams, ARAC.	Field Group activated Call-up by Sierra Dispatchers.	Disaster Cont. Director Field Group, ARAC PIO FBI if applicable DOE if applicable RACES
Not activated	Activated by Emergency Control Coordinator -optional in some Security operations.	Program, Fire, Security, Safety Team Leader, Plant Engineering, Hazards Control	Optional as applicable by order of Emergency Control Coordinator. Call-up by Sierra.	Deputy Disaster Control Director, Hazards Control Plant Engineering Safety Team Leader Security, Fire.
Not activated	Not Activated	Program	Not Activated	Fire Department Security Hazards Control Plant Engineering

FIG. 2. (continued)

immediately, as may be the case in the event of a severe earthquake, nuclear attack, or terrorist intrusion. Figure 2 sets forth the following information for each level:

- incident level
- classification of the level
- incident level criteria
- overall incident command transition (who is in charge at each level)
- Field Operations Commander at each level
- EOC status
- Field Command Post status
- entities involved at each level
- Disaster Control Plan Activation by Group (Field and Administrative)
- necessary notifications.

ORGANIZATION TRANSITION MATRIX

The incident level designator provides a guide to assist emergency service personnel in understanding the mobilization sequence. This will key other Disaster Control Organization members, including dispatchers, as to what level of activation is occurring and what can be expected.

Figure 2 is a guide. Any level can be activated by the senior person in charge at any point in the incident as the situation warrants. The key is the understanding of what level is in effect.

At Level 3, the EOC is activated by the individual in charge of directing the emergency operations on instructions from the Deputy Disaster Control Director. The Deputy Disaster Control Director can order activation during Level 2 if desired. A severe earthquake triggers automatic activation.

Command transition will occur as described below. The levels of response to all Laboratory emergencies are outlined in Figure 2. This response builds up in accordance with the following steps:

Level 0 — The first employee to become aware of an accident must either report the accident immediately or have someone report it.

↓

Level 0 — Immediately after an accident occurs, the Program Director of the involved area is responsible for safeguarding his personnel and taking control actions his group can accomplish safely.

↓

Level 1 — Once the Fire Department arrives, the Senior Fire Officer coordinates the control efforts of all personnel present. He relinquishes this responsibility to an Emergency Control Coordinator when he arrives at the scene.

Level 1 — Level 2 — Level 3 — If the Emergency Control Coordinator considers the accident to be a major emergency or a disaster, the Head of the Hazards Control Department (or Site Manager if incident is at Site 300) is called and serves as the Deputy Disaster Control Director to coordinate all field activities. At level 3, the Manager of Plant Services becomes the Disaster Control Director and takes administrative control of the entire operation through the activation and operation of the LLNL Emergency Operations Center.

LLNL EOC

Upon activation by direction of the individual in charge of emergency operations, the EOC will operate as the primary command center for the disaster operation. The Administrative Group will operate in the EOC. The EOC activities will include the following:

- command of overall incident;
- coordinate all elements of the Disaster Control Organization;
- collect and display damage assessment information;
- collect and display situation status information;
- establish incident strategy and priorities, and allocate resources;
- coordinate the inter-agency interface and liaison;
- manage media interface and media releases;
- request resources from off-site (public and private sector);
- ensure continuity of operations; and
- manage recovery operations.

The currrent EOC location is in the basement of Bldg. 271 (Police Department). The EOC may have to be relocated during a disaster if it is rendered inopèrative by earthquake, hazardous gases, terrorism, fire, etc. An alternate EOC will be designated by the Disaster Control Director.

Self-Help Plans

If the disaster involves all or a major area of the laboratory and the emergency service elements are over-committed, the departments and divisions will implement their self-help plans which will provide for collection, control, and assistance to employees at designated assembly areas. Departments and divisions will establish communication with the EOC and advise of the status of personnel and facilities.

COMMUNICATIONS

GENERAL

The Emergency Communications System serves three purposes. First, it provides a means for notifying proper authorities that an emergency exists. Second, it is used to alert emergency control forces, as well as Laboratory employees. Third, it provides tactical communication lines between various units and personnel combating the emergency. The communications system (Fig. 3) which includes radio, telephone, manual and automatic alarm systems, and messengers tie into a variety of on-site facilities as well as local, state, and federal agencies.

NOTIFICATION

The Emergency Dispatcher is responsible for notifying individuals of the Administrative and Field Groups whenever a major emergency or disaster has occurred or is imminent.

This function may be handed off to the Police Department Dispatcher by the Emergency Dispatcher if the latter is overloaded. Call up is requested by the person in command of the incident.

When notifying the groups, the dispatcher calls the first member of the particular team being activated. The contacted member, in turn, is responsible for notifying other members of his group. (LLNL Disaster Control Plan Supplement 2 lists these groups.)

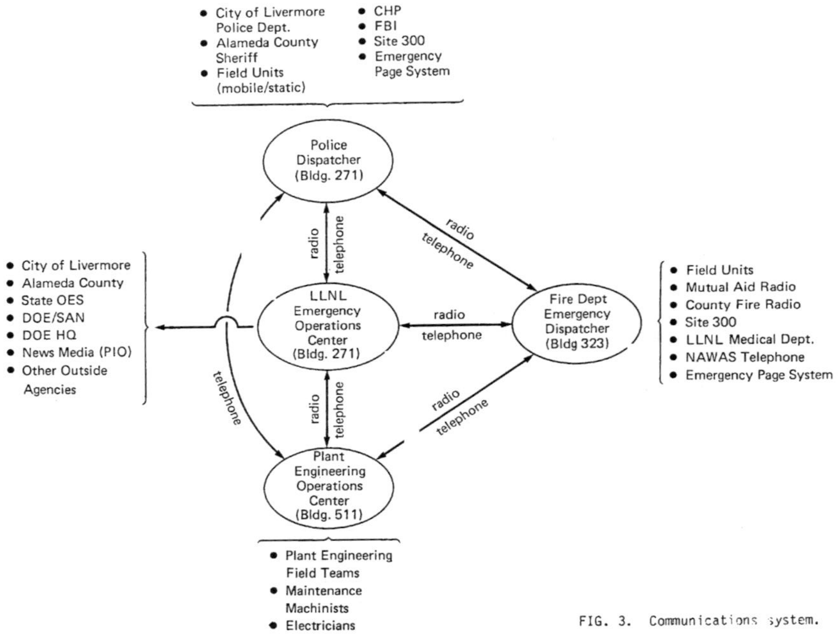

FIG. 3. Communications system.

EMERGENCY CALL LIST

Both Police and Emergency Dispatchers have a current Emergency Call List that is kept up-to-date by the Emergency Control Coordinator. Members of the Disaster Control Organization are responsible for informing the Emergency Control Coordinator of changes to the Call List. All changes are coordinated through the Emergency Preparedness Program Leader.

EMERGENCY ALARMS

Most emergency alarms are received by the Fire Department through emergency telephone extension 2-7333 (Ext. 333 at Site 300). Other alarms are received through automatic alarm systems.

A diagram of the emergency alarm systems is presented in Fig. 4. A special telephone communicating system is used to alert emergency forces at the Laboratory. In addition, speakers connected to emergency telephone number 2-7333 permit emergency calls to be monitored. The Channel B radio system also is used to announce emergencies. A disaster paging system at the LLNL, air raid sirens, or both, announce large-scale accidents or imminent air raids. Radios and telephones are used exclusively at Site 300 to alert personnel of emergencies. Warnings of imminent enemy attack are received either through a special telephone connection with the North American Warning Alert System (NAWAS). Figure 5 diagrams the systems to be used to alert personnel at Livermore and Site 300. Disaster Control Plan Supplement 1 provides further details on the LLNL Emergency Communication System.

OFF-HOURS EMERGENCIES

In the event of a major emergency or disaster occurring at a time other than during the normal workday, the operations will generally follow the transition sequence previously described. The Fire Department, Security Department, and Plant Engineering Department maintain groups responsible for responding to Laboratory emergencies on an around-the-clock basis. The Police Department Watch Commander will take charge initially in incidents involving security; otherwise, the Fire Department Duty Chief will take initial response action. In either instance, the individual in charge will advise their

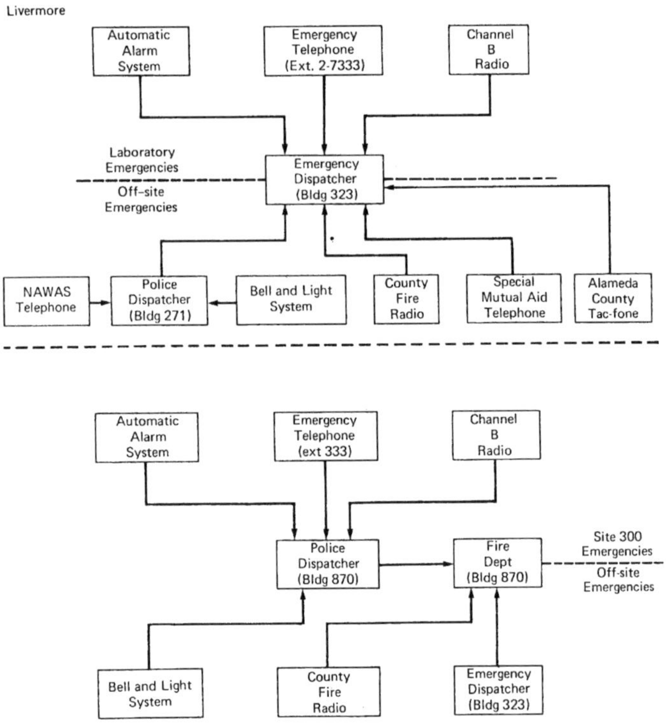

FIG. 4. Emergency alarm systems.

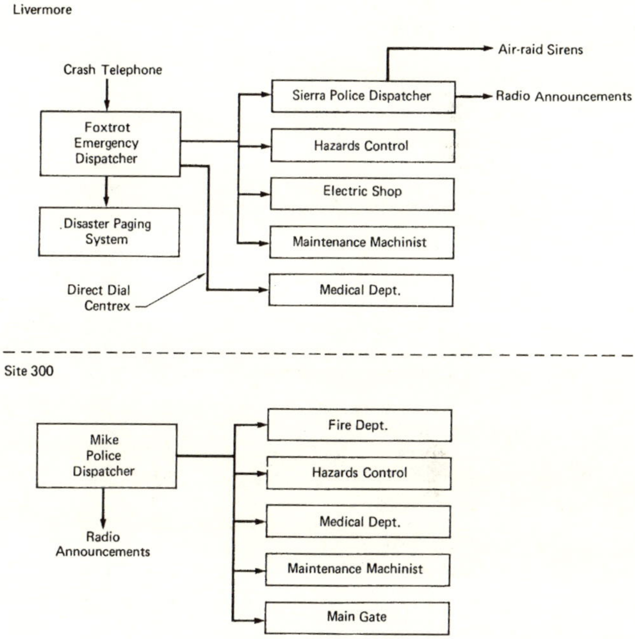

FIG. 5. Group-alerting system.

immediate supervisor and determine what further emergency response personnel and/or resources are required.

SUPPLY AND LOGISTICS

Many special purpose and common types of vehicles at the Laboratory are available for use during emergencies. The Emergency Control Coordinator maintains a complete inventory of this equipment in Supplement 13 to this Disaster Control Plan. It is recommended that Members of the Disaster Control Organization will become familiar with this inventory list.

FALLOUT SHELTERS

The Laboratory maintains a number of fallout shelters capable of housing approximately 11,000 people. The shelters are stocked with necessary medical supplies and radiological instruments (bring food). Fire Safety Division is responsible for marking and stocking these shelters.

Shelters are managed by the responsible Laboratory departments and divisions. They are activated by the Laboratory Disaster Control Director. The Shelter Managers may refer to the Shelter Manager's Handbook (Supplement 9) as necessary. Shelter locations are shown on the map (Fig. 6).

Shelter locations and travel routes are included in the Self-Help Plans for each program. Each program is assigned specific shelter locations. Lab shelters are also designated for use during relocation of citizens from the City of Livermore.

DISASTER CONTROL PLAN SUPPLEMENTS

The basic Disaster Control Plan is augmented by a number of supplements that describe in more detail the equipment and disaster control systems available during emergencies. The following supplements, when combined with this basic manual, comprise the complete Plan. Copies of the supplements may be obtained from the Fire Safety Division of the Hazards Control Department (Ext. 2-5194).

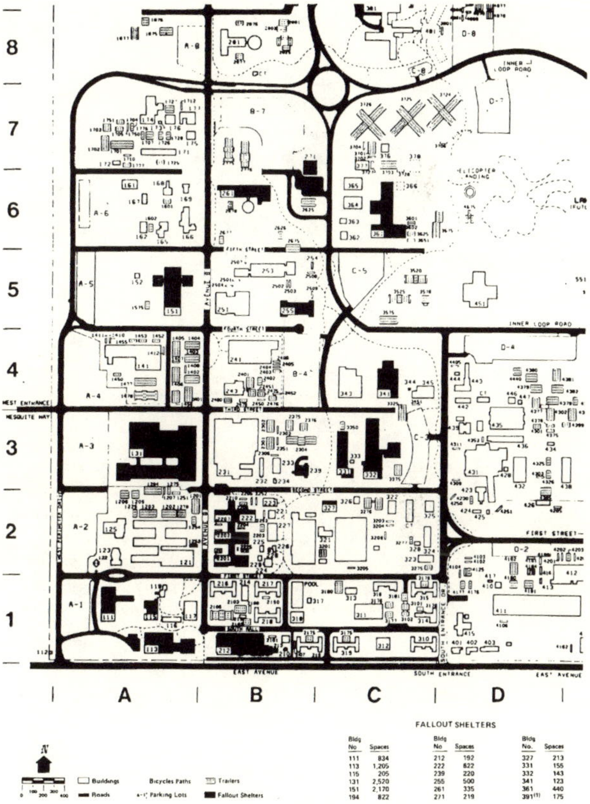

FALLOUT SHELTERS

Bldg No	Spaces	Bldg No	Spaces	Bldg No.	Spaces
111	834	212	192	327	213
113	1,205	222	822	331	155
115	205	239	220	332	143
131	2,520	255	500	341	123
151	2,170	261	335	361	440
194	822	271	219	391[1]	175
					11,093

FIG. 6. Fallout shelter locations and accommodations.

Supplement	Title
1	LLNL Emergency Communications
2	Emergency Callout List
3	Heavy Equipment Available for Emergencies
4	LLNL Water Supply System--Emergency Water Supply Plans
5	Respiratory and Other Protective Equipment for Emergencies
6	Emergency Assistance Team
7	Environmental Evaluations Team
8	Operations Plan for Emergency Operations Center
9	Shelter Manager's Handbook
10	Public Information
11	Traffic Control Plan
12	Security (Classified)
13	Fire Department Equipment and Facilities
14 a&b	LLNL Contract/Charter Aircraft Emergency Procedures
15	Response Plan for Fire in an Explosive Area
16	Bomb Threat Response Procedures
17	Medical Emergency Plan
18	Hazardous Materials Spill Plan

GLOSSARY

ALCO	Alameda County Civic Offices
ARAC	Atmopsheric Release Advisory Capability
ECC	Emergency Control Coordinator
EOC	Emergency Operations Center
EOG	Emergency Operations Guide
DCD	Disaster Control Director
DDCD	Deputy Disaster Control Director
DOE	Department of Energy
FBI	Federal Bureau of Investigation
FEMA	Federal Emergency Management Administration
NAWAS	North American Warning Alert System
NRC	Nuclear Regulatory Commission
OES	Office of Emergency Service--State of California
PIO	Public Information Officer
RACES	Radio Amateur Civil Emergency Service

* U.S. GOVERNMENT PRINTING OFFICE: 1982 361-076/4507

GR/s

Spotted something that isn't quite right?

Let us know and we'll fix it for future reprints. And as a thank you for your diligence, we'll send you a free Sothis book of your choice.

publisher@sothis.press

This page intentionally left blank

Made in United States
Orlando, FL
04 November 2026

90209908R10425